CULTURAL TRAITS
OF
CHINESE UNIVERSITIES

www.royalcollins.com

CULTURAL TRAITS OF CHINESE UNIVERSITIES

JIA JIA & WANG JIANHUA

Books Beyond Boundaries
ROYAL COLLINS

Cultural Traits of Chinese Universities

JIA JIA & WANG JIANHUA

First published in 2021 by Royal Collins Publishing Group Inc.
Groupe Publication Royal Collins Inc.
BKM Royalcollins Publishers Private Limited

Headquarters: 550-555 boul. René-Lévesque O Montréal (Québec) H2Z1B1 Canada
India office: 805 Hemkunt House, 8th Floor, Rajendra Place, New Delhi 110 008

ISBN: 978-1-4878-0484-8

To find out more about our publications, please visit www.royalcollins.com

Contents

Introduction

1. The Reasons for Research

a) Reason 1: Unfair Narration of Chinese Universities – Restating Their Origin

In 1944, a speech titled *Science and Civilisation in China* brought up the historical question of "why modern science had not developed in Chinese civilization and only developed in Europe" into the discussion. This question was later named after Joseph Needham, a British biochemist and science historian, as "Needham's Grand Question." In his studies, he challenged the Eurocentric concept of "modern science" by redefining the term as "a collection of scientific knowledge of many different civilizations." To a certain extent, this broke the scientific concept that had a strong sense of Eurocentrism. At the same time, Needham has inspired the declining Chinese national confidence because he placed traditional Chinese science on a vantage point in his comparison of Chinese and Western science histories. Some scholars even started to worry that a form of cultural arrogance would be developed within China, under the "traditional Chinese science superiority theory" promoted by Needham's monumental work. In fact, a scholar, Chen Fangzheng, held this superior theory in his book *Heritage and Betrayal: A Treatise on the Emergence of Modern Science in Western Civilization*, when attempting to answer Needham's Grand Question.

However, it turns out that Needham's question that bore a great sentiment for China has brought about a "Needham Effect," which was an effect that was almost the complete opposite of its intention. In the comparative studies between China and the West, the focus has been limited to the backward status of modern Chinese science. "The most common mistake in comparative studies is that observers confuse ready-made ideas and concepts with common truths. This has, with few exceptions, shown a Eurocentric approach: culture-specific theories, categories, classifications and concepts derived from Western histories and experiences are generally accepted and subsequently regarded as universal rules."[1] Most studies attempting to answer Needham's question have been reduced to "the study of the backwardness of Chinese modern science."

However, the question of "why modern science had not developed in Chinese civilization but only did so in Europe" itself contains Eurocentric values. Firstly, there was a superior assumption, that "modern science developed in Europe." This assumption virtually named modern science after Europe, which in turn established the superiority of Western science, and set up a subconscious evaluation standard for modern Chinese science. Secondly, there was a presupposition, that modern science "should have" developed in China. This presupposition is a representation of how modern Chinese science is positioned as "backward" in the standard of Western science. From this point of view, the so-called "Needham's Grand Question" bears typical characteristics of a Western question, if not being completely Eurocentric. When this unfair question, under the limitation of the Grand Question's framework, regarding Chinese science history extended to the field of Chinese education, the question of "why Universities had not developed in Chinese civilization but only did so in Europe" came into the picture. Facing the same, or rather a worse, destiny as science, Chinese universities found themselves confined in a rather peculiar understanding, under the shadow of the "history of education" version of "Needham's Grand Question." This understanding could not escape the Eurocentric perspective regarding higher education. Whether the evaluation criteria of Western universities contained in this proposition or the presupposition that universities should be born in China proves that the "Needham Question" is also unfair for the Chinese universities. If the Grand Question on science history was as meaningless as the question "Why your name did not appear on page 3 of today's newspaper?" raised by Sivin, the Grand Question on the history of education is equally illegitimate as the question "why did pears not grow on an apple tree?"

Based on the Needham Effect of science history, the reason for the absence of Chinese universities has been simply attributed to the backwardness of China's political, economic, and cultural environment. Consequently, the traditional Chinese culture was considered as the source of the backwardness that this was constantly blamed on. The Needham Effect in science history and the history of education both lead to the same result, that China's thousand years of cultural heritage was denied simply because of a set of Eurocentric criteria. The reason why the Western concept of *University* can flourish in Chinese soil is also worth studying. This book thus tries to explain the question of "why Chinese universities are *Chinese*," through the quest of Chinese university's cultural roots, from a Chinese cultural perspective, instead of a Eurocentric perspective.

b) *Reason 2: The Unique Charm of Cultural Forces – Why A Cultural Perspective is Adopted*

At the start of the 20th century, German sociologist Max Weber wrote a book called *The Protestant Ethic and the Spirit of Capitalism*. In this book, he unilaterally yet insightfully pointed out the unique effect that protestant ethics possessed in the shaping of the capitalist spirit. With this, he virtually turned around the public's view on the religions in the era of science. By thoroughly digging through, even exaggerating at times, the rational characteristics of the asceticism within the predestinarianism of the protestant ethics, Weber succeeded in establishing a rather rational and logical relationship between the protestant's conception of the calling and the modern spirit of capitalism. To some extent, his work, *the Protestant Ethic and the Spirit of Capitalism*, could be interpreted as a review of the religious and cultural characters and the spirit of capitalism, hence, the unique charm of traditional religious culture in the process of modernization was clearly demonstrated. It was greatly supported by the reasoning and thinking process of his work that this book in your hand took "the cultural characters of Chinese universities" as its theme, and its inspiration mainly came from three aspects:

First, Weber had a very unique understanding of the spirit of capitalism. According to him, "rational behaviors based on the conception of the calling is one of the basic elements of the modern spirit of capitalism, or even of our modern culture. And it is from Christian asceticism that such rational behaviors have originated from."[2] This was exactly the thesis that Weber tried to argue and prove in *the Protestant Ethic and the Spirit of Capitalism*. In his arguments, we could feel the explanatory power that lied within traditional religious culture when it came to modern Western capitalist society, and we had to admit that Weber's cultural argument was highly convincing. This was one of the major reasons why this book chose to study Chinese universities from a cultural viewpoint.

Second, Weber had prescribed a highly prudent range for the explanation of protestant doctrines. In his arguments, the vague and ambiguous dynamics between protestant ethics and the spirit of capitalism were slowly stripped away and replaced with a clear relationship. Meanwhile, on the other hand, we could still constantly perceive the elaboration from the author with a backdrop of borderline desperate justification. "Despite the fact that we had no intention whatsoever to adhere to a preposterous and dogmatic argument, which was 'the spirit of capitalism could only be derived from some effects caused by the religious reformation', or 'capitalism, as an economic system, was created by religious reformation.'"[3] Just as Weber stated, the research "tries to only approach and study one aspect of this problem starting from one single point, which is also the relationship between the spirit of our modern economic life and the rational ethics of the ascetic protestants. Hence, our discussion here merely touches on one single link of the whole chain of causalities."[4] It was exactly this precise and academic Weber's mindset that inspired this book in your hands in trying to find and confirm some form of "link" between traditional Chinese culture and Chinese universities while trying to remain as objective as possible in the process of prescribing a range for reasoning that "some characteristic of a university could be reasoned to originate from the influence of traditional Chinese culture." Also, this book considers in what ways such an explanation could be seen as reasonable.

The third and one of the most important inspirations for this book was the fact that in *The Protestant Ethic and the Spirit of Capitalism*, Weber discarded the stereotypical mindset of social recognition, and established a "unified" relationship between the spirit of capitalism in the era of science and the "anti-scientific" religious culture. To some extent, this deconstructed the rigid "border" of science in a positivist world. In Weber's arguments, the bourgeoisie had always labeled themselves as the main body of "the capitalist system, the manifestation of modern science," and "the representation of the advanced productivity of the modern society." At the same time, and most of the time, they were reluctant to admit that they did possess some obscurant characteristics from the religious culture. After all, religion had always had negative connotations since humanity entered modern times. It was constantly "disenchanted" by our society, while most outcomes and products of the science era would also distance us from it. It was not a coincidence that the traditional Chinese culture came under fire after the May Fourth Movement, marked by the progressive intellectuals of "science" and "democracy" as the "vestiges of feudalism" and a target for criticism. Universities, as a critical "infrastructure" of the modern Chinese society, were also unwilling to associate themselves with traditional Chinese culture, especially Confucianism. Weber's "unification theory" of religions and the spirit of capitalism serves as a reminder that we should probably reflect on our "contradictory theory" regarding the traditional Chinese culture and Chinese universities. Based on this "unification theory," this book focuses on the fact that although it was obvious that Chinese universities had greatly deviated from traditional Chinese culture, it was still a logical development of traditional culture within modern society. And the objective of this research is to thoroughly explore the power that traditional cultural resources possess in their explanation of the issues of Chinese universities.

c) Reason 3: Plurality of Western University Modes – Exploring the References of Chinese University Mode

In the 1930s, a book, *Universities: American, English, German*, revealed to us three different modes of universities through the three different cultural personalities, America, England, and Germany, and reflected the plurality of university modes in the Western world. The author pointed out that "The reader will observe that my discussion of existing universities is unsymmetrical. I have not tried to pour universities into one mold, to view them from a single point of view, or to ask the same questions about all of them."[5] Therefore, Flexner explained three different university modes based on the difference between the three cultural personalities of the three countries. To Flexner, "struggle and instability are at this moment the striking characteristics of American life. Tradition—good and bad—is a stabilizing influence; America, for better or for worse, has practically no traditions either to slow progress or to uphold cultural ideas."[6] With this as a beginning, the author revealed the cultural character of American universities that formed within American traditions. Based on the same logic, English and German universities, too, have unique cultural characters due to the different nations and traditions they belong to.

It is worth noting that Flexner creatively interpreted three different modes of the Western universities, and then regretted that he did not include French universities in his book. He did not intend to leave the French universities out of the picture and has said that he would like to write a book specifically about them. In fact, as of now, with the development of history, Flexner's discourse of modern university theory is missing not only the French university mode. With the rise of China's economy, Chinese universities have received more attention and acknowledgment. In recent years, both Eastern and Western scholars have proposed various Chinese modes of the university system. Putting aside the question of whether the modes can be established, at least Chinese universities have become a unique and indispensable "scene" on the stage of modern universities. This is yet another practical reason for the present study.

Undeniably, nowadays, the horizon of the modern university remains in the West, especially in the US. This has to lead to a phenomenon that "almost all the scholars regard America as a place of strategic importance for modern universities."[7] In comparison, Chinese universities never seemed to be a legitimate member of "modern universities," although Ruth Hayhoe, a Canadian scholar, has proposed the concept of "the Chinese university mode" long ago. We have to admit that, as of now, "the Chinese university mode" is gradually gaining importance in China, and it has made some progress on the theoretical level. Still, it is not widely recognized in the world compared to Western universities.

The plurality of Western modes of the university has "pushed" for the rise of Chinese university mode, while the maturation of Western modes has provided great frames of reference for its establishment. Based on the analysis above, the present study believes that the opportunity for the rise of the Chinese university has arrived, although its maturity is still in the future.

d) *Reason 4: The Unique History of the Chinese University – Why It Is Necessary to Study the Cultural characters of Chinese University*

"The current Chinese university system is the result of *Pang Cai Tai Xi* (adopting Western ideas) instead of *Shang Fa San Dai* (sticking to the traditions of previous generations)."[8] This is only partially true. In the modern era, under the shadow of invasion, it was indeed true that the Chinese university was born under the pressure of Western colonialism. However, this historical tag has hindered or even prevented the Chinese from getting to understand the uniqueness of the Chinese university culture. The most common belief is that Chinese universities were merely universities founded in China. "The triumph of the medieval European university," "bonsai art," "university that cannot be taken seriously" were used to describe Chinese universities. "Universities mimicked Germany and Japan in the late Qing, Europe, and America in the 1920s, the Soviet Union in the 1950s. In the past two decades, American universities were given the most superior status."[9] Chen Pingyuan pointed out that the major problem of the Chinese university education in this century is still being "unable to inherit the traditional Chinese way of 'great learning,' although the Western education system was adapted successfully."[10] When Gan Yang talked about "the concept of Chinese curriculum universities," he also pointed out that the root to the problem of such a university is that Chinese cultural confidence and cultural awareness are still lacking, therefore the concept of "the Mandarin's university" is far established.

From this point of view, based on the "adaptiveness" of Chinese universities, it is mostly agreed that the Chinese university is lacking its own cultural specificity. While on the other hand, "since the start of this century, Chinese university education mimicked Japan, America, France and the Soviet Union, while in some of these stages, the foreign systems were almost completely adapted. However, Chinese university education retained its own characteristics." Just as Liu Haifeng stated, "within the traditional Chinese cultural background with Confucianism as its kernel and foundation, the traditional Chinese 'university' has developed some traits that are distinct from Western universities. Even until now, traditional culture still exerts considerable influence on Chinese university."[11] The cultural specificity of a Chinese university is a highly complicated proposition that involves far more than a negative criticism or an argument on its necessity.

The cultural specificity of a Chinese university is a given fact, whether historically or logically speaking. Firstly, Chinese university develops in China. Secondly, it has a century of history since the late Qing. Just as "it is impossible for a society to completely get away from its traditions, to start afresh, or to substitute its culture with a new set of tradition. Traditions can only get creatively modified based on old traditions."[12] Neither can the fact that modern Chinese university is the product of a history of "horizontal adaptation" stimulated by outer factor allow it to get away from Chinese tradition, nor can this be regarded as absolute evidence to deny or criticize the cultural specificity of the Chinese university.

Therefore, the Chinese cultural character is not a "romantic hope or encouragement," but a given fact. At the same time, history has proven that the cultural characters of Chinese universities do not have an absolute value such as "anything actual is real." Historical facts cannot go without rational value judgments to benefit reality. The cultural explanation of Chinese university would be superficial if it was based purely on historical factual descriptions. The understanding of the Chinese university's cultural characters would be tainted by personal subjectivity and get confined in biased facts through the over-emphasis on critical reflection.

The relationship between Chinese universities and traditional culture has long been a vague point in the concept of Chinese universities. Whether or not the culture specificity of Chinese universities exists has not yet been agreed on. At the same time, while the value judgment of the cultural characters of Chinese university lacks rational thinking and consequently tends to be negative.

Based on the problems above, this book aims to reconstruct the objective features of the cultural characters of Chinese universities, from the historical perspective, followed by value reflection and reconstruction of universities' ideas. Most importantly, a relationship has to be clarified – that traditional culture is always integrated with Chinese universities, sometimes it is hard to detect, yet it is undeniable.

A good cultural heritage is an important backbone of the modern reform of Chinese universities. It is impossible to understand the concept of the Chinese university without considering culture, while the study of Chinese cultural characters would be rendered pointless if there was no rational understanding of the cultural characters of Chinese universities.

e) Reason 5: Research Tendencies of Chinese Universities – Urgency of Studying Its Cultural Characters

At present, there are two special tendencies among scholars in the field of research on Chinese universities. The first is to study Chinese universities using Western university theories. This means that when scholars research some unique phenomena of Chinese universities, what they have in mind are Western university mindsets. Consequently, many of these studies tried to stuff Chinese universities into a Western university framework, and solve problems unique to Chinese universities using Western concepts. However, few have thought about whether the Western modes work in Chinese reality, or to what extent can Western university theories describe Chinese universities. In fact, more and more research on Chinese universities bears a Western feeling, which can be shown especially in reference to Western masterworks in an attempt to show the studies' scientificity. Books like Newman's *The Idea of a University*, Brubeck's *On the Philosophy of Higher Education*, or Kerr's *The Uses of the University* are highly sought after by Chinese researchers. It is rather clear that famous books on Western universities are preferred in terms of their citing rates. In contrast, traditional Chinese cultural classics are rarely favored by Chinese researchers. From this perspective, many domestic studies on Chinese universities introduced works and ideas of Western universities in the name of Chinese universities.

The second is that scholars tend to study Chinese universities from an economic point of view. From the Western idea of "the use of the university" in the past to the Chinese "the adaptability of higher education" in the present, these debates were showing university effects caused by the socio-economic developments. "The use of the university" and "the adaptability of higher education" became the hottest topics in the era when the relationship between universities and the economy became closer. As a result, the era calls for researches on the university concepts from an economic point of view. The globalization, marketization, and commercialization of the discourse in the economic field became the keywords in the research of the university modes, and occupied an absolute advantage in the field of education, especially in higher education. The research on the Chinese university, of course, is no exception. However, it is worth considering that, with globalization, marketization, commercialization as a common background, the question is to what extent can they explain the uniqueness of Chinese university effectively.

The two above-mentioned tendencies within the studies of Chinese universities are getting more and more dominant, therefore, the present discussion of the cultural characters of Chinese universities is most urgent.

2. *Literature Review*

In the theoretical research of higher education, there are various trains of thought regarding the cultural interpretation of higher education or universities, involving many different aspects. Domestically, there are some very representative works studying Chinese higher education from cultural perspectives, such as *Shidu Daxue: Zuzhi Wenhua De Shijiao* (*Understanding Universities: From an Organizational-Cultural Viewpoint)* by Yan Guangcai, *Wenhua Shiye Zhong De Gaodeng Jiaoyu* (*Higher Education from a Cultural View)* by Zhang Yingqiang, *Xiandai Daxue Zhidu Yanjin De Wenhua Luoji (The Cultural Logic in the Institutional Progression of Modern Universities)* by Gao Guijuan.

Based on the perspective of organization culture, in *Shidu Daxue: Zuzhi Wenhua De Shijiao* by Yan, the nature of the university as a spiritual substantive organization has been discussed. Yan argued that universities are unique organizations with rich historical and cultural backgrounds, along with their various traditions. However, in a complex social environment, such as when uniqueness in cultural personality is gradually lost, and universities became a purely worldly place.[13] With such reflection and criticism regarding the current state of universities, the author looked back at medieval universities. He examined the inherent spiritual connotations of universities as academic organizations and established a basic ground for understanding the cultural character within university systems.

Using the cultural view as an anchor in his work, *Wenhua Shiye Zhong De Gaodeng Jiaoyu*, Zhang elaborated on the logical relationship between higher education and culture, and subsequently "extracted" culture from its bilateral relationship with education, elevating it to a "viewpoint" in understanding higher education. Using culture as their "standpoint to move the earth," the author analyzed and demonstrated the relationship among cultural traditions, cultural turns, and higher education, and hence explored the cultural properties of higher education.[14]

Different from the two books mentioned above, Gao instead focused her *Xiandai Daxue Zhidu Yanjin De Wenhua Luoji* on the subject of the university system. From a cultural viewpoint, the author explored Christian cultural characters in medieval university systems, the renaissance cultural characters of modern university systems. She did so while conducting a case study on the national cultural characters of modern British universities.[15]

All the works mentioned above can be considered as typical research works on higher education from a cultural perspective, emphasizing the cultural properties of higher education or universities. In this book, the cultural viewpoint was also adopted as a basic standpoint, while the main focus lies in Chinese universities. Given the considerable leeway that lies within the concept of Chinese universities and the fact that the cultural viewpoint comes with multiple dimensions and high complexities, research on Chinese universities is based on a cultural viewpoint that has shown impressive variety has produced rich results.

a) The Chinese university studied under Chinese and Western cultural viewpoints

1. Research on the history of Chinese universities within the Chinese-Western cultural viewpoints

In this aspect, one of the most typical and representative works would be *China's Universities, 1895–1995: A Century of Cultural Conflict* by Hayhoe. This book was based on a temporal dimension spanning through the historical frame of a century of Chinese universities, starting with the chapter "Concepts and Frameworks for Telling the Story," and followed by "The Nationalist Story, 1911–1949," "The Socialist Story, 1949–1978," "The Story of the Reform Decade, 1978–1990," "Perspectives from the Central South Region," and "Perspectives from the Northwest Region" from a spatial dimension. The book finished with "Mass Higher Education and the Chinese University," focusing on the current reality of Chinese universities. The author regarded the birth of Chinese universities as the "triumphant return of the Medieval European universities," and emphasized the important role played by Chinese traditional culture in the development of Chinese universities. Based on a viewpoint of Chinese and Western cultural research, Hayhoe interpreted the 100 years of Chinese university history as the manifestation of a history of conflict between Chinese and Western culture. On such a basis, she went on and proposed a "Chinese University Model," in which Chinese universities facilitate the integration of Chinese and Western culture while setting their roots within Chinese traditional culture.[16]

Similarly, Chen Pingyuan also took a Chinese-Western cultural approach in his research of the 100 years history of Chinese universities. In his article *Zhongguo Daxue Bainian?* (*100 years of Chinese University?*), he discussed the cultural character of Chinese universities, namely *Pang Cai Tai Xi* and *Shang Fa San Dai*, in a thematic structure. In the article, Chen argued that the most Westernized part of Chinese thought and culture in the 20th century is its higher education of China, to the extent that *Shang Fa San Dai* was practically abandoned.[17] He emphasized the "adaptiveness" of Chinese universities compared with Western universities, while also exclaimed over the decline of traditional cultural character within Chinese universities, especially the absence of "traditional Chinese academic culture" within modern Chinese universities.

2. Research on the system of Chinese universities under Chinese-Western cultural viewpoints

In Fan Yanyan's book *Dual Origin and System Formation*, the system of modern Chinese universities was reconstructed from a Chinese-Western cultural perspective. According to Fan, the system of Chinese universities has dual origins, one being the historical origin developed from traditional Chinese education, the other being the practical origin derived from the introduction of the concept of the Western university into China. As an anti-eurocentrism scholar, she specifically put her emphasis on the opinion that the system of modern Chinese university was essentially rooted in the traditional culture of China.[18]

Differing from Yan's idea, Wang Yongfang's master's thesis, *Jiyu Zuzhi Wenhua Moshi De Zhongguo Daxue Zuzhi Wenhua Jianshe* (*The Construction of Chinese University Organizational Culture Based on Organizational Culture Models),* constructed the organizational culture of Chinese universities based on an analysis of major models of its Western counterparts. By such construction, she emphasized the fundamental role played by Western culture in the foundation of Chinese university organizations.

3. Research on Chinese universities under Chinese-Western cultural viewpoints

Daxue Linian Zai Zhongguo (The Idea of University in China) by Wang Jisheng is a typical piece of work on this topic. According to Wang, the idea of Chinese university not only contains the traditional Chinese character of utilizing Confucian moral principles as a standard, but it also contains the modern Western character of Western universities.

Under the same "Chinese-Western cultural integration" theory of Chinese university ideals, Wang Shu pointed out in her *Moushi Yu Moudao: Zhongguo Daxue Linian Zhi Jueze (For Food or For Truth: The Choice of Chinese University Ideal)* that we could form a harmonious Chinese university ideal only if we use the traditional idea of "searching for truth" as the base, and combine it with the Western idea of "working for food."[19]

Ru Ning and Yan Guangfen, in their *The Change between Modes and the Conflict between Cultures: Thoughts on the Modernization of Chinese University Education Ideas*, proposed an idea different from the aforementioned. They focused on the conflicts between Chinese and Western culture displayed in Chinese university education ideas. The article stated that even though the 100-year progression was explicitly led by Western models, it was implicitly operated with a thinking mode that was heavily based on traditional Chinese culture. Hence, massive conflicts and contradictions were present during the development of the ideas behind Chinese universities.[20]

b) Chinese university studied under traditional Chinese cultural perspective

1. Research on the national properties of Chinese universities

In Liu Haifeng's article, *Chuantong Wenhua Yu Zhongguo Daxue De Tese* (*Traditional Culture and the Specialties of Chinese University*), he pointed out that the long-standing Chinese traditional culture cast a significant influence over Chinese universities. Using this as an entry point, he further explored the national properties of Chinese universities. According to him, on the backdrop of Chinese traditional culture with Confucian as its base and core, ancient Chinese universities had already developed a significant difference from their Western counterparts. This in turn had significantly affected Chinese universities. Hence, even though Chinese university education had undergone multiple phases in which it tried to follow the examples of the Japanese, American, French and Soviet universities, while completely adopting Western ways in a few of these phases, modern Chinese university education still retained its own specialties under the implicit influence of Chinese traditional culture.[21]

Besides Liu's work, there are some other explorative pieces on the national properties of Chinese universities. For example, Pang Rui, based on an international perspective, discussed the national properties of Chinese universities in her *Zhongguo Daxue Jiaoyu Guojihua Yu Minzuhua De Guanxi Pingxi* (*Comments and Analyses on the Internationalization and Nationalization of Chinese University Education*). In this article, she pointed out that the internationalization of higher education had become an irreversible global trend. Under such circumstances, China should consider how, on the level of "true nature of education", to preserve the nationalization of its education when also thriving and promoting the internationalization of its university education.[22]

2. Research of the system of Chinese universities within the traditional cultural viewpoints

In his master's thesis *The Influence of the political leanings of Traditional Culture on the System of Chinese University*, Wang Lijun analyzed and commented on the system of Chinese universities, based on Chinese traditional political culture. The author reckoned that China had yet to establish a systematic structure for universities that were commonly accepted and well-received by society. This phenomenon was caused by the lack of thought given to the inherent cultural traditions when constructing the system for modern Chinese universities. Using the political leaning of traditional culture as an entry point, he emphasized the effect that the "unity of politics and education" and *Da Yi Tong* (Grand Unification) ideas had on the construction of the system of universities. Similarly, in Yi Jianliu's Study on the *Self-rule of Chinese Universities under the Globalization Backdrop from a Traditional Cultural View*, he also emphasized the value of traditional culture to the self-ruling system of Chinese universities, based on a cultural viewpoint. The article pointed out that, excellent educational culture and spirit would have a significantly positive influence in the survival of free thought under the centralized rule, and hence, universities should try and locate the source for the inability to attain self-rule themselves, and try to retain the independent spiritual properties of Chinese universities by re-learning their traditional culture.

3. Research on the idea of Chinese universities within the traditional cultural viewpoints

Ji Guan and Guo Li Jun pointed out in their *Zhongguo Chuantong Wenhua Yu Daxue Linian* (*Chinese Traditional Culture and Ideas of University*) that even though Chinese universities were essentially the result of *Xi Xue Dong Jian* (the gradual eastward spreading of Western culture and science), they were still deeply rooted within the cultural and educational traditions of China. Using the educational ideas in *Daxue* and *Xue Ji* as their entry point, the author argued the historical validity of multiple ideas and tendencies in modern Chinese universities, namely the idea of *Xue Er You Ze Shi* (pursuing a political/administrative career after achieving academic success), the idea of *De Yu Wei Xian* (ethical education comes first) and the practical tendency of treatment of knowledge. Similar studies include Li Yongli and Zhao Weiguo's *Qianxi Zhongguo Chuantong Wenhua Dui Zhongguo Daxue Linian De Yingxiang* (*A Brief Analysis of the Influence of Chinese Traditional Culture on the Ideas of Chinese University*) and Ji Liangjing's *Chuantong Wenhua Siwei Fangshi Dui Zhongguo Daxue Linian De Yingxiang* (*the Influence of Traditional Cultural Modes of Thinking on the Ideas of Chinese University*).

Besides this, the "Idea of Mandarin University" discussion was initiated in the academic circle in 2000, and it was essentially a typical concept of "establishing an idea for Chinese universities based on a traditional cultural viewpoint." The concept was first proposed by Gan Yang, when he used it in a commentary on King Yeo-Chi's *The Idea of a University*.

In 2003, Gan quoted this concept again when discussing the reformation of Peking University. In *Huaren Daxue Linian Yu Beida Gaige (The Idea of Mandarin University and the Reformation of Peking University),* Gan pointed out that the core of the idea of a university for the ethnic Chinese, which was the fundamental mission of Mandarin universities, required such universities to learn from Western universities regarding their superior systems and their excellent achievements. While on the other hand, the goal of such a learning process also lay with reinforcing the independence and autonomy of the mind, academic, cultural, and educational aspects of the Chinese ethnic groups rather than the turning of Chinese people into a subsidiary of the Western universities. Quoting Ding Bangxin's *Xianggang Jiaoyu Hequ Hecong* (*Hong Kong's Higher Education: Where Was It From and Where Will It Go*), Gan emphasized the importance of unique evaluation standards for Chinese journals, academic papers expressed in Chinese, along with Chinese experts. It is now safe to say that, standing on the traditional culture of China, Gan's "Idea of Mandarin universities," on its macroscopic and manifestation level, showed its urge for a perfect construction for a "university for the Mandarin people."

Different from Gan's *Ying Ran* (theory/theoretical) understanding of this concept, Wang Jianhua utilized the *Shi Ran* (reality/realistic) approach and redefined the practical meaning of the "Idea of Mandarin universities." Using "Ideas of Western universities" as a comparison, the author stated that "it seems that the so-called 'idea of universities for the ethnic Chinese' could be concluded as *Xue Er You Ze Shi, Shi Er You Ze Xue* (to pursue a political/administrative career after achieving academic success and to pursue academic advances after achieving political/administrative success)."[23] Taking this as a basis, he then criticized the lack of academic freedom and the lack of self-rule in Chinese universities, on the backdrop of said universities being part of a government-run system.

In conclusion, both Gan's "theoretical" idea or Wang's "realistic" idea could be seen as a "declarations of independence" of Chinese universities, as they both emphasized the importance of the independence of Chinese universities on both the inner and outer level. They shall neither become the "subsidiaries" of Western universities, nor the country or the regime's "subordinates."

c) *Chinese university studied from Confucian perspectives*

I. Research that analyzes Chinese universities according to classic Confucian literature.

Mei Yiqi, a master scholar from the Republic of China, wrote *Daxue Yijie* (*On University/A Solution for University*), a classic critical piece that used Confucian culture as the standard for the evaluation of universities. The article argued that the ancient way of universities lies within *Ming Ming De* (promoting noble ethics) and *Xin Min* (enlightening the people), however, "the universities nowadays still lack in recognition/understanding and implementation/practice."[24] When commenting on Mei's article, Tu

Youguang pointed out that Mei used to live and work in American institutions of higher learning for a considerable amount of time. Tu was highly impressed by the fact that Mei thoroughly understood the reality, history, and theories of Western university education, yet still specifically and distinctively quoted *Daxue* (classic Confucian literature, later became the namesake of universities in China) when discussing Chinese universities.[25]

Following Mei's path of analyzing Chinese universities with classic Confucian works of literature, some scholars reflected on the hardship faced by Chinese universities using the Confucian backdrop. He Liping's *Cong Liang Qichao De 'Lun Junzi' Tan Dangqian Zhongguo Daxue Jingshen De Chongzu* (*Discussing the Reconstruction of the Spirit of Chinese University Basing on Leung Kai Chiu's 'On Intelligentleman'*) is such typical piece of work. Using Leung's speech in 1914 at Tsinghua University *Lun Junzi* (*On Intelligentleman*) as the entry point, the article traced back to the classic Confucian ideas of *Zi Qiang Bu Xi, Hou De Zai Wu* (prosper by endless thriving, embrace the world with boundless morality), and argued that Chinese universities should reconstruct their spirit accordingly under the "intelligentleman" idea.[26]

2. Research that analyzes Chinese universities based on Confucian culture.

Huang Chengliang's *Rujia Wenhua: Zhongguo Daxue De Jingshen Zuobiao* (*Confucianism: The Spiritual Coordinates of Chinese University*) highly praised the value of Confucian culture and the spirit of Chinese universities. In the article, the author pointed out that Confucian culture should become the spiritual coordinate of a Chinese university, namely it should be the think tank of the general education of Chinese university, the draft of speech when Chinese universities are participating in the international discussion, the arbitrator between the instrumental rationality and value rationality of Chinese universities, and the compass to guide Chinese universities to a world-leading status.[27] Even though many pieces of research regarding Chinese universities would involve Confucian culture to some degree, research that interprets Chinese universities solely based on Confucian culture are still rather rare.

According to the result of this review, it was evident that such research could be split into the two categories mentioned above, while both categories share the same attitude towards Confucian culture, which is that "it is highly valuable to Chinese universities."

In the paragraphs above, the research of Chinese universities on cultural viewpoints was briefly sorted into three dimensions, namely "Western-Chinese culture," "traditional culture" and "Confucian culture, and a descriptive analysis was carried out regarding the history, systems, and ideas of Chinese universities in these respective dimensions. This book took the cultural character of China as its theme, re-interpreting Chinese university from a traditional cultural viewpoint, to construct a model of a Chinese university with Chinese cultural character based on traditional Chinese culture. In recent years, the concept of the "model of Chinese university" has developed into an epochal theme in the field of higher education research. By now, the research on this aspect has achieved some success, which will be briefly reviewed below.

d) The conceptual expression of the "model of the university"

1. Hayhoe's "Chinese Model of University"

Hayhoe first mentioned the concept of the "mode of Chinese university" in her book *China's Universities 1895–1995: A Century of Cultural Conflict*, and officially raised the idea later in 2009 in her report *Chinese Model of University: an East-West Dialogue*. Hayhoe stated that, against the backdrop of globalization, Western universities should put more effort into their dialogue with Chinese civilization to gain more wisdom, while Chinese universities should develop their unique ways to promote the ideas of Chinese civilization. It can hence be argued that the essence of Hayhoe's "model of Chinese university" was meant to absorb the core advantages and ideas of Western universities while retaining the historically accumulated wisdom of Chinese culture, hence transcending it over Western universities in the process.

2. Kaneko Motohisa's "Chinese Model for Higher Education Development."

Japanese scholar Kaneko Motohisa first mentioned the concept of "Chinese Model for Higher Education Development" in his article *the Chinese Model of Higher Education Development: An Observation from Japan* and the concept included the diode of "government-run" and "marketized" nature of Chinese universities' operation. The concept revealed the reality of Chinese universities' affinity towards both the government and generic corporations.

3. Tu Youguang's "a University of China."

In his *Localization of Civilization and University*, Tu mentioned two main concepts, "a university in China" and "a university of China."[28] To a great extent, the latter referred to the model of a Chinese university that possesses a local cultural character.

4. Wang Jianhua's "Chinese Model of University".

In his *Cong Zhongguoshi Daxue Dao Daxue De Zhongguo Shji (From Chinese University to the Chinese model of University)*, Wang Jianhua first mentioned the concept, which involved two aspects of university: the system and the idea. The core idea of the concept was "seeking similarity in the idea" and "seeking variety in the system."[29] The former emphasized the absorption and integration of Western university ideas like self-rule and academic freedom into Chinese universities, while the latter emphasized the inheritance of Chinese traditional cultural heritage. To some extent, the "Chinese model of universities" could be seen as the nationalization of the system and the culture of universities.

5. Zhang Jiming and Fang Hua's "Cultural Character of Chinese University."

In their *Research Review on Modes for University*, Zhang Jiming and Fang Hua collected and analyzed the theories regarding the model of Chinese universities, and formed a practical conclusion. In the article, they pointed out that "all these research reckoned that the model of the Chinese university must be based on Chinese culture, and the so-called model of a Chinese university is, to a great extent, the cultural character of Chinese university."[30]

All the analyses above showed that the academic circle still has a rather diverse understanding and differing expressions regarding the "model of a Chinese university," each with different emphasis on each concept. Hayhoe's "model of Chinese university" and Tu's "a university of China" emphasized the traditional cultural properties of Chinese universities, which could be called "localized Chinese universities." Kaneko's "model of Chinese higher education" emphasized the adaptive trend of the development of Chinese higher education, which could be called "marketized and politicized Chinese higher education." Wang's "Chinese model of the university" emphasized the innovations of the Chinese university system under the reformation of traditional culture, which could be called "innovative Chinese university." Zhang and Fang's "cultural character of Chinese university" emphasized the cultural nature of Chinese universities as an entire entity, which could be called "culturally nationalized Chinese university." The concepts mentioned above could all be understood as "the cultural uniqueness of the Chinese university." In other words, all these concepts are meant to distinguish Chinese universities from their Chinese character. Except for Kaneko's "model of Chinese higher education," all other concepts would fit inside the conclusion made by Zhang and Fang in their "cultural character of the Chinese university."

e) The Traits of "Chinese Model of University"

1. Adaptiveness and Transcendency

Hayhoe expressed in her *China's Universities 1895–1995: A Century of Cultural Conflict* that the model of Chinese university should absorb and integrate the core ideas and advantages of the Western model of the University while retaining the historical accumulated wisdom of Chinese culture. Hence, it would be a transcendence over Western universities, instead of an adaption. In Hayhoe's view, the model of Chinese universities should not only learn from the advanced Western culture in the process of development, but it should also surpass the model of the Western university on this basis. Hence, the model of the Chinese university should include the unification of adaptiveness and transcendence.

2. Localization and Internationalization

Wang Hongcai pointed out in his *Bentuhua Yu Guojihua: Zhongguo Daxue Moshi De Jiannan Xuanze (Internationalization and Localization: The Hard Choice of the Model of Chinese University)* that internationalization and localization are not essentially different, but their difference only lies within the point of emphasis.[31] The core of the Chinese universities' model is meant to handle the balance and the relationship between "learning from foreign examples" and "putting down roots in the local culture." Hence, the model of the Chinese university should include the unification of localization and internationalization.

3. Tradition and Innovation

In *Cong Zhongguoshi Daxue Dao Daxue De Zhongguo Shji* (*From Chinese University to Chinese Model of University)*, Wang Jianhua pointed out that university is the product of civilization, and cultural traditions are the origin for innovations of university systems. Hence, Chinese universities should look for new points in their system innovation, and those should come from within their cultural traditions. The article stated that the creation of any modes for university must root themselves within the unique cultural traditions of their ethnicity. Hence, the model of Chinese university should include the unification of tradition and innovation.

4. Uniqueness and Alternativity

In *Zhongguo Daxue Moshi: Suqiu, Kunjingy Yu Goujian Lujing (Chinese Model of University: Appeals, Difficulties, and Paths of Establishment)*, Wu Libao and Jiang Ning pointed out that the equal emphasis on teaching and researching supports the propagation of the German model of the university, while the main feature of the American university is its extension towards social functions. Hence, Chinese universities should have their supporting theory, and this theory should serve as the inherent character of Chinese universities, exhibiting the uniqueness of Chinese universities. The article also pointed out that if Chinese universities could not find a substitute for their current model, which is the American model of universities, the construction of the model of Chinese university would lose its practical significance.[32] Such "alternativity" is different from Hayhoe's "transcendence" based on Western-Chinese dialogue and could be interpreted as the property that guides Chinese universities in becoming the center of universities in the world. It is a path to leading their development from a superior state. From this viewpoint, the model of the Chinese university should include unification of uniqueness and alternativity.

5. Ideality and Reality

Also demonstrated in *Zhongguo Daxue Moshi: Suqiu, Kunjingy Yu Goujian Lujing* is the point that the model of the university could be identified, propagated, and applied in different cultural environments, and its core must be the idea of the university. Hence, the model of Chinese university needs to have a core idea. On the other hand, the article also stated that the construction of the model of Chinese universities should not stray from the reality of the successful transformation of China's economic and social development. Instead, it should try to find the breakthrough point within the development itself. Based on this, the model of Chinese university should include the unification of ideality and reality.

It could be discovered via this review, that the "model of the Chinese university" has a different character to different scholars with different standpoints, however, these characters still implicitly showed consistency. If boiled down to bare forms, they are all circumstantial expressions of the "national uniqueness" and "international universality" included by the model of Chinese university.

f) The idea construction of the Chinese university model

1. The Theory of "Two Dimensions"

In *Bentuhua Yu Guojihua: Zhongguo Daxue Moshi De Jiannan Xuanze*, Wang Hongcai set the key to constructing the model of a Chinese university to be the unification of localization and internalization. From this point of view, the ideal model of Chinese universities is meant to integrate the adapted experience into the host culture and to achieve an inner balance where the latter would be the dominant factor. In *Cong Zhongguo Daxue Dao Daxue De Zhongguo Moshi*, Wang Jianhua also discussed the formation path of the model of Chinese universities in a two-dimensional way. Based on the observation of the "similar explicitly, different implicitly" phenomenon in the progression of the system of Chinese universities, the author reckoned that "seeking similarity in the ideal, seeking variety in the system" is the only path that the "Chinese university" could shift to the "Chinese model of universities." From this point of view, the ideal model of the Chinese university would retain self-rule and academic freedom as its ideal value, and would have innovations while using its inherent cultural traditions as the entry point within the system.

2. The Theory of "Three Dimensions"

Zheng Wen and Chen Wei constructed an ideal Chinese model of higher education from a three-dimensional point of view in their *Woguo Gaodeng Jiaoyu Fazhan De Duowei Tese: Zhongguo Moshi Tansuo (The Multidimensional Character of the Development of Higher Education in China: The Exploration of the Chinese Mode)*. They utilized "catching up and surpassing" as their theme in the mode of the target, "impact and reaction" as their theme in the method of reformation, and "keypoint to the trial point" as their theme in the strategy of practice.[33]

3. The Theory of "Four Dimensions"

In *Zhongguo Daxue Moshi: Suqiu, Kunjingy Yu Goujian Lujing*, Wu Libao and Jiang Ning set their eyes on the rational discussion of the lack of theories, lack of practice, and lack of cultural support in the formation of "the model of Chinese university." They suggested a path for the construction of the model of Chinese universities in four aspects, namely "to build a higher education thought system with the Chinese character," "to form an innovation-driven way of economic development," "to build prototype universities with the Chinese character" and "to reinforce cultural innovation and cultural export."

The ideal construction methods of the model of Chinese universities of different researchers are based on different cognitive dimensions: some are more conclusive and macroscopic, while others are detailed and microscopic. However, if explored from their very essence, every one of these construction strategies of the model of Chinese universities is centered around the same theme "how can we handle the relationship between Chinese character and adapted modes?" This could be seen as the universal goal of this topic.

Concluding all that was mentioned above, it could be seen that research regarding the model of Chinese universities is still lacking, while most of the research were dissertations or articles in academic journals. Generally speaking, the research regarding this idea has yet to form a robust theoretical framework. On the other hand, most research could be categorized as comprehensive and macroscopic discussions, leaving many practical problems and questions for further discussion.

By collating and analyzing literature that involves the theme of this research, it could be observed that the works Researching Chinese universities from cultural viewpoints are highly diverse. Many of the research papers yielded great results and possess great theoretical and practical value. However, on a comprehensive level, it is clear that much is left to be done. One, regarding the interpretation and practical usage of cultural viewpoints, some of the research claimed that they discussed university education or higher education from cultural viewpoint. While in fact, they had shown signs of repeated arguments on the relationship between education and culture. They failed to promote culture from the level of "an influential factor in the development of the university and higher education" to the level of "a viewpoint to understand university and higher education." They lack a precise understanding of cultural viewpoints. Two, from the perspective of the value of traditional culture, the evaluation of traditional culture by different researchers could be split into three categories. Group one labeled it as "outstanding traditional culture," while positively praising the basic and supporting effects of traditional culture towards Chinese universities. Group two labeled it as "outdated historical residue" while emphasizing the negative effects of the traditional culture of Chinese universities. And group three took a dialectical approach, having both positive and negative views on the effects of traditional culture on Chinese universities. However, no matter which group these research papers belonged to, they all had a common problem: their understandings of traditional culture was too abstract and vague, while their discussions regarding Chinese universities were too concrete and detailed. In other words, many of these articles can be argued to be "trying to explain everything within Chinese universities with only an abstract concept of traditional culture. In addition, during the research review of the model of Chinese universities, a very obvious problem was revealed – the model of a Chinese university has great alignment and emphasis on its cultural basis, while the proposition of cultural basis itself has never been extensively explored and discussed. Meanwhile, reverse research that discussed the model of a Chinese university via cultural basis is even less in number. To put it another way, most research derived the concept of "Chinese culture" from the proposition of the "model of a Chinese university," instead of using "Chinese culture" as their starting point to form a "model of Chinese university."

3. Relevant Concepts

a) Chinese University

"Chinese University" is the concept most directly relevant to the research of "the cultural character of the Chinese university," while "university" is the concept most directly related to the research of the "Chinese university." However, the definition of "university" and "Chinese university" could be vastly different within the academic circle, so the definition for these terms within this book must be explained.

"University" is an old yet timeless concept. From the birth of medieval European universities to this very day, the history of the university has last over 1,000 years. As of now, universities are regarded as one of the most important social institutions in countries all over the world. There are various definitions of the university in the academic circles. The following are some examples that are thought to possess the most authority. In *Encyclopædia Britannica*, the definition of a "university" is "institution of higher education, usually comprising a college of liberal arts and sciences and graduate and professional schools and having the authority to confer degrees in various fields of study. A university differs from a college in that it is usually larger, has a broader curriculum, and offers graduate and professional degrees in addition to undergraduate degrees." According to *Cihai*, the definition of "*Daxue*" (university) is "school that implements higher education. Universities can be categorized into comprehensive universities and vocational colleges." In the *Jiaoyu Da Cidian* (*The Grand Dictionary of Education*) edited by Gu Mingyuan, the definition of a university is given as "(1) ancient institute of higher education, originating from the book, *The Book of Rites: Wang Zhi*, written in the Western Zhou dynasty: 'The place of great learning is located at the outskirt of the capital city – for the emperor, it is called *Piyong*, while for high officials, it is called *Pangong*.' After Emperor *Wu* of *Han*, *Taixue*, *Guozixue*, and *Guozijian* established in different dynasties can all be considered as "places of great learning." Secondly, it is a type of institution for higher learning. Universities in the modern sense originated from the guild of teachers and students that formed in Medieval Europe."[34] This book has a rather broad definition for the word "university," and no definitive description will be given specifically. However, the meaning of "university" within this book shall follow the two points presented in the definitions listed above: One, an institution that implements higher education; Two, it is clearly distinguished from other institutions of higher learning that do not focus on undergraduate education.

Burton Clark mentioned that the definition and purpose of the university could vary according to the time and location, and that "everyone can discuss the idea of the university, however university is a place for teaching, researching and conducting community services for scholars, so we can only start to understand what these missions for university really stand for based on the specific environments of different eras and places."[35] So, what on earth does the word "*daxue*" mean in China? And how should we understand the words "Chinese university?" In *Cihai*, the word "*daxue*" is explained as: "Chinese university is primarily consisted of its undergraduate department, with some opening different subsidiary colleges and postgraduate organizations. According to the needs of the construction of socialism and the nature of the university itself, the undergraduate department is usually split into different specializations, while affiliated or similar specializations would be grouped as a school. These specializations would admit students that graduated from high school or possess equivalent certifications of learning, with the curriculum usually spanning across four years for common specializations and five years for some specializations such as Medicine." *Piyong* from the Western Zhou dynasty, *Taixue* starting from the Han dynasty, and *Guozixue* starting from the Jin dynasty could all be categorized as universities. The establishment of modern Chinese universities began with the founding of the Imperial University of Peking in 1898. After its birth, some additional universities were also gradually formed by the government, foreign churches, and individuals. As mentioned before, in *Jiaoyu Da Cidian*, the first definition for "*Daxue*" is the historical description of the university in the Chinese context, which can be seen as an extension of the "Chinese university" in ancient times. The "Chinese university" mentioned in this book is specifically the "university" of "China," which could be understood on two levels. One, considering its property of being "Chinese," Chinese university is different from the Western university while it is also a direct descendant of the ancient higher education of China, which could date back to the birth of Confucianism. Two, considering its property of being a "university," Chinese university is borrowed and adapted from the modern Western university. Counting from the establishment of the Imperial University of Peking in 1898, the history of modern Chinese university has only lasted for about a century.

b) Chinese Culture

"Chinese culture" is another concept that is highly relevant to the research of "the cultural character of the Chinese university." "Culture" is a core concept of "Chinese culture," while both "culture" and "Chinese culture" are considered to be concepts that are highly complex within the academic circles. Hence, it is necessary to briefly explain the meanings of "culture" and "Chinese culture" mentioned in this book.

"Culture", with the same spelling in English and French, originated from the Latin word "*Colere.*" It means the farming and cultivation of plants, which is further extended to represent "developing the mind, intellect, sentiment, and style of a human being." Japanese scholars translated this word borrowing from the word "*Wenhua*" from ancient Chinese, which later spread to China and formed the word "*Wenhua*" in the modern Chinese language. The definition of culture is highly diverse. *Culture: A Critical Review of Concepts and Definitions* written by American anthropologists Alfred Kroeber and Clyde Kluckhohn mentioned that 164 versions of definitions of culture were presented in the academic theory circles during the period between 1871 and 1951, with even more generated afterward. Hence, some people made the statement that there are currently over 200 or over 1,000 definitions for the concept of culture.[36] Within the Chinese academic circle, the discussion regarding the concept of "culture" first gained momentum during the period between the late Qing dynasty and the Republic of China era. By then, many scholars expressed their understanding regarding the term "culture." For example, Leung Kai-Chiu once said that "Culture is the common cause of all that's valuable that's generated from human beings' hearts and minds." Cai Yuanpei said that "Culture is the status of development of the human being." Liang Shuming stated that Culture "is the model for life"[37] and that "Culture is all that we, as human beings, depend on in our life."[38] Qian Mu expressed his similar view in *Wenhua Yu Shenghuo (Culture and Life),* "Culture must be derived from the life of human beings. Without human life, there shall be no culture whatsoever. Culture is the entirety of the living of human beings. Gather the entirety of human beings' lives, and you will get culture."[39] Until now, definitions of culture given by the author can still be found within all sorts of cultural literature, amounting to a near-infinite number. There are also some authoritative explanations. For example, the definition of "culture" in *Cihai* is given as "First, in a broader sense, culture refers to the summation of all the material and spiritual wealth that has been created in the process of the historical practice of the human society. In a narrower sense, culture refers to the ideology of the society, along with all its accommodative systems, institutions, and organizations. Second, it broadly refers to general knowledge, including linguistic knowledge. Third, it is a general term used to represent the rule and indoctrination of the ancient feudal dynasties of China." Generally speaking, "culture" mentioned in this book is a broad concept. It includes not only values, thoughts, and rather abstract ideologies, but also detailed material cultural symbols that are derived from such abstract values.

The term "Chinese culture" is rather self-explanatory. In a broader sense, it refers to the traditional culture and the modern and contemporary culture of China. In this book, the term is used in a narrower sense. The meaning of the term is confined to the traditional culture of China, while not including its modern and contemporary counterpart. Traditional culture, as the major part of Chinese culture, is usually used interchangeably with the term "Chinese culture." Many works of literature that discuss "Chinese culture" can be seen as pieces that specifically explore "traditional Chinese culture." For instance, *Zhongguo Wenhua Gailun (An Introduction to Chinese Culture)* edited by Zhang Dainian and Fang Keli and *Zhongguo Wenhuashi* Gangyao (An Outline of the History of Chinese Culture) edited by Wu Xiaoru both stopped their discussions at the period of *Xi Xue Dong Jian*, without touching on the modern and contemporary culture of China.

So, what is traditional Chinese culture? In *Zhongguo Jiaoyu De Wenhua* Jichu (The Cultural Basis of Chinese Education), Gu Mingyuan gave a concise and comprehensive explanation of traditional Chinese culture – "traditional Chinese culture is the ancient culture of China, which is the culture of China before China's modernization." He also pointed out that "Modern and contemporary Chinese culture are developed based on the ancient culture."[40] In *Guoxue Yu Chuantong Wenhua* (*Sinology and Traditional Culture*), Liu Mengxi explained "the entirety of the culture of the traditional society can be given the name of traditional culture. Usually, the interval of 'traditional society' is defined to be the period that starts from Zhou and Qin, and ends with the abdication of the last emperor of Qing, before Xinhai Revolution in 1911." Culture should include the general way of life and values of the entirety of the people. Hence, in a broader sense, traditional Chinese culture refers to the general way of life and values of the Chinese people within the traditional Chinese society.[41]

Different from the definitions given above, Liu Yizheng based traditional Chinese culture around Confucian culture, "Confucius is the center of Chinese culture. Without him, the origins and existence of Chinese culture would be impossible. The Chinese culture from thousands of years before him is passed down because of him, while the Chinese culture from thousands of years after him is started by him."[42] In this book, the understanding of "Chinese culture" mainly follows the two key points from the definitions mentioned above. One, it refers to the culture of traditional Chinese society before the Xinhai Revolution. Two, it mainly refers to the Confucian culture with Confucius at its center. In a nutshell, it refers to the traditional Chinese culture with Confucianism at its core before the Xinhai Revolution of 1911.

c) Cultural Characters of Chinese Universities

"Cultural character of Chinese universities" is the main topic of this book containing two core concepts, namely "Chinese universities" and "Chinese culture." In addition, "character" and "cultural character" are the key to understanding the thesis of this book.

The word "*Xingge*" (character) means the personality and quality of a person, and it is originally a concept borrowed from psychology. In *Cihai*, it is explained as "the stable and personalized psychological features of an individual within the attitude towards reality and the ways of behavior of an individual. It is the core of personality, which shows the most significant difference between individuals, and it has a complex structure. Generally speaking, the structure can be split into 4 components: (1) the features of one's attitude towards reality and themselves. For example, honest versus hypocritical, humble versus hubristic; (2) the features of one's will. For example, brave versus cowardly, decisive versus indecisive; (3) the features of one's moods. For example, passionate versus indifferent, cheerful versus gloomy; (4) the rational features of one's moods. For example, optimistic, tough, fearful, rough, etc." The explanation of the *Modern Chinese Dictionary* outlines the psychological characteristics shown through the people's attitudes, such as cheerfulness, strength, cowardice, rudeness, and so on. Concluding from the definitions given above, it can be derived that the main features of "character" are stability, internalization, and differentiability.

Usage of the word "character" in the academic circle is not constrained within psychology research, as it is gradually being introduced into different fields and disciplines, and applied to different objects of research. For example, Gao Xinmin used the term "the character of Chinese culture" in his *Renxin Yu Rensheng: Guangyi Xinling Zhexue Lungang* (*Heart and Life: An Outline for General Mind Philosophy*) while using "Chinese culture" as his object of research. In the field of higher education, King Yeo-Chi used the expression of "the ideas and character of universities" in his book the *Idea of a University*, and discussed the "ideas and characters of universities" in different eras from different countries, such as Britain, Germany, and America. In his book, "the character of universities" is semantically interchangeable with the term "the ideas of universities," and it emphasized the differentiability or uniqueness of each model of universities of different eras from different countries. This book focuses its research on "the cultural character of the Chinese university," which is mainly the core features demonstrated by "universities" in "China" due to "cultural" differences in modern and contemporary times that are stable, internalized, and differentiable from others.

"Cultural character" is closely related to the ethnic features. Cultural characters are the most basic content of ethnic features, so "cultural character" can be interpreted as "ethnic cultural character" in a considerable amount of circumstances. At present, there are many works named after the idea of the "cultural character." For example, this phenomenon is present in *Zhongguo Wenhua Xingge (Chinese Cultural Character)* edited and written by Qin Yu, *Zhongguoren De Wenhua Xingge (The Cultural Character of Chinese People)* by Fan Yong, *Mao Zedong De Wenhua Xingge* (*The Cultural Character of Mao Zedong)* by Chen Jin, and *Yige Chengshi De Wenhua Xingge (The Cultural Character of a City by Chen Yi)*, among others. With nations, people, individuals, and cities as the determining element, the term "cultural character" is broadly used in the research of many areas and themes. One of the most significant works that introduced the term "cultural character" into the field of education is *Jiaoyuxue De Wenhua Xingge* (*The Cultural Character in Pedagogy)* by Shi Zhongying. With ground-breaking innovation, Shi combined "character," "culture" and "pedagogy" into the concept of "cultural character in pedagogy." In this book, Shi explained that "in the Chinese language, 'character' is 'the stable psychological features of one's attitudes and behaviors', 'a crucial component of one's personality.' Basing this on physical qualities, 'character' is gradually and progressively developed within the process of social practice. It comes with great differentiability and provides the basic backdrop to all actions of an individual. In English, 'character' means the 'quality' of a person, while it could also refer to the features and specialties of things or persons. We used the term '*Xingge*' (character) in a Chinese linguistic context. Based on its definition, '*Xingge*' has its properties of object, inherence, stasis, identity, and nature. However, in a more major aspect, it belongs to humans instead of objects, and it is not natural but created. Within '*Xingge*' lies a great power of motivation.

Hence, the introduction of the aforementioned features of '*Xingge*' to pedagogical practices, and the combination of them with the concept of 'culture,' and will get us a vivid expression of our understanding of basic pedagogical questions and our interpretation of the essence of pedagogical practices hidden beneath its explicit logics and techniques. Hence, it will provide a general summary of the cultural features of all the practical elements mentioned above. In more detail, 'the cultural characters in pedagogy' refers to the fact that in essence, pedagogy is not 'a scientific activity on a value-neutral, not culturally-involved premise, with factual discovery and knowledge accumulation as its goal and a rigorous logic system as its support.' Instead, it is 'a science of value or science of culture whose goals lie in value construction and meaning elucidation.'"[43]

Using Shi's research on "the cultural characters in pedagogy" as a reference, this book combines "character," "culture" and "Chinese universities" into the concept of "cultural character of Chinese universities," emphasizing the statement that Chinese universities are not essentially just "a type of organization that functions in education, research and community service" that is directly borrowed from the Western model of universities. Instead, Chinese universities are a type of cultural entity that is based on Chinese culture and they are inherently different from any other university organization of other countries. Conceptually, it could be defined as "the fundamental features that make Chinese universities what they are, using Chinese culture as its basis and 'culture inheritors' as its practical body."

4. *Research Methods*

a) *Historical Documents*

This book is, in its nature, a demonstration of the cultural uniqueness of the Chinese university from a historical perspective. Starting the research from seeking Chinese university's cultural roots, this book seeks to establish its argument with history as its foundation from the very start. In the process of the study, this book follows the historical trajectory of Chinese university's development and divides the analysis of the cultural characters of Chinese university into four stages – the late Qing, Republican China, the first seventeen years of the People's Republic of China (PRC), and post-Reform-and-Opening-Up.

Some historical events closely related to the topic of this book were reviewed and re-examined. Events that relate closely to traditional culture, for example, the Westernization Movement in the late Qing, the May Fourth Movement in early Republican China, the Anti-Rightist Campaign in the first seventeen years of PRC, were key research targets. Therefore, this book involves plenty of historical studies. A variety of materials had to be gathered, including traditional Chinese cultural classics, historical materials about modern and contemporary China, as well as historical records on Chinese universities.

In order to understand the formation and development of the cultural character of Chinese universities, one has to read and organize a huge amount of materials. Therefore, historical document analysis is this book's main research method.

b) Comparative Analysis

This book interprets Chinese universities based on traditional Chinese culture. Its main purpose is to highlight and emphasize the traditional cultural characters of Chinese universities. Therefore, the influence of Western culture on Chinese universities in modern times is intentionally left out. However, this does not mean that this book completely excludes the research method of Chinese and Western comparative analysis. On the contrary, in the discussion, it is necessary to make Chinese and Western comparisons relevant to the argument.

It is a given that this book involves mainly vertical historical comparisons. When combing the development characteristics and trends of Chinese universities' cultural characters in different historical periods, it is necessary to carry out comparative research during each stage. Only through a comparative analysis of the historical fate of Chinese culture during different historical periods and the path of formation of university's cultural characters can we clearly understand the development characteristics of Chinese university's cultural characters during each period and we can further explore the possible development trend of Chinese universities in a cultural perspective. Therefore, a comparative analysis is an indispensable research method for the present study.

c) Ideal Type

The "Ideal type" is a sociological methodology proposed by Max Weber, adopted in his book *Protestant Ethics and the Spirit of Capitalism*. Its original purpose was to overcome the over-individualization and over-specialization research tendencies of German humanists and historical schools. Later on, many scholars further developed this method at the theoretical level, together with practical demonstration. At present, the "ideal type" has become a common research method in many subject areas. There are many studies in the field of higher education, and there are many studies that also tend to use the "ideal type" to examine the "most prominent and unique characteristics" of some universities.

The reason for choosing "ideal type" as one of the research methods for the present study is because the main research subject, "the cultural characters of Chinese universities," is rich in its connotations, which means that there are many ways and angles towards understanding the study of the cultural characters of Chinese universities:

The cultural characters of Chinese universities at the macro-level are divided between the domestic cultural characters and adapted Western cultural characters. At the meso-level, area the ancient cultural characters of Chinese "*Daxue*" and the modern cultural characters of Chinese "university." The cultural characters of the Chinese university at the micro-level can be differentiated between traditional cultural characters such as Confucian, Taoist, or even Mohist.

Due to the multi-dimensional nature of "culture" itself, the cultural character of Chinese universities is bound to be a complex proposition. Using "ideal type" as theoretical support, this book can extract a fundamental cultural "nature" of Chinese universities, among the various cultural character phenomena, and establish a logical connection between traditional Chinese culture and Chinese universities. At the same time, it is also conducive for showing a basic standpoint that although the arguments in this book highlight and emphasize the important role of traditional Chinese culture in the cultural character of Chinese universities, it does not deny the influence of other factors or other cultural connotations within it. Therefore, the "ideal type" is a particularly important research method for the present study.

Notes

1. Shi Z. *Jiaoyuxue De Wenhua Xingge*. Taiyuan: Shanxi Education Press, 1999. pp. 355–356.
2. Weber, M. the Protestant Ethic and the Spirit of Capitalism. Trans, Ma Qiyan et al. Beijing: Peking University Press, 2012: 182.
3. Ibid: 87.
4. Ibid: 17.
5. Flexner, A. *Universities: American, English, German*. Trans. Xu Hui, Chen Xiaofei. Hangzhou: Zhejiang Education Publishing Group, 2002: 2.
6. Ibid: 30.
7. Jin, Y. *The Idea of a University*. Beijing: Joint Publishing, 2008: 6.
8. Chen, P. *Daxue Hewei*. Beijing: Peking University Press, 2006: 3.
9. Ibid: 185.
10. Chen, P. *Zhongguo Daxue Shijiang*. Shanghai: Fudan Press, 2002: 8.

11. Liu, H. Chuantong Wenhua Yu Zhongguo Daxue De Tese. *Journal of Qingdao Institute of Chemical Technology (Social Sciences)*. 1999(2): 12, 10.
12. Shils, E. *Tradition*. Trans. Fu, K. and Lv L. Shanghai: Shanghai People's Press, 2009. Translator's Foreword: 2.
13. Yan, G. *Shidu Daxue: Zuzhi Wenhua De Shijiao*. Beijing: Educational Science Publishing House, 2002. Abstract.
14. Zhang, Y. *Wenhua Shiye Zhong De Gaodeng Jiaoyu*. Nanjing: Nanjing Normal University Press, 1999. Introduction.
15. Gao, G. *Xiandai Daxue Zhidu Yanjin De Wenhua Luoji*. Qingdao: China Ocean University Press, 2007. Introduction.
16. Hayhoe, R. E. S. *China's Universities, 1895–1995: A Century of Cultural Conflict*. Trans, Xu Jieying. Beijing: Educational Science Publishing House, 2000.
17. Chen, P. *Zhongguo Daxue Shijiang*. Shanghai: Fudan Press, 2002: 5.
18. Fan, Y. *Dual Origin and System Formation*. Wuhan: Huazhong University of Science & Technology Press, 2011.
19. Wang, S. Moushi Yu Moudao: Zhongguo Daxue Linian Zhi Jueze. *Journal of Shenyang Teachers College*. 2012(1): 5–7.
20. Ru, N. & Yan, G. Moshi De Zhuanhuan Yu Wenhua De Chongtu: Dui Zhongguo Daxue Banxue Linian Xiandaihua Jincheng De Sikao. *Tsinghua Journal of Education*. 2012(3): 1–7.
21. Liu, H. Chuantong Wenhua Yu Zhongguo Daxue De Tese. *Journal of Qingdao Institute of Chemical Technology (Social Sciences)*. 1999(2): 10–13.
22. Pang, R. Zhongguo Daxue Jiaoyu Guojihua Yu Minzuhua De Guanxi Pingxi. *China Electric Power Education*. 2012(23): 3–4.
23. Wang, J. Huaren Daxue Linian Yu Zhongguo Daxue Gaige. *Journal of Jimei University*. 2005(3): 28.
24. Sui, Y. *Xuefu Zhihun: Zhongwai Zhuming Daxue Xiaozhang Jiaoyu Linian*. Nanchang: Jiangxi Education Publishing House, 2001: 28.
25. Tu, Y. *Zhong Guo Gao Deng Jiao Yu Shi Lun*. Wuhan: Hubei Education Publishing House, 2002: 331.
26. He, L. Cong Liang Qichao De 'Lun Junzi' Tan Dangqian Zhongguo Daxue Jingshen De Chongzu. Chuangxin Yanjiu. 2012(10): 14–15.
27. Huang, C. Rujia Wenhua: Zhongguo Daxue De Jingshen Zuobiao. *Education Research Monthly*. 2009(2): 90–92.
28. Tu, Y. Wenming Bentuhua Yu Daxue. *Journal of Higher Education*. 1998(6): 6–7.
29. Wang, J. Cong Zhongguoshi Daxue Dao Daxue De Zhongguo Shiji. *Modern University Education*. 2008(1): 26.
30. Zhang, J. & Fang, H. Daxue Moshi De Yanjiu Zongshu. *Jiaoyu Yu Kaoshi*. 2012(5): 55.
31. Wang, H. Bentuhua Yu Guojihua: Zhongguo Daxue Moshi De Jiannan Xuanze. *Higher Education of Science*. 2013(5): 2–3.
32. Wu, L. & Jiang, N. Zhongguo Daxue Moshi: Suqiu, Kunjingy Yu Goujian Lujing. Jianghai Academic Journal. 2013(2): 218.
33. Zheng, W. & Chen, W. Woguo Gaodeng Jiaoyu Fazhan De Duowei Tese: Zhongguo Moshi Tansuo. *Educational Research*. 2012(7): 71–76.
34. Gu, M. Jiaoyu Da Cidian. Shanghai: Shanghai Educational Publishing House, 1998: 212.
35. Clark, B. Perspectives on Higher Education: Eight Disciplinary and Comparative Views. Trans. Wang Chengxu. Hangzhou: Zhejiang Education Publishing House. 1988: 24.
36. Shao, H. *Zhongguo Wenhua Yanjiu Shinian*. Beijing: People's Publishing House. 2003: 413.

37. Liang, S. *Dongxi Wenhua Ji Qi Zhexue*. Shijiazhuang: Hebei Education Press, 1996: 33.
38. Liang, S. *Zhongguo Wenhua Zhi Yaoyi*. Shijiazhuang: Hebei Education Press, 1996: 237.
39. Qian, M. Wenhua Yu Shenghuo. Taiwan: Taiwan Letian Publishing House. 1963.
40. Gu, M. *Zhongguo Jiaoyu De Wenhua Jichu*. Taiyuan: Shanxi Education Press, 2004: 59.
41. Liu, M. *Dashi Yu Chuantong: Zhongguo Wenhua Yu Chuantong 40 Xiaojiang*. Beijing: China Youth Publishing Group. 2007: 5.
42. Liu, Y. & Lv, S. *Zhongguo Wenhua Shiliu Jiang*. Beijing: Changzheng Publishing House. 2008: 28.
43. Shi, Z. Jiaoyuxue De Wenhua Xingge. Taiyuan: Shanxi Education Press, 1999: 187–188.

Chapter 1

Cultural Roots of Chinese Universities

In the modern era, the influence of the eastward spread of Western culture led to the quick development and founding of Chinese universities. This process was called "the triumph of European universities." However, modern Chinese universities are still first of all "Chinese" universities, since they are rooted in Chinese soil. They can't exist completely devoid of Chinese traditions. There is a solid historical and cultural foundation for the triumph of European universities in China, but the root of Chinese universities still lies in Chinese culture. This is the fundamental reason for the formation of the cultural characteristics of Chinese universities.

Section 1: Chinese culture and Chinese universities

The proposition of "the cultural character of Chinese universities" involves two core concepts" 1) Chinese culture, and 2) Chinese universities. The former is the inner building block of Chinese universities' cultural character, while the latter is the outer, subjective product of construction. The "Chinese culture" in this book is a concept of the past. That is, traditional Chinese culture, the totality of Chinese social customs and ideologies, spanned from the fall of the *Zhou* dynasty to the abdication of the last emperor of the *Qing* dynasty (when using the 1911 Xinhai Revolution as a marker). Spatially speaking, it differs from non-Chinese culture, especially Western culture. It contains a special connotation of why China is China, as well as an inner logic on why a Chinese university is called a Chinese university.

Strictly speaking, the term Chinese university in the present study is not a spatial or temporal concept. It has clearly changed meaning from the past to the present, and the course of interaction between China and the West. From an objective point of view, if we take the founding of the Imperial University of Peking in 1898 as its beginning, it has only been a century since Chinese universities adapted Western ideas. From the viewpoint of internal traditions, Chinese universities are rooted in Chinese culture, therefore, to a certain extent, they contain the idea of "*Daxue,*" the traditional Chinese perception of higher education. From this angle, the arguments of "a century of Chinese universities" versus "millenniums of Chinese universities" are both unilateral yet legitimate, and this is exactly where the uniqueness of Chinese universities lie – they were never a unified concept.

Using "Chinese culture" and "Chinese university" as core concepts, the present study centers its discussion around the relationship between them, in an attempt to understand and demonstrate the role of Chinese culture in the shaping of Chinese universities' cultural character from a historical perspective. Due to the complexity of history and the tacit nature of cultural characteristics that are hard to verify, this book might only be able to tackle certain aspects of this question by meticulously using "Webber's magnifying glass." It might also fail to discuss it with a full and comprehensive manner, or view the question in a much too understanding and sympathetic way, wearing "Kant's glasses," and fail to initiate a strictly rational and objective discussion.

1. The Key Ideas of Chinese Culture

"Culture" is a complex concept, indeed. However, to talk about Chinese culture, it is vital to deal with it. Some scholars claim that the definition of "culture" alone can be a discipline – Cultural Orismology – the study of the backgrounds, thoughts and reasons of the differences behind the formation of various cultural definitions. This claim is, of course, made humorously, but it still reflects the current disparity of culture's definition in academia. This situation arises because firstly, culture itself is mysterious. People are too used to it to realize its existence and culture is usually taken for granted. Therefore, culture has become a "senseless sense." It can be explained in every way, yet none of them seem like a full explanation. As a result, in academia, the number of definitions for "culture" keeps increasing, with a decrease in their internal consistency.

Secondly, the persons who define culture have different cultural understandings affected by various factors, from their socio-cultural backgrounds, academic specializations, to their own cultural accomplishments. Even their gender, preferences and personalities might affect their perspectives on culture. Therefore, it seems that the definition of culture can be accepted if it sounds logical or self-justifiable.

Another term that is similar and easily mixed up with "culture" is "civilization." It is generally believed that civilization addresses the outer, material aspects, while culture tends to refer to the inner, spiritual aspects. Civilization can spread and be accepted by another civilization, but culture can only generate through the accumulation of a nation's inner spirit.[1]

The present study sticks to the inward, spiritual feature of culture, and will not give any operational definition because firstly, as mentioned above, the definitions of culture are already plural, the present study cannot and does not aim to surpass these numerous definitions. Secondly, the present study does not specialize in cultural studies, therefore there is no need to pull out another definition for culture. Instead, it will try to understand the concept of culture based on the already existing definitions made by previous studies.

There are three common ideas of Chinese culture. They are summarized as follows:

1) Based on the Classical School of thought, Chinese culture equals to Confucian culture. It is believed that Confucian thought of ethical standards is the foundation of Chinese culture. Confucius is the center of Chinese culture, or even of Chinese history. Confucian thought has remained dominant in China for thousands of years, even though there was a period of *Baijia Zhengming* (Contention of a Hundred Schools of Thought) in ancient times.
2) Based on the time scale, Chinese culture is regarded as "traditional Chinese culture." This lasted from the *Zhou* dynasty to the downfall of the *Qing* dynasty, including schools of thought like Confucianism, Taoism and Mohism. The outer nationality and independence and the inner amalgamation and complementarity of Chinese culture are underlined in this discourse, emphasizing its historical superiority. Furthermore, it is believed that in the recent century, with the invasion of Western culture, the weaknesses of Chinse culture started to show. As a result, it can no longer be regarded as "Chinese culture," as traditional Chinese culture is shattered, if not was completely lost over the recent century.
3) Based on spatial differences, Chinese culture is believed to include both domestic traditional Chinese culture and foreign cultures that influenced China (mainly Western cultures in the modern era). This discourse emphasized the strong assimilatory power of Chinese culture. The idea that Chinese culture is not lost, instead, it is supplemented by Western cultures, although the former posed a shock to Chinese culture in the modern era. Therefore, so long as none of the cultures that exist on Chinese soil can escape the fate of assimilation, they can all be regarded as "Chinese culture."

The three ideas above show three different cultural views from different perspectives, and each demonstrates one side of a key feature of Chinese culture. Each tap into key concepts, such as Confucian culture, traditional culture and modern Western culture.

Centering around these three core concepts, the present study understands Chinese culture as, temporally speaking, a predominantly Confucian culture that spans from the *Zhou* dynasty to the abdication of the last *Qing* emperor (taking the 1911 *Xinhai* Revolution as a marker). Spatially speaking, a culture that differs from the Western culture – Western culture is but a background of Chinese historical vicissitude in the modern era, instead of a part of Chinese culture. This is a rough operational definition of Chinese culture, to set a certain limit to the use of the term "Chinese culture" in the present study and to avoid ambiguity.

However, what is the true essence of Chinese culture? How can we understand Chinese culture? These questions are far more important than a formal definition. The past is already gone, we cannot go back. However, this also provides an opportunity for later generations to objectively perceive traditional culture. Ruth Benedict sees the end of the religious era in the West as an essential prerequisite to the start of modern religious studies and remarked that religions can only be discussed objectively when they are no longer a major influence on our culture.[2] The traditional Chinese culture has become a part of history instead of a realistic problem after the downfall of the Qing dynasty. We are still deeply influenced by it, but as the temporal difference between traditional and contemporary society becomes more apparent, this influence might tone down.

The Republic of China was established after the fall of the Qing dynasty, and this became the first era in China when traditional culture could be discussed as history. Great scholars in the field of Chinese cultural studies emerged during this period. An excerpt of Liu Mengxi's *Zhongguo Xiandai Xueshu Yaolve* (*An Overview on Modern Chinese Academia*) comprehensively explained the unprecedented relationship between great scholars of the Republic of China and Chinese traditions:

> The achievement of modern Chinese academia in the May Fourth Period made us believe that it was yet another peak and a flourishing period for Chinese academia after Emperor Jiaqing and Qianlong in the mid-*Qing* dynasty. The master scholars during that time – their personalities, their studies, their achievements, their stories – should be remembered by the later generations. Their academic works were broad and profound in the constructions of knowledge, while at the same time glimmered in the light of rationality of the era. These works can be considered as modern academic classics in terms of their pioneering significance and spiritual value. One can even say that the top tier scholars during that time have both inherited the past and inaugurated the present, and they remain unprecedented in terms of personal intellectual accomplishments. They were the unprecedented pioneers because they benefited from the historical era when they could communicate with new ideas from the West – an opportunity the scholars during mid-*Qing* could not have had. They were also the unparalleled masters, their reserves of traditional knowledge, that

is, their heredity of culture and understanding of traditional Chinese studies were incomparable to contemporary scholars.[3]

What I was trying to do by quoting from Liu is not to "borrow" from his ideas, but rather, to expand on his claims and change their angle. The scholars from the Republic of China had extraordinary advantages in terms of traditional Chinese cultural studies – they were far more objective than mid-Qing scholars, and far more educated by traditional culture than contemporary scholars who are relatively more distant from the past. Based on this, some classic works left by master scholars of the Republic of China are selected in the following section as important texts for understanding "what is Chinese culture," in an attempt to further understand the key ideas of Chinese culture.

a) Social Perspective: The Uniqueness of Chinese Culture – Liang Shuming's Discussion on the Key Ideas to Chinese Culture

"Culture is everything that we rely on in our lives. This is to say, *culture* is something solid. The original meaning of culture should include everything, including the economy and politics."[4] This is Liang's definition of culture in his book *Zhongguo Wenhua Yaoyi* (*The Key Idea to Chinese Culture*). In short, Liang believes that culture originates from life, and is something solid, emphasizing the reality of culture.

In terms of Chinese culture, Liang pointed out that, "In the recent century of globalization, China has been changed by the West to such an extent that it has almost lost its tradition. Therefore, things that remain unchanged in the influence of this century of upheavals were regarded as Chinese culture."[5] It can be seen that the Chinese culture that Liang talked about was, in fact, traditional Chinese culture, in tune with the second idea of Chinese culture mentioned above.

In this book, Liang started with Liu Yezheng's "Three questions on Chinese culture," and subsequently summarized 14 key features of Chinese culture form different scholars' opinions. The strong uniqueness of Chinese culture was considered as exclamatory. "The strong Chinese cultural personality makes people think of its sturdy foundation – the reason why what it emitted was so great and magnificent. There must be a meaning or spirit in it, from the root to the branch, the surface to the kernel."[6] The essential significance behind this feature, as according to Liang, is the general feature of Chinese culture – "the precocity of Chinese culture" – what the "key idea" was referred to in the title of his book. Liang's discourse on Chinese culture's precocity was first brought up and analyzed in his earlier work *Dongxi Wenhua Ji Qi Zhexue* (Eastern and Western Culture and Philosophy). In summary, it discussed the following: the stages of development of culture is a process from the surface to the core. It was supposed to be based on physical culture, followed by the development of the spiritual world after the material life becomes abundant. This exactly the development process of Western culture – it spread out from the body, therefore its survival tools developed first, and what is now pursued after, is spiritual development. However, in contrast, Chinese culture developed from the heart (rationality) and exerted its force towards the inner aspects. As a result, Chinese ethics were well-developed, forming a precocious spiritual world, while the material world lagged. Therefore, Chinese culture is precocious compared to Western culture. In reality, the foundation of traditional culture is *Wulun* (the Five Ethics). Its inner spiritual cultivation is been underlined, therefore China was claimed to be the country of rites, the development of the business economy and science was neglected, if not suppressed. Consequently, China was ravaged by the Western world due to its economic backwardness in the modern era.

All in all, Liang was trying to search for the inner spiritual key idea of Chinese culture based on its uniqueness, taking "Chinese family" as the starting point, and initiating the discussion with the 14 key features of Chinese culture. Liang's argument is layered and paced from the surface to the core. We need to understand that the Chinese culture in Liang's eyes is an inevitable outcome of history, a fruit that is precocious yet still underdeveloped.

b) Philosophical Perspective: The Ideological Content of Chinese Culture – Feng Yu-Lan's Discussion on Chinese Philosophy

"The place which philosophy has occupied in Chinese civilization has been comparable to that of religion in other civilizations."[7] To Feng Yu-Lan, Western culture revolves around religion, while Chinese culture had philosophy, instead of religion, at its center. From this perspective, the studies of Western religion and Chinese philosophy are equivalent to the studies of Western and Chinese culture, respectively. Feng's book, *A Short History of Chinese Philosophy*, is at the same a book on Chinese philosophy and Chinese culture. The spirit of Chinese culture is interpreted using Chinese philosophy, even more so, Feng uses Chinese culture to narrate Chinese philosophy.

In this book, Feng has two basic standpoints: 1) Chinese philosophy underlines the elevation of spiritual states, paying no attention to any real knowledge; 2) schools of philosophy inherited from and were fused with no absolute opposition or mutual exclusiveness, while Confucianism occupied a dominant position

Feng believed that "According to the tradition of Chinese philosophy, its function is not the increase of positive knowledge, but the elevation of the mind – a reaching out for what is beyond the present real world, but for the values that are higher than the moral ones."[8]

Exploring culture through Chinese philosophical traditions, Feng revealed the fundamental feature of Chinese culture – emphasizing its spirit and ethics, neglecting material construction. Feng talked about Confucianism, Mohism, Taoism, and even the School of Names, School of Naturalists, Legalism, and Buddhism. He drew attention to the interconnectivity between the thought of each school and believed that there is no such thing as a distinctive or pure school of thought, be it Confucianism, Taoism, or Mohism. For example, the thought of *Wuwei Er Wubuwei* (Doing nothing that is not in accord with the natural course of nature and the world) belongs to both Taoism and Legalism; there are commonalities between the Confucian idea of *Zhongyong* (the 'mean') and the Taoist idea that "things will reverse to the opposite direction if developed to the extreme;" Neo-Confucianism has even merged with the Buddhist Zen as well as the Naturalist concept of Taoism.

However, on the other hand, the dominance of Confucianism is again emphasized in the discourse of the interconnectivity between Chinese schools of thought. Feng pointed out that Confucianism is the orthodox philosophy of China and it remained dominant until the invasion of modern Western industrialism, which transformed the economic foundation of Chinese living.[9] To Feng, the establishment of Confucian orthodoxy is a result of the solid foundation of the Chinese family system that was given rise by the unique geographic environment and economic conditions of China.

In a nutshell, in *Zhongguo Zhexue Jianshi*, Feng talked about Chinese culture from the perspective of Chinese philosophy, from Confucianism, followed by Mohism, Taoism, School of Names, School of Naturalists, Legalism, Buddhism, all the way until Neo-Taoism and Neo-Confucianism. This is "thought on the thoughts," which interpreted the profoundness of Chinese culture from a metaphysical perspective. Chinese culture as it is to Feng is a process of the development and fusion of different schools of thought, an elevation of the minds instead of a gain in positive knowledge.

c) Historical Perspective: The Historical Continuity of Chinese Culture – Qian Mu's Discussion on Chinese Cultural History

"What is Chinese Culture? This question has to be answered from not only from philosophical, but also historical perspectives."[10] Qian Mu remarked that "Chinese culture is manifested in China's entire historical process. There is no way to talk about culture without referring to history. We should uncover the truth of Chinese culture from the objective aspects of the entire Chinese history."[11] Qian approached Chinese culture neither sociologically nor philosophically, instead, he used a historical standpoint. Therefore, Qian stressed continuity on the scale of time in his definition of culture. "Human life is what we usually referred to as 'culture.' Life itself is the various aspects of culture. However, these aspects of life do not lay on a flat cross-section of time – the continuity of time has to be added in... By adding in the continuity of a long period, it turns into 'living.'"[12] From there, Qian pointed out that "Our race and nation have lived for five thousand years."[13] In his book, *Zhongguo Wenhuashi Daolun* (*An Introduction to Chinese Cultural History*), Qian divided Chinese culture into four epochs with their characteristics, starting from the first emergence of Chinese history. These included the pre-*Qin* epoch when the development of religion and philosophy took the upper hand; From *Qin* to *Tang* dynasty, when the development of politics and economy was the main focus; From *Tang* to late *Qing*, when the development of literature and the arts was most prominent; And finally now, the fourth epoch, the development has turned to science and industries. Judging from the above division of epochs, the "Chinese culture" Qian talked about was more than traditional culture, as it included the current (The Republic of China's) culture, quite similar to the third concept of Chinese culture mentioned in the previous section. However, Qian's emphasis remained on the inner integrity and historical continuity of Chinese culture. It was focused on an inner character of Chinese culture incomparable with others, even though he divided Chinese history into different epochs.

A rhetorical comparison was jokingly made by Qian when he was comparing Chinese and Western cultures. He said that European history is a continuous drama played by different theoretical troupes – a constant iteration, from Greece to Rome, followed by the northern barbarians. What about the Chinese, then? Ever since the remote antiquity when different sage kings took control of the land, the drama is always played by the Chinese.[14]

Therefore, to Qian, Chinese cultural history is a "consubstantial" process of transformation and continuation in the same stages, whereby Western cultural history is a "substantial" change and development from one stage to another. Qian remained exceptionally calm in the wave of anti-traditional thoughts, probably due to his unique cultural identity. He remarked that "the future of our culture should be saved by our power from within. It is a given that we should learn from new sciences from the West, yet it should not affect our vitality. Our own life should be contained and preserved."[15] His remark was indeed sincere and precise. Qian took history as his position and insisted that the Chinese culture is "a whole" with dynastical iterations being only a process of cultural amalgamation throughout his book, as the main characters are always Chinese. To Qian, Chinese culture meant the development and continuation of history, containing mainly self-transformation.

In fact, there are countless academic works regarding Chinese culture produced both before and after the founding of the People's Republic of China. Apart from the books mentioned above, Liu Yezheng's studies on Chinese cultural history, Li Zehou's studies on Chinese ideological history, and Fei Xiaotong's studies in the field of cultural anthropology could all be regarded as masterpieces. I am not going to elaborate on them in the present book. With the three examples illustrated above, Liang Shuming's Chinese cultural studies based on social reality and emphasized the uniqueness of Chinese cultural characters from its surface to the core. Feng Yu-Lan's studies on Chinese philosophical history underlined the ideological content of Chinese cultural history from "here" to "there." While Qian Mu took a historical approach in his studies on Chinese cultural history and demonstrated the continuity of Chinese cultural characters.

Though their studies were conducted from different perspectives, they share certain similarities: 1) the emphasis of Chinese culture's inner spirit – bringing about the profoundness of Chinese thoughts; 2) the acknowledgment of the great differences between Chinese and Western cultures – showing Chinese culture's distinct qualities; 3) the recognition of Chinese culture's superiority – improving the practical value of studies on Chinese culture. In conclusion, Chinese culture is a unique social phenomenon, a continual history, as well as a set of deep and profound philosophical thoughts.

2. The Abstrusity of the Chinese University

One must understand what "*daxue* 大学 (university)" is before talking about Chinese universities. And before that, it is necessary to understand the concept of science. At first sight, "university" seems closely related to "science." In "*Kexue* 科学 (Science): (it was defined as) a concept that changes from the past to the present and with the interaction between China and the West." In one of Feng Tianyu's speeches made in Wuhan University, the concept of "*kexue*" was the center of the discussion. Feng described "*kexue*" as follows:

> "A lot of academic works and dictionaries about loan words listed "*kexue*" as a word with Japanese origin – a word created in modern Japan and borrowed by Chinese during the late Qing and the early People's Republic of China. However, this is a common misconception. In fact, the word "*kexue*" is not a new word created by the Japanese; it has a long history in ancient Chinese classics. What the Japanese scholars did during the Meiji era was to borrow an ancient Chinese term, inherited and extended its meaning, in order to translate the Western word 'science.' This borrowed word was again imported into China during the late Qing and early Chinese Republican time to become '*kexue*' as it is understood in the contemporary era, that is, 'science.' The travel across time and space of the term '*kexue*' is a typical example of the changes of meanings of concepts from the past to the present and with the interaction between China and the West."[16]

If the term "*kexue*" is substituted by "*daxue*," we can find out that some of the argument still holds: 1) "*Daxue*" is not newly created, but a term with a long history in ancient classics; 2) What the Chinese scholars did during the late Qing and early People's Republic of China was borrow an ancient Chinese term, inherit and extend its meaning, in order to translate the Western word 'university;' 3) "*Daxue*" is a typical example of the changes of meanings of concepts from the past to the present and with the interaction between China and the West. These three points are going to be discussed in detail in the following paragraphs, in order to explore the profound historical heritage of the Chinese term "*daxue*," how well its meanings were inherited and extended, and what has been lost during the process of the past-present transformation and the China-West interaction.

First of all, it is indisputable that the word "*daxue*" has existed in China for a very long time. "Characters similar to '*daxue*' can be found on the oracle bones, so it can be confirmed that this term is already been established during the Xia and Shang dynasties."[17] It was untraceable what exactly *daxue* was back then, but it can be determined that the exact term was already in use. During the Spring and Autumn and Warring States eras, the term "*daxue*" consisted of two, more or less fixed meanings: 1) "*daxue* education" was compared to "*xiaoxue* education," referring to higher education in the ancient times. There are two layers of meanings regarding "*daxue* education" – "education after the age of 15" and "education of profound knowledge if one is 'dedicated to learning.'" There was an ancient saying that goes, "After the age of 15, the grown-up student would determine his aspiration of learning. He would then enter *daxue* to learn about the classics and method." Therefore, *daxue* education can be understood as "education after the age of 15" – what Zhu Xi annotated as "*daren*'s (adult's) learning." This idea can be traced back to Confucius who once said, "I became dedicated to learning at the age of 15" (ref *The Analects of Confucius, Good Government*). Therefore, it could be deduced that Confucius' higher education started at the age of 15. By "dedicated to learning," when one starts to learn profound knowledge – this has been called "the way of *daxue*." Zhu Xi once said, "the contents of *xiaoxue* (primary learning) is shallow, and shall only be applied to lesser matters", while "the substance of *daxue* is profound, which is used to accomplish greater causes." The opening line of *Daxue* (Great Learning), a Confucian classic, made it clear that "What the Great Learning teaches, is to illustrate illustrious virtue; to renovate the people, and to rest in the highest excellence." 2) Another meaning of *daxue* refers specifically to "*taixue*," an official higher education institution first found in the Han dynasty. The institution teaches primarily Confucian knowledge, as compared to private institutions. This concept is in tune with the definition of *daxue* in *Ciyuan* (*The Origin of Words*). In *Ciyuan, daxue* is "where aristocrats" children used to study." *Daxue* was first established under the rule of Emperor Wu of the Han dynasty. A famous government official, Dong Zhongshu, suggested Emperor Wu to "rise *taixue*," in order to realize his aspiration to rule everything under Heaven with Confucian principles. In the first chapter of *Duice* (Strategies), Dong suggested to "(Great rulers in ancient times) to establish *daxue* to educate the country, implement schools to educate the towns, infiltrate the people with benevolence, train the people with righteousness, constrain the people with moral codes. Therefore, only light penalties were required as the people were stopped from wrongdoings, to begin with. The edification was effective and people had good conventions." (ref. *Book of Han*) The word *daxue* here referred to *taixue*. As for the use of "*tai* (great)" and "*da* (big)" in ancient Chinese language, Duan Yucai remarked, "what is so great that '*da*' cannot suffice must be described by '*tai*' in the later generations. For example, '*dazai* (grand chancellor)' is conventionally referred to as '*taizai*;' '*dazi* (the crown prince),' '*taizi*;' '*dawang* (great emperor)' of the Zhou dynasty, '*taiwang*.'" (ref. annotation of the character *tai* of the section *shui* of *Shuowen*

Jiezi Zhu (*Shuowen Jiezi and Its Annotations*) Therefore, *taixue* is the conventional name of *daxue*, while the *daxue* is the proper name. According to Dong Zhongshu, *taixue* aims to cultivate *shi* (noble scholars) for the enlightenment of everything under Heaven. This is more of a political idea, differing greatly from the *daxue* proposed by Confucius.

The paragraph above briefly summarized two specific meanings of *daxue* in ancient China: 1) "Education after the age of 15" and "education of profound knowledge," the stage after *xiaoxue*; 2) *Taixue*, the official higher education institution, as compared with private education institutions.

Tu Youguang once made a comprehensive summary of *daxue*'s meaning in ancient China, namely: 1) Life-long learning of grown-ups; 2) Adult education; 3) Great knowledge; 4) Higher education institution.[18] While the emphasis leans towards the third and fourth meanings. In the present book, *daxue* refers primarily to higher education and higher education institutions. The former includes what Tu summarized as "life-long learning of the grown-ups," "adult education" and "great knowledge," while the latter refers to "higher education institutions."

Secondly, in modern China, the meaning of *daxue* was inherited and extended to translate to the Western word "university," endowing *daxue* with new meanings. The modern concept of the university would not exist without the "Eastward Spread of Western Culture" during the late Ming and early Qing dynasties, or without the Opium War in the late Qing dynasty. When the Western "university" took root in China, the Chinese started to consider its proper translation. A similar way of translating "science" was adopted to translate the European "university" – using a long-existing term, *daxue* translated "university," in an attempt to open a new chapter of Chinese history for higher education. The paradigm of the construction of the Chinese history of science and technology is "extracting traditional knowledge of science and technology from ancient classics with reference to modern scientific knowledge, while at the same time using Western scientific knowledge of the same kind to corroborate with Chinese findings."[19] This is also how the modern *daxue* came about, by extracting commonalities from the traditional concept of *daxue* regarding the Western concept of the university and replacing the original meaning of *daxue* with its Western meaning. In a nutshell, using *daxue* as a translation of "university" is both a result of the Eastward Spread of Western Culture and an independent choice of Chinese culture itself, to continue the thousand-year history of *daxue*. Therefore, this is beyond just a simple question of translation, but in fact a contest of discourse's rights. The scholars subconsciously wanted to give the ancient *daxue* a modern identity as a "university." Just as the question of whether the discipline of science existed in ancient China, "it is not a historical question, but a philosophical question. It cannot be solved via historical research, as it represents a cultural strategy and standpoint."[20] From this point of view, the hot debate on whether Chinese universities have existed for a century or a millennium is also merely a matter of a cultural standpoint, it is a philosophical question instead of a historical one.

Therefore, there is no point arguing whether "a century of Chinese universities" or "a millennium of Chinese universities" is right or wrong, as these two statements are not presented in the same context. "A century of Chinese universities" is placed within the historical context, from the real perspective of university's organization and system; while "a millennium of Chinese universities" is placed within the philosophical context – it is to be understood from a cultural perspective, based on the spirit of a university. After this idea is understood, a lot of hot topics of discussion in Chinese academia can be automatically resolved, such as the "Three Questions about Chinese Universities:" Does China have universities? What about the century of Chinese university? When did the earliest university emerge in China?

All in all, the Chinese term *daxue* is a typical example of the changes in meaning from the past to the present and its interaction between China and the West. This change and transformation of meaning is ingenious, however, it comes with a price. The concept of *daxue* inevitably ends up in a self-confusion, which is also the exact reason why the "Three Questions about Chinese Universities" exist. From this point of view, if *daxue* was not borrowed to translate the word "university," or rather if "university" was directly transliterated, there would not be so many pointless academic debates. On the other hand, just as "using modern science to measure and evaluate the traditional knowledge system is like inlaying precious pearls of traditional science and technology into the rigid frame of modern science. It can help us to understand traditional knowledge from a whole new angle indeed, yet to 'tradition' itself, it might be a misunderstanding".[21]

There was a strong emotional factor behind the adoption of *daxue* as the translation for "university." However, from deep within, it still shows that Western universities were regarded as the orthodox, making us misunderstand, even forget about tradition. When we closely examine our contemporary academia, we can see that the mainstream idea regarding Chinese universities is "a century of Chinese university." This is a piece of indirect evidence that the concept of *daxue* is gradually being constrained by the framework of a "modern higher education institution." One can even conclude that *daxue* has already lost its traditional meaning and became a mere antonomasia for "university." In *Xiandai Hanyu Cidian* (*Dictionary of Modern Chinese Words*), *daxue* was defined as "a tertiary institution. In China, it usually refers to comprehensive universities." This is a sad sign that the traditional meaning of *daxue* is gradually being lost. Some once described modern Chinese *daxue* as "new wine in an old bottle," now that we realized that its real meaning is to pour out the old wine to fill in a glass of new wine, we can only see the wine bottle and the new wine.

The paragraphs above examined the term *kexue* to discuss *daxue*, and preliminarily studied the development of *daxue* concept in China, as well as its pros and cons. Chinese universities, specifically, is not only a theoretical concept but also a real problem. The name *daxue* can be determined with the express provision, however, it is very difficult to define the substance of a Chinese university. Different concepts about Chinese universities

can be drawn based on different standpoints. The paragraphs below is a brief summary of several basic and representative "Chinese universities" concepts in modern times:
1) Defining Chinese universities as *taixue*. According to Chen Pingyuan, many scholars positioned the historical prototype of Chinese universities as ancient *taixue* due to "national dignity." Ji Xianlin held this view when he narrated the history of Peking University:

> "The education heritage of China dates back to *Taixue*, followed by *Guozijian* (Imperial College after the Sui dynasty), Imperial University of Peking, and finally Peking University. The history is continued without interruption. This is a unique phenomenon in global education history – something that the Chinese should be very proud of."[22]

Hu Shi, too, held the same view in his talk, *The Fiftieth Anniversary of Peking University*. He claimed that Peking University is the official heir of *Taixue*. If one wants to show how long the Peking University history is, he can trace it back to the fifth year of the Yuanshuo Era under Emperor Wu of Han dynasty's reign (124 B.C.) when Gongsun Hong pleaded to set up 50 students/apprentice positions for the *boshi* (the doctor).[23] Feng Yu-Lan also made a clear argument in his essay, *My Studenthood in Peking University*, that "I believe the history of Peking University started in the Han dynasty." Using the idea that Peking University originated from *Taixue* as evidence, people holding the idea of "a millennium of Chinese university" underlined the historical continuity of Chinese higher education from the past to the present. Cultural legitimacy surpassed systematic legitimacy.

2) Discussing Chinese universities with reference to Western universities. This is a conventional belief in the modern and contemporary era. The differences between the past and present are meant to be highlighted, to emphasize the China-West differences. Cai Yuanpei, a prestigious educator from the People's Republic of China spoke about Chinese universities in his article '*Daxue Jiaoyu* (*University Education*):'

> "University education is what students receive after they graduate from high schools. The subjects are humanities, science, theology, law, medicine, agronomy, engineering, business, pedagogy, music, art, military, etc. The first five subjects, except for theology, are universal subjects taught in every university. While in the old system, humanities and science are combined to be a subject called 'philosophy.' German-speaking countries are still using this old system… There was once a form of the university in the history of our country conventionally called *Taixue*; It was originally called *Shangxiang*, followed by *Biyong*, and then *Guozijian*. Its purpose was similar as the universities today. There were students, lecturers; different subjects were taught; a scoring system was implemented; one

> had to meet certain criteria so that they could be admitted; an academic degree could be attained. Its way of organization was very similar to the universities in the present. However, in the recent era, the so-called *Guozijian* was already titular. Therefore, our universities in the present are the direct imitations of the European university system, instead of the evolution of the ancient *Taixue*."[24]

From a realistic perspective, Cai believed that "our universities in the present" were the result of adopting and imitating European university systems. Inheriting the same viewpoint, Chen Pingyuan also expressed something similar in his book *Zhongguo Daxue Bainian* (*Hundred Years of Chinese Universities*): In the twentieth-century China, the westernization of Chinese higher education was at its most severe. Chinese universities nowadays have a value orientation and basic pathway of development towards becoming a University instead of *Taixue*.[25] At the same time, he pointed out that the exact problem of Chinese university education in this century is that it has successfully adopted the Western education system, yet it did not inherit the ancient Chinese "substance of *daxue*."[26] King Yeo-Chi also stated in his *The Idea of a University* that, "Peking University was the beginning of modern Chinese universities, however, the system and spirit of Peking University were borrowed from Western universities. Therefore, modern Chinese universities were a 'horizontal adaptation' instead of 'vertical inheritance.'"[27]

3) Dual arguments regarding Chinese universities. Mei Yiqi, the president of National Tsinghua University in The Republic of China, was one of the first scholars to hold a dual argument regarding Chinese universities. This dual argument is more profound and objective than the previous two concepts. In *Daxue Yi Jie* (*An Explanation of University*), he stated that:

> "Chinese university education nowadays, tracing back to its origin, is actually adopted from the West. Therefore, the system is one issue, while the spirit belongs to another. System-wise, there was no similar organization or institution in Chinese education history; Spirit-wise, it is universal in the experiences of civilized human societies – there are things in common. The lives of civilized humans cannot escape the two categories: the self or group, or putting it in another way, the individual or society. The main purpose of education is to enable either the individuals in a group or the groups made up of various individuals to acquire the ways to live securely and peacefully. They can advance further to position and nurture each other, mimic and harbor each other. Then there is no spatial difference between China and the West, and no time difference between the past and the present – everything can be interconnected.
>
> Western university education has some eight or nine hundred years of history. Few can decrypt its goal, however, if we dig in, its origin can be clearly observed.

> That is a Greek life philosophy. And the essence of the Greek life philosophy is to 'know thyself.' How is this different from the substance of our Confucian thoughts? In chapter 14 'Good and Bad Governance' of the Analects, Confucius said, 'Students of old fixed their eyes upon themselves: now they learn with their eyes upon others.' ..."[28]

Differing from how Cai Yuanpei focused on the difference between the past and present Chinese *daxue*, Mei focused more on the commonalities between China and the West. Mei believed that Chinese universities adopted the western system, therefore on the outside, Chinese and Western universities have things in common. At the same time, he also pointed out that there was no difference between the essence of Greek life philosophy and Confucian thoughts, therefore there was something universal about the inner spirit of Chinese and Western universities. Adopting a dual viewpoint from both history and philosophy to deconstruct the concept of a Chinese university and analyzing the problem of Chinese universities from both ideality and their reality is the unique characteristic of Mei's argument regarding Chinese universities. Currently, *Daxue Yi Jie* has already become a classical title about modern Chinese universities. A lot of statements proposed nowadays can be regarded as annotations of Mei's idea of Chinese universities.

4) Analyzing Chinese universities using university spirit. In the book, *A Study on the Spirits of Chinese University History and Reflection*, an edited version of Chu Zhaohui's Ph.D. dissertation, Chu redefined the concept of Chinese universities. His definition is truly unique. It is quoted as follows:

> "Laying Chinese and Western universities on the same level and measuring them with commonly agreed standards, Chinese university is an educational institution which continued since the Xia, Shang, and Zhou dynasties. Due to various historical reasons, there was no uninterrupted heritage of one specific university. The institution appeared in various forms, showing a dynamic and developing feature. However, to a certain extent, they have all inherited a consistent spirit, including what we called '*xuetong* (education heritage)'. The substance of '*Dao* (the way)' was sought after and re-created. They also share the function of cultivating elite talents and studying the most profound knowledge of their times..."[29]

Differing from Cai's system-based definition of Chinese universities, Chu kept emphasizing the inner spirit of Chinese universities and pointed out that university cannot exist without its spirit. Chu's idea was also different from Mei Yiqi's idea of the commonalities between Chinese and Western university spirits, as he is more interested in the uniqueness of Chinese university spirits instead of their universality. From this point of view, Chu did not take a purely philosophical approach, at least not using universal philosophical ideas as his evidence to demonstrate them.

The present book holds a viewpoint that is different from, yet also related to, the four concepts listed above, the substance of a Chinese university was constructed from two main dimensions, namely the inner (tradition) and the outer (reality). The inner dimension has a deep root in traditional Chinese culture, which refers to the unique cultural character of Chinese universities, and the continuation and development of traditional Chinese higher education. The outer dimension is placed in the social reality of modern China, that is, Chinese universities are the adoption and imitation of Western universities, there are certain universalities between the former and the latter. Basing on the dual connotations of Chinese universities, the history of their cultural characters are also to be narrated, from the outer dimension, the founding of the Imperial University of Peking in 1898 and the inner dimension, from Confucius.

3. *The Relationship between Chinese Culture and Chinese Universities*

Chinese culture and Chinese universities are the two core concepts in the discourse of Chinese culture's characteristics. The reason why the proposition of Chinese universities' cultural characteristics can be established was mainly because of the positive connection and close relationship between Chinese culture and Chinese universities. The present book takes Chinese culture as its basic standpoint, Chinese universities as the research subject, and hackles the process of development of Chinese universities' cultural characteristics in the modern era. In the demonstration of the relationship between the two concepts, Chinese culture is the foundation of Chinese universities, while Chinese universities are the result of Chinese culture. This is the essential connotation of the cultural characteristics of Chinese universities.

a) Chinese Culture as the Foundation for Chinese Universities

In the modern era, we keep emphasizing that Chinese universities are born due to the needs of the times. They emerged in the period of crisis, adopted the Western systems, and were motivated by external sources. However, it is not entirely right to constrain the emergence of Chinese universities in the political and economic aspects, however realistic this might seem. In fact, the emergence and establishment of Chinese universities were not only due to external factors but also because of its cultural characteristics. Therefore, the so-called "adoption" is not a disorderly behavior. What governs the inner order of this adoption is Chinese culture. From this perspective, the reason why Chinese universities are "Chinese universities" is because of the Chinese cultural characteristics, instead of the unstoppable spread of Western culture or the forceful invasion of Western culture in other countries.

In the formation and development of modern Chinese universities, Chinese culture pushed for the modernization of its higher education with its focus on inclusiveness and assimilation.

On one hand, Chinese culture is inclusive towards the idea of "university," therefore Chinse universities were established. The former is inclusive, while the latter is included. The idea of binary opposition is always lacking in Chinese culture, its inclusiveness surpasses any other race or nation in history. What Chinese culture emphasizes is "*tianxia taiping* (peace and order of the world)." Liang Shuming once said that in traditional Chinese thinking, the idea of a "nation" is greatly lacking. No inter-national antagonism could be observed, and it does not behave like a nation at all. Therefore, when modern Western culture invaded, universities started to enter China. The Chinese quickly accepted the idea and actively imitated it, with little hostility. It is obvious that there was a certain degree of political helplessness, yet it was also the result of the Chinese of a highly inclusive Chinese culture. Qian Mu once remarked in his *Zhongguo Wenhuashi Daolun* (An Introduction of Chinese Cultural History):

> China is a relatively culturally-isolated country in the world. However, China kept communicating and interacting with neighboring countries. China has two main westward transportation routes, namely the land route in the Northwest, and the sea route in the Southwest. It was historically proven that the two routes were prosperous, especially during the Han and the Tang dynasties. Moreover, the Chinese are always curious and open-minded about foreign cultures, they are willing to accept and digest them. The new materials from the outside world are taken to nourish their old traditions. The grand idea of "*tian ren he yi* (harmony and unity between the universe and the earthly beings)" is always present in the Chinese minds, they believe that every scenery or value that is strange or new can eventually harmonize and unite into one. This is one of the primary characteristics of Chinese cultural spirit.[30]

That was how Western "universities" came to be established in such an inclusive nation. Without the inclusive attitude within Chinese culture, universities could never be established in China, no matter how unstoppable the spread of Western culture was. This was the basic prerequisite of the universities becoming "Chinese universities."

On the other hand, Chinese culture assimilates "universities," while universities get assimilated. This was the reason why Chinese universities lasted. It was generally believed that being inclusive is as good as being passive, its nature is to compromise, and it is, in fact, harmful to a country's cultural independence. However, Chinese culture has further demonstrated its independence with its great power of assimilation while taking in the Western university.

This great assimilation power is not only where the unique charm of Chinese culture lies, but also the fundamental reason why Chinese universities, as an exotic concept, eventually harmonized and united with Chinese culture. Liang Shuming made a detailed recount of the unique charm of Chinese culture's assimilation power in his book *Zhongguo Wenhua Yaoyi*:

> "When Christianity first spread to China, two distinctive cultures had their first encounter. 'Here' was never changed because of 'there.' Inversely, 'there' has compromised for 'here.' The missionaries accepted the Chinese tradition of ancestors' worship and Confucius' worship, apart from making necessary amendments to the translation of the *New Testament*. These compromises were once reversed due to disagreements and conflicts (in 1742, the Pope banned the Chinese salute), but they were eventually accepted (1939)… The same extended to Buddhism. The Buddhist spirit was contradictive with Chinese filial piety, yet when Buddhism came to China, it was changed by China."[31]

Liang Qichao also made similar remarks:

> "…It is a loss that China is often invaded by the foreigners; it is a gain that the ones that invaded us were soon assimilated. To calculate the gains and the losses, we can find out that the former could make up for the latter, even with a bit of extra (help). As a result, the elements of 'Chineseness' increased. The Chinese idea of '*Tianxia* (Everything under Heaven)' kept expanding."[32]

Deducing from what Liang Shuming said, "universities" joined with Chinese culture and became "Chinese universities." According to Liang Qichao, the intake of "universities" merely added a new element into indigenous Chinese higher education. If the inclusiveness of Chinese culture granted "universities" entry to the country, the assimilation power of Chinese culture has legitimized Chinese universities so that they became lawful residents of the land. The Western idea of the university has grown to become the universities that belong to China.

All in all, Chinese culture is the foundation of Chinese universities. Without Chinese culture's unique inclusiveness and assimilation power, Chinese universities as they are now would never exist.

b) Chinese Universities as the Result of Chinese Culture

Judging from the development process of Chinese universities, it can be observed that Chinese universities were formed under the strong inclusiveness and assimilation of Chinese culture's power, and are still heavily influenced by it. Therefore, it is not only that

Chinese culture gave birth to and shaped Chinese universities, but Chinese universities by themselves also became the tangible entities of Chinese culture.

In conventional thinking, the idea of "*xue er you ze shi* (do well in academics to pursue an official career)" is the most prominent. "There was not a single scholar in China who did not wish to become a government official. They pursued official careers like how others pursue their religions."[33] Scholars in the ancient times used to study for positions in the court right under the emperor's eyes and for a chance to bring honor to their families. This "religious belief" is retained among the contemporary university students' minds. The trend for university graduates to sign up for civil service examinations has, to some extent, demonstrated the traditional Chinese cultural character of "*xue er you ze shi.*" It is no doubt that this trend is one of the reasons held against the utilitarian tendency of contemporary university education, but objectively speaking, there is nothing wrong with pursuing an official career after university graduation. The main problem here is to uncover the sublime educational prospects of "*xiushen* (cultivating morality)" before "*zhiguo* (administering the country)."

System-wise, the gaokao (college entrance examination) system is a significant symbol of the traditional higher education heritage of Chinese universities. Ever since 1977 when gaokao resumed, it has taken an important position in both Chinese education and society as a whole. Just as Liu Haifeng stated, "Limited by tradition and reality, the Chinese have gradually turned gaokao into culture, economy, industry, as well as a grand ritual, a societal activity that concerns many, a routine civil mobilization."[34] That is how uniquely Chinese it is. Liu has given a speech at PKU Education Forum titled *Keju Pingjia Yu Gaokao Gaige* (Imperial Examination Remarks and Gaokao Reform). In this speech, a similarity analysis was conducted between contemporary Chinese gaokao and ancient *keju* (imperial examination). He concluded that:

> "The first similarity is the debate on whether to select talents via examinations. A lot of problems were exposed during the application of the imperial examination system, just like how contemporary gaokao gives rise to problems such as exam-oriented education. This debate regarding imperial examination is highly similar to what we have regarding gaokao.
>
> The second is the scientific experience gained during the implementation of imperial examinations, which can, in turn, inspire us now – the measures and methods to prevent cheating. This similarity is easy to understand, as cheating might happen during any examination.
>
> The third is the debate on whether to admit candidates based on examination results or regions. The way imperial examination developed from free competition to a fixed number of enrollments based on regions is very similar to gaokao today.

> The fourth is how the rule of thesis proposition develops and evolves. The imperial examination is highly similar to gaokao, in a way that they both went from diversity to unity – how the examined contents and subjects changed."[35]

It was indeed that the imperial examination has been abolished since the late Qing. However, the imperial examination culture that lasted for a millennium is abolished, yet persistent. Apart from the second point summarized by Liu, which is universal to all examinations, the contemporary gaokao system still shares a high degree of similarity with the traditional imperial examination. Just as Liu remarked: The imperial examination was like the ancient gaokao, gaokao was like the contemporary imperial examination.[36]

c) Chinese Culture as a Perspective to the Study of Chinese Universities

Based on the above analysis, Chines culture has played a fundamental role in the forming and development of Chinese universities and their cultural character. This point is focused on the idea that Chinese universities are rooted in Chinese culture. Therefore, when studies are conducted around this topic, one has to understand Chinese universities from a cultural perspective. That is to say, Chinese culture is a basic perspective to the study of Chinese universities. In contemporary society, Chinese culture is an essential perspective for a better understanding of Chinese universities.

On one hand, along with the increased attention on universities with Chinese characteristics and the Chinese model of university education, a need of being able to understand and uncover the uniqueness of Chinese universities from a cultural perspective arises. These so-called studies on Chinese universities under a cultural perspective are beyond just a mere description of surface phenomena about the uniqueness, but instead, is a study of explorations of the deep underlying nature of Chinese universities based on cultural understanding.

In some relevant discussions, many scholars used to strongly claim that there is an inevitable relationship between Chinese universities and Chinese culture, and they list the unique characterizations of Chinese universities' culture. However, they rarely stand on the ground of specific social-historical backgrounds and go into the deep analysis at a cultural level on exactly which elements of Chinese culture played a role in the formation and development of Chinese universities, and how these elements were expressed. The present book conducted a deep analysis of the inner mechanism of Chinese universities by describing their particularities to understand the formation of Chinese universities' unique characteristics.

On the other hand, the reform of Chinese universities is heated, yet full of obstacles. There is also a new idea regarding the reform needed along the Chinese cultural horizon. Chinese universities have always been receiving too much attention from society, therefore they became the focus of the society's criticism every time they undergo reform. The much-disputed Peking University Reform and the heated piloting of the new Southern University of Science and Technology system all ended with no clear conclusion. Nowadays, the so-called university reform has already ended up notorious in the eyes of the public due to the conflicts between the ideal and reality.

The problem of a Chinese university seems to have become more problematic with the more attempts that have been made to solve it. Chen Pingyuan stressed in his article *The 3 Questions about Chinese Universities*, "What we are lacking now is not the 'international vision,' but the understanding and respect of 'traditional China' and 'contemporary China,' when discussing university reform theories."[37] Through this statement, he gently yet seriously criticized the westernization tendency of university reformation today.

The present book does not plan to make any value judgements against the discourse of Chinese university reform ideas. Instead, it aims to study Chinese universities from the Chinese cultural perspective, in order to convey an idea that the cultural character of Chinese universities might be able to act as a reference to current or future university reforms. Where does the future path of Chinese universities lie? The Chinese culture has to be its crucial standpoint.

Section 2: The Social Basis for the Cultural Character of Chinese Universities

Initially, Chinese culture was used to refer to traditional Chinese culture. Since the introduction of Western culture during China's modern period, the term has been further divided into traditional Chinese culture and modern Chinese culture. On such basis, the Chinese society contains two discourses, which are traditional Chinese society and modern Chinese society. The former uses traditional Chinese culture as its main entity, while the latter mainly discusses the conflicts between Chinese and Western culture. Chinese universities are intrinsically connected with Chinese society and were formed and developed during the modern period, and are therefore a result of the integration of heritage and atmosphere. In general, the cultural character of Chinese universities is in the "modernized tradition" (according to Du Weiming), and hence it should be analyzed under two contexts: the traditional social context and the modern social context. On such grounds, this section of the study would attempt to discuss the social basis of the cultural character of Chinese universities in two aspects. The first being the historical roots of the cultural character of Chinese universities, and the second being the realistic basis of the cultural character of Chinese universities.

1. The historical roots of the cultural character of Chinese universities

"The history of Chinese culture is but the history of Confucius himself." While this quote is intentionally exaggerating the facts, it is not far from the truth. According to present research, the emphasis and acknowledgment of the central position of Confucian culture should be used as a basic standpoint. Hence, discussion of the historical roots of the cultural character of Chinese universities, to a great extent, needs to dig deeper into the historical connotations of its Confucian culture. Chinese culture, or Confucian culture, has two basic forms of existence within the traditional Chinese society, one being social conventional views and the other being social ideology. Under the guidance of these two forms, traditional Chinese education developed into two sections that are interconnected yet are also greatly different – the private education culture and the official education culture. These two cultural examples will be the historical basis for the construction of the cultural character of Chinese universities. In other words, the cultural character of Chinese universities is deeply rooted in the historical traditions of Chinese private education and Chinese official education. The culture of private education lies with civilians, while the culture of official education lies with the royal court. These two entities seem opposites, and this is also the view that Ruth Hayhoe took in her research regarding the history of Chinese universities within a century of conflict. However, the present research would take a different stand regarding this idea. Chinese culture does not have the notions of confrontation and conflict, and it does not have the concept of countries since it reckons that humanity is a part of the world and nature itself. Such is also the cultural character of Chinese education. In the Confucian "*Jia Tianxia*" (family-governed monarchic country), even though the education was indeed divided into the private sector and the official sector, and even though there had been multiple cultural conflicts and standoffs between them, they did not oppose each other. The differences between them were not made to compete but were there for the sake of complementing each other. They completed each other, and ancient Chinese education would have been incomplete without them.

a) The culture of private education under social conventional views.

One cannot discuss private education without discussing Confucius. Feng Youlan claimed Confucius was a very influential mentor. More importantly and uniquely, Confucius is China's first-ever private mentor.[38] Others think this too, Qian Mu also claimed that Confucius was the pioneer in Chinese mass education. Qian claimed in his *Zhongguo Wenhuashi Daolun*:

> "The most eminent of civilian scholars in China mainly came from two schools of thought: Confucianism and Mohism. Confucianism was created by Confucius. "Ru" is the appellation of Confucian scholars. They would practice the "Six

> arts," namely Li (ceremony), Yue (music), She (archery), Yu (driving), Shu (calligraphy), Shu (math)...Usually, it is a tradition for the noble class to practice and master these arts; for civilians to serve noble families, they would need to master at least one or two of those six arts. And these people from the then concept of "Shi." At first, "Shi" mostly came from the noble concubines' children and the lower classes of noble descendants; later on, it gradually included the civilian society. Confucius is the first person ever to officially pass such ancient aristocracy into civilian society."[39]

From a connotation's viewpoint, the primary cause of the private education culture of Confucian is "*Zhiyu Xue*" (dedication to learning). The only condition requirement, which is also the only sufficient and necessary one, to enter a university, is to be "*Zhiyu Xue*."[40] This is also one of the basic characters that define ancient university education as a university education. It is the counterpart of the "*Xue Qishi*" (to learn how things are) motto of primary education, while also its continuation at the same time. "*Li Ji*, also known as *Xiao Dai Li Ji*, has a chapter *Daxue*. It starts with *Gewu Zhizhi* (understanding through examination and observation) and ends with *Zhiguo Pingtianxia* (unifying and ruling the world). These are the principles that are greater than life itself. Those who commit to learning are indeed committing themselves to these principles, which are different from the smaller education where pettier principles are studied and practiced. The true achievement lies within education. Put your faith in doing good and never falter; you must never become extravagant in wealth, you must never lose your ambition in poverty, and you must never yield to superior power.[41]" Using *Zhiyu Xue* as its core value, the ethical basis of the culture of private education is therefore established.

Confucian culture of private education is also unique in the aspect of the audience's education since its motto is "*Youjiao Wulei*" (education is for everyone). "Confucius giving private education to everyone was the start of the popularization of education, and this led to the situation after him where even the highest officials could be borne from a common background."[42] This is also the essence of private education's differences from official education. Compared with official education, "the uniqueness of private education lies in *Youjiao Wulei*."[43] Confucius said, "I have never denied education to anyone who brought their *Shuxiu* (dried meat, a form of payment to teachers in ancient China and a common token gift) to me" (Quoted from *Lun Yu, Shu Er.)* In other words, as long as the students bring ten pieces of the dried meat as a gift to show that they are willing to learn and willing to admit themselves to mentorship, Confucius would accept them as a student. There was also another quote from the same chapter, "If one purifies oneself and makes progress, then we shall acknowledge the progress and ignore their past." This means that if a person is willing to learn and be diligent in learning, Confucius would look over their past and educate the person without discrimination. Hence, there is no distinction of nationality or ethnicity among Confucius' students, while wealth and intelligence would not matter, either. This is why he went on to have over 3000 disciples. It is stated in *Xun Zi: Fa Xing* that "Hui Zi from Nanguo asked Zi Gong, 'why is there so much variety among His disciples?' Zi Gong answered, 'The righteous man waits with integrity, he wouldn't turn away anyone that approaches, while he also wouldn't stop anyone that leaves. Other than this, you always see many patients at the door of a good doctor, and you always see bentwood pieces at the side of a straightening tool. The reasoning is the same for the variety.'"

On the knowledge aspect, a Confucian culture of private education emphasized: "*Zhongdao Qingyi*" (*Dao* over art). Tu Youguang reckons that the Confucian theories on higher education had two principal contradictions, the first one being the contradiction between "*Dao*" and "art." The main contradiction of Confucianism puts *Dao* over art. Confucius once said, "Build your will around *Dao*, regulate yourself with *De*, base your actions on *Ren*, and act within the bounds of *Yi*." (Quoted from *Lun Yu: Shu Er.*) The "*Dao*," "*De*," "*Ren*," "*Yi*" are all part of "*Zhiyu Xue*," while the objects of build, regulate, base are different from the object of acting. According to Tu's understanding, "*Dao*," "*De*" and "*Ren*" are considered as "*Dadao*" (greater principles), while "*Yi*" is considered as a "*Xiaodao*" (lesser principle). These are two opposing concepts. By Confucian definition, "*Da Dao*" is the study of righteous gentlemen, while "*Xiao Dao*" is the study of lesser men. In the story of "*Fanchi Qing Jiaqiang*" in *Lun Yu*, Confucius defined Fan Chi as a "lesser man," expressing his tendency of "*Zhongdao Qingyi*." At the same time, it is evident that the Confucian "*Dao*" is not opposed to "*Yi*." For example, when discussing the method of "*Chengren*" (becoming a real human), Confucius stated that "*Yi*" is one of the basic qualities of "*Dao*." However, it is still undeniable that the concept of *Zhongdao Qingyi* is the dominant idea within the Confucian culture of private education.

By utilizing self-admission education Confucius pioneered in private lecturing, and hence established the foundation for the culture of Chinese private education. However, private education facilities were not regular education institutes. By the Eastern Han dynasty, traditional private education had been further developed, and private education organizations called "*Jingshe*" appeared. Compared with the Qin dynasty and the dynasties before, such organizations had developed a fixed location of operations, but still could not be considered as institutionalized organizations. It was not until the Song dynasty, when academies became popular, that Chinese private education developed to a new phase. Within the academic circles, whether these academies counted as official or private organizations was still controversial. In the present research, the academy culture is categorized as a form of private education culture during discussions, mainly because these academies were established and developed within the civilian circle, which was outside the national education institution. It proceeds to retain the heritage and embedded spiritual values of the private education culture, even though academies were gradually officialized starting from the intermediate period of the Ming dynasty. There are numerous research papers and descriptions regarding such academies, and Qian

Mu's description is rather comprehensive and accurate. The following is a quotation from Qian's "casual definition" of academies, to help the reader grasp the essence of the academy culture:

> During the Han and Tang dynasties, the official schools of the country came with highly detailed regulations and systems, and a ton of students. Only during the Six Dynasties period were official schools nominal. The official schools of that time would utilize stringent styles of teaching dominated by temples of Buddhism. However, during the Song, Yuan, Ming, and Qing dynasties, the academy system became a system of private schools, replacing the stringent teaching of temples. These schools mainly originated from famous mountains and resorts, sponsored by individuals within the society. The most important component of these schools was the library, with the dormitory for students being its second. Usually, these academies would feature altars with idols' memorial tablets of great scholars from earlier times, and hold ceremonies for them at special times. It can hence be observed that these academies were built with the image of temples in mind. Later on, most major cities built their academies. Among these academies, some were built under the initiative of major government officials, some were maintained under government funding. However, given all these examples, the academies still retained their extra-political, free and independent style in their teachings. During that period, the government still had official schools, ranging from national universities to town schools. Many of these official schools, especially the ones from the Song and Ming dynasties, would copy the system of private academies and make adaptations and modifications to them. With this being said, the rights to provide education were still generally owned by private academies with private teachings. It could be said that within the 1000 years after the Song dynasty, China was occupied by civilian scholars and private education, when the rights to provide education was no longer in the hands of government officials or religious monks.[44]

According to Qian's depiction of the history of academies, the essence of Chinese academy culture lies within:

One, the extra-political, free and independent style of teaching. From the private education provided by Confucius, the *Jixia Xuegong* from the Contention of a Hundred Schools of Thought, to the *Jingshe* education of the scholars from the Han dynasty, they all exuded the spirit of academic independence and free lectures. The establishment of academies inherited such a spirit. Historically speaking, academies were not only a place for Confucian scholars to do their academic research, but they were also places for academic communication and exchange. It is especially worth noting that the formation and development of the "*Jianghui* system" provided a great platform for the exchange and mutual teachings among different schools of thought. The system first emerged during the Southern Song dynasty. In the year 1167, Zhu Xi and Zhang Shi met at the Yue Lu Academy, and hence established the convention of academic exchange. One of the most famous exchanges of such would be "the meeting at Ehu Temple", an academic debate in Xinzhou, Ehu Temple between Zhu Xi, Lu Jiuyuan, etc. Even though the exchange failed to eliminate the academic conflict between Zhu and Lu, it still served as an event of academic exchange and facilitated the progress of academic research. After this, especially after the intermediate period of the Ming dynasty, many renaissance academies such as the one under Wang Shouren would frequently host lecture events, and hence the fashion of academic teaching in academies reached its peak.

Two, it coexisted with official schools founded by the government. The academies are independent of the government, but it did not mean that they opposed it. Historically speaking, academies first appeared when official schools were in a status of neglect and decline. Their purpose was to complement the lacking in popularity and duty official schools, rather than to replace them. As imperial education became more and more utilitarian, academies that lived outside the official education system thrived. Hence, the establishment of academies was not to achieve in the imperial examination. Even if the academies did not express any opposition when their students attended the imperial exam, their purpose did not align to claim the top spot in this exam. At the same time, it was obvious that official education was integral to the imperial education system. In this sense, academy education was parallel to official education. The two complemented each other and interdepended on each other. During the Northern and Southern Song dynasties, academies achieved great success and popularity. The well-known "four greatest academies in the world" (Bailudong Academy, Shigu Academy, Yingtian Academy, and Yuelu Academy) all appeared during this time. And at the same time, the official education system also thrived. At some certain points, *Tai Xue* became the most prosperous central education institute.

Three, the rights to provide education did not belong to government officials, nor religious monks. When compared with official education, academies did not belong to the government; when compared with the Buddhism traces that lied within education, academies did not possess such religious properties, either. While exploring the roots of Chinese academies, we can see that their establishment was indeed under the influence of Buddhist culture. The forming of the earliest academy system occurred as a result of the attempt to replace temple teaching with private schools. However, as stated within the introduction, its influence was constrained to famous mountains and resorts, along with the form character of admiring sacred tablets and idols. Fundamentally speaking, academy education had always put its faith in Confucianism, especially when Confucianism obtained the dominating status after *Sishu Wujing* was designed to be the official topic on the imperial exam. If Confucianism was not considered as a Chinese religion, it was almost safe to say that academies had zero connection with any religion.

b) The culture of official education under the guidance of social ideology.

In ancient China where "politics and education go hand in hand," all rulers took the matters of official education with great seriousness. Every dynasty of China had its official education system, ranging from the central to the local level. Such official schools were led and developed by the government; hence their prosperity and failure were highly linked to the political situation of the time. The schools thrived when the government strived, and the schools were neglected when the government was chaotic and unruly. In Xiong Mingan's *Zhongguo Gaodeng Jiaoyushi*, they traced Chinese universities back to the ancient "Xiao" in the Xia dynasty and the "Xiang" in the Shang dynasty, which were both official education organizations of their times. In the ancient history of China, the most prominent examples of central official education systems would be *Tai Xue* from the Han dynasty, and the *Guozi Jian* after the Sui and Tang dynasties. Below is a divided analysis of the major principles of Chinese official education culture.

Tai Xue is called "the starting point in history where China had its official national university" (Quote by Qian Mu), while it is also considered as one of the earliest and largest instances of officially established universities with specifically indicated written records in the world history of higher education. During the Han dynasty, the establishment of Tai Xue laid the institutional foundation for the Chinese official higher education. 140 B.C., Dong Zhongshu suggested to Emperor Wu of Han that *Tai Xue* should be established. Between the time when the suggestion was made and the time *Tai Xue* was officially established, only 16 years passed. As one of the most prominent Confucian scholars of the Han dynasty, Dong Zhongshu was highly familiar with the classic pieces of Confucianism, while he was also quite knowledgeable in the books of the Hundred Schools of Thought. He went on to build the thought system where "the unity of the world and humans" was its core. To a great extent, the establishment of *Tai Xue* reflected Dong's Confucian values and thoughts. According to *Han Shu: Dong Zhongshu Zhuan*, "Humans'" lives were a gift from nature, and hence they were superior to, and different from, other life forms. We as humans have the intimate concept of families and the political and friendly concepts of the relationship between the Emperor and his court members. When we join each other in gatherings, we have norms according to our age, we have certain codes and etiquette in the way we treat each other, and we love each other with grace and morality. This is why we as humans are superior. We grow crops for food; we grow plants and harvest their fabrics for clothes, we raise animals as well. We keep cows and horses for riding and we put leopards and tigers behind bars. This is proof that we humans have inherited the spirit of nature, and hence we are superior to all others." Judging by this, Dong Zhongshu inherited Confucius' idea of "Humanity is the best part of nature" (Quoted from *Xiao Jing: Sheng Zhi*) and established *Tai Xue* within the framework of "*Wu Lun*" (five ethics). It can be observed within it, its detailed characters are:

The function of *Daxue* is to "gather all the talents and use them." In the second chapter of *Dui Ce*, Dong Zhongshan mentioned, "If one does not focus on the cultivation of talents yet still wants to find them, it would be like asking a piece of jade to be gorgeous without carving it. Hence, to cultivate great talents, there is no place better than *Tai Xue. Tai Xue* is the source of outstanding talents and the origin of education. (…) This lowly one wishes that the Emperor would establish *Tai Xue* and hire excellent teachers to cultivate the talents in our world. We should frequently test them to ensure their abilities, and hence we can gather all the great talents in the world." (Quoted from *Han Shu: Ben Zhuan*) It is hence evident that Dong Zhongshu took a worldly standpoint to explain the importance of the establishment of Tai Xue to Emperor Wu of Han. Its logic is fairly clear – if the country wants to prosper, it must find talent. If the country wants to find talent, it must cultivate it first. If the country wants to cultivate talent, it needs to establish *Tai Xue. Tai Xue* prospers and the country would be able to harvest talent and such talent would be put into the governance of the country. Following Confucius' idea of "*Xiushen, Qijia, Zhiguo, Pingtianxia,*" Dong Zhongshu emphasized the importance of achieving "*Xiushen*" via the cultivation of talent from a "*Zhiguo, Pingtianxia*" viewpoint.

The education of *Tai Xue* was not universally available. The students in *Tai Xue* were called "*Tai Xue Sheng,*" and they had to undergo selection procedures to become part of the system, while their upbringing and background also played an important part in this selection. The sources of how *Tai Xue Sheng* was found during the Han dynasty were highly varied. Some of them were recommended by Tai Chang (who was the official of ceremonies in ancient Chinese court), some of them were elected from different states, some of them were selected via exams, while others were admitted for their fathers' achievements and status. As for the admission requirements and age restrictions of *Tai Xue*, the admission's quota was only 50 during its establishment under the Emperor Wu of Han. These 50 students had to be "over 18 years old and decent looking" intellectuals from the landlord class, regulated to be selected by the Tai Chang. Other than this, other knowledgeable youths that were "good at literature, respectful to seniors and elderlies, compliant to education and political ruling, obedient within their hometown, abided by the rules and etiquettes that they were taught" were to be elected from lower states and admitted as "special students" ("*Shouye Wei Dizi*"). For these "special students," there was no specific quota.[45] By the end of the Western Han dynasty, Wang Mang was in power, and he granted the status of "special student" to the sons of "Shi," the lower officials of the government. After the Eastern Han dynasty, more and more descendants of government officials were admitted. However, generally speaking, *Tai Xue Sheng* still mainly consisted of the descendants of nobles, while sectarian and family-oriented views were still heavily present.

The extent of the political involvement rights of *Tai Xue* was regulated by the government. Official schools had a prevalent history of political involvement. During the Spring and Autumn period, there already was an example of "local schools involving themselves in politics" within the state of Zheng. During the Western and Eastern Han dynasties, the students of *Tai Xue* inherited the proud tradition and eagerly participated in the political world, upholding justice in the process. Some of them even dared to oppose the injustice and corruption within the government. However, as government interference intensified, such rights were gradually subdued. By the end of the Eastern Han dynasty, the country was held and run by weak and unintelligent eunuchs. They brutally repressed the political movements of *Tai Xue* students, and this chaotic period was also when the famous, or rather infamous "*Danggu Zhi Huo*" happened. It was truly not a rare sight that academies that were involved in politics were repressed by the government. However, as academies were based in the civilian world and lay outside the system of the country, they persisted through this severe destruction. However, the government had direct control over *Tai Xue*, and hence the extent of freedom of *Tai Xue* was completely decided by the government, as well.

After the six dynasties period, the Sui dynasty united the country, however, its ruling was short-lived, leaving behind its greatest contribution to Chinese history – the imperial examination system. By the Tang dynasty, the system was fully developed and was therefore merged with the official education system. After Sui and Tang, government-established institutions that specialized in the management of education that was phased into existence. During the Sui dynasty, this institution was called *Guozi Si*. There was one "*Ji Jiu*" within *Guozi Si*, mainly in charge of the education matters. The *Guozi Xue, Tai Xue, Simen Xue, Shu Xue,* and *Suan Xue* were all managed by this *Ji Jiu*. Later, *Guozi Si* was renamed as *Guozi Jian* and the name persisted till the Qing dynasty. The Sui dynasty fell at its second emperor, and *Guozi Jian* also fell into practical disuse, but the education system was inherited by the prosperous Tang dynasty and saw massive development facilitated by its prosperity. The *Guozi Jian* of Tang was split into six departments called *Liu Xue* (namely *Guozi Xue, Tai Xue, Simen Xue, Shu Xue, Suan Xue* and *Lv Xue*) and two institutes called *Er Guan* (*Hongwenguan* and *Chongwenguan*), constituting the core of the central and official education system. This system was followed and developed by the Song, Yuan, Ming and Qing dynasties, and was finally almost completed. The system of *Guozi Jian* started in Sui and ended in Qing. Within its duration of over a thousand years, it was heavily modified along the way with the rising of every new dynasty, but its internal cultural character of official education persisted. In general, its significant characteristics are:

1) The schools paralleled the imperial exam, with *Xue Er You Ze Shi* as their goal. Before Sui and Tang, the system of national education paralleled the schools with selections, and since Sui and Tang, the schools paralleled the imperial exam instead. The imperial exam was created in Sui, but by that time, the system consisted only of the subject of *Jin Shi*, and the institution was not yet established. Also, given the fact that the Sui dynasty was rather short and turbulent, the imperial

exam system was merely started in its primary form, and *Guozi Jian* also fell into practical disuse. During the Tang dynasty, detailed institutions and systems of the imperial exam were established, many more subjects were added, and the imperial exam system was regarded as the only way of success for the Shi. Especially during the Ming dynasty, Zhu Yuanzhang applied the policy that one had to go through the system of schools if they wanted to participate in the imperial exam, and this further tied the school education and the imperial exam together at an institutional level. By the Qing dynasty, the imperial exam had become the only way to become a Jian Sheng in *Guozi Jian*. In general, paired with the imperial exam system, the legitimacy of school education was strictly restricted to the purpose of training future members of the bureaucracy. This also meant that the tradition of "unity of politics and education" had reached its peak.

2) Teaching and research paralleled management and both were gradually standardized and institutionalized. Generally, the *Guozi Jian* of Tang was regarded as a union of education, research and administrative institutions, and this structure was carried on in later dynasties. Take the *Guozi Jian* of Song as an example, the department which administrated the school was called *Guozi Jian*, and the department which was in charge of teaching the students was called *Guozi Xue*. *Guozi Jian* oversaw the general operation of the school, and was in charge of the administration, while *Guozi Xue*, as the highest national institution of education, was tasked with educating the descendants of government officials that were higher than Qi Pin (the seventh rank). All the while, *Guozi Jian*'s subsidiary called *Tai Xue* took charge of educating the descendants of government officials that were below Qi Pin. From this viewpoint, the system of central *Guozi Jian* was highly organized, with a clear indication of duty among its subsidiaries. *Guozi Jian* included institutions for education, research, and administrative management, and this was to demonstrate the institutionalization of the central official education system.
3) Authority centralization paralleled democracy, showing a democratic and popularized trend. While the official education system of Tang had a highly detailed institutional organization, it also featured strict hierarchy, with a high trace of politics within its education. Higher education instituted of Tang, such as *Hongwenguan*, *Chongwenguan*, *Guozi Xue*, *Tai Xue*, and *Si Men Xue*, had strict admission rules regarding the government official ranks' of their students' fathers. Hierarchy not only existed in the admission process but it also existed among different institutes.[46] However, since Tang, the influence of hierarchy within school education gradually receded, as some of the commoners' descendants were allowed to be admitted into the official education system, showing signs of popularization. During Song, Yuan, Ming and Qing, a significant increase in the chances for commoner descendants to receive an education was observed, and

hence these dynasties saw an increase of chances for commoners to be involved in national political matters. This generally aligned with the purposes and the aims of the imperial exam, which was to select government officials among commoners.

In the paragraphs above, this research used the systems of *Tai Xue* and *Guozi Jian* as examples to explore the cultural basis of official education of Chinese universities under the central official education system. During the mentioned dynasties, local official education institutes also existed. However, as the local institutes were in fact subsidiaries of the central institutes, they were highly aligned with central institutes in many major aspects such as administration and content of education, and this research shall not give further discussion regarding this matter.

c) Chinese classic higher education as part of the archaic cultural system

Based on the difference between dominant forces of different nature and from different sources, traditional Chinese education has two categories, namely, official education and private education. However, both categories, which constitute of the traditional Chinese education, were generated from the same cultural tradition of Confucian ethics. In *Zhongguo Chuantong Jiaoyu De Jiegou, Texing He Tezheng Jiqi Yu Wenhua De Guanxi* (*Structure, Properties and Character of Traditional Chinese Education, And Their Connection with Culture*), Ding Gang stated that the Chinese education's tradition could be broken down into a ternary system consisting of Confucianism, Buddhism, and Taoism, where the three elements complement each other and exist in harmony. But at the same time, Ding also admitted that this diverse and mixed character of knowledge did not overshadow the basic character of Chinese education's traditions, which were ethical and political in their nature. This research believes that the root character of Chinese education's tradition can be summarized in one element, which is its ethical nature. In ancient China, the idea that "ethics and politics are inherently the same fields"[47] is non-arguably true. The differences within Chinese politics, in the so-called "politics" in ancient China, were merely extensions of ethical values within the ideological fields and should be regarded as "ethical-ized politics," as in, integrated into the ethics themselves. Hence, politics were not the individual characteristics of Chinese education's tradition, but a subcategory of ethics within its context. The private education or Confucius took on the ideal of "*Ming Mingde, Xin Min, Zhiyu Zhishan*," the *Tai Xue* of Dong Zhongshu prospered by the motto of "*Ren Shouming Yutian Er Guiyu Wu*" (The people are ordered by heaven and expensive things), and the academy of Zhu Xi set "*Wujiao Zhi Mu*" (the five ethics, namely affection between father and son, respect between the emperor and the subject, different duties between husband and wife, order between seniority and juniority, and honor between friends) as its first and most important rule. The creation of private education or the rise of official education both took ethics as their basic groundwork. As Western academics reckoned, Chinese philosophy is a subcategory of ethics, and the philosophy of higher education in ancient China is more set in an ethics' context or at least used ethics as its core. However, in a practical sense, the development of Chinese higher education has always existed in two forms – official and private. Historically speaking, a class of people that was specifically the product of Chinese society, Shi, was the key connection between the two. Exploring this specificity, it could be observed that it resulted from the fact that it acted as the main body of the official education, as well as the private education culture. Hence, they were the embodiment of ethical values. Private education focused on "Min," which meant common farmers within the context of ancient Chinese agricultural culture, and official education focused on "*Shi*" (士), which in the governance system meant the scholars *Shi* (士). According to Zhang Yinlin, the definition of "*Shi*" (士) initially meant the warriors armed with spears, bows and arrows, and later it took on the meaning of scholars that focused on reading books and discussed matters. This showed the significant difference between the period before the Spring and Autumn Period and the period after the Qin and Han dynasty. In the former era, education specifically meant the education of warriors, and warriors were regarded as the group that had to be educated. In the latter era, education meant the education of scholars, and only scholars were the ones that had to be educated.[48] In simpler words, *Shi* (士) meant the scholars from ancient China, and it was exactly the *Shi* who was the dominant force of dividing official and private education when it came to the higher education of ancient China. Most of the scholars hailed from the agricultural roots, and they usually ended up as members of the government. Hence, the scholars connected the "official" and the "private," and private education and official education were then joint together because of them. Liang Shuming once said, "In China, agriculture and academics, like scholars and farmers, have no borders between them, and they are inherently connected."[49] Qian Mu also reckoned that those who participated in the imperial exam mostly came from rural villages, and such was the background of most "*Shi*." In China, scholars are the most eager to become ruling officials, as "By becoming a ruling official, they could bring a better life to the people, and realize their ambitions and ideals. Hence, becoming a government official was the best way to benefit the people. Becoming a teacher, professor or author was all inferior compared with becoming an official."[50] Such is the purpose of "*Shi*:" To become a government official if they succeed in the imperial exam, and to become a teacher if they did not. Confucius was a *Shi* himself, and he served as both, a government official and a teacher. When working as officials, *Shi* became the main body of official education. They served the government, taught at official schools, and they sometimes utilized their political and economic status to promote the establishment of academies. When working as teachers, they become the main body of private education. They gave lectures to common folks, researched different objects, and wrote countless books – they kept private education among commoners alive. In general, private education culture and official education culture were divided by

Shi, while at the same time they coexisted because of *Shi*. In the end, they combined into one complete system, with ethics at its very core. In conclusion, on a philosophical level, the higher education of ancient China was monistic around its "ethics." On a practical level, the existence of *Shi* divided the higher education of ancient China into two forms, official education and private education, which was also the manifestation of the division between "conventionalization" and "politicization." Based on this, it can be said that the higher education philosophy of ancient China was based on the concept of "*Yiti Liangyi*" (one body, two wings), which was different from the higher education philosophy of the Western world.

There are significant differences between these two sets of philosophies, and three of them will be discussed here:

1) The difference between monism and dualism. "Chinese culture is monistic, as it is based on the comprehensive description by Confucius of ancient times. Meanwhile, Western culture originated from two sources, one is the Hebrew religion, and the other is the academics and laws of Greece and Rome."[51] Hence, higher education in China is also monistic. It was discussed before that the base of the legitimacy of higher education in China came from social ethics. Western higher education has always been built around dualism. When discussing the philosophy of higher education in *On the Philosophy of Higher Education*, John Seiler Brubacher reckoned that there were two roots of Western higher education, one epistemological and one political, and there were plenty of conflicts and contraries between the two. In fact, this is a matter of difference between Chinese and Western culture, where the worldview of both sides possesses serious influence. Qian Mu once made a comparison:

> "Westerners often see the world in a dualistic way. Even in their religion, there is the opposition between the duo of "Heaven" and "human world." However, there is only one world to the Chinese. The Chinese people do not think or believe that there is another "Heaven," so they always seek eternal life, to exist in this world forever; they want to be immortal, and their immortality still stays in this world.
>
> Westerners are not only dualistic when they see the world, they often see themselves in the same way. According to ancient Western theories, it was assumed that humans consisted of their flesh and their soul. The "soul" part is in contact with the rational "mental realm," while the "flesh" part was in contact with the sensory "material realm." Based on this, the traditional Western philosophy of dualism was developed...[52]"

2) The difference between using humans and using knowledge as the logical starting point. In ancient China, higher education was centered around ethics. Ethics meant the

relationship between humans, and hence, the higher education philosophy of ancient China used "the human" as its logical starting point. When analyzing Western higher education philosophy, Brubacher used "advanced knowledge" as the logical starting point when constructing the philosophy of higher education. This difference was caused by the dissimilar views of culture and knowledge between Chinese and Western culture. Qian Mu stated that there have always been three major sub-systems within the grand Chinese academic system. The first was "human," with humans at its center. In China, there is an ancient saying of "The purpose of scholars is to learn how to be a human." Whatever knowledge, its ultimate purpose was for scholars to learn to become a human, with the right ideals and the right values. The second sub-system is "practicality," meaning that utilization was the core of all knowledge, hence the saying of "*Xue Yi Zhiyong*" (learn for the sake of using). The third sub-system was "learning (knowledge)," which referred to the system of learning itself. There is a common saying among modern Chinese people, "learning for the sake of knowledge," which is the manifestation of this system.[53] To the Chinese people, the most important system within knowledge is "human." In *Daxue*, it was stated that "*Daxue Zhidao Zai Ming Mingde, Zai Xinmin, Zai Zhiyu Zhishan*" (The way of greater learning is to promote noble ethics, to enlighten the people, and only rest when the highest good is achieved). This aligns with the notion of putting "human" as the priority of knowledge. The concept of modern Western universities mostly focuses on the third sub-system, which is "learning." And this is the reason why Newman claimed the mission of universities to seek out "knowledge, instead of morality."[54] This would explain the differences between the starting points of the philosophical logic of Chinese and Western higher education.

3) The difference between learning from "teachers" and "priests." As mentioned above, ancient Chinese higher education relied on the class of Shi, and Confucius, the first teacher in private education of China, was one of them. The first teachers of medieval Western universities also had the same origin, they were mostly priests. Abelard, the first teacher in the history of Western universities, was a devout Christian priest. "The Shi of the Chinese are different from Western priests. They do not have the organizational system of a church or a diocese, nor the formal missionary organs of a church, nor do they have regular and frequent meetings of religions, and hence the difference (between the two)."[55] Because of the non-religious nature of ancient Chinese higher education, two major characteristics of ancient Chinese higher education can be derived from, first of all, ancient Chinese higher education was non-social. Ancient Chinese higher education systems, both official and private, were not the same as Western communities. Western communities originated from the folk and were originally a kind of guild organization that urban professionals formed to safeguard their interests. Hence, they were non-governmental organizations in nature. In ancient China, private schools among commoners were relatively free and loosely formed, lacking formal organization. The high level of institutionalization existed

in official schools in the court, which had little to do with the commoners. In short, ancient Chinese higher education did not form a Western-style organizational system. But without a community, there shall be no internal contradictions, conflicts and oppositions, and hence personal freedoms did not exist. This is why Hayhoe stated that Chinese higher education has always lacked the tradition of academic freedom and autonomy. In ancient China, higher education did not have a community, so there was no struggle for freedom. It promoted the concept of respecting teachers, following rules, and providing education for everyone. Second of all, ancient Chinese higher education was non-scientific. Spinger told us that religion was the predecessor of natural science. Whitehead also said that the occurrence of modern science was related to medieval religion. Explained from this perspective, Chinese higher education had little connection with religion, and this was one of the major reasons for its lack of natural science knowledge. "Chinese people talk about learning, but they are more focused on human affairs than in the working mechanism of the world."[56] Higher education in ancient China favored humanities and ignored natural science. When talking about the general trend of the development of higher education in China, Tu Youguang also classified ancient Chinese higher education as a "humanistic" stage of education. As Liang Shuming stated, the reason that China had no science "was neither the stupidity of the Chinese people nor the slow cultural progression, but the fact that cultural development had gone another way."[57] And hence, the lack of production and dispersion of natural science knowledge within ancient Chinese higher education was explained.

Finally, to summarize the general characteristics of ancient Chinese higher education, it is better to follow Liang Shuming's way of thinking and call it "precocious higher education." In his book *Dongxi Wenhua Jiqi Zhexue* (*Eastern and Western Cultures and Their Philosophies*), Liang Shuming stated that the general feature of Chinese culture was its precocity. The above-mentioned differences between Chinese and Western higher education can also be understood from this perspective, that is, Chinese higher education is not inferior to Western higher education, but its sequence of development is inverted. Two points need clarification here: First, Chinese culture develops inwardly, and Western culture develops in an outward fashion. This notion has already been well studied and accepted. Western higher education was the first to receive systematization – the medieval universities were created from communities and gained autonomy, and the idea of higher education saw massive development. Newman's idea of a university and Jaspers' idea of the university were both works in modern times. Ancient Chinese higher education established an ethical standard ever since Confucius' time and did not see any fundamental changes for a millennium (until the Opium War in modern times). The institutionalization of Chinese higher education into modern universities was something that happened in modern times. In short, "Chinese scholars would first have a spiritual value, then create and operate a university accordingly; while Westerners created universities first, increased their values, and the idea of the university would be generated based on practice."[58] This is the basic logic of the development of higher education in China and the West, and the two contradict each other. Second, the inherent law of Chinese higher education lies in *Xiushen, Qijia, Zhiguo,* and *Pingtianxia* (self-cultivation, family harmony, governance, and unity of the world), as described in *Daxue (The Great Learning)*. The emphasis lies on the "from the inside out" idea, starting from the person, to their home, their country, and eventually the world. As Du Weiming said, "The humanistic spirit embodied in *Daxue* is a concentric circle that gradually expands outward. The outer circle of this concentric circle should be open; from individual to family, to society, to the country to the world, and even to the human race and the universe, it expands outward; at the same time, it goes deeper, from our heart to our inspiration, to our gods ..."[59] The logic in the development of Western higher education starts from the knowledge itself. First, it is epistemology and politics, and then the emphasis shifts to serving the society, and finally humanism. This is an outside-in process. Therefore, the process of Chinese higher education is different from that of Western higher education. These are the inherent logic of the development of Chinese and Western higher education.

Based on the two points above, one of the basic aims of the present study is to show that ancient Chinese higher education emphasized the internal concepts and humanism, which is the exact opposite of Western higher education. Therefore, the most precious heritage of ancient Chinese higher education lies in the ideas and ideals of higher education. Although modern Chinese universities are built in compliance with Western university systems, these traditional Chinese cultural values are still indispensable. The idea of higher education in ancient China should be the root of modern Chinese universities.

2. *The realistic foundation of the cultural character of Chinese universities*

The cultural character of Chinese universities should be regarded as "modern traditions." Without the introduction of Western culture, China would not have spontaneously produced universities, in their modern sense. The invasion of Western civilization into China in modern times was, internally, a loss of classical Chinese higher education culture, and externally, an introduction of Western higher education culture. The cultural character of Chinese universities is formed in this cultural conflict between China and the West.

a) The loss of Chinese classical higher education culture

Chinese classical higher education is rooted within Chinese culture, and it is itself a part of Chinese culture. The development and prosperity of Chinese culture depend on the social environment, including the country's political stability, economic prosperity, and the general safety of its people. There is no shortage of such glory in the history of China, and it once was a paradise in the eyes of Westerners. The Venetian Marco Polo, who came to China in the early days, traveled in China and wrote *The Travels of Marco Polo*, which incited strong reactions all over Europe, and made the Europeans gradually understand that there is a large country with land so vast and a population so large, as China. A stable and harmonious social environment is a major reason for the Chinese culture's prosperity. In short, there are roughly three elements within the ecological environment of Chinese culture. The first is its relatively independent geographical environment, the second is its natural economy based on agriculture, and the third is its monarchy characterized by centralized power. The relatively closed geographical environment made Chinese culture more isolated and unified. The consistent farming culture made Chinese culture agriculturally-oriented and human-oriented. While the centralized rule regarded the country as an extension of the family and therefore made Chinese culture strong and unified. Chinese culture survived for thousands of years in such a social environment with economic prosperity and political stability, with virtually no outside interference at all. However, since there was no external disturbance, it was easy for Chinese culture to become self-important and narrow-minded. The agriculture-based economy was stable but weak, while the people struggled in poverty, and centralized power led to dictatorship, and if the monarch was not excellent, it would be difficult to strengthen the political and military strength of the country. With the rise of modern Western nations and colonialism, the various disadvantages of Chinese society began to appear during the 19th century. At this point, the ecological environment on which Chinese culture depended had been nearly destroyed, and the loss of Chinese classical higher education culture had become inevitable. Looking back at the history of the 19th century, it all seems painfully real:

> The outstanding feature of Chinese society in the first half of the 19th century was that traditional society was on its last limb, and the prosperity of Kangxi and Qianlong had passed. On the contrary, the high centralization of land, assisted by the increasing rent exploitation and population pressure, brought constant peasant uprisings. Secret societies acted as the pushing force behind these uprisings, and they were on the rise. For instance, *Tiandihui* (the Heaven and Earth Society) had a massive presence in south China during this period. At the same time, the so-called "foreign goods" and opium trade had led to a large outflow of silver from China, which severely dried up the Chinese economy. Internal worries and external difficulties had indeed pushed all kinds of conflicts in the country to a level of imminent danger.[60]

The so-called "internal worries and external difficulties" were part of the objective situation of Chinese society at that time, to which the classical Chinese higher education was lost.

First, the economy was stranded in poverty, and the foundation of higher education was no more. The economy is the foundation of life and society, and its influence on culture is the most fundamental. Economic poverty caused political instability and cultural damage. The profound force of the economy played the most important role in higher education. Since modern times, China had lost its natural geographic barriers, and its economy had undergone major changes in the face of internal and external difficulties. The main manifestations of this included: Internally, the Qing government was extremely corrupt, and farmers were suffering from economic difficulties. Gong Zizhen pointed out in the *Pingjun Pian* (*On Equality and Averageness*) that the inequality of social wealth and the opposition between the rich and the poor at the time was the root cause of the dynasty's decline and the upheaval. Successive peasant uprisings continued to testify Gong's assertions. History always focuses on the criticism of external factors. In fact, the Qing government itself already had shown a tendency of self-destruction. A corrupt bureaucracy and a weak central leadership mechanism joined together, and the innocent people were the first to suffer. Countless corrupt officials hoarded land in the Qing Dynasty. During Qianlong and Jiaqing's era, the extremely powerful minister He Shen alone gathered more than 120 million Liang of silver, along with over 8000 Qing of land. Until the early stages of the Opium War, with the increase of feudal exploitation of farmers via land rents, taxes, usury, etc., the peasants' natural economy became more and more impoverished to the point of near bankruptcy. Externally, the opium trade made China's economy even worse. In modern times, with the rise of the world capitalist economy and the increase in European and American demand for Chinese products, despite the restrictions imposed by the Qing government on foreign trade, Sino-foreign trade continued to increase. In legitimate Sino-foreign trade, China was constantly in a position of surplus. However, since opium was imported into China, the long-term advantage of China's foreign trade gradually changed, resulting in a large outflow of Chinese silver. From the nineteenth century, the country had been struggling with a trade deficit, and a large amount of silver had flown out. The outflow of silver caused China to suffer the consequences of expensive silver and cheap currency. At the same time, the outflow of silver and the rise in silver's value caused difficulty in tax collection, resulting in increasing arrears in various provinces, and a decrease in the state treasury reserve, which led to a financial crisis for the Qing government.[61]

Second, governance struggled in the state of war, and the logistics of higher education were waning. "China was suffering through difficult times, its politics were corrupted, its law and order were disrupted, and the people were struggling with their living."[62] In a sense, due to political decay, cultural and educational chaos was inevitable. The difficult survival of modern Chinese culture in the political environment of war became another social reality encountered by ancient Chinese higher education. Modern China was suffering, with frequent wars and unrest, from both the inside and the outside. The internal wars were mostly peasant uprisings, with constant battling between resistance and repression. The external wars were full of bare and cruel invasion, which were indeed part of a history of aggression and submission. As far as internal warfare was concerned, throughout the Qing Dynasty, the people of all ethnic groups in China had always marched wave after wave, trying to topple the rule of the Qing Dynasty. On the eve of the Opium War, two large-scale uprisings broke out, namely the White Lotus Uprising from 1796 to 1804 and its tribe, *Tianli Jiao*, in 1813. The uprising spread to many provinces and lasted for more than ten years. The Taiping Tianguo Movement, which began in the 1850s, surpassed all previous civil uprisings and established its political power for more than ten years. Although it eventually failed and disintegrated, it was a fatal blow to the long-faltering Qing Dynasty. As far as the external wars of aggression were concerned, in 1840 the British fleet forcibly invaded China's border on the grounds of the destruction of opium at Humen, becoming the culprit of modern aggression against China. The Opium War revealed the weakness of the Qing military, the "Nanjing Treaty" was signed, and the status of Chinese society changed from feudal to semi-colonial. It was at this time that the Western interest in aggression against China saw a surge. The Second Opium War, the Sino-French War, and the Sino-Japanese War soon ensued, and China's regime became the prey.

Third, enlightenment was initiated, and the trust in classical higher education was gradually lost. Due to feudal economic exploitation, political decay, and military weakness, social conflicts were becoming increasingly acute, and the higher education tradition inevitably degraded. In the late Qing Dynasty, feudal education became empty and corrupted. First, the schools became a tool for imperial examinations, and official education existed in name only. Second, the imperial examinations were corrupted, with cheating and fraud becoming commonplace. Third, the mind control was unprecedentedly strict, while the content of education was regarded as nihil.[63] In the first half of the 19th century, a group of enlightened landlords, bureaucrats, and intellectuals began to awaken. Stimulated by Western culture, they reflected on the reality of higher education at that time. Representatives of this period include Gong Zizhen, Lin Zexu, and Wei Yuan. Gong Zizhen was a progressive thinker of the landlord class in the late Qing Dynasty. He was extremely dissatisfied with the reality of the late Qing Dynasty. He advocated "*Jingshi Zhiyong*" (application of experience and knowledge in the real world) and urged for changes within the education system to break the status quo. Feeling that the content of the imperial examination had deviated from practicality and was extremely dark and corrupt, he advocated for the abolition of the imperial examination. Liang Qichao spoke highly of Gong Zizhen, saying that "the liberation of thought in the late Qing Dynasty must be accredited to Gong Zizhen to a great extent. Most of the so-called new scholars in the Guangxu era had worshipped Gong sometime during their career."[64] Lin Zexu was called "the first person in the Qing Dynasty to open his eyes to the world." He was dissatisfied with the vacancy and uselessness of education at the time, and advocated "learning from the West." And he asked his retinues to "learn about two things, translate two books, and buy their newspaper every day" from the Westerners. He compiled the translated materials on Western history, geography, and politics into *Sizhou Zhi* (*The*

Records of Four Continents), which became one of the earliest works in modern China to introduce Western countries. Wei Yuan was a close friend of Gong and Lin. He also criticized the current problems and promoted "*Jingshi Zhiyong*" and the reformation of the imperial examination. He advocated for the abolition of the calligraphic test in the imperial examination, and its substitution with practical knowledge, and believed that if the country wanted to thrive, it had to train talent that could utilize their knowledge in practice.

To sum up, China's higher education was gradually lost in the objective situation of dramatic changes in politics, economy, and ideology in modern China. However, while the development trend of Chinese higher education could be changed by the reality of internal and external difficulties, it was still virtually impossible to eliminate the influence of the Chinese higher education culture that had lasted for thousands of years.

b) The introduction of the Western higher education's system and culture

The tradition of Chinese classical higher education was caught in a downward spiral, among the political, economic, and even ideological difficulties of the late Qing Dynasty. The greater reality was the transmission of Western systems and culture, which happened earlier than at the end of the Qing Dynasty. Indeed, China's higher education culture would not simply give in to the objective reality at the time, but the introduction of Western systems and cultures had, to a certain extent, broken the monocultural characteristics of ancient Chinese higher education with Confucian standards at its core, and even directly affected its future developmental trends. "Culture" in the "cultural characteristics of Chinese universities" discussed in the present study is not a complete concept, but a concept that is independently extracted from traditional Chinese culture, and does not include Western cultural elements after the late Qing Dynasty. This is merely one of the perspectives taken by the present study. As far as reality is concerned, the cultural character of Chinese universities has taken on parts of Western culture since the modern period. The discussion of the Western higher education system and culture along with its introduction not only serves to reveal the other side of the cultural characteristics of Chinese universities that are discussed in the present study but more importantly, it is regarded as a realistic basis for the formation and development of these characteristics, for the sake of better understanding them.

"In modern times, the relationship between the East and the West lies in culture, but the input of Western culture was started by Christian missionaries."[65] The development and transformation of higher education in modern China were primarily driven by Christian missionaries. Western missionaries came to China in the late Ming and early Qing dynasties, which brought information about Western education to China. Earlier works that introduced Western education during this period included Alfonso Vagnoni's "*Tongyou Jiaoyu*"(*The Education of Children*) (1620), Giulio Aleni's "*Xixue Fan*"(*An Introduction to Western Learning*) (1623), and "*Zhifang Waiji*" (*A Brief Introduction to Foreign Geography*) (1623). Among them, "*Xixue Fan*" introduced the situation of Western universities at the time in a more detailed fashion, including the majors, curriculum outlines, teaching processes, teaching methods, and examinations. It was a book about Western universities in the 16th century. There were also descriptions of Western universities in books such as *Zhifang Waiji*.[66] However, it is regrettable that these introductions about Western education did not attract the attention of the Chinese people at the time, let alone have any direct impact on China's higher education. In the end, it was ended by policies such as "prohibition of religious teaching" and "seclusion" in the late Qing Dynasty. By this point, the first attempt of introducing Western learning to China came to an early end under the influence of politics, and the concepts of Western university education that were introduced were limited to China's translation of the one or two books mentioned above.

In the late Qing Dynasty, the trend of introducing Western learning gradually rose again. In 1807, Robert Morrison came to China on a mission to preach, which was considered to be the prelude of Protestant missionary activities in China. Western higher education systems and culture were able to enter China once again, and Chinese universities began to formally modernize. During this period, many bureaucrats and intellectuals who actively promoted the studying and imitation of Western higher education emerged throughout China. One result of this was the establishment of westernized schools during the Self-strengthening Movement. In addition, missionaries from the West also contributed to the modern transformation of Chinese higher education. Many missionaries directly participated in presiding over the establishment of modern Chinese colleges and universities. Many priests also served as university faculty members or presidents, and what's more, there was no shortage of outstanding people. The following are some examples:

As a major representative of the introduction of Western learning in modern times, John Fryer was more prominent as a facilitator of the development of modern Chinese education in modern times, rather than a missionary that he primarily was. In Sun Banghua's book "*Xixue Dongjian Yu Zhongguo Jindai Jiaoyu Bianqian*" (*The introduction of Western Learning to the East and the Evolution of Modern Chinese Education*), Fryer was only the research object of the first section of the first chapter, yet he took up about one-third of the entire book. This says a lot about the affirmation and attention Fryer got from the author. Fryer, a giant in the eastward introduction of Western learning, was born in England in 1861 and came to China in 1861. He made two major contributions to the development of modern Chinese higher education. First, he was employed by the Translation Department of Kiangnan Arsenal. Fryer worked in the Translation Department of the Kiangnan Arsenal since 1868. Up until 1896, he had made outstanding contributions to the translations of Western learning into Chinese, many of which were used directly as textbooks for colleges and universities. The number of Western books translated and published by Fryer was as high as 160, and he was considered to be the person who has translated the most books in the modern period. The list of Fryer's translations of Western books was appended in Sun Banghua's book *Xixue Dongjian Yu Zhongguo Jindai Jiaoyu Bianqian*, which filled 28 pages (107–134). What is even rarer is that although Fryer was a missionary, most of the Western books he translated were on Western science and technology, mainly including natural sciences, applied sciences, and military sciences, and these books even attracted Japanese scholars to visit China for the sake of purchasing them. Fryer dedicated his prime years (29–57 years) to the introduction of Western learning to China. As he said in 1880, "I have lived in China for twenty years, and I only have one hope, that is China will be able to achieve the same level of learning and practice as the Western world, and that is the reason why I dedicated my life to this cause."[67]

Second, he founded Shanghai Gezhi Academy, which adhered to the ideas of Western education. In addition to translation work, Fryer also actively engaged in educational practice during his stay in China and established the Shanghai Gezhi Academy, which became another important way for him to spread Western learning. Westerners living in China by this time mainly founded missionary schools, whose main purpose was to spread Christianity and cultivate Chinese Christians. But it is commendable that the purpose of Fryer's founding of Shanghai Gezhi Academy was not a missionary one, but it was dedicated to promoting Western education. During his tenure as the president of Gezhi Academy, he always insisted on diluting the idea of religious education, making the academy's education "dedicated to knowledge and practice, with no missionary work involved." It was with the efforts and persistence of Fryer that Shanghai Gezhi Academy became an early modern school dedicated to teaching Western studies.

Another fine example of a Westerner who worked tirelessly for China's modern higher education was John Leighton Stuart. Although he was an American descendant, he was born in China, with more of his life spent in China than in the US. If it was not for political reasons, he might have chosen to die and be buried in China, as well. Stuart loved China so much that he claimed to be a Chinese more than an American, and his actions in China have been affirmed and understood by many Chinese people. Wen Yiduo commented that Stuart was the best friend of the Chinese, and the author Bing Xin expressed her deep remembrance and respect for the respectable Chinese university president. In 1949, Stuart left China as a failed U.S. ambassador. What he missed and cared for the most was Yenching University, the university which he founded. It was the passion of his life, to the point that he urged to be buried on its grounds on his deathbed in the United States. Stuart was a missionary, but he was more of an educator in China and was regarded as the ideal president for Chinese universities. Stuart was commissioned to start Yenching University in the critical year of 1918. Since then, he spent over 20 years in the university, which were the golden years of Yenching University and the greatest achievement of his life. The university that he founded was unique. It believed in academic freedoms rather than religious faith. Its goal was to be Chinese rather than American, giving it a unique Stuart-like personality and character. During his tenure, Yenching University consistently adhered to the sinicization, and the campus was filled with a cosmopolitan rather than religious atmosphere. Stuart founded the university with his Chinese faith and established its spirit, which has cultivated many outstanding talents for China and influenced many later generations.

In short, with the missionary's translation and education in China as a major method, Western higher education culture began to take root in China. Since then, Chinese universities were gradually established. Taking this as an opportunity, the lost classical Chinese higher education culture finally found a new carrier, and the cultural characters of Chinese classical higher education were restored within modern Chinese universities, and the cultural character of Chinese universities gradually formed.

c) Chinese universities in cultural conflicts

The essence of Chinese classical higher education lay in "one body and two wings." It was distinguished from Western higher education by its ethics-based monocultural character. The emergence of modern Chinese universities in cultural conflicts, and to what extent their relationship with classical Chinese higher education is established, are both questions that need to be further clarified. In the formation and development of classical Chinese higher education, the class of Shi of the ancient times connected private education and official education, integrating classical Chinese higher education into a unified system. This was the logical growth of classical Chinese higher education. Modern Chinese universities were born in an age where classical Chinese higher education was lost and Western higher education culture was introduced. It was also true that missionaries pioneered in coordinating Chinese culture with Western culture even earlier and established modern Chinese colleges and universities by imitating Western universities. This was the objective logic of the generation of modern Chinese universities. In the book *China's Universities 1895–1995: A Century of Cultural Conflict*, Hayhoe placed the century-old history of Chinese universities in the context of the cultural conflict between Chinese and the West in the modern period, mainly deconstructing Chinese universities based on the perspective of the contrast between Chinese and Western culture. The present study acknowledges that Chinese universities were born out of the cultural conflict between China and the West. But at the same time, it is believed that the birth of Chinese universities itself has proved that the conflict between Chinese and Western cultures has transcended its explicit opposition, into a state of coordination and integration. In a certain sense, Chinese and Western cultural conflicts are synonymous with Chinese and Western cultural fusions. Fusion is only possible with the presence of conflicts, and conflicts are not the opposite of fusion, as they are a prerequisite for such fusion. In short, the cultural conflict and integration of Chinese and Western culture is the objective premise for the formation and development of the cultural character of

Chinese universities. Without cultural conflicts and integration, it would be impossible and worthless to explain or discuss the cultural character of Chinese universities presented in the present study.

When it comes to the question of how to understand the role of classical Chinese higher education culture and modern Western higher education culture in the construction of Chinese university culture, different answers can be generated from different perspectives. A basic standpoint of the present study is that modern Western higher education system and culture have directly constructed modern Chinese universities, but this does not symbolize the demise of classical Chinese higher education culture. The establishment of modern Chinese universities also provides a modern habitat for the once-lost classical Chinese higher education. Observing the argument from this perspective, modern Chinese universities follow the development procedures of Western universities, as the establishment of an organizational system comes first, and the rejuvenation and development of the inner spirit come second. The so-called rejuvenation of inner spirit refers to the inheriting of classical Chinese higher education culture, which is referred to as the cultural character of Chinese universities in the present study. The so-called development of the inner spirit refers to the absorption of Western higher education culture, which is the internal manifestation of the conflicts between Chinese and Western culture and their integration. From this point of view, the philosophy of modern Chinese universities is a special kind of science.

First of all, it deviates from the "one body, two wings" characteristics of classical Chinese higher educational philosophy. Second of all, it is different from the Western higher educational philosophy of dualism. The cultural character of modern Chinese universities aligns with the philosophy of dualistic unity. First, the so-called dualistic culture has always existed, while it did fluctuate in magnitude during different historical periods. As for what kind of culture should have more/less presence to achieve the ideal cultural character of Chinese universities, the present study can only make a supposedly balanced assumption, while looking in history for the experience and lessons. Secondly, although there is no difference in status between the so-called duality, there is a fundamental and objective distinction. The cultural character of Chinese universities, shaped by classical Chinese higher education culture, is the fundamental character of modern Chinese universities, and the essential connotation of the particularity of Chinese universities. In contrast, in the context of Chinese universities, modern Western higher education culture is more objective than internal, while also being more common than special. It is undeniable that universities in most parts of the world today have the characteristics of Western university culture. Dualistic unity is not a unique philosophical character possessed by only Chinese universities, as many universities in non-Western countries are likely to have such a philosophy. For example, modern Japanese universities and Korean universities are a combination or a blend of local and Western cultures. The present study agrees with the dualistic unity concepts of Chinese universities, but its fundamental premise is still the root of Chinese universities that is Chinese culture. Binary non-oppositions are not parallel in the absolute sense. Chinese universities have gradually eliminated the conflict between Chinese and Western culture during the past century, while at the same time, they have strengthened the fundamental role of Chinese culture. Even though this is arguably non-intentional, it is still the inevitable logic of the development of Chinese universities.

Section 3: Formation Paths of Chinese Universities' Cultural Characteristics

As mentioned above, the 'Chinese culture' referred to in the present book is a concept of the past. To some extent, it refers to the cultural tradition of China. "Cultural tradition" is different from "traditional culture." According to Pang Pu, tradition is dead, it belongs to the past, while culture possesses no time constraints. From this perspective, Chinese cultural tradition cannot directly influence Chinese universities. How does Chinese universities' cultural character form, how does Chinese culture impact Chinese universities, what is the bridge between the former and the latter? How can we understand Chinese culture and the Chinese university at both ends of the bridge, their history, and their reality? This section explores the formation path of Chinese universities' cultural character, aiming to embody Chinese universities' cultural character, attempting to construct an analytical framework on the realistic level to understand Chinese universities' cultural character to further unravel the inner logic of Chinese universities' cultural character formation.

1. The Basis of the Formation of Chinese Universities' Cultural Character

"Chinese culture" is a metaphysical philosophical concept, it inevitably bears a sense of emptiness. This book understands Chinese universities' cultural characteristics based mainly on the "*daxue* view" (University view) within Chinese culture. "University view" refers to the basic thoughts and concepts about higher education in Chinese culture – where the spirit of traditional higher education culture lies. Here, the term "*daxue* view" is used to indicate the traditional Chinese idea of higher education, because the emphasis is intended to be placed on the interconnectivity of the ancient higher education idea and the contemporary idea of a university. Although the "university view" originated from the traditional Chinese idea of higher education, it continued to the present day in contemporary Chinese universities. Moreover, the word "*daxue*" is borrowed to imply that this "*daxue* view" shares similarities with the Confucian "substance of great learning." The ancient Chinese idea of higher education has a close relationship with Confucian education's thoughts, or at least the latter is the core of the former.

a) The Beginning of Ancient Chinese Higher Education: Learning for Oneself

Chinese education's tradition is inward, "*ji* (self)" is underlined as the starting point. For example, traditional wisdom such as "*yi ji duo ren* (judge others by oneself)," "*shi ren ru ji* (see others like oneself)," "*xiu ji an ren* (cultivate oneself to bring peace to others)," "*fan qiu zhu ji* (rely on oneself)," "*ke ji fu li* (constrain oneself so that his behavior is according to etiquette)..." In the previous sections, the logical starting point of Chinese traditional higher education's philosophy was different from Western higher education's philosophy. It started with "*ren* (human)." Strictly speaking, the "human" referred to the "self." That is, coming from oneself. This is different from the Western concept of an individual within a group or an organization. The Western emphasis on the individual, positively demonstrated the personal rights and freedoms, while at the same time magnified or even legitimized an individual's selfishness. When the Chinese talk about the "self," they aim to achieve an entirely selfless status – "*zhi shan* (complete goodness)." Exactly as the saying went, "cultivate oneself to unite one's family and subsequently bring peace and order to the nation."

"Learning for oneself is a core concept in traditional Chinese education thought dating back to Confucius, and it dominated the ideal of Chinese scholars for almost three thousand years. During the Southern Song dynasty, it became a common belief due to Zhu Xi's advocation."[68] Confucius was not the only advocator of this idea, but he was one of the first people who raised and practiced it. Outside of the Confucian school, many held the same idea, but most of them used the Confucian idea as support, therefore the present book would not go into detail about their ideas. Within the Confucian school, Confucius, Mencius, and Xunzi have all made statements regarding "learning for oneself":

> "Students of old fixed their eyes upon themselves: now they learn with their eyes upon others." (*The Analects of Confucius*)

> "'The superior man makes his advances in what he is learning with deep earnestness and by the proper course, wishing to get hold of it as in himself. Having got hold of it in himself, he abides in it calmly and firmly. Abiding in it calmly and firmly, he re-poses a deep reliance on it. Reposing a deep reliance on it, he seizes it on the left and right, meeting everywhere with it as a fountain from which things flow. It is on this account that the superior man wishes to get hold of what he is learning as in himself.'" (*The Analects of Mencius*)

> "Students of old fixed their eyes upon themselves: now they learn with their eyes upon others. An intelligentleman (*junzi*) studies to perfect himself." (*The Analects of Xunzi*)

The quotes above have collectively shown that the spine of Confucian education was to enrich oneself instead of pleasing others to gain benefits. Lee Hong Chi believed that learning for oneself defined the purpose of education with concise language – the purpose of education came from personal development.[69] The present book inclines to call it the starting point of (higher) education with a dynamic idea that the meaning of (higher) education begins with personal development. With the understanding of the Confucian belief of "learning for oneself," the present book summarized a few points regarding how an individual can learn for himself.

1) Learning for oneself and regard learning as the basis. We should rather explain "learning for oneself" as a learning pattern instead of a motivational motto. Education is quiet and still, while learning is an actual active behavior. Confucius loved to study, he was dedicated to learning at the age of 15, and through his whole life, he regarded learning as his hobby. He believed that "learning" was the most important feature of human's education. This belief came from his self-identification of his learning journey. There are countless quotes from Confucius about learning:

> "In a hamlet of ten families, there may be found one honorable and sincere as I am, but not so fond of learning." (*The Analects of Confucius*)

> "There is the love of being benevolent without the love of learning – the beclouding here leads to a foolish simplicity. There is the love of knowing without the love of learning – the beclouding here leads to dissipation of mind. There is the love of being sincere without the love of learning – the beclouding here leads to an injurious disregard of consequences. There is the love of straightforwardness without the love of learning – the beclouding here leads to rudeness. There is the love of boldness without the love of learning – the beclouding here leads to insubordination. There is the love of firmness without the love of learning – the beclouding here leads to extravagant conduct." (*The Analects of Confucius*)

> "Is it not pleasant to learn with a constant perseverance and application?" (*The Analects of Confucius*)

> "Learn as if you could not reach your object, and were always fearing also lest you should lose it." (*The Analects of Confucius*)

To Confucius, learning is the most important thing in the world. He kept persuading his students to learn diligently and be constantly mindful that they must "learn as if they could not reach their object." Some scholars believed that Confucius learned from his predecessors' "six arts" and composed the *Spring and Autumn Annals*, which became a classic for later generations' learning.

2) Learning for oneself and cultivating one's body with virtues. The reason to learn for oneself is that learning should be regarded as the basis for everything, which is in turn because that one would be able to cultivate oneself with virtues. "The learning virtue without proper cultivation; the not thoroughly discussing what is learned; not being able to move towards righteousness of which a knowledge is gained, and not being able to change what is not good – these are the things which occasion me solicitude." (The Analects of Confucius) "The most important feature of learning for oneself is that learning is for one's moral cultivation,"[70] the fundamental requirement of learning is to perfect one's virtues.

Liang Shuming studied Chinese culture and believed that what was so unique about China is that the Chinese replaced religion with virtues. Adding on to this statement, classical Chinese higher education is an extremely rare case in the world which lead education with morality and virtues. From this perspective, "learning for oneself" meant to "cultivate and shape oneself with virtues." True learning only happens when one cultivates oneself with virtues because it is only through self-cultivation that one can become a complete "self." There are two main questions in understanding the Confucian "*de* (virtue and morality):"

- What is *de*?

The core to the Confucian idea of *de* is *ren* (benevolence) and *li* (etiquette). *Ren* tends inward, an inner feature of moral cultivation; *Li* tends outward, it is the outer representation of moral cultivation. Confucius said, "To subdue one's self and return to propriety, is *ren*." It is only through *li* that the gain of *ren* could happen.

- What is a person with *de* like?

A person with *de* is one who reflects on his moral cultivation. Confucius addresses one with *de* in two ways, *junzi* (intelligentleman) and *shengren* (sage). Comparatively speaking, Confucius tends more towards reality. He believed that "education knows no class distinction," everyone could become an intelligentleman. Sages mostly appear in ideality, they possess even greater *de* than the intelligentlemen, yet few can achieve this state. Of course, "to Confucius, the purpose of education is all about morality and virtue, yet this can only be achieved in the field of politics in the real world."[71] Therefore, learning for oneself is not a goal. Instead, serving society is the goal of learning.

3) Learning for oneself and adopting the responsibility of serving the society. "There are various reasons why an individual pursues morality and virtue. However, this pursuit impacts society greatly. Although the Confucian moral education took personal moral responsibilities as the starting point, Confucius always discusses this topic under the vein of social functions. Personal cultivation is the basic purpose of education, but it can only be effective when moral achievements realize social functions."[72] From this perspective, regarding learning as the basis of everything and cultivating oneself with morality is only the inner requirement of "learning for oneself," while realizing its realistic values – administering the country and bringing peace to everything under Heaven – is its ultimate goal.

So far, the connotation of "learning for oneself" has been more or less unraveled. "Learning for oneself" regards learning as the basis, cultivating morality, and aims to serve society. There is a gradual development contained within.

If we compare Fei Xiaotong's "*chaxu geju* (differential mode of association)" with ancient Chinese higher education, "learning for oneself" took "self" as the starting point and progressively interpreted the pattern of higher education. In *From the Soil—The Foundations of Chinese Society*, Fei described the ethical society of the countryside in China with "differential mode of association." He pointed out that Chinese society "centered around 'self.' Just like a pebble thrown into the water, the social connections established with others were not like an element in a group which exists on the same plane as its counterparts, but like the ripple of water, going further and further in concentric circles. It grows thinner the further it goes."[73] This the basic feature of Chinese social structure. The basis of Fei's statement is exactly the Confucian thought of "Self – Family – Country – Everything under Heaven," "What Confucius paid most attention to was the pushing force of ripples."[74] From this angle, Fei's "differential mode of association" of Chinese society can also be transferred and applied to the Confucian idea of "moral cultivation," educational thoughts mentioned in *Daxue* (Great Learning). "Cultivating oneself to unite one's family and subsequently administer the nation, thereby bringing peace and order to everything under Heaven. "Learning for oneself" takes "self" as the starting point, while it is in fact learning for personal moral cultivation. This acts as the center of the ripple. As the ripple spreads out, the first circle is the family, followed by the country and everything under Heaven.

b) *The Destination of Ancient Chinese Higher Education:* "Xue Er You Ze Shi *(Succeed in academics to pursue an official career)*"

Confucius said, "With learning – emolument may be found in it." (*The Analects of Confucius*) "The most important feature of Chinese education is that it aims to cultivate talents for the government (or society)," "Ever since Confucius, Chinese education aimed to cultivate a group of so-called 'intelligentlemen' and let them take leadership in society.

They have to be role models of the uneducated."[75] If the idea of "learning for oneself" in the Analects focused on the happiness in learning and the moral superiority within oneself, demonstrating an "aesthetics" of education or learning, then, in comparison, "succeeding in academics to pursue an official career" is a very realistic "practical technique." It is the destination of all scholars who have "learned for themselves," the most important characterization of serving the society and the thorough demonstration of classical Chinese higher education's political philosophy. This is a special product of Chinese culture, as well as important evidence that Confucianism is a school of philosophy instead of a religion. Western religions practiced philosophies of spiritual ministry. They did not pursue after fame, wealth, and power, while Chinese Confucianism followed the ideal of integrating politics and beliefs and encouraged scholars to actively participate in the secular world. Therefore, if one must regard Chinese Confucianism as a religion, it can only be categorized as "a religion of reality" (said Qian Mu) – a religion that exists only on the level of realistic society and politics.

"Xue Er You Ze Shi" is a line in *the Analects of Confucius*, a record of Confucius and his students' deeds and conversations. The original meaning of "*you* (excellence)" was "*rao* (abundance)," which signifies abundance, wealth, and extra (effort). While "shi (official-scholar)" means to become an official."[76] "Confucius was the first scholar in Chinese history, the first scholar who pursued the official career, and the first person who pursued the official career using the method of 'running for a career.'"[77]

Confucius was "well-read yet less-known." To achieve his ideal of "*Xue Er You Ze Shi*," he ran between the nobles around different kingdoms. Some scholars called Confucius "the Greatest Runner for Official Career."[78] This nickname is indeed reasonable. After Confucius, a lot of scholars started to run for official careers, and "*Xue Er You Ze Shi*" became the "religious" belief of Chinese scholars. Qian Mu once stated in *Zhongguo Wenhuashi Daolun*:

> "China is a country of 'great unification.' The government officials are the most honorable of all. A county head governs hundreds of square *li* of land and more than ten thousand families. There could be as many as more than one thousand clerks in the county government, who were all governed by the county head. Therefore, a county head was already like a small feudal duke. If one becomes the head of a prefecture who rules over thousands of square *li* of land and millions of families, there was much more that he could do… Therefore, there was not a single scholar in China who do not wish to become a government official. They pursue official careers like how others pursue their religions."[79]

This is an example of Chinese scholars pursuing official careers for fame and emolument. *Xue Er You Ze Shi* was also closely related to the strong sense of family in China. Chinese society places a strong emphasis on blood relatives, which is the center of

Chinese culture. Therefore, individualism is rarely seen in Chinese culture. "Families can benefit from education." This belief placed a great responsibility on the scholars to honor and revitalize their families, which is the other aspect of why Chinese scholars pursue the official career.

Indeed, after Confucius, official positions were already highly sought after by Chinese scholars. However, what tied the scholars onto the political career path was the imperial examination system after the Sui and Tang dynasties, which have systemized "*Xue Er You Ze Shi.*"

After the implementation of the imperial examination system, "*Xue Er You Ze Shi*" transcended beyond the scholars' ideals and family responsibility. It became the political philosophy adopted by the rulers to administer the country. Employing talents from around the country and putting them in use has been one of the most important statecrafts, no matter which emperor was sitting on the throne, as long as they wanted to achieve a stable government. Therefore, all of the ancient rulers encouraged scholars to participate in the imperial examination. Emperor Zhen of Song dynasty has written a poem, "*Quanxue Pian* (*Encouraging Learning*)," to win over the scholars. In the poem, the lines went "For books will promise a bumper harvest,/ For books will build a luxurious mansion at your nearest,/ For books will pair you with the fairest,/ For books will bring about entourages and carriages like a moving forest," laid out the biggest temptation for the scholars to take part in the imperial examination.

From this point of view, not only had the imperial examination strengthened the willingness of Chinese scholars to pursue official careers, but also made what Confucius said – "students of old fixed their eyes upon themselves: now they learn with their eyes upon others" – truer. At this stage of development of Confucius' "*Xue Er You Ze Shi,*" it can be even more regarded as the country's will than the scholars' aspirations. When the reality of "farming in the field in the morning and facing the emperor himself in the evening" kept replaying, the saying "there is nothing more valuable than studying" has become the highest belief of the entire Chinese society.

"*Xue Er You Ze Shi*" was the main reason why Confucianism has been the official orthodox ruling in China for thousands of years ever since its establishment during the reign of Emperor Wu of Han dynasty. There was no exception, not even during the periods of foreign rule, such as the Yuan and Qing dynasties. All rulers willingly adopted Confucianism as their belief and protected the orthodoxy of Confucianism thought. By nature, this was because Confucianism met the interest of the rulers.

c) *The Ideal of Ancient Chinese Higher Education: To Illustrate Illustrious Virtue, to Renovate the People, to Rest in the Highest Excellence*

It was generally believed that Chines culture is a set of social-ministry philosophies, however, it was not as simple as it seemed. Surpassing secularity and reality, Chinese culture was full of idealistic pursuits. There is an ideal society within every Chinese person's hearts. Chapter Liyun (The conveyance of rites) of the *Book of Rites* stated, "Hence, men do not regard as parents only their own parents, nor do they treat as children only their own children. Provision is secured for the aged till death, employment for the able-bodied, and the mean of growing up for the young. Helpless widows and widowers, orphans, and the lonely, as well as the sick and the disabled, are well cared for." This originated from the secular world and, therefore, belongs to reality, while at the same time it is so hard to achieve that it sounds unrealistic.

Apart from realistic pursuits such as "learning for oneself" and "succeeding in academics to pursue an official career," ancient Chinese higher education also had ideals that transcended reality, as expressed in *the Great Learning*:

> "What the Great Learning teaches is: to illustrate illustrious virtue; to renovate the people; and to rest in the highest excellence. The point where to rest being known, the object of pursuit is then determined; and, that being determined, a calm unperturbedness may be attained to. To that calmness, there will succeed a tranquil repose. In that repose, there may be careful deliberation, and that deliberation will be followed by the attainment of the desired end. Things have their root and their branches. Affairs have their end and their beginning. To know what is first and what is last will lead near to what is taught in the Great Learning.
>
> The ancients who wished to illustrate illustrious virtue throughout the kingdom first ordered well their States. Wishing to order well their states, they first regulated their families. Wishing to regulate their families, they first cultivated their persons. Wishing to cultivate their persons, they first rectified their hearts. Wishing to rectify their hearts, they first sought to be sincere in their thoughts. Wishing to be sincere in their thoughts, they first extended to the utmost their knowledge. Such an extension of knowledge lay in the investigation of things. Things being investigated, knowledge became complete. Their knowledge being complete, their thoughts were sincere. Their thoughts being sincere, their hearts were then rectified. Their hearts being rectified, their persons were cultivated. Their persons being cultivated, their families were regulated. Their families being regulated, their States were rightly governed. Their States being rightly governed, the whole kingdom was made tranquil and happy. From the Son of Heaven down to the mass of the people, all must consider the cultivation of the person the root of everything besides. It cannot be, when the root is neglected, that what should spring from it will be well ordered. It never has been the case that what was of great importance has been slightly cared for, and, at the same time, that what was of slight importance has been greatly cared for."

In *Zhongguo Jiaoyu Shilun*, Tu Youguang stated the above ways of great learning as the general rules of ancient Chinese higher education. He pointed out, "calling it a rule because it is what Chinese higher education abides to. It is regarded as the 'general rule' because it existed in every stage of Chinese higher education history."[80] The present study tends to summarize the Confucian way of great learning with the ideals of higher education. It is called an ideal because Chinese higher education abides by it but has yet to realize it. There is usually an inner necessity within rules. When each element or behavior achieves unity, the differential mode of association of Chinese higher education illustrated above will reveal the inner-to-outer rule of education. Ancient Chinese higher education has always been following the rule of "to illustrate illustrious virtue and to renovate the people," yet "to rest in the highest excellence" is clearly beyond reality and outside of the rule. *The Great Learning* has connected the three principles, however, it can only appear logical on the theoretical level. Experiences have proven that this is more of an ideal model of higher education, with "highest excellence" being the ultimate pursuit.

In the modern period, Chinese universities were established. Many attempted to interpret Chinese university with *The Great Learning*. However, most have focused on the idea of "illustrate illustrious virtue and to renovate the people" to underline the moral education and social service function of modern universities. For example, Mei Yiqi's *Daxue Yi Jie* (*An Explanation of University*) bore this tendency – it used the concept "to illustrate illustrious virtue and to renovate the people" as the two criteria to criticize the universities then, while the criteria of "highest excellence" only appeared once: "It is hard to explain the state of the highest excellence, therefore I am not going to talk about it."[81] This is understandable, though. "To illustrate illustrious virtue and to renovate the people" can be realized on eight levels. These are *gewu* (study the physical world), *zhizhi* (exhaust one's knowledge), *chengyi* (maintain sincere intention), *zhengxin* (regulate one's mind), *xiushen* (cultivate oneself), *qijia* (unite one's family), *zhiguo* (administer the nation), *ping tianxia* (bringing peace and order to everything under Heaven). However, "resting in the highest excellence" does not have corresponding concepts in *The Great Learning*, it is inevitable, then, to discuss it. Therefore, "highest excellence" exists beyond our reality due to its intangibility with itself, and therefore it becomes a meaningless proposition. This is also the reason why scholars intentionally avoided or neglected this concept. However, "highest excellence" was not a meaningless logical decoration when the ancient scholars talked about the substance of great learning. It was also far from a meaningless proposition as it is nowadays. Inversely, it is the key to understanding ancient Chinese higher education.

"Highest excellence" is fundamentally different from the concept "to illustrate illustrious virtue and to renovate the people," it is usually outside of the rule, yet it is always within the ideal. The following paragraphs are going to talk about the unique charm of the "highest excellence" ideal of higher education from three different aspects.

1) "Highest excellence" made "to illustrate illustrious virtue and to renovate the people" the two basic goals of studying, because it is much too superior. The latter two belong to the secular world, and are the basic requirements of higher education, while "highest excellence" is beyond secularity, it pursues excellence – the highest ideal of higher education. Logically speaking, the pursuit of "highest excellence" is to realize the basic requirements of the concept "to illustrate illustrious virtue and to renovate the people." In other words, "to illustrate illustrious virtue and to renovate the people" are the fundamental lessons that have to be learned before achieving the "highest excellence."
2) "Highest excellence" makes "to illustrate illustrious virtue and to renovate the people" a life-long learning process as it is too hard to realize. Indeed, "highest excellence" originates from the reality, yet it is too superior for people to easily achieve. If one is dedicated to "resting in highest excellence," he must keep cultivating "to illustrate illustrious virtue and to renovate the people." Therefore, "highest excellence" motivates people to never stop practicing "to illustrate illustrious virtue and to renovate the people."
3) "Highest excellence" makes "to illustrate illustrious virtue and to renovate the people" autonomous due to its immanence. In *The Great Learning*, "to illustrate illustrious virtue" is to *gewu* (study the physical world), *zhizhi* (exhaust one's knowledge), *chengyi* (maintain sincere intention), *zhengxin* (regulate one's mind), *xiushen* (cultivate oneself); "To renovate the people" is to *qijia* (unite one's family), *zhiguo* (administer the nation), *ping tianxia* (bring peace and order to everything under Heaven). Only "highest excellence" does not exist in the reality. If "to illustrate illustrious virtue" is a realistic inner cultivation, "to renovate the people" is a realistic outer practice, "highest excellence" should have been an unworldly inner spirit. This inner spirit is not cultivated with outer forces but emerged from the willingness of within. Hence, it is only possible to "rest in highest excellence" if one makes "to illustrate illustrious virtue and to renovate the people" autonomous.

In short, "highest excellence" makes the ancient Chinese ideal of higher education a combination of ideal and concepts grounded in reality due to its idealistic feature.

In conclusion, ancient Chinese higher education took "learning for oneself" as the starting point, demonstrating the ethicality of "*daxue* view," "*Xue er you ze shi*" as the destination, demonstrating the practicality of "*daxue* view," "to illustrate illustrious virtue, to renovate the people, to rest in the highest excellence" as the ideal, demonstrating the transcendency of "*daxue* view." Based on these characteristics, the "*daxue* view" of ancient Chinese higher education promotes *de* (morality and virtue), *shi* (fact) and *shan* (perfection). Of course, success or failure can be caused by the same thing. The emphasis on *de* led to the lack of *wu* (physical/scientific) studies, "succeeding in academics to pursue an official career" lead to a disadvantage in technology advancement, adopting "to illustrate illustrious virtue, to renovate the people, to rest in the highest excellence" as the ideals led to a loss in institutional construction.

2. *The connecting "Bridges" of the formation of the cultural character of Chinese universities*

Chinese culture is a basic point for the growth of the cultural character of Chinese universities. How and how much Chinese culture or *Daxue* view can influence today's Chinese universities depends largely on the role of "cultural inheritors." In the present study, the concept of "cultural inheritors" is narrow, that is, the actual subject that connects Chinese culture with Chinese universities (these two concepts are limited to the definition of the present study), which is an important bridge for the formation of the cultural character of Chinese universities. The reason why the cultural character of Chinese universities fluctuates in explicitness and strength during different historical periods is mostly and directly related to the "cultural inheritors." The following analyses will explore the relationship among "cultural inheritors," Chinese culture, and Chinese universities, and the interaction among them the three, to sort out the nature and category of "cultural inheritors," along with its basic character and fundamental roles.

a) The internal connection between "Chinese culture" and "cultural inheritors"

Chinese culture, as the foundation of the cultural character of Chinese universities, plays a major role in the shaping of the cultural character of "cultural inheritors." The cultural character of the "cultural inheritors," in turn, reflects the internal connection between Chinese culture and the "cultural inheritors." The cultural character of "cultural inheritors" has two meanings: on the one hand, the cultural character of "cultural inheritors" is the product of how Chinese culture acts on people, and the inherent coercive force of Chinese culture plays a leading role in this proposition. On the other hand, the cultural character of "cultural inheritors" is the result of self-selection by "cultural inheritors" themselves. The subjective initiative of "cultural inheritors" plays a major role in this proposition. The former determines the two basic properties of "cultural inheritors," while the latter distinguishes three different categories of "cultural inheritors."

First, the cultural character of "cultural inheritors" is the product of how Chinese culture influences people. "Cultural inheritors" that are born in Chinese culture are bound to be influenced by it. There is no doubt about this. Although in modern times, our country "may have encountered unprecedented changes in politics, but the cultural traditions of the past three thousand years have not disappeared, nor have they abruptly transformed into unrecognizable ones."[82] From this point of view, Chinese culture has always had uninterrupted internal coercion for the character formation of "cultural inheritors." Therefore, the cultural character of "cultural inheritors" may vary to a certain degree without any interruption in terms of its continuity. As a product of Chinese culture, the "cultural inheritors" are in their absolute sense. Specifically, in the field of education, the "cultural inheritors" inheriting the tradition of Chinese education are also absolute propositions. In the aforementioned discussion of the ancient Chinese educational culture, it was concluded that there were two types of educational traditions: private education culture and official education culture. Today's Chinese universities are nothing more than the competition and coexistence of two leading forces of social-cultural customs, and political ideology. Intellectuals belong to commoner's society, and they often pursue the inherent value of knowledge or education, while officials and political parties belong to the social ruling class, and they represent the will of the government. Therefore, in the discussions of the present study, the "cultural inheritors" in modern society are mainly divided into two categories: one is the "cultural inheritors" with strong sociality (as opposed to politics), and the other is the "cultural Inheritors" with obvious political tendencies. The two types of "cultural inheritors" coexist, and they take turns in playing major roles in the shaping of the cultural character of Chinese universities. However, neither of them can be in absolute control for a long period, which will render the cultural character of Chinese universities entirely political or social. This is also a basic feature of the cultural character of Chinese universities.

Second, the cultural character of "cultural inheritors" is also the result of the "cultural inheritors" making their own choices. The Chinese culture has shaped the cultural character of "cultural inheritors" with its special internal coercive forces, making the cultural character of "cultural inheritors" an inevitable consequence of Chinese culture. However, the relationship between Chinese culture and "cultural inheritors" is not simply linear. The cultural character of the "cultural inheritors" is formed by the influence of Chinese culture, but on the other hand, the "cultural inheritors" as active subjects, also react to the coercive influence of Chinese culture. In short, the cultural character of "cultural inheritors" is not only an inevitable product of Chinese culture but also a result of the "cultural inheritors" making their own choices. In the process of interaction, the two factors complement each other and coordinate with each other, jointly building the cultural character of the "cultural inheritors." In the formation of the cultural character of "cultural inheritors," the initiative of the "cultural inheritors" is mainly manifested in different positions and attitudes towards the Chinese educational tradition. Since modern times, Western learning has been introduced to China, bringing the integration of Chinese and Western culture. There are roughly three types of "cultural inheritors" in modern Chinese history. The first type is the one that respects and promotes Chinese cultural traditions, who shows strong and obvious traditional cultural character. The second type is one that inherits Chinese culture critically, and the traditional cultural characteristics of this type are relatively "moderate," they respect the fine traditions of Chinese culture and inherit them while drawing on foreign cultures at the same time.

The third type rejects Chinese culture altogether, their traditional cultural personality completely opposes that of the first type, showing little to no signs of Chinese cultural character. However, judging from the facts in historical development, no matter what position they take or what attitude they have, Chinese culture has planted its roots in the "cultural inheritors." Even if they completely reject it, they cannot escape the imprint of Chinese culture. In the end, the exertion of the autonomy of any "cultural inheritors" is based on the inevitable proposition of Chinese culture. There is no unconditional freedom.

b) The symbiotic structure between "cultural inheritors" and Chinese universities

The "cultural inheritors" are inherently an active subject that interacts with Chinese culture in the shaping of its cultural character. On another level, this is manifested through their dominant status in the symbiotic structure with Chinese universities. Throughout history, when a "cultural inheritor" of a certain era guided a Chinese university to a stable concept of a university, this university often had the characteristics of the "cultural inheritor" themselves. Of course, the reason why Chinese universities can be shaped by the "cultural inheritor" is not only because of the irresistible personal charm and external power of the "cultural inheritor," but also because of the Chinese universities' great plasticity. In a sense, the plasticity of universities is the exact reason that the role of "cultural inheritors" has so much weight, and that universities can adapt to society and become an everlasting concept in human history. Therefore, with the dominance of "cultural inheritors" and the plasticity of Chinese universities themselves and their basic features, a symbiotic structure formed between them, which became an important part of the cultural characteristics path and the formation of Chinese universities. The relationship between the two is mainly manifested in a few ways.

First, there would have been no Chinese universities if there were no cultural inheritors. Since the modern period, the initial formation and establishment of Chinese universities relied on the active operation of Western missionaries. But overall, most missionaries aimed at the dissemination of religious teachings, not the development of higher education or construction of universities in China. Although many made major contributions to the establishment of Chinese universities during this period, they were at most merely constructors of Chinese universities, with no possibilities of becoming inheritors of Chinese culture. The history of modern Chinese universities is composed of the experience of the Chinese people constructing universities on their own. They grew up in Chinese society. They were not only the constructors of Chinese universities but also the shapers of their cultural characteristics. Even though the "cultural inheritors" were not the only external factor in the formation and development of the cultural character of Chinese universities, there would not be any Chinese universities today without Chinese culture. From the perspective of the development history of modern Chinese universities, in the late Qing

Dynasty, Chinese universities had just been established. As the heirs of traditional Chinese culture and the direct founders of Chinese universities, bureaucrats in the late Qing Dynasty played an important role in forming the cultural character of Chinese universities. They were the first batch of "cultural inheritors" in the evolution of the cultural character of Chinese universities. For more than a hundred years since then, numerous socio-political changes and cultural changes ensued, but Chinese university education had always maintained its cultural characteristics as a Chinese university, even after countless transformations. The "cultural inheritors" in each period played an important role in this process. In short, Chinese universities were gradually formed and developed under the influence and the work of "cultural inheritors." Without "cultural inheritors," there would be no "Chinese universities" in its true sense, and only "Western universities in China" would exist.

Second, the "cultural inheritors" alternated among themselves, forming the centennial of Chinese universities. The past 100 years have been an eventful period for Chinese society. The entirety of China has seen constant external harassment and endless internal unrest. In different historical stages, the leading forces of Chinese universities frequently changed due to the influence of the political situation. In the process, the formation of the cultural character of Chinese universities experienced different "cultural inheritors." Objectively speaking, the "cultural inheritors" in different periods may have had opposite political stands and different attitudes towards tradition, but they all played important roles in the construction of Chinese universities nonetheless. Under their influence, Chinese universities have exhibited cultural characteristics of different times throughout different historical periods, and have now been developing for more than a century. Among them are some famous centennial universities. For example, the well-known Peking University and Tsinghua University, which have survived social changes from the end of the Qing Dynasty and have survived to this day, are the result of the joint efforts of many "cultural inheritors" throughout history. Peking University has a history of over 110 years. In 1898, under the auspices of Emperor Guangxu, the Imperial University of Peking was founded in Beijing, presided by Sun Jianai. During this historical period, officials of the late Qing Dynasty served as the first "cultural inheritors" in the construction of Chinese universities and the formation of their cultural character. In May 1912, Imperial University of Peking was renamed as National Peking University. In 1917, Cai Yuanpei became the president of Peking University and reshaped its spirit with the concept of "*Jianrong Bingbao*" (compatible and inclusive). In the following 20 years, Peking University rose to a golden era of development. During this period, the intellectuals of the Republic of China, especially the presidents of universities, played key roles in the historical reshaping of the cultural characteristics of Chinese universities as "cultural inheritors." After the founding of the People's Republic of China, through the complete Sovietization and adjustment of departments, reform and opening up, and university reconstruction, new "cultural inheritors" have emerged, and the development of Peking University and its cultural character has entered a new era. The same case applies to Tsinghua University.

Tsinghua Academy was founded in 1911, with a history of more than 100 years. It is also the result of the alternating yet consecutive construction of "cultural inheritors" of each period. Therefore, from this perspective, Chinese universities are the products of "cultural inheritors" taking turns in leading these universities, and the cultural character of Chinese universities incorporates the character of these "cultural inheritors."

Third, not all Chinese universities need to be shaped by "cultural inheritors." The dominant position of "cultural inheritors" in the cultural character of Chinese universities has a decisive role in the development of Chinese universities, but on the other hand, there is always an invisible tension between "cultural inheritors" and Chinese universities. The "cultural inheritors" are dominant but their control is not absolute, and the passive shaping of Chinese universities is not a complete adaptation. If it is true that all Chinese universities are shaped by the "cultural inheritors," then when the "cultural inheritors" in a certain period totally deny the Chinese tradition, the Chinese university should have followed suit, and the cultural character of Chinese universities would have no longer existed. As repeatedly emphasized in the present study, the cultural characteristics of Chinese universities is not an existential proposition, but a concept of degree. It is not a question of "presence or absence," but of the "more or less" degrees. "Cultural inheritors" that oppose traditions can only at most weaken the cultural character of Chinese universities, while "cultural inheritors" that promote traditions can at most just strengthen the cultural character of Chinese universities. Neither can completely dissolve the cultural character of Chinese universities or make it absolute. Therefore, there is a natural tension between Chinese universities and "culture inheritors," and the extremes of the cultural character development of Chinese universities are hence avoided.

c) *The interactive relationship among Chinese culture, "cultural inheritors" and Chinese universities*

"Cultural inheritors" are intrinsically connected with Chinese culture and coexist with Chinese universities. They are the "mediators" for the formation of the cultural character of Chinese universities. In the Chinese culture – "cultural inheritors" exist as a result of Chinese culture, and for the "cultural inheritors" – "cultural inheritors" exist as leaders of Chinese universities. Therefore, in the interactions among Chinese culture and "cultural inheritors," vs. "cultural inheritors" and Chinese universities, the main connotation of "cultural inheritors" is to inherit Chinese culture and shape the cultural character of Chinese universities. In the interaction of the three, the different attitudes of "cultural inheritors" towards Chinese culture directly influence or even determine the cultural character of Chinese universities.

First, the "cultural inheritors" respect Chinese culture, and hence the cultural character of Chinese universities is obvious. Historically, Confucian thought had been regarded as orthodox ever since the Han Dynasty, and this remained unchanged for thousands of years. It has only been less than a century since this was changed by Western culture. It can hence be observed that the roots of Chinese culture would not be fundamentally shaken by Western culture. This rang especially true among the last group of intellectuals or bureaucrats who lived in cultural traditions, who received traditional education since their childhood and were deeply influenced by Chinese culture. During the late Qing Dynasty, social disadvantages were laid bare, and Western learning continued to deepen in the East. Consequently, Chinese cultural traditions suffered unprecedented shocks. However, it was also during this period that the atmosphere of traditional Chinese culture was the strongest. This may have been an instinctive act of resistance to the outside world, or it may have been borne out of the emotional reaction of protecting the weak. Therefore, under the popularity of Western learning, there was an implicit preference and sense of protection towards Chinese cultural traditions. Taking officials in the late Qing Dynasty as an example – they constructed academies featuring Western learning, but it can be argued that their main purpose of doing so was to maintain Chinese cultural traditions and that they wanted to use the "weapon" of Western learning to revive the essence of Chinese culture. The Qing court officials during the Self-strengthening Movement and the revolutionaries during the Hundred Days' Reform all shared this same motivation. Therefore, in the late Qing Dynasty, the cultural character of Chinese universities was strongly present.

Second, the "cultural inheritors" inherit Chinese culture critically, and the cultural character of Chinese universities receives ideal development. History has proven that "cultural inheritors" overly believing in Chinese culture regardless of its strengths and weaknesses would inject Chinese universities with strong traditional culture, and this was not an ideal way of developing Chinese universities. Chinese universities had the strongest cultural character in the late Qing period, which to some extent, even hindered the construction of modern Chinese universities. In the subsequent period of the Republic of China, the cultural character of Chinese universities gradually diminished, but it was once considered to be the golden age of the development of modern Chinese universities. When further exploring this phenomenon, the reason behind this was the fact that the cultural character of Chinese universities during this period only selectively inherited the essence of Chinese culture. Intellectuals from the Republic of China who controlled the destiny of the universities played an important role in this process. It is said that the intellectuals of the Republic of China were an "unprecedentedly brilliant generation which the world will never see again." They were well versed in traditional culture while also were extensively knowledgeable in Western culture. Therefore, in the construction of the cultural character of Chinese universities, they could simultaneously rationally recognize traditions and learn from the West. The so-called "compatible and inclusive" motto was an important declaration of the cultural orientation of the universities at the time. With the responsibility of promoting the integration of Chinese and Western cultures, the intellectuals in Chinese universities strived to maintain a balanced state of the cultural character in Chinese universities. This was mainly because the presidents of the universities during the Republic of China period had more sincerity and tolerance towards Western culture than the officials of the Qing court and the fact that they had more respect and understanding for traditional culture than the ruling parties. For example, Cai Yuanpei, while advocating and promoting the concept of Western universities, also took full advantage of the non-mainstream tradition of ancient Chinese higher education, that is, promoting the strong academic atmosphere of ancient academies, the rapport and friendly competitiveness between teachers and students, along with the status of relative independence.[83]

Third, the "cultural inheritors" completely deny traditions, and the cultural character of Chinese universities appears to be weak. There has always been a trend in history: too many twists and turns usually lead to extremes. The development of modern Chinese history alone has seen plenty of examples of manifesting in this trend. From the May Fourth Movement and the slogan "Down with Confucius teachings" to the unprecedented Cultural Revolution and its radical criticism of Confucius, Chinese traditional culture was once the object of criticism and denial. This radical behavior seemed to seek a thorough relief from the dilemma of Chinese and Western cultures, and the cultural character of Chinese universities had once gone to extremes in the tide of the times. When the anti-Confucian stance was developed to the extreme and the era of the legitimacy of traditional Chinese culture was completely denied, the cultural character of Chinese universities fell into decline or even stagnation.

To sum up, there are two extremes of the cultural character of Chinese universities: one is to follow Chinese culture blindly, and the cultural character appears extremely strong; the other is to completely reject Chinese culture, and the cultural character appears extremely weak. The ideal state is to take an intermediate point, that is, to rationally recognize Chinese culture so that the cultural character of Chinese universities can selectively inherit the high-quality ingredients in traditional culture and develop in a balanced manner. In this process, the role of "cultural inheritors" is the most fundamental.

3. *The results of the formation of the cultural character of Chinese universities*

It is generally believed that "the modern universities in China are the result of 'horizontal adoption,' not 'vertical inheritance,'"[84] which can be regarded as "externally introduced and retroactive." While this is historically true, it is also lopsided. This is roughly the case in modern university systems, as well as the university philosophy of university autonomy and academic freedom. The present study considers that Chinese universities are "internally generated and artificial" in terms of their cultural character. The so-called "internal" factors refer to the fact that the foundation of the cultural character of Chinese universities lies in Chinese culture. The word "artificial" refers to the fact that the cultural character of Chinese universities also comes from "Cultural inheritors," and the key question is, therefore "who runs the university." This is not a negation of the "externally introduced and retroactive" statement, as the two judgments are not opposed, but complement each other, making the structure of Chinese universities more comprehensive. So far, the character of Chinese universities can be understood in two aspects. In terms of the organizational form of Chinese universities, they are mainly forced by external modalities to adopt and imitate the form of Western universities, hence they are "externally introduced and retroactive." As far as the cultural character is concerned, they mainly inherit Chinese culture, sharing certain properties from Chinese educational traditions, hence they are also "internally generated and artificial." The latter has a broader meaning, as the influence of Western culture on Chinese universities mainly lies in the organizational system, while Chinese culture is the root of Chinese universities. Hence, Chinese culture has a more comprehensive impact on Chinese universities, leaving its marks in the ideas, systems, and fields of Chinese universities.

First, let's discuss the cultural connotations of the idea of Chinese universities. At the conceptual level, in his book *Daxue Linian Lungang* (*Outline of Theories Regarding University Ideas*), Han Yanming defined "idea" as a superior and comprehensive philosophical concept at the spiritual and conscious level, which refers to people's rational understanding and ideal pursuit of a certain thing or phenomenon, along with the idea system that is formed by them.[85] Therefore, the "university idea" refers to people's rational knowledge and ideal pursuit of universities, and the certain concept system that is formed based on such understanding and pursuit.[86] In terms of significance, Xiao Haitao pointed out in the book *Daxue De Linian* (*The Idea of University*), "The idea of a university is the most concentrated expression of its country, its society, and its national cultural spirit."[87] When brought down to the more specific level of "idea of modern Chinese universities," "It is a university in China, with the Chinese character and Chinese spirit; at the same time, it also has modern character, combined with the trend of global modernization, and connecting with world civilization and the world's modern universities."[88] The present study treats the concept of Chinese universities as the ambition of the cultural character of Chinese universities, which is the core expression of the cultural character of Chinese universities, and the root of the will of Chinese universities. At present, in the academic discussion of the university concept, the "Idea of Chinese Universities" has gradually become a hot topic. In the process, the "cultural character of the Idea of Chinese Universities" has been continuously demonstrated and legitimized. In the book *Daxue Zhi Linian* (*The Ideas of Universities*), although Jin Yaoji clearly stated in the start that Chinese universities were adopted from the West, he did not deny the Chinese cultural character of the university idea. He wrote in the author's preface of the book:

> "It is true that temporal, social, and cultural changes will affect the order and nature of universities, and will also change our expectations and views on universities. However, on the other hand, some basic ideas embraced by brilliant

> figures of the past, such as the "Ming Mingde," "Xinmin," "Zhiyu Zhishan," and the sub-system of "humans" (as opposed to the sub-system of "practicality" and "learning." Qian Mu made a very sophisticated elaboration regarding this) as educational ideals, the world spirit of the universities that were formed since the Middle Ages in the West; the freedom and independence in academics and minds that were insisted by Weber, Jaspers, Cai Yuanpei... They can all be considered as sources of vitality for the universities today, and they still serve as the conceptual power that shapes the character of universities."[89]

Reading this, it is clear that Confucius' thought of *Daxue* is also a conceptual force that shapes the character of Chinese universities. In the book *Daxue Linian Zai Zhongguo* (*University Ideas in China*), Wang Jisheng directly confronted the idea of a university in China, and put Confucius educational ideas (listed by Jin Yaoji in the quote above) at the center of Chinese university ideas, emphasizing and demonstrating that Chinese culture is the root of Chinese university ideas. In the preface of the abovementioned book, Pan Maoyuan summarized the author's viewpoint as follows:

> "The mainline throughout the book, in my humble opinion, is that the university idea, as a system of ideas, is deeply rooted in the soil of national culture. The development of the university idea in China-based itself on Confucian's "ethics-oriented" educational ideal while absorbing the Western university philosophy of "emphasis on rationality and academic freedom," combined with the intricate exploration of the concept of socialist education with Chinese character while following the road of "taking the excellent culture of the Chinese nation as the main body to promote the harmonious development of Chinese and Western innovation."[90]

Wang Jisheng's book can hence be called, to a certain extent, a book devoted to the study of the cultural character of Chinese universities' idea. The author repeatedly emphasized that "from the Emperor Hanwu to the late Qing Dynasty, Confucianism's ethics-based education thought and the corresponding imperial examination system and academy education played an extremely important role in developing the personality ideals of intelligentlemen and scholars in China. It served as a spiritual adhesive to the entire Chinese nation for a long time, cultivating its people and elites, and created a large number of people with lofty ideals. It composed a great chapter of the glorious history of the Chinese nation, and it is a very precious gem in the grand vault of Chinese university ideas."[91] This is also a basic stand of the present study when discussing the idea and cultural character of Chinese universities.

Second, let's look at the cultural imprint of the Chinese university system. Since Mei Yiqi divided the Chinese university into two in *Daxue Yijie* (*An Understanding of*

Universities), he pointed out that the Chinese university system mainly stemmed from the adoption of its Western counterparts, and the Chinese university spirit is a result of the integration of the East and the West. From then on, the assertion that the Chinese university system originated from the West has constantly been brought up. Chen Pingyuan refuted the theorists claiming "millennium of Chinese universities" with the claim of "100 years of Chinese universities, and the basis of his argument was that Mei Yiqi's Chinese university system was indeed a product imported from the West. Jin Yaoji also clearly stated in *Daxue Zhi Linian* that modern Chinese universities are the result of "horizontal adoption" rather than "vertical inheritance." The academic community generally acknowledges and focuses on the "adoption" of the Chinese university system, while ignoring or denying the traditional cultural properties of the Chinese university system. As a result, the Chinese university system is considered to be directly equivalent to the Western university system, and the concept of the Chinese university system is absolutized and simplified. However, acknowledging the traditional cultural properties of the Chinese university spirit and the Western cultural attributes of the Chinese university system does not equal to the denial of traditional cultural properties of the Chinese university system. The university spirit inevitably acts on the university system. The Chinese university system cannot be a simple adoption of its Western counterpart, without being affected by Chinese education traditions and culture. Therefore, in terms of their system, Chinese universities are not just the result of the adoption of Western universities. Many recent scholars have begun to rethink the Chinese university system and tried to redefine the cultural origin of the Chinese university system. Fan Yanyan's book, *Shuangchong Qiyuan Yu Zhidu Shengcheng: Zhongguo Xiandai Daxue Zhidu Qiyuan Yanjiu* (*Double Origins and Institutional Generation: A Research on the Origin of Modern Chinese University System*) is a relatively representative example. The author believes that the Chinese university system that seems to be completely adopted is not that simple:

> "In fact, even during the creation of the Chinese university system, that is, from the 1920s to 1940s when learning from the West was prevalent and westernization of the university system was commonplace, it was not entirely adopted and copied from the West, and there were choices and adjustments. Whether it is the reference and promotion of the academy system by the university research institutions represented by the Chinese Studies departments of Tsinghua University and Peking University, or the purpose of Peking University, the "localization" policy and specific management system of Nankai University, or the academic style and moral education of Southeast University, they were all inevitably affected by some traditional systems. That generation of scholars was very familiar with traditions, and some traditional systems provided an empirical basis for teaching, rendering the system, management, teaching, examination,

> and other specific systems closer to "common sense," or even in a status of *Riyong Er Buzizhi* (invisible despite daily usage). Nobody discussed such matters with great fanfare, hence its importance seemed obscured. Therefore, when the education of traditional form became a thing of the past, a feeling of absence of the roots of modern university culture emerged, along with the pain of the losing ancient teachings and national culture, and the current reflection on the over-Westernization of the entire education system of that time."[92]

Admittedly, "Although there were many disadvantages or limitations in the traditional education system, the action of finding their roots, and the re-discovery of valuable and usable thought resources such as the educational system, educational ideas, and educational methods that were largely abandoned in the long-term westernization, can help Chinese universities find their cultural roots."[93] In short, Chinese universities were born and raised in China, and the Chinese university system has never been a simple Western concept. The Chinese university system has its cultural character in Chinese culture.

Third, the cultural symbol of the field of Chinese university. The term "field" here is proposed by French sociologist Pierre Bourdieu. He regarded the field as a web-like structure of objective relationships, including various "symbolic goods" in the physical environment, as well as the interrelationship of different parties related to the generation of "symbolic goods." The present book uses the concept of "field" for the meaning of "the construction of concrete matters." "Field of a university" is a narrow concept, which refers specifically to physical symbols such as campus buildings, university badges, mottos, uniforms, etc., as well as various ceremonies and activities. By applying this concept, the present book aims to examine the Chinese university's cultural characteristics at the material level. The cultural character of Chinese university concepts tends comparatively inward, the cultural character of the Chinese university system is more filled ideas, while the cultural character of the Chinese university's field is its most realistic outer presence. To this day, a lot of Chinese universities still retained and collected antique sites and items in many corners of their campuses. For example, Nanjing Normal University was built on the site Nanjing Jinling Woman's College. The classical sense in the campus buildings and the Chinese features in the campus layout is the true portrayal of the features of Chinese university's cultural characteristics.

In a nutshell, the field of a Chinese university is the most basic aspect, as well as the most essential dimension, of examining Chinese university's cultural characteristics. Pang Pu once divided culture into three levels, which could also be regarded as three basic forms of existence of culture. He believed that in a general sense, the cultural structure includes physical matters, psychological matters, and a combination of physical and psychological matters. What is shown at the outer surface are the physical matters, with the physical and psychological combination in the middle, and the psychological matters in the deepest or innermost part. The present book examines the manifestations of Chinese cultural characters following these three dimensions. The psychological matters are the concepts of Chinese university. The Chinese university system is a combination of both psychological and physical matters. While the physical matters refer to the concrete existences in the field of Chinese university. These are all basic manifestations of Chinese university's cultural characters.

In conclusion, the formation of the cultural character of Chinese universities is an "internally generated" and "artificial" process. Using Chinese culture as its foundation, "cultural inheritors" as its connecting bridge, the cultural-symbolic characters of the idea, system, and field of Chinese universities are formed. Therefore, the line of Chinese culture and cultural inheritors and Chinese universities is not only the formational path of the cultural character of Chinese universities but also its internal logic. The basic train of thought of this book's research on the cultural characters of China follows this line as well.

First, using "Chinese culture" as the topic, the root of the cultural characters of Chinese universities during different historic periods are explored, which is the historical destiny of Chinese culture. On such a base, the progression and changes of cultural characters of Chinese universities in the context of a culturally changing China are also discussed. The Chinese culture has a long history and it is deeply rooted within Chinese society, but it is not an invariable element. Especially since modern times, the social changes and causes of such changes in Chinese culture have been extremely complicated and unprecedentedly coercive. Hence, exploring the real historic status of Chinese culture within different periods is the starting point and necessary prerequisite of this book's research on the cultural character of Chinese universities.

Second, by using "cultural inheritors" as the topic, the basic standpoints and major roles of "cultural inheritors" regarding Chinese universities in different historical periods are also discussed. Through an analysis of the personal and educational background of "cultural inheritors," the deeper reasonings of different cultural characters of Chinese universities are revealed. "Cultural inheritors" are the reason for the "artificial" elements of cultural characters of Chinese universities, and they play a leading role in strengthening and weakening the cultural characters of Chinese universities. Hence, researching the identities and activities of the "cultural inheritors" within the formation of cultural characters of Chinese universities during different periods is another critical compartment of this research.

Third, using "Chinese universities" as the topic, the detailed expressions of cultural characters of Chinese universities within different historical periods are explored in three dimensions: the idea of Chinese universities, the system of Chinese universities, and the cultural symbols within the fields of Chinese universities. Even though cultural characters of Chinese universities were "internally generated" by the abstract main body of "Chinese culture," they are not an implicit feature or a metaphysical concept. On a realistic level, the expression of cultural characters of Chinese universities is detailed and observable.

By researching this idea, system, and cultural symbols of Chinese universities on multiple dimensions, it was proven that Chinese culture had a comprehensive, multi-leveled, and profound influence on Chinese universities.

Notes

1. Qian M. *Zhongguo Wenhuashi Daolun*. Beijing: Jiuzhou Publishing House, 2011: 1.
2. Benedict, R. *Patterns of Culture*. Trn, Wang Wei, et al. Beijing: Social Sciences Academic Press, 2009: 163.
3. Liu, M. *Zhongguo Xiandai Xueshu Yaolve*. Beijing: Joint Publishing, 2008: 123–124.
4. Liang, S. *Zhongguo Wenhua Yaoyi*. Shanghai: Shanghai People's Press, 2011: 7.
5. Ibid, p, 7.
6. Ibid, p. 10.
7. Feng, Y. *A Short History of Chinese Philosophy*. Trans. Tu Youguang. Beijing: Peking University Press, 2013: 1.
8. Ibid, p. 5.
9. Ibid, p. 22.
10. Qian M. *Zhongguo Wenhuashi Daolun*. Beijing: Jiuzhou Publishing House, 2011: 220.
11. Ibid, p. 5.
12. Ibid, p. 219
13. Ibid, p. 220
14. Ibid, p. 222.
15. Ibid, p. 241.
16. Feng, T. *Zhongguo Renwen Chuantong Yu Zhongxi Renwen Jingshen Jiangyan Lu* (A Collection of Speeches regarding Chinese Humanistic Tradition and Chinese and West Humanistic Spirit). Changsha: Hunan Education Publishing House, 2010: 168.
17. Liu, H. Liu Haifeng Yanjiang Lu (A Collection of Liu Haifeng's Speeches). Wuhan: Huazhong University of Science and Technology, 2012: 5.
18. Tu, Y. *A Critical History of Chinese Higher Education*. Wuhan: Hubei Education Press, 2002: 28.
19. Tian, S. *Kexue* Huayuquan De Zhengduo Ji Celve (On the Contest of Scientiric Discourse Right and Its Stragegies). Reading. 2001 (9): 35.
20. Ibid, p. 32.
21. Ibid, p. 35.
22. Hao, P. Beijing *Daxue* Chuangbanshi Kaoyuan (Textual Research of the Founding History of Peking University). Beijing: Peking University Press, 2008: Preface 4.
23. Chen, P., & Xia, X. Beida Jiushi (Nostalgic Stories of Peking University) Beijing: Joint Publishing, 1998: 283–284.
24. Zhang, J. Minguo *Daxue*: Yaoxiang *Daxue* Dangnian (Chinese Republican Universities: Throwing Back to the Univerties in the Past). Beijing: Orient Publishing Center, 2012: 265.
25. Chen, P. Zhongguo Daxue Shijiang (Hundred Years of Chinese Universities). Shanghai: Fudan University Press, 2002: 24.
26. Ibid, p. 8–9.
27. King, Y. The Idea of a University. Beijing: Joint Publishing, 2008: Oxford Version Preface 3.
28. Zhang, J. Minguo *Daxue*: Yaoxiang *Daxue* Dangnian (Chinese Republican Universities: Throwing Back to the Univerties in the Past). Beijing: Orient Publishing Center, 2012: 331.

29. Chu, Z. History and the Spirit of the Chinese University of Reflection. Taiyuan: Shanxi Education Press, 2006: 23.
30. Qian, M. *Zhongguo Wenhuashi Daolun* (An Introduction of Chinese Cultural History). Beijing: Jiuzhou Press, 2011: 193.
31. Liang, S. *Zhongguo Wenhua Yaoyi* (The Key Idea to Chinese Culture). Shanghai: Shanghai People's Press, 2011: 74.
32. Cited from ibid, p. 155.
33. Qian, M. *Zhongguo Wenhuashi Daolun* (An Introduction of Chinese Cultural History). Beijing: Jiuzhou Press, 2011: 120.
34. Liu, H. *Liu Haifeng Yanjiang Lu* (A Collection of Liu Haifeng's Speeches). Wuhan: Huazhong University of Science and Technology, 2012: 81.
35. Ibid, pp. 179–182.
36. Ibid, pp. 178.
37. Chen, P. *Daxue Hewei* (What University Does). Beijing: Peking University Press, 2006: 186.
38. Feng, Y. *A Short History of Chinese Philosophy*. Trans. Tu Youguang. Beijing: Peking University Press, 2013: 40.
39. Qian, M. *Zhongguo Wenhuashi Daolun* (An Introduction of Chinese Cultural History). Beijing: Jiuzhou Press, 2011: 71.
40. Tu, Y. *Zhongguo Gaodeng Jiaoyu Shilun*. Wuhan: Hubei Education Publishing House, 2002: 29.
41. Yu, J. *Kongzi Jiaoyu Xueshuo* (Theories of Confucian Education). Beijing: Capital Normal University Press, 2010: 28–29
42. Liang, S. *Zhongguo Wenhua Yaoyi*. Shanghai: Shanghai People's Press, 2011: 169.
43. Tu Y. Zhongguo Gaodeng Jiaoyu Shilun. Wuhan: Hubei Education Publishing House, 2002: 61.
44. Qian, M. *Zhongguo Wenhuashi Daolun* (An Introduction of Chinese Cultural History). Beijing: Jiuzhou Press, 2011: 178–179.
45. Xiong, M. *Zhongguo Gaodeng Jiaoyushi* (The History of Chinese Higher Education). Chongqing: Chongqing Publishing House, 1988: 104.
46. Ibid, p. 211.
47. Liang, S. *Zhongguo Wenhua Yaoyi*. Shanghai: Shanghai People's Press, 2011: 22–23.
48. Ibid, p. 169.
49. Ibid, p. 147.
50. Qian, M. *Zhongguo Wenhuashi Daolun* (An Introduction of Chinese Cultural History). Beijing: Jiuzhou Press, 2011: 120.
51. Liang, S. *Zhongguo Wenhua Yaoyi*. Shanghai: Shanghai People's Press, 2011: 204.
52. Qian, M. *Zhongguo Wenhuashi Daolun* (An Introduction of Chinese Cultural History). Beijing: Jiuzhou Press, 2011: 17–18.
53. Qian, M. *Zhongguo Xueshu Tongyi* (General Points of Chinese Academics). Taipei: Student Books, 1977: 225–226.
54. Jin, Y. *Daxue Zhi Linian* (The Ideas of Universities). Beijing: SDX Joint Publishing Company, 2008: 15.
55. Liang, S. Zhongguo Wenhua Yaoyi. Shanghai: Shanghai People's Press, 2011: 197.
56. Liang, S. Zhongguo Wenhua Yaoyi. Shanghai: Shanghai People's Press, 2011: 255.
57. Ibid, p. 256.
58. Chu, Z. *History and the Spirit of the Chinese University of Reflection*. Taiyuan: Shanxi Education Press, 2006: 316.
59. Du, W. *Rujia Renwen Jingshen Yu Wenming Duihua* (The Talks of Civilization and Humanistic Spirit of Confucianism). Wuhan: Huazhong University of Science and Technology, 2000: 86–87.

60. Cao, X. Zhongxi Wenhua Duibi Daolun: Guanyu Zhongguo Wenhua Xuanze De Zaijiantao (An Introduction to Comparison between Chinese and Western Cultures: Another Reflection on Chinese Cultural Choices). Beijing: China Youth Press, 1992: 65.
61. Zhi, J. Zhongguo Jinbainian Shi (The History of China during the Recent 100 Years). Harbin: Heilongjiang People's Press, 1983: 13.
62. Wang, E. Wanqing Zhgengzhi Sixiang Shilun (History and Comments on the Political Thoughts of the Late Qing Dynasty). Guilin: Guangxi Normal University Press, 2007: 38.
63. Chen, J. Zhongguo Jindai Jiaoyushi (History of Modern Chinese Education). Beijing: People's Education Press, 2003: 12–14
64. Cited from Ibid, p. 18
65. Lv, S. Zhongguo Jindaishi (History of Modern China) Changsha: Yuelu Publishing House, 2011: 7.
66. Zhu, G. Xixue Dongjian Yu Zhongguo Gaodeng Jiaoyu Jindaihua (The Eastward Spreading of Western Learning and the Modernization of Chinese Higher Education). Xiamen: Xiamen University Press, 1996: 16.
67. Zhang, J. Zhongguo Jindai Chuban Shiliao Chubian (A Draft Edit of Published Historic Materials of Modern China). Shanghai: Qunlian Press, 1953: 9.
68. Lee, H. Xueyiweiji: Chuantong Zhongguo De Jiaoyu (Learning for Oneself: Traditional Chinese Education). Hong Kong: The Chinese University of Hong Kong Press, 2012: 632.
69. Ibid, p. 2.
70. Ibid, p. 632.
71. Ibid, p. 173.
72. Ibid, p. 8.
73. Fei, X. From the Soil—The Foundations of Chinese Society. Beijing: Peking University Press, 2012: 43–44.
74. Ibid, p. 44.
75. Lee, H. *Xueyiweiji: Chuantong Zhongguo De Jiaoyu* (Learning for Oneself: Traditional Chinese Education). Hong Kong: The Chinese University of Hong Kong Press, 2012: 623.
76. Liu, H., & Li, B. Xue You Ze Shi: Jiaoyu Yu Keju (Do well in academics in order to pursue an official career: Education and imperial examination). Changchun: Changchun Publishing House, 2004: 155.
77. Zou, J. *Xue Er You Ze Shi* (Do well in academics in order to pursue an official career). Beijing: China Federation of Literary & Art Circles Publishing Corp, 2006: 4.
78. Ibid, p. 4.
79. Qian, M. *Zhongguo Wenhuashi Daolun* (An Introduction of Chinese Cultural History). Beijing: Jiuzhou Press, 2011: 120.
80. Tu, Y. *Zhongguo Gaodeng Jiaoyu Shilun* (History and comments on Chinese higher education). Wuhan: Hubei Education Publishing House, 2002: 359.
81. Zhang, J. Minguo *Daxue*: Yaoxiang *Daxue* Dangnian (Chinese Republican Universities: Throwing Back to the Univerties in the Past). Beijing: Orient Publishing Center, 2012: 340.
82. Li, H. Xue Yiwei Ji: Chuantong Zhongguo De Jiaoyu (Studying for Self: The Education of Traditional China) Hong Kong: The Chinese University of Hong Kong Press, 2012: 1.
83. Tian, Z., Shang, L. Zhongguo Gaodeng Jiaoyu Bainian Shilun: Zhidu Bianqian, Caizheng Yunzuo Yu Jiaoshi Liudong (History and Comments of A Century of Chinese Higher Education: The Shifting of Institution, the Operation of Finance and the Turnover of Teachers) Beijing: People's Education Press, 2006: 11.
84. Jin, Y. *Daxue Zhi Linian* (The Ideas of Universities). Beijing: SDX Joint Publishing Company, 2008: Preface 3.

85. Han, Y. *Daxue* Linian Lungang (Outline of Theories Regarding University Ideas). Beijing: People's Education Press, 2003: 58
86. Ibid, Preface 1.
87. Xiao, H. *Daxue* De Linian (The Idea of University). Wuhan: Huazhong University of Science and Technology, 2001: 5
88. Ibid.
89. Jin, Y. *Daxue Zhi Linian* (The Ideas of Universities). Beijing: SDX Joint Publishing Company, 2008: Self-preface 5.
90. Wang, J. *Daxue* Linian Zai Zhongguo (The Ideas of University in China). Beijing: Higher Education Press, 2007: Preface 1.
91. Ibid, Foreword 4.
92. Fan, Y. Shuangchong Qiyuan Yu Zhidu Shengcheng: Zhongguo Xiandai *Daxue* Zhidu Qiyuan Yanjiu (Double Origins and Institutional Generation: A Research on the Origin of Modern Chinese University System). Wuhan: Huazhong University of Science and Technology, 2011: 234.
93. Ibid, p. 220.

CHAPTER 2

Cultural Characteristics of Chinese Universities during the Late Qing Dynasty

The Qing Dynasty was the last feudal dynasty in Chinese history. The late Qing society, as the ending point of traditional society, unconsciously embarked on the modernization process in the conflict between modern Chinese and Western cultures. The three historical events, namely the Self-strengthening Movement, the Wuxu Reform, and the New Policies reform (the Late Qing Reform), officially started the evolution of social culture in the late Qing Dynasty. It is worth noting that Chinese universities, in the modern sense, also emerged at this time, and they also conceived and formed the original cultural characteristics of Chinese universities. In this process, the scholars in the late Qing Dynasty, as the last group of scholars of the traditional society, inherited the traditions of Chinese culture and developed modern Chinese education. Hence, they became the "driving force" of the cultural characteristics of Chinese universities during the late Qing Dynasty. In short, China's modern universities and their cultural characteristics sprouted from the Self-strengthening Movement, which was originated during the Wuxu era and further developed in the late Qing Reform under the facilitation of the scholars of the late Qing Dynasty. This is the basic understanding of the Chinese universities' cultural characteristics in the late Qing Dynasty that is used throughout this book.

Section 1: The social and cultural evolution of the late Qing Dynasty and the rise of Chinese universities

The continuation of Chinese history for thousands of years is not without turbulent social changes, but the social changes in the late Qing period are "unprecedented in three thousand years" of Chinese history. "In Chinese society during the thousands of years prior, although there was no lack of internal or inter-ethnic wars and frequent changes in dynasties, its cultural life continued. But in the 19th century, the survival of the ethnicity and the nation faced enormous difficulties, and an unprecedented crisis of trust rose against the ethnic culture."[1] The ethnic culture and the nation on which it depends were forced to embark on a journey of modernization, which brought about many changes in the current reality. "As a nation that was 'exogenously' modernized, the nation itself unconsciously acted as the leading force of modernization, due to the lack of internal motivation and mechanisms for modernization within the society. It can be argued that the nation trying to use its centralized political authority in the effort of confronting Western challenges is the historical starting point for modernization for this traditional and autocratic nation."[2] At the end of the 19th century, with the promotion and support of the late Qing government, Chinese society gradually moved towards the path of reform that saved the country and can be seen as the prelude to modernization.

The political changes in the late Qing Dynasty indeed had little effect on slowing the decline of the Qing Dynasty, and even more some, they could have been the disguise that accelerated the dissolution of the feudal dynasty. However, in this era of change, it is worth noting and further researching that the modernization of traditional Chinese culture began at this exact point – Chinese universities in the modern sense were also born then. We can say that the major reforms of the late Qing Dynasty created opportunities for the evolution of modern culture and the rise of Chinese universities, and this phenomenon was prevalent in the three historical events mentioned above. This section attempts to reproduce the actual state of "Chinese culture" and "Chinese universities" during the three major social changes in the context of the cultural conflict between China and the West. It does so through the historical investigation of the three major political reform movements and the exploration of the relationship between Chinese culture and Chinese universities in this particular historical period. This chapter serves as a rough outline of the cultural characteristics of Chinese universities in the late Qing Dynasty.

1. *The social and cultural evolution and the birth of Chinese universities during the Self-strengthening Movement.*

There were two historical reasons for the occurrence of the Self-strengthening Movement, one being the Taiping Heavenly Kingdom Movement, and the other being the Second Opium War. Although the Taiping Heavenly Kingdom Movement failed, it severely shook the orthodox Confucian cultural foundation of the Qing Dynasty. A leader of "Yangwu Pai" (the faction for Westernization supporters) Zeng Guofan painfully stated in his *Tao Yuefei Xi* (*Denounciation of the Canton Bandits*) that "these bandits took on foreign ruling structures and adopted Catholicism" so that "the ethics, etiquettes, rules, and culture that persisted through thousands of years in China were utterly abandoned and disgraced."[3] It is possible the impact of this "internal strife" on traditional society and culture led the ruling class to interpret this fight against peasant uprising as a battle to defend traditional culture. On the one hand, the elimination of cultural traditions within the Taiping Heavenly Kingdom scared the Qing government, while on the other hand, the re-invasion of Western powers also severely intimidated the Qing government. The flames of the Second Opium War subsided in the compromises made by the Qing government, but this political defeat inspired the consciousness of a group of enlightened scholars within the ruling class. *Fuzou Haifang Shiyi Shu* (*Re-Proposal to the Throne Regarding Coastal Defense*) says that after the Second Opium War, Li Hongzhang was shocked and touched by "the speed of Western telegraphs and ships, traveling thousands of miles in a blink of the eye; the power of military armaments, hundreds of times stronger than ours – anywhere within the reach of their artillery shells are vulnerable to total destruction, while our keeps and walls, no matter on water or land, are not enough to stop them." Li Hongzhang thought that these factors made Western countries "unprecedentedly dangerous enemies unseen in thousands of years" to China, showing a subtle hint of fear within his words. It is against this backdrop that the Self-strengthening Movement started. Chinese culture shifted along with the social changes, and Chinese universities have begun to sprout in these cultural shifts.

a) *Cultural shifts within social changes.*

The Confucian culture was the official ideology of the late Qing rulers. The Qing dynasty was a Manchu regime, but since Kangxi, the rationalistic teachings of the Cheng-Zhu school were respected for their "opening a new generation with Confucianism,"[4] and the Emperor Tongzhi even promoted that "our dynasty worships Confucianism and its ways, which are the ultimate ways of teaching" and urged Chinese scholars to "know and respect the teachings of Zong, Shang, Cheng, and Zhu, for the sake of better understanding the holy ways of Confucianism."[5] After the Opium War, accompanied by the mighty ships and cannons of the Western powers, China set off another wave of the introduction of Western learning to the East since the end of the Ming Dynasty and the beginning of the Qing Dynasty. This completely broke the thousand-year-old legacy whereby the Confucian culture had solemn respect in Chinese society. Chinese history officially entered a "century of cultural conflict." "The rise of the Self-strengthening Movement means the beginning of the evolution of Chinese culture. It is the beginning of the evolution of modern Chinese culture."[6] As far as the development and transformation of the word "Westernization" is concerned (Self-strengthening Movement is also known as Yangwu Yundong, or Westernization Movement), it was a breakthrough in the traditional concept of "Neixia Waiyi" (China shall be defined as "Xia," and the rest of the world shall be called "Yi," "Yi" being a derogatory term). The term "Yangwu" (affairs of "Yang", which is a more positive term for the outside world) was originally transformed from "Yi Wu." Since the Ming Dynasty, the term "Yi" was customarily used to refer to foreign countries.[7] During the era of Daoguang of the Qing Dynasty, the word "Yangwu" was only occasionally seen in official documentation, and it was from the era of Xianfeng that it was more generally accepted. At that time, although there were still some conservative scholars who repeatedly requested that "within customs and other authorities, the term 'Yiwu' should be used" to "cultivate a sense of pride," the change from "Yiwu" to "Yangwu" was still forced by both the external political negotiations and the acceptance by internal culture, making it inevitable. Even though this was merely a change of wording, it shows the change of the royal court's attitude towards Western culture.

With the rise of the Self-strengthening Movement, the question of learning Western culture became the focus of cultural debates. Although the promotion of Western learning in the Self-strengthening Movement was supported by the government, it had many twists and turns on the traditional cultural level, and it always encountered doubt and provocation from die-hard conservatives ("Wangu Pai"). These conservatives were represented by a chief government scholar called Wo Ren, who resolutely opposed the "Yangwu Pai" for their "learning from and working under foreigners," saying that this approach should "weaken the roots of the country and lose the hearts of the people." The Westernization supporters, represented by Li Hongzhang and Zeng Guofan, advocated that if China wanted to pursue self-improvement and prosperity, it must "learn from foreigners for the sake of competing with them." The dispute between the Westernization supporters and the conservatives regarding Chinese and Western cultures lasted for decades, with the establishment of Suanshu Guan within Tongwen Guan marking its fiercest peak. In 1866, Yi Xin (Aisin Gioro I Hin) submitted the request for the establishment of a special mathematics school. Due to strong xenophobia and their sense of superiority regarding Chinese culture, the conservatives launched the largest attack on Westernization supporters.

In *Qingba Tongwen Guan Yong Zhengtu Renyuan Xi Tiansuan Zhe* (*Petition to the Throne to Stop Scholars From Studying Astronomy and Calculus in Tongwen Guan*) (1867),

Wo Ren said: "As I have previously learned, the way of building a country should be based on etiquette and righteousness, not games of power; and the ultimate goal lies in the heart of the people, not techniques. But now we are frantically embarking on a journey to pursue a lesser technique while giving the honorable title of 'our teacher' to foreigners. It has to be argued that these foreigners might try to trick us, not teaching us the real essence of their learning. Even if they teach us with the utmost sincerity while we learn with the utmost diligence in return, what we achieve is merely some math tricks. In the thousands of years of history, I have never heard any examples where math played an important part in strengthening the weak. China is a vast country, and we should not worry about not having enough talent. If we need teachers in math and astronomy, we could simply search among our people, and I am sure we can find excellent candidates. Hence, why foreigners? And why must we learn from and work under them?"[8]

Yang Tingxi in *Qing Chexiao Tongwen Guan Yi Mi Tianbian Zhe* (*Petition to the Throne to Revoke Tongwen Guan to Prevent the Heaven from Raging*) (1867) also said, "Ever since the time of Xi, Xuan, Yao, Shun, Yu, Tang, Emperor Wen and Wu of Zhou, Zhougong, Confucius, Mencius and countless prominent Confucian and other philosophers, they have either carried out careful observation for the ultimate Tao, or developed on previous theories, and hence inherited the reasons of the world. They have established the theory of one ultimate truth ('Yi Yuan'), the mechanism of two 'Wu' ('Wu Xing' and 'Wu Qi') and the Tao of three 'Ji' (heaven, earth, and humans), and hence managed to see the truth of many disciplines. They have converted such knowledge into teachings that can be applied to all things. No matter if it is the record for the emperor, the strategies for officials, the research of ultimate learnings or the studies of great knowledge, this set of teachings can handle all subjects and explain even the most obscure details. And this is the reason why China has been the top achiever in astronomy, math, techniques and technologies since ancient times."[9]

Yi Xin and his fellows replied, "Due to the fact that we are exchanging correspondence and negotiating commercial deals, the request for finding teachers in astronomy and math is made out of desperation. The reason why we suggested hiring foreigners was done for the sake of observing the capabilities of foreign countries, and subsequently comparing them with our own knowledge. Currently, China can't make our own ships, guns and artillery weapons, as we do not possess the technology. If we can have scholars researching their books and their language, and hence translating the crucial parts, it would present us with the possibilities of training amongst our people, instead of having to use foreigners all the time."[10]

As a result of the debate, the Westernization supporters won with the support from the central ruling system, and Suanxue Guan was finally established. In this era of the conflict and integration of Chinese and Western cultures, the Westernization supporters gradually formed their own ideological system – "Zhongti Xiyong" (Chinese essence and Western utility). This system almost established the entirety of basic principles for the integration of Chinese and Western cultures throughout the late Qing Dynasty. Since then, Chinese traditional culture was no longer in the equivalence of Chinese culture, but its "main and most significant" part.

b) Chinese universities within cultural changes.

The Self-strengthening Movement "was a turning point in the history of China's education system and opened the prelude to new education in China."[11] China's modern universities sprouted during the Self-strengthening Movement. Westernized education is different from traditional education, which laid the first cornerstone for the modernization of Chinese higher education. First, modernized schools were established, which laid the groundwork for the establishment of modern Chinese institutions of higher learning. It is as Sheng Xuanhuai said, "The way of self-improvement is based on the cultivation of talents. The most basic way to seek talent is to set up schools."[12] According to statistics, during the 30 years between the founding of the Jingshi Tongwen Guan in 1862 and the eve of the Sino-Japanese War, the Westernization supporters established more than 30 new schools of various types. These included language schools to train a variety of foreign language talents, military schools for engineering, weapon manufacturing, ship driving and cultivation of other talents, and specialized schools to train talents in telegraph, communications, mining, medical and other fields.[13] During this period, the Westernized school generally provided a version of education where primary, middle, and higher education were integrated into one. It was also accurately assumed that modern Chinese higher education was brewed within these Westernized Academies.

Zhu Guoren pointed out in his book *Xixue Dongjian Yu Gaodeng Jiaoyu Jindaihua* (*Western Learning Spreading to the East and the Modernization of Chinese Higher Education*) that "The Westernized Schools were not schools for higher education in the strict sense, but they were the starting point for the development of modern higher education in China. Some schools later became, or were incorporated, into colleges and universities its strictest sense."[14] After, multi-disciplinary education using Western languages and techniques was promoted, building the foundation for modern China's multidisciplinary universities. According to Li Hongzhang, "Chinese scholars are obsessed with calligraphy and flowery sentences," leading to the result of "what they use is not what they have learned, and what they learn is not what they will use."[15] He believes that the most crucial point of Westernized education is to seek practicality in the studies, which is based on Western languages and techniques. To a certain extent, this broke the pattern of traditional Chinese education in which "Sishu Wujing" (the four fundamentals and five classics) dominate the world, and instead, the Westernized school that uses Western languages and techniques to accommodate a multidisciplinary nature became dominant.

For example, Beijing Normal University Tongwen Museum was established by the Westernization School. At first, it was only a foreign language education institution. In 1866, Yi Xin asked to set up a math school in addition to foreign languages. It was established in 1867. Since the establishment of the School of Computing, the Planetarium, Gezhi School, Medical School, Chemistry School, and Surveying and Mapping School have been gradually established. This roughly has the germination of later branch universities.[16] Mr. Pan Maoyuan believes that the Suanshu Guan can be regarded as a modern higher education institution if one judges by the division of disciplines and courses according to modern scientific differentiation. Tian Zhengping et al. stated in *Zhongguo Jiaoyu Bainian Shilun: Zhidu Bianqian, Caizheng Yunzuo Yu Jiaoshi Liudong* (*Hundred Years of Higher Education in China: Institutional Changes, Financial Operation and Teacher Mobility*) that if we look at the historical process of the development of China's modern new education system, there should be a consensus. That is, whether in theory, or practice, it is both the landmark of China's early modernization and the bud of China's modern higher education system.[17]

In summary, the Self-strengthening Movement actively introduced Western learning to set off the tide of modern Chinese cultural evolution. The idea of "*Zhongti Xiyong*" began to guide China's social changes. Of course, although the late Qing government acknowledged the use of Western culture, it still emphasized the utilization of Chinese culture as its system and roots. Therefore, "the evolution of Chinese culture at this stage is only carried out at the surface level, and there have been no fundamental changes in traditional culture."[18] However, Chinese universities have begun to sprout during this transformation of the conflict and integration of Chinese and Western cultures, and the brand of traditional culture was destined to become part of the innate nature of Chinese universities. In other words, although the cultural character of Chinese universities during this period was still an unfounded concept, the final result was rather predictable.

2. *The evolution of society and culture during the Wuxu Reform and the birth of Chinese universities*

In the Sino-Japanese War of 1894, the great nation of China crumbled in the hands of the small nation in a shockingly short period. The shock and humiliation brought by this defeat are equivalent, if not worse than the disgrace China suffered in the Opium War. The Opium War opened China's door and made China realize that the millennium of Chinese civilization was inferior to the Western gunboats, and China was put in a delicate situation. Even if China suffered invasion and humiliation, it still recognized the power of Western civilization and submitted to it. However, Japan, which had been a vassal to China from ancient times and had constantly faced China's contempt, was a country that suffered the same fate as China. It too became the object of Western aggression. Suffering defeat by Japan, which developed to an advanced state by adopting Western civilization, was extremely and extraordinarily humiliating for China. As a result, under great social turbulence and stimulation, new social changes were coming, and the Wuxu Reform was born following the tide of the times.

a) Cultural shifts within social changes.

If the evolution of Chinese culture during the Self-strengthening Movement was considered superficial, then it can be argued that the Chinese culture began to undergo profound changes during the Wuxu Reform. The emergence of the Wuxu Reform may be at odds with the Self-strengthening Movement at the political level, but it was in alignment with the direction of the Chinese culture's evolution. Moreover, it can be further affirmed that during the cultural evolution, the Wuxu Reform was undoubtedly more advanced than the Self-strengthening Movement. As some of the relevant scholars stated, during the Wuxu Reform, "brand new mediums of modern new culture appeared and were gradually formed into the age-old land of China – a group of new bourgeois intellectuals, promoting the development of the new cultural movement in China."[19]

Different from the Self-strengthening Movement, the Wuxu Reform was a relatively comprehensive enlightenment movement. It transcended the concept of "equipment and instrument" from Western culture. Comprehensive learning from Western culture became the cultural trend of the movement. It was this attempt to break the traditional cultural concepts that led the reformers to be attacked by both conservatives and Westernization supporters. Whether and how to learn from the West became the focal question of the trilateral cultural debate. The specific debate was mainly centered around the following topics.

First, it was concerning the carrying-out of reform. The conservatives believed that the traditions of the ancestors should be immutable, and they even put forward the term *Ningke Wangguo, Buke Bianfa* (let the nation die if it must, but the traditions shall not be altered), advocating for the sacred inviolability of traditions. Kang Youwei responded with "according to common sense, new things are strong while old things are weak; new things are fresh while old things are stagnant; new things are flexible while old things are rigid; new things are smooth while old things are obscure. This is the mechanism of things. The same applies to traditions, as old traditions will surely accumulate corruption as they age. And this is the reason why no traditions shall be immutable." He also stated that "if you observe the affairs of all nations in the world, you will see that the nations that are willing to change will survive, while nations that are not, will die. Those who change more shall thrive, and those who change less still could not escape their doom."[20] This statement not only scorned the stubbornness of the conservatives, but also the disadvantages of the "small changes" mentality of the Westernization supporters. It also encapsulated the basic viewpoint of the reformists, which was to advocate for "total changes" regarding Chinese and Western cultures.

The second question was about whether Western systems should be adopted. Although the Westernization supporters advocated learning from the West, they only adopted some specific methods of modern science, technology, culture, and education. The so-called "Western learning" in the Westernization discourse only referred to Western languages and techniques, while the political system and doctrines from Western society were left out. This was also the fundamental difference between the Westernization supporters and the reformers under the common premise of "change." From the standpoint of "total change," Liang Qichao accused the Westernization supporters of "an obsession with the so-called 'Western techniques,' which was merely their languages and military studies, while the greater knowledge was left out and fundamental issues were not addressed. In this sense, even if they managed to achieve a full-scale success, it would not be much."[21] We can hence observe that the reformists placed particular emphasis on the importance of the comprehensive adoption of Western learning.

The third question was whether to change the imperial examinations. The reformists believed that the root of the reform was in establishing schools that could cultivate talents, and to achieve this, the first change had to be the imperial examination system. Liang Qichao pointed out in *Lun Keju* (*On the Imperial Examinations*) that "to establish schools and cultivate talents for the sake of strengthening China, the most crucial action is to change the imperial examination system. The effect is proportional to the scale of changes."[22] There was no fundamental conflict between the reformists and the Westernization supporters regarding the reform of imperial examinations. The reform theories of the reformists, to a great extent, were inherited from the Westernization supporters' ideas that were not realized because of their "precocity." Since as early as the Tongzhi years, enlightened officials within the Westernization supporters movement had constantly proposed to change the imperial examination system. Zhang Zhidong's *Quanxue Pian* (*On Encouraging Learning*) also proposed changing of the imperial examination system. In contrast, the conservatives, as unconditional worshippers of feudal rule, always strongly supported the old imperial examination system from the Self-strengthening Movement to the Wuxu Reform. However, reforming the imperial examination system had become an inevitability by this time.

In short, the reformers showed a deeper understanding of Chinese and Western cultures in their cultural disputes with the conservatives and Westernization supporters. However, this did not mean that they were promoting a complete denial of Chinese culture and its substitution by Western culture, as Chinese culture was still the fundamental standpoint for all the changes they suggested.

b) Chinese universities within cultural changes.

"The Sino-Japanese War actually served as a powerful booster in the history of our new education. Since then, our people have come to know that to compete with foreign countries, merely guns and battleships would not be enough, neither should the basic understanding of foreign languages suffice. The key point lies in the training of talent that is familiar with both Chinese and Western knowledge."[23] Although the Wuxu Reform only lasted around 100 days, it cast a lasting impact on modern education. Liang Qichao stated in *Wuxu Zhengbian Ji* (*Coup on Wuxu Reform*) that "after the coup d'état, the emperor ordered schools in various provinces to be abolished, but many private schools still persisted. It can hence be observed that the people have been enlightened, and this process cannot be suppressed."[24] Some important education system reforms during the reform period laid the foundation for the birth of Chinese universities.

First was the abolition of the eight-part essay and the reform of the imperial examination system. These were the prelude to the birth of Chinese universities. In 1898, Kang Youwei wrote to Emperor Guangxu the "*Qingfei Bagu Shitie Kaifa Shishi Gaiyong Celun Zhe* (*Petition to the Throne on Replacing the Talent Selection Method of Using Eight-Part Essay, Political Poetry and Caligraphy with Discourse on Polities*) Emperor Guangxu granted his request and issued an edict stating that "beginning with the next round of imperial examination, all examinations of township level and below that used to test the content of Sishu shall change their subject to writing an argumentative thesis (a discourse analysis on polities). Detailed topics and process of the examination are to be decided by relevant officials and reported to me. This edict aims to abolish the enormous disadvantages within the old subjects of testing, and to promote changes that are in accordance with the present, for the sake of discarding harmful old habits and traditions."[25] Subsequently, Emperor Guangxu promulgated other edicts such as "Sui and Ke exams (economic examination held every year) of Jingji are to be merged with the main subject test, and the Sui and Ke exams of all provinces must shift their subject to the argumentative thesis, effective immediately" and "to promote the reform of imperial examination system, from now on, official posts are to be granted to the examinee accordingly immediately after they pass the test," as well as other orders that intended to reform the imperial examination system in an all-round way.

Second, was that academies were changed into schools, and traditional higher education underwent modernization transformations. In 1898, Kang Youwei sent a petition to Emperor Guangxu inviting him to establish schools and cultivate talent. Emperor Guangxu followed the suggestions made by Kang Youwei, and issued an edict to change academies into schools. It read, "Officials of all administrative levels must report the budget of academies within their jurisdiction to the central government within two months, and convert academies of all levels into schools that teach both Chinese and Western knowledge."[26]

Third, the Imperial University of Peking was reopened, and the first modern Chinese university was born. The Wuxu Reform only lasted around 100 days, and Empress Dowager Cixi assumed the ruling position. She abolished almost all the edicts and policies created during the reform, leaving only the Imperial University of Peking as "it started early and could not be abolished." As early as in 1896, Li Duanfen proposed the establishment of a "Peking Imperial University" for the first time in *Qing Tuiguang Xuexiao Zhe* (*Petition to the Throne on the Popularization of Schools*), and Sun Jianai also wrote to Emperor Guangxu pleading a grant for the reopening of the Imperial University of Peking. During the reform in 1898, Kang Youwei and his team brought up the matters of establishing the Imperial University of Peking again. In the same year, Emperor Guangxu released an order reading, "After much urging and pleading from officials, it is deemed that the Imperial University of Peking should be established. It is hereby approved, and the process is to be started immediately."[27] He ordered the Grand Minister of State to work in conjunction with the Minister of Foreign Affairs to establish the Imperial University of Peking, and the rules of conduct and prohibitions of the university were released the following year. This year marked the institutionalization and standardization of the Imperial University of Peking.

In short, although the reform of the education system during the Wuxu Reform failed, it indeed spawned the first university in modern China, and hence the history of Chinese universities officially begun.

To sum up, the Wuxu Reform took the standpoint of "total change" and tried to rejuvenate the great nation through comprehensive social changes with its immense passion and enthusiasm. Regarding its political result, the reform was undoubtedly a tragic failure, but as Liang Qichao said, after the reform, the social trend of openness was successfully established. The reform introduced Western learning on a comprehensive level, facilitating the modernization of the late Qing society. However, as a political shakeup of the feudal dynasty, maintaining the feudal rule of the Qing dynasty was still its fundamental purpose. This was the only aspect that was considered immutable in its scheme of "total change." It is worth noting that with the birth of Chinese universities, the cultural character of Chinese universities gradually became a clear concept in this social change.

3. *The social and cultural evolution and the development of Chinese universities during the New Policies Reform of the late Qing Dynasty.*

During the war of aggression against China with the eight major countries, China suffered a crushing defeat. Its capital fell, and the royal family was forced into exile. The supreme rulers felt the embarrassment and hardship of expulsion as the country broke down around them. After the Gengzi Guobian, or the War of Aggression against China, the mentality of the entire Chinese society underwent huge and profound changes, and reform became the basic consensus for the society of that time. By then, the political environment was filled with changes and it was no longer comparable with that of the period of the Self-strengthening Movement and the Wuxu Reform. During this period, stubborn conservatives almost disappeared within the political decision-making group, and the legitimacy of change was no longer severely questioned or hindered. Therefore, the New Policies reform at the end of the Qing Dynasty coincided with unprecedented opportunities for change, and it was historically inevitable for the rulers to follow the trend of the times and carry out political reform. In 1901, to solidify the basis of Chinese traditions, the rulers of the Qing Dynasty released *Xinchou Bianfa Zhaoshu* (*Imperial Edict on 1901 Xinchou Political Reform*) under the trend of social reform, starting the prelude to the New Policies Reform of the late Qing Dynasty.

a) Cultural shifts within social changes.

The New Policies Reform of the late Qing Dynasty at the beginning of the 20th century was the last-ditch effort of the late Qing government, as a traditional feudal autocracy, to break traditions and to modernize. Slightly different from the two previous political reforms, this reform had neither obvious party disputes nor repression by the supreme governing group. Instead, it was a social reform initiated directly by the highest powers. In the last ten years of the Qing Dynasty, the New Policies Reform led to the fundamental trend of social and cultural evolution. During this period, the concepts regarding the Chinese and Western cultures mainly adhered to *Zhongti Xiyong* that originated during the Self-strengthening Movement. Some scholars believed that, strictly speaking, the idea of *Zhongti Xiyong* had not reached its maturity during the Self-strengthening Movement. As such, it could not be taken for granted as the political framework of the Self-strengthening Movement, and in the meantime, "during the New Policies Reform (1901–1911), *Zhongti Xiyong* was the core idea of the official ideology of Qing."[28] Su Yunfeng also pointed out that it took more than thirty years for the late Qing Dynasty to conclude *Zhongti Xiyong*, laying out the foundation for the new education of the late Qing Dynasty.[29] Therefore, in both political discourse and educational discourse, it was almost recognized across the board that *Zhongti Xiyong* was the core concept of the New Policies Reform.

The idea of *Zhongti Xiyong* first appeared in the 1860s. Feng Guifen is currently considered to be the earliest proposer of the term. During the Self-strengthening Movement, Zeng Guofan and Li Hongzhang became the actual practitioners of this idea. After the Sino-Japanese War, *Zhongti Xiyong* in Zhang Zhidong's *On Encouraging Learning* (1898) was finally systemized and established as an official ideology. We can say that the idea permeated the entirety of the late Qing society, either for individual doctrine or an official discourse, as a newly sprouted bud, or a formally established idea, and it almost acted as the backdrop for the reforms during the late Qing dynasty. Undoubtedly, during the New Policies Reform of the late Qing Dynasty, the cultural concept of *Zhongti Xiyong* had penetrated all levels of society. There were no obvious bipolar cultural disputes, and there was no fierce dispute over party interests. As a political ideology, it gradually transformed into universal socio-cultural consciousness. In this sense, the New Policies reform preceded the two that came before.

The cultural dispute regarding the question of whether China should learn from Western civilization that happened between the Westernization supporters and the conservatives lasted throughout the Self-strengthening Movement, while Wuxu Reform was riddled with cultural arguments and disputes among the three factions of reformists, Westernization supporters, and conservatives. After the Sino-Japanese War of 1894, the Westernization supporters stepped down from the stage of history. The Wuxu Reformists were merely a short-lived flash in the dark, and the conservatives vanished from the political structure during the battle of Gengzi Guobian. The idea of *Zhongti Xiyong* gradually matured after two political reforms, and it became a social consensus in the tide of social reform at the time. To a certain extent, the debate between Chinese and Western cultures was no longer the main theme or the main concern of the New Policies Reform.

However, it is worth noting that while the society's prejudice of the incompatibility of *Zhong* (Chinese) and *Xi* (Western) was gradually fading away, the internal logic of *Ti* (system) and *Yong* (techniques) was further strengthened instead. During the New Policies Reform, it was not so much the concept of the fusion of the Chinese and Western cultures that became more prosperous, but rather the concept of *Ti* and *Yong*. It can be understood that Chinese cultural ideas have always maintained their ingrained dominant status in the cultural conflict between China and the West in the late Qing Dynasty. It can also be said that Chinese culture has always been a complete concept for the late Qing society.

b) Chinese universities and cultural changes.

The New Policies Reform was an important period of major changes, reorganizations, and divisions within the traditional feudal education system. During this time, several Chinese universities (in the modern sense) were newly established and developed. As Wuxu Reform failed, the conservatives were at once returned to the forefront of history, and all educational measures were abolished. However, just three years later, many education reform policies of the Wuxu era were realized in the New Policies Reform. During this period, more education reform policies were promulgated, which provided a good opportunity for the initial development of Chinese universities.

The first change concerned the transformation of academies into schools. This change meant that colleges and universities were revitalized. In 1901, Emperor Guangxu released the edict *Gai Shuyuan Wei Xuetang* (*On Transforming Private Academies into Public Schools*): The Imperial University of Peking has already been established, but it must undergo further adjustments and improvements. For all other academies within all provinces, those located in the capitals of provinces should be converted into universities, those located in cities and the state of Zhili must be converted into middle schools, while those located in counties should be converted into primary schools. Apart from this, pre-school institutions should also be established.[30] Many people were dissatisfied with the abolition of the academy system, but after all, they couldn't defeat the trend of the times.

The second was the abolition of the Imperial Examination System and the establishment of schools, and the further promotion of university institutions. Since 1904, people including Yuan Shikai, Zhang Zhidong, Zhang Baixi had submitted multiple requests for the abolishment of the imperial examination system, listing the disadvantages of the system as "it hinders the progress of schools and impedes the cultivation of talents." In 1905, Emperor Guangxu granted their requests in *Liting Keju Yi Guang Xuexiao* (*Abolish the imperial examination system immediately to popularize public schools*): "All intellectuals could see that the victory of Japan against Russia should be attributed to teachers of their primary schools. Apart from this, it can be argued that the prosperity of all strong powers and nations are based on their schools. The reason for China being left behind is that we still have the imperial examination system, schools are not yet widely accepted, the scholars cannot achieve a sure mind, the wisdom of the people cannot be improved, and hence it is difficult to renew and evolve our level of knowledge. Therefore, to remedy the difficulties, the establishment of schools must be promoted. To achieve this, the imperial examination system must be abolished first.[31]

The third was the promulgation of the "Renyin School System" and the "Guimao School System." This aided in the final establishment of the university system. In 1902, the Qing government promulgated the *Qinding Xuetang Zhangcheng* (*Imperial Endorsed Constitution of Educational Institutions*), which was the first academic constitution in the history of Chinese education, but it was not implemented. In 1904, the first school system was promulgated and implemented in modern China, by which the *Zouding Xuetang Zhangcheng* (*Imperial Endorsed Petition on the Constitution of Educational Institutions*) was formally introduced. It contained 20 chapters, covering various levels and types of education systems. It included the independent *Xuewu Gangyao* (*University Administrative Outline*), and reflected on the guiding ideology and academic purposes of the school system. The *University Administrative Outline* stated that all schools, both large and small, outside Beijing, must follow the orders issued by the emperor, to correctly operate and foster renaissance talent, which is compliant with the emphasis of the three generations of schools for cultivating talent that excels *in De, Xing, Dao* and *Yi* studies. Provincial schools should also be established with this in mind.[32]

In general, the education reform over the final ten years of the New Policies Reform, especially the promulgation of the modern academic systems, helped China's education tp develop at a rapid pace and it had put it on the right track. According to statistics, in 1907, there were three colleges and universities in the country with a total of 516 students, along with 76 colleges and specialized schools with a total of 13,601 students.

In 1908, there were three universities in the country, with a total of 643 students, along with 88 colleges and specialized schools with a total of 18,059 students. In 1909, there were three universities in the country with a total of 749 students, along with 108 colleges and specialized schools with a total of 19,899 students.[33] The three universities were the Imperial University of Peking, the Peiyang University, and the Shansi Imperial University. They have persisted since their establishment in the late Qing Dynasty to this day.

In short, the education reform of the New Policies Reform gradually led modern education in China towards institutionalization and standardization, and China's higher education system also began to take shape at this time.

In conclusion, the New Policies Reform of the late Qing Dynasty, as the last link in the history of the social evolution of the late Qing society, made a greater breakthrough than the two previous political reforms. It relied on its top-down political authority and promoted the modernization of social culture. However, the political goal of the New Policies Reform, the Wuxu Reform, and the Self-strengthening Movement remained highly consistent, which maintained the traditional cultural foundation of feudal rule. Although Western learning gradually entered many levels of the late Qing's society and has continued to penetrate Chinese society after many reforms since modern times, strengthening the foundation of traditional Chinese culture had always been the fundamental direction of values for the cultural development of the late Qing society. With the emergence of the modern academic system, Chinese universities gained their initial development, and the cultural character of Chinese universities complemented the Western academic system.

4. *General characteristics of the cultural character of Chinese universities in the late Qing Dynasty.*

In the late Qing Dynasty, along with the Western powers' ships and guns, Western culture entered China on a great scale and the late Qing government embarked on the road of continuous independent reform to maintain its feudal rule that was on the verge of extinction. The three successive social changes became the most important social foundations for the social and cultural evolution of the late Qing Dynasty and the rise of Chinese universities. Cultural and social changes also gradually formed the most realistic springboard for the rise of Chinese universities. Chinese universities sprouted from the Self-strengthening Movement; they were officially born during the Wuxu era; they saw initial development during the New Policies Reform at the end of the Qing Dynasty, and maintained a certain consistency in their development. The following section summarizes the specific characteristics exhibited by Chinese universities in the late Qing Dynasty, further clarifies the relationship between Chinese culture and Chinese universities, and interprets the general characteristics of the cultural character of Chinese universities in the late Qing Dynasty. A base point for consideration is that Chinese culture occupied a dominant position in Chinese universities, which virtually stipulated the general characteristics of the cultural character of Chinese universities in the late Qing Dynasty.

First of all, Chinese universities started with "Chinese learning," and their cultural characteristics bore heavy traces of traditional ethics. It is true that since the beginning of the Self-strengthening Movement, Western culture had already entered the field of Chinese education in the form of "equipment and instruments." The Wuxu Reform and the New Policies Reform legitimized Western culture in modern Chinese universities. Along with the social changes in the late Qing Dynasty, it was an indisputable fact that Western learning continued to deepen its roots in Chinese universities. On the one hand, the fundamental role of Chinese learning was also further strengthened. In the trend of *Zhongti Xiyong*, the deepening of Western learning was not contradictive to the strengthening of Chinese learning. The two influenced each other and showed a directly-proportional relationship. On the other hand, the government of the late Qing dynasty actively advocated "learning from the Westerners" and "learning from the Westerners for the sake of competing with them." Still, this emphasized that "regardless of the size of the schools outside Beijing, more attention should be paid to self-cultivation of ethics rather than other subjects, for they are the basis for the cultivation of talent."[34] Zhang Zhidong paid particular attention to the foundational role of Chinese learning. In his work *On Encouraging Learning*, there was a saying, "As of now, if we want to strengthen China and preserve Chinese learning, we would have to teach Western knowledge. However, we must not abandon the root of Chinese learning, and we must adjust the Western knowledge according to our Chinese learning, or we risk falling into a situation where the strong become bandits and the weak become preys and slaves. If that turns out to be the case, we will be better off without Western learning." He also said that "today's scholars must first master the Scriptures of our previous philosophers and teachers, to know the true purpose of education."[35] The above remarks were intended to emphasize the point that, although Western learning was needed, it was only a minor part of education, as the basic ethics of Chinese culture were the essence. Chinese universities were based on Chinese learning, the "ethics of self-cultivation" was the main content of Chinese universities in the late Qing Dynasty, and it became a product of this era.

Secondly, Chinese universities set their goal as "strengthening the nations," which brought prominent political logic into their cultural features. The military aggression of the Western powers in modern times initiated unprecedented changes in modern China. China's modern history is full of defeat and humiliation, and self-reliance became the theme of the times for modern China. The government of the late Qing Dynasty suffered the humiliation of invasions and the cession of lands. Seeking talent for the sake of survival, and developing education for the sake of talent became an inevitable historical choice. Westernized schools were established during the Self-strengthening Movement, but their purpose was only to "learn from Westerners for the sake of competing with them." The rise of China's universities inherited this basic goal of academic development.

Zhang Baixi set up the mission for the Imperial University of Peking, which was based on the theory of "Zhiyong Yitu" (the integration of theory and practice). Starting from "grow our intelligence for competing with the world, search for better ways of ruling for achieving prosperity. The royal court seeks talents for the sake of renewal of knowledge, and it builds schools for the sake of seeking talent."[36] Zhang Baixi further clarified the logic of "strengthen the nation – seek talent – establish schools" of the late Qing Dynasty up to modern times. It can be argued that Chinese universities in the late Qing dynasty, to varying degrees, had the goal of instantly strengthening the nation. The political function of higher education had always been the basic tenet of the academic establishment, and "strengthening the nation" became the main driving force for the rise and development of Chinese universities in the late Qing Dynasty.

Based on the above two points, we can conclude that Chinese culture was the main body of Chinese universities in the late Qing Dynasty. Chinese universities are based on Chinese learning, and the ethics of Confucian classics became the foundation of Chinese universities; Chinese universities aimed to strengthen the nation, and the integration of politics and education became the main feature of Chinese universities.

Section 2: The Path of Formation of the Cultural Character of Chinese Universities in the Late Qing Dynasty

Chinese culture was, of course, important as the intrinsic quality of the cultural characteristics of Chinese universities in the late Qing Dynasty. However, without strong external support, the cultural character of Chinese universities would not have spontaneously formed. Who played a leading role in the formation of the cultural characteristics of Chinese universities in the late Qing Dynasty? Who connected Chinese culture and Chinese universities? One of the major reasons for the formation of the cultural characteristics of Chinese universities in the late Qing Dynasty was that the scholars in the late Qing Dynasty acted as its main external driving force. If we say that Chinese culture provided the possibility for the formation of the cultural character of Chinese universities in the late Qing Dynasty, then we can say that it was the scholars who turned this possibility into reality. During the formation of the cultural characteristics of Chinese universities in the late Qing Dynasty, both were indispensable.

The scholars were collectively referred to as the *Shi* of the late Qing Dynasty. *Shi* not only included bureaucrats and officials, but also included teachers, scholars, and gentry among commoners. Regarding the concept of *Shi*, "if we count from the era of Confucius, the tradition of China's '*Shi*' continued for at least 2,500 years, and it continues to linger till this day. This is a unique phenomenon in the history of world culture."[37] The scholars in the late Qing Dynasty can be regarded as the last group of *Shi* in traditional Chinese society. Following Xinhai Revolution of 1911 and the demise of the Qing Dynasty, the traditional Chinese society ended, and traditional scholars conceptually ceased to exist. Almost overnight, the scholars in the late Qing Dynasty turned into intellectuals in the Republic of China, and the scholar class officially withdrew from the historical stage of Chinese society. However, it is worth investigating that the last batch of *Shi* in Chinese history played an important role in the social reform and cultural changes of the late Qing Dynasty, and they were also the main builders, developers, and the first batch of "cultural inheritors" within the process of formation of the cultural character of Chinese universities.

Therefore, to thoroughly understand the unique "cultural inheritor" status of these scholars regarding the Chinese culture and Chinese universities, and explore the path of formation of the cultural characters of Chinese universities in the late Qing Dynasty, this section attempts to analyze their relationship in three steps. First, by reexamining the main cultural views held by these scholars, we can find out the internal relationship between the scholars and Chinese culture, and dig out the cultural characteristics of these scholars. Second, to summarize and analyze the main characters of Chinese universities that were under the leadership of these scholars, we need to analyze the symbiotic structure between these scholars and Chinese universities, to understand the cultural characters of Chinese universities based on the cultural characters of the scholars. The third step is to focus on the late Qing scholars who played an important role in the political structure of the late Qing dynasty, and, with some examples, analyze the influence of some representative late Qing scholars on the cultural character of Chinese universities led by them on a practical level.

1. Late-Qing scholars and Chinese culture

"When Western knowledge and instruments were first introduced to China, Chinese scholars engaged in interpretation and critical discussion regarding these new matters and their knowledge. That is to say, they took subjective illustrations over objective reception. This is almost a destined natural trend. Due to historical conditions and the objective environment at that time, the path that Chinese scholars could take was destined to be rather traditional, without the possibility of elimination or leaping forward from traditions."[38] Wang Ermin believes that the scholars of late Qing confined themselves by trying to understand Western things with their Chinese learning-based cognition. From the perspective of culture, the reason why the scholar class "engaged in interpretation and critical discussion with its inherent knowledge base" and "took subjective illustrations over objective reception" and hence formed a "destined natural trend" is that they were under the heavy influence of their strong Chinese cultural characters, which were difficult to avoid and control. As some of the later scholars pointed out, "Late Qing scholars tried to explain Western matters based on their traditional knowledge, and the subjective ideas within often dominated their views unknowingly. If we can first affirm that their doctrine was not deliberately self-deceiving, then the sincerity of their interpretation and discussions is worthy of our attention, as it is possible to understand the basic qualities of the ideological trend of their era."[39] Therefore, if we avoid the secular perspective of "self-deception," we should re-examine the theories and thoughts that were popular among these scholars in the late Qing Dynasty, as these theories and thoughts were the "sincere" cultural ideas of the scholars of the late Qing era. The popular theoretical thought is the "sincere" Chinese cultural concept of scholars in the late Qing Dynasty. Xiong Yuezhi analyzed the social response of China to Western learning in his book *Xixue Dongjian Yu Wanqing Shehui* (*The Eastward Introduction of Western Learning and the Society of the Late Qing Dynasty*) and concluded that there are three kinds of doctrines, namely "the debate of Yuan (source) and Liu (stream)," "the theory of Ti and Yong," and "opinion of extremes." Based on this thought, this book analyzes the theories of "*Xixue Zhongyuan*" (Western learning originated from China), "*Zhongti Xiyong*," and "Zhongxue Duzun" (Chinese learning rules supreme), and the views on Chinese and Western cultures of the late Qing Dynasty. All of these will be carefully examined to thoroughly understand the Chinese cultural sentiments that the scholars in the late Qing Dynasty adhered to.

a) The theory of "Zhongxue Duzun."

The so-called "opinion of extremes" refers to the attitude of complete rejection of Western learning along with total admiration for Chinese culture. Throughout the Qing Dynasty, many scholars adhered to this mindset. Xiong Yuezhi presented the example that Yang Guangxian of the early Qing Dynasty "would prefer to have no decent calendar in China than to have Westerners in China." He also mentioned the dispute between the late-Qing conservative scholars such as Wo Ren and the Westernization supporters regarding the establishment of Tongwen Guan. He pointed out that the rejection of Western culture was influenced by China-centrism, which respected only China and despised foreign states. This was caused by China's long-term seclusion and isolation, along with its lack of basic understanding of Western culture.[40] Boiled down, the phenomenon was, to a great extent caused by the "superior mentality" of scholars in the late Qing dynasty. This mood was rather understandable. The so-called sense of cultural superiority has existed in China since its ancient times, and all dynasties have regarded China as the *Tian Xia* (literally translated as "under the sky," meaning the entire world). In modern times, even though Western culture forcibly entered China, the long-standing cultural superiority of Chinese people still could not be instantly abolished. Therefore, it was reasonable for the Chinese to reject Western learning at this time. Xiong Yuezhi called this kind of cultural reaction of the scholars in the late Qing Dynasty as "opinion of extremes," which itself seemed to contain a certain hint of prejudice.

By reviewing the cultural psychology of scholars in the late Qing Dynasty, this book summarizes this concept as the "Chinese-culture-as-center view" of the scholars in the late Qing Dynasty. The notion of using Chinese culture as the center was not simply an act of "self-deception," but an act of maintaining and adhering to traditional culture. From this perspective, the scholars of the late Qing Dynasty, who are centered around Chinese culture, can also be considered as the inheritors and loyal guardians of traditional Chinese culture.

b) The theory of **Xixue Zhongyuan.**

The so-called *Xixue Zhongyuan* theory was very popular among scholars in the late Qing Dynasty. The basic point of this theory was that certain sciences, technologies, and various aspects in the Western world actually originated from China and that they were introduced into the Western world or were acquired by Westerners by learning from China. Hence, according to this theory, China was restoring its own older knowledge rather than learning from the West.[41] Most scholars in the late Qing Dynasty held this view, and many social theories of the period were also derived from this theory. For example, the theories of *Zhongti Xiyong* and *Tuogu Gaizhi* (inheriting from ancient times with adjustments to the system) are all variants and extensions of *Xixue Zhongyuan*. In contrast to "opinion of extremes," this theory does not reject Western learning, but at the same time, it does not acknowledge Western learning as a concept. Many scholars of the period only accepted Western learning as "old knowledge" from Chinese learning and maintained that the essence of Chinese learning was their fundamental purpose. Through this, we can sense a hint of scholars' cultural self-esteem. When analyzing the supporters of this theory, Xiong Yuezhi pointed out that "this is a highly complicated mentality of China, as it once had a glorious history of civilization, which appeared to be outdated under the impact and contrast generated by Western culture. But it is not willing to remain outdated. Hence, it started learning from the West while shying away from actually acknowledging the fact that they were indeed trying to learn from the West. People with a shallow history of civilizations and traditions would not have such mentality, and nations that are open-minded or standing at the forefront of world civilization would not have it as well."[42] The long history of Chinese culture and the backwardness of its reality were the unavoidable facts of China during the late Qing Dynasty. And the phenomenon of the scholars of the time learning from the West, while still feeling shame in acknowledging their actions was rather understandable. From the standpoint of Chinese culture, this is mainly the external manifestation of the strong cultural self-esteem of the scholars of the late Qing Dynasty. The theory of *Xixue Zhongyuan* lacked historical research and appeared to be rather imperious with minimal academic value, but it did revive Chinese culture to some extent. "Under the influence of the theory of *Xixue Zhongyuan*, a trend of researching Chinese science, technology, and democratic thoughts emerged in the academic circles of the late Qing Dynasty."[43] From this point of view, even though the theory appeared to be rather far-fetched, to some extent, it still maintained the dignity of Chinese culture and encouraged scholars to start learning Western knowledge while using Chinese culture as their base. For example, the "opinion of extremes" has been constantly reproached, and people usually consider "the debate of Yuan and Liu" as "ridiculous," "biased," "far-fetched" or even "fake." It could be argued that these opinions were also unjust.

This book believes that "the debate of the Yuan and Liu", as a "Chinese-culture-as-origin view," demonstrates the strong cultural self-esteem of the scholars of the late Qing Dynasty.

c) The theory of Zhongti Xiyong.

Zhongti Xiyong was one of the most important theoretical views among scholars in the late Qing Dynasty. From Feng Guifen, Shen Yugui to Zeng Guofan, Li Hongzhang, and Zhang Zhidong, they all believed in *Zhongti Xiyong*. "The theory of *Zhongti Xiyong* is like a very flexible rubber bag. Since the content of both Chinese learning and Western learning is very extensive, the questions of what parts of Chinese learning should be considered as 'Ti' and what parts of Western learning should be considered as 'Yong' became open-ended, since the answers could vary from individual to individual, as this is a matter of personal opinion and wisdom."[44] Therefore, to explain this theory from different perspectives, *Zhongti Xiyong* was highly diversified. However, no matter what perspective you take, the dominant status of Chinese culture is inherently unchanged.

Under the strong impact of Western learning, the scholars of the late Qing Dynasty felt the imminent crisis of Chinese learning. "Maintaining the dominant status of Chinese learning" became their utmost concern, which was almost an instinct for the scholars in the late Qing Dynasty. From this perspective, the concept of *Zhongti Xiyong* was mainly a cultural self-defense mechanism generated by the crisis of the time. However, sharing the same fate with the "opinion of extremes" and "debate of Yuan and Liu," *Zhongti Xiyong* is often regarded as a fallacy of the scholars during the late Qing Dynasty. Some even argued that it did not make any sense even on a semantic level. As Wang Ermin said, "Whenever someone talks about the late-Qing scholars and their theory of *Zhongti Xiyong*, they usually use a sarcastic and scornful tone. And hence, few have ever explored it on a deeper level and given it a fair judgment."[45] As a matter of fact, beyond the theoretical discussion, the so-called theory of *Zhongti Xiyong* was merely a "Chinese-culture-as-main-body view" that was born by the cultural defensiveness of the scholars in the late Qing Dynasty.

To sum up, the late-Qing scholars' views on Chinese culture can all be basically categorized into the three points mentioned above, the "Chinese-culture-as-center view," the "Chinese-culture-as-origin view," and the "Chinese-culture-as-main-body view." Looking at the commonality of the three cultural concepts, we can obtain a few impressions. First, the scholars of the late Qing Dynasty always took Chinese culture as an orthodox idea. Second, these scholars took the responsibility to revive traditional culture as their duty. Third, the prerequisite for accepting Western culture by scholars in late Qing Dynasty remains the fundamental starting point of Chinese culture. Anyhow, scholars in late Qing Dynasty saw Chinese culture as the center, the origin or the main body. This point may be subjective but it is reasonable.

Firstly, they were well-versed in Confucianism from a young age, and they were well-trained in Chinese learning. *Shi* came out of Confucianism, and since the Han Dynasty, most of the ancient Chinese scholars were considered to be *Rushi* (Confucian *Shi*). In the late Qing Dynasty, as a class of *Shi* in traditional society, most of these scholars learned Confucianism from a young age and possessed a profound knowledge of it. For example, Liang Qichao, a gifted scholar during the Wuxu Reform – "from the age of four or five, he would sit on his mother's knee and learn the content of *Sishu* and *The Book of Songs*; at night, he slept with his father, who taught him great tales and teachings of ancient heroes and philosophers." And hence, he "knew Wujing by heart at the age of six, and was capable of writing thousand-word-long essays at an instant from the age of nine."[46] Another example is Wang Guowei, a great tutor of the Emperor Puyi, who wrote in a self-prologue, "we had five or six boxes of books in my family. I would read all of them after I return home from the academy, except for the book *Shisan Jing Zhushu*, as I did not like it as a child. When I was sixteen, I saw a friend of mine reading the book *Hanshu* (*Book of the Han*, history of the Han Dynasty), and I liked the book so much, I spent all my savings accumulated from the gift money from Chinese New Year and bought *Qian Sishi* in Hangzhou. And hence began my journey of reading."[47]

To some extent, this deep basis of Chinese learning and philosophical culture of Confucianism even promoted the acceptance of Western learning among the scholars of the late Qing. Following the Sino-Japanese War, Liang Qichao and Wang Guowei both "strived hard to acquire new knowledge" and took the initiative to accept the Western culture. As some scholars have said, "For the seventy years of the late Qing Dynasty, traditional thoughts and Confucianism provided the basic motivation for modernization and provided intellectuals with the courage and theoretical basis to accept Westernization."[48] This does make sense. Confucius once said, *Min Er Haoxue, Buchi Xiawen* (A smart and studious person never feels ashamed learning from those intellectually inferior to him). He also said, *Sanren Xing Biyou Woshi* (When three are walking together, I am sure to find something I could learn from among them). All these mottos were to teach the world to be humble, eager and willing to learn from others. From this perspective, it is understandable that scholars in the late Qing dynasty would refuse Western learning because of their profound experience in Chinese learning, and it is also understandable that they would accept Western learning because of the same reason. This perspective helps us understand that the scholars' various Chinese cultural concepts in the late Qing Dynasty originated from their deep-rooted inherent culture of Chinese learning, which contained an unconscious sense of cultural belonging.

Second, they were dedicated to self-cultivation and ruling the world, and had a strong sense of loyalty and patriotism. Self-cultivation, the establishment of family and ruling the world were the pursuits of ancient scholars. The traditional *Shi* would be bestowed the title of *Dafu* as they became government officials. As this was achieved, loyalty to the emperor and protection of the country would become their life-long responsibility. Those who did not succeed in the imperial examination would either step down and resign to research, or become a teacher, but they would never abandon their loyalty to the country. Therefore, as loyal Confucian worshippers, it was their fundamental responsibility to enter the ruling class and serve the country. In the minds of scholars in the late Qing Dynasty, there was a firm concept of respecting Confucianism and remaining loyal to the emperor, and the two concepts are interconnected. The so-called Chinese cultural concept of scholars in the late Qing Dynasty was, to some extent, also a kind of national concept, and its purpose was to stabilize the foundation of the country. In their eyes, the solidification of China's lay in the strengthening of its basis in Confucian culture. Every social reform in the late Qing Dynasty was carried out with this purpose. Judging from the speeches and remarks made by scholars in the late Qing Dynasty, they frequently quoted Confucius' speeches to rejuvenate the country. When Western learning was violently introduced into China, it was understandable that late Qing scholars became hostile to Western learning due to their patriotism. It was also understandable that for political purposes, late Qing scholars began to accept Western learning and actively introduced Western ideas. It was again also understandable that due to their "sense of China," scholars in the late Qing dynasty emphasized retaining the solid foundation of Chinese culture while actively promoting Western ideas in all fields. From this point of view, the various Chinese cultural concepts of the scholars in the late Qing Dynasty were expressions of their political emotions, and they contained their sense of national responsibility as Chinese nationals and subjects of the Qing Dynasty.

Third, Chinese learning was suppressed by Western learning, which stimulated the scholars' cultural emotions. In the late Qing society, the impact of Western learning on Chinese culture was unprecedented. Under the influence of Western ideas, the gradual decline of Chinese learning became an undeniable fact. However, on the other hand, the comprehensive introduction of Western learning also virtually inspired the complicated Chinese cultural sentiments within the scholars of the late Qing Dynasty. The so-called *Xixue Zhongyuan*, *Zhongti Xiyong* and *Zhongxue Duzun* theories that emphasized maintaining Chinese learning all expressed the scholars' complicated Chinese cultural sentiments. As far as the real value of such cultural ideas themselves is concerned, these theories might not have much to boast about, but their cultural value cannot be erased. Wang Ermin's evaluation of such doctrines is fairly just. He believes that "these kinds of theories that are created by inspirations do tend to be self-explanatory, self-justifying, and sometimes even speculative. They surely are shallow, (their ideas) mimicking and immaturely judging (the world) from the perspective of historical progression, but they do possess a considerable force of influence, which constitutes the motivational power for the era to progress."[49] As far as cultural continuity is concerned, regardless of whether such theories are shallow, mimicking, or immature, they still successfully preserved Chinese tradition to some extent, even under the strong influence of Western learning. From this perspective, the Chinese cultural concept of the scholars of the late Qing Dynasty was a true expression of their Chinese cultural sentiments, which contained intense personal and Chinese cultural emotions.

The above analysis can be concluded into one point, which is that the Chinese cultural concept of the scholars of the late Qing Dynasty was a result of their cultural characters. The so-called views of "Chinese-culture-as-center," "Chinese-culture-as-origin", and the "Chinese-culture-as-main-body" belong only to their times. They traditionally looked at Western matters, and even explained Western learning with Confucius' doctrine. However, the two were naturally integrated, achieving a near-seamless merge. The root cause of this phenomenon laid in its inherent Chinese cultural characteristics.

2. *Late-Qing scholars and Chinese universities*

The book *A Hundred Years of Chinese Higher Education: Institutional Changes, Financial Operation and Teacher Mobility* by Tian Zhengping et al. discussed the relationship between bureaucrats of the late Qing and the modern higher education system. It mentioned that "the emergence of the initial form of the modern higher education system (quoter's note: this refers to the system that was started by the establishment of the Imperial University of Peking in 1862 and ended by China's defeat in the Sino-Japanese War in 1895) is also based on traditional feudal education. Most of the people who promoted the establishment of the modern higher education system were a group of feudal bureaucrats and gentry with a capitalist tendency. Their foothold was, for the most part, feudal. They did not want to fundamentally change the feudal education system, but only felt the inevitable capitalist trend of the world earlier than others. They tried to 'slightly alter the traditions' and introduce some parts of the Western higher education system to meet the needs of the changing situation. This determined that the higher education they advocated was still deeply imprinted with feudal education."[50]

From a cultural perspective, scholars in the late Qing Dynasty took Chinese culture as the main body, which determined that the Chinese universities they built would inevitably come with deep cultural imprints, as well. The scholars in the late Qing Dynasty, as the last batch of "Shi" in the traditional society, directly influenced the modernization process of Chinese universities and were the first "cultural inheritors" in the formation of the cultural characteristic of Chinese universities in modern times. When analyzing the relationship between these scholars and Chinese universities, and we can see that, in a sense, Chinese universities of late Qing were highly aligned with the scholars themselves. Based on the values adhered to by the scholars in the late Qing Dynasty, this book will try to analyze the symbiotic relationship between the Shi and Chinese universities by examining the main educational concepts of this era, which are *Zhongjun Zunkong* (loyalty to the Emperor and respect for Confucius) *Xueshi Yiti* (the combination of official career and education), *Jingxue Weibe* (using the study of classics as the foundation). This would help to specifically understand the symbiotic significance of scholars and Chinese universities in the late Qing Dynasty.

a) Zhongjun Zunkong

Zhongjun Zunkong was a core concept of Chinese universities in the late Qing Dynasty. It mainly referred to the basic tenet of Chinese universities which was to be loyal to the emperor and to follow the teachings of Confucius. In the late Qing Dynasty, all scholars were students of Confucius. They abided by the three *Gang* and five *Chang*, emphasizing the ethics and hierarchism. Therefore, under the guidance of scholars in the late Qing Dynasty, Chinese universities possessed the essence of Confucian education, which was evident in their respect for Confucius and the emperor. When the Chinese universities of this period were established, the idea of *Zhongjun Zunkong* became their most fundamental educational concept, and it was eventually established as the educational purpose of the whole country.

In 1906, *the Zouchen Jiaoyu Zongzhi Zhe* (*Statement to the Throne on the Purposes of Education*) was formally proposed by the Ministry of Education to establish *Zhongjun* and *Zunkong* as the purpose of Chinese education. The document reflected the sentiment of *Zhongjun Zunkong* among the scholars of the late Qing. The document used *Zhongjun* as its main point, stating that "China is known as the nation of etiquette. Loyalty and love are rooted in our hearts, and it is particularly easy to feel their power. To promote education, it is better to take ideas such as the difficulties faced by the founding fathers of the country, the greatness of their ambitions and achievements, the events in recent years, the labor and toil underwent by our emperors, the cause of external troubles and the urgent points of internal affairs, redact the taboo and pick out the most crucial parts, and turn these parts into textbooks. We must make sure that students across the country do not forget the importance of loyalty. They shall remember our martyrs, and they shall marvel at the graciousness of the heavens and the earth. They shall see the turbulence and difficulties of the modern world. Hence, there will be no room for evil doctrines to grow in their hearts. Such is our idea of the notion *Zhongjun*."[51] Then the document made another statement of *Zunkong*, demanding that "regardless of the size of the school, Confucian classics should be a compulsory subject. The students shall write songs of praise to Confucius, to eliminate the inferior habits in their minds. When paying tribute to Confucius on his birthday or the day of school commencement, the students shall perform a ritual of respect and play music, to show their excitement. The best part of Confucian classics that are explanatory of the world and its mechanism, along with those well-accepted and well-tested interpreting pieces of these classics shall be chosen, edited into textbooks with great clarity, and these textbooks are to be treated as the ultimate treasure within schools."[52]

The national educational concept was hence set, and Chinese universities followed suit. The scholars of late Qing took *Zhongjun* and *Zunkong* as their educational concepts and they were at the cover of Chinese universities' education systems.

b) Xueshi Yiti

Xueshi Yiti was another important educational concept of Chinese universities in the late Qing Dynasty. It referred to the fundamental function of Chinese universities, which was training government officials. This function had two layers of meaning, one was *Xueyou Zeshi* (do well in academics to enter officialdom) for students, and the other was *Shiyou Zexue* (enter the field of academics after succeeding in officialdom) for officials. In the traditional Chinese idea, *Xueyou Zeshi* is the correct goal for students, while *Shiyou Zexue* is the correct way for officials. One of the basic purposes of scholars' education reform in the late Qing Dynasty was to educate officials. The earliest university in modern China, the Imperial University of Peking, was established to cultivate government officials from the beginning of their studies. It was both an institute for officials to receive primary training and an institute for officials to receive higher education. The following is an analysis, taking Sun Jianai's *Zou Choubei Jingshi Daxuetang Dagai Qingkuang Zhe* (*Statement to the Throne on the General Situation of Imperial University Preparation*) as an example.

In July 1898, the Imperial University of Peking was established, and Sun Jianai proposed the *Jingshi Daxuetang Zhangcheng* (*Constitution of Imperial University of Peking.*)" The following month, Sun submitted another report of *Statement to the Throne on the General Situation of Imperial University Preparation* following up on related matters. Among the suggestions, two were related to the education of officials.

First, it proposed that "everyone who has an outstanding academic performance in the school shall be hired as an official." It also suggested that "Politic students shall be allocated to the Ministry of Personnel; business and mining students shall be allocated to the Ministry of Revenue; law students should be allocated to Ministry of Justice; military students shall be allocated to the Ministry of Defence and other Army or Navy departments; manufacturing students shall be allocated to the Ministry of Works and manufacturing bureaus; language students shall be allocated to the Ministry of Foreign Affairs and other embassies. Throughout their careers, they shall stay within the same field and relative departments, so that their education can be put to good use." This provided systematic support for the conversion of the students from learners to officials, and the Imperial University of Peking practically became a channel for students to achieve *Xueyou Zeshi.*

Secondly, the document proposed that "A Shi Xueyuan (academy for officials) shall be established for those who became officials as *Jinshi* (those who passed the official examination) and *Juren* (those who achieved the highest degree)." Shi Xueyuan was specifically established for officials in Beijing, and hence the Imperial University of Peking officially became an institute of higher education for officials. The document states that "since these officials were chosen by the imperial examination system, they must have already mastered Chinese learning. Hence, the school shall mainly admit officials who are expecting to receive training in Western learning, and the school shall provide specific Western training. As for Chinese learning, the officials shall still keep up their good effort."[53]

In short, under the guidance of the *Xueyou Zeshi, Shiyou Zexue* the mentality of scholars of the late Qing dynasty, the university education, and official training maintained a huge internal consistency, and the characters of Chinese universities contained a great number of official education features.

c) Jingxue Weiben

Jingxue Weiben was one of the main characteristics of Chinese universities in the late Qing Dynasty. It referred to the basic and most important educational idea of Chinese classics and Confucian ethics in Chinese universities. Tu Youguang believed that there were three stages in the development of the history of higher education in China: From the legend of the Five Emperors to the end of the Qing Dynasty was the "humanity" stage; the past century was the "science" stage, and it is currently developing into a "humanity plus science" stage.[54] Although the Chinese University of the late Qing Dynasty intentionally added subjects to spread Western science, China's inherent knowledge of the humanities was still the foundation of its study. Using the *Imperial Endorsed Petition on the Constitution of Educational Institutions* drafted by Zhang Zhidong et al. as an example, the Imperial University of Peking had eight disciplines.

The school of Jingxue (the study of classics) ranked first, followed by political science and law, liberal arts, medicine, Gezhi, agriculture, engineering, and business. The school of Jingxue had a total of 11 courses, including Zhouyi, Shangshu, Maoshi etc. It specialized in Chinese classics while supplemented by foreign literature and history. For example, the main subject of Zhouyi is the research of Zhouyi, while the supplementary courses including the history of Chinese and foreign education, the history of Chinese and foreign geography, and foreign languages. The school of political sciences and law was divided into political and legal disciplines, specializing in Chinese and foreign politics and law. The discipline of political sciences included courses on general politics, records of the Qing dynasty, the examination of legal systems of ancient and modern China, and the comparison of the legal systems of Eastern and Western countries. The discipline of law included main courses such as the principles of law, the essence of the laws and regulations of the Qing dynasty, the examination of criminal law in all Chinese dynasties, the examination of legal systems in ancient and modern China, and the comparison of legal systems in Eastern and Western countries. The school of liberal arts was divided into nine disciplines, including Chinese History, International History, Chinese and Foreign Geography, and another six departments of Chinese and foreign literature. The three categories above belonged to the category of humanities education and were the most important educational content of the late Qing universities. The main reason for this was that the scholars of the late Qing Dynasty trained themselves with Confucianism for the sake of ruling the world, and they only learned about humanities. Most of them excelled at humanities while having little to no knowledge about science. Zhang Zhidong, as an excellent example of the Confucian scholars in the late Qing Dynasty, drafted the *Imperial Endorsed Petition on the Constitution of Educational Institutions*, which was limited by his literati status. Just as Su Yunfeng said, Zhang Zhidong himself lacked knowledge in science, industry, agriculture, and medicine, which was also the reason why he completely copied from others.[55] As a matter of fact, these copied disciplines only existed in name for many higher education institutions in the late Qing Dynasty, and the main body of Chinese universities in the late Qing Dynasty was still humanities (or classical) education.

To sum up, as the last batch of Confucian *Shi* who respected Confucianism and stayed loyal to the emperor, and the scholars of late Qing were the ones who created the cultural character of *Zhongjun Zunkong* in Chinese universities. As the last batch of "feudal bureaucrats" of the traditional society, they created the cultural character of the *Xueshi Yiti* of Chinese universities. As the last group of "literati" in the traditional society, they also shaped the cultural character of *Jingxue Weiben* of Chinese universities. In this sense, these scholars were symbiotic with Chinese universities. The identity and the position of these scholars determined what Chinese universities were. Under the leadership of these scholars, Chinese culture had always taken the leading position in Chinese universities, and the cultural character of Chinese universities was particularly visible. In other words, the strong cultural characteristics of Chinese universities in the late Qing dynasty was mainly due to the dominant role of Chinese culture. Understanding the "main body" status of Chinese culture within Chinese universities means that Chinese culture is neither "full" nor "partial" in Chinese universities. In the special historical era of the late Qing society, although Chinese universities were adopted from Western universities in the tide of the times, they were, after all, built by the Chinese in China. Therefore, Chinese universities can't treat Chinese learning and Western learning equally as "partial" constituent elements. For the same reason, even though the cultural characteristics of Chinese universities were distinct in the late Qing Dynasty, they were different from those of the traditional Chinese higher education. Therefore, Chinese universities will no longer regard Chinese learning as the "all" of its studies. In short, Chinese universities in the late Qing dynasty favored tradition between tradition and modernity, and this is the basic core that defined the cultural character of Chinese universities in the late Qing Dynasty.

3. *Late-Qing Scholar-Officials and Cultural Characteristics of Chinese Universities.*

The more liberal scholar-officials who held important political positions and enjoyed a high reputation across all sectors of society had the closest connections with Chinese universities among all the scholars in the late Qing dynasty. Most of them excelled in academics so that they could enter officialdom. They occupied high positions in court and were the backbone of political reformations in the late Qing Dynasty. In education, late Qing scholar-officials leveraged their political power and social influence to put their ideas of education into best practices. They played an important role in the development and reformation of Chinese universities. Throughout the late-Qing history, scholar-officials contributed greatly to the budding, rising, and shaping of the development of Chinese universities. Generally speaking, late-Qing scholar-officials who influenced the cultural characteristics of Chinese universities shared two obvious similarities.

Firstly, they were liberal and open-minded and were completely in contrast with the stubborn conservatives. Their main view was that "Chinese essence and Western utility." Therefore, what they had in common was their attitude towards Chinese and Western culture. They were firm regarding the cultural subjectivity of Chinese culture while they also advocated learning to accommodate Western cultures.

Secondly, as students of the Confucian court officials, loyalty to the throne and respect to the sage were the doctrines of their lives and the universal starting point of their careers. Therefore, in terms of life values, it was their common mission and responsibility to maintain the official orthodoxy of Chinese culture.

The above characteristics were fundamental in the formation of the cultural characters of Chinese universities in the late Qing Dynasty. The following are the selections of the three influential late Qing scholars, namely Zhang Zhidong, Sheng Xuanhuai, and Kang Youwei, who were not only politicians but also real education entrepreneurs.

a) Zhang Zhidong and the Imperial University of Peking.

"Zhang Zhidong scored the first rank in his imperial exam (*tanhua* (second best overall), in the second year of Tongzhi, and was awarded the position as Classics Compiler). Since the eleventh year of Tongzhi (1872), he served as the Literary Chancellor in Sichuan and remained a prominent and prestigious official for 40 years. His profound knowledge topped all the intellectuals at that time and he alone was more than enough to represent all Chinese scholars. Zhang's great achievements and prestige had been respected in the country in the late Qing dynasty. As a role model of the scholar-official class, his opinions always carry great influences. Zhang's thoughts were deeply influenced by traditional Chinese academic knowledge. Supposedly, he would have retained the conservative attitude. However, his tendency to adopt new things, as well as his high regard towards Western knowledge since the opening up of the Qing dynasty were shown in administrative governance.[56]

Later, generations passed varied judgments on Zhang Zhidong, while Wang Ermin's comment on Zhang Zhidong was quite fair and objective. Zhang Zhidong, as a representative figure of the late-Qing scholars, embodied the cultural characteristics of scholars in the late Qing Dynasty more comprehensively and profoundly. First of all, Zhang Zhidong was a representative of intellectuals and traditional literati in the late Qing Dynasty and his status was deeply cultivated in traditional academic culture. Therefore, his literatus personality was evident. Secondly, Zhang Zhidong was a model of "*xian huan* (prominent and prestigious official)" for 40 years and was a role model for "scholar-officials." Therefore, he had a great influence in the political field and his bureaucratic character was particularly strong. Also, Zhang Zhidong was conservative and liberal at the same time. He could consolidate the tendency to stick to the old and explore the new. Therefore, although he saw the preservation of Chinese culture as his responsibility, he did not reject Western learnings.

Zhang Zhidong's cultural concept was mainly reflected in his "Chinese system and Western usage, or Chinese essence and Western utility" ideology. The thought of 'Chinese essence and Western utility' does not originate from Zhang Zhidong, but Zhang Zhidong was the central figure of the idea. In terms of national politics, it laid the social foundation for the reign of the late Qing Dynasty.

In terms of educational innovation, it constructed the guiding ideology of modern new education. In terms of Chinese universities, the idea served as the theoretical basis of Zhang Zhidong's higher education philosophy. Zhang's education philosophy was summarized in his *Quanxue Pian* (*On Encouraging Learning*), which was also where his higher educational philosophy originated from. The first thing that we need to know to understand the essence of his education philosophy was that it was state-oriented and it was an educational idea that tended to serve the politics.

There was a saying in *On Encouraging Learning* that went, "I heard that there were three ways to save the world nowadays from the great upheavals: to save the country, to pass on the Confucian sages' heritage, to retain the Chinese core. These three ways were essentially the three faces of one agenda. To save the country, to pass on the Confucian sages' heritage, to retain the Chinese core – when these three things will be united, there would be concentricity. To retain the Chinese core, one must first save the Confucian sages' heritage; to pass on the Confucian sages' heritage, one must first save the country."[57]

From this, it could be inferred that the ultimate goal in Zhang's idea of concentricity was "to save the country." Reflected in the purpose of education, that is, to cultivate the talents for the court to save the country. The second point to understanding Zhang's educational philosophy was that it was based on traditional Chinese learning with an obvious leaning tendency to teaching the classics and ethics. To save the country, Zhang Zhidong's thoughts on "Chinese essence" contained the intention of studying the classics first to strengthen the government. In *On Encouraging Learning*, Zhang mentioned that scholars "must first master the classics to clarify the purpose for the sages' first establishment of Confucianism; read through the historical texts to learn about China's iteration between states of peace and chaos, and understand different geography and cultures in different regions of 'the Nine Provinces (China)'; get acquainted with great philosophical and literary writings as references to the academic writings of China."

He also said, "A Chinese scholar not proficient in Chinese learning is as bad as a man who does not know his family name, a horse without a bridle, a boat without a helm. The more familiar he is with Western learning, the more he despises China. How could this kind of person be used by the country, regardless of how knowledgeable or capable he is!"[58] He was Chinese-oriented and Zhang's higher education philosophy was destined to revolve around the classics and the ethics. In a broad sense, the above two points are also the basic footholds of Zhang Zhidong's higher education philosophy.

Zhang's philosophy of higher education was realized to a large extent in the Imperial University of Peking, which was not built by Zhang Zhidong himself, but was owed its final institutionalization to Zhang's *Zouding Xuetang Zhangcheng* (*Imperial Endorced Petition on the Constitution of Educational Institutions*). The characteristics of the Imperial University of Peking clearly reflected Zhang's Chinese cultural complex in the following two aspects. First, the Imperial University of Peking had a special discipline on the great learning of Confucian classics. Zhang Baixi initially drafted the *Qinding Xuetang Zhangcheng* (*Imperial Endorsed Constitution of Educational Institutions*) to follow the Western university system of seven disciplines. The Confucian classics were not listed as one of them. However, *Imperial Endorsed Petition on the Constitution of Educational Institutions* formulated by Zhang Zhidong especially set up discipline on the great learning of Confucian classics as the most important. Wang Guowei disagreed with the absolute superiority of the classics and literature disciplines in his petition.

Yet, he also remarked that "I can't help but admire Minister Zhang, who attached such great importance on these two disciplines. He is not afraid to faithfully write his academic opinions, never afraid of expressing his opinion frankly. In addition, Minister Zhang is not only famous for his academic capabilities but also his loyalty to the country and his great sense of responsibility in bringing the world back to order. Therefore, his fear of the rampant heterodox theories and the loss of national spirit are overflowing in his words and expressions. This is especially so in his two petitions."[59] Although this statement has a sarcastic tone, it also shows Zhang's special emotional tendency is setting up the classics discipline.

Secondly, there was a lack of philosophy courses at the Imperial University of Peking. The lack of philosophy was regarded as a "fundamental error" by Wang Guowei. Wang Guowei attributed the reasons for this as such: Zhang Zhidong "stubbornly regarded philosophy as a negative discipline," "stubbornly regarded philosophy as a useless discipline" and "stubbornly thought that foreign philosophies are incompatible with the traditional studies in China." Fundamentally, these three points lay in Zhang Zhidong's deep-rooted Chinese cultural complex. However, with a similar level of strong Chinese cultural sentiments, Wang Guowei highly valued philosophy and even believed that philosophy must be specially set up as an individual discipline. This difference was mainly because of their educational backgrounds. Zhang Zhidong was not good at philosophy and was less exposed to Western philosophy. Therefore, the Imperial University of Peking did not set up a philosophy discipline. From another aspect of the same reason, Wang Guowei once loved philosophy. He even admired Kant's thoughts and memorized Schopenhauer's thoughts by heart. Therefore, philosophy took up an important part in Wang's idea of higher education.

From this perspective, Imperial University of Peking's obvious feature of emphasizing on Confucian classics and neglecting philosophy was due to Zhang Zhidong's cultural character. If we take one step further, it is derived from the characters of Chinese culture.

b) Sheng Xuanhuai with Peiyang University Hall and Nanyang Public University (Nanyang Gongxue).

Sheng Xuanhuai is a special interpreter of Chinese cultural characteristics. Growing up in a scholar-official family, Sheng Xuanhuai was, too, a master of Confucian studies. However, he did not follow the conventional path in engaging in imperial examinations and entering officialdom. Therefore, he did not attach any importance to the examination but instead focused on talent. He placed a great emphasis on practical learning that could make an impact on the world. He interpreted the subjectivity of Chinese culture from another angle.

Sheng Xuanhuai's higher education philosophy was reflected in his school-building advice in his petitions to the throne. Sheng was one of the first few figures who realized that the current westernized education has lost the essence of Chinese learning, which was supposed to act as the core. In *Zouqing Choushe Nanyang Gongxue* (*Petition to the Throne for Establishing Nanyang Public University*) (1896), Sheng stated that "China has been sending envoys to neighboring countries for more than two decades, raising countless talents at Tongwen Guan (School of Combined Learning) with outstanding proficiency and experience in foreign languages and studies. However, we are still grieving that we do not have enough talents – why is that so? The reason is none other than Confucian and Mencian learnings were uprooted – students do not get the greater substance of domestic and foreign governance and administration. Although they were well-educated in foreign languages, they were still unable to walk on the far-reaching path of greatness."[60] From this point of view, Sheng's so-called "practical learnings" were still based on Confucian and Mencius thoughts.

At the same time, Sheng also emphasized the importance of spiritual cultivation as a solid foundation. He believed that "Confucianism prioritizes morality, while Western learning is based on self-cultivation, so one should keep himself in the right way first."[61] From this perspective, true talent with practical knowledge must first cultivate the internal spirit, rather than pragmatic skills. It can be inferred that Sheng's pragmatic thinking was not a westernized thought that only seeks Western application, but it was still based on the concept of "Chinese essence."

Two late-Qing higher education institutions closely related to Sheng Xuanhuai are Peiyang University and Nanyang Public University. These two universities were built near the end of the Self-Strengthening Movement, before the founding of the Imperial University of Peking. Many scholars believe that Tianjin Beiyang Xixue Tang (Tianjin Peiyang University of Western learning) (renamed as Peiyang University in 1896) established in 1895 was a legitimate university, to begin with. It was the earliest college in modern China. Hayhoe's *China's Universities, 1895–1995: A Century of Cultural Conflict* set the starting point of "Chinese universities" in 1895, based on the founding of Tianjin Beiyang Xixue Tang. Regardless of whether it can be regarded as the first university in modern China, these two institutions were the prototypes of Chinese universities. Under the influence of Sheng Xuanhuai, both Peiyang University and Nanyang Public University demonstrated distinct cultural characters. Both Nanyang Public University and the later Imperial University of Peking were run based on "Chinese essence and Western utility."

Say, Zhang Zhidong eventually shaped the cultural character of the Imperial University of Peking with "Chinese essence and Western utility," then the cultural character of Nanyang Public University would have relied heavily on Sheng's cultural idea on this concept. The first chapter of the Constitution of *Nanyang Public University* set the purpose of the university, stating that "the program offered by the Public University is based on the aim to let students get comprehensive knowledge on the deep root of Chinese classics' great meanings. The programs are guided by Western political ideas and Japanese law and literature disciplines, intending to mimic the French political universities."[62] This purpose was the same as the later founded the Imperial University of Peking, which was "established primarily on Chinese studies, with a supplement on Western learning."

From this point of view, Sheng was one of the earliest to adopt the idea of "Chinese essence, Western Utility" as the founding principle of late-Qing universities, which was later established as the fundamental characteristic of Chinese universities, that is, the subjectivity of Chinese culture.

c) Kang Youwei and Wan Mu Caotang (Thatched Cottage of Woods)

Kang Youwei was born in a gentry-official family. He was well-educated with Confucian studies and also knew classics and history very well. In *The Biography of Kang Youwei*, Liang Qichao talked about his mentor of Chinese learning and Kang's cultivation on Chinese learning, "When he was a grown child, he was interested in the studies of the sages. The village folk laughed at him, and nicknamed him as 'Sage Wei,' (…) when he was 18, he started to study under Mr Zhu Jiujiang. Mr Zhu's given name was Ciqi, and his style name was Zixiang. He was a prestigious Confucian scholar in Canton. (…) After the passing of Mr Zhu, Kang lived in the west of the South Sea, where Xiqiao

Mountain was and studied on his own for another four years. In the meantime, he read a considerable amount of Chinese education books among which history books inspired him the most. He was indulged in the rise and fall of eras in the past – tracing their trajectories, analyzing the gains and losses, even undergoing textual research on the texts and chapters."[63] Compared with Zhang and Sheng, Kang Youwei's Confucian scholar personality weighted significantly more than his bureaucratic personality, which was especially reflected in his respect to Confucianism, as well as his Confucius complex. As Liang Qichao commented, "Master Kang was like Mr Martin Luther of Confucianism." Kang's *Tuogu Gaizhi* (*Reform with regards to Ancient Rules*) was entirely based on Confucianism. The *Kongzi Gaizhi Kao* (*Textual Research on Confucius Reform*) and *Xinxue Weijing Kao* (*Textual Research and Identification on New Learnings on Pseudo-Confucian Classics*) were all using Confucianism as a foothold to defend the legitimacy of reform. Memorials presented to the emperor by Kang were also filled with Confucian ideas. He tried his best to express his opinions according to Confucius, which was evident in his expressions frequented with the phrase, "Confucius said." As for Western learning, Kang Youwei came into contact with it in 1879 and began to study the translated works of a variety of Western books in detail in 1882.

Datong Shu (*Book of a Unified World*) written by Kang Youwei could act as a great reference for the examination of his education's thoughts. *Datong Shu* was Kang Youwei's description of an ideal society. In this book, Kang constructed an ideal education system showing the characteristics of his educational philosophy.

First, he emphasized moral cultivation and a strong sense of ethic-centrism. The ideal education in a unified world attached great importance to moral cultivation, which would be the foundation of all institutions, from primary schools to middle schools. The focus of primary schools would be moral education. Mild and benevolent female teachers should be chosen to cultivate the children's virtues. Middle school would still place a great emphasis on moral education because middle school is where a student's academic ability and moral standard are determined."[64] Universities attach even greater importance on moral education, "There would be songs and poems teaching students to cultivate good virtues every day to improve their moral ethics, train their characters. As such, they will become wise."[65]

Second, he emphasized traditional learning with traditional knowledge as the foundation. The educational system designed by Kang was based on the classification of traditional knowledge, retaining traditional learning discipline. Students in primary schools "learn about themselves." They were supposed to learn about the commonsense, apart from the necessary self-cultivation, calculus, and history. Besides cultivating the body and broadening wisdom, middle school students learned about morality and ethics as one of their focuses. They could also learn about *li* (rites and etiquette) and music, using *li* to empower their outer behaviors and "music" to nurture their temperament. University students learn for the primary goal to develop their intellectual abilities, therefore, they major in specialized disciplines, including politics, law, education, philosophy, and agriculture, etc.

In summary, Kang Youwei's tradition-oriented educational philosophy was the extension of his Confucius complex in the field of education, where the core of his higher education philosophy also lay.

The most famous modern higher education institution founded by Kang Youwei is none other than Wan Mu Caotang. From the perspective of its time of founding and its characteristics, Wan Mu Caotang cannot be counted into the category of late-Qing "Chinese universities." However, as far as its cultural character is concerned, it had no essential differences between late-Qing Chinese universities.

First of all, Wan Mu Caotang was established thanks to Confucius. Kang Youwei's *Changxing Xue Ji* (*Learning Experience in Changxing County*) stated the theoretical basis of establishing educational institutions, in which Confucius said, "people are similar by nature," "learning" is what people value. He went on to quote the next phrase, that "but through people's habits (characteristics), people become quite different from each other." "Learning" is also what makes people different. Subsequently, he quoted that "studying and not research, that is what I am worried about." Kang Youwei pursued the teaching convention of Confucius, therefore we saw the emergence of Wan Mu Caotang.

Secondly, Wan Mu Caotang was structured based on Confucius. Kang Youwei pointed out in *Changxing Xue Ji* that "there are countless ways of thinking and methods of application, while Confucius stands right in the middle; there are countless sayings of Confucius, with the Analects as the orthodox; there are countless principles in the Analects, with understanding *dao* (the way) as the ultimate goal, *de* (morality) as the guidance while leveraging on *ren* (benevolence) and traveling with *yi* (skills)."[66] There were four orders under the class of pursuing *dao*: studying the physical world, being upright, analyzing feelings and disciplining oneself. There were four orders under the class of being guided by morality: remaining calm to avoid being proud, cultivating the heart so that one's mind does not waver, changing the temperament and constantly examining and reflecting on one's manner. There were four orders under the class of leveraging on *ren*: abiding by filial piety, advocating charity, edifying the country and sharing pain and suffering with others. There were also four orders under the class of travelling with *yi*: studying Confucian principles, studying statesmanship, studying to authenticate texts, and studying literature. In Kang Youwei's old system, he listed four guiding principles with a total of sixteen orders for Wan Mu Caotang to promote the Confucian way of *daxue*.

Again, Wan Mu Caotang respected Confucius's teaching. In Liang Qichao's recollection of Wan Mu Caotang, he mentioned the master's teaching, "When he teaches, he is enticing and sincere. Just like how Confucius taught others without weariness," "about seven-tenths of his teaching was about morality, with about three-tenths about intellectual development. He also firmly believed in the importance of physical education."[67] Kang

Youwei respected Confucius's principles of teaching with patience and enthusiasm and his placement of morality before any other learnings. With these principles, he shaped the inside teaching spirit of Wan Mu Caotang and constructed its education program on the outside. In short, Wan Mu Caotang bore strong Confucian characteristics because of Kang Youwei's unique Confucian complex immersed in unique Chinese cultural ideas.

To sum up, although late-Qing scholars' cultural concepts and higher education philosophy were expressed in different ways with different characteristics, their foothold remained the same – Chinese cultural subjectivity was the essence. In short, with late-Qing scholars as "cultural inheritors," late-Qing Chinese universities developed a strong cultural character with Chinese cultural subjectivity.

Section 3: Analysis of Cultural Characters of Chinese Universities in the Late Qing Dynasty – Using the Imperial University of Peking as an example

The Imperial University of Peking has a special status in the history of modern education in China. The establishment of the Imperial University of Peking by the Qing government in 1898 was one of the most important measures for education reform during The Hundred Days' Reform. It also marked the birth of the earliest national university in modern China. As the earliest national university in China, the Imperial University of Peking was a special historical product of the late-Qing era. Today, when the Qing dynasty is long gone, the Imperial University of Peking has become the current Peking University. However, history records know the past of the Imperial University of Peking. This section is based on historical records about the Imperial University of Peking, using text analysis as an attempt to comprehensively analyze the cultural character of the Imperial University of Peking at different stages to deeply understand the cultural characters of Chinese universities in the late Qing dynasty.

1. Educational Concepts of Imperial University of Peking

Imperial University of Peking's educational concept was the most direct expression of its cultural character, and it was also the guiding ideology for the establishment of a school system and its field design. The educational concept of the Imperial University of Peking is mainly reflected in the memorials presented to the throne by late-Qing scholar-officials and the relevant rules, regulations, and provisions introduced by the government.

1) Sun Jianai's *Fuyi Kaiban Jingshi Daxuetang Zhe* (*Petition to Reconsider the Founding of Imperial University of Peking*) (1896):

> Over the past five thousand years in China, sages and divines arose, and politics and edification became prosperous. We must not give in to Western learning and abandon our own completely as the Japanese did. Now, since we are going to establish a university in our capital, Peking, it is natural to set Chinese learnings as the emphasis, with Western learnings as supplements. (We must use) Chinese essence and Western utility. Whenever there is something that cannot be explained by Chinese learning, Western learning can be leveraged to fill up the gap. Whenever an aspect of Chinese learning is lost in history, we can trace it back with the help of Western learning. The educational concept of the school is to include Western learning in Chinese learning, but not to override the latter with the former. In the future, when we decide on the specific disciplines to be taught and popularize this system in other provinces, no matter how many amendments and changes we are going to make, this principle shall remain unchanged.[68]

2) Ministry of Foreign Affair's proposal – *Constitution of Imperial University of Peking* (1898):

> There is absolutely no school, be it Eastern or Western, that abandons its native learning completely or has no idea of its native learning while still being able to master a foreign system of learning. The great malpractice of Chinese scholars is that scholars who adopted Chinese learning refuse to talk about Western learning, and vice versa. As a result, like fire and water, these two systems could never fuse. Scholars of the two camps are merely criticizing each other. Chinese and Western learnings are both necessary. Chinese essence and Western utility (must be used). One can never grow to be a true talent overlooking Chinese essence and Western utility. Now, we would like to rectify the wrongs and present two principles: 1) Both Chinese and Western learning are necessary. We need to look at their interconnections. Neither of which can be disregarded; 2) Western languages should be one of the disciplines in the university, instead of its teaching language. We learn Western languages to leverage Western learning, not the other way around. Adopting Western languages should never be the ultimate purpose of learning Western knowledge.[69]

3) Zhang Baixi's *Qinding Jingshi Daxuetang Zhangcheng* (*Imperial Endorsed Constitution of Imperial University of Peking*) (1902):

> The establishment of the Imperial University of Peking is to inspire loyalty and love to the emperor, enlighten bright minds and rejuvenate the real economy. We will humbly adhere to the imperial order as the principle of this institution, stay on the right track, and nurture generalists.

> Chinese classics written by sages emphasize morality before everything else; foreign schools also attach great importance to moral education outside of intellectual and physical education. Therefore, Chinese and foreign schools share some common principles. It is advisable now for all of the schools and education institutions outside the capital to pay greater attention to moral education, as it is the foundation for nurturing talent.[70]

4) Zhang Zhidong's *Zouding Daxuetang Zhangcheng* (*Imperial Endorsed Petition on the Constitution of the Imperial College*) (with appendix: Constitution of Tongru Yuan (Graduate School of Master Scholars)) (1904):

> Establish a university to enroll high school graduates. Set up a 'Tongru Yuan' (so-called 'graduate school' in foreign countries, which is usually within the university premise) in the university to enroll university graduates. The university will humbly adhere to the imperial order as its principle, stay on the right track, and nurture generalists.[71]

5) Imperial Censor Chen Zengyou's *Zouqing Biantong Xuetang Biye Jiangli Chushen Shiyi Zhe* (*Petition to the Throne on the Revision to Award to University Graduates by Qualification*) (1905):

> There are four main purposes for a government to populate the country with schools. First, to nurture ethics and morality. The social ethos would be pure and positive as everybody knows the right ethics and morality when the populace is educated. Second, to nurture imperial subjects. The country would have a solid foundation as everybody will understand politics when educated Third, to make the whole country combat-ready. Conscription orders would be feasible because the people can be qualified for the army when primary schools are popularized. Fourth, to provide for the people and make the country thrive. The people would have more ways to make their living as they possess more skills when the real economy thrives. Above are the objectives of establishing schools. Therefore, it is not entirely for pursuing government careers. The best thing about the country is that everyone understands the importance of studying; the worst thing is that everyone fixates on positions in the government.[72]

6) Ministry of Education's *Statement to the Throne on the Purposes of Education* (1906):

> Education plays an important role in and is closely related to a country and its governance. If we want to examine the purpose and set a direction, we must thor-

> oughly observe the reasons for national trends, ethos, strengths, and weaknesses. It is only after which we could eliminate negative conventions and shape the people of the country. In our humble opinion, two inherent aspects in Chinese politics and education that make it distinct from others: loyalty to the emperor and respect for Confucius. There are also three aspects that the Chinese (education) is lacking the most and where it requires immediate changes for the country to thrive: *shanggong, shangwu* and *shangshi* (the pursuit of public service, military and martial strength, and practicality). Recently, some parochialistic figures, who have learned merely the surface of Western politics and education, proposed to completely abandon our inherent cultural and customs. By doing so, they are not trying to make the country better but are trying to bring chaos upon this land. Although the political systems of different countries across the world are different, there is not a single one with a substance of disrespecting its ruler.[73]

The above memorials and constitutions were either specifically dedicated to the Imperial University of Peking or nationwide education. Nonetheless, they could all be regarded as an obvious demonstration of the university's educational concept. The first two examples shown above were before and during the Reform Movement of 1898 (Hundred Days' Reform), while the last four cases were important texts of educational reform during the New Policies period of the late Qing dynasty. In terms of ideas, *Petition to Reconsider the Founding of the Imperial University of Peking* and *Constitution of Imperial University of Peking* emphasizes the basic idea of "Chinese essence and Western utility." The former stated that the Imperial University of Peking should set Chinese learning as the emphasis, with Western learnings as a supplement, in essence, follow "Chinese essence and Western utility. Again, the latter stated that education should keep Chinese learning as the substance, Western learning as an application. One can never grow to be a true talent overlooking either the substance or the application." These two texts invariably criticized countries such as Japan, which "gave in to Western learning and abandoned its own completely," to strengthen the importance of "Chinese learning as essence."

The *Imperial Endorsed Constitution of Imperial University of Peking* and *Imperial Endorsed Petition to the Throne on the Constitution of the Imperial College* show the beginnings of the modern Chinese academic system. Both of them emphasized the basic function of "stay on the right track and nurture generalists." The former stated that the principle of the Imperial University of Peking is to "stay on the right track and nurture generalists," and the latter also stated that the university was "to enroll university graduates. The university will humbly adhere to the imperial order as its principle, stay on the right track, and nurture generalists." The two texts were almost the same in their emphasis on the principle of "stay on the right track and nurture generalists."

Petition to the Throne on the Revision to Award to University Graduates by Qualification and *Statement to the Throne on the Purposes of Education*, as national education documents, eventually established *zhongjun, zunkong, shanggong, shangwu* and *shangshi* as the ultimate code of conduct and the ideological guidelines for all the educational institutions across the country, including the Imperial University of Peking. The former stated that the Universities had to "nurture ethics and morality" so that people know the right ethics and morality; "nurture imperial subjects" so that everybody understands politics, make the whole country combat-ready so that the country stays strong and make the people wealthy with thriving real economy. The latter also used *zunkong, zhongjun, shangwu* and *shangshi* respectively, with an additional principle of *shanggong*. The two texts are very similar, as they linked education with politics at the national level. To sum up, there are three main expressions to the official educational philosophy of the Imperial University of Peking: 1) "Chinese essence and Western utility;" 2) "Staying on the right track and nurturing generalists"; 3) *zhongjun, zunkong, shanggong, shangwu* and *shangshi*. Based on this, the cultural character of the Imperial University of Peking could be understood through the following aspects.

a) *It has a strong Confucian culture orientation based on the theory of* Zhongti Xiyong.

It is an established statement in the academia that the Imperial University of Peking was directly established on the cornerstone of "*Zhongti Xiyong*." It the three principles aforementioned were to be summarized into one point, the four characters, "*Zhongti Xiyong*," would be enough. "Staying on the right track" is but the purpose of "Chinese essence" while "nurturing generalists" is but the practical aspect of "Western utility." "Zhongjun" and "zunkong" were but the outer criteria of "Chinese essence." "Shanggong," "shangwu," "shangshi" were but the realistic requirement of "Western utility." For further explanation, "Western utility" was merely a "vassal" under "Chinese essence" during the late-Qing period. What the Imperial University of Peking was striving to maintain were the fundamentals of "Chinese learning," while the adoption of "Western learning" was only for consolidation.

On the surface, Imperial University of Peking has always advocated "*Zhongti Xiyong*" as its principle, while the *Constitution of the Imperial University of Peking* drafted during the Hundred Days' Reform clearly put forward the policy of "emphasizing both Chinese and Western learning," but "Chinese learning" clearly surpassed "Western learning" in terms of importance. "The substance was the Chinese moral system of *Sangang Wuchang* (Three Cardinal Guides and Five Constant Virtues) – a value that cannot be denied. "*Zhongti Xiyong*" was meant for the scholars to learn from Western sciences and technologies based on their original value orientation while retaining the core of classical Confucian studies in their education."[74]

The Imperial Endorsed Constitution of the Imperial University of Peking stated that "Chinese classics written by sages emphasize morality before everything else," and that

"It is advisable now to all of the schools and education institutions outside the capital to pay greater attention to moral education, as it is the foundation for nurturing talent."

The first of the four purposes of popularizing education stated in *Petition to the Throne on the Revision to Award to University Graduates by Qualification* was "The social ethos would be pure and positive as everybody knows the right ethics and morality when the populace is educated." From this point of view, Imperial University of Peking took *Zhongti Xiyong* as its educational concept only to strengthen the fundamental "Chinese essence," which was in turn only to strengthen the "moral-centrism."

b) Its strong cultural orientation of Zhengjiao Heyi *(integration of learning and officialdom)" based on the basic feature of associating education with politics.*

Zhengjiao heyi was a basic feature of ancient Chinese education, and "excelling in academics to enter officialdom" was not only the political pursuit of Chinese scholars but also the ruler's strategy for governing the country. The idea of "excelling in academics to enter officialdom" did not appear in the educational concept of the Imperial University of Peking. Moreover, in *Petition to the Throne on the Revision to Award to University Graduates by Qualification*, it clearly stated that "the best thing about the country is that everyone understands the importance of studying; the worst thing is that everyone fixates on officialdom." On the surface, it seemed that education was to be separated from politics. However, the reason for the government to condemn the fixation on government positions was only to persuade scholars to study Western knowledge. Engaging in a government administrative position remained most scholars' career path.

On the one hand, the late-Qing government advocated that one should not study just for the sake of entering officialdom. On the other, it also induced them to serve the government. *The Imperial Endorsed Constitution of Imperial University of Peking* pointed out that "the establishment of the Imperial University of Peking is to inspire loyalty and love to the emperor, enlighten bright minds and rejuvenate real economy." It is worth noting that "to inspire loyalty and love to the emperor" was listed as the top priority.

Petition to the Throne on the Revision to Award to University Graduates by Qualification talked about the educational function of "nurturing imperial subjects" so that "the country would have a solid foundation as everybody understands politics" as one of the main purposes of education.

Statement to the Throne on the Purposes of Education declared that "education plays an important role in and is closely related to a country and its governance." It centered on politics by listing *zhongjun* as the first of the five purposes of education. Borrowing Brubacher's theory on political philosophy and epistemology in the book *On the Philosophy of Higher Education*, the philosophy that dominated late-Qing modern Chinese higher education was political rather than epistemological. "China learned from the West for practical purposes."[75] The so-called "practical purpose" was essentially both a political appeal of modern China and a modern expression of the political nature of classical Chinese higher education.

c) It has a strong cultural orientation of Zhongjun, Zunkong *based on the basic bottom-up pattern.*

For thousands of years, China's education maintained an internal order, that is, a bottom-up logical relationship, from the individual to the country, from the internal to the external. From this perspective, *Zhongti Xiyong* contains an inside-out internal order. The *ti* (substance) was oriented towards internal ethics and moral cultivation, while the *yong* (application) is oriented towards the utility in the physical society. *Zhengjiao heyi* contained a bottom-up internal order, that is, from the individual to the country. *Jiao* (education) leaned towards the individual – the goal of becoming a generalist, while *zheng* (politics) was more about the country-the realization of one's ideal on governance. "Substance" came before "application;" "individual" came before "country", this is the internal logic of the Imperial University of Peking's philosophy.

This "individual to country" idea was very evident in the four purposes stated in *Petition to the Throne on the Revision to Award to University Graduates by Qualification,* The first principle was about people, popularizing education to "nurture ethics and morality." The second principle turned from the "people" to the "country," that popularizing education is to "nurture imperial subjects." The third and fourth principle stated that the reason for popularizing education is to make the country combat-ready and provide for the people and make the country thrive. The establishment of the Imperial University of Peking was an important measure in late Qing to save the fading imperial dynasty. It was often regarded as a hasty program that reflected only "the country" but not "the individual" due to its strong political connotation.

It is true that since modern times, "the Chinese have been learning about Western culture with the attitude of seeking quick benefits to varying degrees, to save the country from perishing."[76] But after all, political goals and educational logic are two different things. The political intention of its establishment is unquestionable, and its educational function is equally worthy of recognition. From the perspective of culture or education, taking the ideas of "emphasize morality before everything else," subsequently "nurture ethics and morality" to make people "know the right ethics and morality" as its purpose, Imperial University of Peking, as an educational institution, inherited classical Chinese higher education's cultural character of using "people" as the starting point of its logic chain.

2. *Organization and Management of Imperial University of Peking*

Constitution of the Imperial University of Peking issued by the late-Qing government in 1898 was the first official document on the Imperial University of Peking. In the *Constitution of the Imperial University of Peking*, eight chapters contained 54 sections, including General Outline, Student Assignments, Student Admission, Student Qualification, Teaching Staff Employment, Relevant Government Officials, and Budgets. In 1902, during the late-Qing New Policies period, Zhang Baixi presided over the construction of the first educational system in modern China, the *Imperial Endorsed Constitution of Educational Institutions*, consisting of six constitutions of different levels of education. *Imperial Endorsed Constitution of the Imperial University of* Peking was specially listed as the first constitution, with a total of eight chapters containing 84 sections. The eight chapters were General Outline, Student Admission, Student Qualification, Relevant Government Officials, Teaching Staff Employment, School Rules and Organizational System. Although this system was not be implemented, it became an important reference for Zhang Zhidong's composition of the *Imperial Endorsed Petition on the Constitution of Educational Institutions.*

In 1904, Zhang promulgated the *Imperial Endorsed Petition on the Constitution of Educational Institutions.* He did not specifically draft the constitution of the Imperial University of Peking, but there were *Zouding Gaodeng Xuetang Zhangcheng* (*Imperial Endorsed Petition on the Constitution of Higher Educational Institutions*) and *Imperial Endorsed Petition on the Constitution of the Imperial College* (with appendix: *Constitution of Tongru Yuan*), of which the title of the final chapter was *Current Regulations of the Imperial University of Peking.*" Afterward, two documents were added specifically for the aspects that the original document did not tap into *Statement to the Throne on the Purposes of Education and Petition to the Throne on the Revision to Award to University Graduates by Qualification*. These two documents were also part of the organization and management of the Imperial University of Peking. This section examines the cultural character of the Imperial University of Peking's management and organization mainly based on the aforementioned documents. The main areas of study are curriculum design, student qualification, and school management. The basis of the study is the cultural character of the University of Peking's educational concept.

a) Curriculum design.

From the perspective of curriculum design, the Imperial University of Peking had moral education as the foundation; Confucian principles as the substance. It strived to maintain the fundamental "Chinese learning." Three documents clearly stated the organization and management rules of the Imperial University of Peking, namely*: Constitution of Imperial University of Peking* (1898), *Imperial Endorsed Constitution of Imperial University of Peking* (1902), and *Imperial Endorsed Petition on the Constitution of the Imperial College* (1904). Although these documents made certain references to the Japanese system and copied a considerable portion of curriculum design, the Confucianism roots of Chinese education were never shaken. Ever since the Imperial University of Peking was established,

Sun Jianai made it clear that "there should be strictly no amendment to classics that used to be compulsory texts for learning. However, books of Western learning should be compiled and edited quickly by the Compilation and Translation Bureau."[77] In 1898, the *Constitution of the Imperial University of Peking* was conferred and Confucian classics were placed atop all other disciplines. It contained the following:

> The majors and disciplines are set with reference to the Western and Japanese educational system, as well as the traditional Chinese learning system as listed below: 1) Confucian Classics; 2) Neo-Confucianism; 3) Chinese and Western History; 4) Chinese Philosophy; 5) Elementary Maths; 6) Elementary Science; 7) Elementary Political Studies; 8) Elementary Geography; 9) Literature; 10) Physical Education. The above are all compulsory lessons to be taught according to schedule. Shanghai Compilation and Translation Bureau would publish relevant textbooks... 11) English; 12) French; 13) Russian; 14) German linguistics; 15) Japanese...[78]

Four years later, after Zhang Baixi formulated the *Imperial Endorsed Constitution of the Imperial University of Peking*, the curriculum transformed into 7 disciplines: Politics, Arts, Science, Agriculture, Engineering, Business, and Medicine. Confucian classics were placed atop all other majors in the arts discipline. Taking the preparatory course subjects as an example, the relevant provisions of the *Imperial Endorsed Constitution of Imperial University of Peking* were as follows:

> The preparatory course is divided into two disciplines: *Zheng* (Politics) and *Yi* (Skills). *Zheng* Students would be promoted into either politics, arts or business disciplines upon graduation from the preparatory course; *Yi* students would be promoted into either agriculture, science, engineering or medicine discipline. Higher education institutions at the provincial level should also follow this curriculum.
>
> *Zheng* discipline: 1) Ethics; 2) Confucian Classics; 3) Chinese Philosophy; 4) Literature; 5) Maths; 6) Chinese and Western History; 7) Chinese and Foreign Geography; 8) Foreign Languages; 9) Physics; 10) Logic; 11) Law; 12) Finance; 13) Physical Education.
>
> *Yi* discipline: 1) Ethics; 2) Chinese and Foreign History; 3) Foreign Languages; 4) Calculus; 5) Physics; 6) Chemistry; 7) Biology; 8) Geology; 9) Art; 10) Physical Education.[79]

Judging from the content of the constitution, *Zheng* discipline placed Ethics and Classics as its top two majors, while *Yi* discipline placed Ethics as its top major. We can see that although Confucian classics were categorized as an art major, it still occupied a central position in all majors. In 1904, Zhang Zhidong reformulated the *Imperial Endorsed Petition on the Constitution of Educational Institutions*, which further separated Confucian Classics from arts into an individual discipline, and placed it at the top of the curriculum system of the university. *Imperial Endorsed Petition on the Constitution of Educational Institutions* (Chapter 7: Current Regulations of Imperial University of Peking) stated that:

> University disciplines are set as follows: Daxue of Classics, Politics, Arts, Medicine, Science, Agriculture, Engineer, and Business. The curriculum of Classics: *Zhou Yi (Book of Change), Shang Shu (Book of Documents), Mao Shi (Classic of Poetry with Mao Commentaries), Chunqiu Zuozhuan (Spring and Autumn Annals with Zuo Commentaries), Chunqiu Sanzhuan (Spring and Autumn Annals with 3 Schools of Commentaries), Zhou Li (Rites of Zhou), Yi Li (Etiquette and Ceremonial), Li Ji (Book of Rites), Lunyu (the Analects of Confucius), Mengzi (the Analects of Mencius), Lixue (Neo-Confucianism).*[80]

In the *Imperial Endorsed Petition on the Constitution of Educational Institutions*, the Confucian Classics discipline had 11 majors, which made it the discipline with the most majors. This greatly strengthened the supreme status of this discipline. The biggest feature of the *Imperial Endorsed Petition on the Constitution of Educational Institutions* was that it highlighted the status of Confucian classics. Although the discipline of business appeared in the curriculum, it still ranked last. *Imperial Endorsed Constitution of the Imperial University of Peking* coined seven disciplines, business being the sixth subject. Classics ranked first and consisted of 11 majors, while Business ranked last with only 3 majors. Chinese social hierarchy consisted of *shi* (scholar-officials or gentry-scholars), *nong* (farmers or peasants), *gong* (craftsmen) and *shang* (merchants), with *shi* ranking first and *shang* ranking the last. The curriculum design of the Imperial University of Peking course was based on this tradition.

b) Student Qualifications.

Award policy based on student qualifications was a key theme running through the various versions of the *Constitution of the Imperial University of Peking*. The fact that reward was given with due consideration to qualification means that the University's administration was grounded on the traditional politics-centric principle. The relevant provisions on the Imperial University of Peking award policy based on qualification were mainly reflected in three historical texts, namely, *Constitution of the Imperial University of Peking, Imperial Endorsed Constitution of Imperial University of Peking* and *Petition to the Throne on the Revision to Award to University Graduates by Qualification*. The earliest record of specific rules and regulations governing the award can be found in the 1898

Constitution of the Imperial University of Peking. Its content reads as follows:

> Imperial edict issued on the 7th day of the first lunar month of this year: Titles for Current Affairs *Juren* (provincial graduate), Current Affairs *Gongshi* (candidates sitting for provincial examinations) have been established for each province. By imperial order, all provinces, from provincial capital down to the various administrative divisions of *Fu* (prefecture), *Zhou* (Independent Department) and *Xian* (District) shall set up schools within a year. Schools at *Fu, Zhou,* and *Xian* levels are to be called primary schools; at the provincial capital, middle schools; at the capital, universities. Holders of primary school graduation certificates may proceed to enroll as economic students at middle school. Holders of secondary school graduation certificate, or *Juren*, may be promoted to the university. Upon graduation from the university, *Juren* shall be awarded the rank of *Jinshi. Jinshi* shall be granted an audience by the throne and be assigned an official position.[81]

The Imperial Endorsed Constitution of the Imperial University of Peking of 1902 stated that:

> Referring respectfully to previous imperial edicts on the subject, graduated students were duly awarded qualifications of *Shenyuan* (graduate of primary school), *Juren* (graduate of middle school), and *Jinshi* (graduate of imperial university). This time, the Throne has approved my suggestion to award graduates of the preparatory and express classes *Juren* and *Jinshi* respectively.
>
> All certificates for *fusheng* (appended student, i.e. students admitted on supplementary quota and without allowance), *gongsheng* (the top of the allowance recipients aiming for imperial university, a level higher than *Juren*), *Juren, Jinshi* shall be administered by the Imperial University of Peking who is responsible for designing the printing plates, print, and seal setting among others concerning certificates issued by the imperial court. Certificates for candidates below the *Gongsheng* qualifications shall be dispatched to various provinces for administration at the provincial level. At the end of each year, each province shall submit a list of candidates qualified as *Gongsheng* with personal particulars as follow: name of *Fusheng*, place of birth, age and description of past three generations, first to the University for verification and then through the University to the Ministry of Rites for their records.[82]

In 1905, then Censor Chen Zengyou submitted a proposal to the Throne. In his *Petition to the Throne on the Revision to Award to University Graduates by Qualification*, he opined that:

> In awarding University graduates, it is recommended that the cream should be appointed to the post of Junior Compiler (*Bianxiu Jiantao*) of the Imperial Academy (*Hanlin Yuan*), and those with excellent results, should be called *Shujishi* (scholar on short term attachment to the Imperial academy whose function is to help draft edicts and read to the Emperor). Those at the lower end of the score should be placed in the talent pool for appointment as district magistrate to various provinces.
>
> Concerning the graduates of various practical disciplines, it is recommended that the top, as *Juren*, be included in the talent reserve pool for appointment as middle to the low ranking officials at the Independent Department level. Those with excellent results, as *Juren*, be included in the talent pool for selection in the appointment of middle to low-rank positions.
>
> Concerning the graduates of preparation classes as well as higher learning institutions at the provincial level, it is recommended that the cream, as *Juren*, be deployed in two ways: internally, included in the reserve pool for *Neige Zhongshu* (cabinet correspondence) and externally, be included in the talent reserve pool for posting to various provinces as district magistrate. Those with excellent results, as *Juren,* may be deployed in two ways: internally, be included in the talent reserve pool for *Zhongshu for Zhongshuke* (administrative support to Cabinet correspondence) and externally, in the talent reserve pool for posting to various provinces as officials at the district level. Those in the middle range, as *Juren*, may be deployed in two ways: internally, they may be included in the talent reserve pool for administrative appointments at Ministry, Branch or Department levels; externally, in the talent reserve pool for posting to various provinces as *Tongpan* (controller-general).[83]

From the *Constitution of the Imperial University of Peking* to *Petition to the Throne on the Revision to Award to University Graduates by Qualification*, the Confucian thought of "excel in academics to enter officialdom" is still clearly reflected. The policy of awarding university graduates by qualification assumed that students of the Imperial University of Peking were to take up an official post eventually after their graduation. The titles of *gongsheng, juren* and *jinshi* were all coined terms of the imperial examination system. The graduation awards ha at most transformed "pursuing an official post through imperial examinations" into "pursuing an official post through the university." The tradition of learning for official posts never changed. The imperial examination system was abolished in 1905. It was replaced by the policy of university graduate awards by qualification. Because of that, entering a university had become a must for late-Qing scholars. In history, many figures have entered university for the sake of getting into politics. There were even those who gave up their teaching positions and became students to get official titles. For example, Chen Hanzhang was a well-known late-Qing scholar for his erudition. In 1907, he was invited to become a lecturer at the Imperial University of Peking. However, to attain a position in the Imperial Academy, which would be awarded after graduating from the Imperial University of Peking, he decided that he would rather become a student than a lecturer. It can be said that all of the lecturers and students of the Imperial University of Peking taught or learned just for the sake of advancing in their official careers. It was, after all, about "officialdom."

In short, the Imperial University of Peking had integrated learning with officialdom since the beginning, heightening the sense of bureaucracy. The situation did not begin to change until early Republican China when Cai Yuapei took charge of Peking University.

c) School management

The management of the Imperial University of Peking was copied from the governance style of the Qing imperial court. From the Minister-in-charge to the Supervisor and Branch head – these were all political appointees. The 1898 *Constitution of Imperial University of Peking* stipulated that:

> There shall be a Minister-in-charge who must be a *Da Xueshi* (grand scholar from the Imperial Academy), a minister or vice-minister, just like *guozijian shiwu daceng* (Chancellor of the Directorate of the Imperial Academy).
>
> There shall be a Principal, a post which can be assumed by an officer of any rank appointed by special edict, just like *guozijian, jijiu* (Chief of staff, Imperial Academy) or *Siye* (Dean of Studies, Imperial Academy).
>
> There shall be 24 Instructor posts to be appointed by the Principal. Just like, Doctor of Five Classics, Assistant to instructors. Western Instructors shall not be appointed to official positions (but can still take on sub-work).
>
> There shall be a Chief of Administration to be assumed by officials of rank sixth and above.
>
> There shall be eight Controllers to be assumed by officials of fifth grade and above – one in charge of logistics, five in charge of supervision, two in charge of miscellaneous activities.
>
> There shall be 16 Heads and eight Transcribers.[84]

The Imperial Endorsed Constitution of the Imperial University of Peking of 1902 stated that:

> There shall be a Minister-in-charge who shall be appointed by imperial edict to oversee the Academy and give directions. There shall be one Chief of Administration and two Deputy Chief of Administration to oversee the administration of the university in consultation with the Minister-in-charge.[85]

> There shall be four Controllers to take care of the attendance and welfare of the students. The Controller in charge of internal affairs shall mediate disputes between students and handle other major incidents in consultation with the Chief of Administration. The Controller in charge of judicial affairs shall also handle the discipline of low-rank officers and non-official staff, and determine the punishment to be metered out to any breach of rules and disorderly behavior within the Academy.[86]

Imperial Endorsed Petition on the Constitution of the Imperial College of 1904 stated that:

> The Academy shall have the following positions: Chief supervisor, subject supervisor, controller of education, instructor, assistant instructor, Controller of logistics, planning officer, financial officer, clerical officer, Controller of discipline and hostel, Dean of studies, Dean of discipline, Dean of health, Dean of observatory management, Dean of botany management, Dean of zoo management, Dean of martial art site management, Dean of Medical clinic, Dean of the library.[87]

When overviewing the above provisions about the organization and management of the university, a few main characteristics can be derived: First, the strong sentiment of centralized power. The Imperial University of Peking was established directly by the central government. Initially, there was a Minister-in-charge. From 1904, after the *Imperial Endorsed Petition on the Constitution of the Imperial College,* the post was renamed as the Chairman of the university. The Minister-in-charge or the Chairman was the highest manager of the university, directly responsible to the central government. They resided in the power center of the Imperial University of Peking. There were three Ministers-in-charge in the history of the Imperial University of Peking, Sun Jianai, Xu Jingcheng, and Zhang Baixi. In addition to eight (including interim) Chairmen of the university since 1904, these 11 figures in charge of the university were all important members of the court. It can be derived that the Imperial University of Peking was directly controlled by senior government officials and is a subsidiary body of the centralized government.

Second, there was a strong sense of bureaucracy. All members of the university were called *guan* (official). There were 18 administrative positions listed in the *Imperial Endorsed Petition on the Constitution of the Imperial College*, 12 of which were called *guan*.

Third, the hierarchical relationship was clear. Let's take the *Constitution of the Imperial University of Peking* as an example. The Minister-in-charge was at the highest position, followed by the Principal, the Instructor, the Chief of Administration, the Controller, and the Heads in descending order. The administrative affiliation was established by the constitution and the 24 members sub-teaching class, showing strong characteristics of government-run universities. In summary, the curriculum of Jingshi University Hall had moral education as the foundation; Confucian principles as the substance. This was the annotation of Imperial University of Peking's "Confucian-centric" cultural character. The graduation reward policy, as well as the set up of its administrative structure, conveyed a strong sense of bureaucracy, which was also the explanation for Imperial University of Peking's cultural character of "integrating learning and officialdom."

In a nutshell, the organization and management of the Imperial University of Peking, as a product of traditional society, was a special marker of late-Qing universities' cultural characteristics.

3. Cultural Symbols of the Imperial University of Peking

The cultural symbol of the Imperial University of Peking is more tangible compared to the cultural characters of the ideals, organizations, and management styles. This section further explores the cultural character of the Imperial University of Peking by examining names, etiquettes, and rites, as well as school activities.

a) Names.

The various "names" in the Imperial University of Peking were one of the most prominent symbols of its cultural characteristics. The following will examine the classic cultural references behind the titles for the school (*Tongru Yuan*), major (*Gezhi Xue*) and discipline (*Zheng* and *Yi*).

Tongru Yuan was the highest educational institution within the higher education system of the Imperial University of Peking. *Hanyu Cidian* (the Chinese Dictionary) defined *Tongru* as follows: "*Ru,* the *dao* of Coinfucius. E.g. 'Those who escaped from Yangzi's School of philosophy would definitely turn to *Ru*. (Mencius)' '*Tongru*', accomplished Confucian scholar who mastered the Confucian classics." Tracing back to its ancient meaning, Mencius said, "Those who escaped from the Mohist school of philosophy would turn to Yangzi; those who escaped from Yangzi's School of philosophy would definitely turn to *Ru*. Turn to, that is, *gui*, means acceptance. Arguing with the followers of Mozi and Yangzi is as good as chasing a loose pig. The pig is already back in its pigsty, yet one still wants to chain its legs." Biography of Jia Kui, *Book of Later Han* stated that "Jia has written millions of characters of annotations and analyses of the meanings and principles in the classics. He has also composed *shi* (poetry), *song* (prose), *lei* (funeral oration), *shu* (essay), *lianzhu* (lianzhu-style poem) and *jiuling* (poem written during drinking) with a total of nine chapters. He was highly valued by other scholars. Later generations called him *tongru*."

Gezhixue was an important major in the Imperial University of Peking's curriculum structure. *Hanyu Cidian* defined *Gezhi* as follows: "*Gezhi* refers to the deep and thorough exploration of the meanings and mechanisms of things, to attain the knowledge behind them and extend one's knowledge. *The Book of Great Learning* stated, *zhizhi zai gewu* (understanding comes after thorough examination and observation). Tracing its origin, the *Book of Great Learning* stated that "(those who are) wishing to cultivate their persons, they (must) first rectify their hearts. Wishing to rectify their hearts, they first sought to be sincere in their thoughts. Wishing to be sincere in their thoughts, they (must) first extended to the utmost of their knowledge. Such an extension of knowledge lies in the investigation of things. The character becomes the known, the knowledge is then sincere, the sincerity and the heart is then right, the heart is right and the body is cultivated." Zhu Xi annotated this statement, "By saying that extension of knowledge lies in the investigation, it means that to extend my own knowledge, I have to exhaustively explore the principles behind all aspects. As all hearts of men contain the knowledge and all things under Heaven contain principles. There are infinite principles, just as there is no end for the extension of knowledge. Therefore, what the *Book of Great Learning* teaches is that scholars should exhaustively examine and explore the principles behind all things under Heaven in pursuit of the ultimate knowledge. It does not matter how much effort it would take. Once the sudden enlightenment dawns on us, the inside and outside, the general shape and the small details of things would all be presented in front of our eyes. At this time, the uses for everything would be clear in our hearts. This is called 'things investigated' and 'knowledge extended.'" Wang Yangming explained this statement that, "*Zhizhi* is not what we used to call 'the extension of knowledge.' In fact, it refers to our virtue," "*Wu* means 'things,' whenever there is a thought, there must be some 'thing' that appears. Therefore, *wu* is where the thoughts lie. *Ge* means 'right', that is, to right the wrong and return things to the right path. Righting the wrong, that is, eliminating the evil. Returning things to the right path, that is, being virtuous. This is what we call *Ge*."

Zheng and *Yi* were two general disciplines coined by the Imperial University of Peking. *The Analects of Confucius* defined *zheng* as correctness, "If you were to lead the people with correctness, who would dare to be right?" "If you are not in the correct position, you should not make plans for the respective administration." *The Analects of Confucius* also mentioned *Yi*, "Confucius said: understanding *dao* (the way) as the ultimate goal, *de* (morality) as the guidance while leveraging on *ren* (benevolence) and traveling with *yi* (skills)", "Qiu is skillful. What difficulty would he have in handling government work?"

In summary, if we briefly trace back to the ancient meaning of the names in the Imperial University of Peking, we can find out that, regardless of the modern and ancient semantic meanings of the words, the characters stayed the same. Just like the word *daxue* in modern times, which is derived from the Confucian concept of "greater learning." The word *gezhi* has the same origin as *daxue*, which is in the *Book of Greater Learning*. *Zheng* and *Yi* are classic Confucian concepts, while the word *Tongru* is undoubtedly the highest ideal of Confucian education. Judging solely from the word choice, the host of the Imperial University of Peking tended to find corresponding words from Confucian classics, and use the old words to represent new things.

For example, in 1898, when the Imperial University of Peking was first established, there were four halls named *Shi* (*Shi Jing*, Classic of Poetry), Book (*Shang Shu*, Book of Documents), *Yi* (*Zhou Yi*, Book of Change) and *Li* (*Li Ji*, Book of Rites), which were four of the Five Classics in Confucianism. Later, in order to "better convey the meaning to the scholars, encourage their moral and intellectual cultivation, as well as to stop the people from questioning,"[88] the names of the four halls were changed to *Liben* (Rooted), *Qiuzhi* (Pursuit), *Dunxing* (Hardworking), *Shouyue* (Credible). The changed names were still based on Confucian concepts. The late-Qing government also clearly. stipulated the choice of vocabulary.

In *Imperial Endorsed Petition on the Constitution of Educational Institutions*, there were two statements in the University Administrative Outline, one stating that "the university must not abandon Chinese dictions so that ancient classics can still be read." The lecturers and students were required to choose words that "can express the principles and meanings clearly, preferably borrowed from classics or history records."[89] The other one stated that "the use of unnecessary foreign terms should be avoided, to preserve the national language and promote moral integrity." In addition, "except for chemistry, engineering and other specific fields where there are new concepts and new laws, which we should create new characters to represent, all common nouns should not be copied or mixed up with foreign languages," "there are inherent Chinese common nouns to describe and explain things, why adopt others' languages instead of using our own?"[90]

In short, the new use of old words in the Imperial University of Peking was intentional and it adhered to certain rules and regulations. Indeed, the meaning of *daxue* in ancient and modern times is no longer the same. The current debate in academia regarding *daxue* is just a struggle for discursive power. But this kind of meaningless dispute over discursive power has, in a sense, retained the Chinese tradition. *Tongru, Gezhi, Zheng,* and *Yi,* are the remnants of tradition in modern times, are also the most direct expression of the cultural character of the Imperial University of Peking.

b) School manners.

The Imperial University of Peking had a strict set of requirements regarding school manners which emphasized the order of human relations and was very particular about the external relationships between people. In the following, specific regulations regarding school manners in the official documents of the *Constitution of the Imperial University of Peking* (1899) and *the Imperial Endorsed Constitution of the Imperial University of Peking* (1902) will be used as subjects to study the cultural characters of Imperial University of Peking's school manners. *Constitution of the Imperial University of Peking* (1899) stipulated that:

> The ancestor teacher, Confucius, must be respected. His memorial tablet shall be displayed in the main hall of the university. On the first day of lunar calendar in February and August each year (Confucius sacrificial Day), the Minister-in-charge, the Chinese Principals, the Chief of Administration, the Controllers, the Instructors shall lead the students to perform the sacrificial ritual, and worship Confucius with *Sanbai Jiukou* (the ritual of three kneels and nine kowtows). On the syzygy day of each month, Controllers and Instructors shall lead students of respective disciplines to perform *Sanbai Jiukou.* When school reopens, every member of the school, from the Minister-in-charge to the students, shall gather in front of Confucius' memorial tablet and perform *Sanbai Jiukou.*
>
> Every day when school begins, one of the administrative staff, one the Controllers, or the Dean of Studies (in rotation) should give a lecture on a section of one of the *Four Books*, or *Zizheng Yaolan (Notes of Emperor Shunzhi*), or *Quanshan Yaoyan* (*Imperial Compiled Persuasions to Do Good*), or other rules passed down by the Qing imperial family. The speaker shall take a seat at the front of the lecture hall, while the students shall listen silently, and read the books. If there are students who can give such lectures, the Instructor can also nominate them for the morning speech.[91]

The Imperial Endorsed Constitution of the Imperial University of Peking of 1902 stated that:

> Every time the school reopens from or closes for holidays, as well as on the syzygy days of the months, students shall be led to the memorial tablet of Confucius by the Principals and Chiefs, and Deputy Chiefs of Administration to perform the ritual. After the ritual, students shall salute the Principals, Vice-Principals and Chiefs of Administration three times and return to their classes.
>
> Every year, at the Empress Dowager, the Emperor, the Queen, and Confucius' birthdays, as well as on the Confucius Sacrificial Day, the Principals, Vice-Principals, and Chiefs of Administration shall lead the students to the main hall to perform the ritual.
>
> Whenever a student meets the Minister-in-charge, Principal, Vice-Principal, or Instructor, he shall perform a *Dizi Li* (Student Salute); when he meets other officials and superior administrative staff, he shall salute once to show respect.[92]

Based on the content of the quotations, first of all, it can be inferred that the Imperial University of Peking emphasized the manners between teachers and students, and maintained the order between teachers and students with the idea of *Zunshi Zhongjiao* (respecting the teacher and valuing education). The statement in the *Imperial University of Peking Provisions*, that "the ancestor teacher, Confucius, shall be respected. His memorial tablet should be displayed in the main hall of the university" was intended to show respect for both Confucius and teachers. There were similar statements in the *Imperial Endorsed Constitution of the Imperial University of Peking*, that when school reopens, "students shall be led to the memorial tablet of Confucius by the Principals and Chiefs of Administration to perform the ritual" first.

Secondly, the Imperial University of Peking stressed manners and the relationship between the emperor and the subordinates and maintained the order between the emperor and the subordinates with the concept of *Zhongjun Jingzhu* (Loyalty to the emperor and respect for the ruler). The *Imperial Endorsed Constitution of Imperial University of Peking* clearly stated that "Every year, at the Empress Dowager, the Emperor, the Queen and Confucius' birthdays," the administrative staff of the university "shall lead the students to the main hall to perform the ritual." Besides, the Imperial University of Peking also attached importance to maintaining social hierarchies and respect. According to the above rules, Confucius enjoyed a supreme status. All members of the university, regardless of their positions, when school reopens, "shall gather in front of Confucius' memorial tablet and perform *Sanbai Jiukou*." The emperor assumed supreme status. All members of the university, regardless of their positions, "shall lead the students to the main hall to perform the ritual" for every important national celebration. The administrative staff of the school is superior to the students. "Whenever a student meets the Minister-in-charge, Principal, Vice-Principal, or Instructor, he shall perform a *Dizi Li*."

In short, the above school manners of the Imperial University of Peking inherited and promoted the Confucian idea of *Sangang Wuchang*, which adhered to the Confucian life principle of nurturing *ren* with *li*. This is the best example of the university's cultural character of *Zhongjun* and *Zunkong*, that is, loyalty to the emperor and respect for Confucius.

c) School Activities – Example of university sports games.

Sports games were important activities for the Imperial University of Peking. They intended to fulfill the "purpose of education" and to implement the *Shangwu* policy of the court. According to the records of *Historical Materials of Peking University*, the Imperial University of Peking hosted three sports games in the spring season of 1905, 1906, and 1907, respectively. In 1905, the Imperial University of Peking hosted its first sports games, and "Chief superintendent's address to the guests of the first sports games" recorded:

> Today, our university holds its first sports games, and I would like to thank all our guests for taking the time to attend. This is not only an honor for our University but an event worthy of the celebration of the entire Chinese academic community. And here, I would like to give a speech regarding my thoughts. The purpose of university education is to cultivate talents. And to cultivate

> talent, ethical and physical education are the two indispensable elements. All the content taught in the lecture halls and all the rules inside and outside the lecture halls, are all parts of ethical education. However, people may vary in strength and talent, and to make everyone willing to undertake responsibilities and even die for their duties to serve the emperor is no easy task. All of the countries in the world already know this, and that is why they all treat physical training as one of the most fundamental parts of education.
>
> In ancient China, most of the people's skills were related to martial arts, so *Cuju* (a form of football in ancient China) was invented in the era of Emperor Xuan, and the swing started from the Shan Rong tribe and was promoted during Emperor Qi Wei's crusade. Emperor Wu of Han engaged in *Juedi* (wrestling) in his palace, while Huo Jinghuan did the same in his army camp. There are many poems in the Tang Dynasty where emperors and their subjects played *Jiqiu* (polo), while seven ministers, two emperor's sons-in-law, and five generals played the tug-of-war without any regards to their position and identity. This trend lasted for many years, and for many generations during this time, the people were strong and skillful in battle. The reason for our dynasty to keep *Shanpu Ying* (the battalion of wrestlers) is not only for retaining the tradition but also for this purpose, as well.[93]

In 1906, the second sports games of the Imperial University of Peking were held, and *Address to the guests of the second sports games* recorded:

> The purpose for th establishment of the Husbandry Games was to put the emphasis on sports and military affairs and to place them as one of the most important aspects of national education. For those who do not do this, the school must clearly set up the purpose of education, declare the world, and mark it in throwing, wrestling, sports, and walking and lifting, and consider it a martial art. Fengzhao said that everyone has the spirit of encouraging martial arts, and he is self-improving, and he admires the court's desire to save the weak and to be strong ... or to hear it, what is more valuable to the brave, and to dare have good manners. Therefore, those who are brave and powerful, if there is nothing in the world, they use it for courtesy. If there is something in the world, they use it for victory. It is invincible when used for victory, and *Shunzhi* for courtesy. Invincible outside *Shunzhi* is called *Shengde*.[94]

When using the materials cited above as a basis to analyze the cultural connotation of the sports games of the Imperial University of Peking, it can be observed that it was mainly manifested in two ways. First, China had always been strong in sports and military tactics since ancient times, and the sports games were originated from the traditions of

China. The event of sports games itself is the inheritance of "national customs." The *Chief superintendent's address to the guests of the first sports games* pointed out that "in ancient China, most of the people's skills were related to martial arts," and cited the examples of Emperor Xuan's Cuju, the Jiqiu and tug-of-war games of Tang Dynasty officials. Although these are historical facts, the speech still bore a slight hint of *Tuogu Gaizhi*, with a potential intent on proving or emphasizing that even though the form of sports games was adopted from Japan, its legitimacy was still rooted in Chinese tradition since ancient times.

Secondly, the purpose of the Games was to achieve strength for etiquettes and righteousness internally and for battling skills externally, achieve *Shengde*. *Address to the guests of the second sports games* mentioned that the actual purpose of the sports games was to achieve *Shunzhi*, "external victory and internal peace and order," for the sake of achieving ultimate ethics of the entire society – *Shengde*. As this book's understanding, the so-called *Shengde* with the meaning of "external victory combined with internal peace and order" is similar to Confucius' *Zhishan*, his idea of achieving an ethical *Zhishan* by *Ming Mingde* and *Xin Min*. From this perspective, it can be argued that while the university's *Xiuti Er Qiangguo* (strengthening the country through the strengthening of its body) emphasized sports and the country itself, it was in fact still compliant with the cultural traditions with Confucian ethics at its core. In addition, in terms of linguistic expressions alone, these paragraphs of text possessed obvious features of Confucian culture. The terms mentioned such as *Liyi* (etiquette and righteousness), *Shunzhi* (peace and order), *Shengde* (ultimate ethics), and *Tianxia* (the world) were all derived directly or indirectly from Confucianism. The indispensability of ethical and physical education regarding the cultivation of talents, along with the expression of "willing to undertake responsibilities and even die for their duties to serve the emperor" were both teachings of Confucius.

To sum up, as an event of sports, the sports games were held by the Imperial University of Peking when it picked up pace in China. Their goal was to achieve a culture of ethics, and peace and order of the nation. It also followed the traditional logic of *Youji Jiguo* (from individuals to the nation). Hence, it can be interpreted to be a realistic manifestation of the cultural character of the Imperial University of Peking, which is *Zhongjun Zunkong*.

Summary

Several features can be observed in the formation of the cultural characteristics of Chinese universities in the late Qing Dynasty:

1. Chinese culture.

In the late Qing Dynasty, Chinese society was troubled both externally and internally, and the Qing government underwent frequent political reforms. From the Self-strengthening Movement, the One Hundred Days' Reform to the New Policies Reform, each reform came with drastic social and cultural changes. It is true that the introduction of Western learning into the East had gradually become a trend of the time. However, the three reforms used Western learning as the means to strengthen the nation, so the fundamental status of Chinese culture within Chinese society was still rather intact.

2. Scholars in the late Qing Dynasty.

In the late Qing Dynasty, the scholars, as the last batch of *Shi* in traditional society, had a relatively strong cultural character. In the conflict and integration of Chinese and Western cultures, the mainstream cultural views included the theory of *Zhongxue Duzun*, *Xixue Zhongyuan*, and *Zhongti Xiyong*. They all shared some properties in the following aspects: first, the scholars of the late Qing Dynasty have always taken Chinese culture as the orthodox view; second, these scholars took the responsibility to revive traditional culture as their duty; and third, these scholars were under the of accepting western culture in late Qing Dynasty only when they took Chinese culture as their fundamental starting point.

3. Chinese universities.

Under the guidance of the aforementioned scholars, Chinese universities showed relatively obvious cultural characters, especially *Zhongjun Zunkong*, *Xueshi Yiti*, and *Jingxue Weiben*.

In general, the cultural character of Chinese universities in the late Qing Dynasty was relatively obvious. One reason was that the foundation of Chinese culture in the late Qing society had not been shaken, and another was the strong traditional cultural character of the scholars in the late Qing Dynasty. In short, Chinese universities in this period were still in their infancy, with traditional scholars holding the dominant status. Their property of the "cultural" was stronger than their property of "university," which also, in a sense, hindered Chinese universities' transformation to modernity.

Notes

1. Office of Chinese Philosophy Research, Department of Philosophy and Religious Studies, Peking University. *Zhongguo Zhexueshi* (History of Chinese Philosophy). Beijing: Peking University Press, 2003: 508.
2. Xiao, G. *Weiji Zhongde Biange: Qingmo Xiandaihua Zhongde Jijin Yu Baoshou* (Changes within Crysis: Radicalism and Conservatism within the Modernization of the Late Qing Dynasty). Shanghai: Shanghai Joint Publishing, 1999: 18.
3. Zeng, G. *Zeng Guofan Quanji* (Collected Works of Zeng Guofan). Changsha: Yuelu Publishing House, 1985: 232.
4. First Historical Archives of China. *Xianfeng Tongzhi Liangchao Shangyu Dang* (Archive of Orders from the Emperors Xianfeng and Tongzhi). Guilin: Guangxi Normal University Press, 2000: 132
5. Meng, S. *Qingshi Jiangyi* (Lecture Notes on History of the Qing Dynasty). Hangzhou: Zhejiang People's Publishing House, 1998: 182.
6. An, Y. *Chongzhuang Yu Ronghe: Zhongguo Jindai Wenhuashi Lun* (Conflict and Integration: A Discussion of Modern Chinese Cultural History). Shanghai: Xuelin Press, 2001: 22.
7. Qi, Q. *Wanqing Shehui Sichao Yanjin Shi* (The History of Ideological Trend Progression of the Late Qing Dynasty). Beijing: Zhonghua Book Company, 2012: 218.
8. Gao, S. *Zhongguo Jindai Jiaoyushi Ziliao Huibian: Yangwu Yundong Shiqi Jiaoyu* (Collection of Materials regarding Modern Chinese Education History: Education of the Self-Strengthening Movement Era). Shanghai: Shanghai Education Press, 1992: 9.
9. Ibid, pp. 20–21.
10. Ibid, p. 14.
11. Li, G., Wang, B. *Zhongguo Jiaoyu Zhidu Tongshi* (General History of Chinese Education System). Jinan: Shandong Education Press, 2000: 147.
12. Zhu, Y. Zhongguo Jindai Xuezhi Shiliao Diyiji Xiace (Historical Materials of Modern Chinese Education System, Vol. 1, Part 2). Shanghai: East China Normal University Press, 1986: 490.
13. Tian, Z., Shang, L. *Zhongguo Gaodeng Jiaoyu Bainian Shilun: Zhidu Bianqian, Caizheng Yunzuo Yu Jiaoshi Liudong* (History and Comments of A Century of Chinese Higher Education: The Shifting of Institution, the Operation of Finance and the Turnover of Teachers) Beijing: People's Education Press, 2006: 39.
14. Zhu, G. *Xixue Dongjian Yu Zhongguo Gaodeng Jiaoyu Jindaihua* (The Eastward Spreading of Western Learning and the Modernization of Chinese Higher Education). Xiamen: Xiamen University Press, 1996: 25.
15. Cao, X. *Zhongxi Wenhua Duibi Daolun: Guanyu Zhongguo Wenhua Xuanze De Zaijiantao* (An Introduction to Comparison between Chinese and Western Cultures: Another Reflection on Chinese Cultural Choices). Beijing: China Youth Press, 1992: 150.
16. Tian, Z., Shang, L. *Zhongguo Gaodeng Jiaoyu Bainian Shilun: Zhidu Bianqian, Caizheng Yunzuo Yu Jiaoshi Liudong* (History and Comments of A Century of Chinese Higher Education: The Shifting of Institution, the Operation of Finance and the Turnover of Teachers) Beijing: People's Education Press, 2006: 44.
17. Ibid, p. 47.
18. An, Y. Chongzhuang Yu Ronghe: Zhongguo Jindai Wenhua Shilun (Conflict and Integration: History and Comments on Modern Chinese Cultural History). Shanghai: Xuelin Press, 2001: 24.
19. Ibid, p. 26.

20. Association of Chinese Historians. *Wuxu Bianfa* (The Wuxu Reform). Shanghai: Shanghai Bookstore Publishing House, 2000: 197–198.
21. Tang, Z., Chen, Z. *Zhongguo Jindai Jiaoyushi Ziliao Huibian: Wuxu Shiqi Jiaoyu* (Collection of Materials of Modern Chinese Education History: The Education of the Wuxu Era). Shanghai: Shanghai Education Press, 1993: 7.
22. Ibid, p. 10.
23. Zhuang, Y. *Zuijin Sanwushinian Zhi Zhongguo Jiaoyu* (Education of China during the Past 30–50 Years). Shanghai: The Commercial Press, 1931: 64.
24. Qu, S. *Zhongguo Daxue Jiaoyu Fazhanshi* (The History of the Development of Chinese Universities). Beijing: Peking University Press, 2006: 203.
25. Tang, Z., Chen, Z. *Zhongguo Jindai Jiaoyushi Ziliao Huibian: Wuxu Shiqi Jiaoyu* (Collection of Materials of Modern Chinese Education History: The Education of the Wuxu Era). Shanghai: Shanghai Education Press, 1993: 47.
26. Ibid, p. 55.
27. Zhu, Y. Zhongguo Jindai Xuezhi Shiliao Diyiji Xiace (Historical Materials of Modern Chinese Education System, Vol. 1, Part 2). Shanghai: East China Normal University Press, 1986: 633.
28. Bai, W. Yingbian Yu Kunjing: Qingmo Xinzheng Shiqi De Yishi Xingtai Kongzhi (Adaption and Difficulties: The Ideological Control during the New Policies Reform Era of the Late Qing Dynasty). Beijing: Community University of China Press, 2008: 53.
29. Su, Y. Zhongguo Xinjiaoyu De Mengya Yu Chengzhang (1860–1928) (The Sprouting and Growth of the New Education of China (1860–1928)). Beijing: Peking University Press, 2007: 7.
30. Zhu, Y. *Zhongguo Jindai Xuezhi Shiliao Diyiji Xiace* (Historical Materials of Modern Chinese Education System, Vol. 1, Part 2). Shanghai: East China Normal University Press, 1986: 454.
31. Qu, X., Tang, L. *Zhongguo Jindai Jiaoyushi Ziliao Huibian: Xuezhi Yanbian* (Collection of Materials regarding Modern Chinese Education History: The Shifting of Education System). Shanghai: Shanghai Education Press, 1991: 531.
32. Chen, X. *Zhongguo Jindai Jiaoyushi Jiaoxue Cankao Cailiao* (Referential Materials for Teaching the History of Modern Chinese Education). Beijing: People's Education Press, 1986: 532.
33. Tian, Z., Shang, L. Zhongguo Gaodeng Jiaoyu Bainian Shilun: Zhidu Bianqian, Caizheng Yunzuo Yu Jiaoshi Liudong (History and Comments of A Century of Chinese Higher Education: The Shifting of Institution, the Operation of Finance and the Turnover of Teachers) Beijing: People's Education Press, 2006: 90–91.
34. Qu, X., Tang, L. Zhongguo Jindai Jiaoyushi Ziliao Huibian: Xuezhi Yanbian (Collection of Materials regarding Modern Chinese Education History: The Shifting of Education System). Shanghai: Shanghai Education Press, 1991: 235.
35. Zhang Z. Quanxue Pian (On Encouraging Learning). Guilin: Guangxi Normal University Press, 2008: 43–44.
36. Qu, X., Tang, L. Zhongguo Jindai Jiaoyushi Ziliao Huibian: Xuezhi Yanbian (Collection of Materials regarding Modern Chinese Education History: The Shifting of Education System). Shanghai: Shanghai Education Press, 1991: 233.
37. Yu, Y. Shi Yu Zhongguo Wenhua ("Shi" and Chinese Culture). Shanghai: Shanghai People's Press, 1987: Preface 2.
38. Wang, E. Wanqing Zhengzhi Sixiang Shilun (History and comments on the Political Thoughts of the Late Qing Dynasty). Guilin: Guangxi Normal University Press, 2007: 2.
39. Ibid.
40. Xiong Y. Xixue Dongjian Yu Wanqing Shehui (The Eastward Introduction of Western Learning and the Society of the Late Qing Dynasty). Shanghai: Shanghai People's Press, 1994: 728.

41. Ibid, p. 717.
42. Ibid, p. 723.
43. Ibid, p. 722.
44. Ibid, p. 725.
45. Wang, E. Wanqing Zhengzhi Sixiang Shilun (History and Comments on the Political Thoughts of the Late Qing Dynasty). Guilin: Guangxi Normal University Press, 2007: 38.
46. Qu, X., Tong, F. Zhongguo Jindai Jiaoyushi Ziliao Huibian: Jiaoyu Sixiang (Collection of Materials regarding Modern Chinese Education History: Education Thoughts). Shanghai: Shanghai Education Press, 1997: 283–284.
47. Ibid, p. 617–618.
48. Wang, E. Wanqing Zhengzhi Sixiang Shilun (History and Comments on the Political Thoughts of the Late Qing Dynasty). Guilin: Guangxi Normal University Press, 2007: 20.
49. Ibid, p. 9.
50. Tian, Z., Shang, L. *Zhongguo Gaodeng Jiaoyu Bainian Shilun: Zhidu Bianqian, Caizheng Yunzuo Yu Jiaoshi Liudong* (History and Comments of A Century of Chinese Higher Education: The Shifting of Institution, the Operation of Finance and the Turnover of Teachers) Beijing: People's Education Press, 2006: 21.
51. Qu, X., Tang, L. Zhongguo Jindai Jiaoyushi Ziliao Huibian: Xuezhi Yanbian (Collection of Materials regarding Modern Chinese Education History: The Shifting of Education System). Shanghai: Shanghai Education Press, 1991: 535.
52. Ibid, p. 536.
53. Tang, Z., Chen, Z. Zhongguo Jindai Jiaoyushi Ziliao Huibian: Wuxu Shiqi Jiaoyu (Collection of Materials of Modern Chinese Education History: The Education of the Wuxu Era). Shanghai: Shanghai Education Press, 1993: 137.
54. Tu, Y. Zhongguo Gaodeng Jiaoyu Shilun (History and comments on Chinese higher education). Wuhan: Hubei Education Publishing House, 2002: 1.
55. Su, Y. Zhongguo Xinjiaoyu De Mengya Yu Chengzhang (1860–1928) (The Sprouting and Growth of the New Education of China (1860–1928)). Beijing: Peking University Press, 2007: 95.
56. Wang, E. Wanqing Zhengzhi Sixiang Shilun (History and comments on the Political Thoughts of the Late Qing Dynasty). Guilin: Guangxi Normal University Press, 2007: 67–68.
57. Zhang Z. Quanxue Pian (On Encouraging Learning). Guilin: Guangxi Normal University Press, 2008: 11.
58. Ibid, p. 44–45.
59. Chen, X. Zhongguo Jindai Jiaoyushi Jiaoxue Cankao Cailiao Shangce(Referential Materials for Teaching the History of Modern Chinese Education Part 1). Beijing: People's Education Press, 1986: 552.
60. Tang, Z., Chen, Z. Zhongguo Jindai Jiaoyushi Ziliao Huibian: Wuxu Shiqi Jiaoyu (Collection of Materials of Modern Chinese Education History: The Education of the Wuxu Era). Shanghai: Shanghai Education Press, 1993: 164.
61. Ibid, p. 165.
62. Ibid, p. 168.
63. Qu, X., Tong, F. Zhongguo Jindai Jiaoyushi Ziliao Huibian: Jiaoyu Sixiang (Collection of Materials regarding Modern Chinese Education History: Education Thoughts). Shanghai: Shanghai Education Press, 1997: 170–171.
64. Ibid, p. 165.
65. Ibid, p. 167.

66. Chen, X. Zhongguo Jindai Jiaoyushi Jiaoxue Cankao Cailiao Shangce(Referential Materials for Teaching the History of Modern Chinese Education Part 1). Beijing: People's Education Press, 1986: 349.
67. Qu, X., Tong, F. Zhongguo Jindai Jiaoyushi Ziliao Huibian: Jiaoyu Sixiang (Collection of Materials regarding Modern Chinese Education History: Education Thoughts). Shanghai: Shanghai Education Press, 1997: 174.
68. Tang, Z., Chen, Z. Zhongguo Jindai Jiaoyushi Ziliao Huibian: Wuxu Shiqi Jiaoyu (Collection of Materials of Modern Chinese Education History: The Education of the Wuxu Era). Shanghai: Shanghai Education Press, 1993: 122.
69. Ibid, p. 127–128.
70. Qu, X., Tang, L. Zhongguo Jindai Jiaoyushi Ziliao Huibian: Xuezhi Yanbian (Collection of Materials regarding Modern Chinese Education History: The Shifting of Education System). Shanghai: Shanghai Education Press, 1991: 235.
71. Ibid, p. 339.
72. Ibid, p. 542–543.
73. Ibid, p. 534–535.
74. Zhou, G. et al. Zhongguo Jindai Daxue De Xiandai Zhuanxing: Yizhi, Tiaoshi Yu Fazhan (The Contemporary Transformation of Modern Chinese Universities: Adoption, Adaption and Development). Hangzhou: Zhejiang University Press, 2012: 17.
75. Hayhoe, R. E. S. China's Universities, 1895–1995: A Century of Cultural Conflict. Trans, Xu Jieying. Beijing: Educational Science Publishing House, 2000: 38.
76. Zhu, G. Xixue Dongjian Yu Zhongguo Gaodeng Jiaoyu Jindaihua (The Eastward Spreading of Western Learning and the Modernization of Chinese Higher Education). Xiamen: Xiamen University Press, 1996: 3.
77. Research Office of School History, Peking University. Beijing Daxue Shiliao Diyijuan: 1898–1911 (Historical Materials of Peking University, Vol. 1: 1898–1911). Beijing: Peking University Press, 1993: 68.
78. Tang, Z., Chen, Z. Zhongguo Jindai Jiaoyushi Ziliao Huibian: Wuxu Shiqi Jiaoyu (Collection of Materials of Modern Chinese Education History: The Education of the Wuxu Era). Shanghai: Shanghai Education Press, 1993: 128.
79. Qu, X., Tang, L. Zhongguo Jindai Jiaoyushi Ziliao Huibian: Xuezhi Yanbian (Collection of Materials regarding Modern Chinese Education History: The Shifting of Education System). Shanghai: Shanghai Education Press, 1991: 237–238.
80. Ibid, p. 391.
81. Tang, Z., Chen, Z. Zhongguo Jindai Jiaoyushi Ziliao Huibian: Wuxu Shiqi Jiaoyu (Collection of Materials of Modern Chinese Education History: The Education of the Wuxu Era). Shanghai: Shanghai Education Press, 1993: 131.
82. Qu, X., Tang, L. Zhongguo Jindai Jiaoyushi Ziliao Huibian: Xuezhi Yanbian (Collection of Materials regarding Modern Chinese Education History: The Shifting of Education System). Shanghai: Shanghai Education Press, 1991: 246–247.
83. Ibid, p. 540–541.
84. Tang, Z., Chen, Z. Zhongguo Jindai Jiaoyushi Ziliao Huibian: Wuxu Shiqi Jiaoyu (Collection of Materials of Modern Chinese Education History: The Education of the Wuxu Era). Shanghai: Shanghai Education Press, 1993: 133.
85. Qu, X., Tang, L. Zhongguo Jindai Jiaoyushi Ziliao Huibian: Xuezhi Yanbian (Collection of Materials regarding Modern Chinese Education History: The Shifting of Education System). Shanghai: Shanghai Education Press, 1991: 248.

86. Ibid, p. 248.
87. Ibid, p. 387.
88. Tang, Z., Chen, Z. Zhongguo Jindai Jiaoyushi Ziliao Huibian: Wuxu Shiqi Jiaoyu (Collection of Materials of Modern Chinese Education History: The Education of the Wuxu Era). Shanghai: Shanghai Education Press, 1993: 140–146.
89. Chen, X. Zhongguo Jindai Jiaoyushi Jiaoxue Cankao Cailiao Shangce(Referential Materials for Teaching the History of Modern Chinese Education Part 1). Beijing: People's Education Press, 1986: 536–537.
90. Ibid, p. 537–538.
91. Tang, Z., Chen, Z. Zhongguo Jindai Jiaoyushi Ziliao Huibian: Wuxu Shiqi Jiaoyu (Collection of Materials of Modern Chinese Education History: The Education of the Wuxu Era). Shanghai: Shanghai Education Press, 1993: 140–141.
92. Qu, X., Tang, L. Zhongguo Jindai Jiaoyushi Ziliao Huibian: Xuezhi Yanbian (Collection of Materials regarding Modern Chinese Education History: The Shifting of Education System). Shanghai: Shanghai Education Press, 1991: 250.
93. Research Office of School History, Peking University. Beijing Daxue Shiliao Diyijuan: 1898–1911 (Historical Materials of Peking University, Vol. 1: 1898–1911). Beijing: Peking University Press, 1993: 291.
94. Ibid, p. 293–294.

CHAPTER 3

Analysis of the Cultural Characters of Chinese Universities in Republican China

Republican China was a very important stage in Chinese universities' history. Despite the social turmoil, political changes, cultural agitations, and frequent changes in the education system, Chinese universities still blossomed and made glorious achievements. Heroes emerge from great upheavals. Countless intellectuals appeared during the Republican China era, and hundreds of philosophy schools contended that discussed academics and politics. Brilliance grew in adversity. With the unique charm of Republican Chinese intellectuals, especially presidents of Chinese universities, the universities once gained relatively ideal cultural characteristics in the mutual checks and balances between Chinese and Western cultures. In the development history of Chinese universities' cultural characteristics, this stage was described as "unprecedented and unparalleled."

Section 1: Social and Cultural Evolution during Republican China and the Development of Chinese Universities

"Social change requires the guidance of advanced thought, as well as the counterbalance of cultural conventions. This seems to be a contradictory proposition or a paradox,"[1] yet it was most vividly reflected throughout Republican China. In nearly 40 years from the start of the Revolution of 1911 to the founding of the People's Republic of China in 1949, Western culture has been guiding the social trends in China, but it was also always subjected to the counterbalance of traditional Chinese cultural forces. Chinese culture rose and fell several times in the fierce debate between Chinese and Western cultures, and Chinese universities were subjected to frequent social changes. Just as Lu Xun said, "Since the beginning of the 20th century, Confucius has had bad luck. But in the era of Yuan Shikai, he was brought up again."[2] Soon, his luck was reversed again, and the anti-Confucian ideological trend that had been deposited for a long time since the May 4th Movement reached its peak. Immediately afterward, Xueheng School (School of Constant and Balanced Studies), which was the traditionalist representative, gradually surfaced. We can say that since the 1911 Revolution, Confucius' luck has experienced some ups and downs. The evolution of Chinese culture has never diverged from the model of "divergence to reversion," "reversion to divergence." But in fact, there was no irreconcilable contradiction between the fierce encounter of *Zun Kong* (Confucianism) and *Pi Kong* (Anti-Confucianism) during the 1911 Xinhai Revolution. While the concepts "Democracy" and "Science" that was celebrated during the May Fourth Movement failed to take root in China. There has never been a diametrical confrontation between tradition and modernity. Instead, they communicated with each other and merged into one after countless cultural debates. In general, ideological control was relatively loose throughout Republican China, and the two trends of Westernization and Revivalism were in wane and wax, confronting, counterbalancing, integrating with, and complementing each other.

In Republican China, Chinese universities entered a complex and erratic period of development that was full of opportunities. As far as higher education was concerned, by continuously borrowing and adopting different forms of Western university models, the university system had gradually matured through trials and errors. In terms of cultural characteristics, they gradually abandoned the excessively rigid and conservative cultural model in the late Qing dynasty while at the same time maintained their unique cultural traits. This section aims to discuss the historical background of the cultural character formation of Chinese universities during the Republican China period, with its main focus being the three typical historical periods, namely the Xinhai Revolution period, May Fourth Movement, and the Second Sino-Japanese War period. Tsinghua University flourished around Xinhai Revolution, while Peking University became the fortress of the May Fourth Movement, and during the Second Sino-Japanese War, National Southwestern Associated University became a glorious institution. The basic idea of this section is, therefore, to first, to investigate the evolution of Chinese cultural trends during the changes of Chinese university policies to reconstruct the historical fate of Chinese culture in the special period during Republican China and to understand the formation of Chinese universities' cultural character. Second, to discuss, from the special to the normal periods, the whole time frame by using specific points, to explore on the relationship between Chinese culture and Chinese universities during Chinese Republican era and to summarize the general cultural characters of Chinese universities

1. Chinese culture and Chinese universities during the Xinhai Revolution

Xinhai Revolution was not just a major event in Chinese history, it also represented a historical period of early Republican China. In 1912, *Imperial Edict of the Abdication of the Qing Emperor* was issued to the world. Some three hundred words marked a hasty end of Qing history. With the end of the 2000-year feudal autocratic monarchy, the bourgeois-democratic republic was born, marking the first year of the Republic of China. However, the Xinhai Revolution achieved its success in one battle, and the sudden changes were greater than the gradual nature of change, and thus it inevitably fell into historical limitations. Yuan Shikai reinstated the throne in 1915 and the Manchu Restoration happened in 1917, and so in regards to political performance, ex-dynastic officials' dreams and pursuits of the throne kept replaying. Along with the iteration of political power, there were complex conflicts and reselections of Chinese and Western cultures, as well as frequent changes in the education system. The history of Republican Chinese universities had officially begun in the process of political changes and mutual checks and balances between Chinese and Western cultures.

a) Cultural changes within social changes.

Although the Xinhai Revolution was an overnight success, the political and cultural debates between the Reformists and the Revolutionists did not end. After the revolution, the cultural debate between revivalism and westernizations only intensified. Before the Xinhai Revolution, Sun Yat-Sen established *T'ung-meng Hui* (The United League of China) in 1905 and then used *Min Bao* (*People's Newspaper*) to promote Western capitalist and democratic ideas. The reformists, represented by Kang Youwei and Liang Qichao who possess strong ideas and respect for Confucius and had loyalty to the emperor, leveraged on *Xinmin Cong Bao* (*Newspaper Series of New People*) as a front to fight against Sun. As a result, the revolutionists led by Sun Yat-sen not only prevailed in the ideological and cultural debate but also overthrew the Qing dynasty with the power of revolution and established a democratic republic. However, the Xinhai Revolution was just a new beginning. "After the Xinhai Upheaval, China's politics and academics were almost unified by the new thought. However, as the country is old and loaded with history, the majority still stuck to old thoughts. The dispute between the old and the new has already lasted for decades yet never seemed to end. There is such chaos at home, we are facing very difficult choices."[3] Wang Guowei's remarked negatively on the Xinhai Revolution, yet at the same time, he revealed some facts. After the Revolution, the dispute between Chinese and Western cultures intensified, and Confucius was once again pushed to the heat of the waves.

In 1912, the Nanjing Provisional Government was established and issued a series of laws and regulations that explicitly abolished the rituals of reading Confucian classics and kneeling to Confucius. Although this measure has cleared obstacles for the establishment of the capitalist democratic system, it also becomes a conviction for the conservative forces to fight back once again. In October 1912, the conservative representatives, Chen Huanzhang, Shen Zengzhi and others, established Kongjiao Hui (Confucianist Association) in Shanghai, to "make the Confucian ideology prosper." The ideological differences quickly evolved into a new round of Chinese-Western cultural debate where the Confucianists and Anti-Confucianists' opinions vigorously clashed. The Confucianist camp was represented by late-Qing political reformists such as Kang Youwei, Liang Qichao, and Yan Fu. They probably had different political stances, but they shared the deep and profound solicitude towards traditional culture. Fundamentally, the Confucianists unanimously believed that Confucius' doctrine represented the cultural spirit of the Chinese people and it was the fundamental condition for the restoration and stability of the Chinese social order which does not conflict with the democratic republic. The Anti-Confucianist thoughts were already formed even before the Xinhai Revolution. The main initiators and followers were new intellectuals of modern China. Under the influence of strong Western influence, they criticized Chinese tradition and supported republicanism. In their view, Confucius' theories were contrary to the principles of a democratic republic. The republican government would be in danger, and autocracy will reappear as long as the society still respects Confucius. The confrontation between the two camps and the struggle between the old and the new... What Wang Guowei said about the chaotic cultural scene in China was indeed true.

In April 1912, Yuan Shikai began to deliberately promote Confucian ethics after stealing the fruits of the revolution. Confucianists received official acquiescence and support. It appeared that the Confucianists were in a temporary victory. However, Yuan Shikai's reinstatement of the throne was as brief as the life of a blooming epiphany, and the Manchu Restoration was revoked on the twelfth day, all of which became historical "farce." Confucianists and Anti-Confucianists took turns to become the embarrassment of history during the Xinhai Revolution. In fact, during this period, there was no fundamental opposition between the two camps in the Chinese-Western cultural debate regardless of their different tendencies. Confucianists did not reject Western culture, they were not even against the Western political system. What they repeatedly argued about was that social stability cannot be achieved without Confucianism and that Confucianism was in tune with the democratic ideal of freedom and equality. The critics of Confucius did not reject traditional culture from the bottom of their hearts, either. They resolutely denied the tradition was because of their worries about Confucius's doctrine being used by political careerists. From this perspective, there was no irreconcilable contradiction between Confucianists and Anti-Confucianists. It could be said that the cultural confrontation during the Xinhai Revolution was constrained by political positions. Chinese and Western cultures checked and balanced each other in the debate, and neither of them went to extremes.

In short, Chinese culture has experienced several ups and downs in the erratic political situation during the Xinhai Revolution. It no longer enjoyed a subjective status like it did in late Qing, yet it maintained its foundation in the upheavals.

b) Chinese universities in cultural changes.

After the Xinhai Revolution, educational decrees were promulgated one after another, and the reform of the Chinese higher education system also entered a new era. On January 1, 1912, Sun Yat-Sen became the president of the Nanjing Provisional Government. He soon appointed Cai Yuanpei on 3 January as the first Minister of Education of the Republic of China, who presided over the Ministry of Education established later on January 9. Under the leadership of Cai Yuanpei, an education system that has been conventional since the late Qing dynasty was drastically reformed. Chinese universities have ushered in new development opportunities in the new era of educational reform.

First, the purpose of Republican Chinese education was promulgated, thereby establishing the purposes of raising educational institutions and the objectives of the educational cultivation of Chinese universities. In September 1912, the Ministry of Education promulgated the decree of educational purposes. It emphasized moral education, which is supplemented by utilitarian education (or practical education) and national military education. The system was further completed by aesthetic education.[4] Moral education was put first, replacing the late-Qing educational principle and the educational purpose of "loyalty to the emperor" and "respect for Confucius." On the surface, the utilitarian education and national military education seemed to have continued the late-Qing educational purpose of *shangshi* (the pursuit of the real economy) and *shangwu* (the pursuit of military strength), but they were also endowed with a new spirit of the era, such as emphasizing natural scientific knowledge, developing capitalist economy, recovering lost lands, and suppressing the separatism of warlords. Aesthetic education was the most innovative, bearing a relatively strong Western influence. It was listed among the educational purposes for the first time, reflecting the new value orientation of the construction of the educational system.

Secondly, the promulgation of the Educational Plan of 1912/13 had gradually perfected China's higher education system. In September 1912, the Ministry of Education formulated the Educational System Order (that is, Educational Plan of 1912) and announced its implementation. Afterward, a series of school regulations were promulgated, such as Primary Education Plan, Secondary Education System Plan, Teacher Training and Education System Plan, University Education Plan, and Specialized Education Plan. In 1913, it was combined with the Educational Plan of 1913 and formed a new plan for the educational system, namely the Educational Plan of 1912/13. The revised and endorsed higher education planning at the time was already very different from the late-Qing Educational Plan of 1903.

Taking the University Education Plan as an example, its first article already stated the purpose of university education: "The purpose of the university is to teach advanced academics, cultivate master scholars, with meeting the country's needs as the principle."[5] Taking academics, talents, and country as university education's aspirations, the late-Qing idea of "humbly adhering to the imperial order and staying on the right track." For the first time, the term "advanced academics" entered the constitution of Chinese higher education and was listed as one of the top educational purposes. Article 2 stipulated that there are seven disciplines in university education: "The disciplines are divided into arts, science, law, business, medicine, agricultural science, and engineering."[6] This is entirely based on the Western university discipline system, the independent status of the "Classics" discipline has been completely abolished. Also, in the Educational Plan of 1912/13, the policy of rewarding graduates from various higher education institutions was canceled. It was proposed to establish an evaluation committee and a professors' committee to be responsible for the internal and departmental decisions of the university. The remains of late-Qing imperial examination were washed away, while the Western university administration system was actively brought in. Compared with the 1903 Educational System implemented in the late Qing dynasty, which was a simple mirroring of the Japanese system, the Educational Plan of 1912/13 drew ideas from a range of sources. It not only brought in a more comprehensive Western university system but also began to tap on the spiritual level of Western universities.

The above measures were mostly borrowed from the West, in an attempt to eliminate the shortcomings of higher education in the late Qing dynasty. However, traditional education was broken but not eliminated. At the same time, Confucian education was also revived. Almost at the same time that the Educational Plan of 1912/13 was formulated and promulgated, Yuan Shikai began to advocate moral education with a high profile, intending to revive the popular Confucius education, which, to a certain extent, also played a role in the development of higher education.

In 1913, Yuan Shikai issued the *Order to Pay Attention to Moral Education Regulations*, which pointed out that "the statecraft can be differentiated by dictatorship and republicanism, but the education principle remains the same, that is to prioritize moral education both ancient and modern, Chinese and Western alike."[7] In the following year, *The Educational Plan Drafted by the Ministry of Education* officially stipulated: "Every primary and secondary school should adopt Chinese textbooks as moral cultivation and train students with classics to preserve the inherent morals; Classics discipline should be added to the universities to highlight the ideas of the ancient philosophers." This draft emphasized moral education. It took Confucius as the role model while reiterated the late Qing dynasty's principle of "following the right path and cultivating upright personalities so that the style of learning can be revitalized."[8] In 1915, Yuan Shikai promulgated another policy, the *Specially Formulated Outline of Education*, which clearly stated that "it is appropriate to establish a School of Classics to be independent of the university and divided the subjects according to branches of Classics,"[9] thereby resurrecting the Classics discipline in late-Qing universities. Subsequently, the Principle of Education was promulgated, stating the principles as patriotism, pursuing military strength, valuing realism, learning from Confucius, and Mencius, emphasizing on self-discipline, refraining from greed, contest, the desire to achieve quick success and impulsivity. These principles were a revival of the late-Qing educational purposes of respecting Confucius, pursuing military strength, the real economy, and public opinions. The Confucian education laws and regulations established by Yuan became void along with his forced abdication, but its traces remained in history.

In summary, the political situation changed, Chinese and Western cultures checked and balanced with each other in debates, and Chinese culture experienced ups and downs during the Xinhai Revolution. However, even at the times of Chinese cultural revival, the dominant position of Chinese culture in the late Qing dynasty was no longer recoverable. Even when Chinese culture was experiencing downs, the mark of tradition persisted, even during the periods of the so-called "criticizing of Confucius." In short, in early Republican China, Chinese universities developed in the course of social changes. The Western university system and Confucius's education were used side-by-side with no hard opposition. Chinese universities entered the initial stage of integrating Chinese and Western cultures.

2. *Chinese culture and Chinese universities during the May Fourth Movement*

Yuan Shikai's dream of reinstating the throne fell apart in a few months, and China immediately entered the era of warlordism and hegemony. With the political scuffle, the conflict between Chinese and Western cultures intensified. After the Xinhai Revolution, the traditional social order disintegrated, and Chinese society faced an unprecedented belief crisis. Yuan Shikai and Zhang Xun leveraged on the tradition to stage the restoration farce twice, which worsened the belief of crisis in Chinese society. The New Culture Movement gradually emerged in 1915 and was forced to embark on the journey of seeking light from the West.

a) Cultural changes within social changes.

In the late 1980s, Lin Yusheng's *Zhongguo Yishi De Weiji: 'Wusi' Shiqi Jilie De Fanchuantong Zhuyi* (*Crisis of Chinese Consciousness: Fierce Anti-Traditionalism during the 'May 4th' period*), put a label of "Total Anti-Traditionalism" on the Movement. The book mentioned that during the May Fourth period, "this anti-traditionalist was very fierce, so we have every reason to describe it as total anti-traditionalistic. As far as the social and cultural changes we know, this kind of anti-idolist movement requires a complete destruction of all past ideas, and it was in many ways an unprecedented historical phenomenon."[10] As soon as this argument was formed, it quickly aroused a domestic debate on the "total anti-traditionalist" nature of the May Fourth Movement. Judging from the speeches made by the representatives of the May Fourth period, the Movement was indeed all-out anti-traditionalist – a fundamental position repeatedly demonstrated and adhered to by Chen Duxiu and Hu Shi. However, speech and fact were two different things, after all, there is always a gap between theory and reality. The so-called "total anti-traditionalist" slogan during the May Fourth Movement was loud, but it was neither realized nor did it last. It was largely a temporary discourse victory. In fact, "anti-traditionalist was only one aspect of the spirit of May Fourth Movement, while the other aspect of it was exactly a strong traditional spirit."[11]

In 1915, Chen Duxiu and Li Dazhao, editors-in-chief of *La Jeunesse* magazine, and Du Yaquan, editor-in-chief of *The Eastern Miscellany*, officially opened the prelude to the May Fourth cultural debate. "It was unprecedented that how long this cultural debate lasted, how many people it involved, and how deep the questions were involved," "The May 4th cultural debate presents its national movement pattern in an unprecedented manner."[12] As the Commander-in-Chief of the May Fourth New Cultural Movement, Chen Duxiu had a clear stand on Chinese and Western cultures. In Chen's opinion, "just as the north and the south don't get along, the water and fire don't get along", the Chinese and Western cultures are on opposite sides of binary opposition, and the Western culture has absolute superiority. Chen Duxiu's value judgment and preference in Chinese and Western cultures lead him to a destined path of total anti-tradition. In the essay *Attention: Contemporary Youths*, Chen stated his belief that "I would rather endure the demise of the national essence in the past than to see the demise of our nation in the future because of its inability to survive in the world."[13] Li Dazhao and Chen Duxiu held the same stance and pointed out that the progress of China "can only open up to something new; (it) can never revert to anything from the past". The criticism of old culture by Chen Duxiu and by others was quickly met with opposition from conservative forces. In the conservative camp, there are Gu Hongming and other people who missed the Qing dynasty's former Qing dynasty but had little influence, and they were mainly dominated by new intellectuals such as Du Yaquan, Zhang Shizhao, Liang Qichao, and Liang Shuming. They were well-versed in Chinese and Western learning and had no objection to Western ideas. Du Yaquan earlier retaliated against total anti-traditionalists, criticizing "the envy of Westerners in our country in recent years has affected all aspects of society" and the phenomenon of "the civilization inherent in our country was almost completely neglected." He pointed out that "our inherent civilization is enough to make up for the shortcomings of Western civilizations and reach what Western civilizations could not reach."[14] From 1915 to the mid-20s, as the debate gradually deepened, Li Dazhao, Cai Yuanpei, Zhang Shizhao, Zhang Dongsun, Jiang Menglin, Liang Qichao, Liang Shuming, Hu Shi and other famous scholars all joined the discussion and published nearly a thousand academic works. In the 1930s, echoes of this debate could still be heard.[15]

On the surface, the new cultural propositions proposed by Chen Duxiu and others grasped the main thoughts of the time, but it was hard to say that they won over the discourse. It was difficult for the participants on both sides of the war to separate themselves from the Chinese or Western standpoint. In fact, since the late Qing dynasty, the dual characteristics of Chinese and Western culture had already unconsciously melted into the unconscious consciousness of intellectuals, and it was difficult to differentiate. From this perspective, apart from the conceptual distinction, neither absolute "traditionalist" nor absolute "anti-traditionalist" existed in China. As Liu Mengxi said, "At that time, the outstanding ones who fought at the peak of the wave of the time were all exceptional scholars with a deep foundation in the old studies. Since when did they ever reject all traditional culture?"[16] In the same sense, many of the so-called conservatives "had been abroad for many years and had a systematic Western knowledge structure. During the period of great cultural transformation when imperialism ended, active thinking emerged, and Western culture flooded eastward, were they indifferent to the era of 'cultural reform' and keen to play a role that hinders the construction of Chinese culture?"[17] From this point of view, the result of the May Fourth Chinese-Western cultural debate between the two parties had already been determined from the beginning, that the debate was just a process that pushed for further integration of Chinese and Western cultures.

b) Chinese universities in cultural changes.

Su Yunfeng believes that "the impact of May Fourth on education is more destructive than constructive."[18] This certainly has its basis, but it is noncomprehensive. During the May Fourth period, the Chinese government promulgated the 1922 Educational System and standardized the educational pattern for the next 30 years. Private universities flourished at this time, and the private traditional academies were also revived. This was more or less influenced by the May Fourth Cultural Movement. In short, the development of Chinese universities during this period was mainly reflected in the following two aspects.

First, at the policy level, the American culture was striking, and the Western academic system had become mainstream. Mainly manifested in the setting of "seven standards" for education and the promulgation of the "1922 Educational System" as well as the "National University Regulations." In 1922, the Peiyang government promulgated the School System Reformation Bill, which listed the "seven standards" to wipe away the feudal legacy left by Yuan's educational purposes. The specific content was as follows: (1) adapt to the needs of social evolution; (2) exert the spirit of civilian education; (3) seek the development of personality; (4) pay attention to the economic power of the Republic of China; (5) pay attention to life education; (6) make education easy to popularize; (7) leave more room of improvisation for local governments.[19]

These standards were largely influenced by Western education and cultural trends such as civilian education, pragmatist education, and vocational education brought by the May Fourth Movement. Western educational terms such as personality development and life education entered the official Chinese educational discourse for the first time, while concepts such as morality and ethics were withdrawn from the Chinese educational principles for the first time. Based on this, the 1922 Educational System was promulgated and implemented as the second Chinese Republican educational system after the Educational Plan of 1912/13. Two years later, higher education legislation was introduced specifically to replace the University Order and University Regulations implemented at the beginning of the Republic with the National University Regulations. The regulations re-emphasized the purpose of running a national university, "The purpose of a national university is to teach advanced academics, develop master scholars, and meet the needs of the country."[20] It bore little difference from the University Order. It is worth mentioning that the regulations clearly stated that national universities should establish a board of directors to administer important matters, which caused a huge uproar. At that time, the professors of Peking University and its evaluation council publicly opposed the government's intention to interfere in the school's internal administration by using a "board of directors." It can be seen that since Cai Yuanpei's reform of Peking University, it has adopted the style of self-governing. The unity of politics and education was no longer unconditional. According to relevant statistics, the number of universities had increased significantly since the 1922 Educational System. The number increased from 19 in 1922 to 52 in 1927. These new universities were either newly established private universities or upgraded specialized schools. A considerable number of private universities emerged during this period later became famous universities in China. For example, Nankai University, founded by Zhang Boling in 1919, and Xiamen University, founded by Chen Jiageng and officially opened in 1921.

Second, at the reality level, the ancient style persisted and traditional academies revived. "After May Fourth, people's attention and research on traditional academies' educational experience were the main content of reflection on Chinese higher education issues."[21] In 1898 Emperor Guangxu issued an edict to replace traditional academies with schools, which marked an official end to the thousand-year Chinese academy system. But it was miraculously partially restored during the May Fourth period. What was even more curious was that both traditionalists and anti-traditionalists shared the same nostalgic attitude towards traditional academies. As a representative of total anti-traditionalism, Hu Shi also grieved that "the abolition of the academy is an unfortunate event in China. The spirit of scholars' independent studies for a thousand years would no longer exist today."[22] Therefore, In the Western cultural wave of the early twentieth century, a not-so-dazzling but not-to-be-ignored landscape appeared in Chinese higher education. That is: either borrow the spirit of the academy to transform a modern university (such as Cai Yuanpei, Hu Shi), or try to rebuild the academy that has been lost (such as Zhang Taiyan, Ma Yifu)[23]. In the climax of the May Fourth New Cultural Movement, Tang Wenzhi saw that the study of Confucius and Mencius at the university was completely abandoned, and felt that "our scientific progress is still unknown,yet we have already abandoned our own culture. How painful."[24] He then abandoned the post as the president of Nanyang University and was later known by the establishment of the Wuxi Guoxue Zhuanxiu Guan (Wuxi Specialized Academy of Chinese Studies) in 1920 (later renamed as Wuxi Guoxue Zhuanxiu Xuexiao). After this, other traditional-style academies also emerged. For example, Tianyou College founded by Kang Youwei in Shanghai in 1926, and the Chinese Learning Seminar Classroom founded by Zhang Taiyan in Suzhou in 1935, were both silent symbols against the celebrated "new culture" with Chinese learning as their ethos. In a sense, the revival of the traditional academy could also be regarded as another result of the full Westernization brought by the May Fourth Movement.

In summary, the May Fourth New Culture period was an important period for further conflict and integration between Chinese and Western cultures. Western culture and Chinese culture checked and balanced each other out. Although Chinese culture was no longer dominant in the wave of Western culture, it had not lost its influence. The modern Western education system ran in parallel with the ancient Chinese higher education system. Although Chinese universities mostly followed the Western university system, there were plenty of higher institutions with a classical atmosphere.

3. *Chinese Culture and Chinese Universities during the Second Sino-Japanese War*

The July 7th Incident (Lugou Bridge Incident) broke out in 1937, and Japan completely invaded China. The national conflict had risen to become the main conflict of the country. Politics-wise, the Chinese Nationalist Party and the Chinese Communist Party chose to cooperate and fought unanimously with the invader. At the dawn of a critical national war, the cultural field was ushered into an unprecedented "peace," but at least open verbal disputes were no longer mainstream. On the one hand, due to the overwhelming importance of the war, cultural issues relegated to a secondary position. On the other hand, the enduring and intense cultural debate between Chinese and Western culture during the May Fourth period had indeed reached a period of sedimenting thoughts. During this period, Chinese universities did not decline due to wars but became a historical miracle in adversity.

a) Cultural changes within social changes.

At the 25th Anniversary Lecture of the Chinese University of Hong Kong, Yu Ying-shih talked about the state of culture during the Second Sino-Japanese War and pointed out that "at that time everyone seemed to have stopped talking about cultural issues, and the cultural issues between China and the West seemed to have been resolved." Then it was mentioned that "in the mainstream academia, it was generally believed that Chinese culture hinders modernization."[25] Since modern times, Chinese and Western cultures have continuously integrated, even after many conflicts. The Chinese-Western cultural debate was only a means to an end, not a goal. The ultimate goal was national prosperity. Both, the advocators of Westernization and the conservatives, spoke on behalf of national interests. When discussing the May Fourth culture, Li Zehou proposed that the movement was a double variation of enlightenment and national salvation, and national salvation dominates over enlightenment. Enlightenment, the transformation of culture, and the abandonment of traditions were still for the sake of the country, the nation, and the change of China's political situation and society.[26] From this perspective, there is no fundamental conflict between the so-called Chinese and Western cultural debates. The period of the Second Sino-Japanese War was a special and important period for the further integration of Chinese and Western cultures. The outbreak of war has made national salvation the only aim of society. The social trend at this time was no longer the ups and downs of Chinese culture in Western culture, but the further integration of Chinese and Western culture in the name of national salvation. Before the war, Chen Yinque wrote, "I personally suspect that, from today onwards, although North American or Eastern European thoughts could be imported faithfully into China, it would end up just like Xuanzang's theory of consciousness-only. In the history of thought of my country, they could never occupy the highest position, and would ultimately renunciate. The only way to construct a true system of thought and provide something new is to absorb the imported doctrine on the one hand, and not retain the status of our nation on the other hand. These two opposite and complementary attitudes were the true spirit of Taoism, the old way of Neo-Confucianism, and what has been revealed in our history contact with other nations for two thousand years."[27] His words were regarded by some scholars as an introspective summary of the May Fourth Movement. This statement also laid an internal tone for the cultural situation during the Second Sino-Japanese War. During the war against Japan, Western studies flourished, with Kant and Hegel's philosophies being the most popular, while Chinese studies were also flourishing, which reflected in *Guoshi Dagang* (*An Outline of Chinese History*) written by Qian Mu, *Zhongguo Wenhuashi* (*Chinese Cultural History*) written by Liu Yezhi and *Wenhua Yu Zhexue* (*Culture and Philosophy*) written by Zhang Shenfu. In particular, Feng Yu-lan's successive publications such as *Xin Lixue* (*A New Treatise on Neo-Confucianism*), *Xin Shilun* (*On New Affairs*), *Xin Shixun* (*Explanation of the New World*), *A New Treatise on the Nature of Man*, *Xin Yuandao* (*The Spirit of Chinese Philosophy*), and *Xin Zhiyan* (*A New Treatise on the Methodology of Metaphysics*), which studied Chinese Confucianism based on Western philosophical knowledge. These work had annotated Chen Yinque's cultural integration on the academic level. This academic thought once again verified the cultural atmosphere at the time. China's cultural issues were no longer just superficial conservative or Westernization choices, but how to integrate the two. Seeking a balance between Chinese and Western cultures had become the main theme of cultural development.

b) Chinese universities in cultural changes.

After the complete Japanese invasion, China's education became turbulent. Almost all formal educational institutions were in the Nationalist-ruled region, while most of the stronger universities in the country concentrated in Nanjing, Shanghai and Beijing. These universities first lost their campuses in the rampant bombing of Japan. During this period, higher education had generally gone through three stages: major migration, restoration and improvement, as well as consolidation and development. What was gratifying is that when the war against Japan was finally won, China's higher education did not fall into the disuse of Western cultures, and instead, it developed.

At the beginning of the war, in the face of Japan's frenzied and devastating destruction of Chinese higher institutions, schools in the warzone, especially some important universities, were forced to embark on a difficult migration and mergers. For example, Peking University, Tsinghua University, and Nankai University were the first three schools to be destroyed by Japanese invaders after the war began. In 1937, some teachers and students arrived in Changsha and formed Changsha Provisional University. The departments in the original schools merged with slight adjustments, such as the mergers of history and sociology, philosophy and psychology education, and geology and meteorology. There were 17 departments in 4 schools (Literature, Science, Engineering, Law, and Business).[28] Due to the war, the university moved to Kunming again, forming the famous National Southwestern Associated University in modern history. From October 1938 to December 1941, before the outbreak of the Pacific War, it was at the stage of the restoration and adjustment for the higher institutions in the rear area. At that time, except for some higher institutes that were still relocating, most of the colleges and universities that had moved to the rear and had resumed classes while adjusting their departments. As of the first half of 1941, there were nearly 20 adjusted higher institutions set up in the rear area. Among them, two were the most famous: one was the National Southwestern Associated University located in Kunming, Yunan, with a total of 3000 students, which was the merger of Peking University, Tsinghua University, and Nankai University, and the other was the National Northwest University, which was the merger of Beiping University, National Beiping Normal University and Peiyang Institute of Technology, located in Chenggu, Shaanxi, with 800 students. It was formerly known as Northwest United University and subsequently reorganized as National Northwest University in September 1939.[29] During the war against Japan, the Chinese Nationalist government promulgated a policy to strongly support the academic work of universities. Since then, the number of Chinese universities and enrollment has been steadily increasing throughout the Second Sino-Japanese War. In 1930, there were only 85 universities, colleges, and specialized schools in China, and the number of students in the school was only 37,566. By 1945, the number of colleges and students had risen to 141 and 83,498 respectively.[30]

From a cultural point of view, at that time, "during the entire period of the Nationalist rule, Chinese universities have already gone through the stage of adaptation and absorption of a foreign culture."[31] During the war against Japan, the total Westernization theory could no longer hold in Chinese universities. Hayhoe's pointed out in her research on Chinese universities in this period, "At that time, China was experiencing a political and economic crisis. Therefore, no matter from a theoretical or practical perspective, it was difficult for Chinese universities to fully accept the academic freedom and self-governing idea of European universities. But no matter what, it could be seen that during the development of modern Chinese universities during this period, based on absorbing the ideas of European and American universities, combined with Chinese tradition and the realistic situation, they finally formed their unique intellectual freedom and social responsibility in the idea of running a university.[32] Hayhoe's so-called "Chinese and Western Cultural Conflict" proposition was temporarily resolved in Chinese universities during the war. From this perspective, the Chinese universities during the war against Japan not only paid attention to absorbing the European and American system but also combined them with traditions. Chinese universities seemed to be intentionally searching for a point of equilibrium between Chinese and Western culture. History proved that during this period, in some sense, the most successful universities of modern China had emerged. Of course, these were the product of a special era. During this period, the reason why Chinese universities could better handle the relationship between "absorbing European and American university ideas" and "integrating Chinese traditions" was mainly due to the impact of war. The debate within the academia regarding culture was temporarily suspended, and the aggressive theory of total Westernization gradually receded. As a result, Chinese and Western cultures had entered a relatively balanced period of development. This became an important opportunity for the development of Chinese universities during the war against Japan.

In summary, during the Second Sino-Japanese War, Chinese and Western cultures shifted from a superficial confrontation to a relatively balanced period of development. Chinese culture was a symbol of traditional spirit, and Western culture a symbol of modernization – and they started to merge. Chinese universities blended traditional spirit with modern university forms, effectively reconciling Chinese and Western cultures and achieved brilliance in adversity.

4. *General characteristics of Chinese universities' cultural characters development during Republican China*

Thirty years of the Republic of China were the most drastic and volatile periods in modern Chinese history. Chinese culture and Chinese universities have been given special connotations of the time during republican China. From a historical perspective, Chinese culture held its ground in the wave of the eastward spread of Western learnings.

In Republican China, the Chinese-Western cultural discourse started in late Qing had continued. Throughout the Xinhai Revolution, the May Fourth Movement period, and the Second Sino-Japanese War period, Chinese and Western cultures gradually changed from waning and waxing in mutual confrontation to gradual integration in mutual checks and balances. The foundation of Chinese culture had never been lost. Tu Youguang pointed out in his book *Zhongguo Jiaoyu Shilun* (*History of Chinese Higher Education*) that "Western culture, through propaganda, has become an external factor that induces the inherent energy of Chinese culture. Its contribution has to be acknowledged. But in comparison, during the Xinhai Revolution, which one played a greater role? Western or Chinese culture? Which one was fundamental? Of course, it is Chinese culture."[33] He also said, "As an internal factor, Chinese culture has cultivated a strong driving force for criticizing Confucianism with Tao in Chinese cultural psychology. However, under the influence of Western culture, which acted as an external cause, it has produced an unprecedented new cultural movement. Without the internal cause of criticizing Confucianism using Taoism, the new cultural movement couldn't emerge."[34] It was precisely because of this that Chinese universities had to learn from others, and grow in the cultural changes and yet, retain the traditional style. Historically, early Chinese Republican universities were still influenced by Japan, while in the 1920s, they mainly drew ideas from the United States, as well as Germany and France. It seemed that there was no trace of Chinese traditional culture, but this was not the case. The previous review of the history of Chinese universities was sufficient to prove that although Chinese universities in this period no longer insisted on having Chinese culture as their core, they had always adhered to Chinese culture as the basis and made attempts to find a balance between Chinese and Western cultures. History has shown that an ideal Chinese university model did appear during the Republican China era. They successfully found a balance between Chinese and Western cultures, which became a typical example of the ideal cultural character of Chinese universities. According to Hayhoe, "In this historical period, China adopted a compromised approach to the educational ideas of Western universities."[35] During Republican China, Chinese universities have indeed chosen a middle road between Chinese and Western cultures, both in ideology and systems.

First of all, the cultural characters of Republican Chinese universities demonstrated an ideal development trend. The reason why the ideal cultural characters of Chinese universities appeared in Republican China could be summarized as follows: First, in the transition process from traditional to modern society, the integration of Chinese and Western cultures became the inevitable trend. Although the eastward spread of Western learnings has gradually become an irresistible trend in the late Qing dynasty, the idea of having Chinese culture as the main body was deeply entrenched. Therefore, the Chinese and Western cultures have not been effectively integrated into Chinese universities. Republican China continued the Chinese-Western cultural disputes between intellectuals since the late Qing dynasty. Between extreme anti-traditionalism and conservatism, the fusion of Chinese and Western cultures became an inevitable trend. This became the fundamental prerequisite for Chinese universities to maintain a balance between tradition and Westernization. Second, during the period of transition from traditional to modern education, intellectuals dominated Chinese universities. Xie Yong summed up the reasons why the process of transforming traditional Chinese education into modern education was relatively smooth. He mentioned two points: 1) The designers of the university system had a global vision, such as Cai Yuanpei and Jiang Menglin; 2) The designers of the university system occupied dominant positions in education, to begin with.[36] Compared with the late-Qing scholars, the Republican Chinese intellectuals had a broader vision of the world, which means that they no longer bound Chinese universities within the mainframe of Chinese culture. Compared with the intellectuals of the early People's Republic of China, the Republican Chinese intellectuals enjoyed the dominance of universities, which made it possible for their ideas of running schools to directly turn into reality. This was also a key factor in the formation of the ideal cultural characteristics of Chinese universities. From this perspective, the formation and development of the cultural characters of Republican Chinese universities were the product of a specific era and had historical inevitability.

Secondly, the cultural characters of Chinese universities fell into a pattern during the Republic of China, especially the National Southwestern Associated University during the war against Japan, which represented the ideal type of Republican Chinese universities. The 1920s and 1930s were known as the golden age of Chinese universities. Peking University and Tsinghua University also established their core positions in the field of higher education in China during this period. If it is said that the Western university system has enabled the Republican Chinese universities to smoothly transition, then the formation of the Chinese cultural characteristics had eventually shaped the basic form of Republican Chinese universities. From a cultural point of view, the establishment of Republican Chinese universities' tradition was based on the formation of its cultural characters. Therefore, it can be concluded that the rudimentary cultural characters of Chinese universities have been established in Republican China.

Lastly, it should be pointed out that the formation and development of the cultural characters of Chinese universities during Republican China was the product of a specific era, and this is not replicable. The cultural characters of Republican Chinese universities were formed under specific historical conditions. Republican Chinese intellectuals possessed thorough knowledge across Chinese and Western culture. Such cultural cultivation, together with their relatively independent relationship with the government, became the main reason for their development. Free intellectuals born in the era gradually withdrew from history after Republican China and became an eternal memory of this historical period. Even though the cultural characters of Republican Chinese universities were ideal, objectively speaking, it is impossible for Chinese universities today to return to the old path to achieve the ideal characters of future Chinese universities.

Section 2: The Formation Path of Republican Chinese Universities' Cultural Characters

The cultural characters of Chinese universities are "self-generating" and "artificial." Republican Chinese intellectuals played an important role in the formation and development of Chinese universities' cultural characters. As the dominators of Chinese universities' cultural characters during this period, Republican Chinese intellectuals were very special. Republican Chinese Intellectuals were intrinsically connected with Chinese culture and bore considerable Western cultural characteristics. They were an unprecedented generation in modern Chinese history. The first reason is that, "In terms of the accumulation of traditional knowledge, that is, the origin of family studies and the foundation of Chinese studies (the academy of Chinese traditional ideology and culture), the latecomers may not be able to compare with them."[37] The second reason being that "There was an opportunity to absorb the new Western methods in terms of academic concepts, which was not available for scholars during Emperor Qianlong and Jiaqing's reign."[38]

Intellectuals and Chinese universities were in symbiosis. Republican Chinese universities could also be described as "unprecedented." Republican Chinese intellectuals had profound traditional knowledge, therefore the Chinese universities' cultural characters were especially prominent, which could not be achieved by later universities. Republican Chinese intellectuals were accomplished in both Chinese and Western learnings, therefore Chinese universities' cultures were prominent yet unbiased, which was what previous universities failed to achieve. Republican Chinese intellectuals were another group of important "cultural inheritors" in the formation of Chinese university's cultural characters after the late-Qing scholars. This is exactly where their uniqueness lay. Among them, there was a group, who had the closest relationship with Chinese universities and even influenced universities throughout Republican China with their special ideas and methods. They were the presidents of Republican Chinese universities, such as Cai Yuanpei and Mei Yiqi. It could be said that they single-handedly shaped the entire university with their resolutions, or rather their cultural characters. Under their influence, Chinese universities were committed to the conciliation of Chinese culture and Western culture.

Revolving around the key concept of Republican Chinese intellectuals, this chapter takes the basic path of the formation of Chinese universities' cultural characters during the Republic of China. It looks at the Chinese culture-Republican Chinese intellectuals-Chinese universities as the analytical framework, and it deconstructs the cultural characters of Chinese universities in this period in depth. There are three basic steps: 1) By analyzing the Chinese and Western cultural concepts popular in the society during

Republican China, it explores the emotional entanglement between the intellectuals and Chinese culture behind the cultural view, and conducts an in-depth scan on the cultural characteristics of Republican Chinese intellectuals. 2) By taking the intellectual-centric core university outlook as the object of investigation, this section discusses the specific characteristics of Chinese university cultural characters under the influence of intellectuals and analyzes its internal basis. 3) By taking individual presidents of Republican Chinese universities as an example, this section analyzes the unique achievements of the cultural character of Chinese universities by several famous presidents of Chinese universities.

1. Republican Chinese intellectuals and Chinese Culture

Born in the late Qing dynasty and educated in Europe and America, intellectuals in early Republican China possessed a thorough knowledge of both Chinese and Western learning. Traditional and Western culture both conflicted and integrated with them. They expressed their opinions boldly and wrote books. Some were radical and rebellious, and vigorously criticized Confucianism. Others were conservative and loyal, and tried their best to protect traditional culture or dedicated themselves in the conciliation of Chinese and Western cultures while being rational and sympathetic. The Chinese-Western cultural discourse became an unavoidable theme of the period when the intellectuals discussed academics and commented on politics. It was no wonder Liang Shuming commented that "Chinese-Western culture" has become a very "abused" term, yet no one could say for sure what it was.

Dongxi Wenhua Ji Qi Zhexue (*East-West Culture and Their Philosophies*) was Liang Shuming's "go with the times" piece during the May Fourth New Culture period, which discussed in detail the society's understandings of the concept of "Chinese-Western culture." The book mentioned three ways to deal with Chinese and Western cultures and contained three mainstream Chinese-Western cultural concepts. One was that Eastern culture was not co-existent with Western cultures. There was no interconnectivity between these cultures, therefore Eastern culture must be uprooted today. The second was that it was not a big deal that Eastern culture was getting oppressed by Western culture, the former can indeed turn itself over. The third was that there are ways for conciliation between Eastern and Western cultures.[39] The first standpoint put Eastern and Western cultures in opposition and regarded the latter as the world culture. The second standpoint drew a line that separated both cultures and regarded Eastern culture as the world culture. The third regarded both cultures as world culture and integrated them. These three views could be summarized as total westernization, revivalism and cultural conciliationism. Later scholars often criticized rather than empathized with each of these three theories. The general idea was that the total westernization was too radical and almost bigoted. Revivalism and conciliationism were homologous, and they tended to be conservative and unconstructive. It was far from what Chen Yinque advocated, that when commenting on our predecessor's theory, one should have "compassion of understanding." In fact, in a review of the cultural views of Republican Chinese intellectuals, it could be seen that all views were, after all, generated from the spirit of a particular era. They were all full of intellectuals' sophisticated Chinese cultural complex.

a) Total westernizations.

All total westernizations believed in the Western social evolution theory. They regarded Western culture as "superior" and Chinese culture as "inferior." "The fittest survive," therefore the Chinese culture cannot be retained. These total westernizations, on the one hand, equated Chinese culture with feudal monarchism – the root of China's backwardness. They no longer recognized the superiority or even transformability of Chinese culture. On the other hand, they equated Western culture with world culture – a symbol of modern society. They repeatedly emphasized and demonstrated the absolute superiority and inevitability of Western culture. With this as the keynote, Chinese and Western cultures were in diametrical opposition and were irreconcilable. It is impossible to build up a Western cultural system without abolishing Chinese culture, therefore total westernization becomes a logical necessity. On the surface, total westernizations did not possess any traditional cultural character. But this was not the case. No matter how they promoted and proved their identity of being fully westernized in verbal disputes, they still could not get rid of their inborn Chinese cultural imprint. Sometimes they even found it hard to justify their own total anti-traditionalist standpoint. On the contrary, there is a sense of helplessness in their critical discourse, revealing a sentimental feeling of being trapped in a dilemma. Still, they vigorously promoted that "national quintessence definitely cannot be retained." They tried their best to show their determination and attitude to completely break away from Chinese culture, yet at the same time, it seemed that they wanted to defend themselves and make some additional remarks on their conclusions. This was intriguing.

Chen Duxiu opposed Confucius, but he still unconsciously persuaded young people to make progress with Confucian ideas such as *Xiu Shen* (cultivating oneself) and *Zhi Guo* (ruling the country). On the first page of the first issue of *La Jeunesse*, there was a statement, "The country is in decline, the academics are falling. All responsibilities in the future rest on today's youth. This periodical intends to discuss with our youths on how to cultivate ourselves and rule the country in the future."[40] It was no wonder Lin Yusheng replied that "it seemed illogical when a person chose the standpoint of a historical figure whom he completely opposed to illustrating his point of view."[41] When we think about it carefully, it seemed illogical at first, yet, deep down, it was completely logical. This was due to his inherent cultural characters.

Li Dazhao also opposed Confucius, but he also explained that "What I denounced about Confucius was not Confucius himself, but the authority of the idols carved by

Confucianism for the emperors, the spirit of authoritarian politics."[42] Although this sounded anti-Confucian, it was also very much an explanation of his anti-Confucian stand. The "but" fully expressed the author's helplessness, and at the same time, it proved that Confucius' theory was not all undesirable.

In another example, Lu Xun was one of the biggest opposers to "compiling national heritage," but he collated *Ji Kang Ji* (*Complete Collection of Ji Kang*) and published *Xiaoshuo Jiuwen Chao* (*Selected Novels and Old Stories*).

From this perspective, the so-called total anti-traditionalists were not well-deserved in many ways, at least not in reality. This was largely limited by their sophisticated Chinese cultural complex, or it could be understood as the result of the extreme sense of cultural inferiority of intellectuals. The root of understanding the sense of cultural inferiority of Republican Chinse intellectuals lay in their idealistic expectations of Chinese culture rather than their true belief in Western culture. The ideal might have been shattered, the expectation could be transferred, but the Chinese cultural beliefs in their hearts were hard to eradicate. The so-called slogan of "total westernization" could not eliminate the Chinese cultural imprint. Total westernizations, loaded with intellectuals' sense of cultural inferiority, was a typical "Chinese cultural backwardness theory."

b) Revivalism.

Revivalism had long been a stigmatized concept. Whether from the perspectives of total westernizations or cultural conciliationists, the revivalist theory was more of a guise used by late-Qing imperial loyalists in an attempt to restore the imperial system. It is also difficult for today's scholars to understand this theory. They believed that revivalism was the vicious wave of regression disguised under the name of the revival of traditions. Cao Xiren holds this view in the book *Zhongxi Wenhua Bijiao Daolun* (*Introduction to the Comparison of Chinese and Western Cultures*). Although there were certain bases to such views, they are, to some extent, biased.

In the demonstration Chinese cultural superiority, the revivalists emphasized that the Chinese culture has been passed down for thousands of years, its inherent superiority is beyond doubt and definitely unsurpassed by Western culture. Their purpose was to prove the blindness of total westernization. This is fundamentally different from the purpose of the late-Qing conservatives who leveraged the Chinese culture to strengthen the foundation and cultivate the hearts of the people. One of the main points of the theory was that although Chinese culture was oppressed by Western culture, it was not that big of a deal. The shortcomings of Western culture are gradually revealed, therefore the world culture of the future must be traditional Chinese culture. Chen Jiayi held this view in his essay *Dongfang Wenhua Yu Wuren Zhi Daren* (*Eastern Culture and the Great Responsibilities of Our People*). He pointed out that, "in essence, our nation's traditional morality is in fact the international morality and human morality, not just national morality. Therefore, it can be safely said that the world culture of the future must be created by the spirit of our Eastern culture (Author's note: specifically, "the whole world as a family," "love others and all things," and principles of virtues, benevolence, etc.). Therefore, I think that Eastern culture is not only the culture of the Eastern countries, but also world culture of the future."[43] This remark was extremely inappropriate at the time and was regarded as a conservatism "fallacy." Just as Liang Shuming said, society at the time "judging from the general situation, we could only foresee the extinction of orientalization, but not any way to turn over."[44]

Liang Qichao returned from a journey to the west in 1919. He witnessed the disaster brought to the Western countries by the First World War. He went against the tide of the new cultural movement and changed his previous advocation for Western culture. Based on his European experience, he wrote *Ouyou Xinying Lu* (*Thoughts on My European Trip*) and revealed the decline and shortcomings of Western culture during the wars, and called for the rescue of Western culture with Chinese inherent culture.

Looking at the examples cited above, the theory of Chinese cultural superiority is not a simple traditional cultural revivalism. It was actually inspired by the inherent superiority of Chinese culture. The so-called conservatives were not stubborn old antiques, instead, they actually retained Chinese cultural confidence. Cultural revivalists were a group of intellectuals who retained cultural confidence. To some extent, they inherited the late-Qing "Chinese cultural superiority theory."

c) Cultural conciliationism.

The cultural conciliationists exuded a strong traditional cultural complex, therefore they were once regarded to be singing the old late-Qing tune of Chinese essence and Western utility. They were even equated with the late-Qing conservatism forces and the aforementioned cultural revivalists. But in fact, this was the wishful thinking of a small group of scholars. Although the theory was based on the concept of "Western materialistic civilization, Eastern spiritual civilization." It was different from the late-Qing concept of "Chinese essence and Western utility."

The so-called cultural conciliationists were mostly well-read scholars indulged in both Chinese and Western cultures. Rationality and sympathy were their main characteristics. Their defense of Confucianism stemmed from an instinctive sympathy and a sense of responsibility. It was no longer the blind loyalty bearing strong political sentiments, therefore they were different from late-Qing conservatives. Although they retained their loyalty in traditional culture, they did not regard Chinese culture as the world culture of the future, so they were also different from the revivalists. The basic stance of conciliationists: reconciliation of the old and the new, and letting society make its own choices. That is to say, Chinese and Western cultures were different types of cultures. Compared with Western cultures, Chinese culture had its own strengths, but the shortcomings of Western cultures had long been concerned by Chinese traditions. Therefore, there should not be a total westernization, but a cultural conciliation instead.[45]

There are were quite a few cultural conciliation theorists in the Republic of China, as well as a considerable amount of academic works. Liang Shuming's *Dongxi Wenhua Ji Qi Zhexue* (*Eastern and Western Culture and its Philosophy*) was very representative of these titles and scholars. He defended Chinese culture, and in the trend of total westernization, he endeavored to promote the true spirit of Confucian culture. He also defended Western culture, sincerely recognized and praised the advantages of Western culture and he stood between Chinese and Western cultures, devoting his whole life to the integration of Chinese and Western cultures. He strove to find a balance between Chinese and Western cultures. One of the main points stated in the book was that Chinese culture was not inferior to Western culture, but that it has taken a different path. There was no such thing as advantages and disadvantages. Liang Shuming's cultural theory had changed the model of how the westernizationists distinguished Chinese and Western cultures based on their advantages and disadvantages, thereby fundamentally denied the "Chinese cultural backwardness theory." It also got rid of the revivalist argument that Eastern culture was superior to Western culture, which virtually resolved the "Chinese cultural superiority theory."

In a certain sense, cultural conciliation theory has always been the basic tone in Republican China, either hidden or demonstrated. It was the path both total westernizations or cultural revivalists agreed on. This theory embodied the enduring Chinese cultural self-improvement emotions of intellectuals. The disappointment of total westernizations and the self-confidence of the revivalists could both be seen. The confidence surpassed the disappointment, therefore a way of integrating Chinese and Western culture was chosen. Cultural conciliationists bore strong cultural self-improvement psychology, their theory could be regarded as a "Chinese cultural eclectic theory."

In summary, the ideas about Chinese culture during Republican China mainly involved three theories, namely, Chinese cultural backwardness theory, Chinese cultural superiority theory, and Chinese cultural eclectic theory. On the surface, it seems that the three theories were different, and two were opposite. But in fact, they were all loaded by Chinese intellectuals' thick and sophisticated Chinese cultural complex. In terms of Chinese cultural emotions, there was no essential difference, but only a different path was taken in reality. Deep in the hearts of the intellectuals, Chinese culture always occupied a special space. They long destined to bear the imprint of Chinese culture. The core values of traditional cultural ethics and politics have become their shared life tone. The main reasons were:

First, traditional ethics were deeply ingrained in them since childhood. At the beginning of Republican China, intellectuals were the inheritors of late-Qing scholars. They learned from scholar-officials and were indulged in Confucianism learnings from childhood. Concepts of Confucian ethics laid the foundation for their lives. Even in the anti-traditional cultural upsurge, intellectuals' Confucian ethics always existed. In view of the May Fourth intellectuals' Confucian backgrounds, the nature of the New Cultural Movement was also increasingly reconsidered. For example, Liu Mengxi objected to blaming the cultural discontinuity on the May Fourth Movement. In the article *Wenhua Yishi De Juexing* (*Awakening of Cultural Consciousness*), it was pointed out that "was there any pioneer in the May Fourth Movement who was not familiar with Confucian classics and Confucius' doctrine?"[46] This really highlighted the internal reason why the May Fourth Movement could not be totally anti-traditional. For example, Cai Yuanpei, a supporter and participant of the May Fourth Movement, was enrolled in a traditional academy to study Confucianism from an early age and he once became an official of the late Qing dynasty. The traditional values were deep-rooted within him and demonstrated by his behavior. For example, he was extremely particular about and abode by Confucius' ethical etiquette. According to historical records, before the age of 20, he admired Confucian scholars of the Song dynasty the most, and therefore he was devoted in filial piety. When his mother was ill, he not only served medicine for her, but also scraped flesh from his own arm as an ingredient for the medicine. After the passing of his mother, Cai insisted on the ancient ritual of sleeping on a straw bed and used a soil block as his pillow. His family stopped him from doing so, but he took a pillow and a mat to sleep by the coffin side at night when no one was watching. The family realized that they could not stop Cai, so they placed a bed in the mourning hall and let his brothers sleep beside him.[47] Another example was Hu Shi, a representative of total anti-traditionalism, who was also a faithful believer in human ethics. From this point of view, indulging in Confucianism since childhood, possessing profound Chinese learning knowledge, the idea of Confucian ethics was deep-rooted in Republican Chinese intellectuals' minds. Furthermore, the intellectuals believed in self-cultivation and rule the country, they possessed a heavy traditional political complex.

The abolishment of the imperial examination system in the late Qing dynasty seemed to have cut off the intellectuals' path to officialdom. Since the beginning of the Republic of China, scholars and officials gradually differentiated into two independent groups. However, political responsibility of intellectuals to worry about the country and the people did not diminish. Although many Republican Chinese intellectuals decided to concern themselves only with academics and distance themselves away from politics, they still unconsciously cared about the fate of the country and were keen to make comments on current affairs. History proved that in Republican China where wars were frequent, it was difficult for intellectuals to hide themselves away from politics. Intellectuals in the Republican China "usually participated in the revolution in their early years, focused on learning after their middle age, and became more peaceful in their later years."[48] However, regardless of being detached from politics, it was difficult to conceal their feelings for the world, even in the peaceful old age. In his later years, Zhang Taiyan hated the corrupted politics and was "a scholar who retired to tranquillity," however, throughout his whole life actually "endeavored himself in the advocation of total resistance against Japanese aggression."[49] In the autumn of Yan Fu's life, he "closed the door and refused guests, not caring about the weather outside his doors", but "in the letter, he wrote to Xiong Chunru, he said that 'China's future is indeed unknown, but its greatest challenge is that there are too many bureaucratic practices, yet lacking a practical law.'"[50] We can see from this that although Republican Chinese intellectuals tried their best to draw a clear line to differentiate themselves from politics, it was still difficult to truly cultivate themselves without caring about the world. If it was difficult for the intellectuals to even enjoy their "quiet old age," it is not hard to imagine their enthusiasm in politics during their "early revolutionary age" and their "middle academic age." Neither would not be inferior in any aspect.

In summary, the distinction or opposition between the cultural theories of Republican Chinese intellectuals was not due to the differences in the degree of their cultural characters, but only in the different paths, they chose with different methods of implementation. No matter what kind of cultural rhetoric was adopted, the fundamental purpose was nothing more than to strengthen the country. Chinese culture can rejuvenate itself when the country is prosperous. When comparing the three cultural theories we can see that the revivalists believed that the country will be strengthened with the revival of Chinese culture, therefore they strongly advocated for the revival of traditions. The conciliationists chose a compromised method, believing that the conciliation of Chinese and Western cultures was the way to strengthen China, so they devoted themselves to the conciliation of Chinese and Western cultures. Total westernizations believed that Chinese culture obstructed the path to the country's prosperity. The most urgent task was to learn from Western culture, but the ultimate goal was still to strengthen China instead of establishing a Western culture in China. Just like Hu Shi's statement that said that Chinese students study abroad now in order not to study abroad in the future. In the same way, the total westernizations learned from the West for the future prosperity of the country so that they no longer had to learn from the West. The horizontal differences were negligible, but there were indeed significant differences in cultural characters between intellectuals in Republican China and late Qing dynasty when compared vertically.

Although Republican Chinese intellectuals were inheritors of late-Qing scholars, they no longer belonged to that special era, therefore their cultural characteristics were weaker than that of the late Qing dynasty. The reasons were:

1) Since Republican China, Western learnings had further spread and deepened in the country. More people had the opportunity to study abroad. Although Republican Chinese intellectuals have indulged in Confucianism from childhood, the more they interacted with and understood Western culture at the same time, the weaker their cultural characteristics developed in their childhood.

2) Most late-Qing scholars took the path of excelling in academics for officialdom. Being a government official meant that they were loyal to the feudal emperor. Therefore, they would naturally choose to maintain the orthodoxy of Confucian culture. However, Republican Chinese intellectuals lacked bureaucratic experience and therefore had a lack of such political pressure. As such, Chinese culture no longer had an absolutely dominant position for Republican Chinese intellectuals. This was the basis for the weakening of the traditional cultural characters in Republican Chinese universities. Of course, born out of late-Qing scholars, Republican Chinese intellectuals were destined to bear the Chinese culture mark.

In short, the Republican Chinese intellectuals still regarded Chinese culture as the foundation. Due to the existence of these intellectuals, the dominant position of Chinese culture in Chinese universities was lost, yet its foundation remained. This was the reason why the traditional cultural characteristics of Chinese universities gradually weakened compared to the late Qing Dynasty. And yet some remained.

2. *Republican Chinese intellectuals and Chinese Universities*

Chen Pingyuan once said that "the relationship between scholars and universities complement each other like the goods and the shop windows. Sometimes each shines more brilliantly in the other's company; sometimes one party becomes overly-dependent on the other."[51] In comparison, nowadays, more scholars now rely on first-class universities for fame and fortune. But back in Republican China, the universities relied on first-class intellectuals to grow their reputation.

During the Republic of China, universities were highly autonomous, governed by university lecturers, which meant that the cultural characters of intellectuals were an important internal basis for the development of Chinese universities. Taking Weber's "ideal types" as a research method, there are four core concepts that we can draw from the university views of Republican Chinese initellectuals, namely *Houde Zaiwu* (holding the world with virtue), *Tianxia Wei Gong* (sharing the world equally with others), *You Rong Nai Da* (being inclusive to attain great achievements), *Wenshi Bingbao* (practicing both idealism and realism) as the distinctive features of Chinese universities during Republican China, which also became the great legacy of Republican Chinese intellectuals' culture characters.

a) Houde Zaiwu

The Book of Changes stated, "*Tianxing Jian, Junzi Yi Ziqiang Buxi, Dishi Kun, Junzi Yi Houde Zaiwu*" (The Heavens are in motion ceaselessly; The enlight'ned exert themselves constantly. While the Earth is supportive and natural, only the virtuous can bear the utmost.) Giving importance to morality is the core value of the Chinese national spirit. After the establishment of the Republic of China, Cai Yuanpei was in charge of education. He completely abolished the late-Qing traditional ethics principles such as *Zhong Jun* and *Zun Kong*. However, moral education still ranked first in the reformed educational principles. In 1912, the Ministry of Education officially announced its education principles as "Emphasizing moral education, which is supplemented by practical education and national military education. The system is further completed by aesthetic education."[52] This statement of purpose places moral education at the center, with utilitarian (or practical) education, national military education, and aesthetic education as its supplements. Utilitarian education and national military education continued the educational principles of the late Qing dynasty, which was *shangshi* and *shangwu*, while aesthetic education was a new concept. These principles were all drawn from Cai Yuanpei's educational ideas. Cai Yuanpei set moral education at the center of Chinese education. He put forward the idea of developing moral education with the development of aesthetic education and first opened aesthetic education lessons in Peking University. In his essay *Meiyu* (*Aesthetic Education*), he pointed out that:

> Aesthetic educators apply aesthetic theories to education. Their purpose is to cultivate feelings. Life is nothing more than will power. The way people interact with each other is nothing beyond behaviors. Therefore, the purpose of education is to make everyone behave properly, that is, make moral education the core. Two things have to be prepared in order to achieve proper behavior. On the one hand, consider the interests, examine the causes and effects, and make judgments with a calm mind; all the virtues of defending oneself and protecting the country belong to this category of intellectual education. On the other hand, regardless of misfortune and fortune, regardless of life and death, rush towards a goal with passion; everybody who shares happiness with others and sacrifices himself for greater good belongs to this category of aesthetic education. Therefore, aesthetic education and intellectual education should go hand in hand in an attempt to accomplish moral education.[53]

"The Father of Nankai," Zhang Boling, also attached great importance to the moral education of universities. He pointed out, "Education is a tool for transforming individuals. But the scope of education should not be limited to the textbook, intellectual education. Instead, personality and moral education should also be paid special attention."[54] Pan Guangdan also indicated that "Education is only complete if it can cultivate characters," "This moral education is extracted from China's original moral education system."[55] In general, under the influence of Republican Chinese intellectuals, moral education became the core educational policy for the reform and development of Chinese universities.

The regulations regarding Chinese university reform during this period paid special attention to students' moral education. For example, Nankai, as a private university, issued the *Tianjin Nankai University Constitution* during this time to urge students to strictly cultivate their morality with serious school discipline and treating all students equally. The constitution emphasized characteristics beyond the *ping* (quality) of personal behaviors. Its Article 2 already specified that "every student in the school should act with dignity if he fails to self-discipline, and he is found to solicit prostitutes, he will be expelled immediately." The *li* (etiquette) during human interactions was also crucial, in Article 11, it was stated that "students must greet teachers of the university with respect, and they must greet their fellow schoolmates."[56] Such rules regarding moral behaviors were not a unique characteristic of Nankai. At this time, many universities had similar school rules. The reason for this is that the idea of Houde Zaiwu maintained its core position in Republican Chinese universities, which was largely driven by the traditional ethical and emotional complex of Republican Chinese intellectuals.

b) The world is equally shared by all.

In Chapter *Liyun* (*Rites and Fortune*) of *Liji* (*Book of Rites*), it stated that "When the great way prevails, the world community is equally shared by all." Confucius said, "the will of even a common man cannot be taken away." Mencius said, "Neither riches nor honors can corrupt him; neither poverty nor humbleness can bend him; neither threats nor forces can subdue him. This is called a great man." This is the ancient concept of *yi* (righteousness). Dong Zhongshu said, "The way of the heaven is to give; the way of the earth is to transform; the way of human is to be righteous." Born in a trying time, Republican Chinese intellectuals possessed a particularly strong complex of "sharing the world equally with all," which greatly influenced the formation of Chinese universities' cultural characters. Ji Xianlin once summarized the patriotic tradition of Peking University as China's *shi* (scholar) spirit and attributed this spirit to the traditional cultural quality of the intellectuals of Peking University.

The fine tradition of Peking University was deeply entrenched in patriotism. It was precise because of this excellent quality of traditional intellectuals that the people of Peking University have always been extremely concerned about the nation and the public. This tradition evolved from the beginning of the Spring and Autumn Period and the Warring States period, "An educated gentleman cannot but be resolute and broad-minded, for he has taken up a heavy responsibility and a long course," to the Ming and Qing motto that "the rise and fall of All Under Heaven is the responsibility of every individual." Finally, in the Qing dynasty when the society experienced a once-in-a-thousand-year great upheaval, this tradition became concentrated in the Imperial University of Peking with the tradition of a millennium of Taixue. It is here that the last generation of traditional intellectuals bore the scholar-official complex. They not only possessed cultural inheritance, but also shouldered the responsibility of social progress without hesitation. Therefore, in the past 100 years, Peking University not only created extremely brilliant academic and cultural achievements but also walked in the forefront of each patriotic movement. The most influential movement was the May Fourth Movement. Two flags, "democracy" and "science," were raised, to achieve the purpose of prospering the country. Therefore, Peking University's 100-year history was a reflection of the patriotic tradition of intellectuals, which was also reflected in countless Peking University teachers and students, that is, they undertook not only the responsibility of cultural creation and inheritance, but also the extra responsibility of national value identification.[57]

Peking University professor Le Daiyun also made a similar statement:

> There are two distinctive features in Peking University's tradition. Firstly, a strong sense of social responsibility and national consciousness. And secondly, a strong sense of personal freedom and inclusiveness. The former was inherited from the traditional spirit of scholar-officials, and the latter was born under the modern enlightenment spirit advocated by President Cai Yuanpei and others.[58]

It can be seen that although Peking University was an important anti-traditionalist base in the new cultural movement, its inheritance was of the scholar-official spirit of sharing the world equally. As another example, during the war against Japan, the characters of National Southwestern Associated University were just as equally remarkable – the world is shared by the people. Brilliance in adversity. Not only was National Southwestern Associated University the higher education base for inheriting and passing down culture, it was also a cultural front for fighting against Japan and saving the country. In order to adapt to the social needs during the war against Japan, many professors of the National Southwestern Associated University adjusted their research direction and fields and produced many new research results. Based on the results of these studies, some new courses were opened, and their academic direction of national salvation became more distinct. In a word, the intellectuals born in a national emergency were determined to save the country. They established their cultural characters with the traditional scholar-official spirit of *Tianxia Wei Gong*.

c) **You Rong Nai Da** *(be inclusive to attain great achievements).*

Chapter *Jun Chen* (Lord Chen) of *Shang Shu* (*Book of Documents*) stated, "Do not be angered by the stubborn ones. Do not expect anyone to be perfect. There must be tolerance so that you would gain; There must inclusiveness so that you would have great morality."[59]

The term *you rong nai da* came from the classics, and later generations were often self-disciplined with mottos including this quote, such as *shou yi wei qian, you rong nai da* (only humbleness leads to gains, be inclusive to attain great achievements) or *hai na bai chuan, you rong nai da*; bi li qian ren, wu yu ze gang (be inclusive like how the ocean accepts thousands of rivers, be inclusive to attain great achievements; the mountain measures a thousand feet, it is upright because it has no earthly desire). There is a character *da* (great) in the Chinese term *daxue* (university) in Republican China. An important layer of connotation was that universities had the spirit to be widely inclusive to master scholars. Republican Chinese intellectuals looked upon their forefathers. They accepted talents from around the world, shaped the *you rong nai da* spirit of Chinese universities with their modesty, prudent, broad-minded traditional spirit. Peking University emerged as the role model of Chinese universities' inclusive spirit with its abundance of talents, in which Cai Yuanpei contributed greatly. In the book *Bainian Zhi Gong: Zhongguo Jindai Daxue Xiaozhang De Jiaoyujia Jingshen* (*Hundred Years of Achievement: The Educator's Spirit of the President of Modern Chinese University*), Zhou Chuan and others approached the question from Cai Yuanpei's traditional education thought of respecting teachers and talents, and commented on the character of Peking University's character of inclusiveness:

> In terms of widely recruiting those who were "passionate about academics" and "life-long scholars" as professors, Cai Yuanpei attached great importance to hiring scholars with different or even opposite ideas, ideologies, schools of thought and styles. Cai Yuanpei highly praised the sayings in the *Liji* (Book of Rites) and *Zhongyong* (*Doctrine of the Mean*) that "all things can be nurtured together without conflicts, and the ways can extend together without contradiction." He believed that "if (the professors) indeed to have their opinions, and can voice them out logically, they can do so at the same time. It does not matter if they are in the same university and have opposing ideas. Let the students compare and make their own decisions, this is how '*daxue*' can be '*da*.'" Therefore, among the famous scholars of Peking University at that time, there were Hu Shi, Qian Xuantong, Liu Bannong, and Lu Xun who advocated for a literary revolution, as well as Huang Kan and Liang Shuming who defended the old learnings and were against the new cultural movement; there were Chen Duxiu and Li Dazhao who promoted Marxism, even Gu Hongming, the imperial restorationist who refused to cut off his pigtail and Liu Shipei, who advocated for imperialism. In addition, due to Cai Yuanpei's eclectic way of talent selection, Peking University's faculty was quickly rejuvenated.[60]

Rooted in Chinese tradition, under the guidance of Cai Yuanpei, Peking University gathered masters from all over the world with an eclectic attitude and accommodated dissidents. This move not only started Republican Chinese universities' spirit of being eclectic and inclusive to all talents but also laid the foundation for their inclusive cultural character. Mei Yiqi later took charge of Tsinghua University, and also insisted on this idea. In his Inaugural Speech (1931), Mei Yiqi emphasized that "the reason why a university is a university lies in whether there are good professors. Mencius said, 'The so-called native country is not about taxes, but about generations of loyal subordinates.' I can now imitate him and say, 'the so-called university is not about buildings and campuses, but about generations of master scholars.' Our knowledge gain depends on our professors' instructions; our spiritual cultivation also depends on the professors' inspiration."[61] When Chen Shi founded Zhonghua Daxue (Private Chinese University of Wuchang), he imitated the example set by Peking University's spirit of inclusiveness established by Cai Yuanpei. He coined the school motto as *Chengde* (establish morality), *Dacai* (grow intelligence), *Duli* (be independent), *Jinqu* (strive for excellence), and widely recruited talents from around the country. Before and after the May Fourth Movement, Chen Shi made full use of his prestige and social relations and created a grand scene in Zhonghua Daxue that "Tagore from India, Cai Yuanpei from China, Jiang Baili in the militia, Vi Kyuin "Wellington" Koo in the field of politics, John Dewey the philosopher, Kang Youwei and Liangqichao the masters of Confucian classics and Chinese history... There wasn't a master scholar of the time who have not visited the school." In short, under the influence of the traditional Chinese culture complex of respecting teachers, intellectuals have fully interpreted the connotation of the character "*da*" in "*daxue*" with the spirit of "you rong nai da."

d) **Wenshi Bingbao** *(Practice both idealism and realism).*

In *Zhongguo Gaodeng Jiaoyu Shilun*, Tu Youguang classified the history of Chinese higher education after Qing dynasty as a stage of science. According to this view, higher education in the Republic of China was clearly at a stage of science. However, as Tu Youguang said, "the boundary between the 'humanity' stage and the 'science' stage was not clear-cut. This is because the humanities and sciences cannot be separated as subjects; they can only be separated as concepts,"[62] Since the end of the Qing dynasty, China's higher education had moved towards the science stage, and it was completely "forced."[63] Republican China was in a social transition period between the old and the new. How could any "force" push the humanistic characteristics of Chinese higher education which lasted for a millennium to extinction? Out of practical need, the Republican Chinese government strengthened practical education, even at the price of restricting humanistic education. Yet it still struggled. In 1932, the Ministry of Education proposed the *Gaige Jiaoyu Fangan* (Educational Reform Plan). Measures were taken to vigorously develop practical subjects. It was even proposed that the universities' humanity subjects should be suspended for 10 years. It was also true that some students followed the trend of the time and were keen to apply for practical subjects. However, instead of being forced by the government and following the trends of the students, professors in the university insisted on carrying out humanities education in universities. It was precisely because of their strong opposition that stopped the government's plan to suspend university humanities education. They eventually had to change "suspension" to "restricting the development of humanities subjects." Zhang Boling once had a good description of the relationship between humanities and science education. He believed that "science is the foundation of modern knowledge, humanities cannot progress without science."[64] Mei Yiqi also attached importance to humanities education. He pointed out in the article *Gongye Jiaoyu Yu Gongye Rencai* (*Industrial Education and Industrial Talents*), that "An industrial education whose purpose is to cultivate organizational talents, should also include most of the humanities and social science subjects, apart from the compulsory engineering and natural science subjects. The more the arts subjects are tapped into, the closer the learners would be to a generalist."[65] Pan Guangdan pointed out the malpractices of the times were based on the humanistic perspective. He also proposed that the first three years of high school and university education should be enriched by humanities courses as much as possible. Thanks to their support and practices, the Chinese humanities education tradition was protected and passed down in Chinese universities. For example, National Southwestern Associated University always paid attention to the protection and inheritance of arts subjects, and was committed to the development and progress of humanities in the new era. In *Xinan Lianda Zhishi Fenzi Qun De Xingcheng Yu Shuailuo* (*Formation and Decline of Intellectual Group of National Southwestern Associated University*), Xie Yong explained this phenomenon by using the educational backgrounds of the professors in the university as a starting point. The article stated:

> Among the professors, intellectuals such as Mei Yiqi, Zhang Boling, Chen Yinque, and Liu Wendian belonged to the older generation. Qian Zhongshu, Fei Xiaotong, Chen Xingshen, and Hua Luogeng were born around the year 1910, they belonged to the younger generation. In terms of educational backgrounds, most of the intellectuals of Chen Yinque's generation possessed a sense of the previous dynasty. Most of them underwent a complete traditional education, while at the same time had the experience of studying in Europe or America. With a relatively complete university education, many of their generations have become the founders of new humanities' disciplines in China.[66]

From this perspective, Republican Chinese universities still adhered to the concept of running a university with "Wenshi Bingbao" when the Western practical education fully entered the Chinese education field. This was due to the internal promotion of the broad Sinology background and the strong traditional cultural complex of the intellectuals of the Republic of China.

To sum up, under the influence of Republican Chinese intellectuals, *Houde Zaiwu* (holding the world with virtue), *Tianxia Wei Gong* (sharing the world equally with others), *You Rong Nai Da* (being tolerant to achieve something big), *Wenshi Bingbao* (being inclusive to both idealism and realism) have become important qualities of Chinese universities. Of course, the traits of Republican Chinese universities were not limited to the above. For example, *Xueshu Zhishang* (academic supremacy), *Daxue Zizhi* (university autonomy), and even *Xueshu Ziyou* (academic freedom) were all prominent signs of Chinese universities during this period. However, as Cai Yuanpei said, "My country has inherited thousands of years of academic autocracy. It was a habit for the scholars to explain what they saw with Confucian doctrine."[67]

Western university concepts like academic freedom were far from the tradition of Chinese academic autocracy. There were indeed ancient sayings such as *Jianrong Bingbao* (inclusiveness to all) and *Baihua Qifang* (hundreds of species of flowers blooming at the same time) in Chinese culture. However, as far as a social reality is concerned, this tradition did not become the mainstream of society nor did it play a lasting and effective role in ancient higher education. Objectively speaking, the concepts of modern academic freedom contained more of the Western cultural tradition. The cultural characteristics of Chinese universities listed above were directly derived from the tradition of Chinese culture and were closely related to the cultural cultivation of Republican Chinese intellectuals. Republican Chinese intellectuals, as disciples of traditional Confucianism, had strong moral ethics, which were reflected in Chinese universities' *Houde Zaiwu*. Their scholar-official characteristics were inherited from late-Qing was reflected in Chinese universities' *Tianxia Wei Gong*, while as the scholars of the traditional society, their literati complex was reflected in Chinese universities' *You Rong Nai Da* and *Wenshi Bingbao*. From the perspective of traditional culture, the origins of the above-mentioned characteristics of Republican Chinese universities were all traceable. Republican Chinese intellectuals were the strongest bridge between Chinese universities and Chinese culture. Compared with the cultural characters of late-Qing Chinese universities, the foundation of Republican Chinese universities insister on the Chinese cultural roots.

First, Chinese universities were based on Chinese culture, which means that Chinese universities took Chinese culture as the most basic "component" rather than the "main body." As "cultural inheritors," Republican Chinese intellectuals did not regard learning classics as the basis for learning, and they lacked feudal thinking, though they had strong humanitarian and ethical complex. They were detached from politics and bore little bureaucratic habits even though they possessed an obvious scholar-official complex. They also prioritized both, humanities and science, though they had an obvious literati complex. In contrast, the late-Qing scholars were the first "cultural inheritors" of Chinese universities' cultural characters, their Confucian classics thinking, bureaucratic style and literati senses were especially strong. Chinese universities in the late Qing dynasty and the Republic of China had different logic of development.

In the late Qing dynasty, Chinese universities established the cornerstone of Chinese learnings. The purpose was to maintain or strengthen the dominant position of Chinese culture in universities. It was a prerequisite for the theory of Chinese cultural subjectivity. Political pressure overwhelmed educational autonomy, and cultural perspective was stronger than the university perspective. During Republican China, Chinese universities still respected Chinese learnings as a foundation but no longer pursued the dominant position of Chinese culture. Instead, universities integrated Chinese and Western cultures, which was the way it was supposed to be. The autonomy of education surpassed political pressure, the cultural and university perspectives co-existed. This was the fundamental difference between the cultural characters of late-Qing and Republican Chinese universities.

Secondly, the cornerstone of Chinese universities was Chinese culture, which means that the traditional nature of ethical and political characteristics was retained in reality. For the cultural characteristics of "cultural inheritors:" The intellectuals of the Republic of China, and their ethics and morals have long been deeply entrenched. Although they were enlightened by Western culture, they had a weakened sense of tradition with strong ethical characteristics, although it was still difficult to shake its foundation. In the Republic of China, there was no longer the official rule of excelling in academics to enter officialdom. Moreover, in the face of political turmoils and government corruption, many intellectuals deliberately detached themselves from politics or abandoned their posts and turned to academics. This kind of background might have weakened universities' traditional bureaucratic characteristics, yet it was difficult to shake their spirit of caring about the world, so there was also a notable sense of politics. In contrast, late-Qing scholars were more deeply influenced by traditional culture and lacked an understanding of Western culture. Their cultural characters were inevitably politicized and bureaucratized, as most of these scholars took the path of excelling in academics to enter officialdom and thus bore a great sense of being loyal to the emperor and respecting Confucius.

Finally, seeing Chinese culture as the cornerstone meant that in Chinese universities' search for a balance between Chinese and Western culture, Chinese culture remained as their first approach. During Republican China, the development of Chinese universities followed a basic law, that is, they used Chinese culture as a starting point, they absorbed and learned from Western culture, and finally integrated the two cultures. During Republican China, the fusion of Chinese and Western cultures became a consensus on the reform and development of Chinese universities, but on the other hand, Chinese culture had always occupied a fundamental position. This was also the reason or basis for the ideal cultural characteristics of Chinese universities during Republican China. History has told us that Republican Chinese universities have indeed blended Chinese and Western cultures with Chinese culture. Many truly remarkable historical miracles have been achieved. Of course, this was, after all, a product of a special era. There were multiple reasons why this is hard to replicate. The free Republican Chinese political environment did not last. Political pressure overwhelmed educational autonomy in the development of Chinese universities and it was hard to re-create the freedom for development of universities. It was also hard to get the hang of the East-West cultural integration in Chinese universities as it was rare for the intellectuals to be generalists across Chinese and Western learnings. As some scholars have lamented, "there will never be another Cai Yuanpei."[68]

3. *The Presidents of Republican Chinese universities and the cultural character of Chinese universities*

Intellectuals played an important role as the "cultural inheritors" in the formation and development of Chinese universities' cultural character in the Republic of China. As an important member of the intellectuals, the Presidents of the Republican Chinese universities had a unique historical contribution to the formation and development of the cultural characters of Chinese universities. "Famous Republican Chinese universities shared a common feature, that is, almost every university had their unique history of struggle. Since each government was busy with political disputes and civil wars, they paid little attention to university education. As a result, almost every university suffered from various setbacks. In this context, the development of each university was inseparable from the support of one or two famous university presidents, who exerted a profound influence on the university."[69]

During the Republic of China, the president alone could represent a university, and they could even dominate the university of the entire era. This was very hard to achieve for normal intellectuals, even normal university presidents. Yet, figures like this still emerged in history. They brought their universities back to life, such as Cai Yuanpei, the president of Peking University. They also suffered together with their universities, such as Mei Yiqi, the president of Tsinghua University. They were willing to live in symbiosis with their universities, such as Zhang Boling, the father of Nankai University. Their outstanding contributions were not only praised by the Chinese people but also highly regarded by Western scholars.

Chen Pingyuan commented on Cai Yuanpei, the president of Peking University, "As Peking University's 'principal forever,' Cai Yuanpei is worthy of constant reminiscence because he single-handedly laid out the basic characters of this university. There have been countless heroes in China in the past 100 years, but none are comparable with President Cai so far, in terms of the profound influence on Peking University. Today, Cai Yuanpei's governance of Peking University has almost become a 'legend' – that his knowledge and talents suited the need of the time so perfectly, it was almost once in a millennium event that cannot be replicated."[70]

Dewey, an American scholar, also said, "Comparing the presidents of universities all over the world, Oxford, Cambridge, Paris, Berlin, Harvard, Columbia, etc. The only one capable of leading the university to transform a nation, an era, was none other than Cai

Yuanpei."[71] Here, we are going to study three presidents of the Republic of China universities, Cai Yuanpei, Mei Yiqi, and Zhang Boling, and interpret their cultural characters in regards to specific aspects together with the corresponding cultural characters of Chinese universities.

a) *Wenshi Bingbao:* ***Cai Yuanpei's literati character and Peking University's humanistic characteristics.***

Cai Yuanpei was a traditional Confucian literati. According to himself, "I was educated in a traditional private academy from the age of 6 to the age of 17; at 18 and 19 years old, I became a private academy tutor."[72] At the same time, his political career went rather smoothly, he became a *Xiucai* (passed county-level imperial examination) at the age of 17, a *Juren* (passed provincial-level imperial examination) at the age of 23, excelled the *Huishi* (central imperial examination) at the age of 24, became a *Jinshi* (passed the highest imperial examination) at the age of 26 and was appointed to a position in the Imperial Academy, and then was appointed to the position of Classics Compiler in the Imperial Academy at the age of 28. After the Reform Movement of 1898, Cai Yuanpei was extremely disappointed with the late Qing dynasty. He resigned from the Imperial Academy and devoted himself to the development of education. He went on multiple learning journeys to Europe and America and accepted the influence of Western culture comprehensively and profoundly. In the first year of the Republic of China, he served as the first Minister of Education. From 1916, he took charge of Peking University for more than ten years and became the veritable "most representative figure of Republican Chinese higher education" (according to Tu Youguang). Cai Yuanpei possessed thorough knowledge of both, Chinese and Western cultures. Therefore, his educational thought was the product of the integration of Chinese and Western cultures. This was an important characteristic that differentiated him from the late-Qing scholars.

Cai Yuanpei gave a speech at the University of California, Berkeley. He pointed out that "University education should adopt the strengths of Europe and America, as well as the Confucian and Mohist spirit." It could be said that although Cai Yuanpei was a "traditional who was familiar with Confucian classics," his university thoughts were influenced by the concepts of Western universities. Conversely, although Cai Yuanpei's university education ideas were influenced by Western university ideas, this did not obliterate the existence of his traditional education background. Furthermore, the fundamental role of traditional culture cannot be ignored.

According to Tu Youguang, "Cai Yuanpei has built such great historical merit, is it enough to leverage on a little influence of Western liberalism? Obviously not [...] No matter how great the Western influence was, it cannot replace the main root of Cai's learning. Not only can it not be replaced, but the Western influences could also only work through the main root of Cai's learning"[73]. There are many academic studies from Peking University on the cultural origins of Cai Yuanpei's reformist thoughts, and the emphasis is on the cultural interpretation of propositions such as *Jiaoshou Zhixiao* (university managed by professors), *Jianrong Bingbao* (inclusiveness to all), and *Sixiang Ziyou* (freedom of thought). The present study assumes that the above attributes demonstrated more Western characteristics than Chinese traditions. Therefore, only Cai's Peking University reform measures and remarks were studies, as an attempt to explore the aspects of where his traditional literati personalities and Peking University's humanistic characteristics corresponded.

First and foremost, Cai Yuanpei's reforms focused on the liberal arts disciplines of Peking University. He gathered master scholars from around the world to expand and enrich the arts education. In the article *Wo Zai Jiaoyujie De Jingyan* (*My Experience in Education*) (1937), he pointed out that, "The rectification of Peking University starts from the arts. Among the old teachers, such as Shen Yinmo, Shen Jianshi, and Qian Xuantong, the spark of reform is already kindled. Since Chen Duxiu came on as a senior, Hu Shizhi, Liu Bannong, Zhou Yucai, Zhou Qiming all came as teachers, the trend of literary revolution and freedom of thought thereby became the mainstream."[74]

Chen Pingyuan summarized four reasons as to why Cai's reform of Peking University started with the arts: 1) Peking University was centered on two disciplines, arts and science. The science discipline was very young, yet the arts disciple was already strong; 2) The amount of money required to reform science is much larger than that of the reform of liberal arts, which the University could not afford; 3) In terms of influences on the society's ideological trend of the era, reconstructing the arts subjects is undoubtedly more direct and more effective – if President Cai chose to monitor the science subjects first, Peking University would never be able to rejuvenate itself within the span of two to three years and lead this trend; 4) Lastly and probably most importantly, to reform the arts, is within the scope of the principal's interests and abilities.[75] Interpreting this statement, "the probably most important last factor" showed that the arts reform of Peking University was closely related to the principal.

In this way, Cai Yuanpei's attitude towards the classical Chinese language in the reform process of Peking University was completely consistent.

In 1936, Cai Yuanpei delivered a speech titled *Zhengdun Beijing Daxue De Jingguo* (*The Process of Rectifying Peking University*), which showed his basic stance on the dispute between the vernacular and the classical Chinese education of Peking University. He said, "Use vernacular Chinese too, but not attacking classical Chinese." He pointed out, [...] At the time in Peking University, Hu Shizhi, Chen Zhongfu, Qian Xuantong, Liu Bannong, and the Shen brothers, actively advocated vernacular literature, while Liu Shipei, Huang Jigang others actively defended classical Chinese. However, I believe that, for practical purposes, vernacular writing must prevail. I practice vernacular writings and advocate for vernacular writing often. However, I have also stated that it is also good to do fine writing in classical Chinese."[76] In the trend of using vernacular Chinese,

Cai Yuanpei advocated the use of both and virtually protected the tradition of classical Chinese. In practical teaching, although Cai Yuanpei supported vernacular text, he also advocated for the use of classical Chinese in university Chinese textbooks and student assignments. To some extent, this was the inevitable choice made by President Cai's literati character.

b) *Houde Zaiwu:* ***Mei Yiqi's "Way of University" and the Confucian legacy of Tsinghua University and National Southwestern Associated University.***

Mei Yiqi was well-educated in Confucian classics and history from his childhood and was very good at reciting works. A foreign colleague once called him a "well-read Chinese Confucian scholar with an exceptional memory." His colleague recalled, "He once told us that if anyone of us recites any Chinese ancient classics with mistakes or omissions, he could immediately continue with the rest of the chapter."[77] Judging from his educational background, Mei Yiqi studied in Yan Shi Jiashu (Family Academy of the Yans) organized by Yan Fansun, a prominent late-Qing Confucian scholar, which laid the foundation for his traditional Chinese studies. Afterward, he became a Nankai student and started engaging with the new learnings. He was selected as one of the Boxer Indemnity Scholars and studied in America for 4 years, during which his cultivation in Western learning greatly progressed, and formed a life-long bond with Tsinghua University.

In *Zhongguo Gaodeng Jiaoyu Shilun* (*On the History of Chinese Higher Education*), Tu Youguang elaborated on the origin of Mei Yiqi's relationship with Tsinghua University, and at the same time raised an interesting "doubt." Mei was a Tsinghua "prehistoric" alumni and was part of the first batch of Boxer Indemnity Scholars. Tsinghua University was only established after this batch of students went to America. He studied electrical engineering in America and returned to China in 1914. He then became a faculty of Tsinghua in the following year and taught mathematics, English and physics, successively. In April, 1926, as the Dean of Physics Department, he was elected by the board of professors to become the Chief Administrator of Tsinghua. In 1928, he served as the Tsinghua Overseas Student Supervisor of the United States and resided in America long-term, when he toured around American universities where Tsinghua scholars studied. In 1931, he returned to China as the President of National Tsinghua University. The above experiences of Mei's demonstrated that his major was science, not humanities, nor Chinese humanities. He had lived (and practiced) in American universities for a long time and was familiar with the current status, history and theories of American university education. However, when Mei's summed up the experience of Chinese university education, he clearly and firmly chose the principles of the Chinese humanity classic *Daxue*, The Great Learning, instead of the principles of America, that is, of the West, which he was also familiar with. He always implemented the former thoroughly and put the latter as a comparison and reference.[78]

One simple line is enough to address the "doubt" raised above: it was an inevitable choice made by the traditional cultural characters of Mei Yiqi. Mei Yiqi's educational thoughts are summarized in the article *Daxue Yijie* (Understanding of the University). He always adhered to the great learning approach of *Ming Mingde* (highest virtue) and *Xinmin* (new democracy). Tu Youguang provided a meticulous and wonderful interpretation of this article in his *Zhongguo Gaodeng Jiaoyu Shilun*. Therefore, I should not do repetitive work here, but to emphasize on one point: although *Daxue Yijie* was the product of a comprehensive dialogue between "the essence of China's traditional (Confucian) educational thoughts and the essence of modern Western philosophical education," Mei Yiqi's personal Confucian cultivation basics were also fundamental. President Mei successively took charge of Tsinghua University and the Southwest Associated University. Both universities never deviated from the Confucian "way to great learning" under the "subtle influence" of President Mei.

Speaking of Tsinghua first, the Confucian way of great learning was first fully realized there. Everyone knew that there were three *zhai* (house) in the boys' dormitory: *Ming* (enlighten), *Xin* (new) and *Shan* (virtue), which were named after the three key points of The Great Learning. Mei's ideas of *Ming Mingde* and *Xinmin* were also reflected in the educational principles of Tsinghua University. Huang Yanfu pointed out that during the period of Tsinghua University, especially after President Mei Yiqi presided over the administration, Tsinghua University adopted "general education" or "free education" as its educational policy. The basic points were the "multi-faceted" cultivation and nurturing of knowledge. On top of that, it was the characters and the ambitions for students in general education (mainly undergraduate level) to improve their "whole personality" (not break their personality), for them to obtain the qualification to actively participate in the "great cause of *Xinmin*" (transforming old conventions and being the society's role models) after graduation or to lay the foundation for further studies.[79] Mei Yiqi's educational ideas of *Mingde* and *Xinmin* became the internal basis for teaching and educating people of Tsinghua University, and have long guided its reform and practices. Moving on to the National Southwest Associated University.

During the war against Japan, the three universities migrated south and merged, and Mei Yiqi became the actual director of all three universities. *Daxue Yijie* was written during that time, which was not only a summary of his previous experiences of being in charge of Tsinghua University but also an attempt to build up the spirits and the heart for the education of National Southwestern Associated University at the time. Under the influence of Mei Yiqi, the Associated University still took the path of "general education," emphasizing the cultivation of students' whole personality. For example, the moral education of the Associated University attached great importance to teaching by example and self-cultivation. This could be seen from the executive committee's attitude towards students' behaviors which violated the moral principles. For example, at the 100th executive meeting, a student who "repeatedly vandalized public property" was expelled. At the 147th meeting, three students who "insulted the teachers with vulgar language" and "behaved abusively" were also expelled.[80] The purpose for the associated University to pay attention to moral education was, as Mei Yiqi said, to make the youth "able to give back to the society once they graduate" and realize the university's function of *Xinmin*. In this context, both Tsinghua and Nankai's Confucian atmospheres were influenced by President Mei's "way of great learning."

c) *Tixanxia Wei Gong*: *Zhang Boling's literati complex and the scholar spirit of Nankai.*

Zhang Boling was born in a late-Qing Xicai family. One cannot discuss Zhang Boling without mentioning Yan Xiu. Hu Shi once commented that no cooperation in education can be more successful than that between Zhang Boling and Yan Xiu. Yan Xiu was a typical open-minded late-Qing scholar, well-versed in Chinese learning, and a great visionary. At the age of 28, he became a *Jinshi*. He was appointed as a Classics Compiler in the Imperial Academy and back-up editor of *National History*. He used to be the Guizhou Provincial Chief of Education. He advocated for education for national salvation and therefore pushed for the establishment of schools. In 1898, Yan Xiu founded Yan Shi Jiashu. Zhang Boling, who was only 22 years old, was hired as a tutor, marking the beginning of nearly 30 years of educational cooperation. Their shared educational ideals led the two to work together to create a "miracle in the history of education" (according to Chen Pingyuan) – Nankai University. From Yan Shi Jiashu to Nankai High School, followed by Nankai University, Zhang Boling was provided with an important platform. From a private academy tutor to the president of Nankai University, Zhang Boling's educational ideas were gradually realized. Nankai University was different from Peking University and Tsinghua University, it was originally the "private property" of Yan Xiu, Zhang Boling, and others. Yet private ownership had its benefits, Zhang Boling enjoyed a greater degree of freedom presiding over Nankai, away from the numerous limitations of public universities. Therefore, to some extent, the original Nankai University interpreted Zhang Boling, and the cultural characters of Nankai University began with him. Objectively speaking, Zhang Boling possessed literati characteristics no less than Cai Yuanpei. Nankai University escaped from Yan Shi Jiashu and Zhang also possessed an abundance of Confucian spirit like Mei Yiqi, shown in Nankai University's "localization" policy. However, the present study believes that its most typical spirit was the literati spirit of *Mingdao Jishi* (find the way and save the world). Some scholars pointed out that "Nankai University was the one with the greatest Chinese *daxue* spirit of the era,"[81] which was largely implying the strong sense of patriotism of the university. This book interprets the unique scholar spirit of Nankai from the perspective of Zhang Boling's strong scholar-official complex, which added an internal dimension to this statement.

Nankai University was born from Zhang Boling's profound patriotic sentiment. The painful national crisis brought by the First Sino-Japanese War of 1894/1895 greatly shocked the Chinese people. Zhang Boling "witnessed that the national flag changed three times. My chest was filled with grief and anger. How painful! I thought of my country's prevailing weakness. How could the country dream of survival if it does not strengthen itself? The way to self-strengthening is through education. Establishment new education, create new talents, Ling will dedicate his life in education to realize the dream of saving the country, starting from this moment onwards."[82] This became the source of Nankai's scholar-official spirit. Taking Zhang Boling's idea of saving the country as the principle, Nankai University held a national aspiration since its establishment and demonstrated a strong scholar-official spirit in all aspects.

In terms of the curriculum arrangement, Nankai University did not have a Chinese department. It emphasized practicality and denounced empty talk. Chen Pingyuan stated, "A notable feature was that, before liberation, the liberal arts discipline in Nankai University focused on politics and economy, which directly influenced the society, there was no room for Chinese literature. This was in stark contrast to old Peking University's emphasis on literature, history, and philosophy." He also stated, "it was a conscious choice that old Nankai did not set up a Chinese department. Future generations could only 'understand and empathize' with President Zhang Boling's 'stubbornness.'"[83]

It is worth mentioning that Zhang Boling prioritized sports. He once said, "People who do not know sports should not preside over a school." That was because Zhang Boling believed that the Chinese nation had five major illnesses: ignorance, weakness, poverty, dividedness, and selfishness. The basis of getting rid of these illnesses and rejuvenating a country lies in education, and sports must be developed to strengthen the country. Therefore, he paid special attention to the physical fitness of students.

In terms of teaching and scientific research, Nankai was one of the first who started research into Japan's invasion of China. According to historical records: In the autumn of 1927, Nankai University established the Northeast Research Association, which was aimed at "investigating the field situation of the Northeast region, the conditions of Japan and Russia, and their various operating profiles in Northeast China, thereby studying solutions to these problems."[84] After the July 7th Incident, the Japanese army first "focused" on bombing Nankai and razed it to the ground in a seemingly revengeful manner. Besides, Nankai scholars demonstrated remarkable spirit in the patriotic student movements guided and supported by Zhang Boling. For example, in 1931, after the 18th September Mukden Incident in which Japanese armed force invaded Northeast China, Zhang Boling gathered the school's teachers and students on the 20th to give a speech, titled The Northeast Incident and Our Right Attitudes, and on the 22nd, Nankai teachers and students organized a national emergency rescue meeting and elected eleven representatives including Le Yongqing, Gu Yuantian, and Mao Guoqi, and decided to immediately participate in the Tianjin Student Congress of National Salvation. On the

29th, *Nanda Zhoukan* (*Nankai Weekly*) published the *Special Issue on Japan Affairs.* On 17 October, Nankai decided to stop the annual school celebration due to a national crisis. On 14 October, a meeting of 357 students decided that all students of Nankai University would go to Nanjing for the petition and invited Zhang Boling as their commander-in-chief.[85] Without the support and protection of President Zhang, the Nankai student movements might not be able to develop in such fashion.

Overall, Zhang Boling's scholar-official complex of "education for national salvation" was especially strong and Nankai University's scholar spirit of "Discipline and Practicality" was also outstanding.

Section 3: An Analysis of the Cultural Characteristics of Chinese Universities in the Republican Period
– A case study of Peking University, Tsinghua University, and National Southwestern Associated University

During the Republican Period, Chinese universities entered a "golden era" of development. Although the history of higher education in China entered the "science" era which focused on studying Europe and the United States, the customs and legacy of traditional culture proved that Chinese universities did not lose their foundation. During this period, Chinese and Western cultures complemented and counterbalanced each other in Chinese universities. Many well-known Chinese universities rose to prosperity during this era of relatively balanced development of Chinese and Western cultures, and at once obtained a rather ideal set of cultural characteristics. Based on the previous theoretical analysis of the cultural characteristics of Chinese universities during the Republic of China period, this section will select three famous universities during the Republic of China period and interpret their cultural characters at specific levels.

These three universities have already been covered in previous examples. The first is Peking University, which was developed from the Imperial University of Peking in the late Qing Dynasty. It was not only the source of the anti-traditional New Culture Movement but also the first Chinese university to establish the Institute of Chinese Studies. The second is Tsinghua University, which was developed from Tsinghua School, a preparatory school for studying in the United States at the end of the Qing Dynasty. Although it was born with the inherent colonial character of "imitating the United States on every level," it was determined to stick to Chinese people's characteristics of "unceasing self-strengthening through practice." The third is National Southwestern Associated University, which was formed by the combination of Peking University, Tsinghua University, and Nankai University during the war after their southward "migration." It was a product of the weakness of the country, a symbol of foreign invasion and humiliation, and the forced migration of these universities. However, it managed to become a miracle in Chinese history and even in the world despite its "hall of shame" status.

In the Republic of China era, they were not Chinese universities in the complete sense, but they were competent as examples of the cultural characters of Chinese universities during this period. They did not have ideal cultural characters throughout the Republic of China era, but during this special period, they were once committed to the integration of Chinese and Western cultures in Chinese universities and achieved considerable success. This section mainly adopts a textual analysis method, which uses government regulations, presidential speeches or articles, school mottos, and school songs, along with relevant scholars' reminiscent descriptions of campus cultural symbols related to the subject as analysis texts, to conduct cultural interpretation of the educational concepts, system designs and cultural symbols of these three universities.

1. *Analysis of the cultural character of Peking University (PKU)*

Peking University, formerly known as the Imperial University of Peking in the late Qing Dynasty, changed several times during the Republic of China, it had achieved brilliance and it has the longest history among the three. In 1912, the Republic of China was established, the Imperial University of Peking was renamed the National Peking University (NPU), and Yan Fu became the president. By the start of 1917, Cai Yuanpei took over the NPU and gave it new life. During the next 10 years, PKU (Peking University) saw rapid development. During the May 4th Movement, PKU became famous as an anti-traditional cultural center. Between 1927 and 1929, PKU fell into social unrest and was severely damaged.

After seizing the Beijing regime, the Fengtian clique abruptly announced the abolition of NPU in 1927 and merged it with eight other national universities in Beijing to form a consolidated university (Jingshi Daxuexiao). In 1928, the Ministry of Education of the National Government of the Republic of China reorganized it into Zhonghua University, and later into Peiping University, which was yet again restructured into "the school of Peking University" under National Peiping University. In 1929, Peking University announced on its own that it would resume school by itself, and the National Government changed "the school of Peking University" to National Peking University on 6 August. By the year 1937 when it moved to the south and was combined with the other two universities, Peking University had already become a veritable model of modern Chinese universities.

It should be pointed out that the cultural analysis of Peking University here mainly refers to the "old Peking University" during the Republic of China period. Chen Pingyuan has a specific definition for "the old Peking University," which is the Peking University from 1898 to 1937. Although this time-division follows the history of the school at its original site, it spans two eras, the late Qing Dynasty and the Republic of China. "The old Peking University" mentioned here overlaps with this concept, while not being completely consistent with it. The concept this book uses also ended in 1937 when the school moved south, but the beginning was chosen to be when the Republic of China was founded. The cultural character of the Imperial University of Peking in the Late Qing Dynasty has been discussed in the previous chapter of this study, and later on, there will also be an analysis of the cultural character of the National Southwestern Associated University from 1937–1945. The cultural character of Peking University explored here mainly refers to the "old Peking University" at a certain point in the historical period from 1912 to 1937.

a) Peking University's educational concept.

Peking University originated in the traditional society of the late Qing Dynasty. Under the leadership of scholars in the late Qing Dynasty, Peking University's cultural character was very strong. Until the beginning of Cai Yuanpei's takeover of Peking University, it was still a school with a "grandmaster" status. After Cai Yuanpei took over the "old Peking University," he intentionally balanced the cultural atmosphere of Peking University, based on the position of "integration of Chinese and Western cultures." Hence, fundamental changes happened at Peking University. During this period, Peking University no longer emphasized, or even intentionally weakened some negative Chinese cultural characters since the late Qing Dynasty, while it was still consistent with the basic standpoint of taking Chinese culture as its foundation. A general feature of the development of higher education during the Republic of China was that education autonomy overwhelmed political coercion, and intellectuals, especially university presidents, played a leading role in the development of Chinese universities.

The educational ideas of "old Peking University" were mainly influenced by two principals during this period, the first was Cai Yuanpei and the other was Jiang Menglin. For over 30 years during the Republic of China era, the two had almost taken charge of the entirety of "old Peking University," and their educational concepts became an important basis for the formation of the cultural character of the "old Peking University." Especially under the leadership of Cai Yuanpei's concept of integration of Chinese and Western cultures, the tone of the "old Peking University" and even the whole idea of educational concepts in universities during the early Republic of China were laid. The documents issued by the Ministry of Education of the Republic of China in the earlier days were mostly formulated and promulgated by Cai Yuanpei's educational thoughts, and no matter how the society changed afterward, the internal thoughts continued. For example, in 1912, the Decree of Educational Purposes of the Ministry of Education stipulated that: "Universities should focus on moral education, supplement it with practical education and military national education, and complete its morality with aesthetic education." In the same year, the first article of the University Education Plan of the Ministry of Education stated that: "Universities should aim to teach advanced academics, develop and cultivate talents of great knowledge, and meet the needs of the country." The promulgation of the two educational regulations stipulated the basic direction of Chinese universities at the national level.

In a nutshell, the core educational concepts of Peking University during this period mainly included *Dili Dexing* (cultivating virtue), *Canzheng Aiguo* (participating in politics and patriotism), and *Nangkuo Dadian*, *Wangluo Zhongjia* (gathering all great learnings and collecting knowledge and merits from all schools of thought). The above concepts may not be unique to the "old Peking University," but as the highest institution of higher education in the country at that time, Peking University was the first to adopt such concepts.

1. *Dili Dexing.*

The Decree of Educational Purposes listed four major themes of education, namely moral education, practical education, military national education, and aesthetic education. It was based on Cai Yuanpei's idea of *Wuyu Bingju* (spontaneous development of five aspects of education), with citizen morality as the center of the five aspects. In the *Opening Address of the National Temporary Education Conference* (1912), Cai Yuanpei pointed out that the task of educators was to develop within the students the ability to fulfill their responsibilities. The specific requirements were as follows:

> Since the Republic of China was founded, the educators have been trying to develop education. Briefly speaking, education is nothing more than five kinds of doctrines, namely military national doctrine, practical doctrine, civilian morality, worldviews, and aesthetic education. Civilian morality acts as their backbone, with worldviews and aesthetic education complementing it, completing the idea of ethics. In the meantime, military national education and practical doctrine must take such ethics as their foundation. Our people are known to the world for doing good business. Overseas, Chinese people often endure incredible hardships, and hence many of them prospered in wealth. This serves as a pertinent example. But The reason why the people of our country have now become poor is that they have no moral education and therefore, it is inevitable that those who are from poor countries would not be able to join their efforts for the sake of fighting against foreign powers. At the same time, they would rather take their gamble with chance, than to work hard and support themselves. Therefore, if you want to promote practical doctrines, you must first cultivate morality and ethics among the people. As for the fact that military national doctrines cannot be separated from morality, this is more visible. Our country has long had the saying of *Yongyu Gongzhan, Qieyu Sidou* (brave when fighting against external powers, and fearful when fighting internally). Now the military has seen

numerous problems, and the prime reason for that is because those who are military professionals could not rule their troops with proper ethics. Educators are working not for the past, not for the present, but for the future. Even in ancient times, there was the saying of *Shinian Shumu, Bainian Shuren* (it takes 10 years to grow a tree, but it takes 100 years to cultivate a talented person) among educators. It can be seen that educators must have solid doctrines that shall not be altered or shaken throughout time, such as citizen morality. As of the others, judging by the needs of the times, shall also be activated, such as practical doctrine and military national doctrine. When we conduct our meetings, we must pay close attention to this.[86]

Cai Yuanpei raised moral education to the level of national responsibility, and hence established the core position of moral education in the education system of the Republic of China. After taking charge of Peking University, one of the major educational concepts that Cai Yuanpei emphasized was "using morality as the standard." In the speech *Address of Inauguration as President of PKU* (1917), Cai set out two major points based on his idea of "holding to the purpose," namely *Dili Dexing* and *Jingai Shiyou* (respect and love for your teachers and friends). Their details are as follows:

> One, hold on to your original purpose. All of our students must have had a certain purpose in mind when they come to us for education. And if they want to know if their purpose is right or wrong, they must know the nature of the university. Nowadays, it is evident that those students will join specific schools for mastering specific skills and obtaining specific knowledge. However, this is not the case for universities, because universities are supposed to be a place for advanced studies.
>
> Two, cultivate virtues. Society nowadays is becoming more perfunctory, morals are lost, and Beijing is particularly bad: actions of evilness and immorality can be seen everywhere, those who are tainted by such practices often find themselves disgraced. When our students finally graduate from universities, they should be able to love themselves without such vulgarity. What's more, the rise and fall of the country depend on the morality of its society. If such is the status of our morality, it is not hard to see that our future is grim. Therefore, we must have distinguished people who lead by example and correct the decadency.
>
> Three, respect, and love for your teachers and friends. Our teachers and staff must facilitate the study of our students. For this, our students shall show their gratitude. Hence, they should treat their teachers and the staff with sincerity and respect. As for their classmates, our students should especially love each other so that they can learn from each other. Not only should the relationship be open and honest, but they should also be willing to lend a helping hand. This

> is because they are studying in the same school, and the honor or disgrace of individual students is shared among all. If there are students who lack in their ethics and behave immorally, we shall all be resented by our society, and the disgrace shall persist even if the rest of us abide by the rules and morals perfectly. Hence, we must advise and encourage each other regarding this matter.[87]

2. *Participating in politics and patriotism.*

A notable feature during the period of the Republic of China is the successive political movements of university students. The strong sense of civic morality and national duty made students of Peking University a major influential force in the political movements in the Republic of China. Chen Pingyuan believes that the strong sense of social responsibility and political participation of Peking University students had to do with the ancient traditions of *Taixue*. On the one hand, Cai Yuanpei intended to weaken the traditional political intentions of *Xue Er You Ze Shi* among Peking University students, and even opposed students 'participation in radical political movements.' But on the other hand, Cai Yuanpai also showed a positive attitude towards the students' patriotism and encouraged students to focus on their academic learning, for the sake of promoting education to rejuvenate the country.

3. *Gathering all great learnings, and collecting knowledge and merits from all schools of thought.*

Peking University's spirit of tolerance is another notable feature in its educational concept. In 1919, Cai Yuanpei pointed out in the article *The Foreword for the Publishing of Peking University Monthly Journal*:

> Universities are supposed to be institutes of education that "gather all great learnings, and collect knowledge and merits from all schools of thought." *The Book of Rites* and *The Doctrine of the Mean* stated that: "All things in the world can grow together without harming each other, and various codes of conduct can be carried out at the same time without contradicting each other." This excerpt is a great description of such a definition. It works the same way as a person. Our organs are divided into right and left sides; air goes in and out as we breathe; we have tissues as soft as flesh and structures as hard as bones. They all seem to be contradictory pairs, while in reality, the two elements from each pair complement each other. As we can see in universities of various countries, idealism and materialism of philosophy, idealism and realism of literature and art, interference theory and laissez-faire theory of statistics, motivation theory and utilitarianism theory of ethics, optimism, and pessimism of world view, these pairs all coexist in contradictory pairs, and this is the general principle of freedom of thought, and the reason universities are institutes of "higher" education.[88]

Jiang Menglin also expressed similar views in *The Spirit of Peking University* (December 1923, 25th Anniversary of Peking University):

> The school has a spirit of generous tolerance. As the saying goes, *Zaixiang Duli Hao Chengchuan* (literally meaning: you can fit a ship in the stomach of a chancellor.) This is to say that a person can only become a competent chancellor when they have an appropriate sense of tolerance. And if you are narrow-minded and cannot tolerate all kinds of people, you are not worthy of such a high position. As seen in history, most of the prominent chancellors were people of tolerance, and they could preserve their being even in great adversities. Thousands of years later, the bones of their opponents and detractors had turned into dust; but the reputation of fame of these great chancellors still shines through the ages, "the longer it endures, the brighter it shines."
>
> This is also true for individuals as well as institutions. Any organization that can only tolerate one group of people or one kind of thinking, shall die out in the end because of the changes in the environment. Academic institutions that are intolerant and petty make little contribution to our society. Even if they do not die out, it would be the same as if they were dead nonetheless.[89]

Based on the above, with the basic philosophy of *Dili Dexing, Canzheng Yizheng* and *Nangkuo Dadian*, *Wangluo Zhongjia*, the "old Peking University" profoundly interpreted the cultural character of *Houde Zaiwu* (holding the world with virtue), *Tianxia Wei Gong* (sharing the world equally with others) and *You Rong Nai Da* (being tolerant to achieve something big) of Chinese universities.

b) The institutional design of Peking University – a case study of the Research Institute of Sinology.

The research institute system only existed in name before the Research Institute of Peking University was established. Cai Yuanpei presided over Peking University and focused on building research institutes, and hence the Graduate Education system of Chinese universities began to be implemented. In 1922, the Peking University Council discussed and adopted the *Organizational Outline of the National Peking University Research Institute.* The outline stipulates that the institute shall be divided into four departments: natural science, social science, Sinology, and foreign literature. Due to the limitations of funds and manpower, only the department of Sinology was opened in 1922. The research subjects of the department included Chinese literature, history, philosophy, linguistics, archaeology, and other fields, and they began to recruit graduate students. And hence, Peking University's research Graduate Education system moved onto the right track. As an important measure for Peking University to sort out the national heritage and protect the quintessence of the country, the system of the Research Institute of Sinology was the most effective evidence of the cultural character of the university.

During May 4th Movement and New Culture Movement, Peking University became the center of anti-traditional culture. A large number of Peking University professors and students were keen on new literature and wrote books to lead the trend. "However, the tradition of textual research still had an unshakable position in academia. Sinology was massively developed in the Republic of China period, and although the new culture was fascinating, the reputation of Sinology in the academic circle was still not to be underestimated."[90] The Research Institute of Sinology, as a bastion of Sinology in Peking University, took the lead in raising the banner of defending Sinology. In terms of the purpose for its establishment, the Research Institute of Sinology was mainly founded due to the reality of the loss of culture and to carry forward the inherent Chinese culture. In 1920, on the eve of the establishment of the Research Institute of Sinology, the *Plan of National Peking University Research Institute to Organize Sinology Materials* was promulgated. Its content is summarized as follows:

> The purpose of our school, regarding the present and future academia of the world, not only lies in the spreading and researching new knowledge but also in the responsibility of playing the role in carrying forward the inherent academics of our own country.
>
> The newly invented academics of the Western world are derived and are further promoted from their inherent academics as well, and hence, our school must carry forward our academics, for the sake of achieving discoveries.
>
> Recently, Western scholars have shifted their attention to the inherent academics of our country, and we are worried that our inherent academics might have little to offer to them. Moreover, our inherent academics are rather chaotic, and hence, Western scholars might become rather confused during their research, causing them to land at wrong conclusions, which may lead to undeserved despise and scorns towards our academics. Hence, Western scholars can't learn the truth of our inherent academics, unless it is carried forward by us. It is for this very reason that our school takes the carrying forward of our inherent academics as one of its greatest responsibilities.
>
> [...]
>
> Today, science is seeing rapid development. We should take the methods of the scholars from the era of Qianlong and Jiaqing, compliment them with a scientific methodology to achieve greater success, (To sort out Sinology, one must refer to scientific methods. Even if the scholars from the era of Qianlong and Jiaqing are still alive by this point, they would also approve such methods. Judging from the views of such scholars towards astronomy and mathematics,

> we can see that they would also understand the knowledge that we recently acquired. For example, Yu Yue, Huang Yizhou, and Sun Yirang are three of the most prominent examples that show this trend) sort them out with haste, and then our inherent academics shall be promoted and discoveries shall be made on its basis. Such will be the contribution we make to the academia of the world, and our culture shall hence be spread across the globe. This is the expectation and goal of our school.[91]

The document repeatedly emphasized that the study of Sinology should "bear the responsibility of carrying forward our inherent academics", and stated that "carrying forward the cultural spirit of our country is the expectation and goal of our school." This would be enough to suggest that the establishment of the School of Sinology of Peking University was a sign of Chinese people's cultural consciousness and a symbol of Chinese cultural renaissance. It is the result of the cultural character of Chinese universities. At the systematic level, it is generally believed that the institute system of the research institutes is based on that of Western universities, which is indeed the case. In ancient China, there was no equivalence to the "research institute" system for higher education. But on the other hand, the research institute system of Peking University also had its Chinese characteristics. For example, the *Announcement of Research Institute of Sinology* clearly stated that:

> We are establishing this school, whose research is based on text rather than discipline. This is mainly because our academia has always lacked the concept of division, and it is not easy to manage it by discipline before it is sorted out. Hence, this school is established to prepare for the division of subjects and disciplines in the future by sorting out our old knowledge, rather than sticking to our "own way" and reserving our broken knowledge, thinking that it can already compete with other disciplines. Although the system is fundamentally based on the three departments of Chinese literature, philosophy, and history, this is only because these departments have the most to do with Sinology. We are currently on a drive to find more talents, and that is the reason why the other departments were not yet established. Our department wholeheartedly welcomes the university to propose more subjects of natural sciences and social sciences accordingly, to research them separately, to find materials from ancient academics that are yet to be closely examined and explored by scientists, or materials that have been examined and explored, but not to the full extent. Hence, we could realize the real values behind these materials, and earn our rightful place in the history of science. This is our utmost wish.[92]

It can be seen from this that the school of Sinology was not trying to copy the Western style of the division of subjects. It intended to follow the Chinese tradition, blurring the boundaries among disciplines. As some scholars have said, "The deep meaning of this guiding concept also lies in the excavation of reasonable factors in the traditional academy system in terms of their cultural views, to preserve the traditional academic spirit, and integrate the two different educational ideals of China and the West."[93] This book believes that the traditional academy is indeed an important source of a system for modern Chinese universities. It is possible to almost accurately trace the Chinese elements of the system of the school of Sinology back to the traditional academy system.

c) Cultural symbols of Peking University.

The school song motto is a universally recognized symbol of university culture. However, Peking University acts with much "obscurity" regarding this point or rather giving off a "free and liberal" vibe. By now, there is still no such things as an official school motto or school song for Peking University. Some people call it the "regret" that lasted for over a century of Peking University, while others think it is an expression of Peking University's free character. This book looked for the cultural symbols of Peking University, and here, some clear and unmistakable and typical campus features and campus life examples are chosen as the subject matter to interpret the connotation behind the "old Peking University" cultural symbols.

1. Campus features – the university next to the Royal Palace.

The campus of Peking University is known as "the university next to the Royal Palace" and it has a long history. Zhang Zhongxing made a detailed examination of Peking University's origin in the article *The Library of Peking University*. The summary is below:

> The so-called school refers to the Imperial University of Peking founded by in the 24 years of Guangxu era (AD 1898). After many twists and turns, it finally became the "Peking University" we know today. The site of the school at the time of its establishment was originally the palace of the fourth daughter of the Emperor Qianlong of the Qing Dynasty (Princess Heshuo Hejia, married to Fu Longan, the son of Fu Heng), located on the north of the Mashenmiao West Street (a name derived from a temple of the same name), to the east of Jingshan. During the fifth year of the Republic of China (1916), a red building was built in the Han Garden of Dongshatan, which was later used as a liberal arts classroom, called the First Academy (School of the Literary) at the time, and the original Mashenmiao (renamed Jingshan East Street, and renamed not long ago as Shatan Back Street) site was renamed as the Second Academy

> (School of Science). Here, the expansion of the First Academy will be discussed. The red building is adjacent to the street facing south and is a 4-story brick-wood building. Behind it is a vacant land belonging to Songgong Mansion, and further northwest is the Songgong Mansion. First, in 1918, the school rented the vacant land as its sports field. By 1931, the school purchased the whole mansion altogether. The mansion had multiple layers of houses in good quality, and after some modification, the library and the Research Institute of Sinology were all moved into it. The library was in the front, and the school was in the back. The library had many precious books, and the school had many relics. Till this very day, these items are still considered to be a significant part of the precious possessions of Peking University.[94] (Zhang Zhonghang; *The Library of Peking University*)

From the red building to Shatan and the library, the architecture of the "old Peking University" always was an antique and exuded a unique temperament of Chinese classical culture. This is very different from the European-style and Westernized campus architecture at Tsinghua University, but it seems to align with that of Yanjing University, which is located right next to Tsinghua University. It is such a coincidence in history that the buildings and styles of the campuses of Peking University and Yan University are similar, and which seems to serve as a prophecy of the relationship between the two. Later, Peking University moved into Yanyuan, and the two merged into one. What remains unchanged is the external flavor of classical culture. The "old Peking University" is similar to Yanjing University while also remaining different from Yanjing University in many ways. Compared with Yanjing University and Tsinghua University, which are located far from the boisterousness of the city, Peking University is built next to the Royal Palace. This special campus makes the Chinese "flavor" of the "old Peking University" more distinctive. The scenery of *Yunli Dicheng Shuangfengque, Yanzhong Yushu Wanrenjia* (Hidden in the clouds, the phoenix eaves of the Forbidden City; covered in the mist and rain, trees among countless homes) may be an exclusively unique cultural symbol of the "old Peking University." Zhu Haitao reproduced the unique classical beauty of the old Peking University in the *article Peking University and the Peking University Insiders.* The following is an excerpt from the article:

> To the west of Shatan is the north exit of Beichizi Pond, which is the smoothest and most beautiful pond exit in Peiping. Along with full blossoms of lotus flowers, is a wide moat, an exquisite turret of the Forbidden City, a vermilion partition board, with windows and eaves with yellow-blue glaze occasionally appearing among the green trees. The flat asphalt road, covered with shades of acacia trees on both sides, stretches to the south, running among mansions with

> red doors. Looking west, the lotus of the moat ran straight along with the roots of the Forbidden City into the boundless cluster of gold, red, and yellow. You can see the stone bridge of the Shenwu Gate, the archway, the official waiting rooms in front of Mountain Jingshan, and the Royal Palace. I especially love wandering here in mist and rain. I saw with my own eyes the description of *Yunli Dicheng Shuangfengque, Yanzhong Yushu Wanrenjia*.
>
> It is in this environment that the students of Peking University are cultivated.[95]

Zhu Haitao's sentence "It is in this environment that the students of Peking University are cultivated" is rather intriguing. "It seems self-evident what kind of psychological expectations were formed when studying in a place where you can see the Royal Palace."[96] It seems that Chen Pingyuan always grasped the peculiar inherent characteristics of Peking University. According to Chen Pingyuan, "Even if the monarchy was abolished, the towering palace is still a kind of cultural symbol. Seeing this symbol every day, it is impossible to completely ignore it. No matter if you regard it with admiration or despise, one thing is certain: the implication of "politics," "power" and "a center" is hard to miss for any beholder. [...] It is rather interesting to think about how the students' political awareness will weaken if the Qing government chose some beautiful site in the suburb that was far away from the center of power when building the Imperial University of Peking."[97] This is indeed a unique perspective to understand the strong national consciousness and the obvious *shi* spirit displayed by the "old Peking University." History has testified that Peking University, as a university right next to the Royal Palace, did not turn a blind eye to politics and power. When observing the aforementioned School of Sinology from the perspective above, the subjective basis for the cultural character of Peking University behind the preservation of the quintessence of Chinese culture and the sorting of ancient Chinese cultural materials can be found. In short, the special royal site, classic architectural styles, and even the political consciousness constituted the "old" of the "old Peking University," and they interpreted the multi-level cultural connotation of "old Peking University."

2. Campus life – "The out-of-place campus culture of Peking University."

"Ideally speaking, Peking University's style is a mixture of the free and traditional Chinese academy style and the highly academic style of German universities in the late 19th century."[98] With this one sentence, Ye Wensin pointed out the two historical sources of the campus culture of Peking University. It is the strong traditional cultural atmosphere that made Peking University's campus life contradict that of other universities during the Republic of China. And sometimes, the campus life of Peking University even contradicted some of its Western characters. In the book *The Alienated Academy: Culture and Politics in Republican China, 1919–1937*, Ye Wensin described the student life of Peking University as follows:

> No matter in style or spirit, the student culture of Peking University is very different from the Westernized style popular in most of the Republic of China universities. This 4-story dormitory with a concrete structure built in 1935 is a typical epitome of this stark contrast. The construction of such a humble building-with 8 independent entrances and 30 fully equipped single rooms-may not be noticed at all at Yanjing University or St. John's University, but it caused a sensation at Peking University as it was Peking University's first dormitory building with modern sanitary equipment and hot water supply. As a metaphor for its social status in the school, this modern building stood alone in an open area, distanced from other buildings.
>
> [...]
>
> In Li Ji's memory of this incident, there is a "status quo" attitude that despises Western comfort. Li Ji was a student of the 1935 class, he prided himself as a "poor scholar," and later became a well-known socialist theorist.
>
> The typical image of Peking University is a "poor scholar" dressed in Chinese robes who perseveres under Spartan-like hardship.[99]

In the same book, Ye Wensin also provided a detailed record of the clothing of the students of Peking University:

> Earlier, during the May 4th Movement, Peking University students marched in their robes, shouted slogans, and took flags to the streets of Beijing. Blue cotton robes and black cloth shoes were the most common dresses in Peking University lecture halls and libraries, and occasionally you'd also see silk, fur, or gabardine. However, by the mid-1920s, it was pointed out that at least half of Peking University students had changed to clothing that resembles military uniforms, in dark green and light beige.
>
> During the Nanjing Decade, the trend of choosing university clothing prevailed. When uniforms were equated to party discipline and suits represented the laid-back urban rich, robes returned as a symbol of cultural identity in the 1930s.[100]

As an important part of campus life, these students living in the "old Peking University" were the most vivid cultural symbols of the university campus. From the turmoil of Peking University dormitory to the return of student robes, through the real and simple records of campus life of Peking University students, the deep Chinese cultural feelings contained in Peking University students were revealed. They called themselves "poor scholars" and despised the comfort of the Western lifestyle. They were born with the mentality of "being content in poverty and devoted to the spiritual," with strong traditional integrity similar to that of traditional scholars. It was for the sake of patriotism that they wore clothing that resembled military uniforms, and they wore traditional Chinese robes for the same reason. Such actions were the manifestation of a unique spirit of *shi*. From this perspective, the campus life of Peking University was filled with a strong sense of patriotism, and it was the most distinctive symbol of the *Tianxia Wei Gong* cultural character of Chinese universities.

In summary, based on the historical investigation and cultural interpretation of Peking University's educational concept, system design, and cultural symbols, it can be concluded that Peking University, as one of the most famous Chinese universities during the Republic of China period, interpreted several core concepts of the cultural character of Chinese universities comprehensively and profoundly. In short, under the influence of intellectuals, especially several university presidents, the cultural character of Peking University showed a relatively ideal state of development, which was finalized during the Republic of China and became the basis for the formation of Peking University models.

2. *Analysis of Tsinghua University's cultural character*

Tsinghua Academy, the predecessor of Tsinghua University, was originally a preparatory school for studying in the United States. Since it was built with the aid of the "refunded" Boxer Indemnity from the United States, it was called "the monument of national shame" by the older generations of teachers and students of Tsinghua University. Tsinghua Academy was founded in 1911. Upon the establishment of the Republic of China in 1912, it was renamed as Tsinghua School. In 1925, its University Department was established. In the same year, the Research Institute (Guoxuemen- Institute of Sinology Research) was opened. In 1928, it was renamed "National Tsinghua University." In 1937, by the time the university moved south, it already had considerable status and quite a reputation. Here, the cultural character of Tsinghua University that underwent examination mainly refers to the Tsinghua University from its establishment until its integration into the National Southwestern Associated University, that is, Tsinghua University during 1925–1937. This was the golden age of Tsinghua University and its ideal cultural character should be traced back to this time. Of course, Tsinghua's history is continuous, and it is difficult to make an effective distinction in terms of time, especially in terms of its educational concepts and its cultural character. Therefore, the materials cited here are not strictly limited to 1925–1937.

a) The educational concept of Tsinghua University.

Unlike Peking University, which has a long history, Tsinghua University, as a preparatory school for studying in the United States, was forced to generate a colonial character of "copying everything from the US." However, since President Cao Yunxiang or even before him, Tsinghua had the ambition to change the serious tendency of Westernization and to change Tsinghua into a Chinese school on its right. Therefore, Tsinghua University's educational concept in this period was very prominent through Chinese culture. The following is a detailed analysis of the two official constitutions along with the speeches and remarks of the three presidents during the period of Tsinghua's transition.

Although Tsinghua University and the "old Peking University" both followed the way of integrating Chinese and Western cultures in their educational concepts during this period, they had their own ways of doing so. Because of its rich history, the "old Peking University" intentionally weakened the elements of Chinese culture while maintaining the roots of Chinese culture. At this time, Tsinghua School, due to its inherent lack of cultural character, began to increase the involvement of Chinese culture right from the beginning of the establishment of its university department. In the words of Chen Pingyuan, "Peking University feared it was not Westernized enough, while Tsinghua feared it was not 'grassroots' enough" during this period.[101] However, their purposes of balancing Chinese and Western cultures were no different.

In the early years of the Republic of China, the *Constitution of Beijing Tsinghua School* (1914) clearly stated that Tsinghua School "was within the scope of making it possible to be admitted to an American university and receive the same education as those from the US."[102] It can be seen that by this time, Tsinghua School was still merely a complete preparatory school for studying in the United States, with strong colonial properties and no obvious cultural character. It was not until more than ten years later that the Tsinghua School established its university department, and the subsequent Regulations of National Tsinghua University (1928) announced that, "The National Tsinghua University, in accordance with the guidance by the Ministry of Education of the Republic of China, seeks the independent development of the Chinese nation in academics for the sake of completing the construction of a New China."[103] With this, Tsinghua University finally ushered in the opportunity for the growth of its cultural character. During this period, the educational concept of Tsinghua University changed, and the three principals Cao Yunxiang, Luo Jialun, and Mei Yiqi played important roles in this transformation.

Cao Yunxiang served as the president of Tsinghua University during 1922–1927. During his tenure, he reformed Tsinghua University and established a university department at Tsinghua School, and the concept of preserving Chinese culture was conceived, and the famous Institute of Sinology Research was established. This indicated that Tsinghua University's aim of changing from a preparatory school in the United States to a Chinese university has been formally put into motion under Cao Yunxiang's leadership. When Tsinghua's Institute of Sinology Research was established in 1925, Cao Yunxiang spoke at the opening ceremony, officially declaring Tsinghua as a university in China. The main ideas were as follows:

> Fourteen years ago, China and the United States agreed to establish a Tsinghua School to prepare students for studying in the United States. However, due to changes in the current situation, the vision of the Chinese education sector

has also changed. Hence, it was decided in the previous year that Tsinghua School should establish a university department, and for it to hopefully become a Chinese university. After spending the past year making preparations, we are finally ready today. From this point on, there shall be fewer and fewer students sent to the US, with more and more students admitted to the university.

The main purpose of the new plan is to grant the new education in China with self-sustaining abilities and gradually spread the new education throughout the nation. It is similar to planting trees for them to grow prosperously day by day. Therefore, to study various sciences, it is not necessary to follow only foreign books. That is, we can also make progress by studying Chinese books.

We must consolidate the foundation of the new university. Nowadays, the so-called new education in China is mostly copied from the education of the Western world. If we want to gain self-sufficiency, we must carefully base our studies on the Chinese cultural spirit. Therefore, the school is also establishing a school of research, dedicated to the classics and philosophy of ancient China.

Education is not merely reading and memorizing knowledge from books. Its purpose is to develop a noble and complete character within people and prepare them to enter society. If this cannot be accomplished, then education has lost its essence.[104]

Based on the above, Cao Yunxiang successfully transformed Tsinghua School into a Chinese university, which laid the first cornerstone for the formation of Tsinghua University's cultural character. In 1928, Luo Jialun took over as the president of Tsinghua University. During his tenure, he reformed Tsinghua from "the life of a preparatory school for the United States" to "the life of a complete national university," and contributed greatly to the formation of Tsinghua University's cultural character. In September 1928, Luo Jialun delivered a speech *Academic Independence and the New Tsinghua* at his inauguration ceremony, which could also be regarded as the declaration of Tsinghua University's independence, reaffirming Tsinghua University's responsibility to promote Chinese culture. The speech was as follows:

In this solemn auditorium, I officially announce the establishment of National Tsinghua University in this beautiful Tsinghua Park on behalf of the government. Starting from today, the life of Tsinghua School as a preparatory school for studying in the United States has transformed into the life of a complete national university.

We are putting a stop to the old system where all graduates would be sent to the United States, and we will recruit foreign professors on a purely academic basis. This is not because we do not pay attention to the goodwill of our friendly

> nations. On the contrary, we pay special attention to them. As a national university, we naturally want to study and promote our beautiful culture, but at the same time, we will also with enthusiasm to accept the Western scientific culture. But the methods we accept are different. We will not teach Chinese students to "come to study" the American standpoint, but we will continue to select a certain number of outstanding students with good grades through public examination to go to the United States for further study. We shall base ourselves on a Chinese standpoint, and hire prominent, first-tier scholars to "teach," rather than having "fourth-fifth-tier scholars." We shall recruit a group of truly accomplished scholars, especially scientists, to support the independence of our scientific education, transplant the "roots" of science into the "garden" of Tsinghua and the "soil" of the whole country of China, where they shall sprout branches, blossom and bear fruits.[105]

Luo Jialun's *Academic Independence and the New Tsinghua* inaugural speech was sincere, and it also emphasized the university's foundation of Chinese culture. Speaking about the fusion of Chinese and Western cultures, Luo Jialun stated, "We are a national university, so we would naturally want to study and promote our beautiful culture, but we also accept Western scientific culture with full enthusiasm" to emphasize Tsinghua University's educational concept of combining Chinese and Western cultures, to reverse and adjust the serious tendency of Tsinghua University's Westernization. From China's standpoint, Luo Jialun pointed out, "We shall recruit a group of truly accomplished scholars, especially scientists, to support the independence of our science education" and "transplant the roots of science into the soil of China." This emphasized the fundamental role of Chinese culture in the fusion of Chinese and Western cultures. After Luo Jialun, Mei Yiqi took over as the president of Tsinghua University from 1931, until he left Beijing for the United States in 1948, spending nearly two decades with Tsinghua University. Following the two, Mei Yiqi continued to adjust the Chinese and Western cultural characters of Tsinghua University, and also put forward some unique educational concepts which led to Tsinghua University's glory. This period was also praised by Tsinghua insiders as the "golden age" (1931–1937). It can be said that Tsinghua University's cultural character was finally formed under Mei Yiqi's dedicated management. Mei Yiqi's educational concepts were mainly reflected in two important documents. One was the *Education Policy of Tsinghua School* published by Mei Yiqi in December 1927:

> Educational concepts of Tsinghua University: Tsinghua University's educational concepts, in a nutshell, can be described as creating specialized personnel for social construction. This purpose is no different from other universities in of itself. However, because of the different circumstances of the schools, or the

> different opinions, the ways they work are also different. Tsinghua University has set up all its plans to meet the needs of the times and the environment to achieve this goal.
>
> [...]
>
> Sports: Tsinghua University still has a very important part of its course, which is sports. It is compulsory for all students, every semester. Even though the credits of sports shall not be counted in the total number of credits, those who do not pass the physical education will not be allowed to attend the graduation exam. During the recent seven or eight years, Tsinghua has abandoned the sense of competition among students in its purpose of physical education and instead has been paying more attention to the students' health. We may never know the general situation of our students if we only watch matches between sports teams, and hence we must ensure that every student can receive appropriate physical training, increase their physical strength, and we can ensure that they meet the needs of future matters by providing them with enough stamina to learn new knowledge. This is the real purpose of sports, and we should treat it as a task that is critical to every single one of our students. As for the sports competitions, our students can learn to cooperate and follow the rules of their teams within the process, and such practice has its value. However, when it comes to inter-school competitions, we tend to pay too much attention to the outcome of winning or losing, while ignoring the real importance of this competition, which is the training received by the participants and the spectators. By ignoring such importance, we are doing more harm than good, so the main purpose of school sports today should be changed accordingly.[106]

And the other was the *Inaugural Speech* where Mei Yiqi officially took office as the president of Tsinghua University in December 1931:

> The operation of a school, especially a university, should have two goals: one is to conduct academic research, and the other to cultivate talent. Tsinghua's economy and environment can achieve both of these goals, so we must work hard in this regard. Some people often use the development of quantity to estimate if the education fees are worth it, but this should be considered rather inappropriate. Because academic attainments cannot be measured in quantity. For us to pursue advanced research, two necessary conditions must be achieved: one, decent equipment; and two, competent professors. In regards to equipment, the issue is relatively easy to resolve. As long as we have the money, and we are willing to use it in this regard, this condition is not difficult to achieve. But the professors' side poses many difficulties. A decent university must have good professors. Mencius once said: "When we talk about our 'old country', we are not referring

> to the tall trees, but the governance and the prominent officials." I can now imitate this saying: "When we talk about 'university', we are not referring to the buildings but its great masters of knowledge." Our attainment of knowledge depends on the teaching and guidance of the professors; and our cultivation of spirits depends on the inspiration of the professors as well. However, to find such great professors is no small feat that can be instantly achieved. What we can do is keep our eyes out for them and recruit them, constantly. At the same time, we should respect the professors at school, which is a method of attracting more great professors, as well.[107]

Based on the texts above, the two outstanding features of Tsinghua University's educational concepts are sports and respect for masters. A basic feature of the *Education Policy of Tsinghua School* prepared by Mei Yiqi is to emphasize the importance of physical education in the university. The tradition of Tsinghua Sports did not start with Mei Yiqi, but was valued and further developed during Mei Yiqi's tenure. The real purpose of Mei Yiqi's promotion of sports was to "increase students' physical strength, ensuring that they meet the needs of future matters." The basic foothold was still the needs of the country. Using Western sports equipment and curricula to strengthen the people of China and the nation itself. It came with a certain mirroring of *Zhongti Xiyong*, but it was showing a kind of Chinese patriotic spirit. Besides, in the *Inaugural Speech* Mei Yiqi also proposed the classic university concept of "When we talk about 'university', we are not referring to the buildings but its great masters of knowledge." The Chinese culture is highly ethical, and its traditional education has always emphasized "respecting teachers and respecting the Tao." The tradition of respecting teachers in China is unmatched by Western culture. The reason why Mei Yiqi's "master" theory was widely accepted and recognized is closely related to traditional culture.

Looking at the information cited above, the three presidents all took the fusion of Chinese and Western cultures as their main stance. Breaking down their basic standpoints, they supported accepting and integrating with Western culture, but they worked towards preserving the foundation of Chinese culture, as well. The cultural character of Tsinghua University's concepts came from the latter.

b) System design of Tsinghua University—a case study of the Institute of Sinology Research at Tsinghua University.

Su Yunfeng pointed out that there are three backgrounds for the establishment of the Institute of Sinology Research at Tsinghua University.

First, during the May 4th New Culture Movement, Hu Shi advocated the use of scientific methods to *Zhengli Guogu* (organize and sort out the national heritage). In 1922, Peking University established the Research Institute of Sinology as a pioneer in the experiment, while hoping that Tsinghua University would follow suit.

Second, to improve the general status of Tsinghua University and achieve academic independence, Cao Yunxiang (the then president of Tsinghua School), planned to set up a university department, including a research institute.

Third, since the establishment of Tsinghua, it had been accused of neglecting Chinese culture and national conditions. Regarding this, Cao Yunxiang tried to make corrections.[108]

The three points above were all generated because of the external environment or external pressure. The establishment of the Research Institute of Tsinghua was a historical necessity in terms of its internal cultural character adjustment. During this period, Tsinghua Research Institute only managed one subject of Sinology, so the so-called "Research Institute" was the same as the "Institute of Sinology Research" in its substance. From 1925, when Wu Mi was appointed by President Cao to start the preparations for the establishment of Tsinghua Research Institute, to the preparation's premature ending in 1929, the preparation process lasted around four years. In September 1925, the director of the Research Institute, Wu Mi, gave a speech on the day of the opening of the Institute of Sinology Research, which was the *Purpose and Process of the establishment of the Research Institute in Tsinghua University*. The main content of the speech is as follows:

> The original intention of our school to set up a research institute is detailed in the booklet *The Relationship between Western Culture and China's Future* written by President Cao (published in May of the 13th year of the Republic of China). As for the detailed purpose and regulations of the Research Institute, they were written in *The Origin and Constitution of the Research Institute*. President Cao's intentions can be divided into three layers: (1) At the time of the evolution, Chinese people should conduct deep research of Western culture, for the sake of adopting and integrating their culture without hindrance; (2) All aspects of Chinese inherent culture (E.g. politics, economics, philosophy) should also be thoroughly studied, and then applied to today's national economy and people's livelihood, to take appropriate measures and solve all kinds of important issues; (3) To achieve the two purposes mentioned above, there must be a high-level academic institution, for university graduates and those who have a solid and considerable foundation to be furtherly educated, saving them the effort and money of going to the Western world and to eliminate the disadvantage of learning knowledge that is not compliant with the situation in China. This is the original intention of the school's establishment of a research institute.
>
> In short, the purpose and effect of the research institute are beyond the educational need of ordinary general specializations. It is appropriate for our school to change its policies, formulate a new set of methods for sending

students to the United States, establish schools of general specializations, and to implement a research institute. The research institute was originally planned to be very considerable in size, with various subjects (such as natural sciences, social sciences, etc.) under its management. Due to financial constraints, it could only run one subject of Sinology first. Moreover, the study of Chinese culture is particularly important nowadays, and everything regarding this matter has been detailed in *The Origin of the Research Institute.*

"Chinese classics since the Han Dynasty have seen considerable interpretations, but most of the research done is still flawed due to the lack of materials and unsound methods, and the existing research must be accordingly complemented and corrected by later generations. Besides, more and more ancient historical materials are being discovered in recent times, and are still waiting to be studied in detail, like newly found materials on lifestyle aspects, such as the state of life in past dynasties, changes in speech, the evolution of customs, the rise and fall in morals, politics, religion, and academics. Along with materials regarding nature, such as the migration of the rivers, the countless names, and properties of animals and plants. Although our predecessors made records, these aspects all need their special classification for the sake of research." And "this kind of career is ultimately beyond the reach of individuals and ordinary schools."

Hence, we shall dedicate the first department of our Research Institute to Sinology. The so-called Sinology refers to the whole of Chinese academic culture, and its way of research pays special attention to the correct and precise methods (the so-called 'scientific method' now) and draws on the achievements of Western scholars in the study of Eastern languages and Chinese culture. And this is the difference of our Research Institute from other domestic research scholars. Here, the status of the Research Institute shall be clarified as: (1) It is not part of Tsinghua University's undergraduate or graduate school, as it is a special institute dedicated to advanced studies; (2) It is not established for the sake of training teachers for any certain school, as its purpose is to cultivate renaissance talents and masters of knowledge.

The nature of the Research Institute shall also be clarified hereby as (1) researching advanced academic learning; (2) focusing on personal guidance (for detailed methods, see the *Constitution of the Research Institute*).[109]

As Cao Yunxiang stated in his *Address at the Start of the Semester*: "Nowadays, the so-called new education in China is mostly copied from the education of the Western world. If we want to gain self-sufficiency, we must study the Chinese cultural spirit carefully." The Institute of Sinology Research of Tsinghua University can be considered as a symbol of the Chinese cultural spirit of Tsinghua University. Wu Mi's *Purpose and*

Process of the establishment of Research Institute in Tsinghua University described in detail the establishment of the Institute of Sinology Research, including the reasons for its establishment, the status, and the nature of the research institute.

In September 1925, the school formally promulgated the *Constitution of the Research Institute*, which listed six major aspects of the Research Institute, including its purpose, its organization, and its subjects, and hence the Research Institute officially became the main institution of Tsinghua University. Generally speaking, as the research institutes of Peking University and Tsinghua University emerged sequentially, and they were both famous universities in China, most commentators would take up the view that they learned from each other. One of the main points of this view is that Tsinghua University's Institute of Sinology Research was founded later than Peking University's Research Institute of Sinology, and so it imitated its counterpart in Peking University and achieved great success, even surpassing its PKU counterpart in some ways. Chen Pingyuan believes that Tsinghua University's Institute is a historical miracle that cannot be copied in future generations, it can be and interpreted as a miracle from three perspectives, the institution, the teacher, and the student.

This book believes that compared with Peking University's establishment of the Research Institute of Sinology, Tsinghua University's founding of the Institute of Sinology Research had more "sincerity," and "determination" with an "older" system. During this period, "Peking University feared it was not Westernized enough, while Tsinghua feared it was not 'grassroots' enough". Imagine how Peking University, which "feared it was not Westernized enough" could have competed with Tsinghua University, which "feared it was not 'grassroots' enough," when it came to being "grassroots?"

Compared with Peking University, Tsinghua University was established with the shameful refund of Boxer Indemnity, and hence, it was born with an inscrutable "sense of humiliation," and the revival of Chinese culture was particularly strong within their will of strengthening the country. However, Peking University, which was born in the late Qing Dynasty, was particularly "distanced" from Chinese culture after the May 4th Movement. And hence, Tsinghua had more "sincerity." Compared with Peking University, Tsinghua University had been severely misunderstood and blamed due to its special American colonial character. As a result, Tsinghua University urgently needed an opportunity to prove its cultural character to highlight its Chinese cultural spirit. Peking University did not have such needs. This led to Tsinghua University having more "determination." Compared with Peking University, Tsinghua University was more daring to act and express their purpose during the establishment of its Institute of Sinology Research, because of the two above-mentioned factors. For example, it was also more formal by following the traditional academy system and writing the rules and regulations. It was mentioned in the *Constitution of the Research Institute* that "Regarding the general system, this institute follows the example of ancient academies and British universities." Since Peking University itself already possessed a strong resemblance to ancient academies, this was not particularly emphasized the "academy" form of the Research Institute of Sinology. And hence, Tsinghua Institute had an "older" system.

c) Cultural symbols of Tsinghua University.

Look at the cultural symbols of Tsinghua University, it can be observed that Tsinghua University was a lot more "well-disciplined" than Peking University. School mottos and school songs were listed in its rules and regulations. It had documented monuments around the campus, and in particular, its campus culture had a unique "serious and neat" style.

1. SCHOOL MOTTO AND SCHOOL SONG.

1) The motto of Tsinghua is *Ziqiang Buxi, Houde Zaiwu* (Always exert oneself in ceaseless betterment, holding the world with virtue).

This sentence was a quote from *Zhouyi: Tianxing Jian, Junzi Yi Ziqiang Buxi* (The Heavens are in motion ceaselessly; The enlightened exert themselves constantly) and *Dishi Kun, Junzi Yi Houde Zaiwu* (While the Earth is supportive and natural, only the virtuous can bear the utmost); In 1914, Liang Qichao came to the school to give a speech on "intelligentleman," quoting *Zhouyi* and encouraging Tsinghua students to cultivate themselves according to the standards of "intelligentlemen." After this speech, the president Zhou Yichun formally decided to use *Ziqiang Buxi, Houde Zaiwu* as the motto of Tsinghua University, laying the tone for Tsinghua's cultural character of self-improvement.

2) Tsinghua School Song.

> *The West Mountain shows its hazy greens, and the East Sea shines its brightest beams. How solemn is our school, sitting in the center with esteem? Eastern and Western cultures in our hall gather, expressing their excellence together; comradery shall expand, bringing glory to our nation land. The students shall embark on a journey, the students shall embark on a journey, to a place where guidance is great and joy is boundless, and their effort must be ceaseless. For the Heaven remains in constant motion, and self-betterment must be achieved with determination.*
>
> *In a campus surrounded by books, and bookshelves, we explore for profound knowledge and trace back to history. The old and the new way of governance integrated into one, like all paths would finally lead to one destination. Enjoy mastering the knowledge as if we enjoy a grand meal, our intelligence plumps up as we feast. Always remember to stick to the virtuous path so that our heart does not sway. Always remember to stick to the virtuous path so that our heart does not sway. Be humble, like the ocean,*

> *so that all rivers converge to us. Shine with a mind full of knowledge. Shine, shine, shine with a mind full of knowledge.*
>
> *Put forth tolerance and experience, followed by aesthetics. Establish virtues and voice out opinions, East and West alike. Who could achieve it? It is none other than our school. Treat everyone equally to demonstrate the magnanimity of a great university. What a great scenery, what a great gathering of exceptional talents. What a great scenery, what a great gathering of exceptional talents. Countless students collectively formed a string of loyalty to the school. The glory to the name of our school is boundless. Boundless, Boundless, the glory to the name of our school is boundless.*

The Tsinghua school song appeared around 1923, and it echoed the school motto. As the Tsinghua School was not satisfied with the over-Americanization of the old school song, it publicly solicited a new school song. Wang Luanxiang, who was a Chinese and Philosophy lecturer at Tsinghua at the time, submitted the entry of *Xishan Cangcang*, and it was finally decided as a school song. It followed the education philosophy of "Fusion of the East and the West, integration of the ancient and the modern." On the one hand, it advocated for the Eastern and Western cultures in our hall gather, expressing their excellence together," and "establishing virtues and voicing out opinions, East and West alike." On the other hand, it emphasized "the old and the new way of governance integrated into one, as all paths would finally lead to one destination." The school song was written in classical Chinese, and many of its words and sentences can be found in famous classic literature, showing the connotation of Chinese traditional culture. For example, *Datong* (together) originated from *Book of Rites: Ritual, Fuying* (always remember) came from *Book of Rites: The Doctrine of the Mean* and the term *Zuotu Youshi* (surrounded by books and bookshelves) can be traced back to the allusion of "Yang Wan's reading" in the Tang Dynasty. In addition to philosophy and style, the excellent traditional spirit of China contained in the school song was also obviously present, such as the fusion of East and West, the spirit of self-improvement ("for the Heaven remains in constant motion, and self-betterment must be achieved with determination"), as well as the spirit of scholarship ("we explore for profound knowledge and trace back to history") and so on.

2. Campus monuments.

Tsinghua's history is full of great talent, ranging from patriotic students with a heart of gold to great masters with timeless status. Tsinghua engraved their stories on the monuments which became the unique cultural symbols of the Tsinghua University campus. For example, the broken monument of March 18th.

At the foot of Tsinghua North Mountain, the monument was restructured from white marble remnants. The front side reads "the broken monument of March 18th." The inscription is as follows: the monument was built in 1926 to commemorate the martyr Wei Jiesan, who was killed by the government under Duan Qirui during the anti-imperialist patriotic demonstration on March 18th. Wei Jiesan, a native of Mengshan, Guangxi, was a first-year student of our university at the time of his sacrifice. He said before his death: "My heart is at ease, but China must become strong!" Death took him when he was only the age of twenty-three. As mentioned in the inscription, the monument commemorates Wei Jiesan. He did not fear the oppressive power of the warlord government and took to the streets to put pressure on the government and to strengthen China. Courage is commendable. It was also commendable that Tsinghua was not afraid of the oppressive government and named him a hero of Tsinghua.

Wang Guowei Monument was built in 1929 at the foot of the back mountain at the northern end of the first classroom building of Tsinghua. The front reads "Monument of Master Wang Jingan from Haining." The inscription was written by Chen Yinke, a professor at Tsinghua Institute of Sinology Research at the time. The inscription reads as follows:

> Two years after the suicide of Master Wang, his fellows at Tsinghua Research Institute still couldn't help but think about him. Many of his disciples were grateful for his years of guidance and cultivation and wished that there was something to remember him by. They all suggested that his story should be inscribed into a monument, to show his moral courage to later generations. Hence, they came to me, Chen Yinke, for a brief article dedicated to him and his life. I tried to reject their request to no avail, so I shall carefully collect the stories of Master Wang, and tell them to the world after his time.
>
> The article is as follows:
>
> When a *Shi* studies and goes into academics, they always aim to free their heart and mind from the prison of secular truth, and hence the truth is revealed. Not having the freedom of the heart and mind is a punishment worse than death. The essence of truth that countless scholars have devoted their lives to and died for, is not something that can be understood by lowly people. You chose the way of death to show the independence and freedom of your heart and mind, not to settle some personal grudge or to maintain the existence of a family. Sadness reigns! We shall put this stone here near our classroom, for all to feel the solemnity and remembrance. It shall tell the world of the courage of this philosopher, and it should tell the hardship of finding the truth, as even two lifetimes would not be enough to discover it. The articles written by him might sometimes be out of chapter order, and the theories developed by him might not be iron-clad, but his spirit of independence, along with his thoughts on freedom

> shall never be forgotten in a million years. They shall shine the eternal light that exists as long as the sky, the earth, the sun, the moon, and the stars.

The death of Wang Guowei, a late Qing dynasty minister, a master of Sinology, and a professor of Tsinghua University shocked many people. Tsinghua's setting up of the monument was not because he was a teacher of the emperor of the late Qing Dynasty, nor because he was a professor at Tsinghua University, but due to the respect towards the vastness of his mastery of Sinology, and his great courage of dying for his country. Chen Yinke's open praising of Wang Guowei's spirit of independence and freedom with "his spirit of independence, along with his thoughts on freedom shall never be forgotten in a million years. They shall shine the eternal light that exists as long as the sky, the earth, the sun, the moon, and the stars" while the government was pushing for party education was truly a commendable effort. Tsinghua did not fear the power of the Government of the Republic of China, and it was also commendable that Tsinghua University dared to erect a monument with such inscriptions on its campus.

3. Campus life.

The campus life of Tsinghua University is very different from that of the "old Peking University." Enthusiastic sports, plain campus robes, and strict student rules marked the distinctive cultural character of Tsinghua life. As mentioned above, one of Tsinghua University's unique educational concepts was the emphasis on sports, which was reflected in campus life in the way of numerous sports activities. In *The Campus Culture of Tsinghua University in the 1920s and 1930s*, Huang Yanfu described the campus sports of Tsinghua University as follows:

> When talking about the campus culture of Tsinghua University in its early years, it is truly unavoidable to talk about sports.
>
> Sports in Tsinghua had a special status ever since the school was established, and their subsequent development was even more prosperous. Physical education in Tsinghua is not so much a course (Tsinghua is one of the earliest schools in China to include physical education as a required course), but rather it was a custom, a habit, a school lifestyle, and a tradition. At that point, Tsinghua University truly achieved a fear – everyone participated. In short, sports were an important part of Tsinghua campus culture during the 1920s and 1930s.
>
> From the beginning, the main purpose of the sports at Tsinghua was not to train a small number of athletes but to improve and cultivate the physical and personal strength of Tsinghua insiders. That is, not only to correct the frail stereotype of Chinese scholars, but also to build with young students the idea of unity, cooperation, courage, tenacity, and the noble spirit of patriotism and collectivism.[110]

Yeh Wen-Hsin once said: "The influence of the United States dominated Tsinghua's physical education classes, even though this was inspired by the patriotism of the Chinese people."[111] Vice versa, Tsinghua's physical education classes were fundamentally dominated by Tsinghua's traditional spirit of *Shi*, even under the influence of American factors. The sports facilities and courses on the Tsinghua campus were indeed from the United States, but without the patriotism of all the teachers and students of Tsinghua University, it would be difficult to tell if these facilities and courses would be as popular. The starting point of the sports in Tsinghua was meant to foster one's personality for the sake of meeting the needs of the country. It was deeply rooted in the traditional Chinese culture of self-cultivation and governing the country, which was a concrete expression of the cultural character of *Tianxia Wei Gong* of Chinese universities.

The clothing of students is an important symbol of campus cultural life. In the book *From Tsinghua School to Tsinghua University*, Su Yunfeng described the clothing of Tsinghua University students as follows:

> "Tsinghua students are spiritually pursuing American culture, but they are not Americanized in their clothes. The school does not have regulations that require students to wear uniforms, so there were different forms of clothing among students, from Eastern to Western, from intellectual to the military, almost all types and kinds of clothing could be found. It can be divided into three types: Chinese, Western, and Chinese-Western. Chinese and Chinese-Western styles were most prevalent. Generally, most of the students would wear blue Chinese gowns or Western suit pants with a Chinese gown or cloth shirt covering the outside. Therefore, they would seem relatively frugal."
>
> In conclusion, the clothes of the students at Tsinghua University were mostly Chinese robes, gowns, shirts, and pants crafted from cotton or silk. In terms of color, black and white were the most common. It was just as Liang Shiqiu said, they seemed quite frugal, indeed.[112]

According to Su Yunfeng, "Tsinghua students are spiritually pursuing American culture, but they are not Americanized in their clothes." It is still unclear whether this statement was accurate. The "not Americanized" part was right, while there might be some problems in the first part of the sentence. This book believes that Tsinghua students, as preparatory students that are planning to study in the United States, would naturally take American culture as their target of pursuit, and hence their minds were certainly deeply affected by American culture. However, it might be a bit too much to say that their spiritual target of pursuit lay within American culture. Tsinghua students were all Chinese. Although their minds were influenced by a considerable amount of American culture and its elements in spirit, they still had the spirit of Chinese culture. As Su Yunfeng said in this quotation, the clothing style of Tsinghua students was quite simple and frugal, and that sentence was trying to brandish the traditional character of Tsinghua students, which was thrift and frugal.

Student rules are a must for campus life. In terms of student rules, Tsinghua University and the "old Peking University" were indeed very different, and at times, fully contradictory. The educational concept of "old Peking University" advocated freedom and leniency, hence its campus discipline was relaxed with very few regulations for students. But Tsinghua was a place where rules were very strict. Judging from this quotation, Tsinghua students were extremely "restricted." Su Yunfeng shared details in *From Tsinghua School to Tsinghua University*:

> Regarding the life management of Tsinghua students, in addition to various systematic management rules, the president also had the power to announce new entries and rules at any time. The faculty members also had the authority of supervising and managing students, but the actual management was handled by *Zhaiwu Chu* (services office), which was later turned into *Xundao Chu* (student's affairs office). Under the Zhaiwu Chu, student self-governing organizations were established. Monitors of different grades, classes, and rooms, the student on duty, community representatives, along with the chief of the middle section and the head of the higher section were elected by students, enforcing self-discipline through a hierarchical structure.
>
> For example, matters such as students' living, eating, taking classes, self-study, sports, extracurricular activities, leaves, school trips, rewards, and penalties, etc., were all within the scope of their management. The above-mentioned life management regulations were indeed strictly enforced by *Zhaiwu Chu*.
>
> Li Xianwen once said: It didn't matter if it is common life affairs, sports, shaving, bathing, miscellaneous expenses (bank passbooks), family letters, etc., they were all under strict management. Normally, you are not allowed to leave the school. When you see the president of the university, you must stand upright with your hands on both sides. The school punished students with excessively strict rules, such as compulsory expulsion if they fail in two subjects under the English course. Those who violated the school rules were also likely to be expelled. Self-study in the evening was monitored by teachers. Students from the higher section were allowed to smoke and enter the city freely, but leave was required for overnight stays.
>
> Liang Shiqiu also stated: The school stipulates to take a bath at least twice a week, but some people still do not comply. The school prohibited reading novels, and offenders would be put in detention on Saturday afternoons. Once someone is caught with theft, they would be immediately expelled ...
>
> Tsinghua had strict management and a high rate of elimination. To maintain the tranquility and order of the campus and to facilitate the smooth process

> of teaching and academic activities, students with poor grades and violations might have faced punishments as harsh as expulsion. A large number of dropouts showed that there were students who simply could not keep up, and expulsions were mostly results of rule violations. There were many reasons for the student movements, and the patriotic sentiment was only one of them. However, it was also likely to be an excuse. For example, students always liked to boycott classes and exams in the name of patriotism during the exam period, especially those with poor grades, misbehaving records, and those who were political enthusiasts. Tsinghua applied the "iron fist" type of management. Although it increased the cost of school education, conversely, if it were not so, Tsinghua would have become a holy place for student unrest like other universities, with noisy protests everywhere and no one calm enough to conduct any academic research. Tsinghua would no longer be Tsinghua.[113]

After reading the texts above, it is evident that the students of Tsinghua University had to abide by very strict rules, which was quite different from the situation of Peking University. However, as Su Yunfeng said, "If it were not so, Tsinghua would have become a holy place for student unrest like other universities, with noisy protests everywhere and no one calm enough to conduct any academic research. Tsinghua would no longer be Tsinghua." This makes sense. Tsinghua did not inherit the free atmosphere of ancient Chinese academies, but it demonstrated the strict spirit of the ancient imperial examination system in which only the superiors were chosen to remain. In short, the reason why Tsinghua University and Peking University are unique by their right is not the difference in the degree of cultural character, but, on the common premise of taking Chinese and Western cultural integration as the basic concept and taking Chinese culture as the foundation, they had different expressions that showed different cultural characters.

3. *Analysis of the cultural character of National Southwestern Associated University (NSAU)*

If National Southwestern Associated University is a miracle in the history of education, then the cultural character of NSAU is an important internal cause of these miracles. NSAU was a university that began and ended with the Second Sino-Japanese War. After the July 7th Incident, National Peking University and National Tsinghua University from Peiping and the private Nankai University from Tianjin were ordered by the Ministry of Education to first move to Changsha in the south to establish the National Changsha Temporary University. Later, as Nanjing fell, the university was moved eve further to Kunming, with its name changed to National Southwestern Associated University. It remained there until its disbandment during the fall of 1946. Before the war, Peking University, Tsinghua University, and Nankai Univerisity were already three of the most prestigious universities in China. They adhered to the concept of fusing Chinese and Western cultures, they safeguarded the foundation of Chinese culture, and they shared a common set of educational concepts. In terms of specific educational concepts, school systems, and campus culture, they each had their unique characteristics, forming their university styles, thus creating a highly diverse landscape. Peking University had its open-mindedness and freedom, Tsinghua had its strict and serious attitude, and Nankai had its *Yungong Yunneng* (fair public, fair abilities). NSAU was composed of three schools, "but after all, it should no longer be just Peking University, just Tsinghua University or just Nankai University, but an independent university with unique spiritual temperament and cultural character."[114] Here, looking at NSAU as the object of the investigation, the work examines the unique cultural character of NSAU as a whole.

a) The educational concept of NSAU.

Zhongbang Sanshizai, Xitu Yiqiannian (China achieved in thirty years what took the Western world a thousand years) NSAU was called a miracle in the history of world education. John Israel of the University of Virginia in the United States pointed out that, "NSAU was the most interesting university in Chinese history. Under the most difficult conditions, it preserved the best education methods and cultivated the best talents."[115] How did NSAU achieve such a great feat? This has become an interesting "mystery of the Sphinx" in the history of education.

The establishment and development of NSAU were directly influenced by the Kuomintang government's educational policies and financial support at the time, and its great success relied on the wisdom of school administrators. Looking back on this glorious history, the educational concepts of NSAU were the foundation of its success. It is worth noting that nominally after the three schools moved south and merged into NSAU, the three respective presidents, Jiang Menglin of Peking University, Mei Yiqi of Tsinghua University, and Zhang Boling of Nankai University, worked as standing committee members and co-chaired NSAU. However, in reality, Zhang and Jiang rarely appeared in the school, and Mei Yiqi was the de facto president of the school for more than eight years. Hence, the educational concepts of NSAU were greatly influenced by Mei Yiqi.

In the Republic of China before 1937, especially during the May 4th New Culture Movement period, the fusion of Chinese and Western cultures in Chinese universities still faced many disputes and conflicts. In contrast, during the Second Sino-Japanese War, Chinese universities enjoyed a much smoother and more successful integration of Chinese and Western cultures. In 1937, the war fully broke out. The Kuomintang established the basic policy of *Zhanshi Yingzuo Pingshi Kan* (treating wartime as usual days) and promulgated a series of education policies.

For example, the *Guidelines for Education Supervisory at the Time of General Mobilization* promulgated in August 1937 stipulated that "when a war occurs, schools and other cultural institutions at all levels throughout the country should remain calm and work under the principle of maintaining coursework at their original site." It also emphasized that "the training of schools of all levels should strive to meet the needs of national defense, but the curriculum changes must still comply with the scope set by the Ministry."[116] *The Outline of the Implementation Plan for Education of All Levels during Wartime* (April 1938) stipulated that "the purpose of education shall align with the purpose of politics, [...] new systems should be created so that everything can remain suitable with the national conditions."[117]

Judging from the two documents of the National Government of the Republic of China, on the one hand, they provided a system guarantee and policy support for the smooth development of education during wartime. On the other hand, they also intended to strengthen the government's control over education. In this intricate and delicate environment, NSAU effectively maintained the balance between university autonomy and government authority, and on the other hand, it also ideally balanced the proportion of Chinese and Western culture in universities. Overall, NSAU maintained the autonomy of university education to a certain extent, and the integration of Chinese and Western cultures in the university ensured the formation of the ideal character of NSU. Among them, the role of Mei Yiqi, the president of NSAU, was extremely important. Mei Yiqi's educational concepts for NSAU were mainly reflected in the article *Daxue Yijie* written in 1941. The following is a brief quote:

> Today's university education in China, when traced back to its origins, is transplanted from the Western world. It is one thing when we examine it from a system viewpoint, and it is another thing when we examine it from a spiritual standpoint. As far as the system is concerned, there are no organizations with similar forms in the history of Chinese education. As for the spirit, the experiences of civilized human beings are roughly the same, and there should be some common elements shared by Chinese and Western cultures. Civilized human life depends on nothing but two major aspects: *Ji* and *Qun*, in other words, "individual" and "group." The biggest purpose of education is to facilitate some level of alignment between the "individual" within the "society" and the "society" filled with "individuals," and hence we let the two elements complement and cultivate each other. If that should be the case, there shall be no difference between China and the Western world, no distinction between the ancient and the new, and the world shall be fully connected as it were one complete entity.
>
> [...]

As *Da Xue* was written, the ultimate goal and the greatest spirit of learning were revealed. In the opening chapter of the book *University*, it was clearly stated, *Daxue Zhidao, Zai Mingmingde, Zai Xinmin, Zai Zhiyu Zhishan* (The way of greater learning is to promote noble ethics, to enlighten the people, and only rest when the highest good is achieved). As far as its purpose is concerned, it is a matter of *Gewu* (observing the world), *Zhizhi* (understanding the world), *Chengyi* (becoming sincere), *Zhengxin* (becoming morally upright), *Xiushen* (cultivating virtues), and these parts belong to *Ming Mingde* (promoting noble ethics). On the other hand, *Qijia* (family harmony), *Zhiguo* (governance), and *Pingtianxia* (unity of the world) belong to *Xinmin* (enlightening the people).

Xue Ji stated, "After years of learning, if one can understand things comprehensively and spread such understanding to other fields, while sticking to their own belief, not being easily shaken, then we say their education is complete. After such completion, they should have enough to change the people and create good ethics. Those who are close will follow them and those who are far away shall yearn to join them in the University way." Within this, *Zhilei Tongda* (understanding things comprehensively and spreading such understanding to other fields) and *Qiangli Bufan* (sticking to own beliefs, not being easily shaken) can be seen as footnotes of *Ming Mingde. Huamin Chengsu* (changing the people and create good ethics) and *Jinyue Yuanhuai* (Those who are close will follow them and those who are far away shall yearn to join them) can be seen as footnotes of *Xinmin*.

Mencius also said in the chapter of *Jin Xin* that one should cultivate themselves and the world would achieve a peaceful rule. Xunzi's theory of "Those who try to understand themselves will be wise, and those who try to surpass themselves will be strong." Also falls within the scope of *Ming Mingde*, and Xunzi also discussed the importance of group life and suggested that the life of a group must be regulated with rules, which can be seen as a further explanation of the true meaning of the word *Xinmin*.

In short, although the ideas of Confucianism are rather diverse, their emphasis on the philosophy of life and the ideals of education such as the two steps of *Ming Mingde* and *Xinmin* remain consistent.

When we look at today's university education, it would seem at the first glance that it does not have much to do with the meaning of *Ming Mingde* and *Xinmin*, but if you look closely, you can see that the various measures of the university education today all fall within the scope of the meaning of these two concepts. However, there is still a lack of understanding and practice. The establishment of university courses, and all other aspects that belong to the scope of teaching affairs, from the teaching of basic academics to the research of specialized subjects, should be considered as a part of *Gewu Zhizhi*, and hence

> a part of *Ming Mingde*. School life outside the curriculum, that is, all kinds of student and teacher affairs such as the teacher's self-cultivation, their pursuit of study, how they treat the world and others around them, these elements shall all be of great benefit to the youth. And such benefits shall be manifested through the process of *Gewu Zhizhi* and other aspects of life. As for the setting of various humanities and social sciences programs, the group extracurricular activities of students, and all the efforts of the teacher to the general society as a citizen, all of these could be seen as the preparation for knowledge, or the preview of fieldwork, or the establishment of an atmosphere. Once a student graduates, leaves school, and contributes to society, they simply cannot deny that the factors above inherently contributed to their effort. This is also the *Xinmin* effect of university education.[118]

Judging from the content of the quotation, *Daxue Yijie* revealed its aim right from the beginning, "Today's university education in China, when traced back to its origins, is transplanted from the Western world. It is one thing when we examine it from a system viewpoint, and it is another thing when we examine it from a spiritual standpoint. As far as the system is concerned, there are no organizations with similar forms in the history of Chinese education. As for the spirit, the experiences of civilized human beings are roughly the same, and there should be some common elements shared by Chinese and Western cultures." Mei Yiqi first affirmed that Chinese universities are the product of the fusion of Chinese and Western cultures. This is also the fundamental idea of all of his ideas regarding universities. *Daxue Yijie* emphasized that Chinese universities have two major purposes, one is *Ming Mingde* and the other is *Xinmin*. This is concrete evidence that Mei Yiqi's university concepts are based on Chinese culture. Some scholars believe that the educational concepts of NSAU are tales of the old path of *Zhongti Xiyong*. "Because among the professors of NSAU, basically all of them had been influenced by traditional Chinese culture since childhood, and those who studied abroad mostly went to Europe and the United States. Therefore, every one of them had in their mind the question about how to treat Western culture. To be fair, the *Zhongti Xiyong* theory by Zhang Zhidong was the motto of most people in NSAU."[119] It is undeniable that from the perspective of Mei Yiqi's educational concepts, they indeed had a hint of *Zhongti Xiyong*. But in fact, it was massively different from Zhang Zhidong's version of *Zhongti Xiyong*. The former emphasized that Chinese culture was the basis, while the latter strived to protect the system of Chinese culture, which was fundamentally different. Since this is not the simple "recycling" of the phrase, it is probably most appropriate if the term *Zhongti Xiyong* was given a new interpretation before it was used to describe the educational concept of Mei Yiqi or the entire NSAU. That is to say, the fundamental value of *Zhongti Xiyong* of NSAU lay in the notion of keeping Chinese culture at its roots while seeking a fusion of Chinese and Western cultures.

Another important document embodying Mei Yiqi's educational concept is *Industrial Education and Industrial Talents* published in 1943. This article is a collaboration between Mei Yiqi and Pan Guangdan, and the ideas in the text mainly were originated from Mei Yiqi. The following quotes are the relevant segments to interpret Mei Yiqi's educational ideas of cultivating "generalist talents:"

> To create a generalist talent, the engineering colleges of universities must add courses on general knowledge, while reducing the courses on specialized techniques. The construction of the industry depends on technology and machinery, but it does not rely on them alone. Without financial resources and raw materials, the machines couldn't achieve anything. So, a generalist talent must have a full understanding of economic geography, economic geology, and even general economic science. Without manpower, or proper coordination and setup of personnel, no matter how many horsepowers the machine possesses, it will still not start, or it may stop abruptly even if it somehow started. Therefore, real industrial-organizational talents should have a full understanding of psychology, sociology, ethics, and all humanities and cultural backgrounds. It is strange to say that strict knowledge of the natural sciences is relatively secondary, although it has a great relationship with industrial theory, it is not closely related to industrial organizations. The importance of human resources has been deeply felt in the West. Therefore, on the one hand, there are scientific settings such as industrial psychology and business management, and on the other hand, there is a recitation of terms such as "personnel engineering." In my humble opinion, China needs to obtain more understanding and training. Due to the complexity of personnel, friction and conflicts are common among the people, and cooperation will become difficult. This is an evident fact. In short, an industrial education aimed at developing organizational talents, in addition to engineering itself and the natural sciences required by engineering, should be supplemented by a large part of the humanities and social sciences. The more the talent comes into contact on these matters, the more open-minded and capable they will become, the fewer difficulties they will encounter in the organization of material resources and manpower.[120]

Mei Yiqi was not the inventor of the idea of general education in the Republic of China, but he was indeed an outstanding implementor. Mei Yiqi's liberal education ideas were gradually formed, as he had a clear tendency of specialized education in the early period when he hosted Tsinghua University. When the previous part of this book analyzed the cultural character of Tsinghua University's educational concepts, it quoted Mei Yiqi's *Education Policy of Tsinghua School* (1927): "Tsinghua University's education policy, in summary, can be described as creating specialized personnel." After more than a decade,

Mei Yiqi was in charge of the NSAU with a clear idea of a generalist education. Based on the quotation from *Industrial Education and Industrial Talents*, it is clearly stated "making generalist talents" was the true goal instead of "making specialized talents," and further stated that university education is "industrial education aimed at developing organizational talents, in addition to engineering itself and the natural sciences required by engineering, should be supplemented by a large part of the humanities and social sciences. The more the talent comes into contact on these matters, the more open-minded and capable they will become."

The Chinese culture has always emphasized humanities, but since the start of the research of Western culture in modern times, the reversed situation appeared where there was too much emphasis on natural science and too little on humanities and social sciences. The practical function of Mei Yiqi's idea of general education was mainly to increase the proportion of humanities in industrial education.

According to the above discussion, the educational concepts of the NSAU can be concluded as emphasizing *Daxue Zhidao* (way of Daxue/university) and practicing "general education." Understanding such concepts from the perspective of traditional culture, it can be seen as the specific elucidation of Chinese universities' cultural characters of *Houde Zaiwu* and *Wenshi Bingbao.*

b) The system design of the NSAU – a case study of the mandatory course First-Year Chinese Language.

An important feature of NSAU's educational ideas was its general education. This was reflected in the curriculum, as NSAU adopted the system of mandatory core courses and elective courses. Its School of Chinese Language had the course of First-Year Chinese Language, which was a mandatory course for students of all departments. According to historical records, NSAU particularly highlighted the humanities courses among the common mandatory courses.

In 1938, a First-Year Chinese Language committee was established in the School of Chinese Language, and its task was to compile a textbook for First-Year Chinese Language. The committee was chaired by Yang Zhensheng and he asked all the teachers part of the course to recommend articles that should be included in the textbook. After this, they added new materials, deleted existing materials, and revised the content of the textbook along with its usage. The textbook was not finalized until 1942.[121]

Before talking about the First-Year Chinese Language, it is also necessary to discuss the "professor governance" system that was popular in Chinese universities during this period. This system can be traced back to Cai Yuanpei's reform of Peking University, after which all major universities followed suit. This is also a point that this book has not discussed when researching the cultural character of Chinese universities during the Republic of China period. The academia generally believes that the system of professor governance originated from Western universities and had no cultural character at all, and it even opposes the idea of the cultural character itself. However, with modern society's new understanding of traditional culture, more and more scholars began to reflect on this view. In the book *History and Comments on Chinese Higher Education*, Tu Youguang summarized the main sources of the system of professor governance in Chinese universities. Among these sources, there are two that belong to traditional cultural characters:

1) It is rooted in the transformation of the national cultural idea of *Zunshi Zhongdao*, respecting teachers and the truth (this is extremely important as it is the root of the idea. Using it as the root, the system should be able to penetrate the hearts of the people and obtain heartfelt support). Lots of heroic figures violated this national cultural idea and were met with opposition and criticism from all generations. Of course, the national cultural idea of *Zunshi Zhongdao* was also a product of history, and it was created by the long history of the Chinese nation. Although it was severely damaged in the early twentieth century, it was not destroyed. And hence, when universities such as PKU implied the system of professor governance, it could be used as the root of this cultural idea.

2) It inherited the tradition of "teacher management" in original Chinese schools.[122] The First-Year Chinese Language course of NSAU was similar to the system of professor governance, which was often interpreted as a sign that Chinese universities had abandoned traditional culture for the sake of adopting a new culture. This is not the case. Just as the system of professor governance was not entirely Western in of itself, the First-Year Chinese Language was not purely modern. There was never a clear distinction between China and the West, or between the ancient and the modern. An overview of the selected texts with the textbook for First-Year Chinese Language, reveals that it was not focusing on vernacular Chinese, and the school poured their heart into teaching classical Chinese. NSAU was committed to striking a balance between the proportion of Chinese and Western cultures in universities, and it was the same for old and new cultures, and there was no intention of bias. This was one of the features of the cultural character of NSAU. This book believes that the establishment of the First-Year Chinese Language of NSAU did not simply proclaim the legitimacy of vernacular language within universities. The following is a related record about the First-Year Chinese Language:

> The textbook's content that was finished last is roughly: 15 articles from classics, 11 articles of styles, 44 ancient poems, and 1 appendix. The classics include *The Analects of Confucius* (excerpts), *The Tso Chuan: the Battle of An*, *Records of the Grand Historian of China: Records of Sima Rangju*, *Records of the Three Kingdoms: Records of Zhuge Liang*, *The Literary Mind and the Carving of Dragons: Shen Si*, Li Qingzhao's *Jinshulu Houxu* (Preface to a Records on Stone and Metal Inscriptions), Wang Guowei's *Renjian Cihua* (Notes on Ci Poems in the World), etc., and the ancient poems are selected from the *Book of Songs*,

> there are *Shiwu Congjun Xing*, Tao's Poetry *Yong Jing Ke*, etc., the *San Li* (three depictions of lower officials) and *San Bie* (three depictions of farewells) by Du Fu, along with other poems by Li Bai, Ouyang Xiu, Xin Qiji, Qin Guan, Li Qingzhao and others. Articles of styles: Hu Shih's *Wenxue Gailiang Zouyi* (*A Preliminary Discussion of Literature Reform*), Lu Xun's *Shi Zhong* (*A Public Example*), Xu Zhimo's *Wo Suozhidaode Kangqiao* (*Cambridge as I Knew It*), Lin Huiyin's *Chuangzi Yiwai* (*Outside of the Window*) and Ding Xilin's *Ya Po* (*Oppression*; single-act drama).
>
> In the autumn of 1944, the Ministry of Education again stipulated that the First-Year Chinese Language course must adopt the department-set textbooks, but NSAU "did not bow to the retro forces." While having to use the department-ordered textbooks, the First Year Chinese Language Committee also compiled another book *Xinan Lianhe Daxue Dayi Guowen Xizuo Cankao Wenxuan* (*Selected Works of Reference for Writing Practices of the First-year Chinese Language of NSAU*) as a supplementary textbook in retaliation. It did not only include those modern literary works in the original First-Year Chinese Language textbook, but also Hu Shih's *Jianshe De Wenxue Geming Lun* (*Constructive Literary Revolution*; excerpt), Lu Xun's *Kuangren Riji* (*Diary of a Madman*), Xu Zhimo's *Si Cheng* (*Dead City*; excerpt), Zong Baihua's *Lun Shishuo Xinyu He Jinren Zhi Me* (*On 'Shishuo Xinyu' and the Beauty of Jin People*), Zhu Guangqian's *Wenyi Yu Daode* (*Literature and Morality*) and *Wuyan Zhi Mei* (*The Beauty of Speechlessness*); Liang Zongdai's *Gete Yu Li Bai* (*Goethe and Li Bai*), *Shi · Shiren · Pipingjia* (*Poems, Poets and Critics*), Xie Bingxin's *Wangshi* (*Past Events*; excerpt), etc.[123]

Under the mandatory textbooks issued by the Ministry of Education, NSAU prepared a volume of *Xinan Lianhe Daxue Dayi Guowen Xizuo Cankao Wenxuan*, and it was not just a sign of "not bowing to the retro forces." One, First-Year Chinese Language was a compulsory course for all departments of the school, and its purpose was to provide general education, especially to supplement the balance of humanities knowledge of natural science majors. Although the professor of NSAU deliberately increased the length of the vernacular text, the First-Year Chinese Language was not designed to promote vernacular Chinese, which should be self-evident. Two, the textbook compilation of the First-Year Chinese Language was still based on classical Chinese literature and ancient poetry. It can be seen that within the textbooks compiled by the First Year Chinese Language Committee, there were "15 articles from classics, 11 articles of styles, 44 ancient poems." Compared with the recent university textbooks of Chinese language and literature, it was still rather old-fashioned. The last and the most important point is, the so-called vernacular text was ultimately a derivation from classical Chinese language, instead of its opposition. And hence, it should be considered a modern extension of traditional literature. Based on the three reasons above, this book is more inclined to classify the *First-Year Chinese Language* into the category of institutional expression of the cultural character of the United University.

c) The cultural symbols of NSAU.

Now, when we mention words such as *Gang Yi Jian Zhuo* (Fortitude, Courage, Resilience and Salience) or *Pao Chaguan* (lounging in tea house), people are immediately reminded of NSAU. As a special product of a special period, NSAU only lasted eight years, but it did leave a permanent mark in history. The NSAU's school motto and school song shall always remain in the annals of history. At the time of the separation of NSAU into the three original universities, Feng Youlan wrote on the "Monument of National Southwestern Associated University," which to this very day is still standing in all three of the universities. The unique campus life of NSAU has been constantly recalled and described by its students. All of the cultural symbols of NSAU have unique and unusual general connotations.

1. School motto and school song.

1) School motto: *Gang Yi Jian Zhuo* (Fortitude, Courage, Resilience, and Salience).
The Book of Changes: Qian Gua: "How grand is the universe! With great fortitude and upright of character." *The Analects of Confucius*: "The scholar must be courageous and resilient, as his burden is heavy and his course is long." *Gang Yi Jian Zhuo* means strong, resilient, courageous, and salient. The school motto of NSAU, *Gang Yi Jian Zhuo* was taken from classic Confucian scripture, while it was also similar to Tsinghua's motto of *Ziqiang Buxi, Houde Zaiwu*. Therefore, no matter from what point of view, the school motto of NSAU was still focused on inheriting Chinese culture, demonstrating a traditional spirit of "fortitude." NSAU inherited the ancient motto of *Gang Yi Jian Zhuo*, encouraging and cultivating the strong character of the university students in a difficult environment.

2) School song.
Tune: *Manjiang Hong* (*The River All Red*). The school song of NSAU was written by Luo Yong, a professor in the School of Chinese Language of NSAU. The use of the ancient text showed the passionate patriotism of the faculty and students of NSAU. The lyrics were as follows:

> *For thousands of miles we marched. We bid the palace of five dynasties farewell. Among the mountains and rivers of Changsha we inhabited, which shortly after became another farewell. To the distant border, we went when the people shed their blood all across our country. Though we are studying here, in the hilly city of Kunming, our minds grow even more fervent.*

> *The humiliation would eventually be avenged. Great talents are needed to make the country prosper. Even if we fight till the last one of our kind, our assertion will never bend. In this trying time, we worry about the future of our new nation. We train ourselves with hardship and look upon our great forefathers. The time will come, when we rid the invaders, liberate the great capital, and bring the country back to glory.*

As the lyrics say, "For thousands of miles we marched. We bid the palace of five dynasties farewell. Among the mountains and rivers of Changsha we inhabited, which shortly after became another farewell," the faculty and students of NSAU first moved south and later moved to the west, and their journey was filled with hardship and troubles. "In this trying time, we worry about the future of our new nation," the faculty and students of NSAU still saw the survival of the nation as their responsibility, hoping to restore the country one day. Their strong will, their worry for the world, and their resolution to drive out the enemy are very clear, and it is the result of their traditional cultural character.

2. The Monument of National Southwestern Associated University.

The Monument of National Southwestern Associated University was created by professors of NSAU. The title was compiled by Wen Yiduo and Tang Lan, the calligraphy was created by Luo Yong, the text on its front was written by Feng Youlan, and the calligraphy for the list of enlisted students on its back was created by Liu Jinnian. In 1946, after the victory of the Second Sino-Japanese War, the three universities of NSAU were instructed to return to their sites in the north. During their farewell, this monument was erected in the name of the 8 years of cooperation among the three universities. In terms of its style, the text written by Feng Youlan was highly classical, commenting on the present by quoting ancient times. Luo Yong's calligraphy was exquisite and beautiful, and the monument itself was an outstanding artwork of Chinese culture. In terms of its meaning, the monument expressed the four reasons why NSAU should be commemorated, and its significant mark of traditional Chinese culture was hard to miss. Feng Youlan truly was a master of Chinese studies. When he wrote about the history of the school and praised the spirit of NSAU, he was tracing it back to the traditional meaning of Chinese culture. The content of the front inscription is as follows (an excerpt):

> Our nation is finally restored, and the sun and the moon shall shine brightly again. NSAU has officially fulfilled its duty during the time of war, and it shall now end under official orders on May Fourth, Year 35 of the Republic of China. NSAU consisted of three universities, and they shall go back to their old homes, and carry on with their journeys. Now that we look back upon the hardship and efforts of the past 8 years, and we can see that, there are four reasons why we should commemorate the cooperation of our three universities: Our country

is one of the oldest in the world, located on the fertile land of East Asia. If we inherit the merits of the dynasties of Han and Tang, we shall achieve the status of the elite in the world. By the time our nation is thoroughly constructed, we would take an exclusively special place in the history of the world. As far as we can see, the strong powers in the world do not lack history; and while Greece and Rome had their brilliant ancient times, they are now nowhere to be found. Only China survived from ancient times to this day. We have a rich history, and we are still going strong today. This is exactly like the ancient script from *Book of Songs*, "Our nation is an old one, but our country is constantly renewed!" Through the eight years of arduous fighting, the foundation and standards have been laid for a great nation. Our victory today shall bring a new age of brilliance to our nation. The duty of NSAU, after all, aligns with our fight against the enemy, and this is the first reason for commemoration. It has been commonly known that literati always looked down on each other since ancient times. At this point, we indeed have a new perspective on this. The three universities each had their history and their styles. During these eight years, they collaborated with utmost affinity and with virtually no conflicts. We might have had our differences, but still united we stood. All our colors mixed and complemented each other, shining brightest beams of brilliance, and all our tones played in harmony, making the most beautiful music. And this would be the second reason for commemoration. All things can be nurtured together without conflict, and different ways can extend together without contradiction. Minor ethics flow around us like a river, while major ethics cast their influence like the invisible air. And that is why our world is grand. These are the words of our ancient ancestors, but they are indeed words of truth for democracy. NSAU, holding its spirit of "inclusiveness for all," shaped the ethos of our country, set the standards for internal academic freedom, and was externally given the name of "bastion of democracy." Our school breached through the obedience of countless people and revealed the truth. And this is the third reason for commemoration. Looking at Chinese history, there were several incidents where our nation could not hold its Northern territory and had to retreat to the South. Such action was given the name *Nan Du* (crossing the river to the South). Throughout Chinese history, there never was an example where a nation that crossed the Yangtze River and went to the South could return to the North. The people of Jin, Song, Ming, they all failed to return to their home. The unfamiliar scenery reminded the people of Jin of such sadness and the wish of retrieving their homeland lingered in the hearts of the people of Song. Our journey is the fourth *Nan Du* in history, and we managed to recover within merely ten years. Our sentiment is the same as Yu Xin getting the news of the retrieval of his homeland, and Du Fu when hearing that Ji Bei was recovered. And this is the fourth reason for commemoration.

After reading the above text, there are two major affirmations of Chinese culture that can be observed. First, the victory of the Second Sino-Japanese war was traced back to the long history of China. The text said, "As far as we can see, the strong powers in the world do not lack history; and while Greece and Rome had their brilliant ancient times, they are now nowhere to be found. Only China survived from ancient times to this day. We have a rich history, and we are still going strong today. This is exactly like the ancient script from *Book of Songs*: "Our nation is an old one, but our country is constantly renewed!"

Second, he traced the spirit of "inclusiveness for all" of NSAU to the true meaning of Chinese culture. It is written in the text that "All things can be nurtured together without conflict, and different ways can extend together without contradiction. Minor ethics flow around us like a river, while major ethics cast their influence like the invisible air. And that is why our world is grand. These are the words of our ancient ancestors, but they are indeed words of truth for democracy."

Of course, Feng Youlan also mentioned some of the disadvantages of Chinese culture such as "literati always looked down on each other since ancient times." In short, regardless of the form of expression or the content of the inscriptions, the Monument of National Southwestern Associated University is a precious cultural heritage left by the NSAU to future generations.

3. Campus life.

Terms such as "Anniversary celebration of NSAU," "*Shisheng Congyou*"(teachers and students taking a trip together), and "*Pao Chaguan*" can be used interchangeably with the name of National Southwestern Associated University. In the first three years (1937–1940) since the establishment of the Southwestern United University, there was no event to commemorate the anniversary of NSAU, and Peking University, Tsinghua University, and Nankai University held activities to commemorate their anniversaries. On March 7, 1941, the Committee held its 170th meeting to discuss this matter and decided that, "We shall take the date when National Changsha Temporary University, the predecessor of this university, started its classes in Changsha in 1937 as the date of the anniversary, which is 1 November." In 1941, NSAU started the custom of the joint-celebration of three universities. The school history records show:

> On November 1, 1941, the first-anniversary celebration was held. At 9 a.m. that day, a meeting was held in the new school building. Miao Yuntai, a celebrity from Yunnan Province, was invited to give a speech, and Huang Yusheng gave a lecture on *Memories of the Four Years in NSAU.*
>
> On November 1, 1942, the fifth anniversary of NSAU was held in the new school building. Mei Yiqi, a member of the Standing Committee, described the important changes and the funding income of NSAU over the past five years,

> encouraging students to persevere through tough times and push on. At the meeting, a celebrity from Yunnan, Mao Tangchen, was invited to give a speech.
>
> After that, every year on 1 November, there would a routine holiday, along with a commemorative meeting and other celebrations (such as dinners), until the end of the Second Sino-Japanese War.[124]

The joint celebration of the anniversary of NSAU was an authentic depiction of the idea that "The three universities each had their history and their styles. During these eight years, they collaborated with utmost affinity and with virtually no conflicts. We might have had our differences, but still united we stood. All our colors mixed and complemented each other, shining brightest beams of brilliance, and all our tones played in harmony, making the most beautiful music," written on the Monument of National Southwestern Associated University. As the cultural symbol of NSAU, the joint celebration symbolized the spirit of unity among the three universities, and it continued the ancient cultural tradition of *Datong*.

The phenomenon of *Shisheng Congyou* was another cultural symbol of the NSAU campus life. When talking about the relationship between teachers and students, Zhao Ruihong said, "Teachers and students can feel free to contact and talk with each other, and they can also help and debate with each other. During the spring and autumn holidays, teachers and students would roam together, drink tea, play chess, and chat freely."[125] This turned the seriously and rigorously "beneficial interaction" into an intimate and natural *Congyou* (trip together). When Qian Mu was teaching the course of General Chinese History at NSAU, he lived in the dormitory of NSAU on Fridays and Saturdays. During these days, many students went to "pay their respects and seek advice." "The students either sat on the bed or stood against the wall. As some left, some more would go in, and the flow of people seemed neverending." In this regard, Qian Mu "did not hold any feeling of boredom or resentment."[126] From the perspective of later generations, *Shisheng Congyou* was a special backdrop of NSAU. President Mei Yiqi had a good explanation for this cultural symbol. Or, it could be said that it is essentially Mei Yiqi's concept of *Congyou* that created the "both new and old" cultural symbols of NSAU.

Daxue Yijie stated that "During ancient times, students would learn from their teachers, and this action was called *Congyou*. Mencius said, 'It's hard to say who wanders through the door of a saint.' If we think about it, much meaning is contained by the term *You* (travel/swim). The school is like water, and the teachers and students are like fish. And hence, this action could be called *Congyou* (swimming together). The larger fish lead the way, and the smaller fish follow suit. are also from the swim. As time passes, the smaller fish shall learn from the larger fish's example, and hence they would have learned knowledge without actively trying" Mei Yiqi was inspired by Mencius' saying of "It's hard to say who wanders through the door of a saint," and produced the thought of *Congyou* among teachers and students. From this perspective, Mencius can be regarded as the theoretical source of the *Congyou* among teachers and students of NSAU. The sight of *Congyou* among teachers and students was also a common phenomenon in traditional Chinese academies. It can hence be observed from the NSAU phenomenon of *Congyou* that even though ancient academies are gone, their spirit lives on.

Pao Chaguan was another manifestation of the cultural character of NSAU. Teahouses were originally a traditional Chinese place for drinking tea and leisure, but they also became an off-campus "library" for NSAU students. Wang Zengqi specially wrote an article called *Pao Chaguan*, stating that *Pao Chaguan* was a language unique to NSAU students. The local people did not have such a phrase, as they would only use *Zuo Chaguan* (sitting in tea house). He recalled the student experience of *Pao Chaguan* at NSAU as follows:

> In the second year of university, I and a few foreign language classmates often sat at a table near the window of this tea house early in the morning, reading our books, and sometimes sat all afternoon, without speaking to each other. That was when I started writing. My first novels were written in this teahouse. [...]
>
> What effect does *Pao Chaguan* have on the students of the NSAU? Here is the answer: First, you can cultivate your noble spirit. The students of NSAU were naturally diverse in their intelligence, but most of them were decent. It was a dirty and chaotic era, and student life was almost impoverished. However, many people were able to pride themselves in their pureness. They despised vulgarity, and maintained a good sense of humor, to deal with the wicked poverty, and not be discouraged from life. This has something to do with the act of *Pao Chaguan*. Second, the tea houses helped in the cultivation of talents. The students of NSAU who went to the tea houses were not there just to kill time. Apart from chatting, they would spend most of their time reading. There weren't many seats in the NSAU Library, and there were no tables or stools in the dormitory. And hence, most of our reading was done in the tea house. The students of the NSAU rarely went to the tea houses without holding one, or even a few, books. Many people wrote their thesis and reading reports in the tea houses. [...] During the eight years during which NSAU was operating, a lot of talents were produced. If you want to study the history of NSAU or its "talent studies," you would have to learn more about the tea houses near NSAU. Third, the tea houses can help the students connect with society. I am interested in all kinds of people and all kinds of life. So, I just have to make some connections with and within the tea house. If I can still count as a novelist, then I am a novelist who was brewed in a tea house in Kunming.[127]

Judging from the author's memories, NSAU students used tea houses as a place to study, discuss academics, and talk about world affairs. There is a certain hint of the hardship from ancient tales of *Nangying Yingxue* (using the light of fireflies and the reflection of snow to read), a hint of the academy students who *Guoshi Jiashi Tianxiashi, Shishi Guanxin* (care about everything that is going on with their family, their nation, and the world), and a hint of the "hermit scholars" who *Xinyuan Di Zipian* (find peace anywhere if the heart is at peace). The Chinese cultural connotations of *Pao Chaguan* are self-evident. Later, many scientists and writers, such as Yang Zhenning and Wang Zengqi, claimed that they were "made" in the tea houses. What they deeply missed was still the experience of *Pao Chaguan* in NSAU. It is enough for us to see the unique charm of *Pao Chaguan* as a cultural symbol of NSAU.

Summary

Several features of Chinese university during the Republic of China's cultural character formation are:

1) For the over 30 years of the Republic of China, Chinese culture indeed entered an era of extremely strong Westernized atmosphere, but Chinese culture maintained its strong vitality and stroke a dynamic balance with Western culture. Throughout the Xinhai Revolution, the May Fourth Movement, and the Second Sino-Japanese War, Chinese and Western cultures gradually evolved from mutual confrontation to mutual integration, and the foundation of Chinese culture was never lost.
2) Intellectuals in the Republic of China era were an "unprecedented" generation in Chinese history, learning from China and the West for deep, national cultivation. During the period of the Republic of China, the Chinese-Western cultural disputes between intellectuals since the late Qing Dynasty continued. Between extremes of anti-traditionalism (total Westernizationism) and conservatism (cultural revivalism), the fusion of Chinese and Western cultures (cultural conciliationism) became the most fundamental cultural concepts for the intellectuals in the Republic of China.
3) Under the leadership of the intellectuals in the Republic of China, especially the presidents of Chinese universities, the cultural character of Chinese universities showed some ideal cultural characters in the era of the fusion of Chinese and Western cultures, especially the most typical ones *of Houde Zaiwu, Tianxia Wei Gong, You Rong Nai Da* and *Wenshi Bingbao.*

During the Republic of China, intellectuals came out in large numbers and dominated Chinese universities. Therefore, Chinese universities not only inherited some excellent traditions of Chinese culture but also succeeded in weakening the disadvantageous influences of Chinese culture under the enlightenment of Western culture. In general, Chinese universities in the special historical period of the Republic of China showed an ideal cultural character. First, it was influenced by the social and cultural atmosphere at the time, and second, it was affected by the personal charm of the intellectuals of the Republic of China, especially the presidents of the universities.

Notes

1. Liu, M., Chuantong De Wudu (Misinterpretation of Traditions). Shijiazhuang: Hebei Education Press, 1996: 2.
2. Lu, X., Lu Xun Quanji (Collected Works of Lu Xun). Beijing: The People's Literature Press, 1981: 252.
3. Yuan, Y., Liu, Y., Wang Guowei Nianpu Changbian: 1877–1927 (A Chronical Record of Wang Guowei: 1877–1927). Tianjin: Tianjin People's Publishing House, 2005: 517.
4. Chen, X. Zhongguo Jindai Jiaoyushi Jiaoxue Cankao Zailiao Zhongce (Referential Materials for Teaching the History of Modern Chinese Education Part 2). Beijing: People's Education Press, 1987: 178.
5. Ibid, p. 198.
6. Ibid.
7. Ibid, p. 201.
8. Ibid, p. 210–211.
9. Ibid, p. 231.
10. Lin, Y., Zhongguo Yishi De Weiji: "Wusi" Shiqi Jilie De Fanchuantong Zhuyi (The Crisis of Chinese Sense: Radical Anti-Traditionalism during May 4th Period). Guiyang: Guizhou People's Publishing House, 1988: 6.
11. Cao, X. Zhongxi Wenhua Duibi Daolun: Guanyu Zhongguo Wenhua Xuanze De Zaijiantao (An Introduction to Comparison between Chinese and Western Cultures: Another Reflection on Chinese Cultural Choices). Beijing: China Youth Press, 1992: 435.
12. Ibid, p. 329.
13. Qi, X., Shao, Z., Chen Duxiu Jiaoyu Lunzhu Xuan (A Selection of Works by Chen Duxiu on Education). Beijing: People's Education Press, 1995: 21.
14. Xu, J., Tian, J., Du Yaquan Wencun (Record of Works of Du Yaquan). Shanghai: Shanghai Education Publishing House, 2003: 338.
15. Hu, F., Shehui Biange Yu Wenhua Chuantong: Zhongguo Jindai Wenhua Baoshou Zhuyi Sichao Yanjiu (Social Changes and Cultural Traditions: As Research on the Conservatism Ideological Trend of Modern China). Shanghai: Shanghai People's Press, 2000: 106–107.
16. Liu, M., Chuantong De Wudu (Misinterpretation of Traditions). Shijiazhuang: Hebei Education Press, 1996: 303.
17. Liu, L., Wusi Wenhua Baoshou Zhuyi Sichao Yanjiu (Research on the Cultural Conservatism Ideological Trend of May 4th Period). Beijing: The China Social Sciences Press, 2006: 1.
18. Su, Y., Zhongguo Xinjiaoyu De Mengya Yu Chengzhang (1860–1928) (The Sprouting and Growth of the New Education of China (1860–1928)). Beijing: Peking University Press, 2007: 102.
19. The Second Historical Archives of China, Zhonghua Minguoshi Dangan Ziliao Huibian Disanji Jiaoyu (Collection of Historical Archives and Materials of the History of Republic of China Vol.3 Education). Nanjing: Jiangsu Ancient Book Publishing House, 1991: 102–103.

20. Ibid, p. 173.
21. Zhu, G. Xixue Dongjian Yu Zhongguo Gaodeng Jiaoyu Jindaihua (The Eastward Spreading of Western Learning and the Modernization of Chinese Higher Education). Xiamen: Xiamen University Press, 1996: 71.
22. Bai, J., Liu, Y., Hu Shi Jiaoyu Lunzhu Xuan (A Selection of Works by Hu Shih on Education). Beijing: People's Education Press, 1994: 193.
23. Chen, P., Zhongguo Daxue Shijiang (Ten Lectures on Chinese Universities). Shanghai: Fudan University Press, 2002: 71.
24. Cited from: Ibid, p. 77.
25. Yu, Y., Qian Mu Yu Zhongguo Wenhua (Qian Mu and Chinese Culture). Shanghai: Shanghai Far-East Press, 1994: 204.
26. Li, Z., Zou Woziji De Lu (Going My Own Way). Shanghai: Shanghai SDX Joint Publishing Company, 1986: 240.
27. Chen Y., Jinmingguan Conggao Erbian (The Second Editing of Articles from Jinmingguan). Shanghai: Shanghai Ancient Books Publishing House, 1980: 252.
28. Xiong, M., Zhongguo Gaodeng Jiaoyushi (History of Chinese Higher Education). Chongqing: Chongqing Publishing House: 1988: 342.
29. Ibid, p. 340.
30. Hayhoe, R. China's Universities 1895–1995: A Century of Cultural Conflict. Trans. Xu, J. Beijing: Educational Science Publishing House, 2000: 82.
31. Ibid, p. 85.
32. Ibid, p. 85–86.
33. Tu, Y. Zhongguo Gaodeng Jiaoyu Shilun (History and comments on Chinese higher education). Wuhan: Hubei Education Publishing House, 2002: 242.
34. Ibid, p. 243.
35. Hayhoe, R. China's Universities 1895–1995: A Century of Cultural Conflict. Trans. Xu, J. Beijing: Educational Science Publishing House, 2000: 90.
36. Chen, Y., Shiqu De Daxue (Universities That Died Away). Beijing: Tongxin Publishing House, 2005: 234.
37. Liu, M., Zhongguo Xiandai Xueshu Yaolue (A Brief Framework of Contemporary Chinese Academics). Beijing: SDX Joint Publishing Company, 2008: 124.
38. Ibid.
39. Liang, S., Dongxi Wenhua Jiqi Zhexue (Eastern and Western Cultures and Their Philosophies). Beijing: The Commercial Press, 2010: 17.
40. Lin, Y., Zhongguo Yishi De Weiji: "Wusi" Shiqi Jilie De Fanchuantong Zhuyi (The Crisis of Chinese Sense: Radical Anti-Traditionalism during May 4th Period). Guiyang: Guizhou People's Publishing House, 1988: 108.
41. Ibid, p. 109.
42. Li, D., Li Dazhao Xuanji (Selected Works of Li Dazhao). Beijing: People's Publishing House, 1959: 72–80.
43. Qian, J., Guoxue Bidu Xia (Must-Reads of Sinology Part 2). Shanghai: Shanghai Ancient Books Publishing House, 2011: 381
44. Liang, S., Dongxi Wenhua Jiqi Zhexue (Eastern and Western Cultures and Their Philosophies). Beijing: The Commercial Press, 2010: 19.
45. Cao, X. Zhongxi Wenhua Duibi Daolun: Guanyu Zhongguo Wenhua Xuanze De Zaijiantao (An Introduction to Comparison between Chinese and Western Cultures: Another Reflection on Chinese Cultural Choices). Beijing: China Youth Press, 1992: 398.

46. Liu, M., Chuantong De Wudu (Misinterpretation of Traditions). Shijiazhuang: Hebei Education Press, 1996: 303.
47. Tang, Z., Cai Yuanpei Zhuan (A Biography of Cai Yuanpei). Shanghai: Shanghai People's Press, 1985: 3.
48. Liu, M., Chuantong De Wudu (Misinterpretation of Traditions). Shijiazhuang: Hebei Education Press, 1996: 184.
49. Ibid, p. 186.
50. Ibid.
51. Chen, P., Zhongguo Daxue Shijiang (Ten Lectures on Chinese Universities). Shanghai: Fudan University Press, 2002: Self-preface 5.
52. Chen, X. Zhongguo Jindai Jiaoyushi Jiaoxue Cankao Zailiao Zhongce (Referential Materials for Teaching the History of Modern Chinese Education Part 2). Beijing: People's Education Press, 1987: 178.
53. Gao, P., Cai Yuanpei Jiaoyu Lunji (Collected Works of Cai Yuanpei on Education). Changsha: Hunan Education Publishing House, 1987: 490.
54. Cui, G., Zhang Boling Jiaoyu Lunzhu Xuan (Selected Works of Zhang Boling on Education). Beijing: People's Education Press, 1997: 309.
55. Pan, N., Zhang, H., Xunqiu Zhongguoren Weiyu Zhidao: Pan Guangdan Wenxuan (Looking for the Way of Position Education for Chinese People: Selected Works of Pan Guangdan). Beijing: International Culture Publishing Company, 1997: 309
56. Editing Group of School History of Nankai University. Nankai Daxue Xiaoshi (1919–1949) (The School History of Nankai University (1919–1949)). Tianjin: Nankai University Publishing House, 1989: 17–18.
57. Li, X., Beida Binfen Yibainian (The Colorful Century of Peking University). Beijing: Peking University Press, 1999: 347–348.
58. Ibid, p. 350–351.
59. Li, M., Wang, J., Shangshu Yizhu (Translation and Annotation of Book of Documents). Shanghai: Shanghai Ancient Books Publishing House, 2016: 369.
60. Zhou, C., Huang, X., Bainian Zhi Gong: Zhongguo Jindai Daxue Xiaozhang De Jiaoyujia Jingshen (Effort of a Hundred Years: The Educator Spirit of Presidents of Modern Chinese Universities). Fuzhou: Fujian Education Press, 2005: 88–89.
61. Liu, S., Huang, Y., Mei Yiqi Jiaoyu Lunzhu Xuan (Selected Works of Mei Yiqi on Education). Beijing: People's Education Press, 1993: 11.
62. Tu, Y. Zhongguo Gaodeng Jiaoyu Shilun (History and comments on Chinese higher education). Wuhan: Hubei Education Publishing House, 2002: 1.247v
63. Ibid, p. 245.
64. Liang J., Yungong Yunneng Rixin Yueyi: Nankai Daxue Xiaozhang Zhang Boling (Discipline and Practicality, New Progress by the Day: Zhang Boling, The President of Nankai University). Jinan: Shandong Education Press, 2003: 102.
65. Yang, D., Daxue Jingshen (The Spirit of University). Shenyang: Liaohai Publishing House, 1999: 245.
66. Xie, Y., Shiqu De Nianday: Zhongguo Ziyou Zhishifenzi De Mingyun (The Age Gone: The Fate of Liberal Intellectuals of China). Beijing: Culture and Art Publishing House, 1999: 235.
67. Gao, P., Cai Yuanpei Jiaoyu Lunji (Collected Works of Cai Yuanpei on Education). Changsha: Hunan Education Publishing House, 1987: 213.
68. Han, S., Shishang Yiwu Cai Yuanpei (There Will Never Be Another Cai Yuanpei). Dushu, 2005 (4).

69. Liu, K., Fang, M., Beida Yu Qinghua: Zhongguo Liangsuo Zhuming Gaodeng Xuefu De Lishi Yu Fengge (PKU and THU: The History and Style of Two Famous Institutes of Higher Education in China). Beijing: National Administrative Academy Publishing House, 1998: 277.
70. Chen, P., Zhongguo Daxue Shijiang (Ten Lectures on Chinese Universities). Shanghai: Fudan University Press, 2002: 40.
71. Feng, Y., Zhongguo Xiandai Zhexueshi (History of Contemporary Chinese Philosophy). Hong Kong: Chung Hwa Book Company (H.K.), 1992: 57.
72. Gao, P., Cai Yuanpei Jiaoyu Lunji (Collected Works of Cai Yuanpei on Education). Changsha: Hunan Education Publishing House, 1987: 612.
73. Tu, Y. Zhongguo Gaodeng Jiaoyu Shilun (History and comments on Chinese higher education). Wuhan: Hubei Education Publishing House, 2002: 307.
74. Gao, P., Cai Yuanpei Jiaoyu Lunji (Collected Works of Cai Yuanpei on Education). Changsha: Hunan Education Publishing House, 1987: 618.
75. Chen, P., Zhongguo Daxue Shijiang (Ten Lectures on Chinese Universities). Shanghai: Fudan University Press, 2002: 48.
76. Gao, P., Cai Yuanpei Jiaoyu Lunji (Collected Works of Cai Yuanpei on Education). Changsha: Hunan Education Publishing House, 1987: 589–590.
77. Huang, Y., Mei Yiqi Jiaoyu Sixiang Yanjiu (A Research on the Educational Thoughts of Mei Yiqi). Shenyang: Liaoning Education Press, 1994: 7.
78. Tu, Y. Zhongguo Gaodeng Jiaoyu Shilun (History and comments on Chinese higher education). Wuhan: Hubei Education Publishing House, 2002: 331.
79. Huang, Y., Qinghua Chuantong Jingshen (The Traditional Spirit of Tsinghua). Beijing: Tsinghua University Press, 2006: 40.
80. Zhang, A., Guo, J., Guoli Xinan Lianhe Daxue Shiliao (Er) (Historical Material of National Southwestern Associated University Vol.2). Kunming: Yunnan Education Publishing House, 1998: 83, 142.
81. Chu, Z. Zhongguo Daxue Jingshen De Lishi Yu Xingsi (History and the Spirit of the Chinese University of Reflection). Taiyuan: Shanxi Education Press, 2006: 153.
82. Wang, W., Zhang Boling Jiaoyu Yanlun Xuanji (Selected Statements of Zhang Boling on Education). Tianjin: Nankai University Press, 1984: 243.
83. Chen, P., Zhongguo Daxue Shijiang (Ten Lectures on Chinese Universities). Shanghai: Fudan University Press, 2002: 236.
84. Yu, Z., Minzu Weiji Xiade Jiaoyu Yingdui (Educational Response during a National Crisis). Wuhan: Central China Normal University Press, 2001: 133.
85. Editing Group of School History of Nankai University. Nankai Daxue Xiaoshi (1919–1949) (The School History of Nankai University (1919–1949)). Tianjin: Nankai University Publishing House, 1989: 403.
86. Gao, P., Cai Yuanpei Jiaoyu Lunji (Collected Works of Cai Yuanpei on Education). Changsha: Hunan Education Publishing House, 1987: 54–55.
87. Yang, D., Daxue Jingshen (The Spirit of University). Shenyang: Liaohai Publishing House, 1999: 324–326.
88. Gao, P., Cai Yuanpei Jiaoyu Lunji (Collected Works of Cai Yuanpei on Education). Changsha: Hunan Education Publishing House, 1987: 213.
89. Yang, D., Daxue Jingshen (The Spirit of University). Shenyang: Liaohai Publishing House, 1999: 23.
90. Yeh, W., The Alienated Academy: Culture and Politics in Republican China, 1919–1937. Trans. Feng, X. et al. Beijing: China Renmin University Press, 2012: 11.

91. Research Office of School History, Peking University. Beijing Daxue Shiliao Dierjuan: 1912–1937 (Historical Materials of Peking University, Vol. 2: 1912–1937). Beijing: Peking University Press, 2000: 1437.
92. Ibid, p. 1444.
93. Cited from: Fan, Y. Shuangchong Qiyuan Yu Zhidu Shengcheng: Zhongguo Xiandai Daxue Zhidu Qiyuan Yanjiu (Double Origins and Institutional Generation: A Research on the Origin of Modern Chinese University System). Wuhan: Huazhong University of Science and Technology, 2011: 175.
94. Mu, Z., Mu, X. Beida Gushi (Stories of Peking University). Beijing: China Market Press, 1998: 3.
95. Ibid, p. 5.
96. Chen, P., Xia, X., Beida Jiushi (The Old Stories of Peking University). Beijing: SDX Joint Publishing Company, 1998: 12.
97. Ibid.
98. Yeh, W., The Alienated Academy: Culture and Politics in Republican China, 1919–1937. Trans. Feng, X. et al. Beijing: China Renmin University Press, 2012: 149.
99. Ibid, p. 148–152.
100. Ibid, p. 153–155.
101. Chen, P. Daxue Hewei (What University Does). Beijing: Peking University Press, 2006: 25.
102. Research Office of School History, Tsinghua University. Qinghua Daxue Shiliao Xuanbian Diyijuan (An Edited Selection of Historical Materials of Tsinghua University Vol.1). Beijing: Tsinghua University Press, 1991: 259.
103. Research Office of School History, Tsinghua University. Qinghua Daxue Shiliao Xuanbian Dierjuan (Shang) (An Edited Selection of Historical Materials of Tsinghua University Vol.2 Part A). Beijing: Tsinghua University Press, 1991: 138.
104. Research Office of School History, Tsinghua University. Qinghua Daxue Shiliao Xuanbian Diyijuan (An Edited Selection of Historical Materials of Tsinghua University Vol.1). Beijing: Tsinghua University Press, 1991: 262–263.
105. Yang, D., Daxue Jingshen (The Spirit of University). Shenyang: Liaohai Publishing House, 1999: 344–345.
106. Liu, S., Huang, Y., Mei Yiqi Jiaoyu Lunzhu Xuan (Selected Works of Mei Yiqi on Education). Beijing: People's Education Press, 1993: 5–7.
107. Ibid, p. 9–11.
108. Su, Y., Cong Qinghua Xuetang Dao Qinghua Daxue 1911–1929 (From Tsinghua School to Tsinghua University 1911–1929). Beijing: SDX Joint Publishing Company, 2001: 282–283.
109. Research Office of School History, Tsinghua University. Qinghua Daxue Shiliao Xuanbian Diyijuan (An Edited Selection of Historical Materials of Tsinghua University Vol.1). Beijing: Tsinghua University Press, 1991: 373–374.
110. Huang, Y., Ersanshi Niandai Qinghua Xiaoyuan Wenhua (The Campus Culture of Tsinghua University in 1920s and 1930s). Guilin: Guangxi Normal University Press, 2000: 214.
111. Yeh, W., The Alienated Academy: Culture and Politics in Republican China, 1919–1937. Trans. Feng, X. et al. Beijing: China Renmin University Press, 2012: 146.
112. Su, Y., Cong Qinghua Xuetang Dao Qinghua Daxue 1911–1929 (From Tsinghua School to Tsinghua University 1911–1929). Beijing: SDX Joint Publishing Company, 2001: 234–235.
113. Ibid, p. 214–229.
114. Jiang, Y., Xinan Lianda: Teding Lishi Shiqi De Daxue Wenhua (National Southwestern Associated University: The University Culture of a Specific Period of Time). Chengdu: Publishing House of UESTC, 2010: 35.

115. Ishijima, N., History of the Second Sino-Japanese War. Trans. Zheng, Y. et al. Changchun: Jilin Education Press, 1990: 61.
116. National Institute of Education Sciences. Zhongguo Xiandai Jiaoyu Dashiji (1919–1949) (Chronicle of Contemporary Chinese Education (1919–1949)). Beijing: Educational Science Publishing House, 1988: 374.
117. Editing Committee of Education Yearbooks, Ministry of Education, China. Dierci Zhongguo Jiaoyu Nianjian (Diyibian) (2nd Yearbook for Chinese Education (1st Edit)). Shanghai: The Commercial Press, 1948: 9.
118. Yang, D., Daxue Jingshen (The Spirit of University). Shenyang: Liaohai Publishing House, 1999: 68–70.
119. Yang, L., Xinan Lianda De Sifenkesi Zhimi (The "Mystery of Sphinx" of National Southwestern Associated University). Kunming: Yunnan People's Publishing House, 2005: 149.
120. Yang, D., Daxue Jingshen (The Spirit of University). Shenyang: Liaohai Publishing House, 1999: 245.
121. Jiang, Y., Xinan Lianda: Teding Lishi Shiqi De Daxue Wenhua (National Southwestern Associated University: The University Culture of a Specific Period of Time). Chengdu: Publishing House of UESTC, 2010: 272–273.
122. Tu, Y. Zhongguo Gaodeng Jiaoyu Shilun (History and comments on Chinese higher education). Wuhan: Hubei Education Publishing House, 2002: 315.
123. Jiang, Y., Xinan Lianda: Teding Lishi Shiqi De Daxue Wenhua (National Southwestern Associated University: The University Culture of a Specific Period of Time). Chengdu: Publishing House of UESTC, 2010: 272–273.
124. Beijing Alumni Club, National Southwestern Associated University. Guoli Xinan Lianhe Daxue Xiaoshi: Yijiusanqi Zhi Yijiusiliu Nian De Beida, Qinghua, Nankai (History of National Southwestern Associated University: Peking University, Tsinghua University and Nankai University From 1937 To 1946). Beijing: Peking University Press, 1996: 95–96.
125. Zhao, R., Liluan Xiange Yi Jiuyou: Cong Xinan Lianda Dao Jinse De Wanqiu (Remembrance of Old Trips in Wandering String Music and Songs: From National Southwestern Associated University to the Golden Late Autumn). Shanghai: Wenhui Press, 2000: 67.
126. Jiang, Y., Xinan Lianda: Teding Lishi Shiqi De Daxue Wenhua (National Southwestern Associated University: The University Culture of a Specific Period of Time). Chengdu: Publishing House of UESTC, 2010: 87.
127. Cited from Ibid, p. 258–259.

CHAPTER 4

The Cultural Character of Chinese Universities in the First 17 Years of People's Republic of China

On October 1, 1949, the People's Republic of China (PRC) was established. The Communist Party of China transformed from a revolutionary party into a ruling party and began to carry out drastic reforms in China. The first seventeen years after the founding of the PRC (thereinafter referred to as the Seventeen Years) was an important period of social transformation and development in China. Influenced by its ideology, the Communist Party's attitude towards Chinese cultural traditions was more critical than affirming, and therefore, the ruling party of the People's Republic of China replaced the Republican Chinese intellectuals and became the leader of universities. As a political barometer, Chinese universities had entered a special period of development. As such, politics was a key point in helping us to understand the cultural character of Chinese universities during this period.

Section 1: The social and cultural evolution during the Seventeen Years and the transformation of Chinese universities

"The iteration of eras in 1949 was unprecedented in Chinese history. Because of the impact on the whole society's daily life brought by previous iterations of regimes were not abrupt, the basic structure and cultural tradition of society could continue in the same way in general. However, this time, the transformation of the times has changed the basic structure and cultural traditions of Chinese society."[1] While the overall negation of traditional culture during the May Fourth New Culture Movement was still more of a slogan and lacked depth, at some point from the founding of the New China to the Reform and Opening-up, even the root of Chinese culture was facing an existential crisis. During the May Fourth anti-traditional period, conservatives who protected traditional culture and radicals who supported Western culture emerged and fought against each other in the free and fierce Chinese-Western cultural debate. However, during this period, Chinese traditional culture and Western culture, as the respective representatives of feudalism and capitalism, were both reduced to the "scum" of the times, while all voices of opposition were contained. Looking at this from a general perspective, at the time when New China was founded, many things were waiting to be done. In the tide of abolishing the old and establishing the new, anti-traditionalism, as an inevitable political choice, laid the cultural tone for the new era.

The Seventeen Years was a special period of frequent changes and an old-new iteration of Chinese society. Although Chinese culture has generally declined in the vigorous cultural criticism, there were still traces of deep-seated traditional culture. Following the Seventeen Years, there was the ten-year Cultural Revolution, a period of stagnation for the development of Chinese culture and its education. On the one hand, the "Cultural Revolution posed unprecedented destruction to culture. At that time, not only the traditional culture was denied, but also Western culture. Everything that was culture had to be uprooted. The culture was no longer wanted."[2] The destruction of education was also unprecedented. During the Cultural Revolution, Chinese universities were virtually non-existent. Formal universities were closed and abandoned, while July 21 Universities became prevalent. As Hayhoe stated, "they have little to do with universities in the original sense, and there was little connection with the university system that has been developed in China for a hundred years."[3] "Chinese culture" faulted, "Chinese universities" disappeared, not to mention their cultural character.

Therefore, the study of the cultural character of Chinese universities in this chapter is mainly limited to the Seventeen Years. This was an important period for China's preliminary exploration and tortuous development. Radical changes and restoration adjustments were alternately connected. Overall, it seemed that the fluctuation was huge, but it did not enter the extreme stages of development. Due to repeated changes in policies, the evolution of Chinese culture was extremely irregular, basically showing a characteristic of sometimes popular, sometimes depreciated, sometimes declining, sometimes blooming, while its overall decline was still evident. Due to frequent cultural revolutions, Chinese universities underwent a superficial rebirth with high irregularity, yet they were still regarded as "Chinese" universities.

The main task of this section is to review the fate of "Chinese culture" from a historical perspective, and then examine the development status of "Chinese universities" in the context of cultural changes. Finally, based on this, it will discuss the overall cultural character of Chinese universities during this period. The following intercepts three historical segments of Full-Scale Sovietization, Double Hundred Guidelines, and Great Leap Forward in the Seventeen Years, to comb through the historical background and characteristics of the formation of Chinese universities' cultural character in the '50s and '60s.

1. Chinese Culture and Chinese Universities during the Full-Scale Sovietization Period

On October 1, 1949, the People's Republic of China was established. In the face of the complicated international situation, the Chinese government chose to "lean to one side." On the surface, Soviet culture had replaced the traditional Confucian culture as the official culture of New China. In contrast, both traditional Chinese culture with Confucianism as its core and Western culture characterized by capitalism had fallen into an impasse in the wave of "anti-feudalism" and "anti-capitalism." Objectively speaking, in the early period of the founding of PRC, the main purpose of the government's radical reform was to "reform" the "old culture" rather than to "revolutionize." Therefore, during this period of Full-Scale Sovietization, Chinese culture surged in the process with many undercurrents, and the traditional characteristics of Chinese universities loomed in the cultural changes.

a) Cultural changes within social changes.

Influenced by political ideology, Full-Scale Sovietization became the main historical background of the social and cultural changes in China during the early days of the founding of the People's Republic of China. In October 1951, the article *Celebrating the 34th Anniversary of the October Revolution in the Soviet Union and Strengthening the Friendly Unity of the Chinese and Soviet Peoples* pointed out, "The extremely powerful and extremely happy Soviet Union proved that the path pointed out by the October Revolution was the correct path for the people of the whole world to attain complete liberation and happiness, as well as the incomparable superiority of socialism (...) We must further learn from the advanced experience of Soviet construction and completely break the conservative thinking, especially the wrong thinking of 'Britain's and American superiority.'"[4]

During this period, China imported and learned from the Soviet culture by hiring Soviet experts, sending a huge amount of students to the Soviet Union, translating a large number of Soviet books, and showing Soviet films. According to relevant statistics, in the 1950s, 38,000 scientists, technicians, teachers, students, and workers went to the Soviet Union for study and immersion, and 10,000 Soviet experts, consultants, and teachers came to China to guide the work. The *article Introduction to the Sino-Soviet Friendship Association* in 1951 pointed out that in the past two years "more than 500 books and brochures have been published to promote Sino-Soviet friendship and advocate for the

Soviet Union. Last year, more than 690 works, including Lenin and Stalin's books and Soviet philosophical and literary works were translated and published all over China. In 1951, "the state-run film factory produced 26 feature films" and "translated 43 Soviet feature films."[5] From this perspective, it could be seen that Soviet culture had comprehensively and deeply penetrated many areas of Chinese society. The Full-Scale Sovietization policy did allow China's social reforms, especially in the economic field, to achieve great results in a short time. At a cultural level, the full invasion of Soviet culture inevitably left out the Chinese culture, but it did not suffer substantial damage. Moreover, although China in this period was en route to Sovietization, to some extent, Chinese culture was still affirmed or even protected.

At the beginning of the founding of the People's Republic of China, *Baihua Qifang, Tuichen Chuxin* (Let a hundred flowers blossom; Getting rid of the old, developing the new) became the government's prominent cultural slogan. *Baihua Qifang, Tuichen Chuxin* contained an attitude of "taking the best of Chinese culture and discarding its dross." On April 13, 1951, the China Academy of Traditional Chinese Opera was established with Mao Zedong's inscription of *Baihua Qifang, Tuichen Chuxin.* In the same year, Zhou Enlai approved the *Instructions on the Reform of Traditional Opera* issued by the Government Administration Council and pointed out that, "All drama propagating against aggression, or about the resistance to oppression, the love for the motherland, the love for freedom, the love for labor, and the praise for people's justice and their good characters should be encouraged, promoted, and multiplied; any drama that advocates the morality of feudal forces, brutal terror, obscene or vulgar behavior, and that denigrates and insults the working people should be opposed."[6] Looking at the above policies, Chinese culture was still recognized and affirmed during this period. What hurt and damaged Chinese culture was the ideological reform movement initiated by the government against the intellectuals. As the main heir and transmitter of Chinese culture, the misfortune brought by the times upon the intellectuals directly affected the development of Chinese culture.

Objectively speaking, in the process of carrying out the ideological remolding of intellectuals, both the Central Committee of the Communist Party of China and Mao Zedong had some good claims, such as, "No one is entitled to any privilege in academic criticism and discussion," "Academic criticism and discussion should be rational and truth-seeking," "arbitrary, rude attitude should be discouraged," "for academic workers who have serious wrong bourgeois views on academic thinking, as long as he is not counterrevolutionary in politics, they should be guaranteed a suitable working position... Respect and give play to their expertise that is useful to society," etc. These propositions were highly consistent with the slogan of *Baihua Qifang, Tuichen Chuxin.* However, with the development of cultural criticism, intellectuals' ideological reform movement deviated from, or even went completely against, the starting point of *Baihua Qifang, Tuichen Chuxin*, many behaviors went too far.

On May 20, 1951, *People's Daily* published an editorial written by Mao Zedong, *The Need to Pay Attention to the Discussion in the movie 'Wuxun Zhuan,'* and then triggered a national wave of criticism. *Wuxun Zhuan* was a typical example of "fanatic propaganda of feudal culture" and "counterrevolutionary propaganda that slanders the Chinese nation" that caused the first wave of great cultural criticism since the founding of the People's Republic of China. Influenced by the criticism of *Wuxun Zhuan,* literary criticism eventually turned into personal criticisms against intellectuals. On October 23, 1951, Mao Zedong spoke at the third session of the First Chinese People's Political Consultative Conference (CPPCC) Committee and said, "Ideological remolding, first of all, is the ideological remolding of various intellectuals. This is an important condition for our country to completely realize democratic reform and gradual industrialization."[7] Thereafter, the movement of ideological remolding of intellectuals officially kicked off. For example, the criticism of "Liang Shuming's counterrevolutionary thoughts" from 1953 to 1955, criticism of "wrong thoughts" in Yu Pingbo's *Research on the Dream of Red Mansions* in 1954, and the subsequent denunciation of Hu Shi's political and academic thoughts. It is worth mentioning that there were voices against both, literary and art circles and criticisms of the academic fields. For example, Li Shizhao has always defended *Wuxun Zhuan,* and Liang Shuming opposed the cultural dictatorship with "the courage of ordinary people." These contrarian voices, regardless of being weak, defended Chinese culture to some extent. As Hu Sheng said, these criticisms "were not necessary or effective from the perspective of hindsight, and they have not received good results (...) Relying on political power to launch a mass movement cannot solve any problems in the ideological field. Furthermore, it may only lead to a negative impact."[8] From a cultural perspective, the biggest negative impact of this cultural criticism campaign against intellectuals was the one-sided understanding and radical denial of traditional culture.

b) Chinese universities in cultural changes.

A general feature of the changes in Chinese culture during the Full-Scale Sovietization period, that is, the Soviet Union's culture struck invaded in an all-round way. The ideological remolding of intellectuals followed, and Chinese culture struggled to loom in the loss. The mainstream Soviet culture and the lost Chinese culture became the main cultural backgrounds for the development of Chinese universities during this period. In 1952, *People's Education* published an editorial *Further Studying the Advanced Educational Experience of the Soviet Union -Let Us Welcome China-Soviet Friendship Month.* The article pointed out that, "The construction of education in New China in the past three years has achieved a lot from learning the Soviet experience. This also proves that to build a new democratic education, we must first thoroughly and systematically study the advanced education experience of the Soviet Union; in the past, we have not done this thoroughly or systematically enough." At the same time, it was clearly emphasized that

"When we learn from the Soviet Union, we must follow China's actual needs. It should not be a simple imitation, but a constructive adoption. To absorb the experience of the Soviet Union as our nourishment, we must digest it and Sinonize it."[9] This heralded the all-round arrival of the Full-Scale Sovietization period of higher education.

Colleges and departments adjusted to the results that were learned from studying Soviet higher education experience during this period. In the first three years of the founding of the People's Republic of China, although the state's partial adjustments to universities were continuous, they were not carried out under a nationally unified plan. The convening of the Deans' Conference of National Institutes of Engineering in 1952 marked the entrance to the official preparation period of the national college and department adjustments. In May 1952, the national College and department adjustments, *National Higher Education College and Department Adjustment Plan (Draft)* was formally introduced, which systematically proposed principles for the adjustment: "Universities (referring to comprehensive universities) are for training scientific research talents and teachers. There shall be at least one but no more than four institutions of higher learning in each of the major administrative regions of the country; the college level of university administration shall be abolished and regard the department as the teaching administrative unit. The colleges of engineering are the focus of this adjustment. Opening less or none multi-disciplinary engineering colleges but more specialized engineering colleges was the principle for this adjustment. The agricultural colleges currently adopt the principle of a centralized merger. There should be one or two such colleges in each major administrative area, and so on."[10] During the college and department adjustments in the early 1950s, the anti-traditionalistic features of China's higher education reform were particularly obvious, especially showing a heavy tint of Soviet culture. For example:

1. The tendency for the adjustment leaned heavily towards industry-related engineering, while arts and humanities were seriously weakened.

Since the October Revolution, the Soviet Union had adjusted the faculties of colleges and universities to adapt to the development of industrialization. As Alshindev, the then General Counsel of the Ministry of Education, said, "The change in Soviet higher education is to transform the universities from institutes that cultivate abstract generalists to institutes that cultivate specialized talents. In principle, the reform and development of the Chinese education system should follow this direction."[11] A prominent manifestation of this period was that the traditional Tertiary Chinese module that no longer appeared in Chinese universities as a compulsory common course, and would remain absent for nearly thirty years from 1952.

2. The colleges and departments were adjusted to be predominantly single-disciplinary institutions.

The number of comprehensive universities was reduced. China and the Soviet Union walked the same path in terms of reform. Soviet expert Fu Min once described the Soviet university adjustments as, "Separate medical departments and other departments that should not belong to universities, (they should) establish independent colleges based on these disciplines, such as medical colleges, law colleges, financial colleges, and other single-disciplinary colleges. The university itself shall retain half of the departments of natural sciences and humanities..."[12]

3. In the college and department adjustments, the number of training colleges was reduced, while the number of undergraduate universities was increased.

This feature was also largely influenced by the Soviet model. It could be regarded as an attempt of mimicking the feature of "no training colleges" in the Soviet university system. Hu Jianhua pointed out in the book *Xiandai Zhongguo Daxue Zhidu De Yuandian: 50 Niandai Chuqi De Daxue Gaige* (*The Origin of the Modern Chinese University System: University Reform in the Early 1950s*) that, "In the college and department adjustments in 1952, although this kind of system without training colleges could not be copied in its entirety, getting close to this goal was considered as the direction of development for the Chinese university system reform."[13]

Based on the above characteristics, the college and department adjustments in the early 1950s mainly imitated the Soviet model and fundamentally changed the Chinese university system established in the Republic of China. "Overall, under the influence of the Soviet model, the reform of China's higher education system had achieved tremendous results. This was especially true as to how this system met the needs of rapid economic growth."[14] Hayhoe, from the point of view of cultural conflict, believed that, in a certain sense, "the common problem in the adjusted Chinese higher education system was that this system was detached from China's cultural background."[15] In fact, if a Chinese cultural ground that matched the Soviet model was missing, it would be difficult for the Soviet higher education model to be successfully adopted by China. The reforms in this period still bore the characteristics of Chinese culture, and the reform idea of "striving to achieve sinonization" advocated by the Chinese government was not mere lip service. For example:

1. The unified college entrance examination system.

In the early 1950s, "in the upsurge of mainland China learning from the Soviet Union, the college entrance examination system was an exception."[16] Liu Haifeng pointed out that, "Because the Soviet Union, which had implemented a planned economy, it had never implemented a unified national college entrance examination system. However, based on reflecting on the experience of joint admission examinations of national public colleges and universities in the Kuomintang-ruled area after the Second Sino-Japanese War in 1952, China developed a unified college entrance examination system with distinctive Chinese characteristics. It was hard to say that traditional culture did not come into play."[17] And this traditional culture could be traced directly back to the ancient imperial examination system that lasted for thousands of years in ancient China.

2. The system of Universities ran by government departments.

When learning from the Soviet Union in the 1950s, most Chinese colleges established their specialized majors, which were managed by the national ministries and commissions corresponding to their majors. This system of universities ran by government departments shared the same vein of development as the ancient official school management system. For example, the establishment of the *Liu Xue Er Guan* (six disciplines and two schools) in the central government system of the Tang Dynasty were respectively subordinate to the *San Sheng Liu Bu* (three departments and six ministries) of the administrative management system.

Specifically, the central *Liu Xue* (*Guozixue)* (Central academy for offspring of Tier 2 and above officials), *Taixue* (Institution of Great Learning), *Simenxue* (Central academy for offspring of lower-tier officials and commoners), *Shuxue* (Academy of calligraphy), *Suanxue* (Academy of arithmetic and astronomy), *Lvxue* (Academy of laws) were central academies which belonged to the *Guozijian* directly under *Shangshu Sheng* (Department of State Affairs). The *Er Guan* was peripheral, composing of *Hongwen Guan,* under the supervision of *Dong Gong* (East Palace, the Palace of the Crown Prince), and *Chongwen Guan*, which was directly under *Menxia Sheng* (the Chancellery). The medical school was a specialty and was, therefore, a self-contained department. It belonged to *Zhongshu Sheng* (the Secretariat) and was directly under *Taiyi Shu* (Department of the Imperial Doctors). From this perspective, although Chinese higher education in this period used the Soviet model as the main reference, it also, to some extent, inherited the traditional Chinese higher education system.

2. *Chinese culture and Chinese universities during the time of Double-Hundred policy*

The Double-Hundred Policy period from 1956 to 1957, although short-lived, was a major change in China's history. Especially the persecution of intellectuals by the Anti-Rightist Struggle in 1957 caused the most direct impact on the development of Chinese culture and Chinese universities. Generally speaking, after a short period of renaissance, Chinese culture had fallen into a long-term decline. After a short period of freedom, the past glory of Chinese universities no longer existed.

a) Cultural changes within social changes.

In 1956, the Soviet Criticizing of the Stalin Movement intensified and the Chinese government began to consciously adjust the excessive Sovietization tendency of the Full-Scale Sovietization policy. China was still facing the problem of how to deal with "Chinese culture" in the development process of gradually getting rid of the influence of Soviet culture.

The short *Baihua Qifang* era could be summed up in one word as – huge ups and downs. Mao Zedong pointed out in his speech on *On the Ten Major Relations*, "The Soviet Union recently exposed some of their shortcomings and mistakes in the process of socialist construction. Do we still want to take the detour that they have already taken? [...] we should take warnings from that." Since then, the government had put forward some good ideas and suggestions on cultural development and cultural policy issues. In April 1956, at the expanded session of the Politburo meeting, Mao Zedong proposed that *Baihua Qifang* (Let a hundred flowers blossom) and *Baijia Zhengming* (Let a hundred schools of thought contend) that should be our principle. *Baihua Qifang* in the field of arts and *Baijia Zhengming* in the field of academics. On May 26th, Lu Dingyi, Minister of the Publicity Department, wrote a report entitled *Baihua Qifang, Baijia Zhengming*. The report pointed out that, "What we advocate is that 'Let a hundred flowers blossom; let a hundred schools of thought contend.' This is to promote the freedom of independent thinking, freedom of debate, freedom of creation and criticism in literary, artistic and scientific work, and the freedom to express, insist on and retain their opinions."[18] Until February 1957, Mao Zedong continued to affirm and promote the spirit of *Baihua Qifang, Baijia Zhengming*at the Supreme State Conference. At the same time, the critical attitude of the Party and the state towards intellectuals was also different from before.

In 1956, Zhou Enlai pointed out in the *Report on Intellectual Issues* that, "The vast majority of intellectuals in China are already part of the working class." For the first time, intellectuals were regarded as "parts of the working class." It could be said that the proposal and implementation of the Double-Hundred and related cultural policies not only foreshadowed the government's gradual adjustment of the Full-Scale Sovietization policy but also implied that the era of the revival of Chinese culture is coming. Under the guidance of the Double-Hundred Policy, intellectuals were once liberated and actively criticized and suggested ideas to the Party. At the same time, academia had paid attention to the issues of Chinese history and excavated and sorted out a batch of Chinese cultural heritage. However, the Double-Hundred Policy only existed for a brief period, and the central policy soon changed.

The expansion of the Anti-Rightist Struggle in 1957 caused a devastating reversal after a brief renaissance of Chinese culture. In March 1957, Mao Zedong pointed out that, "Our party has a large number of new members who are intellectuals (the number is even greater in the Youth League), and some of them have quite serious revisionist ideas." In May 1957, large-scale Anti-Rightists Struggle began, and intellectuals became the object of criticism once again. According to statistics, more than 550,000 rightists were identified across the country during this movement. On June 29, 1957, the central government instructed that among the rightists, there were about 400 people in Beijing and about 4,000 people across the country who needed to be named and criticized in various areas. Only 10 days later, the number of people instructed by the central government to prepare for the public criticism doubled. In August, it was required by the movement to expand further downwards, and it was proposed to dig deeper for the rightists.[19] "The consequences of this Anti-Rightist Struggle were very serious. A large number of intellectuals, patriots, and Party cadres have been misclassified as rightists, and they and their families have suffered long-term wrongs and blows. They were unable to utilize their talents and intelligence for the socialist construction of the country. This is not only their misfortune but also the misfortune of the country and nation."[20]

In terms of culture, this was a major misfortune of Chinese culture which has been passing down for thousands of years. After this "Big Sweep" against intellectuals, elite intellectuals leftover from the Republic of China withdrew from the stage of history in 1957. The emancipation of intellectuals in the *Baihua Qifang* era and the overall silence since then became a major historical turning point in the development of Chinese culture. After this upheaval, Chinese culture has long found it difficult to recover.

b) Chinese universities in cultural changes.

The ups and downs of Chinese culture in the Double-Hundred era have had the most direct impact on the development of Chinese higher education. In 1956, the *Baihua Qifang* Policy proposed that intellectuals responded to the call for freedom and began to reflect and criticize the excessive admiration and unconditional imitation of Soviet culture in the early stage. "As far as the education system is concerned, they severely criticized the fact that the country has rigidly copied the much-too narrow specialization setting, neglection, and limitation of social sciences in higher education in the Soviet Union, and also that the country regarded Marxism as the doctrine blindly, instead of critically absorbing its rules."[21]

In 1957, Chinese universities ushered in a short period of liberalization, and to some extent restored some characteristics of Chinese traditional education, especially traditional academy education. There were two representative events in this period. The first was the political criticism of the Renmin University of China. In the early days of the Double-Hundred, most of the fierce criticism came from the Renmin University of China. "Some young people from Renmin University called it 'the big hive of dogmatism.' This kind of criticism goes far beyond the scope of academic issues, and constituted a threat towards the Party's authoritarian rule."[22] In fact, in ancient China, the academy had a tradition of close integration with politics. For example, the Donglin Academy in the Ming dynasty was famous for its style of "satire on political affairs and discretion on characters." From this perspective, the criticism of current politics by the Renmin University of China has shown the characteristics of traditional Chinese academy culture. The second was the advocation of academic freedom by Peking University's President, Ma Yinchu. In 1957, Ma Yinchu, the president of Peking University, published the *New Population Theory* in this brief period of freedom. In the Anti-Rightist Struggle, Ma Yinchu received a series of attacks due to this article and was forced to resign in 1960. However, he still refused to withdraw his argument because the article was academic research rather than political speech. Hayhoe interpreted Ma Yinchu's insistence from the perspective of Western culture as a full manifestation of Western academic freedom, but on the other hand, Ma Yinchu's unique *pifu buke duozhi* (you cannot snatch away the will of even the lowliest of men) style as an unbent literati was more of the manifestation of traditional Chinese culture.

The wind of freedom rushed by Chinese universities, but the following blow of anti-rightism was profound and far-reaching. After the Anti-Rightist struggle, "the function of higher education of guiding social development had ended, as it could only unconditionally obey the political and economic system. As a result, higher education had lost its vitality, generability, and energy. From this moment on, for some time, the past glory of Chinese universities no longer existed.[23] A large part of the intellectuals targeted by the Anti-Rightist Struggle belonged to the higher institutions, they became the hardest-hit areas of the struggle. "According to the statistics of the Ministry of Higher Education in August 1957 on 205 colleges and universities across the country (there were 229 colleges and universities at that time, 24 of which did not report relevant materials), there were 17,769 teachers and students designated as rightists, accounting for 3.6% of the total teachers, students, and cadres population. There were 59,641 teachers in the 205 colleges and universities, of which 3911 were deemed as rightists, accounting for 6.56% of the teaching population. Among the 3,911 rightists, there were 789 professors, 375 associate professors, 1216 lecturers, and 1531 teaching assistants. Judging by the numbers, professors and associate professors occupied a considerable proportion."[24] In this turbulence, the more famous universities became the hardest-hit areas. "Among the 205 higher institutions, the more prestigious the institutions, the greater the proportion of rightists, which could be as high as 10.97%. The ratio of rightist teachers was 18.48% in some schools; rightist students, 10.98%."[25] Throughout the prestigious universities of this period, the former tranquillity in the field of academics and respect for teachers had completely disappeared. The most regrettable thing was the complete demise of the National Southwestern Associated University Intellectual Group formed during the war against Japan. If the college and department adjustments in 1952, say, only broke up this huge knowledge group in terms of structure and system, the Anti-Rightist Struggle in 1957 eventually destroyed the remaining spirit of freedom of this intellectual group. As

Xie Yong said, "After 1957, the National Southwestern Associated University intellectual group had the highest proportion of rightists. Since then, this group, as an epitome of Chinese intellectuals in the first half of the 20th century, has never recovered."[26] The Anti-Rightist Struggle effectively suppressed university intellectuals left over from the Chinese Republican period, and the voice of opposition has been completely contained.

3. *Chinese Culture and Chinese Universities during the Great Leap Forward*

In May 1958, at the Second Session of the Eighth National Congress of the Communist Party of China, the Central Committee adopted the general direction of "drumming up, striving forward, and building socialism in a fast, wide, good and economical manner." This marked that China no longer relied on the Soviet model politically and economically. The era of the Great Leap Forward has arrived. In the social development process of blindly fast-forwarding and rectifying, national policies repeatedly swayed and changed. Chinese culture and Chinese universities have once again entered a period of upheavals after the Double-Hundred era.

a) Cultural changes within social changes.

During the Great Leap Forward movement of 1958–1959, the political "leftist" tendency continued to expand, criticism of intellectuals in the cultural field continued unabated, and Chinese culture continued to sink in extreme social changes. Facing the extreme chaos brought about by the Great Leap Forward in 1960, the central government began to adjust its economic development policies and formally proposed the "eight-character" policy of "adjustment, consolidation, enrichment, and improvement." In the cultural field, it mainly manifested in the adjustment of literature and art and the change of intellectual policies.

From the second half of 1961 to the first half of 1962, the central government organized a series of symposiums on cultural ideas, summing up experience and lessons, and trying to correct misconducts. Zhou Enlai pointed out, "Performing modern drama could express the spirit of the times, so could performing historical drama." He severely criticized the extremist and unilateral tendency in the field of arts influenced by the leftist ideological trend. The adjustment of literature and art necessarily involved the adjustment of intellectual policies. At the Guangzhou Conference in March 1962 (that is, the State Scientific and Technological Commission held a national science conference and the Ministry of Culture and China Theatre Association held a national drama, opera, children's drama creation symposium in Guangzhou), Zhou Enlai spoke to the representatives of the two conferences, titled *On Intellectual Issues*. He reiterated the 1956 basic estimation that intellectuals were already part of the working class. In his speech, Chen Yi proposed that the intellectuals who were harmed in the movement should be "redressed and crowned." At the same time, Deng Xiaoping chaired a meeting of the Secretariat of the Communist Party of China to discuss the work of redressing.

The meeting pointed out that "In the past few years, there have been many incidents where people were criticized and punished. Most of them have undergone processes such as "purging of white thoughts," "purging of rightism tendencies," and "purging of incorrect thoughts and trends," most of which were ungrounded."[27] According to statistics, in August 1962, more than 6 million cadres, party members, and the masses were redressed. The adjustment of literature and art and the adjustment of intellectual policies attempted to reverse the long-standing leftist tendency in China, gradually revealing a trend of Chinese culture's revival. However, due to differences within the ruling party, especially the "silence" of the party's top leader Mao Zedong, many correct policies have not been effectively supported and implemented. Under the influence of ideology, Chinese culture has once again lost a precious opportunity for rejuvenation since the Double-Hundred policy. The Tenth Plenary Session of the 8th Central Committee of the Communist Party of China was held in September 1962, the policy of having class struggle as its principle was reiterated. From 1963 to the spring of 1966, a "socialist education movement" was launched at some rural and urban grassroots levels. In this movement, criticism, and denial of Chinese cultural heritage once again dominated the discourse.

The Central Committee of the Communist Party of China's *Resolutions on Several Historical Issues of the Party Since the Founding of the People's Republic of China* made an objective evaluation of this period of history that, "In the field of ideology, some wrong and overindulgent criticisms were placed on some literary works, academic views, and some representatives of the literary and academic circles. There had been an increasingly serious leftist tendency in terms of evaluating the problems of intellectuals, education, science, and culture, which later developed into the catalyst of the Cultural Revolution. However, these errors had not reached the point of dominating the overall situation at the time."[28] As far as the intellectual policies were concerned, although criticism and repression were mainstream during this period, the country had also provided plenty of special care for senior intellectuals. Some scholars conducted historical investigations on the living conditions of senior intellectuals during the Three-Year Famine and pointed out that it was a period when senior intellectuals were favored. The special care from the government persisted until the Cultural Revolution. Lu Jiandong recorded in *The Last Twenty Years of Tschen Yin-koh* that although Tschen was categorized as "middle-right" politically, he still enjoyed special care higher than ordinary people in his life. Objectively speaking, the "leftist" tendency before the Cultural Revolution has not yet brought down intellectuals. However, it was undeniable that the road to the revival of Chinese culture during this period was full of obstacles. The stronger the momentum of criticism was getting, the closer it got to the fate of full-scale denial.

b) Chinese universities in cultural changes.

In 1958, the wind of the Great Leap Forward swept across China. Higher education followed the trend of the times and proposed the "popularization of higher education in about fifteen years." Higher education entered the first period of rapid development since the founding of New China. According to statistics, there were 229 higher institutions in the country in 1957, which grew to 791 in 1958, 841 in 1959, and 1289 in 1960. In three years, the number of higher education institutions has increased by 1,060, which was more than 4.6 times as before. However, the result of blindly developing higher education ultimately led to a serious decline in its quality. In 1961, higher institutions implemented the "eight-character policy," reflected from past experiences, and comprehensively adjusted and rectified the order of higher institutions. In particular, the formulation and implementation of Sixty Articles of Higher Education once brought Chinese higher education back on track. However, due to the limitations of special historical conditions, the tide could not be turned. In general, the development of higher education fluctuated greatly during this period, and the radical thought reform once again overwhelmed efforts to restore and adjust the higher institutions. Before the Cultural Revolution, Chinese universities struggled between traditionalism and anti-traditionalism for the last time.

During the Great Leap Forward, a major feature of China's higher education reform was the pilot implementation of the work-study system. Contrary to the educational tradition of belittling labor for thousands of years, combining education with productive labor became the basic concept of higher education during this period. In January 1958, the Central Committee of the Communist Youth League issued the *Decision on Promoting Work-Study Program among Students*, proposing the importance of the work-study scheme and paying for the educational expenses via part-time working. On January 31, Mao Zedong pointed out in the *Sixty Working Methods (Draft)*, "All laboratories and affiliated factories that can produce in higher industrial schools, outside of the needs of teaching and scientific research, should be involved in the production as much as possible."[29] In May 1958, Liu Shaoqi formally proposed the idea of "two education systems" and "two labor systems" at the expanded session of the Politburo. He pointed out, "Some universities could also implement work-study schemes." The scheme could be implemented in all universities, or a few work-study classes could be established. This should also be regarded as a formal school system."[30] There was nothing wrong with the idea of combining labor and education advocated by the work-study system, but in the reality of the Great Leap Forward in education, it had gone further and further. In March and April 1958, the Ministry of Education convened the Fourth National Education Executive Conference in Beijing and put forward the central theme of "Promoting the Great Leap Forward in Education by Opposing Conservative Thoughts." Since then, in colleges and universities, labor has been over-emphasized, and the building of factories and farms became the mainstream. It has drifted away from the concept of learning first that was emphasized in traditional education. In 1961, to implement the "eight-character guideline" to rectify problems that emerged in the rapid development of higher education, the Ministry of Education formulated and piloted the *Temporary Work Regulations in Higher Institutions Directly under the Ministry of Education of the People's Republic of China (Draft)*. There were clear requirements that higher institutions must focus on teaching, and strive to improve the quality of teaching. There should be at least eight months in a school year spent on teaching. Students should participate in productive labor for one to one and a half months.[31] This regulation, in a sense, reaffirmed the tradition of ancient Chinese education which emphasized books and knowledge. During this period, the anti-traditional momentum of the Chinese society intensified, and the resistance almost disappeared. However, the Chinese characteristics in the development process of Chinese higher education were still traceable. For example:

1. The establishment of traditional Chinese medical colleges.

Between 1956 and 1960, a traditional Chinese medical college was established in almost every province and autonomous administrative region. These medical schools were independent of those general medical schools which offered a mix of European and Soviet curriculum models. Besides, the general medical school also offered courses on traditional Chinese medicine, which lead two different scientific streams – Chinese and European – towards convergence in medical education, and influenced each other to develop side-by-side.[32]

2. The rise of local institutions.

During the Great Leap Forward, the decentralization of central education management authority promoted the development of local higher institutions to a certain extent. From a cultural perspective, "these changes were a reaffirmation of local culture and knowledge, as well as a process of reconnecting the huge hierarchical system with Soviet characteristics to China's real cultural background."[33] Of course, as the political situation changed again, these characteristics were short-lived, and soon died off. But on the whole, in the early days of the founding of the People's Republic of China, even in the most radical leftist-leaning period, the characteristics of Chinese culture in the development of Chinese higher education were still valid.

4. *General characteristics of Chinese universities' cultural character development during the Seventeen Years*

The first seventeen years of the founding of the People's Republic of China was a period of great change in Chinese society. The Chinese culture was ill-fated. It loomed within political upheavals. Chinese universities stuck to a lost tradition in the difficult continuity of Chinese culture. From the historical perspective, Chinese culture has undergone social changes, which appeared to be diminishing, yet it had been quietly surging from the inside. During the period of Full-Scale Sovietization, Chinese culture was neglected, and yet, it was not completely denied. During the period of the Double-Hundred Policy, there were both times of criticisms and favors regarding Chinese culture, yet it experienced a short period of renaissance. During the Great Leap Forward, Chinese culture was irrecoverable but still, it was not completely lost. The general characteristics of Chinese universities' cultural character during this period could be summarized as declining overall, but still present.

First, the cultural character of Chinese universities generally declined. This was mainly influenced by the social and cultural atmosphere, or taking one step further, an inevitable result of political revolution. New China was founded, the Communist Party was in power, and political supremacy dominated the formation of Chinese culture. Due to the unstable political views and distortions in practice, the development of Chinese culture was extremely irregular and it gradually declined. During this period, the much-too-frequent movements of the ideological remolding of intellectuals posed the gravest impact on Chinese culture, with the 1957 Anti-Rightist Struggle being the most destructive. The greatest reality of Chinese society in the Seventeen Years was that intellectuals, as representatives of traditional culture, basically remained silent since the Anti-Rightist Struggle in 1957. As a result, Chinese culture had lost its most effective supporters and transmitters, and Chinese universities were no longer the free front for intellectuals. Although there were more underlying factors of the overall decline of Chinese universities' cultural characters, this was indeed the greatest reason.

Second, traces of the cultural characteristics of Chinese universities remained. The historical dilemma of Chinese culture had a profound negative impact on the formation of Chinese universities' cultural characters. The main reason that the cultural character of Chinese universities still survived was that Chinese culture never really died off in China. Firstly, as far as Chinese culture itself was concerned, it had thousands of years of heritage. Its history was so long that it was already written in the genes of the Chinese nation. How could it be eliminated artificially in a short time? Secondly, as far as the external influence of Chinese culture was concerned, on the one hand, the leaders of the Party, as the directors of Chinese culture in the new period, had the closest relationship with Chinese culture, regardless of their backgrounds or personal experiences. On the other hand, although most of the intellectuals in this period "gave up their independent judgment voluntarily because they accepted or adapted to the new government too eagerly,"[34] there were still a few people who maintained their independent personality and defended the fine traditions of Chinese culture.

It was true that governed by the ideology, the ruling party's recognition of Chinese culture was more limited and selective. The intellectuals' support for Chinese culture was also fragile in the wave of anti-traditionalism. However, history proved that this was still necessary for the preservation of Chinese university cultural genes.

Section 2: The Formation Path of Chinese Universities' Cultural Characters in the Seventeen Years

After the founding of the People's Republic of China, the Communist Party of China transformed from a revolutionary party to a ruling party. Party-ruled nation, Party-ruled military, and Party-ruled religion became the main form of organization, while the intellectuals were marginalized. Jin Guantao deconstructed the "super-stable system" of Chinese society, pointing out that "under the conditions of opening to the outside world and increasing diversification of thoughts, schools couldn't impart knowledge (institutions for intellectual creation) to guarantee that all intellectuals have a unified ideological belief. Therefore, another organization must be established to ensure the ideological unity of the social organizers. That is the Lenin-style political party. In short, integrating ideology and establishing political structure under open conditions with the Lenin-style political party as the backbone of the social organization. Intellectuals naturally retreated to the margin."[35] In the first seventeen years of the founding of the People's Republic of China, this kind of conflict between the ruling party and intellectuals manifested intensively. Intellectuals' ideological remolding movements occurred repeatedly, anti-rightist waves surged. There was a little right of governance or even right to speak for intellectuals in China's universities. They were left with two inevitable choices, to either remain silent or consciously transformed themselves into the Party's spokesperson. However, the forced "disappearance" of intellectuals did not interrupt the continuity of the cultural characters of Chinese universities. Instead, the ruling party began to play a leading role in their formations. Admittedly, as the main body of Chinese universities, intellectuals were still the external impetus for the formation of the cultural character of Chinese universities during the Seventeen Years, such as Ma Yinchu of Peking University and Wu Yuzhang of Renmin University.

But on the whole, they had not been able to exert a lasting and powerful influence, and this influence was still introduced according to the compliance with the political power of the ruling party. In July 1950, the *Decision on the Leaders' Relationship within Higher Education Institutions* established the principle that "national higher institutions are under the unified leadership of the Ministry of Education of the Central People's Government." Since then, the supreme management power of national higher institutions was firmly controlled by the party and the state. Objectively speaking, there was no irreconcilable conflict between the ruling party and intellectuals at the Chinese cultural level due to their common cultural background. Therefore, the conflict might have existed, yet the former and the latter were not in binary opposition. This was manifested in the fact that the cultural character of the Chinese university still existed during this period. For the same reason, the ruling members of the party were closely related to and intertwined with the Chinese culture, but only to a limited extent. The decline of Chinese universities' cultural character was good evidence for this fact. Therefore, under the influence of the special cultural characteristics of the ruling members of the party, there was an overall decline of the Chinese universities' cultural character in the Seventeen Years. And yet, traces of the universities' cultural character persisted and carried on.

Based on the above analysis, this section takes the Chinese culture, the ruling party, and the Chinese university as the analytical framework, and step-by-step studies the basic formation path of Chinese universities' cultural character in the Seventeen Years. There are three main steps to this analysis. First, examining the cultural views of the ruling party and digging out the internal connection between the Party and Chinese culture from a historical perspective, all based on the analysis of the cultural propositions and policies promoted or established by the state during this period. Second, analyzing the Party rulers' university view and sorting out the basic characteristics of Chinese universities' cultural characters, based on the typical external characteristics of Chinese universities during this period. And third, concretely analyzing the internal consistency between Mao Zedong's and Chinese university's cultural characters, and reaffirming the present book's judgment on the characteristics of Chinese university's cultural character, by taking Mao Zedong, the core leader of the Party as the object of this research.

1. The Party Rulers and Chinese culture

"The disintegration of China's 'tradition' in the early 20th century first occurred in terms of 'hardware,' with the most obvious being the abolition of the two-Millenium imperial system [...] However, the value system belongs to the 'software' part of 'tradition.' Though 'invisible' and 'intangible,' it directly regulated people's thoughts and behaviors. After 1911, the 'hardware' of 'tradition' collapsed, yet the 'software' as a value system entered a state of 'dead without perishing.'"[36] After the founding of the People's Republic of China, the socialist political system was regarded as supreme. The ruling party especially loathed the "hardware" of traditional society, and this attitude even seriously affected the status of the "software" as a value system in people's minds. The state of "dead without perishing" remained the same in the new period. In the evolution of the times, Chinese culture had found new sustenance among the ruling party members.

In the Seventeen Years, due to the collective silence of intellectuals, especially intellectuals from the Republican Chinese period, Chinese culture mainly affected social changes through the ruling members of the party. The rulers were inseparable from Chinese culture, and many scholars systematically and comprehensively demonstrated and analyzed this. Zhao Chuanhai's *Wenhua Jiyin Yu Shehui Bianqian-Zhongguo Shehuizhuyi Lujing Zouxiang De Minzu Wenhua Jiexi* (*Cultural Genes and Social Changes – An Analysis of the National Culture Led by the Path of Chinese Socialism*) has a detailed description of the cultural genes of the Communists: "The Chinese blood, which carried and accumulated Chinese cultural genes, ran in the Chinese Communist Party, both on the level of individuals and the party as a whole," "Although the Communist Party of China once raised the banner of anti-traditionalism, on the whole, it still 'had a rich heritage of traditional culture.'"[37] The Seventeen Years was a special period in which the ruling party demonstrated strong anti-traditionalist momentum, but the heritage of Chinese culture could not be denied. The reason was largely due to "the founders and early leaders of the Chinese Communist Party received relatively good traditional education to a varying degree."[38] But on the other hand, due to the interference of the leftist path, in the first seventeen years after the founding of the People's Republic of China, the reality of Chinese society was that traditional Chinese culture had already been neglected for a long time. This was an important reason why the cultural characters of the Party leaders were queried. The serious deviation between reality and theory made an objective evaluation of the ruling party's cultural characters by future generations more obscure. Throughout the Seventeen Years, the cultural propositions or cultural policies advocated by the leaders of the Communist Party of China have largely reflected the true attitude of the ruling party towards Chinese culture.

a) The new democratic cultural concept.

The concept of the new democratic culture was put forward before the founding of the People's Republic of China. "From 1940 until the 30 years after the founding of New China, it has been highly regarded by Chinese Communists and advanced intellectuals."[39] In the Seventeen Years, the new democratic cultural concept, as the most basic cultural policy of New China, was a concentrated expression of the ruling party's cultural characters.

The ideological origin of the new democratic culture could be traced back to the cultural debate during the May Fourth New Culture Movement. During the Movement, Western culture and Chinese culture were in a fierce confrontation. The total-Westernizationists confronted the conservatives, but they failed to produce lasting influence due to their overcorrection. The Chinese Communists and non-Party Marxists had overcome the extreme leftist and rightist biases and put forward a new concept of cultural issues, namely "popular literature of the national revolutionary war." "Popular Literature of the National Revolutionary War" was first proposed by Lu Xun and others in June 1936. In *On Our Present Literature Movement*, Lu Xun pointed out, "What the 'League of Left-Wing Writers' has led and fought over the past five or six years was the movement of proletarian revolutionary literature. This literature and movement had been developing. Until now, more specifically and practically, it has developed into popular literature in the National revolutionary war."[40] On the issue of traditional culture, Lu Xun pointed out, when discussing woodcuts, that "Other publishers are reproducing ancient Chinese woodcuts while introducing new works in Europe and America. These are also new wings of Chinese woodcuts. It is a way to adopt good foreign practices and give play to making our works richer. It is also a way to adopt Chinese heritage and integrate new elements to make future works unique."[41] This largely revealed the true meaning of the word "national" in "popular literature of the national revolutionary war." "Lu Xun's direction was the direction of the new culture of the Chinese nation." Lu Xun's cultural propositions mentioned above were further developed in the New Enlightenment Movement in 1937.

Zhang Shenfu pointed out in the article *May Fourth Movement and New Enlightenment Movement*, "The emergence of a truly new culture is logically the combination of two different cultures. Transplantation of a foreign culture (or civilization) will not grow if it does not adapt to the local soil. Or in other words, to meet today's needs, the cultural movement brought by this New Enlightenment Movement should not only be popular but also bear some national characters."[42] In Zhang Shenfu's exposition, the basic characteristics of the new democratic culture were adequately expressed nationally, scientifically, and popularly. In February 1940, Mao Zedong published the famous *The Theory of New Democracy*, which made a scientific summary of the Sino-Western cultural debate over the past 100 years, and formally summarized the culture of new democracy as "national, scientific, popular culture." Mao Zedong pointed out that the so-called new-democratic culture was the people's anti-imperialist and anti-feudal culture, and it was characterized by being "national, scientific, popular." Although this expression was the product of the political situation at that time, it also reflected the Communist Party's cultural view before the founding of the country. After the founding of the People's Republic of China in 1949, the new democratic culture was formally established as the cultural policy of the ruling party to govern the country and prosper the industries. The words, "national" and "scientific" collectively expressed the connotation of "Chinese culture" in the proposition of the new democratic culture. From a cultural perspective, the word "national" was mainly referred to in terms of Chinese and Western cultures. It emphasized that Western cultures should be absorbed as nutrients of China's own culture, and we should see Chinese culture as the basis for transplanting Western cultures. "Scientific" was mainly used in terms of the new and old culture. It emphasized eliminating the dross of feudal culture and absorbing its democratic essence. Chinese culture (traditional culture) was both the object of criticism and the subject of inheritance. In this sense, the new democratic culture interpreted a "critical inheritance" of Chinese culture, which laid the cultural tone of the early New China in theory and policy. In a certain sense, the theory expressed the Communists' macroscopic or overall Chinese cultural standpoint, which was the dialectical interpretation of the Communists' cultural concepts.

b) The cultural view of Baijia Zhengming.

Baihua Qifang, Baijia Zhengming in short, *Shuang Bai* (Double-Hundred) policy, as an important cultural policy, put forward by the ruling party in the early days of the founding of the People's Republic of China, was a concrete expression of the new democratic cultural concept in the art and academic fields. It was also an important theoretical reference for studying the ruling party's cultural characters.

In April 1956, at the expanded session of the Politburo meeting, Mao Zedong was the first one who proposed that *Baihua Qifang* (Let a hundred flowers blossom) and *Baijia Zhengming* (Let a hundred schools of thought contend) should be our principles. *Baihua Qifang* in the field of arts and *Baijia Zhengming* in the field of academics. This marked the formal introduction of the Double-Hundred policy. In May, at the seventh session of the Supreme State Conference, Mao Zedong once again said, "Now the spring season has dawned on us, let a hundred kinds of flowers bloom do not let only a few kinds of flowers bloom. This is called the blooming of hundreds of flowers. The struggle of hundred schools of thought was during the Spring and Autumn Period and the Warring States period two thousand years ago. There were many doctrines at that time, everyone argued freely, and this is also what we need now."[43]

Mao Zedong had made a similar statement as early as the founding of the People's Republic of China. For example, in April 1951, the Chinese Academy of Traditional Chinese Opera was established, and Mao Zedong wrote the inscription *Baihua Qifang, Tuichen Chuxi*n, and established it as the general guideline for the reform of Chinese traditional opera. The proposal of the Double-Hundred policy in 1956 was largely a further development and a wider range of popularization of the idea of *Baihua Qifang, Tuichen Chuxin*. According to Mao Zedong's speech at the expanded session of the Politburo, in May of the same year, the then Minister of the Publicity Department of the CPC Central Committee, Lu Dingyi, made a report to intellectuals, titled *Baihua Qifang, Baijia Zhengming*, making in-depth and comprehensive interpretations of the Double-Hundred policy. The report pointed out, "What we advocate is that we 'Let a hundred flowers blossom; let a hundred schools of thought contend.' This is to promote the freedom of independent thinking, freedom of debate, freedom of creation and criticism in literary, artistic and scientific work, and the freedom to express, insist on and retain their opinions."[44] In February 1957, Mao Zedong once again emphasized in his speech at the 11th (expanded) session of the Supreme State Conference, "The policy of *Baihua Qifang, Baijia Zhengming* is a policy to promote artistic development and scientific progress, and it was to promote the socialist cultural prosperity of China Policy. Different forms and styles of art could develop freely, and different schools of science could contend freely."[45] At this point, the Double-Hundred policy had become quite mature on the theoretical level. From the perspective of traditional culture, "the proposal and implementation of the Double-Hundred policy did not only herald the arrival of the spring of modern cultural construction but also implied that the spring of the resurrection of Chinese cultural genes."[46]

In August 1956, Mao Zedong's speech entitled *A Chat with Musicians* was of landmark significance. He emphasized, "The appearance of China, be it political, economic or cultural, should not be old and should be changed, but the characteristics of China should be preserved. It should be based on China and [it should] absorb foreign ideas. They should be integrated and organically combined."[47] Taking Chinese culture as the foundation, being inclusive, and learning from others, was an important part of the Double Hundred policy. This fully affirmed the fundamental value of Chinese culture in the process of cultural construction in the new period. In a sense, the Chinese cultural concept embodied in the Double-Hundred policy was the first direct expression of the ruling party's cultural characters in national policies.

c) A brief review of the Chinese cultural concepts of the ruling members of the Party.

The new democratic cultural view and the *Baijia Zhengming* cultural theory, as the most fundamental macro-cultural policy and specific literary and the arts policy in the Seventeen Years, were the intensive expressions of the ruling party's cultural characters. Looking at the cultural policies of the ruling party during this period, one of the main standpoints was the repeated confirmation of the foundation of Chinese culture. This meant that the reform and development of Chinese universities should also reasonably inherit the fine traditions of Chinese culture. It was true that these cultural policies and guidelines were largely dominated by ideology, but they also reflected the basic cultural positions of the ruling party. Even in extreme social changes, Chinese universities still maintained the characteristics of Chinese culture. It could be largely attributed to the implicit restrictive role played by the Party leaders' cultural characteristics. Although the ruling party deviated further and further away from the cultural policy at the realistic level, it was still true that their cultural characters loomed throughout the period. Undeniably, they indeed formed a realistic basis for the cultural characters of Chinese universities. Conversely, although the ruling party had established a more reasonable cultural development direction in terms of policy guidelines, it had failed to adhere to most of them in actual practice, or even the opposite. This was also the reason why in the Seventeen Years, the cultural character of Chinese universities declined overall, yet they persisted.

2. *The ruling members of the Party and Chinese universities*

Based on the analysis of the main cultural policies over the Seventeen Years, one of the main reasons for the establishment of the cultural character of the ruling party was the establishment of the 'foundation' of Chinese culture. Furthermore, to what extent and how was this Chinese cultural value applied to the reality of Chinese universities? Under the leadership of the ruling party, which were the aspects of Chinese culture that were accepted and then influenced Chinese universities? This is a key point for us to deeply understand the cultural character of Chinese universities during this period. The following section discusses the specific relationship between Chinese universities and Chinese culture based on the main university-running concepts of the ruling party in university reform. Taking Weber's "ideal type" as the basic research method, three core concepts were extracted from the ruling party's university-running ideas throughout the Seventeen Years. These were *Yi Min Wei Ben* (People-orientedness), *Yi Dang Zhi Xiao* (Party-ruled universities), and *Sixiang Geming* (Ideology revolution). These characteristics could all find their roots in Chinese culture.

a) People-orientedness.

People-orientedness was a basic starting point for the ruling party's university-running concept. The people-orientedness idea regarded serving the people, especially the workers and peasants, as the fundamental task of Chinese universities. During this period, the education policy was repeatedly emphasized on the educational principle of "serving the people," including the concepts of *Dazhong* (the masses), *Renmin* (people), and *Qunzhong* (the populace), which were mainly reflected in the working guidelines for the students and the people in charge of education. In September 1949, the First Plenary Session of the Chinese People's Political Consultative Conference convened and adopted the *Common Guidelines of the Chinese People's Political Consultative Conference.* In the fifth chapter, the Guidelines put forward the cultural education policy of New China:

> The cultural education of the People's Republic of China is a new democratic, national, scientific, and popular cultural education. The cultural and educational work of the people's government should focus on raising the people's cultural levels, cultivating talents for national construction, purging feudal, comprador or fascist ideas, and developing the thought of serving the people.[48]

To serve the people, popular cultural education became one of the development goals and basic characteristics of Chinese university education in the new period. In his speech at the opening of the first National Higher Education Conference in 1950, Ma Xulun established the idea of "Higher institutions preparing and beginning to open doors for workers and peasants" as one of the basic policies for rectifying and strengthening higher education. In the same year, the Ministry of Education formulated the *Interim Regulations for Higher Education*, which required the below:

> Universities and training colleges should enroll and provide special assistance for the following students with the equivalent of high school graduation: (1) revolutionary cadres with considerable work experience; (2) young workers and peasants; (3) students of minority races; (4) overseas Chinese students.[49]

The establishment of the "public" higher education policy not only diversified the types of higher institutions, such as the emergence and prevalence of correspondence schools and evening schools but also made sure that universities, as the country's major higher education institutions, continued to lean towards graduates from fast-track workers and peasants high schools. According to statistics, under the promotion and support of national policies, the percentage of students with worker and peasant backgrounds in the total higher institution population increased from 20.5% in 1953 to 36.4% in 1957. Although "children of national cadres and intellectuals still monopolized the enrollment of higher institutions," this was, after all, a breakthrough. Besides, the educational concept of people-orientedness was also reflected in the policy of Schools Ran by the People Nationwide. In 1958, Lu Dingyi pointed out in the article *Education Must Be Combined with Productive Labor:*

> We believe that the masses need education for the sake of the socialist revolution and socialist construction. Since the masses could do revolutionary and construction work, they not only could receive an education but also run education. To run education, a team of professionals is a must. Now we should greatly enhance this specialized team by the means of mobilizing cadres and establishing normal universities. However, the special education team must be integrated with the masses, and the running of education must rely more on the masses. Only under the leadership of the Party can we integrate professional educators with the masses. It is only through adopting the popular path of 'coming from the masses, going back to the masses,' and implementing the Schools Ran by the People Nationwide, could China's education develop in a fast, wide, good and economical manner.[50]

Based on this concept, during the Great Leap Forward, the power of university-running was decentralized, and Chinese universities leveraged on the power of the people to rapidly develop. According to statistics, there were 229 higher institutions in the country in 1957, which grew to 791 in 1958, 841 in 1959, and 1289 in 1960. In three years, the number of higher education institutions had increased by 1,060 – by more than 4.6 times. Under the guidance of the concept of Schools Ran by the People Nationwide, the enthusiasm for running schools at the grass-roots level had risen and many local universities with local characteristics emerged. In short, the general education policy of the ruling party and the policy of Schools Ran by the People Nationwide might have had various problems in the specific practice, but the starting point of "people-orientedness" was beyond reproach.

From a cultural perspective, the ruling party's people-oriented university education concept was in line with the people-oriented thought in Chinese culture. A core concept in the Chinese cultural tradition is people-orientedness, most typically reflected in Mencius' thought of *Min Gui Jun Qing* (the masses are superior and the emperor is inferior). Although the people-oriented thought belonged to the traditional ruling class' policy of governing the people, what was manifested in the ancient private education was a democratic spirit. Confucius founded private academies, which flourished among the people. Learning was then no longer restricted by class. He was one of the first who practiced this democratic and equal people-oriented thought in the field of higher education. The academies of later generations inherited the legacy of Confucius, and there were also higher institutions that relied mainly on private power and provided education for the public. From this perspective, there was every reason to believe that the ruling party aimed at the masses and advocated the idea of running a university "coming from the masses, going back to the masses," based on Confucius' ideal of private education. Specifically, at least in the following aspects, it could be considered that Chinese universities' basic characteristic of people-orientedness was rooted in Chinese culture. Others include:

1. Education for the people.

One of the core concepts in the Confucian classic *Daxue* is *Xinmin,* which emphasized that the practical purpose of higher education was to teach the people to be good and to enlighten the wisdom of the people. Chinese universities were people-oriented, and they fulfilled the social responsibilities and obligations of the *Xinmin* of ancient *daxue.*

2. Teaching without class distinctions.

Higher education was for the general public, regardless of social hierarchies. This was one of the main characteristics of private education institutions in ancient China. Since the establishment of Chinese universities in modern times, they had followed the path of elitist education of Western universities, with obvious characteristics of class and selection. During this period, to a certain extent, the open policy of workers and peasants restored the traditional Chinese private education, which bore a quality of teaching without class distinctions.

3. People-run education.

Although unified leadership of the central government was emphasized in Chinese universities since the founding of the People's Republic of China, they also supported and encouraged the people to actively participate in running education. Since ancient times, China has had the tradition of running private schools, most typically the traditional academies as the ancient Chinese higher institutions had private origins.

In short, people-orientedness was the fundamental university-running concept of the ruling party that was rooted in Chinese culture. It has become a basic characteristic of Chinese university cultural characters.

b) Party-ruled universities.

Party-ruled universities was another important concept behind the university-running ideas of the ruling party during this period. Contrary to the educational concept of independent universities pursued by intellectuals in the Republic of China, Party-ruled university was a university-running concept of centralized management and unified planning that the ruling party came up with based on the needs of the country. Universities were nationalized based on the national authority and political power. Party-ruled universities were characterized by a high degree of uniformity and planning, involving two aspects: the first was the national unified examination for university admissions, that is, university admissions were controlled by the state; the second was the national unified work allocation upon graduation, which was the allocation of university graduates that belonged to the state.

After the founding of New China, with many things still to be done, the primary task was to build the country. To meet the needs of the country's construction, establishing the Party's leadership in education in the new period became the top priority. Party-ruled universities were gradually raised to the top of the agenda. In 1950, the Minister of Education, Ma Xulun, pointed out in his *Opening Speech of the First National Higher Education Conference:*

> Our higher education should gradually get on the same track with the construction of the country and gradually move towards "plannedness." China used to be a semi-colonial and semi-feudal country. Its economic and political inconsistency manifested in the extreme anarchy in higher education. Each institution governed themselves. Now that New China has a strong political and economic unification, our education work should be planned and carried out based on this background, under the principle of unification.

He also declared that:

> At this stage, because of the shortcomings of objective and subjective conditions, the Central Ministry of Education had temporarily entrusted the regional Departments of Education or Cultural Education to govern higher institutions in

> each of the administrative regions. And through the necessities and possibilities, the central government would gradually implement direct governance of higher institutions across the country.[51]

To realize unified management of the national higher education by the central government, the transformation to public-ownership of private universities and church universities had become an inevitable choice and a core measure for the country to transform universities. At the beginning of the founding of the People's Republic of China, the state already started to accept and transform public and private universities and church universities leftover from the Republic of China in a planned manner. By the end of 1951, all church universities receiving foreign subsidies were merged by the national universities and their original names were canceled. During the college and department adjustments in 1952, all private universities were also incorporated. legalized and transformed to public-owned schools. With the end of private and church universities, Chinese universities entered a fully public-owned era. During this period, universities' main features were that they were highly centralized with unified management.

Under the unified public-ownership system, Chinese universities had gradually established a systematic national service mechanism. There were two key systems, and the first was the national unified examination system. In 1955, to ensure that all universities provided fair opportunities and enrolled candidates based on their academic status, the country formulated a unified national examination system. Until today, the national Gaokao (college entrance examination system) is still a major feature of China. The second was the work allocation policy for university graduates. In 1951, in the *Decision on Educational System Reform*, the government had stipulated: "The work of higher institution graduates will be allocated by the government." This system emphasized the absolute obedience to the country, and it was not withdrawn until the mid or late 1990s. The significance of these two systems was that the former unified the entrance method for Chinese universities through the national examination, and the latter ensured the social service value of Chinese universities through the work allocation of university graduates. From the perspective of university students, participating in the college entrance examination and then entering state-owned enterprises became an ideal life path. To some extent, entering the university meant direct entry to state-owned enterprises upon graduation.

Indeed, the high degree of centralization and standardization of Chinese universities was largely due to the influence of the Soviet model of the higher education management, but if this model was incompatible with the Chinese cultural soil, it would have been hard to reform the university model so smoothly in such a short period. The traits of a high degree of unity and consistency of Chinese universities during this period had a greater inherent isomorphism with the cultural character formed by the ruling party members in that special era. This was mainly manifested as follows:

1. It largely coincided with the concept of "excelling in academics to enter officialdom" in Chinese culture.

Under the control of centralized power, ancient Chinese higher education established a strict national service system. Although there were official and private schools in ancient society, unlike the total officialization of Chinese universities in this period, most of the students in both official and private studies took the path of Imperial Examination going to Officialdom, which was regarded as the right track in life. As a result, the imperial examination system for a unified talent selection prospered for over a millennium. In comparison, the unified examination system of Chinese universities during this period and the ancient national examination system, as well as the unified work allocation system for university graduates, and the ancient "imperial examination for officialdom" system seemed to coincide.

2. This was in great agreement with the concept of unity in Chinese culture that centered on unified power.

A unified power center was established after Qin Shi Huang (The First Emperor of the Qin Dynasty) unified China. Since then, the traditional Chinese society has operated for a millennium under a highly unified feudal imperial power. In the reunification of China by the Communist Party, the unified power center remained unchanged, and the highly unified management method remained the same. From this perspective, when the one-party dictatorship of New China was established, the centralization of state management of Chinese universities was still consistent with the traditional Chinese concept of unity. In short, Party-ruled universities as the ruling party's basic university-running concept had become another characteristic of Chinese universities' cultural character.

c) Ideology revolution.

The ideology revolution was a key feature given to Chinese universities by the ruling party during this period. This idea supplemented the most fundamental internal premise of the Chinese universities' people-oriented and party-based university-running concepts, reflecting the most essential cultural character of the ruling party. This was the soul of Chinese universities.

Contrary to the idea of freedom of thought advocated by intellectuals during Republican China, the revolutionary mindset referred to the criticism and remolding of the original thought itself and its main carriers, such as university intellectuals, by the ruling party, to better implement the proletarian political ideology. The educational ideas within the revolutionary mindset were mainly reflected in the specific reform measures such as the setting of political courses and the transformational movement of university teachers' ideology.

The classical works of Confucianism in the late Qing Dynasty were kept as the only type of knowledge, and based on this, a series of narrowly defined expertise disciplines were arranged to achieve the aims of the state machine. Similarly, in New China, Marxism-Leninism and Mao Zedong Thought became the new orthodox and leading concepts of the new higher education system. Curriculum design became a major method for the new orthodox ideas to lead the higher education system. In 1952, the Ministry of Education formulated the *Instructions on Marxism-Leninism and Mao Zedong Thought Courses in National Higher Institutes*, which made specific provisions for the establishment of Marxism-Leninism and Mao Zedong Thought courses in colleges and universities in the country. The three courses of Theories of New Democracy, Theories of Political Economy and Dialectical Materialism, and Historical Materialism were established as mandatory courses in colleges and universities. The instructions demanded that:

> Comprehensive universities and colleges of finance and arts should set up theories of a new democracy, theories of political economy and dialectical materialism and historical materialism in the order of the first, second, and third grades respectively. For industrial, agricultural, and medical colleges, they should set up theories of a new democracy and theories of political economy during the first and second grades respectively.[52]

What paralleled the reform of the ideology courses was the ideological remolding of intellectuals. According to Mao Zedong, the so-called "ideological remolding" was "one of the important conditions for the complete realization of democratic reform and the gradual implementation of industrialization in all aspects of our country." And according to Qian Junrui, it was "the key to higher education reform." From 1951 to 1952, higher institutes across the country launched a learning campaign aimed at "transforming teachers' ideas and reforming higher education." During the campaign, many university professors actively studied Marxist-Leninist courses and conducted self-examination and self-criticism. In 1953, in the summary report of *Improvement of Higher Education over the Past Three Years*, Zeng Zhaolun summarized the early ideological reform movement:

> This is a movement where all teachers applied criticism and self-criticism, to achieve self-transformation. The purpose of our study is to clear the counterrevolutionary thoughts and to draw a clear line between our enemies and allies; to criticize the bourgeois ideology, and to make a clear distinction between the working class ideology and the bourgeois ideology, to establish the leading position of the working class ideology in schools and lay the ideological foundation for reforming the old education.

He also pointed out that:

> By combining the ideological remolding and the Three-anti Campaign, teachers in higher institutes generally made a great step forward in their way of thinking.[53]

In the same year, the Minister of Education Ma Xulun delivered a speech, *Regarding the Principles and Tasks of Higher Education* at the forum of heads of higher institutes in Northern China. It established that the ideological remolding of the teachers of higher institutes should be considered as the priority of the national reform of higher education in 1953. From the above analysis, it is not difficult to see that revolutionary transformation in ideology was a core concept of the reform of Chinese universities during this period. The higher education reforms since the establishment of PRC have always been accompanied by the ideological remolding of intellectuals, and the ideology revolution became the theme of the time for university reform. In terms of its thoroughness and comprehensiveness, this ideological revolution was radical. In terms of its political coercion and ideological unification, this ideological revolution was also authoritarian. Because of its profound radicalism, the ideological revolution tried to abolish everything and inevitably pointed the finger at Chinese culture, while because of its strong authoritarian nature, this impact was further strengthened by political protection. From this perspective, the idea of universities of the time was based on ideological revolution and anti-tradition, which seemed to be quite different from Chinese culture. However, this was only one aspect of the whole truth.

From the perspective of its methods, it was not coincidental that the idea of an ideological revolution of universities regarded ideological remolding as the base point of Chinese universities' reform. From the perspective of purpose, it was also reasonable that such an idea established the starting point of Chinese university reform on the ideological side. In a sense, the ideological revolution still followed the traditional thinking mode of Chinese culture. Specifically:

1. The basic point of traditional Chinese reform was thought, and utilizing ideological reform as the entry point was the basic law of Chinese social change.

"The way to solve problems by ideology and culture was influenced by the deep-rooted traditional Chinese cultural tendency of monism and intellectualism."[54] Lin Yusheng claimed during the interpretation of the Chinese cultural roots of the fully anti-traditional ways utilized by the May Fourth Movement. For the same reason, the ideological revolution in Chinese universities, as another anti-traditional climax after the May Fourth Movement, still applied the same way of "solving problems with ideas." This was indeed the same as the tradition of "ideas first" of the ancient Chinese reforms.

2. The starting point of higher education in ancient China was *Xiushen* (self-cultivation).

"*Xiushen* first, *Zhiguo* (governing the country) second" was the fundamental rule of ancient Chinese higher education. The so-called "self-cultivation" was the establishment of a personal ideological and moral foundation. The fundamental purpose of ideological criticism was to reshape the values of intellectuals with the new official orthodoxy and to achieve the purpose of "self-cultivation" within the proletarian ideology. From this perspective, as a basic way of self-cultivation for university education, ideological criticism had the ultimate goal of governing the country, and the value pursuit was no different from that of ancient Chinese universities.

To sum up, people-orientedness, party-ruled universities, and ideological revolution were the main university concepts that were established and promoted by the ruling party during the Seventeen Years. The three concepts did not exist independently. Chinese universities took people-orientedness as their starting point, the party-rule as their essential feature, and the ideological revolution as their most basic way or realization, hence they integrated the three. As proven above, these characters were closely related to Chinese culture and constituted the specific content of the cultural character of Chinese universities during this period. Objectively speaking, these so-called Chinese university concepts were mainly the one-sided manifestations of the traditional characteristics of Chinese culture under the special ideological background of the ruling party and the needs of the national ideology. Due to the established national standpoint of the ruling party, this one-sided cultural character was extremely macroscopic. Looking at the above core concepts of Chinese universities, we can see that the ruling party, as the builder of the cultural character of Chinese universities, paid little attention to the specific university spirit and the knowledge itself, so it lacked the pursuit of the inner spirit of the institution shown by the Republican Chinese universities. It and did not emphasize the autonomy of universities. It also lacked the pursuit of the value of knowledge itself, and hence it did not value academic freedom. From this point of view, the main focus of the ruling party in constructing the concept of Chinese university lay in the macro-political levels of state and power, mass, and responsibility, etc. Therefore, all the concepts involved in the university-running concepts were the "bigger" ones, such as the "people" in people-orientedness, and the "political party" in the party-ruled universities.

It is worth noting that it did not matter if it was the people-oriented education policy for workers and farmers, or the adjustment of departments based on the premise of party-rule, or the ideological reform movement characterized by the ideological revolution, the determination to overthrow everything was unprecedented in the history of Chinese universities. Therefore, the one-sidedness and the macroscopic nature of the cultural character of Chinese universities during this period also showed an unprecedented revolutionary nature. In short, the basic characteristics of the cultural character of Chinese universities during the Seventeen Years can be roughly described as three characters: one-sidedness, macroscopic nature, and the revolutionary character. The three characters' reign, in reality, was the product of a special era. The fundamental reason for them was that the ruling party wanted to build a higher education service institution that was highly consistent with the national ideology. Due to this point, it was fundamentally different from the academic position of the intellectuals of the Republican China universities. Instead, it was quite consistent with the establishment of Chinese-style universities by the scholars in the late Qing Dynasty to maintain Confucian ideology.

3. *Mao Zedong and the cultural character of Chinese universities*

As the highest leader of the ruling party, Mao Zedong was the core of China's political power during the Seventeen Years. Therefore, many scholars refer to this period as the Mao Zedong Era. Due to the special nature of the period, Mao Zedong's cultural character had a direct, even decisive, impact on the development of China's education. Mao Zedong's selective acceptance of Chinese culture became an important factor in the formation of the cultural character of Chinese universities. Mao Zedong was enlightened in Confucianism and possessed considerable knowledge regarding the development of ancient and modern China, and it was inevitable for him to accept Chinese culture. This is an inherent premise in the exploration of Mao Zedong's important role in the cultural character of Chinese universities. Based on the reality of the country, Mao Zedong had a strong revolutionary spirit. It was also inevitable that his acceptance of Chinese culture was extremely selective and critical. This is a key point for continuing the study of Mao Zedong's influence on the cultural character of Chinese universities. During this period, some of the main educational policies were drafted or reviewed by Mao Zedong himself.

In 1957, Mao Zedong made a report at the 11th (Expanded) Meeting of the Supreme State Conference, *Regarding the Proper Handling of the Internal Conflicts among the People*, stating: "Our education policy should enable the people who receive it to improve in moral, intellectual and physical properties, allowing them to become enlightened and cultured socialist workers."[55] In 1958, Mao Zedong further proposed in his speech, education policy of "education serving proletarian politics and must be combined with productive labor." Through these two educational talks, the fundamental nature of Chinese higher education "serving proletarian politics" was finally established. The following analysis will start from the three core concepts of the Chinese university's cultural character of people-orientedness, party-ruled universities, and ideological revolution, to find arguments within Mao Zedong's educational thoughts. The purpose of this is to explain the decisive role of Mao Zedong's traditional cultural thoughts in the real cultural character of Chinese universities, regarding their consistencies in people-oriented thought, centralized thought, and ideological revolution thought.

a) People-orientedness.

The education policy proposed by Mao Zedong emphasized that education served the proletariat. The so-called proletariat in the political dictionary of the Mao Zedong era mainly referred to the masses of workers and farmers. Mao Zedong pointed out in *On the People's Democratic Dictatorship:* "The foundation of the People's Democratic Dictatorship is the union of the working class, the farmer class, and the urban petty bourgeoisie, but mainly the union of the workers and farmers because these two classes account for 80% to 90%."[56] In Mao Zedong's view, "Among these four types of people, workers, farmers, and soldiers are the main force, the number of the petty bourgeoisie is relatively small, their revolution is less resolute, and they are more educated and cultured compared to the farmers, workers, and soldiers."[57] Therefore, making education systems serve the education for the people and establishing universities serving the masses of workers and farmers became the fundamental point for Mao Zedong's reform of education and Chinese universities. From a cultural perspective, the formation and construction of Mao Zedong's theory of "people's education" stemmed largely from his acceptance of the Chinese culture, especially the Chinese cultural character of "peopleness." When reviewing Lu Dingyi's article *Education must be combined with productive labor*, Mao Zedong added this passage:

> The history of Chinese education has a character of "peopleness." Confucius' *Youjiao Wulei* (indiscriminating education); Mencius' *Mingui Junqing* (the people matter more than the emperor); Xunzi's *Rending Shengtian* (the people shall triumph over the sky); Qu Yuan's criticism of the wrong of the ruler; Sima Qian's tribute to resistance; ancient materialism of Wang Chong, Fan Zhen, Liu Zongyuan, Zhang Zai, Wang Fuzhi's ancient materialism; democratic literature of Guan Hanqing, Shi Naian, Wu Chengen, and Cao Xueqin; and the democratic revolution of Sun Yat-sen; they all differed from each other, and many of them did not author any educational monographs. However, they still inherently affected the education of the people. When discussing the history of Chinese education, they should be mentioned.[58]

Mao Zedong's educational thought of serving the proletariat indeed had strong political tendencies and purpose, but it was undeniable that Mao Zedong's affirmation and acceptance of Chinese people-oriented thoughts, whatever the purpose, were a matter of fact. And this is largely based on his profound understanding of Chinese culture. Besides, Mao Zedong's history as a farmer seemed to make his acceptance of the ancient people-oriented thought more natural. Based on the analysis above, Mao Zedong's people-oriented thought was the fundamental starting point of his educational thought, and this was the main theoretical basis for the formation of Chinese universities' cultural character.

b) Party-ruled universities.

A fundamental position of Mao Zedong's educational thought was to uphold the party's unified leadership of education. In Mao Zedong's view, the primary condition for "education to serve proletarian politics" was that the party must lead to education. At the beginning of the founding of New China, Mao Zedong solemnly declared at the first meeting of the First National People's Congress, "The core force leading our cause is the Communist Party of China. The theoretical basis for guiding our thinking is Marxism-Leninism." Mao Zedong made it clear that on the seven aspects of the industry, agriculture, commerce, education, military, politics, and the party, the Party shall lead in everything. The party must lead the industry, agriculture, commerce, culture, education, the army, and the government. As far as the leadership of higher institutions is concerned, Mao Zedong pointed out in 1958, "Higher institutions should seize three things: the first is the leadership of the party committee; the second is the route of the people; the third is the combination of education and productive labor." He placed the unified rule of the party as the primary condition for the development of higher institutions. From Mao Zedong's point of view, "Whether a school runs well or not depends on the president of the school and its party committee, and how competent they are on a political level."

Based on Mao Zedong's exposition on strengthening the party's leadership in education, Chinese universities gradually became nationalized during the Seventeen Years – they became national universities. Although Mao Zedong had always criticized feudal totalitarianism in politics, his insistence on the unified leadership of the education party directly and inevitably introduced the centralized system of traditional Chinese politics into Chinese universities. It is also worth noting that although Mao Zedong tried to unify the education of the entirety of China with power in the reform of the educational system, he was particularly sensitive against the feudal bureaucracy brought by the unification of power. Therefore, Mao Zedong proposed that an important issue for the party to become an education expert was learning. Mao Zedong's *Speech at the Yan'an Literature and Art Forum* pointed out that, "We must not refuse to inherit and learn from the ancients and foreigners, even [from the] content with feudal and bourgeois backgrounds." He called on party members to actively learn from the experience of old times and foreign countries for them to competently lead in education.

The above analysis proves that Mao Zedong's thought of state-owned education not only continued the system of China's monolithic centralized management but also used the history of Chinese culture as a basis for learning. The above-mentioned thought of Mao Zedong had an important impact on the formation and practice of the idea of party-rule in Chinese universities.

c) Ideology revolution.

Following Mao Zedong's educational policy of "education serves the proletariat's politics" and based on the traditional Chinese people-oriented thought, Chinese universities established the educational concept of "serving the proletariat with education." This was based on traditional Chinese management, and Chinese universities established an educational system where "education served politics." However, without unified thought, it was difficult to achieve either of the two. To ensure that education served proletarian politics, the ideology revolution became a fundamental inner premise. One of the major cultural reforms in the Mao Zedong era was the ideological remolding of intellectuals. Mao Zedong believed that "ideological remolding, first of all, is the ideological remolding of various groups of intellectuals. It is one of the important conditions for China to thoroughly implement democratic reforms and gradually implement industrialization on all aspects."[59] In 1957, Mao Zedong's *About the Correct Handling of Contradictions Among the People* specifically talked about the ideological remolding of intellectuals:

> Recently there has been a falling off in ideological and political upkeep among students and intellectuals, and some unhealthy tendencies have appeared. In the eyes of some people, it seems that politics, the future of the motherland, human ideals are none of their concerns ... Given this situation, it is now necessary to strengthen ideological and political upkeep. Both intellectuals and young students should study hard. In addition to studying their disciplines, they must progress in ideology and politics. This requires learning Marxism and current affairs and politics. Not having a correct political viewpoint is comparable to having no soul.[60]

Mao Zedong opposed the ideological dictatorship of Confucianism on the Chinese people and replaced it with an ideological monopoly of Marxist-Leninist culture. The intellectual transformation movement indeed caused harm to the vast number of intellectuals, however, it was inevitable for the unification of national ideology. As a core content of Mao Zedong's educational thought, the ideology revolution was, to some extent, the acceptance of China's monocultural character, which directly affected the ideological reform of Chinese universities.

In summary, in Mao Zedong's education philosophy, Chinese universities should belong to the people, the country, and the proletariat. These concepts were also consistent with Mao Zedong's traditional ideas such as people-orientedness, centralization of power, and thought-orientedness. Although the above-mentioned cultural concepts and measures of Chinese universities cannot be completely attributed to Mao Zedong's personal cultural preferences, it is still reasonable to believe that Mao Zedong's educational thoughts played a key role in shaping the cultural character of Chinese universities. In other words, the cultural character of Chinese universities was largely the result of Mao Zedong's selective acceptance of traditional culture. During the Seventeen Years, Mao Zedong quickly changed the appearance of Chinese universities since the Republican China era with his personal cultural preferences and successfully created the Mao Zedong era of a Chinese university. He encountered minimal resistance while receiving overwhelmingly positive responses. Apart from factors such as his core position in politics and his personal "charisma," there was also an important point which was the profound influence of Chinese culture within Chinese society. It is almost a consensus that during the Seventeen Years, the coercive political force of university reform greatly overwhelmed educational autonomy. However, this phenomenon was the great alignment of some reform thought and Chinese culture, which was concealed by history for a long time. The reason why Mao Zedong's educational thought (which can also be called the ruling party's ideas and measures of university reform) progressed smoothly during this period could be greatly attributed to the fact that even though Chinese culture had died in Chinese society, it did not fade out entirely.

Section 3: Analysis of Chinese Universities' Cultural Character during the Seventeen Years: A Case Study of Renmin University of China (RUC)

Considered the first university after the founding of New China, Renmin University of China was an iconic school in the history of the reform and development of Chinese higher education during the Seventeen Years. For a long time, RUC was a national model for comprehensively learning from the Soviet Union. It was often regarded as an anti-traditional representative. Admittedly, RUC was a political benchmark set by the ruling party in the early days of the founding of the People's Republic of China. For the sake of abolishing the old and establishing the new it inevitably had a strong anti-traditional political consciousness. However, RUC, born in Chinese culture, could not achieve a complete change of its nature, and it was precisely because of the special cultural traits that were endowed by this political force that RUC was destined not to be a "brand new" university from its very beginning. Maturing before PRC and established at the beginning of PRC, RUC was different from PKU and THU, which were established in the late Qing Dynasty and developed in Republican China. It was a new starting point for modern Chinese universities. Before the founding of the PRC, from its days as the Northern Shaanxi Public School to its life as North China University, RUC grew up in the baptism of blood and fire before the establishment of the People's Republic of China. It was therefore established and rapidly developed under the support of the ruling party. From the Northern Shaanxi Public School of the Revolutionary University (founded in

Yan'an in August 1937) during the Second Sino-Japanese War to the establishment of the first new socialist university, the People's University of China, in 1950, for over ten years, it was developed under the direct care of the leaders of the party and the country. This was unprecedented in the history of Chinese universities. As a university directly established by the Central Committee, RUC was the concentrated manifestation of the ruling party's university-running concepts, which embodied the cultural character of Chinese universities during this period. Therefore, this section chose RUC as an example of the cultural character of Chinese universities during the Seventeen Years to analyze in detail the aforementioned cultural character of Chinese universities and their reality. In the following part, text analysis will be applied to generate a comprehensive cultural overview of RUC on three levels: university concept, the university system, and university cultural symbols. The content of the above investigation will mainly be limited to the RUC from its official establishment in 1950 to the Cultural Revolution in 1966. The materials were obtained from national policies, historical records of RUC, memoirs of alumni, along with other historical documents.

1. The university-running concepts of RUC

The university-running concept of RUC came directly from the leaders of the Central Committee, and at the same time, it depended on the active implementation and practice of school leaders, especially its first president, Wu Yuzhang. Based on government documents or individual speeches issued by relevant leaders, the unique university-running concepts of RUC during this period can be summarized as follows:

a) RUC is a university of the nation.

When PRC was first founded, Mao Zedong and other party leaders, while planning to build a new China was considering building a "new type" university led by the Communist Party of China. From June to August 1949, Liu Shaoqi secretly visited the Soviet Union and decided to establish the university in Peiping. In December 1949, on the eve of the founding of RUC, Liu Shaoqi, the deputy chairman of the Central People's Government, personally issued the *Decision of the Establishment of Renmin University of China* by the CPC Central Committee at the 11th meeting of the Government Administration Council. This could also be seen as the first-ever formal mentioning of the university-running concept of RUC. The relevant content of the decision is summarized as follows:

> The People's Republic of China has already been born, and we are about to achieve a comprehensive and thorough victory of the People's War. The great construction of our new country has begun. To accommodate the needs of the construction of our country, the People's Central Government has decided to

> establish the Renmin University of China to receive advanced experience from the Soviet Union, and to hire Soviet professors for the sake of training various officials for the construction of our young country in a planned and step-by-step manner. The university's educational policy should be a combination of teaching and practice, combining Soviet experience with China's situation.[61]

As stated in the above document, the university's educational policy was to combine the Soviet experience with the situation in China. And the so-called Chinese situation was that "the great construction of our new country has begun." Based on the purpose of "training various officials for the construction of our young country," the Central Committee represented by Liu Shaoqi defined the establishment of RUC to be on the "national affairs" level. This was the most fundamental and most important point. Starting from the fundamental purpose of the founding of RUC, one of the university-running concepts of RUC could be summarized as governing the country, that is, RUC was, first of all, a university of the country, and its fundamental purpose was to serve national construction.

b) The Renmin University of China was a university of the people.

In October 1950, when the Renmin University of China was officially established, Liu Shaoqi gave a more in-depth explanation of its founding at the opening ceremony:

> The People's Republic of China has won. It broke through the rule of imperialism. Feudalism and bureaucracy were eliminated. The people's country was established with the working class as its leader and the worker-farmer union as its basis. We are here to serve the workers and farmers. Therefore, the education of our country should also serve this purpose. Our university should educate officials who serve the people. Therefore, we cannot build a new type of university-based entirely on the old universities – and hence the Renmin University of China [was born.] The policies of those old universities are to be reformed, but they cannot be reformed instantly, and it is impossible to correct them at once. The transformation of the old university must be carried out slowly and step by step, and it will take a considerable time. But we can't wait any longer, we have to start a new university.[62]

After the founding of New China, the people became the main body of the country, and serving the people became the main task of the Communist Party. Interpreting Liu Shaoqi's speech, one of the main points was that RUC, as "the first new university established by the new China," was fundamentally different from the old universities, since RUC was dedicated to serving the people. From the perspective of social service, this concept can be summarized as *Xinmin,* that is, RUC belonged to the people and served the people as its purpose. In fact, RUC was founded based on the revolutionary school in the old liberated area and had a fine tradition of serving the people throughout history. This had always been consistent. On the practical level, this was also the result of the direct promotion of the ruling party, who led the construction of RUC in the new era. "Renmin University of China was established under the cordial care of Comrade Liu Shaoqi. From organizing the preparatory committee to formulating specific plans, he participated in and presided over the work."[63] This is what, Vice President of RUC, Cheng Fangwu later said. As the leader of the party, Liu Shaoqi played an important role before and after the founding of RUC and he constructed the initial macro-level university-running concept for RUC.

c) RUC was the base for proletarian ideology.

In October 1951, RUC held its first anniversary. The then-Minister of Education, Ma Xulun, mentioned in his speech that he hoped that RUC could strengthen its patriotic education and hoped it could continue to strengthen its political education. He emphasized the political and ideological education function of RUC. To serve the country and the people, RUC took the spreading and learning of Marxism-Leninism and Mao Zedong Thought as its fundamental task from its very establishment. As the former president of North China University and the first president of RUC, Wu Yuzhang always insisted on Marxism-Leninism and Mao Zedong Thought as the fundamental guiding ideologies for running the school. In the article *Fighting to Implement the Policy of Improving the Quality of Education-Commemorating the 5th Anniversary of the Establishment of Renmin University of China*, Wu Yuzhang pointed out that:

> The school will further implement on all aspects the educational policy that theories come from practice, pay attention to the content of the five-year plan and the reality of national construction in teaching and research, and criticize the bourgeois ideology. It is necessary to strengthen the political and ideological education of students so that the political theory education in the class system and the regular ideological upkeep outside the class could be better combined.[64]

Based on this thought perspective, Wu Yuzhang reiterated the educational policy of combining theory and practice, striving to "make RUC a strong fortress for studying and propagating Marxism-Leninism and Mao Zedong Thought." Using this as the basis, the third university-running concept of RUC can be summarized as *Zhengyi* (shaping the right ideas), that is, RUC was a university of proletarian ideology, and it spread the ideas of Marxism-Leninism and Mao Zedong Thought. It shaped these right ideas to educate and cultivate the people. History proved that as the first new university in New China,

RUC always adhered to the party's multiple-identities design as a national construction machine, an institution of people's service, and the fortress of political and ideological thought, and it trained a large number of talent for the country and society. Wu Yuzhang, the president of the RUC, urged students to:

> Arm the mind with Marxist-Leninist knowledge and establish a worldview of dialectical materialism and historical materialism; be proficient in science, technology, and business; acquire the skills to participate in various constructions; connect theory with practice, and be able to correctly master policies on the economy, culture, education, and foreign affairs; acquire noble qualities, shrewd talents, loyalty, and simplicity, to not be afraid of hardships, to be one with the masses, serve the people, and train to be a talent for the sake of creating a new society.[65]

The above text can be regarded as a comprehensive and specific summary of the university-running concept of RUC. It took the Marxist-Leninist knowledge as the ideological pursuit, served the people as its value orientation, and trained oneself as a talent for national construction. Such was the fundamental purpose of *Zhiguo, Xinmin,* and *Zhengyi* of RUC. On the one hand, this was due to the value orientation indicated by the ruling party of RUC after the founding of the PRC. And on the other hand, this was also closely related to the origin of RUC, which was the revolutionary school before the founding of the PRC. However, no matter the angle, the root cause for this lay in the influence of traditional culture.

Throughout the above sorting and induction of the university-running concepts of RUC, it can be observed that RUC still utilized the ways of ancient Chinese universities. Specifically, RUC set its foundation as *Zhiguo,* and this was inherently related to the ideas of *Xue Yi Zhiyong* (learn for the sake of using), centralization of power, and the combination of politics and education in traditional culture. RUC had set its root as *Xinmin,* which implicitly aligned with the people-orientedness, *Tianxia Datong,* and the equality of people in traditional culture. RUC also set its stand as *Zhengyi*, which was compliant with the ideas of a spiritual revolution, unity of thought, and unity of culture in traditional culture. From this point of view, the ideological origins of the above-mentioned university-running concepts of RUC could be traced back to traditional culture, even though they became pan-politicized due to the control of the ruling party in their practice. Of course, the university-running concepts of RUC are not limited to this, nor do they all take Chinese culture as their historical basis. Its anti-cultural character is even more powerful in practice. However, no matter how obvious the anti-traditional colors in the cultural changes of Chinese universities were during the Seventeen Years, the traditional imprint of Chinese culture still existed.

As the first new university in New China, RUC embodied the cultural character of people-orientedness, party-ruled universities, and ideological revolution in the Seventeen Years through its university-running concept.

2. *The System Design of RUC*

Guided by the university-running concept that was designed by the ruling members of the party, the system design of RUC was determined and implemented strictly by following the educational principles of *Zhiguo, Xinmin,* and *Zhengyi.* Before the Cultural Revolution, under the direct planning of the ruling party, RUC established a systematic, formal, and unique university organization system. In the following part of the book, the relevant system design of RUC will be examined on two levels: the level of the macro national management system and the level of the micro-school teaching system. They would provide an institutional basis for the university-running concepts of RUC and help to annotate a unique traditional cultural feature of the university.

a) Macro-level: National management system.

The relationship between RUC and the government was extraordinary. As a university created by the Government Administration Council instead of the Ministry of Education, RUC was bathed in special attention by the Party from its establishment. From enrollment to distribution, the government provided comprehensive care for RUC and it always occupied a dominant position within RUC. To clarify the relationship between RUC and the government means to understand the basic and key points of the RUC system. Taking the president's responsibility system under the leadership of the Party Committee, the national enrollment system, and the national distribution system as examples, it can be observed that they provided a real guarantee for RUC to better realize the concepts of *Zhiguo, Xinmin,* and *Zhengyi.*

First was the President's Responsibility System under the Leadership of the Party Committee. When PRC was first founded, RUC implemented the president's responsibility system. A university affairs committee was established under the leadership of the president, consisting of the president, the vice president, all department leads, the chief librarian, deans of all schools, the director of the president's office, the chairman of the teachers' labor union and the president of the student union.[66] *The Chronicle of Renmin University of China* recorded:

> Nominated by the Politburo of the Central Committee of the Communist Party of China on February 19, 1950, and approved at the sixth meeting of the Central People's Government Committee, the former president of North China

> University Wu Yuzhang was appointed as the president of the RUC, and Hu Xikui and Cheng Fangwu were appointed as vice presidents. Regarding school management, RUC adopted the president's responsibility system under the leadership of the Party group.[67]

In 1956, this system was changed:

> On October 13, 1956, in accordance with the provisions of the Eighth National Congress of the Communist Party of China and the instructions of the higher-level Party committees, the Party committee of the university convened a plenary meeting to discuss the decision to implement the party committee system and revoke the Party organization of RUC. The leadership system of the university was changed to the president's responsibility system under the leadership of the Party committee. At the meeting, 13 members of the Standing Committee were selected. Hu Xikui served as Party Committee Secretary, Cui Yaoxian served as Deputy Party Committee Secretary, while Nie Zhen and Zou Lufeng served as Deputy Party Committee Secretary for their additional posts.[68]

The shift from the president's responsibility system under the leadership of the Party group to the president's responsibility system under the leadership of the Party committee meant that the secretary of the Party committee of RUC officially replaced the president of the university. This system established the Party's direct and unified supreme leadership over RUC, and it signified that the country ownership had become the fundamental attribute of RUC. On this basis, the implementation of the university-running concepts of *Zhiguo, Xinmin,* and *Zhengyi* of RUC was guaranteed. As Wu Yuzhang, the first president of RUC, said, "Our mission is so important that it cannot be achieved without the concerted efforts of internal and external comrades under the leadership of the Party."[69] The president's responsibility system under the leadership of the Party committee established the Party's highest leadership status for RUC and guaranteed the fundamental development direction of the university.

Second, was the national planned enrollment system. As a university founded and led by the ruling Party, direct allocation by the state was the only enrollment process of RUC. This was another special point that marked RUC's differences from other universities. At the beginning of the establishment of RUC, its enrollment of students was entirely based on state allocation. In 1950, the Central People's Government Ministry of Heavy Industry, Fuel Industry, Textile Industry, Light Industry, Railway, Posts and Telecommunications, Communications and the All-China Federation of Trade Unions jointly issued a notice that allocated employees from various industries in various regions to participate in the phase of enrollment and study at RUC.[70] This system of recommendation by state organizations and direct-entry was the main source of students in RUC in the 1950s. With the establishment and implementation of a unified college entrance examination system, the country gradually nationalized the enrollment rights of higher institutions nationwide. Since 1961, the undergraduate entrance examination for RUC has also joined up with the national unified college entrance examination. From the unified allocation of quota by the nation to the unified college entrance examination, RUC's Congress enrollment always obeyed the arrangements of the nation, reflecting a high degree of planning and uniformity. As far as its function was concerned, on the one hand, it stipulated the goal of the National People's Congress in cultivating national construction talents within a specific range. While on the other hand, it made the people, as the main body of the country (especially the workers and farmers), the legal members of the university. As far as its cultural connotations were concerned, the two characters fully reflected the properties of serving the nation and serving the people within its basic university-running concepts.

Third, was the national unified distribution system. The national distribution system was a special education policy during this period. It mainly referred to a policy that the ruling party allocated work to graduates to fully meet the needs of national construction. The students of RUC were taking up various national construction positions, mostly under the unified arrangement of the nation. In this instance, the 2527 graduates from the 1960 class will be used as an example. Among all graduates, in addition to the 635 graduates who were assigned jobs by their original work organizations, a total of 1892 were uniformly assigned to various jobs by the nation. Among the fresh graduates of that year, a total of 1007 were allocated to central government agencies, scientific research institutions, and other higher institutions, accounting for about 50% of the total amount. At the same time, a total of 283 were allocated to Tibet, Xinjiang, Qinghai, and other border provinces and autonomous regions, accounting for 15% of the total amount. The rest were distributed to other provinces and cities.[71] In a word, the policy of graduates' national distribution enabled graduates to be "used properly," which directly guaranteed the full implementation of the concept of serving the national construction by RUC.

The establishment of the system mentioned above pushed for the realization of the RUC's university-running concepts. With serving the national construction as its basic purpose and obedience to the nation as its basic feature, the above management system showed a high degree of power centralization, planning, and uniformity. This was greatly consistent with the ancient Chinese system of official schools. The ancient official schools were led by the central government in terms of administrative affiliation. The highest decision-making power was concentrated in the hands of the emperor, and hence the centralization of power was achieved. As such, regarding the enrollment system, the country was determined and it allocated the quotas and chose students with the bottom-top examination and selection processes, and hence the planning property was also achieved. In terms of students' utilization, the country selected talents through the national imperial examination system and granted them with official positions, which allowed them to directly serve the construction of the country, and hence the property of unity was achieved, as well. Based on its history, it can be concluded that under the leadership of the ruling party, the institutional characteristics of power centralization, planning, and unity of RUC were all deeply affected by traditional culture.

b) Micro-level: school teaching system.

The school teaching system of RUC permeated its style with the external management system as the guarantee and the internal university-running concept as its guide. In the following part of the book, starting from the teaching body, teaching form and teaching content, the relevant systems of the three aspects will be examined, namely student composition, class setting, and curriculum arrangements. From a cultural perspective, they are all situational expressions of the teaching practice of RUC's *Zhiguo, Xinmin,* and *Zhengyi* of RUC.

The first was student composition. The main task of RUC was to train officials for the government. Therefore, from the very beginning, RUC was a university that mainly recruited workers and revolutionary cadres. Taking the enrollment constitution upon the establishment of the university as an example, in 1950, the Ministry of Education made specific regulations for the RUC admissions in the *Instructions on the Establishment of Renmin University of China:*

> The undergraduate students are divided into four types: A, senior officials who have participated in the army or local work for more than 8 years, who have educational levels equivalent to junior high school, and are under 35 years of age. B, officials who have participated in the revolutionary fighting for more than 3 years, or have worked in the relevant departments in the liberated areas for more than 3 years, who have an education level equivalent to junior high school, and are under the age of 32. When recruiting students from various places, officials who meet the requirements of categories A and B from the army and local governments should be given priority. C, industrial workers with an education level equivalent to junior high school, with more than three years of working experience, who are single, ideologically progressive, and fit for receiving further education, aged 17 to 32. D, young intellectuals who have an education level of high school, who are ideologically progressive and under the age of 27.[72]

Judging from this constitution, the student composition of RUC mainly included officials, workers, and young intellectuals. There were two outstanding features in terms of specific features of the students: First, special preferential treatment was given to officials and workers. For example, age limitations were less strict for them, and they were met with lower academic requirements. In particular, the requirements for officials with rich revolutionary history and work experience were more relaxed. Second, the different requirements for different enrollment targets showed different points of emphasis. For example, the requirements for revolutionary officials' revolutionary experience and work experience were high, and the requirements for the educational level was limited to junior high school. The requirements for workers focused more on seniority, and the requirements for young intellectuals were focused on their education levels. Hence, these prerequisite conditions emphasized the ideological progressiveness of workers and young intellectuals. In summary, RUC mainly took in and trained national officials and industrial workers, and its ideological requirements were higher than academic requirements in terms of admission standards. The former was the main presentation of RUC as a university of the people, and the latter reflected the positioning of RUC as an ideological fortress.

The second was the setting of departments and classes. At the beginning of the RUC's establishment, undergraduate and specialized courses were set, and later tutoring classes were also added, due to the low educational level of workers and farmers. Therefore, during this period, RUC mainly included three levels of education: undergraduate, specialized courses, and tutorial classes. Undergraduate teaching was organized by departments, while specialized courses were organized by classes. It was stated in *People's Education*:

> Eight undergraduate departments: (1) Department of Economic Planning; (2) Department of Finance and Credit; (3) Department of Trade; (4) Department of Cooperation; (5) Department of Factory Management; (6) Department of Law; (7) Department of Foreign Affairs; (8) Department of Russian Studies. The time needed to graduate was four years for departments of law and diplomacy. Two for Russian studies, and three for all the other departments.
>
> Eleven special courses: (1) Class of Economic Planning; (2) Class of Finance and Credit; (3) Class of Domestic Trade; (4) Class of Foreign Trade; (5) Class of Cooperation; (6) Class of Factory Management; (7) Class of Statistics; (8) Class of Law; (9) Class of Foreign Affairs; (10) Class of Education; (11) Class of History and Geography. The completion time for these classes was 8 months.
>
> Tutoring classes for workers and farmers: these courses were focused on teaching cultural and scientific knowledge. Students might graduate in one or two years, and they would directly be accepted as undergraduates upon graduation.[73]

From the very first moment, the establishment of RUC was based on the main feature of the university-department structure. This structure was different from the university-college-department system adopted by other Chinese universities of the same period (before their adjustment of departments).

Judging from the above-mentioned RUC settings, in addition to the eight undergraduate departments, RUC also set up eleven special courses and tutoring classes for workers and farmers. The setting of this flexible system reflected the university-running concept of RUC, which aimed to serve the workers and farmers. Judging from the specific setting of its departments, the eight departments and the specialized RUC courses were basically all related to the economic field, which once again confirmed the purpose of the RUC as serving the national construction. In short, the establishment of RUC followed the basic idea of the ruling party running RUC as a university of the nation and the people.

The third was the arrangement of the curriculum. Under the direct leadership of the Party, an important purpose of the RUC curriculum was to fulfill the task of studying and propagating political ideas. At the beginning of its establishment, RUC was the first higher institution in China to set up four courses of political theories including Basic Marxism-Leninism, History of Chinese Revolution, Political Economics, and Philosophy. In 1951, *People's Daily* released a special report on the school's teaching plan:

> Upon its establishment, Renmin University of China formulated a complete education plan for undergraduate and specialized courses, which stipulated their courses, critical implementation points, schedules, and other steps and procedures. In the teaching plan, Marxism-Leninism, Political Economics Theory of State and Legal Power, the History of the Chinese Revolution, the Mechanisms of People's Democracy, Russian, and Physical Education are common courses for all departments. Each department sets up systematic core courses and professional cultural courses according to their professional training goals. A total of 142 courses are offered in undergraduate courses, of which political theory courses account for 20% to 25%, professional culture basic courses account for 20%, and core courses account for 50% to 55%. There is a total of 83 courses in the specialty courses. For classes of education and classes of history and geography, political theory courses account for 26%, and core courses account for 74%; for the remaining classes, political theory courses account for 37%, and core courses account for 63%.[74]

The characteristics of the RUC curriculum can be attributed to two points. First, the political, ideological, and theoretical courses weighed more than the professional cultural basic courses. This was consistent with the value orientation of the aforementioned admission standards of RUC where ideological requirements were higher than academic requirements. From the above teaching plan, among the 142 courses offered to undergraduates, the proportion of political theory courses was greater than or equal to the professional cultural basic courses. Besides, within the seven common courses of all departments, all were special political theory courses except for Russian and Physical Education. The main purpose of the establishment of political courses was to achieve the unity of thought through ideological remolding and education of school teachers and students. As a new type of university established under the direct care of the Party, RUC had a particularly significant political backdrop, and political subjects were a key point within its curriculum.

Second, the ratio of practical courses was higher than that of theoretical courses. As mentioned above, the establishment of the RUC departments was mainly based around the economic field, and their fundamental purpose was to contribute to the national construction, and so, the proportion of business courses was the highest. RUC, as a university of the nation, aimed to cultivate national construction talents. It was inevitable that practicality rather than theory became the basic standard for the cultivation process.

To sum up, the curriculum design of RUC showed higher requirements on the ideological aspect than the cultural aspect, and it favored practical requirements over theoretical requirements. The former was a concrete manifestation of the idea of running the RUC as an ideological fortress, while the latter served the fundamental purpose of national construction.

Based on the above investigation of the RUC teaching system, its system can be seen as the best example of its concept of *Zhiguo, Xinmin,* and *Zhengyi.* No matter if it was student composition, department setting, or curriculum arrangements, RUC always followed and adhered to the main functions and responsibilities of cultivating talents for the nation, serving the people, and spreading Marxism-Leninism and Mao Zedong Thought.

3. RUC Cultural symbols

RUC was established at the beginning of PRC's founding. It did not have a rich history as Peking University and Tsinghua University, and it lacked the historical monuments of Peking University in terms of campus features. However, this did not affect the formation of traditional qualities within RUC. RUC was born and developed in the wave of reform during the new period, and it expressed its unique cultural character with its own, unique symbols. These symbols were different from Republican China's styles of PKU and THU, but they were not inferior in their cultural connotations.

a) The name of Renmin Daxue (People's University).

RUC was the first university in New China to be named after "the People." In October 1949, the Communist Party formed the new nation, giving it the name of the People's Republic of China, or China for short. In October 1950, the ruling party created Renmin University and combined it with the word China, forming its name of the Renmin University of China, also known as Renmin University of the People's Republic of China. Renmin University, as a Chinese university itself, is a people's university, and it is named after the People. This is indeed very special. The term "people" has existed in China since ancient times. Examining its origin, there are three connotations. First, it referred to human beings. *Guanzi · the Seven Standards*: "The living beings: People, flora, and fauna." Second, it referred to the common folk. *Mengzi · Jinxin II*: "There are three treasures for all kings: Land, People, and Political Affairs." Third, it referred to the counterpart of the "enemy." In different historical periods of different countries or the same country, "people" may have had different connotations according to the times. As far as the concept of China's "people" was concerned during the Seventeen Years, it generally belonged to the third interpretation, which was the antonym to the word "enemy." Since the founding of the PRC, an important ruling idea for the Communist Party of China was class struggle. Therefore, the term "people" was directly linked to the class origin and it had a strong political sense. The concept of "people" in the field of education was also distinguished by class. In 1949, the new democratic education policy established the basic idea that education served the people. In the next year, the policy was fully interpreted by Qian Junrui in *Current Policies Regarding the Construction of Education*. When the article talked about the purpose of education which was serving the people, a simple definition of the concept of "people" at this stage was given as:

> "I want to serve all people, not just the workers and farmers." If you are willing to serve the people, it is very good. But who, exactly, are "the people?" The first group is the working class, the second is the farmer class, the third is the petty bourgeoisie, and the fourth is the national bourgeoisie. Together, these four classes are the people in China at this stage. It is therefore clear that the feudal and bureaucratic bourgeoisie and their political representatives, the Kuomintang reactionaries, are by no means the people of New China. On quite the contrary, they are the enemy of the Chinese people.[75]

From the above text, "people" were more of a political concept in the official discourse, mainly representing the majority of the workers and farmers in Chinese society during this period. However, the ancient words received a new life, and the traditional fervor of "people" that was contained in the word did not completely fade. Many revolutionary cadres during the founding of the country were mostly workers and farmers, inheriting the cultural genes of traditional Chinese farmers. Hence, they were more closely related to the word "people." RUC was named after the "People," and it held the ruling party's urgent expectation of the RUC to serve the people. And a people-oriented feeling that had existed in China for thousands of years was fully visible.

b) Campus movements.

From the "Three-anti" and "Five-anti" campaigns to the comprehensive Anti-Rightist Struggle, the Seventeen Years could be described as an era of frequent political movements. It also manifested on the campus of RUC, mainly in the form of a vigorous campus movement launched by the school in response to the Party's call. Taking 1957 as a specific example:

1) *Jingjian Jieyue Yundong* (Retrench and Economize Movement). In *The Chronicle of the Renmin University of China,* the Retrench and Economize Movement was an important theme of the campus movements of RUC in 1957. The following are some excerpts regarding this matter:

> On March 15 and 21, 1957, Party Secretary and Vice President of RUC, Hu Xikui presided over the 67th school council meeting. The meeting mainly discussed the issues of enrollment, correspondence education, and the matter of retrenching and economizing. It was decided that a retrench and economize committee should be established.
>
> On April 3, 1957, the university formulated a plan for Retrench and Economize.
>
> On December 29, 1957, to implement the policy of "increasing production and to cut spending, [to] practice saving in school running" put forward by the Central Committee of the Party, the school formulated the plan of "reducing institutions and decentralizing cadres," and decided to change the working department of the school from its three-tier system to a two-tier system. The Department of Academic Affairs and the Department of Research were merged into the Department of Academic Affairs; the Department of Administrative Affairs was changed to the General Affairs Office; the school archives were changed to the school archive room, and were put under the management of the president's office. After merging and reorganizing, the number of administrative departments was reduced from 9 to 7.[76]

In 1957, the Central Committee of the Party put forward the policy of "increasing production and savings, and [increasing] diligence in running schools [to] increase production and cut spending, practice saving in school running," and the Retrench and Economize Movement of RUC reached its peak. On the one hand, this was driven by the Party's policy guidelines during this period. On the other hand, RUC always had the tradition of practicing diligence and frugality. Growing up under the baptism of war before its establishment as RUC, the university acquired a revolutionary spirit of putting up with hard conditions. Wu Yuzhang once said, "The spirit of putting up with hard conditions and overcoming difficulties, including the hard and simple style of life, is a fine tradition of the revolutionary army and working people led by our Party." After its official establishment, RUC received special support from the government, but still adhered to the idea of "diligence and frugality." As early as 1951, RUC launched the activity of "Learning and Implementing the Patriotic Convention on Increasing Production and Saving" throughout the university to promote the frugality tradition. In 1957, the

Retrench and Economize Movement entered a new climax at RUC. From a cultural point of view, the Retrench and Economize Movement and the concept of *Zhiguo* and *Xinmin* established by RUC were inseparable. Their purpose was to reduce the economic burden for the country and the people.[77]

2) The ideological remolding movement. In 1957, the anti-rightist struggle swept across the entire intelligence community and even the entirety of China. RUC actively responded to the call for national ideological remolding and launched a series of anti-rightist struggles on the campus. This was recorded in detail by *The Chronicle of Renmin University of China:*

> In the mornings of July 28 and 29, 1957, the school held a summary meeting of the Anti-Rightist Struggle. The Party Committee Secretary and Deputy President of RUC Hu Xikui, the Deputy Secretary of the Party Committee and Deputy President of RUC Zou Lufeng, on behalf of the school Party Committee, made a preliminary summary report regarding the Anti-Rightist Struggle to teachers and students in the city and the western suburbs. From the beginning of June to the end of July, the university launched an Anti-Rightist Struggle. The utilized forms of struggle included symposiums, debates, critical meetings, *Da-Zi-Bao Zhan-Dou-Dui* (Big-character Poster Combat Teams) or Combat Groups, weekly newspapers, comics, etc. In addition to thousands of criticism meetings in all departments and classes, there were also some "major campaigns" against people like Cheng Haiguo (Lin Xiling), Ge Peiqi, Wang Dezhou He An, and Wu Jingchao. According to statistics from the university in 1960, a total of 378 people were given the status of "rightists."[78]

At the beginning of its founding, RUC advocated the occupation of university podiums with Marxism-Leninism and Mao Zedong Thought and established RUC as a strong fortress for the study and spread of Marxism-Leninism and Mao Zedong Thought. This university-running concept was not only reflected in the curriculum design, but it was also manifested as one of the major themes of the ideological remolding in the campus movements. The above material described the detailed situation of the RUC campus during the Anti-Rightist Movement in 1957. In terms of form and content, this movement was profound and extensive. History proved that the Anti-Rightist Struggle itself was not a reasonable move. However, as far as its starting point of unifying ideology and stabilizing national foundation was concerned, it was not incomprehensible. In the final analysis, the issue should still be considered from the perspective of the country and the people.

c) Student life.

The Seventeen Years was a relatively difficult period for the social development of China. Especially after the three years of natural disasters, the national economy was in a critical state. During this period, the conditions of Chinese universities were quite limited and at times, extremely bad. However, RUC still trained a large number of talent for the new China.

In 1959, *Renmin University Weekly* published an editorial *Nine Years of Renmin University of China*, which mentioned that the university had trained 16,984 officials for the nation during the past nine years. Among them, 5,557 were undergraduates, 3,493 were graduates, and 7,934 were specialized students. They had written more than 1,000 scientific papers with a considerable level of quality, along with more than 100 monographs.[79] Based on the life of the RUC students during this period, the students who bathed in the concept of RUC were extremely strict with themselves and took on the responsibility of national construction, which went on to become an important reason for the RUC's fruitful achievements during its many following years. Here are a few examples.

1) Special seats in the reading room.The most vivid memory in the heads of the alumni of the RUC was probably their studying years in the 1950s and the 1960s, during which they needed to "reserve" their seats in the reading room. A 1956 alumnus recalled:

> At that time, in addition to taking classes according to the curriculum, many students were used to carrying a pile of books and notebooks from the dormitory to the reading room if there were no classes at all. Except for the time when they left for meals, they would be there all day. Given the poor conditions of the dormitories, the reading room was the best place to go. Even though the reading room was quite spacious, it was still not enough for the enormous amount of students. Hence, the trick of "reserving seats" naturally appeared. We would often hurry to the reading room and put a pile of books on the table before breakfast. The latecomers had to return to the dormitory or find another place to read. Although this kind of behavior was not very civilized, everyone understood each other, and the management staff of the reading room would also turn a blind eye, so disputes rarely occurred. Over time, this seat-reserving action slowly evolved into a "special seat" system. If anyone wanted to find someone in the reading room, there was no need to look left and right, since most students already knew the common seat for everyone. And when examinations approached, it was even more reasonable for the students to bury their heads in books during the night.[80]

Diligence and hard work were the common memories of all the RUC students. It seems that every university had a scene of "reserving seats for studying." You can see it in the old PKU and THU, while it is also a common sight for many universities nowadays, too. However, this scene was particularly memorable for RUC. Speaking of this, it is rather easy to see its parallelism with National Southwestern Associated University. Although RUC was established in the peaceful years after the founding of the PRC, economic poverty was still not significantly alleviated by this time. Compared with PKU and especially THU during the Republican China era, RUC had it extremely tough. However, the students living in the difficult RUC environment developed a diligent spirit for studying instead. On the one hand, this was related to their background and experience. Most of the RUC students were from the worker and farmer classes, and they had adopted the spirit of diligence and hard work since their childhood. As students of RUC, the great duty that rested on their shoulders made the spirit of hard work even more prevalent and important. The two points above gave the "seat-reserving" of RUC students a unique connotation of the times.

2) The students' little folding stools. Studying the memoirs of the campus life recorded by the alumni of RUC, no matter which topic they were discussing, they would always invariably mention their little folding stools from their RUC days. This is indeed somewhat unique. The following is a summary written by a 1956 alumnus:

> In our dormitory, the research class prepared a little folding stool for each student. It was made from eight short wooden strips, cross-studded, with seven or eight hemp ropes fixed on the upper end. Once unfolded, it became a small bench. Once folded, it could be taken away by gently lifting it with your hands. This kind of living utensil was quite popular in the old liberated zones. Fróm a certain perspective, it also reflected the revolutionary tradition of hard struggle. But in the southern part of China, we rarely saw it.
>
> Since then, the small folding stools accompanied us day and night and served the study and life of everyone in obscurity for two years. To draw an analogy, just as the contemporary trendy university students wear Walkmans around their waist, we were also quite comfortable and proud when we boasted about our folding stools.[81]

According to the alumnus' recount, their little folding stools reflected a revolutionary tradition of hard struggle. The arduous and simple spirit of RUC was indeed ubiquitous, and it was this spirit that was propagated and promoted by the aforementioned Retrench and Economize Movement. In the life of the students, the students' little folding stools once again proved the RUC's hard and simple tradition. In the minds of university students at that time, these folding stools became their deepest memory. The deeper reason behind this was that the concepts of RUC during the 1950s and 1960s were deeply ingrained into their minds.

3) "Three-three systems" on the playground. RUC has always had a rather active life in sports. Just as THU took physical education as its primary task, RUC also attached great importance to students' sports activities. However, the situations of the two were very different. According to the alumni of the 1961 class:

> In the 1960s, China encountered unprecedented natural disasters, food supply was tight, teachers and students were generally undernourished, everyone reduced sports, combined work and rest, to save precious energy and physical strength. Nonetheless, as we lay in our beds, we still felt hungry and couldn't fall asleep. Hence we often chattered on and on, and we all called it our "spiritual buffet." To guide students in overcoming difficulties and ensure normal learning and life, the university promoted the experience of the departments of law and archives. The university urged everyone to participate daily in 30 minutes of light activities, such as gymnastics, Tai-Chi, and walking, which were the so-called "three-three system" exercise.
>
> In a short time, the playground regained its vitality. According to the records of 12 departments of the university, the attendance rate for morning exercises reached 95%, and the simplified *Taijiquan* had a dispersion rate of 90%.[82]

The sports activities of RUC students in the 1950s could be described as colorful. The three years of natural disasters in the 1960s once again tested the students of RUC. As mentioned above, they still entertained themselves under extremely difficult circumstances and invented the interesting "three-three systems" on the playground. What they faced was incomparable with the advanced sports equipment and superior environment of THU. However, even in such a poor situation, RUC students still insisted on keeping up their physical fitness, which was even more commendable. The above analysis shows that the life of RUC students was the most vivid cultural symbol on the RUC campus, and they truly reflected the unique charm and endless influence of RUC concepts within RUC itself.

In short, as a typical representative of Chinese universities in the Seventeen Years, from the university concept to the university system to the cultural symbols, Renmin University of China was always consistent with its special cultural character, that is, people-orientedness, Party-ruled university, and ideological revolution.

Summary

There were several characteristics in the formation of the cultural character of Chinese universities during the Seventeen Years:

1) Chinese culture: political struggles prevailed during the Seventeen Years. Even though the surface of Chinese culture was broken, and the traditions were still inherited on a deeper level. During the period of Full-Scale Sovietization, Chinese culture was unfavored but never been rejected. During the Double-Hundred policy period, Chinese culture rose and fell from time to time, and also saw a brief revival. During the Great Leap Forward period, Chinese culture was heavily lost, but it never went extinct.
2) Ruling members of the Party: "The new democratic culture concept" and the "Hundred Flowers culture concept," were the most fundamental macro-cultural policies and specific literary and arts policies in the Seventeen Years. They were the intensive expression of the ruling party's cultural character. However, although the ruling party established a relatively reasonable direction of cultural development in its policy, it was not able to adhere to it for most of its actual operation, and at times, it even went in a completely different direction.
3) Chinese universities: Along with political movements, the cultural character of Chinese universities showed a strong revolutionary and political character. Serving a specific ideology, people-orientedness, Party-ruled universities, and ideology revolution became the distinctive cultural characters of Chinese universities during this period.

Overall, the Seventeen Years were a special period for the development of Chinese universities. The cultural character of Chinese universities was generally weak and their ideology was strong. One, the situation was influenced by the overall social and cultural atmosphere of the new era. And two, this was mainly the result of the ruling party directly leading and shaping Chinese universities.

Notes

1. Chen, Y. Shiqu De Daxue (Dying Universities). Beijing: Tongxin Publishing House, 2005: 244.
2. A Zheng. Duihua: Wenhua Shanbian Yu Zhongguo Mingyun (A Dialogue: Cultural Change and the Fate of China). Beijing: Xiyuan Publishing House, 2001: 9.
3. Hayhoe, R. China's Universities 1895–1995: A Century of Cultural Conflict. Trans. Xu, J. Beijing: Educational Science Publishing House, 2000: 137.
4. Cited from Feng, J. Mingyun Yu Shiming: Zhongguo Zhishifenzi Wenti Shiji Huimou (Destiny and Responsibility: Rethinking the Problem of Chinese Intellectuals after a Century). Beijing: Sino-Culture Press, 2006: 191.

5. Ibid.
6. Academy of Literature and Arts, Ministry of Culture. Zhou Enlai Lun Wenyi (Zhou Enlai's Duscussion on Literature and Arts). Beijing: People's Literature Publishing House, 1979: 37.
7. Mao Zedong. Opening speech at the Third Session of the First Political Consultative Conference. People's Daily.1951–10–24.
8. Gong, Y. Dangshi Zhaji (Notes on the History of the Party). Hangzhou: Zhejiang People's Publishing House, 2002: 338–339.
9. East China Normal University Advanced Training Class for Cadres, Academy of Educational Science, East China Normal University. Zhonghua Renmin Gongheguo Jianguo Yilai Gaodeng Jiaoyu Zhongyao Wenxian Xuanbian (Shang) (Selection of important higher education documents since the founding of the People's Republic of China (Part 1)). Shanghai: East China Normal University Press, 1979: 21, 24.
10. Su, W. 50 Niandai De Yuanxi Tiaozheng (College and department adjustments in the 1950s). Journal of Higher Education Research, 1989(4): 10.
11. Quoted from Hu, J. Xiandai Zhongguo Daxue Zhidu De Yuandian: 50 Niandai Chuqi De Daxue Gaige (The origin of the modern Chinese university system: university reform in the early 1950s). Nanjing: Nanjing Normal University Press, 2001: 85.
12. Fu, M. Sulian Gaodeng Jiaoyu De Gaige (Higher Education Reform in the Soviet Union). People's Education, 1952(9): 10–11.
13. Hu Jianhua. The origin of the modern Chinese university system: university reform in the early 1950s (M). Nanjing: Nanjing Normal University Press, 2001: 121.
14. Hayhoe, R. China's Universities 1895–1995: A Century of Cultural Conflict. Trans. Xu, J. Beijing: Educational Science Publishing House, 2000: 121.
15. Ibid, p.116.
16. Liu Haifeng. Chuantong Wenhua Yu Zhongguo Daxue De Tese (Traditional culture and the characteristics of Chinese universities). Journal of Qingdao Institute of Chemical Technology (Social Science Edition), 1999 (2): 12.
17. Ibid.
18. Sun, W., et al. Zhongguo Gongchandangren Sixiang Baoku (Treasure Vault of the Thoughts of Chinese Communists). Beijing: Gaige Publishing House, 1991: 663.
19. Dong, B. Zhongguo Jinxiandai Gaodeng Jiaoyu Shi (Higher Education History of Modern and Contemporary China). Wuhan: Huazhong University of Science and Technology Press, 2007: 294–295.
20. Li, W. Huiyi Yu Yanjiu (Xia) (Recollection and Research (Part 2)). Beijing: History of Chinese Communist Party Publishing House, 1986: 839.
21. Hayhoe, R. China's Universities 1895–1995: A Century of Cultural Conflict. Trans. Xu, J. Beijing: Educational Science Publishing House, 2000: 123.
22. Ibid.
23. Dong, B. Zhongguo Jinxiandai Gaodeng Jiaoyu Shi (Higher Education History of Modern and Contemporary China). Wuhan: Huazhong University of Science and Technology Press, 2007: 296.
24. Ibid, p. 295.
25. Ibid.
26. Xu, J. 20 Shiji Zhongguo Zhishifenzi Shilun (Historical Comments on Chinese Intellectuals in the 20th Century). Beijing: New Star Press, 2005: 404.
27. Liu, G. Xin Zhongguo Gaodeng Jiaoyu Dashiji (1949–1987) (Chronicles of New China's Higher Education). Changchun: Northeast Normal University Press, 1991: 188.

28. Party Literature Research Center. Guanyu Jianguo Yilai Dang De Ruogan Lishi Wenti De Jueyi Zhushi Ben (Annotated version of the Party's decisions on several historical issues since the founding of the country). Beijing: People's Publishing House, 1983: 174.
29. Yuan, Z. Zhongguo Dangdai Jiaoyu Sichao 1949–1989. Shanghai: Joint Publishing Company. 1991: 39.
30. Liu Shaoqi Division, Party Literature Research Center. Liu Shaoqi Xuanji (Selected Works of Liu Shaoqi (Part 2)). Beijing: Central Party School Press, 1985: 324–325.
31. East China Normal University Advanced Training Class for Cadres, Academy of Educational Sciende, East China Normal University. Zhonghua Renmin Gongheguo Jianguo Yilai Gaodeng Jiaoyu Zhongyao Wenxian Xuanbian (Shang) (Selection of important higher education documents since the founding of the People's Republic of China (Part 1)). Shanghai: East China Normal University Press, 1979: 263–264.
32. Hayhoe, R. China's Universities 1895–1995: A Century of Cultural Conflict. Trans. Xu, J. Beijing: Educational Science Publishing House, 2000: 127.
33. Ibid, p. 129.
34. Ke, S. & Wang, N. Biange Zhongguo: Shichang Jingji De Zhongguo Zhilu (How China Became Capitalist). Trans, Xu, Y., et al. Beijing: CITIC Press, 2013: 16.
35. Jin, G., & Liu, Q. Kaifang Zhong De Bianqian: Zailun Zhongguo Shehui Chaowending Jiegou (Transformation in Opening Up: Re-discussion the Super-Stable Structure). Beijing: Law Press·China, 2011: 14.
36. Yu, Y. Xiandai Ruxue De Huigu Yu Zhanwang. Beijing: SDX Joint Publishing Company, 2004: Introduction 9.
37. Zhao, C. Wenhua Jiyin Yu Shehui Bianqian: Zhongguo Shehuizhuyi Lujing Zouxiang De Minzu Wenhua Jiexi (Culture Genes and Social Changes: Analysis on the National Culture Lead by the Chinese Socialist Path), 2010: 117,124.
38. Ibid, p. 120.
39. Zhang, D., & Cheng, Y. Zhongguo Wenhua Lunzheng (Chinese Cultural Debate). Beijing: China Renmin University Press, 2006: 314.
40. Lu, X. Qiejieting Zawen Mobian (Latest Edition of Qiejie Pavillion Essays Collection). Beijing: People's Literature Publishing House, 1973: 101.
41. Ibid, p. 36.
42. Cited from Zhang, D., & Cheng, Y. Zhongguo Wenhua Lunzheng (Chinese Cultural Debate). Beijing: China Renmin University Press, 2006: 312.
43. Cited from Lin, Y., & Zhang, G. Kaige Xingjin De Shiji (Period of Triumphant March). Zhengzhou: Henan People's Press, 1996: 657.
44. Sun, W., et all. Zhongguo Gongchandangren Sixiang Baoku (Treasure Vault of the Thoughts of Chinese Communists). Beijing: Gaige Publishing House, 1991: 663.
45. Mao, Z. Mao Zedong Xuanji Diwu Juan (Selected Works of Mao Zedong, Vol. 5). Beijing: People's Publishing House, 1977: 418.
46. Zhao, C. Wenhua Jiyin Yu Shehui Bianqian: Zhongguo Shehuizhuyi Lujing Zouxiang De Minzu Wenhua Jiexi (Culture Genes and Social Changes: Analysis on the National Culture Lead by the Chinese Socialist Path), 2010: 173.
47. Mao, Z. Mao Zedong Zhuzuo Xuandu Xiace (Selected Readings of Mao Zedong, Part 2). Beijing: People's Publishing House, 1986: 752
48. Faculty of Education Archive, East China Normal University. Gaodeng Jiaoyu Wenxian Faling Xuanbian. Shanghai: East China Normal University Press, 1981: 1.

49. Ibid, p. 32.
50. Yuan, Z. Zhongguo Dangdai Jiaoyu Sichao 1949–1989. Shanghai: Joint Publishing Company. 1991: 55–56.
51. Faculty of Education Archive, East China Normal University. Gaodeng Jiaoyu Wenxian Faling Xuanbian (Selection of Higher Educational Legal Documets). Shanghai: East China Normal University Press, 1981: 27.
52. Ibid, p. 44–45.
53. Ibid, p. 47.
54. Lin, Y. Zhongguo Yishi De Weiji: "Wusi" Shiqi Jilie De Fanchuantong Zhuyi (Crisis of Chinese Conscious: Vigorous Anti-Traditionalism during "May Fourth" Period). Guiyang: Guizhou People's Publishing House, 1988: 48.
55. Yuan, Z. Zhongguo Dangdai Jiaoyu Sichao 1949–1989. Shanghai: Joint Publishing Company. 1991: 36.
56. Mao, Z. Mao Zedong Xuanji Yijuan Ben (Selected Works of Mao Zedong, Single Volume Edition). Beijing: People's Publishing House, 1977: 1367.
57. This excerpt is from Mao Zedong's Speech at the Yan'an Literature and Art Forum in May 1942. The full article was published on Jiefang Daily on 19 October 1943. It was deleted when it was selected into Mao Zedong Xuanji, Volume 3, in 1953.
58. Yuan, Z. Zhongguo Dangdai Jiaoyu Sichao 1949–1989. Shanghai: Joint Publishing Company. 1991: 56.
59. Mao Zedong. Opening speech at the Third Session of the First Political Consultative Conference. People's Daily. 1951–10–24.
60. Yuan, Z. Zhongguo Dangdai Jiaoyu Sichao 1949–1989. Shanghai: Joint Publishing Company. 1991: 36.
61. He, D. Zhonghua Renmin Gonghe Guo Zhongyao Jiaoyu Wenxian 1949–1997 (Important Educational Documents of People's Republic of China, 1949–1997). Haikou: Hainan Publishin House, 1998: 3.
62. Liu Shaoqi Division, Party Literature Research Center. Liu Shaoqi Lun Jiaoyu (Liu Shaoqi's Remarks on Education). Beijing: Educational Science Publishing House, 1998: 92.
63. Cheng, F., & Peng, M. Huiyi Liu Shaoyi Tongzhi Dui Renmin Daxue De Guanhuai (Throwbacks to Comrade Liu's Care of Renmin University). Teaching and Research, 1980(21): 2.
64. "History of China Renmin University Research Studies Series" Editorial Board. Zhongguo Renmin Daxue Jishi (1937–2007) Shangjuan (Chronicles of China Renmin University, 1937–2007, Volume 1). Beijing: China Renmin University Press, 2008: 137.
65. Biography of Wu Yuzhang" Editorial Board, Committee of Party History, Sichuan Provincial Communist Committee. Wu Yuzhang Wenji (Complete Collection of Wu Yuzhang). Chongqing: Chongqing Publishing Group, 1987: 418.
66. Hu Jianhua. The origin of the modern Chinese university system: university reform in the early 1950s (M). Nanjing: Nanjing Normal University Press, 2001: 155.
67. "History of China Renmin University Research Studies Series" Editorial Board. Zhongguo Renmin Daxue Jishi (1937–2007) Shangjuan (Chronicles of China Renmin University, 1937–2007, Volume 1). Beijing: China Renmin University Press, 2008: 96.
68. Ibid, p. 145.
69. Cited from Liu, B. Ed. Zai Shenzhou Dadi Shang Jueqi Zhongguo Renmin Daxue Huiyi Lu (1950–2000) Shangjuan (Rising from the Divine Land: Memoir of China Renmin University (1950–2000), Volume 1). Beijing: China Renmin University Press, 2007: 21.

70. "History of China Renmin University Research Studies Series" Editorial Board. Zhongguo Renmin Daxue Jishi (1937–2007) Shangjuan (Chronicles of China Renmin University, 1937–2007, Volume 1). Beijing: China Renmin University Press, 2008: 96.
71. Ibid, p. 181.
72. Quoted from Hu, J. Xiandai Zhongguo Daxue Zhidu De Yuandian: 50 Niandai Chuqi De Daxue Gaige (The origin of the modern Chinese university system: university reform in the early 1950s). Nanjing: Nanjing Normal University Press, 2001: 156–157.
73. Hu, X. Zhongguo Renmin Daxue De Jianlve Jieshoa (A Brief Introduction of China Renmin University). People's Education, 1951.
74. "History of China Renmin University Research Studies Series" Editorial Board. Zhongguo Renmin Daxue Jishi (1937–2007) Shangjuan (Chronicles of China Renmin University, 1937–2007, Volume 1). Beijing: China Renmin University Press, 2008: 106.
75. Faculty of Education Archive, East China Normal University. Gaodeng Jiaoyu Wenxian Faling Xuanbian (Selection of Higher Educational Legal Documets). Shanghai: East China Normal University Press, 1981: 2.
76. "History of China Renmin University Research Studies Series" Editorial Board. Zhongguo Renmin Daxue Jishi (1937–2007) Shangjuan (Chronicles of China Renmin University, 1937–2007, Volume 1). Beijing: China Renmin University Press, 2008: 149,150,157.
77. Liu, B. Zai Shenzhou Dadi Shang Jueqi Zhongguo Renmin Daxue Huiyi Lu (1950–2000) Shangjuan (Rising from the Divine Land: Memoir of China Renmin University (1950–2000), Volume 1). Beijing: China Renmin University Press, 2007: 22.
78. "History of China Renmin University Research Studies Series" Editorial Board. Zhongguo Renmin Daxue Jishi (1937–2007) Shangjuan (Chronicles of China Renmin University, 1937–2007, Volume 1). Beijing: China Renmin University Press, 2008: 153.
79. Ibid, p. 172.
80. Liu, B. Zai Shenzhou Dadi Shang Jueqi Zhongguo Renmin Daxue Huiyi Lu (1950–2000) Shangjuan (Rising from the Divine Land: Memoir of China Renmin University (1950–2000), Volume 1). Beijing: China Renmin University Press, 2007: 252–253
81. Ibid, p. 253.
82. Ibid, p. 398.

CHAPTER 5

Cultural Character of Chinese Universities Since Reform and Opening Up

In 1976, when the Cultural Revolution ended, China gradually deviated from ideological radicalism and turned towards national economic construction. After a decade of devastating silence, especially under the re-emerging impact of Western culture, China successfully set off multiple cultural advancements from the 1980s onwards. With the awakening of cultural consciousness, Chinese universities also began to seek their roots on the road to reform. Indeed, the cultural character of Chinese universities had not yet been fully formed, and the Chinese university model in the cultural sense was still under construction. However, in the reflection and introspection of the times, Chinese universities were gradually showing the future arc of their cultural character.

Section 1: Sociocultural advancements since the Reform and Opening Up and the prosperity of Chinese universities

With the beginning of a new era, economic reform and developments began to occupy the center of Chinese society, and China began to rapidly rise. Commercialization, marketization, and globalization had indeed become the main background of Chinese cultural changes and the development of Chinese universities. In the process of popularization of modern civilization, Chinese culture had once again been impacted by Western culture, and it had become a fact that Chinese universities were affected by utilitarianism. Objectively, this had also become an important opportunity for the rejuvenation of Chinese culture and the development of the cultural character of Chinese universities. On the one hand, Chinese culture had gradually been on the road of rejuvenation since the Reform and Opening Up. In a politically-stable and economically-recovering social environment, Chinese culture was trying to explore and achieve an ideal state through self-identification and self-emphasis in the conflicts and integration of Chinese and Western cultures. To some extent, this trend confirmed Huntington's diagnosis that modernization and economic development are neither necessary nor a possible cause in the westernization of culture, and they shall only lead to the revival of local culture.

The reason behind such a phenomenon was that "At the social level, modernization has improved the overall economic, military and political strength of this society, which encourages its people to have more confidence in their own culture, thus becoming a promoter of the culture."[1] On the other hand, in the revival of Chinese culture or the fusion of Chinese and Western cultures, Chinese universities had gradually formed and developed their characteristics. Regarding this point, the Canadian scholar Ruth Hayhoe constructed an expectation for the development of Chinese universities a long time ago, and proposed a concept of a "Chinese university model." Macroscopically speaking, during the 30 years since the Reform and Opening Up, Chinese culture had exhibited a characteristic of intermittent fluctuations, that is, the development of the entire Chinese culture was not continuously advancing, but it was in a pattern of alternation between tidal advancements of new cultural trends and temporary calm. In general, the pattern showed a trend of gradual recovery. On the whole, the cultural upsurge during the mid-to-late 1980s (1985–1988) can be regarded as the first cultural wave since the Reform and Opening Up. The Sinology upsurge in the 1990s once again set off a wave of Chinese cultural trends.

In the early 21st century, the rise of the Confucius Institute had led to a boom of Chinese culture throughout the world. This intermittent cultural recovery process was largely affected by political and economic aspects. Usually, booms in Chinese culture occurred when political conditions were relaxed and the economy was prosperous; otherwise, it was to fall into a trough.

In this section, we will use the thought of the liberation era (the 1980s), economic era (1990s), and globalization era (since the 21st century) as individual stages and intercept relevant events and scenes, to explore the developmental trends of Chinese culture in each period from a historical perspective. Based on this, we will describe the development of Chinese universities in various eras based on cultural perspectives. Finally, we will summarize the Chinese universities' character since Reform and Opening Up based on the interpretation of the two concepts of Chinese culture and the Chinese university.

1. *Chinese culture and Chinese universities during the "thought liberation" era*

The convening of the Third Plenary Session of the Eleventh Central Committee in 1978 became a turning point in Chinese history. On October 1, 1983, Deng Xiaoping wrote an inscription for the Beijing Jingshan School, "Education should be geared towards the needs of modernization, of the world and the future." Deng Xiaoping's expectations of the "three orientations" in the field of education also represented the basic strategy of Chinese cultural development, which pointed out the direction for the development of Chinese culture in the new era. Under the call of the new era, China returned to the international stage and was ushered into the era of ideological emancipation. It once again faced the test of the conflicts and integration between Chinese and Western cultures. The great discussion about Chinese and Western cultures in the cultural craze in the 1980s was a historical repetition of the "Critical" and "Revival" debate of Chinese culture in the May Fourth Movement. Although "Critical" overwhelmed "Revival" in the end, it still laid the first cornerstone in the foundation for the formation of the cultural character of Chinese universities.

a) Cultural changes within social changes.

Cultural Revolution was finally over like a fever dream, and the Chinese people opened their eyes to the world once again after a whole decade. There was not only a huge gap in the economic field but also a huge contrast in culture. Under the influence of the US and Europe, China set off a new wave of learning from Western culture as it reflected on its backwardness. During this period, China's introduction of Western culture was highlighted in large-scale translation work. In this era of ideological and cultural liberation, the translation and publication of foreign literary works and various theoretical works were unprecedented through China. Liu Dengge et al. described in the book *Western Learning to the East and Eastern Learning to the West*:

> In addition to natural sciences and engineering technologies (whose number of translated works far exceeds the social sciences and humanities), social sciences (excluding art) alone has seen a massive amount of Chinese-translated works during the past 10 years or so. Although there are no precise statistics, it is definite that the amount exceeds 1000. The Commercial Press' Chinese Translation World Academic Masterpieces had begun to include modern works; SDX Joint Publishing's *Culture and World Series, Modern Western Academic Library,* and *Smaller masterpieces* series have all included over 100 different books; Huaxia Publishing House has its *20th Century Library* series; Shanghai Translation Publishing House and People's Publishing House each has one or

> two sets of translated works series; Jiangsu has its *Foreign Studies in China Series;* Zhejiang has its *World Culture Series;* Sichuan has its *Towards Future Series, Western Marxism Research Series* and *Human and Religion Series*; Guizhou has its *Modern Society and Human Series,* etc. It should be said for this period that it was impossible to find another country with so many translated works in the world. Translated works took up a critically important role in Chinese academia.[2]

Foreign academic works, literary-artistic works, and other cultural carriers were introduced into China across all fields, and the ideological upsurges and cultural movements were stirred up in China again and again. Western thoughts and culture were studied and spread in full swing, which made people unconsciously pride themselves on the re-appeared manifestation of the spirit of the May Fourth Movement. "But it was not only the lifting of the ban on Western culture but also the ban removal on and the revival of traditional Chinese culture. Hence, a new round of contention and a cultural confrontation began. Some people reiterated the old theory of *Zhongxue Weiti, Xixue Weiyong,* and cited articles and ancient dogmas to admonish cultural importers. In the 1980s, there was a series of cultural conflicts and confrontations, such as the struggle between East and West, the struggle between ancient and modern times, and the struggle between elegance and vulgarity."[3]

The cultural upsurge that emerged in China in 1985 and reached its climax in the following two years was an important event during this period and was called "the second May Fourth new cultural movement in China in the 20th century." The reason for this was: on the one hand, the cultural fever movement pushed the aforementioned translation and introduction of Western works and theories from the 1980s to the climax, becoming a center of anti-traditionalists in the new era. And on the other hand, it also triggered a new round of debate about Chinese and Western cultures, which brought the long-lost Chinese culture back into the public view. The cultural upsurge started earlier in the literary world when a group of educated young writers who were at the core of the Chinese literary world of the time advocated for the root-seeking literature, which was quickly spread to the art world, film, and other art fields. The choice between Chinese and Western culture became an important topic in this cultural craze.

In 1987, when the cultural upsurge was on the rise, Chen Lai summarized the development trend of Chinese culture at that time in the article *Three Trends of Thinking Outlets.* The article focused on three cultural models, which can be summarized as follows: One was the "going to the future" faction, which referred to the "future-oriented" cultural activities represented by Jin Guantao. This faction used science as the standard for evaluating traditional culture and advocated the idea of "scientific" humanities and social sciences with methods that are similar to those of natural sciences. As the author commented, "the lack of self-conscious cultural awareness brought challenges to their avant-garde status."[4] The second faction was the "Culture: China and the World" faction, which referred to the editorial board of the *Culture: China and the World* series edited by Gan Yang. This faction attached great importance to humanities and was committed to introducing Western culture to develop Chinese culture, but it was obviously biased towards Western culture. As Gan Yang stated in *Some Questions within the Cultural Debates of the 1980s* (1986): "In such a significant era of historical changes, the most powerful way to promote our traditions happens to lie in anti-traditionalism!"[5] And the third was the "Chinese cultural academy" faction, which referred to the cultural academies established by Tang Yijie. Instead of the anti-traditional tendency of the two previously mentioned factions, this third faction took on the mission of promoting the currently existent cultural traditions, and they were more amicable to Chinese culture regarding their values. Some thoughts from masters of Chinese such as Tang Yijie, Li Zehou, and Pang Pu can be used to represent the cultural tendencies of the cultural academy faction. Chen Lai wrote this article in 1987.

In the same year, Zhang Dainian published the *article Integrate and Innovate, Establishing a New Socialist Culture*, which can be classified as the fourth faction, namely the "Integrate and Innovate" faction. The "new culture" of integration and innovation mentioned by Zhang Dainian was to take advantage of both Chinese and Western cultures to create a composite that is neither Chinese culture nor Western culture. This is a great representative of the views that lay between anti-tradition and tradition. In general, compared with anti-traditional thoughts, the voices of promoting traditions were still weak, as Chen Lai said, "This is "inevitable" even if it is not "reasonable." This pattern can only be fundamentally changed after the completion of the historical task of modernization."[6]

In short, in the era trend of cultural upsurge, intellectuals' attitudes toward Chinese culture were still relatively radical, or very immature. However, it indeed accumulated power for the future development of Chinese culture: on the one hand, according to Xu Jilin's viewpoint, the cultural upheavals in the 1980s created China's fifth generation of intellectuals. They had the special experience of the Cultural Revolution and the restoration of the college entrance examination system. Using the root-seeking cultural complex within the cultural upsurge as a breakthrough, they prepared and triggered the Chinese culture boom in the 1990s.

b) Chinese universities in cultural changes.

In the 1980s, Chinese universities were reborn during the era of ideological emancipation. Based on the American university model and by adopting various features from European and American countries, the reform of Chinese universities during this period tried to rearrange and restore some Western university systems prevailing in universities during the Republican China period. The formulation and promulgation of the *Decision of the Central Committee of the Communist Party of China on Education System Reform* in 1985 were of great significance. Many of these regulations were intended to introduce and restore some effective Western university management methods. One of the obvious trends was the deliberate decentralization of the country's educational power, which meant that "university autonomy" was introduced into China once again after the era of Republican China. The document proposed the "expansion of the autonomy of higher institutions." The specific requirements read as follows:

> "Under the premise of implementing national policies, decrees, and plans, higher institutions have the right to accept entrustment to train students and enroll self-paid students within their plan; they shall have the right to adjust their direction of professional services, to formulate teaching plans and syllabuses, to compile and select teaching materials; they shall also have the right to accept entrustment or cooperation with external corporations for scientific research and technology development, to establish teaching, scientific research, and production consortia; they shall have the right to nominate, appoint or remove vice presidents and cadres of other levels; they have the right to specifically arrange infrastructure investments and to manage the funds allocated by the state; they have the right to use self-raised funds in order to carry out international education and academic exchanges, etc. For different higher institutions, the state can also grant other powers as per the situation requires."[7]

The text repeatedly emphasized the "rights" of higher institutions. Although it was based on national macro-control, it was still a leap of progress in the history of education in China. In fact, during the first half of the 1980s, Chinese universities were indeed given more freedom and liberty. In particular, higher institutions were given a certain degree of autonomy in setting their curriculum and the scope of their research work. In Hayhoe's research on Chinese universities, it was also stated that the academic enthusiasm of higher institutions surged during the first five years before the reform in the 1980s, and the Western university model of "conducting academic research for the sake of academics" was once again recognized.

It is also worth mentioning that the selection process of some university presidents in the 1980s was indeed switched from national appointments to Western democratic elections. For example, Zhang Kaiyuan described that his election as the president was "a complete misunderstanding of history," as it was carried out by a secret ballot for the entire university, and the result "shocked everyone."

In addition to institutional referencing and imitation, to better learn from the West, China also resumed exchange programs with Western countries during this time. Many member countries of the Organization for Economic Cooperation and Development funded several development projects in China, providing Chinese scholars with opportunities to study abroad. Besides, a whole set of major projects funded by the World Bank had begun, which funded the training of overseas students in about 180 higher institutions.[8] These college scholars returned to China in the 1980s, forming an important force of leadership in the construction of Chinese universities. Of course, China was not only influenced by Western free academics in the wave of Western learning in the 1980s but it was also inevitably caught in the trap of Western venality. In the late 1980s, the atmosphere of the "business" side became stronger, and the problems of intellectuals' losses and the decline of social morality was starting to show. This situation continued directly into the 1990s.

The reforms in the 1980s were "to a large extent out of self-control," but Chinese universities were not "submerged in the torrent of external changes."[9] In the 1980s, humanistic ideas began to revive in Chinese universities. Just like the rise of Chinese culture in the anti-traditional May Fourth Movement, this was "surprising" and "understandable" at the same time. One of the major manifestations of humanities education in the revival of Chinese universities was the restoration of Chinese university education. During the adjustment of courses within universities in 1952, university-level Chinese, as a public course, was eliminated from the university systems. Since then, university Chinese completely disappeared in Chinese universities for nearly three decades. As the Cultural Revolution ended, the higher education community wanted to reopen the university-level Chinese courses, but it was not implemented. In 1980, university Chinese courses were first reopened at Nanjing University, Fudan University, and East China Normal University. The purpose of the course lay in four aspects: (1) training of communication tools; (2) the penetration and inheritance of the excellent traditional culture; (3) the construction of a common spiritual civilization for modern humans; (4) coping with and solving the cultural confusions of the current open society.[10] Due to the lack of official institutional support, the university Chinese revival work in the 1980s did not continue, and it stagnated in the 1990s. However, it did indeed break the historical dilemma of the long-term absence of university Chinese in Chinese universities, and it briefly provided the most direct way to revive Chinese culture within universities.

In short, the 1980s was a transition period for the development of Chinese society, and Chinese universities began to "restore their memory" in the new era and the new environment. On the one hand, in the process of *Xixue Dongjian,* the autonomy and freedom of universities were gradually restored and developed. On the other hand, traditional Chinese culture was starting to be intentionally restored in the enlightenment of the recovery of Chinese culture. The cultural characteristics of Chinese universities during this period were obviously out of tune, and the westernization transformation was greater than the enlightenment in Chinese learnings. However, this situation indeed laid a realistic foundation for the cultural reconciliation of Chinese universities during the 1990s.

2. *Chinese Culture and Chinese Universities during the economic era*

In the 1990s, the commodity economy became popular in Chinese society under the approval of its official ideology. Gan Yang once commented on the intellectuals in the 1980s: "Compared with the 'Era for Economic Personnel' in the 1990s, the 1980s can be called the last 'Era for Cultural Personnel.'"[11] The Era for Economic Personnel quickly rose and lasted well into the 21st century. It can be said that the Sinology studies boom in the 1990s brought Chinese culture to the foreground of history reasonably and legitimately, and set an important background for the formation and development of the cultural character of Chinese universities.

a) Cultural changes within social changes.

In the 1990s, the Western market economy system was finally legally introduced to China after a long period of disputes and setbacks. While various Western civilizations were knocking on China's door and effectively changed the production, life, social interaction, and behavior of Chinese people, they also inevitably had an impact on the traditional values and thinking patterns of Chinese people and triggered a profound cultural change. When the long-awaited economic commodities tide came in full under the recognition of its official ideology, the development of Chinese culture was brought to an important historical turning point. In this economic age which was full of temptations, culture and economy were rapidly combining and moving towards industrialization, while the development situation of Chinese culture further worsened. On the one hand, the traditional ethical and moral order that was the foundation of the stability of Chinese society was gradually disintegrating under the business logic. As Yin Haiguang said, "Money became a dominant force in society, corroding and even ruling moral, ethical and religious disciplines. The economy determined almost everything, and morality became an empty mantra. This was the unprecedented development of instrumental features, and the normative features were compressed and subsequently lost their normative power over behavior."[12] This discourse, written in the 1980s, became the most authentic depiction of Chinese society in the 1990s.

On the other hand, as the backbone of Chinese cultural inheritance, intellectuals again faced marginalization under the economic pressure of the 1990s. Chen Pingyuan pointed out in the article *The Loss of Chinese Elite Culture in the Past One Hundred Years* that the cultural elites in the 1990s were eliminated or transformed by the commodity economy – perhaps they had never felt the tremendous pressure of money like that. At the same time, they probably had never been so aware of their own insignificance, as their prophetic mentor mentality, their superiority of truth at hand, and their tragic feelings of worrying about the country and the people had become worthless in the circulation of commodities. As a result, the most tragic ending of these Don Quixotes in modern China may not only be the punishment by political authorities for their alienation but also the abandonment by the market because of their "morality," "ideals" and "passions."[13] During the 1990s, there were many examples of elite culture succumbing to popular cultures, such as authors and professor dipping their toes in the sea of commerce. On the surface, enveloped by Western civilization and the rapid development of the commodity economy, the prospects for the development of Chinese culture were not seemingly optimistic. However, history proved that the 1990s were not a traditional Chinese economic era, but instead an important time slot for the revival of Chinese culture. The interference of various external factors was indeed inevitable. However, it also stimulated the long-accumulated vitality of Chinese culture. "Since the 1990s, Chinese academic circles have shown two major trends: one is to reflect on the expansion and hegemony of Western academic discourse, and the other is to try and establish a Chinese school of thought and express a 'Chinese voice' on the world stages of academics and culture."[14]

The Sinology fever in the 1990s was the most typical "Chinese voice" of the intellectuals who tried to establish a Chinese school of thought based on their reflection of Western culture. According to records and materials, the Sinology fever was officially introduced to the public field in 1993. During that year, *People's Daily* posted two articles on Sinology fever on August 16th and 17th respectively, with one of them using the direct call of *It's been a long time, Sinology* as its title. Hence, the attention of the public was shifted to the traditions of Chinese culture. Regarding the term Sinology (*Guoxue*), it was not a new creation of the 1990s, scholars found references to this term in *The Book of Rites of the Learning*: "Regarding the education of ancient times, there was Shu for families, Xiang for parties, Xu for arts, and Xue for nations." Modern scholars such as Kang Youwei, Zhang Taiyan, Yan Fu, Hu Shi, and others all have specialized works in Chinese studies, which gradually fixed the main purpose of this concept to the study of "national classic literature and inherent culture." Therefore, the upsurge of Sinology in the 1990s meant the rise of traditional Chinese culture in a new period.

During this period, Chinese culture became a hot topic in the academic world, which mainly manifested i: the emergence of a large number of modern neo-Confucian works. These included *Xiandai Xin Rujia Xuean* (*Modern Neo-Confucian Studies Materials*) *Xiandai Xin Ruxue Yanjiu Congshu* (*Modern Neo-Confucian Studies Series*), *Xiandai Xin Ruxue Yanjiu Lunji* (*Collection of Modern Neo-Confucian Studies and Research*), and *Xiandai Xin Ruxue Jiyao Congshu* (*Modern New Confucianism Essentials Series*) among others. There was also the emergence of journals with the theme of Chinese culture, such as *Zhongguo Wenhua* (*Chinese Culture*), *Guoxue Yanjiu* (*Sinology Research*), *Xueren* (*People of Academics*), Yuan Xue (*The Original Studies*), and *Yuan Dao* (*The Original Way*), among others. There was also a rise in academic cultural events whose main purpose was to promote and study Chinese culture and the establishment of organizational structures. Such as the establishment of the International Confucianism Federation in 1994, the joint research seminar of "Marxism and Confucianism" jointly held by the Scientific Research Department of the CPC Central Party School and the Academic Committee of the China Confucius Foundation in 1995.

With the fierce upsurge of Sinology, Chinese and Western cultures have once again become the focus of debate, but this time it was obvious that the Chinese culturalists had the upper hand. Among them, Ji Xianlin's Thirty Years on the East and Thirty Years on the West theory and Fei Xiaotong's Cultural Self-consciousness theory were hailed by academics as "a peculiar cultural landscape at the end of the century." In 1992, Ji Xianlin pointed out in *21st Century: The Era of Eastern Culture* that, "From the perspective of the entire history of mankind, I think the relationship between Eastern culture and Western culture is, 'thirty years on the East and thirty years on the West.' The Western culture being popular all over the world had not always been the case, and it would not be the case forever in the future. In the 21st century, Western culture in its 'thirty years on the West' will gradually give way to Eastern culture in its 'thirty years on the East,' and the development of human culture will enter a new era..."[15] Following this in 1997, Fei Xiaotong put forward the viewpoint of "cultural self-consciousness" in his article *Reflection · Dialogue · Cultural Self-consciousness*, which seemed to supplement Ji's "Thirty Years" theory with an important premise. The article pointed out that, "Achieving cultural self-consciousness is a difficult process. First of all, we must recognize our own culture and understand the various cultures we are exposed to. Only through this can we determine our position in this multicultural world that is already being formed. We shall adapt to other cultures, learn from each other's strengths, build a common order with mutual agreements and a set of coexistence codes that enable various cultures to coexist peacefully, utilize their strengths and develop together."[16] The emphasis on the Chinese culture of the Sinology upsurge also encountered a lot of opposition. However, just as the anti-traditional tendency of the cultural upsurge in the 1980s was inevitable, the Chinese cultural tone of the Sinology upsurge in the 1990s also became an irreversible trend.

b) Chinese universities in cultural changes.

On March 4, 1993, the Demolition of the South Wall at Peking University attracted considerable attention. To many scholars, "this move symbolized Peking University's stepping out of the ivory tower, from focusing on politics and academia to emphasizing market and society."[17] In the same year, Peking University issued the slogan "integration of industry, teaching, and research," and Peking University's school-run enterprises quickly developed to achieve economic income. The above-mentioned changes at Peking University can be seen as a microcosm of the development and transformation of Chinese universities in the market economy wave in the 1990s.

During this period, business logic gradually penetrated the field of education, and Chinese universities began a Great Leap Forward to create sufficient economic talents. The campaign of expansion in university enrollment in 1999 was a major event during this period. Chen Pingyuan disclosed the inside story of this "Great Leap Forward" in education: "It is said that the earliest proposal to expand university enrollment was suggested by the economists; this proposal was supported by politicians and was quickly promoted; as for educators, they passively participated."[18] From this perspective, the expansion of university enrolment in the late 1990s was largely an "expansion of commercialization of higher education."

In addition, in the 1990s, among frequent contacts with Western universities, the "building of a world-class university" became a popular discourse in Chinese universities. For example, in 1993, the State Council issued the *Outline of China's Education Reform and Development,* which proposed the "211" project to promote the development of Chinese universities. Its purpose was to cultivate 100 world-renowned Chinese universities in the 21st century. In another example, the wave of universities' mergers in 1998 was also based on the idea of becoming stronger and bigger and striving to become world-class universities. In the same year, the president of Peking University announced that the university would strive to become a "world-class university" by 2015. In short, no matter if it was the university enrollment expansion or the university grading, they both went after the quickness and high-level of education, which inevitably deviated from the developmental laws of higher education itself. These events became a significant symbol of Chinese universities chasing the world trend in the economic era.

The Sinology fever was intended to use traditional culture to balance the serious westernization and commercialization bias that was gradually exposed to Chinese universities. As for cultural quality education, which was a major aspect of the reform of Chinese universities in the 1990s – this is still on the rise today. Although the power of the Sinology fever in the 1990s was limited, "the mid-1990s emphasized the humanistic elements of university education, especially the traditional cultural qualities, which can be understood as part of the action to achieve national 'cultural self-consciousness' from the perspective of cultivation of humanistic values within the younger generation, enhance cultural 'soft power' that matches the rise of economic status, especially from the perspective of the inheritance of the national culture."[19]

During this period, the main measures implemented by the state for the implementation of university cultural quality education were:

1) In 1995, the Higher Education Department of the former State Education Commission conducted a pilot of university students' cultural quality education in 52 higher institutions and stipulated that the pilot schools should formulate a catalog of famous books, famous songs, famous paintings, and famous plays that should be read, known, and watched. In addition to special subject research, the 52 pilot higher institutions would all implement humanistic quality education by offering elective courses and lectures on humanities and social sciences throughout the school.

2) In 1998, the Ministry of Education of the People's Republic of China established the Ministry of Education Steering Committee on Cultural Quality Education for Higher Institutions, inviting relevant leaders and famous scholars from higher institutions across the country to serve as its members, who were in charge of guiding the cultural quality education of university students across the country, as well as researching and solving various problems that are encountered along the way. Academic Yang Shuzi served as the chairman and the secretariat was located in Huazhong University of Science and Technology (HUST).
3) In 1999, with the approval of the Ministry of Education, Peking University, Tsinghua University, HUST, and other universities established 32 "education bases for cultural quality education in higher institutions," and stipulated their tasks as follows: To carry out theoretical research on cultural quality education and organize training for teachers of cultural quality education, etc. With the gradual development of quality education in higher institutions, the country promulgated a series of rules and regulations for the promotion of humanities education in higher institutions in the late 1990s.For example, in 1998, the Ministry of Education issued several *Opinions on Strengthening College Students' Cultural Quality Education*, and in 1999, the CPC Central Committee and the State Council promulgated and implemented the *Decision on Deepening Educational Reform and Comprehensively Promoting Quality Education.*

In short, the cultural quality education of Chinese universities began in the mid-1990s and continues into the 21st century today, effectively balancing the scientific and technological society's bias towards scientific and technological education. From this perspective, Tu Youguang's "science and humanities" model for future Chinese higher education has already emerged.

3. Chinese Culture and Chinese Universities during the Globalization Era

The 21st century is an era of globalization. Since the very beginning of the 21st century, exclamations such as "the world is flat" and "the ivory tower is flat" never ceased. China's successful 2001 entry into the WTO heralded China's comprehensive entry to globalization. As the distance between China and the world closed by the day, Hayhoe's proposition of "conflict between Chinese and Western cultures" began to seem a little narrow. The development of Chinese universities could no longer be measured only from the perspective of Chinese and Western culture. China stepped into the development process with the rest of the whole world. No matter what nationalities or types, no Western university model could dominate China alone. Chinese universities were gradually tapping into their potential on the world stage and were committing to forming their own mode of existence.

a) Cultural changes within social changes.

If the prevalence of Western learning in China in the 1980s could only be called the "Western era" of China, and the 1990s was the era when Chinese cultural awakening began to seek and reshape China, then we can say that China in the 21st century is trying to construct a Chinese era for the world based on Chinese culture. At present, it can be seen that although the imitation of the US and Europe is still required for China's rise, this imitation will not be China's future. From imitation to reflection, the development of Chinese culture has gradually matured in the conflict between and the fusion of Chinese and Western cultures. The 21st century had just begun. It can be seen that the main direction of China has shifted from Western culture to Chinese culture in the early 21st century. When examining the revival of Chinese culture during this period, it can be seen that it is mainly rooted in the context of the times in the following two aspects. First, China is rapidly rising and becoming stronger, it is gradually receiving the attention and respect of the world. It therefore must meet the political needs for the expansion of China's influence and the establishment of its international prestige. China is supporting the revival of Chinese culture and encouraging it to go abroad. Second, the Internet connects the world as a whole, and the concepts of states and nations are gradually fading in the process of globalization. In order to strengthen national identity and social cohesion, China must maintain the existence of the country, and the revival of national culture has become an inevitable choice for the Chinese people. The following is a list of key cultural events in relevant years, and a brief overview of the revival of Chinese culture in the past 10 years.

The year 2004 was the first important year after Chinese culture entered the 21st century. During this year, China ushered in the second round of Sinology fever since the Reform and Opening U. This was also the first Chinese cultural boom in the new century. Hence, it was named the "Year of Cultural Conservatism." Important events of the year were:

1) In May 2004, Higher Education Press published 12 volumes of *Zhonghua Wenhua Jingdian Jichu Jiaoyu Songben* (*Book of Reading for Basic Education of Chinese Cultural Classics*), which was compiled and edited by Jiang Qing, and was to be used for recitation practice of children aged 3–12. The purpose of this book was to revive Chinese culture, and the key to reviving Chinese culture was to revive traditional classics. The first step in reviving traditional classics was through children's reading. With this as the beginning, the society launched a reading movement for children. Some people were supportive, while many others also expressed their doubts and opposition. Regardless of their attitude, there was not much controversy about the intention of cultural-educational children's reading.

2) In September 2004, at the closing meeting of the "2004 Cultural Summit Forum" held in Beijing, five people, Xu Jialu, Ji Xianlin, Yang Zhenning, Ren Jiyu, and Wang Meng, initiated and published the *Jiashen Cultural Declaration.* The core views of the declaration were as follows: We advocate that each country and people has its own rights and obligations to preserve and develop its own traditional culture; they all have the right to independently choose to accept, not fully accept, or completely reject foreign cultural factors in certain specific areas. At the same time, they also have the right to express their own opinions on the cultural issues faced by mankind...

   As soon as the *Declaration* came out, it attracted extensive discussion and attention in the academic world, some called it the "Declaration of Chinese Culture" based on its theme of reviving Chinese culture, while some compared it with the *Declaration of China-based Cultural Construction* of the Republic of China (1935) and Taiwan's *Declaration of Chinese Culture for the rest of the world* (1958), calling it a puppet of official cultural policies. No matter what, it indeed expressed the common expectation and firm determination of officials and intellectuals to revive Chinese culture.
3) In 1994, Chen Ming founded *Yuandao* and worked hard ever since. The year 2004 was the tenth anniversary of *Yuandao.* Chen Ming was known as a representative of cultural conservatives. He founded the *Yuandao* magazine in the upsurge of Sinology in the 1990s. This magazine was known as the main front to promote Chinese cultural traditions. More than ten years of perseverance and existence proved that the road to the revival of Chinese culture has gradually become a legitimate trend.

   The year 2007 was also memorable in the history of Chinese cultural revival. On April 9, 2007, the Confucius Institute was officially established in Beijing as an educational and cultural exchange institution that promoted the Chinese language and spread Chinese culture and national studies. The Confucius Institute was headquartered in Beijing, and overseas Confucius Institutes are all considered its sub-branches, mainly established in the form of Sino-foreign cooperation. The world's first Confucius Institute was listed in Seoul, the capital of South Korea as early as November 21, 2004. As of October 2010, 322 Confucius Institutes and 369 Confucius Classrooms have been established globally, totaling 691, distributed across 96 countries (/regions). Confucius is a representative of Chinese traditional culture. Confucius Institute's choice of Confucius as a Chinese teaching brand is a symbol of the revival of traditional Chinese culture. At the same time, the wide establishment of Confucius Institutes around the world had also become an important way for Chinese culture to go abroad and a good way to build the confidence of the Chinese nation. In addition, the revival of traditional festivals, the rise of private schools, and the holding of various cultural forums at the beginning of this century were all important signs of Chinese cultural revival.

The above examples showed that Chinese culture has grasped the integration of Chinese and Western cultures in the century of conflict and incorporation. Different from the blind or paranoid revivalism in history, the purpose of Chinese cultural revival in the new century is not to unilaterally "strengthen Chinese culture and deny Western culture," but instead, it is highly open and diverse. The main idea behind the Chinese cultural revival is to try to restore the Chinese cultural tradition that has been riddled with the impact of Western culture over the past century. At the same time, it is to learn from each other's strengths and complement each other. The revival of Chinese culture is still on the way, some critics oppose it, and some are blindly old-fashioned. However, in general, both groups have failed to voice or play an effective role in this transformation.

b) Chinese universities in cultural changes.

The highly developed Internet technology of the 21st century announced to universities that "the ivory tower was flat." Connecting with the world has become an important goal for the development of Chinese universities in the new century. It is particularly worth mentioning that MOOC (Massive Open Online Courses) born in American universities have swept the world and successfully entered Chinese universities. With the increasing frequency of world exchanges, Chinese universities entered a new period of development following in the footsteps of the scientific and technological era. However, this is no longer the most noteworthy focus of Chinese universities in the 21st century. Admittedly, the impact of the Western universities' trend on China in the new century is still an important aspect, but it turns out that the reform of Chinese universities solely based on Western models is doomed to be turbulent in the era of Chinese cultural revival. The vigorous reform of Peking University is a landmark event of this period, and its ending is, to some extent, an inevitable product that violates the self-conscious trend of Chinese culture.

In late May 2003, Peking University launched the soliciting opinion draft of the *Reform Program for Teacher Appointment and Position Promotion System of Peking University,* which triggered a heated discussion in the academic circles regarding personnel reform. The result of the discussion was clear, as the voice of opposition overwhelmed the response of the supporters, and the sensational personnel reform of Peking University was eventually forced to shut down due to "concerns and opposition." The reasons behind it were indeed worthy of our consideration. The opposers' view was focused on the point that the relevant system of Peking University reforms had a strong American style and even gave off a sense of blind admiration for the Westerners. It lacked respect and a reference to Chinese traditions and the experience of higher education in other European countries, and it ignored the common rule of independent development of Chinese universities. Based on the first draft of the reform plan of Peking University, two articles within it were criticized according to *Chongyan* (blind admiration for the West). One stipulated that in addition to a few disciplines, newly hired professors should be able to teach in at least one foreign language. While the other stipulated that no less than one-third of the members of the committee shall be professors who have obtained tenure at a well-known overseas university. Among the voices that were against or questioning the reform of Peking University, Gan Yang's *Chinese University Concept and Peking University Reform*, Chen Pingyuan's *International Vision and Local Sensibility*, and Li Meng's *How to Reform the University?—Research regarding a few points within the logics of the plan of Peking University personnel reform* and Li Ling's *Schools are not chicken farms* were all highly representative. A common position was that the international integration of Chinese universities should be based on local adaptation. As Chen Pingyuan said in his comments on the reform of Peking University, the formulation of Peking University's reform plan "lacked the participation of humanity scholars" and "policymakers relied too much on the American experience."[20] Now that a decade has passed since the reform of Peking University, from the perspective of the era's trend of Chinese cultural development, it is clear that the failure of Peking University's reform was historically inevitable. The upsurge of Sinology in the early 21st century hinted that the cultural self-consciousness of Chinese intellectuals has long been different, and China has set its determination to distance itself from the "China's Western Culture Era." The reform incident of Peking University, to some extent, reflected that the Western university model was to face huge difficulties in its implementation in contemporary China. The contribution of Peking University's reform was not so in itself, but it showed this trend in the fact that it caused a century of reexamination of the university-running concept in China by the Chinese academic community. In this reexamination, traditional cultural consciousness was reactivated and highly affirmed. This was indeed the "windfall" of Peking University reforms.

The influence of the Sinology upsurge in higher education at the beginning of the century was rather obvious, and its influence on Chinese universities seemed to be even more profound. The reform of Chinese universities in the 21st century entered a new stage. In stark contrast to the aforementioned difficult reform of Peking University, the promulgation and establishment of relevant Sinology revival plans and institutions during the reform of Chinese universities of this period were widely recognized. For example:

1) On May 28, 2005, the establishment of the School of Chinese Classics in Renmin University of China was officially announced. Relevant reports indicated that as the official establishment of the first School of Chinese Classics since the founding of PRC, it marked that the Renmin University of China will now fully initiate formal

Sinology education and research within China's new situation. It had enrolled over 300 undergraduates and established a basic curriculum system. Systematic textbooks were written, which were highly appreciated by China's academic circles and the rest of the world. Based on professional Sinology education, the School of Chinese Classics was also committed to promoting Sinology in society. It had to be deeply rooted in the hearts of the people and it had to make its due contribution to the future development of Chinese culture.

2) In 2005, the School of Philosophy of Peking University founded the Qianyuan Guoxue Classroom, which became the first adult Sinology training program in China. The birth of Qianyuan Guoxue at Peking University had driven the trend of studying Sinology across society and inspired the social elites to turn to the classroom to solve their confusion. Sinology went from scholar's study to the society, reflecting the cultural self-consciousness and cultural self-confidence of the Chinese people's rejuvenation.
3) On May 5, 2014, Yenching Academy was formally established in Peking University. The academy designed six directional curriculum systems, namely philosophy and religion, history and archaeology, literature and culture, economy and management, law and society, and public policy and international relations with the principle of "cultivating international leaders based on Chinese subjectivity." Through the establishment of chair professors, Yenching Academy was committed to building an international first-class "Chinese studies" academic team, including the joint recruitment of 30 outstanding scholars from Peking University's existing humanities and social sciences scholars, 20 outstanding scholars in related fields from abroad, along with the invitation of 20 top international professors as visiting scholars. Reportedly, the first students of Yenching Academy were to be enrolled in September 2015, and the enrollment target was for them to become the fresh graduates of colleges and universities of the world in 2015.

In short, in the past ten years or so, Chinese universities have been comprehensively studying Sinology. At present, around ten universities have set up Sinology classes or related projects, targeting different groups and involving multiple levels. And the Yenching Academy Project that Peking University has launched has received significant attention and expectations from many parties. Of course, since the emergence of Sinology in the reform of Chinese universities, it has aroused discussion, support, or doubt from all walks of life in the society, but now, more are showing a sense of expectation and hope.

4. *The general characteristics of Chinese universities' cultural character since the Reform and Opening Up*

In the thirty years of Reform and Opening Up, China had entered a new era of reform. Unlike the extremely irregular characteristics of the Seventeen Years, the evolution of Chinese culture had shown a gradual upward trend in the thirty years after the Reform and Opening Up. It went from humbly learning from the West to profound cultural self-consciousness, to a comprehensive cultural revival. Although "criticism" overwhelmed "revival" in the cultural upheaval during the period of ideological emancipation, the long-silent Chinese culture was still officially returned to the public's view. Sinology fever based on Chinese culture in the economic era acted as an effective counterweight to the negative effects of the economic era and the new round of Sinology fever in the era of globalization is still ongoing.Chinese culture began to enter the world stage. At the same time, Chinese universities were constructing their own universities' systems during the revival of Chinese culture. During the period of ideological emancipation, the humanistic spirit of Chinese universities began to recover in the wave of *Xixue Dongjian*. In the economic era, Chinese universities sought solutions to the enormous amount of society's problems, while facing many challenges of quality education. In the era of globalization, the introduction of advanced technology of the world and the maintenance of national local feelings were combined in Chinese universities. Chinese universities have started to show the ideal development model of "science and humanities." Based on the above analysis, a preliminary conclusion can be drawn: the general characteristics of the development of the cultural character of Chinese universities since the Reform and Opening Up can be concluded as "gradual recovery, that is not yet finalized."

First of all, the cultural character of Chinese universities is gradually recovering and reviving, showing an ideal, possible trend. From this perspective, the ideal cultural character of Chinese universities does not seem far away from us. This huge possibility is mainly rooted in the two situational characteristics of the new era: As far as the world environment is concerned, "going along with the process of economic globalization is the relative decline of the status of the nation-state."[21] So the new logic of "country rejuvenation through culture" began to emerge. The key to preserving the concept of the country was to strengthen national consciousness and to strengthen national identity with the revival of local culture was the priority. The revival of Chinese culture is indeed based on these considerations. As far as the situation in the country is concerned, an important fact is that China is becoming stronger. Objectively speaking, this supports and encourages the cultural confidence of the Chinese people. As a unique symbol of China, Chinese culture has become the fundamental starting point for establishing the concept of China in the world. Besides, the formation and development of the cultural character of Chinese universities in the 21st century also have an important social foundation.

First, since the Reform and Opening Up, economic construction has been at the center of the society, and the social atmosphere is therefore relatively loose. Reduced political sensitivity has become a clear development trend. In 1991, Jiang Zemin called this out in his *Speech at the Conference Celebrating the 70th Anniversary of the Founding of the Communist Party of China* saying that "we must carry forward the excellent traditional culture of our people and fully embody the spirit of the socialist era. We shall base on our own country and culture while fully absorbing the outstanding cultural achievements of the world" to establish a "socialist culture with Chinese characteristics." This idea completely reversed the anti-traditional tendency of the Mao Zedong era. This showed that the ruling party is no longer an anti-traditional representative, as it had transformed into a strong supporting force for the Chinese cultural revival. This is a major change in history which is unmatched in the early days of the founding of PRC.

Second, since the Reform and Opening Up, a group of intellectuals in the new era has emerged in a relatively liberal and free, social ideological, and cultural atmosphere. They reflect on reality and rationally call for tradition while also caring about the future of Chinese universities. It is their consensus to reshape the cultural character of Chinese universities based on Chinese culture to build a Chinese university model. Additionally, although the cultural character of Chinese universities has shown an ideal possible trend, it has not yet been realized. From this perspective, the ideal cultural character of Chinese universities still lies in the future.

The formation and development of the cultural character of Chinese universities are also affected or controlled by many factors. It is mainly manifested in two aspects. One, under political intervention, the free space of universities is rather limited. In *How China Became Capitalist*, Coase discussed the crux of China's economic problems but ultimately traced it back to the reality of Chinese culture and education. In his view, "the lack of a free market for ideas undermines China's efforts to build a harmonious society and to rebuild cultural traditions."[22] For now, Chinese universities are fighting for freedom but they are still not free. Without official support, it is difficult for a university to make a difference.

Two, the negative economic effects are flooding Chinese universities. While economic development stimulates and supports the rejuvenation of the cultural character of Chinese universities, it also creates various obstacles for its resurgence. On the one hand, economic logic has spread to the field of education, seriously challenging the educational logic of Chinese universities. The so-called university rankings, university-run enterprises, and even university reforms throughout the entire society are unconsciously controlled by an economic way of thinking, which is beyond the control of the economic era. On the other hand, economic pressure forces intellectuals in universities to be marginalized. Under the temptation of the economy, university professors can hardly remain in solitude. They either seek employment overseas, change their profession, and engage in trade, or become university's income-generating machines. In a sense, this self-degeneration of intellectuals impacts the formation and development of the cultural character of Chinese universities on a level that is no less severe than the ideological remolding of intellectuals.

Based on the above analysis, the formation of the ideal cultural character of Chinese universities still has a very long way to go. However, we are still full of hope. As mentioned above, on the one hand, university freedom is no longer prohibited in China. On the other hand, there indeed are some idealistic educators who have played or are playing an important role in Chinese universities.

Section 2: The Formation Path of Chinese Universities' Cultural Characters since Reform and Opening Up

"In the West, universities are already finalized, and their paths are roughly determined. As an individual intellectual, you can present your voice, but it hardly matters anymore. However, it is different for China. You will find that so many scholars are willing to put their majors on hold temporarily and rush to talk about university issues. That is because they believe that university issues are still solvable by their efforts. Today's '100 schools of thought' may affect the future direction of Chinese universities' development."[23] Chen Pingyuan's remarks have two key points. One is to diagnose the current "unfinalized" status of Chinese universities, and the other is to predict the influence of *Dushuren* (scholars, those who read books) on the future direction of Chinese universities.

These two points unintentionally reveal the reality of the current cultural character of Chinese universities. As in, the cultural character of Chinese universities is still unfinalized, and groups of scholars are destined to become an important influence in the process of their finalization. On the one hand, since the Reform and Opening Up, China has gradually matured under the unified leadership of the party. The mutual understanding and support between the party and intellectuals is the mainstream trend. In particular, the decentralization of state power has expanded the autonomy of Chinese universities, and many daring presidents of the universities came forth in response. On the other hand, Reform and Opening Up has created a group of intellectuals of the new era, and they have accumulated rich experiences during their communication and exchanges with the world and while cherishing unique Chinese cultural feelings at the same time. It does not matter if they live within or outside of the national system. They come from different disciplines and care for Chinese universities. They have become a voice that Chinese universities cannot ignore. In short, the rise of new intellectuals means that the formation of the ideal cultural character of Chinese universities has become possible one again. This is also a fundamental reason why this book firmly believes in the historical inevitability of the achievement of the ideal cultural character of Chinese universities.

According to their life status, Xu Jilin divided the 20th-century Chinese intellectuals into six generations. The first generation was the cross-century intellectuals in the late Qing Dynasty. As the last batch of *Shi* class scholars in the traditional society of China, they had the most profound knowledge of Sinology and maintained tolerance for Western learning. And hence, they were also the main sculptors of the cultural character of Chinese universities at the birth of Chinese universities. The second and third generations of intellectuals were scattered throughout the Republican China period, the former referred to the first generation of Chinese intellectuals in the modern sense since 1915, while the latter were the intellectuals of the 1930s and 1940s. They were well educated in both Chinese and Western cultures and were collectively referred to as "the unprecedented generation" in Chinese history. They created the glorious era of the Republic of China and became the successful shaper of the ideal cultural character of Chinese universities throughout history. The fourth-generation was the intellectuals in the Mao Zedong era after 1949. As the "survivors" of Republican China, they lost their power of speech under the new ideology. This was the reason for the decline in the cultural character of Chinese universities in the early days of PRC's founding. The fifth generation of intellectuals officially appeared in the cultural upsurge of the 1980s. Most of the sixth generation of intellectuals were born after 1960. As intellectuals that came after the start of Reform and Opening Up, they mediate between politics, economy, and academics, and they have the potential of becoming the backbone for the formation of the ideal cultural character of Chinese universities. Although the fourth generation of intellectuals was "reborn" after the Cultural Revolution, their stories of Chinese universities have come to an end and most of them have now passed away. Hence, when discussing the formation path of the cultural character of Chinese universities, this book focuses on the fifth and sixth generation of intellectuals, and it shall refer to them as "new intellectuals" for the time being.

Taking these "new intellectuals" as the research perspective, there are three tasks for this section. First, by analyzing the cultural views popularized in the academic circles since the Reform and Opening Up, it will deconstruct the internal relationship between new intellectuals and Chinese culture, and grasp the cultural character of new intellectuals. Second, using the concept of university advocated and practiced by new intellectuals as the research object, this section will try to understand the isomorphic effect of new intellectuals and Chinese universities from a cultural perspective, as well as predict the specific cultural character of Chinese universities in the future. Third, by focusing on the university presidents that are the most closely related to the shaping of the cultural characteristics of Chinese universities, this section will verify the feasibility of the ideal cultural character of Chinese universities.

1. New Intellectuals and Chinese Culture

From a cultural perspective, the great historical merit of Reform and Opening Up lay in the liberation of intellectuals and the instigation of various cultural thoughts. Until today, with the active participation of new intellectuals, the cultural discussions in the academic world are still happening in full swing, and they show no signs of stopping at all. It seems that it is still too early to make a historical comment on this phenomenon. However, based on the understanding of cultural theories and viewpoints that have emerged or those that are currently popular, it is possible to see a trend of Chinese cultural development. The book, *Twenty Years of Chinese Cultural Studies,* edited by Shao Hanming included a detailed summary of various cultural viewpoints and theories of new intellectuals since the Reform and Opening Up. The book listed seven kinds of Chinese and Western cultural views held by various schools of thought, namely, *Xiti Zhongyong*, "national nihilism and total Westernization," "integration and complementation," "comprehensive creation," "complementation," "harmony in diversity" and "world cultural integration." Each of the viewpoints described in the book had its own characteristics, but in general, everything could be divided into three trends. These are overall Westernization, integration of Chinese and Western cultures, and the integration of world culture. Judging from the current situation, most views fall under the integration category.

With the rise of multiple civilizations in the world, especially since the 21st century, it is possible to still use the conflict and integration of Chinese and Western cultures as the background for the development of Chinese universities. Although after all, it is no longer an accurate argument. Therefore, the following section analyzes the three basic cultural trends of new intellectuals from two perspectives, "Chinese and Western cultures" and "world cultures," in an attempt to explore the inner connection between new intellectuals and Chinese culture.

a) Total Westernization.

The theory of total Westernizationism originated during the May Fourth New Culture Movement, with Chen Duxiu and Hu Shi as the representative figures. It advocated for the complete elimination of Chinese tradition and it was for a complete Westernization. This was the product of a special historical era. In the 1980s, China restored its communication to the world, and Chinese and Western cultures met once again. The question of "How can we deal with the relationship between Chinese and Western cultures?" became the focus of discussion among new intellectuals. In a new round of disputes between Chinese and Western cultures, the theory of total Westernization rose once again. Among the more representative characters were also Fang Lizhi and Liu Xiaobo.

In the late 1980s, Fang Lizhi, the then-vice president of the University of Science and Technology of China, vigorously advocated for overall Westernization. Its main points can be summarized as follows: China's overall cultural level was lagging behind the world's advanced culture, so China should open up on all aspects, and let the advanced culture impact every aspect of China, including its politics, economy, culture, technology, education, etc.[24] Liu Xiaobo was another typical representative of the total anti-traditionalism in the new era. He made a clear statement, "I totally reject traditional culture. I think that traditional culture should not have any successors. "[25] It is fine to criticize tradition, but the remarks of these two deliberately depreciated the shortcomings of Chinese culture with the advantages of Western culture, and eventually completely stigmatized Chinese culture. This is not a fair showdown between Chinese and Western cultures. The extreme anti-traditionalism and even anti-socialism caused a severe backlash, and their remarks eventually drowned in the collective criticism of the public. This also meant that although China widely accepted and imported Western culture after Reform and Opening Up, it did not want the overall acceptance of Western culture, nor the complete abandonment of Chinese traditions.

Zhang Dainian and Cheng Yishan once commented on this theory, "In the 80's cultural forum, 'total Westernization' is not so much a serious theoretical proposition but an emotional slogan." "People who advocated "total Westernization" in the 1980s sometimes affirmed 'total Westernization' as a slogan synonymous with 'omnidirectional opening' and advocated the full introduction of Western culture, including philosophy, politics, economics, and other theories and systems. They planned to bring impact to all the fields of China and keep whatever was left after the impact. This kind of proposition was basically a copy of Hu Shi's theory of "total Westernization." The political meaning of this was to imitate the West and follow its capitalist ways. In the 1980s, when the Chinese people had chosen and embarked on the path of socialism after nearly a hundred years of hard work, reiterating such a proposition only undermined the political situation of unity, stability, and solidarity that was finally formed. It meant interfering with the process of modernization. It's right to talk about opening up in all directions, but it's not right to talk about letting Western culture impact everything we have."[26] In a word, the total Westernization theory exceeded the scope of culture in the 1980s. It was mainly limited to radical individuals and it failed to cause any wide-spread influence. With the growing strength of China, it had withdrawn from history.

b) Integration of Chinese and Western cultures.

The Integration of Chinese and Western cultures was the mainstream contemporary Chinese cultural discourse. It was different from the popular Chinese-Western reconciliation theory advocated during the New Culture Movement, but they shared the same basic starting point, that is, the Chinese and Western cultures were combined into one based on Chinese culture. This was done to achieve a more ideal state of Chinese and Western cultural balance. Since the 1980s, the more representative views are:

1. Chinese and Western cultural integration theory.

This kind of theory advocated for the equality and mutual development between Chinese and Western cultures, and the compatible integration into modern culture. The main theories of this category included Liu Lilin's theory of *Zhonghun Xiti* (Chinese soul and Western body) and Bao Zhicheng's theory of "hybridization" optimization. Taking Liu Lilin's theory of *Zhonghun Xiti* as an example, it was based on the comparative research framework of Chinese and Western cultures by previous researchers. This included *Dongfang Shangdao, Xifang Shangyi* (the East excels in Dao, the West excels in Arts). The so-called *Zhonghun Xiti* meant to take the *Daohun* (Dao and spirits) of Chinese culture and the instruments and systems of Western culture, combining them, and letting them coexist codependently. Looking at the various views under the Chinese cultural integration theory, their fundamental purpose was to make Chinese and Western cultures complement each other through integration. What was certain was that the *Daohun* of Chinese culture was the inner spiritual side of this cooperation.

2. Theory of complementation of Chinese and Western cultures.

This theory appeared in the 1990s, and Tian Jianguo in the field of economics mentioned this point of view in *Random Thoughts on the Comparison of Chinese and Western Culture*. He pointed out that, "The West rules families with country laws, and China rules the country with the family laws. They both had their advantages and disadvantages. Western laws are effective in ruling the country, and Chinese laws are effective in ruling families and corporations. Hence, we should apply Westernization on the macroscopic level, ruling the country with 'rule of law' and market; and apply Sinicization on the microscopic level, ruling families and corporations with moral order. This is my complimentary view of macro-westernization and micro-sinicization." This theory discussed Chinese and Western cultures from an economic perspective. It particularly recognized and emphasized the aspect of China's moral tradition.

3. Synthesis of Chinese and Western cultures.

This theory was represented by the "synthesis of creation" theory proposed by Zhang Dainian and Cheng Yishan in the late 1980s. In the discussions of Zhang Dainian and Cheng Yishan, the so-called "synthesis and creation" was meant to "abandon the dichotomy and the dualistic rigid thinking mode of Chinese and Western cultures, eliminate the interference of blind China-centrism and create a highly developed socialist new Chinese culture that has both national characteristics and fully reflects the spirit of the times in accordance with the actual needs of China's socialist modernization drive. It should be based on the principles of socialism, and formulated with an open mind and a compatible attitude, through scientific and dialectical analysis and prudent screening of the constituent elements and structural forms of the ancient and modern Chinese and foreign cultural systems, while bearing the subjective democratic consciousness in mind, under the guidance of the universal truth of Marxism. The 'synthesis' in the discussion is not an unprincipled compromise, but the result of dialectical consideration."[27] This view was based on Chinese reality and it paid more attention to the innovative spirit of the synthesis of Chinese and Western cultures. As far as Chinese culture was concerned, it emphasized a national feature in a macro sense.

4. *Xiti Zhongyong* (Western systems, Chinese practices).

This theory, represented by Li Zehou, was a highly controversial point of view in the disputes between Chinese and Western cultures in the 1980s. Li Zehou's interpretation of *Xiti Zhongyong* was that the future path should be the combination of modernization of social ontology (production methods, superstructures, and daily real life), along with its ontological consciousness (technological thought, ideology) of social existence (which was originated from the West, such as the Marx Doctrine) and the reality of China (including the reality of Confucianism as the objective existence of Chinese cultural psychology).[28] Many scholars believe that this view has a clear Westernization tendency, and some directly incorporate it into the "total Westernization" category. Objectively speaking, Li Zehou's *Xiti Zhongyong* is still trying to solve the problems of the integration of Chinese and Western cultures. Its focus is not on Western learning, but on the adaptability of Western learning in Chinese culture.

Views on the fusion of Chinese and Western cultures are not limited to the above, and many are still emerging at this moment. However, the thinking behind them is clear, that is, no matter what kind of expression it is or what leaning tendencies they have in their connotations, their purpose is to seek the fusion of Chinese and Western cultures. These thoughts are based on the revival of certain Chinese cultural elements. Compared with the theory of "harmony between Chinese and Western cultures" during the Republican China period, the horizon is broader and the position of Chinese culture is more present.

c) Integration of World Cultures.

Different from the previous idea of using Chinese and Western cultures as the basic place to express Chinese cultural concepts in "total Westernization" and "integration of Chinese and Western cultures," the theory of the integration of world cultures takes on a new perspective. It views China from the world's perspective and discussed Chinese culture according to this idea. At the turn of the century, when Huntington pitted Chinese and Western cultures against each other again with his *Clash of Civilizations and the Reconstruction of the World Order,* Luo Zhitian, who was very experienced overseas, used ancient Chinese to propose the theory of *He Er Butong* (harmony in diversity). According to the theory, the *He Er Butong* was advocated by Confucius and the *Yi Buqi Wei Qi* (unity in diversity) was advocated by Zhuangzi and they were more suitable for the coexistence of different cultures of the world and were more likely to be realized.

Luo Zhitian explained: To work in the direction of *He Er Butong*, we must first be able to fully understand ourselves and produce a genuine "compassion of understanding" for different cultures. The direction of this effort is not to seek common ground, but to distinguish between our and their cultures first, that is, not only to understand the identity problem of "who I am," but also to understand the "non-self" as "others." Because it is practically impossible to remain in solitude due to the integration and interaction of today's world culture. No matter what culture or doctrine, no one is completely pure and not mixed. But to be able to truly absorb the strengths of other countries' cultures, one must build on the solid foundation of the local culture, and one must achieve what Zhi Xi calls *Xu Qixin* (hollow thy heart), which is equivalent to the so-called "open mind" of the Westerners, and one must treat local culture and foreign cultures equally.[29]

Luo Zhitian replaced the fixed expressions of Chinese culture and Western culture with the concepts of local culture and foreign cultures. The field of vision was no longer confined between Chinese and Western cultures, and his fundamental position was based on local culture and therefore was also more distinct.

Dong Xiaochuan was also an advocate of world cultural integration. Also at the time of Huntington's theory of cultural conflict, Dong Xiaochuan made it clear that we did not think that Western culture was to be replaced by Eastern culture, nor did we think that Eastern culture and modernization could not be integrated. Instead, we believed that the general trend of world cultural integration was unstoppable, and it was highly hopeful that human culture would progress towards great unity.[30]

Along with the progress of globalization, more scholars had begun to study Chinese culture in the context of world culture. However, whether from the perspective of Chinese and Western cultures or based on world culture, the Chinese cultural position of the "new intellectuals" was getting clearer. Nowadays, words such as "civilization localization," "national characteristics," "subject consciousness" and "native feelings" had become popular terms in the cultural world. New intellectuals are using their pens to guide the future of Chinese culture.

In summary, although there were still episodes when the Westernization theory reappears since the Reform and Opening Up, these episodes were more political than cultural, and they did not achieve any wide-ranging influence. As such, they were eventually forgotten throughout history. From the previous analysis, the integration of Chinese and Western cultures was undoubtedly the mainstream idea of the new era, which showed that the new intellectuals had a "sympathetic understanding" of Chinese culture. The new intellectuals who were active in academia after the 1980s are indeed a special generation. "Understanding" and "sympathy" connected them closely with Chinese culture. The reason for this can be summarized in the following aspects.

First, as far as their personal experiences were concerned, most of them have experienced special events such as the Cultural Revolution, the restoration of the college entrance examination, the cultural upsurge, and the comprehensive initiation of the market economy. Coming from the declining Chinese culture, they summed up the historical laws of the close connection between Chinese culture and China's fate in the deeply painful lessons of China's abandonment of tradition. Coming from the college entrance examination system that has been stagnant for many years, they became the most diligent students of Chinese universities and accumulated solid cultural knowledge. Coming from the cultural upsurge of *Xixue Dongjian*, most of them had the experience of studying abroad which meant they understood Western learning more comprehensively. Coming from the economic era with its pros and cons, they strengthened their determination to revive Chinese culture during the challenges and crises of marginalization.

Second, in terms of their relationship with the government, since the Reform and Opening Up, the relationship between the Chinese government and intellectuals has been greatly improved. Especially for the revival of Chinese culture, they showed greater consistency in goals, so it was easier to move towards mutual support and cooperation. From this perspective, there were no political pressures and obstacles in the new intellectuals' concepts and practices of cultural revival.

Based on the above two points, it can be considered that the cultural character of new intellectuals presents an ideal possible trend. To some extent, this may be the return of the cultural character of the intellectuals in Republican China, which was located between the two poles: the strong Chinese cultural complex of the scholars in the late Qing Dynasty and the weak Chinese cultural feelings in the Mao Zedong era. Of course, both Republican China's intellectuals and the new intellectuals were products of specific eras, and therefore, new intellectuals can't repeat history, and it is meaningless for them to try to imitate history. Republican China's intellectuals had a profound knowledge of Chinese culture, which new intellectuals could not compete with. While the new intellectuals possess unprecedented knowledge and culture of Western learnings in the era of globalization, which Republican China's intellectuals could not have had, either. New intellectuals and intellectuals of Republican China are not comparable in terms of academic characteristics due to the differences in their backgrounds, but there are no impassable gaps between their ideologies. In a word, they took the same path, that is, to seek the integration of Chinese and Western cultures based on Chinese culture.

2. *New intellectuals and Chinese Universities*

The reform of Peking University in 2003 was an important basis for exploring the relationship between new intellectuals and those of Chinese universities in that era. The failure of Peking University's reform back then was largely due to its failure to gain widespread support from new intellectuals. New intellectuals across various fields and specialties "came together and attacked it," which, exerted invisible pressure on Peking University. Their critical focus was based on the obvious Westernization tendency of Peking University's reform. This was contrary to the mainstream cultural concepts of contemporary new intellectuals. In his work *Daxue Sanwen*, as a response to Peking University's reform, Chen Pingyuan mentioned, "What the university reformists are lacking today is not 'international vision,' but understanding and respect for 'traditional China' and 'modern China.'" He also emphasized, "The 'Chinese experience of 'a millennium of traditional academies,' plus 'a centennial of the university', should not be ignored."[31] This was also a fundamental position of most new intellectuals at that time.

When Peking University's strong America-flavored personnel system reform met the new intellectuals' Chinese cultural complex, it was obvious that the latter had the upper hand. The reason for Peking University reform's failure could be regarded as the objection of new intellectuals' cultural characters, which also reflected the influence of the latter on Chinese universities. The 30 years of Reform and Opening Up was an era of "overflowing" Chinese university reforms. Apart from conducting studies and research, new intellectuals also "read the universities," creating a new fashion in academia.

"Most preciously, more scholars have gone beyond their respective disciplinary horizons and discussed in depth some of the abstract, heavy and ideologically impactful propositions such as the spirit, temperament, and soul of Chinese universities."[32] It was exactly in these profound thinkings where some of the influential concepts of Chinese universities were born. When we think about it now, there were two basic characteristics that the new intellectuals shared in constructing Chinese university concepts: 1) starting from the problems of Chinese universities and criticizing their current malady; 2) starting from the cultural perspective and digging deep into traditions. It was indeed true that most of these university concepts were standing in between the ideal and reality, while some of them were more idealistic than practical and realistic. However, we have all the reasons to believe that, when new intellectuals were gradually returning to the main body of the university, the ideal Chinese university cultural characters were just around the corner.

The following would extract three core concepts from the current diverse university concepts, namely *Yi Ren Wei Ben* (people-orientedness), *Renwen Lishen* (building on humanities), and *Ningjing Zhiyuan* (looking beyond in quietude), to grasp specifically the possible trends of the development of Chinese universities' cultural characters under the influence of new intellectuals.

a) Yi Ren Wei Ben

People-orientedness, is one of the core concepts of the current university concepts of new intellectuals. It refers to taking the "people" as the fundamental starting point and the goal of university education. The subjectivity of people was fully respected and highlighted. There were two aspects of this idea, namely student-orientedness and teacher-orientedness. Enlightened by the people-oriented thoughts in the traditional society, addressing issues while positioning universities on the presence of people has become a common trend of new intellectuals' studies of Chinese universities.

With a higher education perspective, Zhang Liqiang has provided a general theoretical basis for universities' people-oriented concept. In the book, *Gaodeng Jiaoyu Xiandaihua De Fansi Yu Jiangou* (*Reflection and Construction of a Modernized Higher Education*), he raised the slogan:

> "People are the subject and theme of a modernized higher education." He explained that the process of modernization is not without subjectivity or a goal. The real subject of modernization is not the "society," which is merely a form of existence of "people." Similarly, the modernization of higher education is not a process of development with no subject or goal. The subject of higher education's modernization is not "higher education" itself, as it is merely a special way of practicing its idea of the "people." The "people" are the only subject of modernization and the modernization of higher education. Judging from the current times, "people" are also the theme of these two processes.[33]

Wang Jisheng listed the humanistic spirit of people-orientedness as the primary value pursuit of universities from the viewpoint of university spirit. In the *book Daxue Zhi Dao* (*The Way of the University*), he pointed out, "As the spiritual homeland of human civilization, the universities should establish a 'people-oriented' humanistic spirit, which is not only the essence and core of the scientific development but also the essence and core of educational philosophy. It occupies a particularly important position in the spirit of the university."[34] Based on a cultural perspective, Wang Jisheng affirmed the people-oriented tradition of Chinese universities. "Universities have long advocated the humanistic spirit of 'people-orientedness.' As early as in the pre-Qin period, our country has vigorously advocated that 'The way of great learning consists in manifesting one's bright virtue, consists in loving the people, in stopping in perfect goodness.'"[35] He believed that the time to revive the humanistic spirit of Daxue has come.

Sui Yifan defended the university's student-oriented philosophy from the perspective of the university's mission. In the book *Lixing Hanwei Daxue* (*Defending the University with Rationality*), he pointed out that "the cultivation of talents is a cultural heritage that the university cannot give up." He stated, "only universities with a strong mission to cultivate talent will regard students rather than buildings as their most valuable assets, and will, therefore, focus their love, time, energy and all resources to their responsibilities of cultivating talented and virtuous students, as well as the improvement the education environment, which respects, cares and protects the students. This environment would also be conducive to the development of students' characters and the healthy growth of the students' bodies and minds. Emphasizing talent cultivation is both the founding principle and the basic reason for the existence and development of the university."[36]

From the perspective of university composition, Chu Zhaohui put forward the proposition that "teachers and students are the true masters of the university." This proposition emphasized the unique value of teachers and students as the main body of the university. He pointed out in the book *Lixiang Daxue* (*Ideal University*) that, "The reason why *daxue* (great learning, university) is *da* (great) is because of the *xue* (learning). Who is learning? Teachers and students. Teachers and students are always the masters of the university. Only by seeing teachers and students as the masters of the university can we truly establish the value of academic standards and promote academic freedom." "Only when a scholar becomes the master of a university can a university become a real university." "[37]

In the book *Biange Zhong De Daxue* (*Universities in Reformation*), Li Wei also emphasized two "-oriented" school concepts and explained specific measures on how to realize "student-orientedness" and "teacher-orientedness" based on his university running experience. As for "student-orientedness," he believed that "we have to treat our students and their parents with the attitude of 'wishing himself to be established, seeing that others are established, and, wishing himself to be successful, seeing that others are successful,' and 'What you don't want to be done to yourself, don't do to others.'"[38] To insist on student-orientedness and to better serve the students, we must implement the mentor system from the undergraduate level. Let the mentors train students into new talents through the process of demonstrating good examples, learning from each other, and teaching while learning, in accordance with the characteristics of the students. As for the 'teacher-orientedness,' Li Wei pointed out: "Since we must insist on "student-orientedness," teachers in the frontline of students' cultivation are the main body that implements the "student-oriented" education. Therefore, the work of cadres at all levels of the school should serve this purpose, and center their work around all frontline teachers to achieve the goal of 'teacher-orientedness' and 'serving the teachers.'"[39] The fundamental measure for implementing 'teacher-orientedness' was to expand the autonomy of colleges (departments) and achieve flat management.

In summary, in the construction and practice of new intellectuals, the fundamental direction of the reform and development of Chinese universities had been established, that is, the people-oriented university concept. From a cultural perspective, which stemmed from the philosophy of Chinese classical education, ancient Chinese cultural knowledge claimed itself to be "the study of the unity between Heaven and man." The mainstream view believed that there was no such thing as the supreme and immortal way of Heaven. Instead, the idea of "orienting around people and achieving the unity between Heaven and man" was further advocated. In Chapter *Gongsuhn Chou* of Mencius, it was stated that "Reaching appropriate timing is not as good as being in a beneficial place. Being in a beneficial place is not as good as attaining the harmony of the people." Mencius advocated that the harmony between people is better than being in a beneficial place, which is, in turn, better than reaching an appropriate timing. "People" are fundamental. Tracing back to the roots of this idea, at least during the times of Confucius and Mencius, China already had the tradition of putting people first and this belief has been passed down for thousands of years. The various introductions of the concepts of the new intellectuals covered above would be regarded as a theoretical basis. On a practical level, they embodied the following concepts of Chinese classical higher education.

First, teaching students according to their aptitudes. This concept was a basic educational principle of Confucius, that is, to respect the differences between students and to differentiate teaching in a targeted manner. Its traces could be found in the new intellectuals' advocation of the idea of "student-orientedness," which was to promote the comprehensive development of students.

Second, respecting and dignifying the teacher. China has its historical allusion of *Chengmen Lixue* (students stand in the snow to respectfully wait for Master Cheng). All the talented and benevolent emperors in ancient China saw respecting and dignifying the teacher and knowledge as the way to make a country prosper. During the Mao Zedong era, university teachers were confined and besieged by politics, the tradition of university teachers' dignity was completely torn down. New intellectuals re-established the tradition of teacher-oriented education. This was a historical reflection and a return to tradition. From this perspective, the people-oriented university concept of new intellectuals was deeply rooted in Chinese cultural traditions.

b) Building on humanities.

Building on humanities was the new intellectuals' further extension of the people-oriented connotation within the university concept. The so-called "building on humanities" was mainly in contrast with practical sciences. Humanities referred to humanistic knowledge, especially Chinese traditional culture as the main idea to improve the spiritual realm of students through the cultivation of humanistic qualities. Driven by new intellectuals, humanistic education has become an important part of Chinese universities' reform. The new intellectuals' consciousness of humanistic education was not coincidental. Under the impact of pragmatic sciences, "the general silence of the humanistic environment of Chinese universities was in sharp contrast with the now-mainstream practical sciences such as science and technology, economics, business management, and law. The need for this knowledge for social development does not mean that those who have mastered knowledge in these fields are actively contributing (to this development). Nowadays, the development of the economic, cultural, and social fields has involved intellectuals to different degrees. While enjoying the achievements brought by practical knowledge and technology, members of society also suffered from the exhaustion of humanistic care."[40] This became the direct motivation for the new intellectuals to renew humanities education in universities.

Gan Yang was a passionate advocate of humanities education in Chinese universities. At the beginning of the 21st century, Gan Yang had already put forward the concept of "university for the Mandarin" to call for the cultural consciousness and self-confidence of

Chinese universities. Chinese humanities education could be regarded as an operational definition of Gan's university for the Mandarin concept. In the article *Daxue Renwen Jiaoyu De Linian (Idea, Goals, and Models of University Humanities Education),* Gan Yang planned out an ideal path of Chinese humanities education (general education) by comparing Chinese and Western cultures, he used Chinese culture as the fundamental foothold. To cite some of his words:

> "I, therefore, believe that the central task of the general education curriculum in Chinese universities is to reorganize our cultural traditions that have been broken since the Republic of China, and gradually form the tradition of our universities' 'core curriculum.' Therefore, our inspection of the general education experiences in the United States and other countries must look beyond their latest external forms. We must understand how they initially worked after the breakdown of traditional education... What is important is to study Western learnings in-depth. We should not be misled by the most nominal and fashionable things in the West. Instead, we should gradually form the Chinese people's judgment and analysis of Western ideologies and academics through in-depth research. Therefore, we can't build a general education curriculum like the Western countries and the early United States, who placed sole respect for their traditions. We need to take the path of the "simultaneous development of Chinese and Western traditions."
>
> The next two to three decades might be the most critical period for the revival of Chinese civilization and the development of Chinese universities. If the Chinese people themselves have no confidence in the Chinese civilization, if the Chinese people always held a negative attitude towards the tradition of the Chinese civilization and everything in China, certainly, Chinese universities can never be run well. On the contrary, if Chinese people and Chinese university students can have the appropriate cultural consciousness, if Chinese universities are firmly rooted in the depth of Chinese civilization, then we have all the reasons to expect that after a generation of unremitting effort, Chinese universities would become great universities that serve as the leader of the great Chinese civilization, though they are far from satisfactory today.[41]

It can be seen from this that Gan Yang's Chinese humanistic education philosophy takes the path of the simultaneous development of Chinese and Western traditions, that is, a combination of a rational analyst of Western thought and a leader of the Chinese civilization. Based on the reality that Chinese culture has "little remaining" in its modern times, Gan Yang particularly emphasized that Chinese universities should be rooted in traditional culture. From this perspective, what he interpreted was still a Mandarin university idea which saw Chinese culture as the basis, and promoted the absorption of Western culture.

Chen Pingyuan was another constructor of the humanities education concept in Chinese universities. When commenting on the reform of the personnel system of Peking University, Chen Pingyuan believed that an obvious shortcoming in the formulation of the Peking University system was the absence of scholars specializing in the humanities. In the article *Daxue Zhognwenxi De Ziwo Dingwei (Self-positioning of the Chinese Department in a University),* Chen Pingyuan pointed out: "University, as a knowledge community, requires professional skills and cultural ideals. It is the humanities that play a decisive role in creating the campus atmosphere, shaping the style of the university, and reflecting its spiritual values."[42] The essence of Chen Pingyuan's concept of universities' humanities education could be summarized as 'being inclusive to both Chinese and Western, ancient and modern cultures. This virtually incorporated the lost Chinese cultural traditions into a venue for equal dialogue with "Western" and the "present."

One of Tu Youguang's basic views in *Zhongguo Gaodeng Jiaoyu Shilun* was that the development of Chinese higher education had gone through the "humanities" stage of traditional society. It was at that time in the "science" stage and the ideal trend in the future that lay in the "humanities plus science" idea. In his article *Wenming Bentuhua Yu Daxue (Cultural Localization and Universities),* Tu stated that the characteristics of civilization lay in humanities instead of technology. If a Chinese university ignores Chinese humanities, "it can only be regarded as 'a university in China,' instead of 'a university of China.'"[43] Of course, new intellectuals' concepts of university humanities education discourse could be found outside of their words and works. As a pioneer of university humanities education, Yang Shuzi was already committed to the practice of cultural and quality education in the 1990s at Huazhong Technological University (now Huazhong University of Science and Technology).

By seeing "people-orientedness" as the basic starting point, new intellectuals' traditional humanistic complex had become the cultural connotation of the theories and practices of Chinese universities' humanistic education. The philosophy of humanistic education was not from China, nor was it a unique characteristic of Chinese universities. The so-called ideological trend of humanistic education and general education had already entered a relatively mature stage of development in Western universities. However, in different countries and cultural backgrounds, humanities have their unique connotations. The philosophy of humanities education in Chinese universities is also derived from Chinese tradition. According to Tu Youguang, Chinese higher education was in the "humanities" stage from ancient times until the end of the 19th century. Confucius should be regarded as the founder of the humanistic characters of Chinese higher education. Under the millennium of the ancient Confucian idea of excelling in academics for officialdom, it became a historical tradition that China is run by the literati, which lasted until the Qing Dynasty.

It was not until modern times that under the impact of Western scientific and technological civilization, China's humanistic logic gradually disintegrated. Since the

20th century, due to overcorrection, the power of science and technology has almost obscured the traditional humanistic background of China. From the perspective of historical evolution, the construction of humanistic education in Chinese universities today was an intentional return to China's "humanistic" education tradition. It can also be seen that Chinese universities have walked from the "science" era where traditions declined in general to the ideal era of "humanities plus science."

c) Looking beyond in tranquillity.

This is the new intellectuals' ideal expression of their reflections on, and detachment from, reality. The so-called 'looking beyond tranquillity' idea implies that universities, as people-oriented educational institutions, should keep a distance from the secular merits, benefits, and interests of the society. It touches on the basic qualities of those working in tertiary educational institutions and universities. That is, they should maintain the academic spirit under the temptation of power and interests. 'Looking beyond tranquillity' stemmed from the new intellectuals' concerns about the vulgarization and secularization of the universities.

Sui Yifan defined "the vulgarization of universities" in the article *Daxue Yongsuhua Pipan (Criticism of University Vulgarization)* as the unfavorable phenomena and behavior of universities that tended to be non-normative, unethical, unhealthy, non-self-disciplinary, and even deviated from the essential attributes of university organizations. He deeply criticized the bureaucracy-oriented trend, philistine style, academic malpractices, and cynicism demonstrated by higher education institutions and those working there.[44] Chen Pingyuan investigated the crux of the decline of Chinese universities' credibility in *Daxue Gongxinli Weihe Xiajiang-Cong 'Wenhua' De Guandian Kan 'Daxue' (Why does the credibility of universities decline-approaching 'universities' from a 'cultural perspective).* He talked about the vulgarization of universities. In this article, he described: "There are tall and full walls enclosing our campuses, yet we cannot shut the campuses away from the huge wave of commercialization. Secular slogans were all over the place. It was almost impossible for you to even 'hide away in a little building and mind your own business.'" The "zero-distance contact" between universities and the society, plus the over-secularization, made it hard for the professors and students within the walls to maintain a calm heart and study in a down-to-earth manner.[45] In the criticism of Chinese universities' reality, the university administrative concept of "looking beyond tranquillity' was gradually established in new intellectuals' reflection and introspection.

In an interview with journalists, Chen Yi was asked how one should view the criticisms of universities from all walks of life in society. He emphasized solely on one point, that is, "universities can only achieve lasting accomplishments via tranquillity." It contained the following:

> A university should be calm and quiet, it should not follow the trends blindly, nor should it be impetuous. It does not have to pay too much attention to all these kinds of evaluations. Some evaluations were superficial – during the evaluation, everybody is stressed out, yet when the result is released, everything is rated well and everybody is happy. The problems, however, are taken lightly, not to the point. These evaluations are mostly useless, and may even leave negative effects. While some others were highly random, I don't get their points.[46]

Chen Pingyuan also had similar comments in his book, *Zhongguo Daxue Gaige, Lu Zai Hefang? (Chinese Universities Reform, Where Is the Right Path?)*:

> The reason why there are "incessant inspections and evaluations," apart from suspecting teachers for being lazy, is the Great Leap Forward-thinking. I have been saying that repeatedly, admitting that there is still hope for Chinese universities at their current level if they maintain a down-to-earth attitude and move forward progressively. If we keep trying to make progress in a "quick and economical" manner and achieve "ultra-conventional development," the universities would be prone to problems. If the goals are too high, the management too strict, there are going to be falsifications when goals fail. In the end, we would not even be able to keep our bottom line. What a pity. This statement allowed the universities to return to peace.[47]

Admittedly, the university concept of "looking beyond in tranquillity" seemed so outdated in terms of the historical role of universities as a social service device. However, though there were conflicts, there were no fundamental clashes. On the contrary, if the universities maintain the attitude of "looking beyond in tranquillity," they would better serve society. Or rather, this attitude itself is the pre-requisite for the universities to keep to the academic spirit and fulfill social responsibilities. Sui Yifan pointed this out in his book, *Lixing Hanwei Daxue*:

> The persistence of scientific research's mission requires that universities not only focus on the responsibility of innovating knowledge and exploring truth, but they must also create a free atmosphere for academics, which allows teachers and students in the universities to be comfortable with learning, be passionate about learning, be loyal to learning, and devote themselves to learning. At any time, the universities should have enough sobriety to know its mission and direction. Not only should it consciously adhere to and protect the academic attributes of the university, but also have the consciousness, power, and system to arouse and protect the real interest and passion of scholars and students in their pursuit of

> knowledge in their major fields. Also, they would not be disturbed and driven by all kinds of interests other than learning, they are comfortable with being calm and achieve lasting accomplishments via tranquillity in the field of academics.[48]

The present book summarizes new intellectuals concepts of *Danbo Ningjing* (Calm and Quiet) (Chen Yi), *Chonggui Pingjing* (Returning to Peace) (Chen Pingyuan), *Ningjing Zhiyuan* (looking beyond in tranquillity) (Sui Yifan), as the term "looking beyond in tranquillity." Just as the word "lonely" was closely related to the German classical culture as the "German classic university concept," "looking beyond in tranquillity" is closely related to the traditional Chinese ancient teachings of *Mingde* and *Xiushen*, and other Confucian greater learning languages. Liu An in the Western Han Dynasty wrote in Chapter *Zhushu Xun* in the book *Huainan Zi*, "The leader's house is as bright as the sun and the moon. Everyone under Heaven would tilt his head to look, to hear, and extend his neck, tip his toe to see. Therefore, there is no way to demonstrate virtues if one is not calm, no way to look far beyond is one is not in tranquillity, no way to be inclusive if one is not benevolent, no way to make a judgment if one is not just." Zhuge Liang wrote in *Jiezi Shu* that, "An intelligentleman should live in quietude to cultivate his mind, be thrifty to nurture his virtues. There is no way to know one's true aspiration if he is not calm, no way to look far beyond if he is not in tranquillity. Learning requires quietude. Talents require learning. One's talent cannot be broadened without learning; One can never learn successfully without determination." The above words indicate that "looking beyond in tranquillity" was regarded as a basic quality of governing the world by virtue, morality, and self-cultivation. Looking back to how the ancients studied, they all emphasized the quiet environment to achieve the effect of calming down and studying. For example, the traditional academies were usually set up in the mountains, or near farming fields, which were quiet and distant from the secular world. One of the reasons for the choice of location was to provide a quiet place for the scholars so that they could cultivate their minds.

To sum up the basic characteristics of the above-mentioned university concepts, that is, the combination of reality and history, the ideal and practicality. First of all, these concepts originated from reality and returned to reality. Some typical problems of Chinese universities under the economic era were: The universities prioritized scientific and technological education as more important than humanistic education. Criticisms and reflections by the new intellectuals against Chinese universities' malpractices, in reality, followed up and became the mainstream voices in the academic world. It is precisely to find the right solution, that the concepts of the people-oriented idea, building on humanities, and looking beyond in tranquillity were gradually brewing. They were committed to returning to reality to alleviate the crisis of Chinese universities. This is where the realistic factor lay. Secondly, as a special group of people who had experienced the special era since the Reform and Opening Up, international visions and local sentiments had gradually become the main cultural characteristics of new intellectuals. From this point of view, it was the new intellectuals' cultural characters that they sought to return to history and tradition to construct Chinese university concepts. This is where the historical factor lay. Furthermore, objectively speaking, the shaping of Chinese university culture was, after all, a gradual process. On the one hand, the problems of Chinese universities were still very prominent. On the other hand, there were plenty of idealistic factors and personal preferences that were not very mature in the new intellectuals' construction of university concepts. Therefore, from the perspective of reality, there was still a certain distance between these ideals and the reality. This is where the idealistic factor lay. Finally, it should be pointed out that although the realization of ideals faced many difficulties, the dual coercion of power and interests was still the hardest reality of Chinese universities. At the same time, the act of constructing the concepts by new intellectuals was not mature or perfect. However, in the face of the rising new intellectuals, we have reasons to believe that the problem will still eventually be solved. This is where the practicality factor lay. In short, without active theoretical argumentations and practical attempts completed by new intellectuals, it would be difficult for the cultural characteristics of Chinese universities to show a relatively ideal development trend in just over thirty years. The basic logic for the formation of the ideal cultural characters of Chinese universities in the future was to use new intellectuals as intermediaries to reshape the foundation of Chinese culture.

3. *The Presidents of Chinese universities and the cultural character of Chinese universities*

Among the intellectuals, the ones that were most closely related to Chinese universities were the university presidents. Unlike the professors, "as the chief executive of the school, the president of the university is the soul of the school, that is, the president of the university has a decisive influence and the role of the successful creation, smooth operation, innovation and progress of a university." "The president of the university plays a decisive role in the reform of its management system, and what affects him is his unique educational philosophy."[49] Since the Reform and Opening Up, "in the historical process of the iteration between the old and the new, a group of intellectual cadres has taken up the post of university presidents. It was a truly substantial historical progress that the university transformed from a party-run and a cadre-run [institution] to an intellectual-run one."[50]

Since the 1980s, Chinese universities have emerged with many influential and accomplished presidents. They were more reputed as educators and reformers rather than the chief executives of universities. From a cultural point of view, as the backbone of Chinese university reform, they have become an important driving force for the Chinese university's school-running concept of being "people-oriented," "building on humanities," and "looking beyond in tranquillity" from an ideal to a reality. The following part of the book will verify and analyze the reality of the three core university concepts of being "people-oriented," "building on humanities," and "looking beyond in tranquillity" by describing the concepts and practices of the three university presidents who have played an important role in the realization of the cultural characters of Chinese universities. It could be considered that under the influence of the presidents of Chinese universities, the shaping of the ideal cultural characters of the Chinese university was already on the way.

a) Zhang Kaiyuan: Students are the foundation of education.

In the 1980s, Central China Normal University, as a prestigious normal university in Wuhan, was closely related to Zhang Kaiyuan. Born in the Republic of China, Zhang Kaiyuan entered Huazhong Normal University in 1951 (also known as Huazhong University) and served as the President of Huazhong Normal University from 1985 to 1991. Coming from the Mao Zedong era, he had gone through College and Department Adjustments, the Anti-Rightist Struggle, and the Cultural Revolution to become the president of the Chinese University in the era of Reform and Opening Up. Zhang Kaiyuan successfully transformed from an educator into a veritable educator. In the early 1980s, during the initial period of economic transformation and the turbulent interaction between the Chinese and Western cultures, Zhang Kaiyuan became the president of the university elected by teachers and students of Huazhong Normal University via a general election. During his tenure at Central China Normal University, Zhang Kaiyuan had always adhered to the people-oriented concept of running a university. His core idea was to return the subjectivity of the university as well as the nature of education. After being interviewed by reporters and being asked how he could rectify the problems of higher education, Zhang Kaiyuan reiterated the university's "student-oriented" philosophy:

> The object of education is human, not related to objects. Educators and educated people need benign interaction, not unidirectional "indoctrination" and "shaping." The starting point and destination of education are both love and the perfection and improvement of human nature. "Orienting around students" is as good as "orienting around human nature." Today, major measures in all aspects of education are called "projects," this is, in fact, a sign that people have forgotten about the differences between people and objects. Schools are not factories, education is different from the process of manufacturing. After all, education is meticulous enlightenment, not simple production.

He also pointed out that:

> Rather than subjectively and arbitrarily carrying out the so-called "innovation" or "leapfrogging" which tossed university teachers and students through administrative orders, it is better to let the university maintain relative peace, perhaps naturally following the rules left by the predecessors. It is more conducive to the development of higher education than any brazen slogans such us "opening up a new era."[51]

"Insisting on student-orientedness," was what Zhang has said, and also what he had practiced. As he mentioned, he often went to the student canteen to have meals with students and to chat with them. He generally did not bring notes when reporting to students. It was also in his style to give lectures in the form of dialogue and casual communication. Under the influence of Zhang Kaiyuan's example, the idea of students as the main body of education was thoroughly implemented at Huazhong Normal University.

b) Yang Shuzi: Science and humanities, connected yet different.

Yang Shuzi was the soul of HUST. "As a scientist in China, it was very rare for him to have such a humanistic accomplishment because few Chinese scientists who have grown up after the founding of New China to have the same deep humanistic qualities as the senior scientists such as Li Siguang and Hua Luogeng."[52] Rather than the title of a scientist or the President of HUST, Yang had a more prominent identity as an educator with profound humanistic feelings. Yang's profound cultivation of Chinese studies mainly benefited from the personal lessons taught by his father Yang Gengsheng, a former *Xiucai* of the Qing dynasty. The five-year experience of Chinese studies at a young age had benefitted Yang greatly. He bore a special sentiment of Chinese culture throughout his whole life. Yang served as the president of Huazhong Technological University (predecessor of HUST) from 1993 to 1997. He established the concept of "science and humanities, connected yet different" for Huazhong Technological University, and actively advocated classical humanistic education in universities. For example, when he was in charge of HUST, Yang Shuzi proposed to renew the teaching of ancient poetry to cultivate the humanistic spirit of the university. In his speech titled *Kexue Renwen Xiangrong Aiguo Chuangxin Yugong-Zailun Rang Zhonghua Shici Dabu Zoujin Daxue Xiaoyuan (Fusing Science and Humanities, Patriotism and Innovation: A Reproposal to Let Chinese Poetry Take Its Stride into University Campuses*), Yang explained:

> Without advanced science and modern technology, a country or a nation would go backward and decline. It would be defeated and live under other countries' influences forever. It would be miserably dominated by other countries. However, without an excellent national tradition, a national human spirit, the country,

> and the nation would be empty and foreignized. It would defeat and destroy itself. This is as if it willingly lives under other countries' influences and willingly submits to them. The most dangerous word here is "willingly." The reason why humanity's education and poetry education are important lies in it.[53]

Yang's humanistic enthusiasm set off a "humanistic storm" at HUST. Until this day, HUST has retained some rules set by the old president – all students (including science and engineering students), would take an annual Chinese language test. Students who failed the test would not get a graduation certificate. Undergraduate students had to take two academic credits of humanities subjects, otherwise, they could not graduate. The humanities education of the university was revived in the 1990s, and HUST had become an important experimental base for national quality education. This was all thanks to the active advocate work of Yang Shuzi. In short, the era of Yang Shuzi at HUST showed us the ideal characters of "building on humanities" in Chinese universities.

c) Zhu Qingshi: The university for stargazers.

In 2009, Southern University of Science and Technology initiated an election for the president, once again making Zhu Qingshi the focus of everyone's attention. At the turn of the 21st century, Zhu Qingshi did a magnificent job when he was in charge of the University of Science and Technology of China, and his election as president of the Southern University of Science and Technology seemed very logical to everyone, too. Zhu Qingshi, had a chemistry major, and he engaged in scientific research at the early stages of his life. He was transferred to the University of Science and Technology of China in 1994 and began to form a close bond with university education. From 1998 to 2008, he was the President of the University of Science and Technology of China. From a chemist to a real educator and reformer, Zhu Qingshi's Chinese university story is worthy of meticulous research. From a cultural perspective, Zhu Qingshi was also an active builder of the ideal cultural character of contemporary Chinese universities.

Studying Zhu Qingshi's university experience, his belief and perseverance in the university's ivory tower spirit are all worth noting. They are very rare indeed. As for how to understand and deal with the relationship between the university and the market, Zhu Qingshi stated:

> Universities must be placed above the market. The university cannot rush and have quick success, otherwise, it will lose its spirit. The most important function of a university is to lead social culture. It should be a highland of thought, and the advancement of society depends on the leadership of the university. Just as Premier Wen Jiabao has said, universities are for "stargazers." Only stargazers would be able to lead the culture.

He also stated that:

> Universities must support industrial development and economic development, but they do not have to do it themselves or dive into the market itself. After all, running an enterprise is about quick success and maximizing profits, while the university's culture and spirit should be still, clear-headed, and dedicated to succeeding in academics. These two activities completely contradict each other. Academics cannot be disturbed by money and power. Money and power cannot be introduced into academics, otherwise, academics will be compromised.[54]

In the wave of Enrollment Expansion, the University of Science and Technology of China was the only university that did not expand its enrollment. Zhu Qingshi's explanation for this was: "The campus of the Chinese University of Science and Technology is, though not luxurious, quiet. We did not expand the enrollment, did not build a new campus, therefore we saved the teachers from suffering a big loss."[55] When asked if it was worthwhile just for having a "quiet environment," Zhu Qingshi once again emphasized: "A quiet environment is very important." Zhu Qingshi's stubbornness and dedication have given teachers of the Chinese University of Science and Technology as much time as possible to sit down, to read, and think. The quiet University of Science and Technology of China was once a unique figure in the era of the "vulgarization of universities." From here, it can be seen that "looking beyond in tranquillity" had already started to return to Chinese universities.

The presidents of contemporary universities who strived for the bright future of Chinese universities have done far more than what has been mentioned above. They have become an important driving force in realizing the ideal cultural characters of Chinese universities. For example, in the 1980s, Liu Daoyu, President of Wuhan University, Zhu Jiusi, Dean of Huazhong Institute of Technology, and Deng Xuchu, President of Shanghai Jiaotong University, were all believers and practitioners of university ideals such as being "people-oriented," "building on humanities," and "looking beyond in tranquillity." The above examples are sufficient to prove that, with the return of the university president's dominant position in the university, the ideal cultural characters of Chinese universities have gradually changed from an ideal to reality. The Chinese cultural sentiments embedded in the contemporary Presidents of Chinese University were the key elements of this realistic transformation. Of course, to a large extent, their assumptions and practices of the ideal cultural characters of Chinese universities were still immature or excessive. As a result, many measures and systems were not sustainable. However, what was important was not the achievements of these university presidents' courageous attempts. Following these historical experiences, the cultural self-consciousness that has been getting clearer and firmer, as well as the increasingly clear cultural trends contained therein, were the more important result of these attempts. In short, the paths walked by the predecessors, be it success or failure, were necessary, as they would become valuable experiences for future generations to go even further. A new generation of presidents of Chinese universities was rising, standing on the shoulders of giants with firm conviction. They inherited the course, and the ideal Chinese university cultural characters were already foreseeable.

Section 3: Analysis of the Cultural Characters of Chinese Universities since the Reform and Opening Up – Using HUST as an example

HUST was born in the heated wave of university mergers at the turn of the century. It was formed by the merger of the former Huazhong Technological University (formerly Huazhong Institute of Technology), Tongji Medical University, and Wuhan City Construction College on May 26, 2000. As a young university established after the founding of New China, HUST quickly rose to the top after the Reform and Opening Up. It was called "the epitome of the development of higher education in New China." Though named "University of Science and Technology," HUST has led the movement of universities' humanities education. It was famous for being a modern university, yet it had maintained a strong Chinese classical cultural temperament. Cultivating both humanities and technology, modernity and history were the important features of HUST. These features were highly consistent with this book's investigation of the future development trends of Chinese universities' cultural characters. This was also the main reason why the present study selected HUST for the analysis of Chinese universities' cultural characters since the Reform and Opening Up. Of course, using HUST as an example to analyze the cultural characters of Chinese universities is not an attempt to prove that the ideal cultural character has already been formed in Chinese universities. First, HUST is only one case, and it does not represent the current status of most Chinese universities. Second, even though HUST attained outstanding achievements, there is still a clear distance from it and the ideal Chinese university's cultural character. Therefore, the main purpose of this research on the HUST's cultural character is to map the ideal trend of expressing the cultural characters of Chinese universities which has already emerged. The following is a detailed analysis of HUST's cultural character from three aspects: university concepts, the university system, and university cultural symbols. The pieces of evidence used were mainly extracted from the speeches made by university presidents, media interviews, newspaper reports, and the commemorative series published by HUST.

1. HUST's university-running concept

The Constitution of HUST was finalized and promulgated in October 2014. The constitution defined its university-running concept and insisted on the values below: "cultivation of people as the foundation," "innovation as the soul," "act responsibly," implement student-oriented education, and adhere to the integration of science education and humanities education, among other attributes. During the rise of HUST, two presidents were hailed as the soul of HUST, one was Yang Shuzi, who served in 1993–1997, and the other was Li Peigen, who served in 2005–2014. These two figures were important shapers of HUST. HUST formed its unique school-running characteristics in a relatively short period, and it became a famous university in China, thanks to the advanced school-running concepts of these two presidents.

a) Student-orientedness.

In recent years, a fundamental point was repeatedly emphasized by HUST, which was its student-orientedness. Under the university's self-positioning as a place to cultivate talents instead of producing machines, people-orientedness became a deep-rooted idea, and thereby also became the soul of HUST. Yang Shuzi mentioned in one of his speeches, *Shi 'Yuren' Fei 'Zhiqi' (Cultivation of Talents, Not Producing Machines)*, in 2000:

> The main theme of universities should be "cultivating talents," not "producing machines." We need to cultivate advanced talents, not advanced machinery. Everybody has thoughts, emotions, personalities, and spiritual worlds, not to mention advanced talent. Machines are objects, they are lifeless. No matter how advanced they are, even the most advanced intelligent robots, they are merely programs with complex and exquisite functions endowed by human beings. Whatever they do, they could never cross the potential limits set up by humans. The "people" aspect is lost in our education. If we forget that everybody has thoughts, emotions, personalities, and spiritual worlds, we lose everything.
>
> In fact, all of our endeavors see the "people" as the starting point, the ultimate goal, and a factor that weaves through all aspects throughout. Not to mention "education," which is an endeavor that directly cultivates people. The main theme of universities in our country is to cultivate Chinese university graduates.[56]

In 2011, HUST's third-party congress proposed the implementation of "three major strategic changes" – transforming from improving scale development to improving quality. It proposed a move from industrial and medical advantages to comprehensive advantages, and from teacher-oriented education to student-oriented education. The student-oriented educational concept was officially listed as one of the basic items of these strategic changes. In 2020, an interview report titled Huazhong Keda Xiaozhang Li Peigen: *Gaodeng Jiaoyu Dui Xuesheng De Xinling Kaifang* (Li Peigen from HUST: *The Role of Higher Education in Opening Up Students' Minds*) was published in *People's Daily*. President Li Peigen pointed out that:

> The core of student-oriented education was to stimulate students' innovative potential and to let students develop freely. We shall only claim that we have started to pay attention to the opening up of students' minds under this concept.
>
> This should be the original purpose of modern universities. Of course, completing this transformation will mean a long-term process that requires a long period of effort. It is now proposed and raised to the level of school-running strategy, which would play a guiding role in talent cultivation.

As can be seen from these two presidents' speeches and reports, "students" were their most important focus and the basic reference point of their school-running concepts. *The Constitution of HUST University* promulgated in 2014 was based on the "student-oriented education." The constitution mentioned "cultivation of people as the foundation" several times, and formally adopted the "implementation of student-oriented education" as one of its general rules. Seven student rights were listed at the same time. The above analysis shows that from the fundamental standpoint of "students," HUST's primary school-running philosophy lay in being "student-oriented," that is, it regarded the cultivation of people as the foundation, and adhered to the crucial position of the students."

b) Regarding humanities education as the foundation.

At the Ministry of Education Major Social Science Funded Project Releasing Conference, Yang Shuzi talked about four things that "cannot keep up." The first was that, in the rapid development of market economy construction, the development of cultural construction cannot keep up. The second was that, in the rapid development of science and technology, the development of humanities and culture cannot keep up. The third was that in the rapid development of modernization, the inheritance of excellent traditions cannot keep up. The fourth was that in fast learning from the West, the promotion of national spirit cannot keep up. Under the guidance of Yang Shuzi, HUST had gradually grown from an export base of scientific and technological talent to a hub of cultural quality education among Chinese universities. Yang Shuzi contributed tremendously to the development of HUST's unique humanities complex. One of Yang Shuzi's basic educational views was that the integration of humanities and science was an inevitable trend in the development of the times, while humanities always served as its basics. As such, in the speech *Shi 'Yuren' Fei 'Zhiqi'* (*Cultivation of Talents, Not Producing Machines*), Yang Shuzi proposed that:

> In the current situation, science and technology are advancing by leaps and bounds, and achievements are multiplied. Scientific achievements have a huge role and far-reaching impact. In particular, the rapid development of information technology is changing the world with great depth and breadth. The rapid development of life science and technology may also change humanity itself

> with shocking discoveries. Is it our blessing? Or our misfortune? This does not depend on the technology itself, but on the people who research, develop, apply, and advance science and technology. It depends on how people's spiritual and physical worlds are combined, and it depends on their thoughts, feelings, and spiritual worlds.

At the end of the speech, Yang Shuzi reiterated the theme:

> We cannot help stressing the fundamental role of humanistic education again. *The Mean* said this well, "Things would succeed with adequate preparation, and fail without such." The water floats the boat and sinks the boat. Beware! Beware![57]

Since the 1990s, Yang has put down the roots of humanistic education at HUST. After Yang Shuzi, all succeeding presidents followed the tradition and saw humanities education as an important part of the university's reform and development. Today, the rich humanistic atmosphere has become an important symbol of HUST, and the university has been highly commended in the society. In *The Constitution of HUST*, "The integration of science education and humanities education is included in the general principles as the school's basic educational development concept." This indicates that the concept of running a school with the integration of humanities and science and technology education at HUST had become institutionalized. The above analysis shows that, from the perspective of culture, the concept of HUST lies in humanities. It is committed to the comprehensive development of students based on humanistic education.

c) *Rooted in academics.*

In 2006, at the Chinese and Foreign University Presidents' Forum, among the seven schools including Renmin University of China, Beijing Normal University, Beijing Diplomatic College, China Agricultural University, China University of Finance and Economics, Beijing Language and Culture University, HUST expressed its intention to abolish the hard indicator that postgraduate students must publish papers in order to graduate. In fact, before this forum, HUST had already canceled the stipulation of the hard indicator of papers' publication. In response to a reporter's interview, President Li Peigen pointed out:

> Last year, HUST published the largest number of papers in the country. Lifting the hard indicator that "postgraduates must publish a paper" may cause us to lose this title, but it does not matter. The important thing is to be realistic and pragmatic. We are not banning students from writing papers, it was just that we

> changed it from hard indicators into encouraging measures. We are trying to guide them to think more, innovate more, and write more high-quality papers.
>
> In recent years, there seems to always be an impetuous atmosphere in higher education and academia in our society. For example, universities often care about the total amount of education funding, the number of papers published, ranking, and the number of patents. The scholars spent most of their energy not conducting in-depth research but applying for more projects and research funds. Scholars in the scientific and technological fields should have a social conscience and bear social responsibilities. They should regard concentrating on research as their sacred duty.[58]

The above-mentioned materials show that in an increasingly complex social environment, HUST adhered to the idea of running a school with moral principles, and insisted on the modern university's spirit of the ivory tower in its unique way. As we all know, HUST took social service as its responsibility. It is at the forefront among domestic universities in terms of school-enterprise cooperation and international integration. Its students are also extremely active in social activities. However, between merit and academics, HUST would rather lose its highest rank in terms of the number of papers published in the country, instead of focusing on fame. It strives to reserve a free academic space for its students. With policy support, students get to focus on academics without being troubled by the pursuit of fame. The spirit of disregarding fame and focusing on academics was demonstrated by the University of Science and Technology and its students. Based on the above analysis, from the academic point of view, the concept of HUST is scholarship, that is, the return to the academic essence with intensive research as the responsibility.

In summary, the above-mentioned school-running concepts of HUST can be summarized as "student-oriented," "humanities" and "scholarship." As in, student-oriented, humanistic education as its foundation, and its overall academic focus. The interrelationship of the three aspects form HUST's core idea. "Student-orientedness" is the university's leading principle, the inner basis of the concepts of "humanities" and "scholarship." Humanistic education aims to shape students' comprehensive personality, while academic research intends to satisfy students' freedom of academics. Both of them serve the basic positioning of HUST.

Admittedly, "student-orientedness" is not a unique feature of HUST, but more like a collective feature of Chinese universities. No university would say its education is not student-oriented. However, when interpreting the student-oriented cultural connotation of HUST, we can sense that the classic charm of traditional culture is part of its unique charm. Judging from the sources above, the concept of HUST is largely based on the "error-correction" psychology. Both presidents have expressed their worries about the serious bias towards scientific research and the widespread pursuit of fame and profit in university education. Choosing to go back to the tradition and even deliberately strengthen the influence of classical culture to "correct errors" have become the main trends of humanities education and academic research at HUST. Based on the above analysis, the concept of HUST is rooted in traditional Chinese culture. The so-called "student-oriented" idea, "humanities" and "scholarship" are the specific expressions of its cultural character. As Li Peigen had said, it will take some time for Chinese universities to complete its transition to the purpose of opening up student's minds. The cultural character of HUST is still in formation. However, it is undeniable that with the specific university system and cultural symbols as intermediaries, the ideal school-running idea of HUST is transitioning to reality.

2. *System Design of HUST*

With the gradual maturity of its school-running concepts, a series of constitutional systems were formulated on this basis and have been gradually implemented at HUST. On the whole, the establishment of these systems is slowly perfecting through the process of school development, and the results continue to show. Driven by the president of the university and the main leaders of the school, the design of these systems is demonstrated through two main characteristics. One is that the rules are mainly formulated by the school itself, and then supplemented by extensively listening to the opinions from both the inside and outside of the school. While the second is that the rules mainly revolve around the students, intending to maximize the students' interests. The following section will list the relevant policies for specific analysis from the two levels, namely the curriculum and teaching systems.

a) Curriculum design.

As an experimental base for quality cultural education, HUST has integrated humanities education with the student cultivation program, forming three levels and six aspects: the first classroom (primary classroom), the second classroom (extracurricular scientific and cultural activities), and the large classroom of the society (social activities). The specific rules of the cultural quality education curriculum system are as follows:

- Implementing a plan that students are thereafter cultivated without the differentiation of majors and disciplines in the first three semesters, to reinforce basic education and cultural quality education.
- Implementing humanities and social sciences minor system with more than 130 cultural quality education modules.
- Implementing humanities and social sciences as elective courses with clear rules that humanities and science students have to take 6 credits of natural science

modules, while STEM and medicine students have to take 12 credits of humanities and social science modules.

- Implementing the annual "Chinese Language Proficiency Test," requiring all undergraduates and postgraduates to pass this test each year.[59]

From the above, the main theme of the curriculum system reform was to strengthen humanistic education. This was especially shown in the requirement for STEM and medicine students having to take 12 credits of humanities and social science modules. This was focusing on strengthening non-arts students' humanity cultivations. In addition, the Chinese language was listed as a key subject that all students had to take as part of their course examinations, reflecting the university's emphasis on the Chinese culture of the humanities subjects. From this perspective, the main feature of the cultural quality education curriculum was that it focused on humanities subjects, with particular emphasis on Chinese humanities. Based on the above analysis, the design of the quality education curriculum system was intended to enhance the humanistic quality of students and cultivate comprehensively-developed talents. It also intended to inherit and promote Chinese culture and revive Chinese traditional culture. The purposes of the two aspects fully embodied the school-running concept of "student-orientedness" and "humanities."

b) Teaching system.

The teaching system of HUST was and is very unique. Teachers and students, as the main body in the teaching process, are the main objects of teaching system design. Revolving around teachers and students (including undergraduates and graduates), HUST has developed and implemented a series of unique systems, briefly listed as follows:

Firstly, the "teaching professors" system. In 2001, HUST established the "teaching professors" system, institutionalizing the rule that the academics and professors have to teach undergraduates. The university clearly stated that:

> Each year, competitions for the appointment of senior teaching professors and senior lecturers will be held within the school. Those who successfully compete for the positions would be granted a monthly teaching position allowance of about 1,000 *yuan*. Those who compete for the position of "senior teaching professor" must be current professors with a certain academic status in a certain discipline or research field. Those who compete for the position of "senior lecturer" must be current professors or associate professors with a clear research direction in a specialized field, as well as certain research results.[60]

Represented by academics such as Yang Shuzi, Xiong Youlun, Zhang Yongchuan, and the then-President Fan Mingwu, the professors walked onto the teaching podiums and started teaching undergraduates. According to the university, teaching professors can lead undergraduates to the forefront of the discipline and allow them to see the full picture and the future of the discipline. This may not be unique to HUST, but it was indeed worthy of recognition in transforming well-known "scholars" into students' "teachers." As far as the above-mentioned "teaching professors" system was concerned, it is considered from a student-oriented standpoint.

Second, the undergraduate major transfer system. HUST has implemented a credit system reform in 2003. Under this policy, a system of transferring majors with no examination or payment of tuition fees for transferring majors was implemented in 2005. This policy states that:

> Students are granted two chances of transferring to another major after their enrollment. The time for the first transfer to the major is the first semester after entering the university. All freshmen who request for a major transfer due to physical reasons or special interests (except for those who major in information disciplines) can apply for a major transfer (without examination). Upon approval by the department and the educational administration department, they can be transferred to another school (department) in the second semester. The time for the second major transfer is the fourth semester. Students can choose their major within the school they belong to.[61]

The establishment of the HUST undergraduate major transfer system made the students the biggest beneficiaries. The policy stipulated that there were two opportunities for transferring majors with no need to pay tuition fees or take examinations. The choice of majors became more free and reasonable, giving students sufficient time to consider and providing them with some room to choose. This would have added some work to the school when students apply for major transfers, but the school still enjoyed it. Clearly, during the university's policymaking, students' interests were adequately considered.

Third, the graduate student reading seminar system. The Graduate Student Reading Seminar, with the full name of Graduate Student Reading, Results Reporting Seminar, has been held since 2002, and it had become the main form of cultivating master's degree students at HUST. There was a comment regarding this:

> Students are required not to participate in any research projects, not to publish papers, not to take part-time jobs outside the school, but to concentrate on study and read wholeheartedly, creating a quiet, pure, positive, and fulfilling reading atmosphere. We summarized it as "deep mountains and thick forests are the best places for practicing skills," "there is no way to know one's true aspiration if he is not calm, no way to look far beyond if he is not in tranquillity."[62]

The formation of the Graduate Student Reading Seminar system was closely related to the university's lifting of the hard indicator that required graduate students to publish papers before graduation. As President Li Peigen said, canceling the requirement for graduates to publish papers was not to push students away from academics. The establishment of the reading seminar system shifted the students' attention away from the impulsiveness of writing essays in search of fame and profits, to now calming down and reading classics. In 2002, when facing the issue that there were students with complex academic backgrounds and relatively weak foundation, the Graduate Center proposed the cultivation principle of "two no's and one yes" for the enrolled master students, that is, those with no participation in research projects, no published papers, and those who concentrate on reading classics during their studies." This stipulation continued to this day and had achieved remarkable results, forming a unique academic atmosphere of HUST. In an increasingly impetuous social environment, the Chinese University of Science and Technology of China has created a quiet world of reading for university students, once again demonstrating the concept of student-oriented education.

At present, the above-mentioned system of HUST has achieved obvious results, and HUST's school-running philosophy of being "student-oriented," "humanities" and "scholarship" have gradually been realized. It is worth mentioning that HUST's consistent attitude has prevented many system initiatives from being abandoned due to the iteration of school leadership, especially the change of presidents. For example, the aforementioned annual Chinese Language Proficiency Test required formulated by President Yang Shuzi. This rule remained unchanged and was implemented throughout, though it has experienced many iterations under different presidents. On the contrary, with the support of each president and school leader, this system has lasted to this day and is gradually improving. This is an aspect that cannot be ignored in shaping the cultural character of HUST.

3. *Cultural symbols of HUST*

HUST's school running concept not only permeates the school system, but its university cultural symbols are also important expressions of its cultural character. The following section will attempt to search for classical cultural qualities within its campus views and campus activities of HUST, which were the most vivid examples of its cultural character.

a) Campus views.

The campus building of HUST does not have the quaintness of Peking University's Yenching campus, nor the European and American style of Tsinghua University. There was an ordinary wall with an eye-catching sign, *Mingde Houxue, Qiushi Chuangxin* (Demonstration of Virtues, Thick learning, the Search for Truth, Innovation). Within the campus, the *Zhaoxian Lou* (Building of Attracting Talents) and the Professor Building were particularly impressive. Also, the simple administrative building would register and impress all visitors. Last but not least, there was a humble yet lively principle's mailbox. These were the most unique "buildings" of HUST that embodied the rich background of the university.

1. School motto wall.

This school motto was confirmed in 2003. Judging from its language, all words within this motto came from ancient classics. The phrase *Mingde* (demonstrating virtues) came from chapter *Jun Che* of the book *Shang Shu*: "Delicious food is not the most fragrant thing in the world, but the demonstration of virtue." It was also found in chapter *Liji* of the book *Daxue*: "The way of great learning is to clearly demonstrate good virtues. *Houxue* was adapted from chapter *Tuan Zhuan* from the book *Zhou Yi:* "The octogram of Kun is thick and carries everything on it. Its virtue is boundless. It is inclusive to all, allowing everything to go smoothly." *Qiushi* came from chapter *Hejian Xianwang Zhuan* of the book *Han Shu*: "Looking up to the ancient scholars in studying and search for the truths as they are." "Innovation" was adapted from Chapter *Liji* of the book *Daxue*: "If one can discover something new for one day, he can discover something new every day, and something new from the new things discovered." From the perspective of language expression, the motto was intended to carry forward the traditional Chinese spirit. *Mingde* referred to the demonstration of ethics and the perfection of virtues, *Houxue* referred to regarding knowledge highly and studying ceaselessly, *Qiushi* meant the search for truth and the serious attitude when it comes to academics, and *Chuangxin* meant making progress and following the pace of the times.

HUST advocates that humanities should have a special emphasis on Chinese culture. The eight-character school motto of *Mingde Houxue, Qiushi Chuangxin* has become its most significant cultural symbol. It is a tradition for Chinese higher institutions to formulate mottos from ancient Chinese classics. Since the Reform and Opening Up, the Chinese studies fever has led this trend, and the tendency of university mottos quoting from classics has once again been revived. HUST's school motto was established during the Chinese studies fever of the new century, and it was rooted in HUST's strong humanistic feelings. It seemed destined for this motto to be finally presented in its current form. In its specific aspects, the school motto particularly emphasizes the moral and academic spirit of the Chinese cultural tradition. HUST has established the school-running philosophy of being "student-oriented," "humanities" and "scholarship" under the guidance of the traditional thoughts of highlighting virtues and emphasizing academics.

2. Names of the buildings.

Extensively recruiting talents, respecting teachers, and emphasizing teaching is the basis of HUST's prosperity. Revolving around the students, HUST placed the strongest emphasis on teaching. Teachers, as the main body of teaching, directly affect what students learn. By regarding students as the foundation and putting teachers first, HUST has maintained the cultural tradition of respecting teachers and valuing education from ancient times. The so-called Zhaoxian Lou, Jiaoshou Lou (Professor Building), and Yuanshi Lou (Academician Building) stand on the campus of the university, not to show off their strong faculty, but to show respect to all teachers who worked hard at HUST. This is a special treatment not even enjoyed by its presidents. The school leaders have been highly recommended for their efforts in recruiting famous teachers. For example, in 1998, Zhu Yuquan, Zhou Ji, Liu Xianjun, and other school leaders went to Hefei four times to invite Academic Pan Yuan to be the Dean of the School of Electrical Engineering. Stories like this are enough to interpret the true meaning of the names of the "buildings" such as Zhaoxian Lou. In a nutshell, the "buildings" of HUST, as a symbol of "master scholars," carry the ideal pursuit of "student-orientedness" and highlight the traditional way of respecting teachers in the Chinese culture.

3. The humble administrative building.

In the interview record of HUST, there are plenty of interviewer's special reports on its administrative building. Ma Guochuan's recorded in his interview notes: "The office building of HUST is very ordinary, absolutely not as impressive as the office building of some other universities. No ordinary decorations could be found in the corridors. The thin and lean Academic Yang Shuzi was already waiting for me in the office.[63] *Kexue Shibao* (*Science Times*) reporter wrote in the interview record with President Li Peigen's: "The administrative building of HUST is a very inconspicuous old building. President Li Peigen's office is not spacious, very humble, and the area is very small. To avoid telephone interference, President Li changed the interview location to a small conference room."[64] The administrative building, as the office space for the president and other school leaders, is a symbol of administrative power and it occupies a central position in university buildings. The administrative buildings of many universities are known for their magnificent style, but HUST is much inferior in this respect. If one looks through many reports regarding the university, most of them report the construction and improvement of the student dormitory buildings, or that the problem of school teachers' housing has been solved. Going back to the humbleness of the administrative building, one cannot help but be in awe. In short, the humble administrative building was not only a sign of the diligence and frugality of HUST but also the demonstration of the school leaders' focus on the interests of students and teachers. This is an interpretation of HUST's people-oriented cultural idea.

4. The president's mailbox.

The president's mailbox is not a unique innovation of HUST. However, this mailbox is full of stories between the presidents and the students. Here are two famous letters from the president's mailbox. One letter was written by an undergraduate student to President Yang Shuzi in the 1990s. As stated in the letter: "Now we cannot get a degree without passing the CET-4 exam. However, if one cannot write a proper composition, make mistakes writing the characters, and cannot even pass his mother language, does that count as a qualified Chinese university student?" As such, Yang Shuzi, who has always attached great importance to humanistic education, led HUST to take a step that is quite influential in China's higher education community. At the time, students from 1995, college students, undergraduates, and graduate students participated in the Chinese language proficiency test organized by the school for the first time. The other was a letter from a sophomore in 2006 to President Li Peigen, which mentioned two hidden safety problems in the school. Soon the student saw his letter to the president, instructions from the president, and the measures taken by the security department published in the school newspaper, and the so-called security risks were resolved. As an important way of dialogue between the students and the presidents, the president's mailbox is full of love from the president and the university for the students and it has become another typical cultural symbol of HUST.

In summary, the above-mentioned "buildings" of HUST are unique to the campus, and they are ideal tangible markers of HUST's cultural character. Under the concept of "student-orientedness," "humanities" and "scholarship" of HUST, they bear a unique Chinese cultural heritage.

b) Campus events.

HUST is a place with plenty of campus activities. What truly made HUST were the humanities seminars that have continued from the middle of the last century to the present day – they have almost become a unique sign of the school. The rich and colorful social practice activities outside the school also bring about a high social reputation to the university. The following will focus on the humanities seminars and social practice activities outside the campus of HUST to understand their cultural connotations.

1. Humanities seminars.

In 2005, *Zhongguo Jiaoyu Bao* (*China Education Daily*) put out a special report on the campus culture of HUST, that is, its humanities seminars:

> Since 1994, Huazhong Technological University, the predecessor of HUST, has focused on further strengthening students' patriotic consciousness and shaping their patriotic characters via quality cultural education activities such as humanities lectures. At present, there have already been more than 1,000 sessions of this seminar series, master scholars such as Yang Zhenning, Du Weiming, Yang Shuzi, Zhang Kaiyuan took the stage to teach, attracting 500,000 college

> students. The seminar series has become the university's most distinctively-featured second classroom with its long duration, rich content, wide audience, and great influence.[65]

The media spoke highly of the humanities seminars of HUST with sixteen Chinese characters, which translates as follows: "long duration, rich content, wide audience, and great influence." HUST deserved this high commendation. This also reflected the society's affirmation and support of the humanities education concept at HUST. As mentioned above, the lectures on humanities began in 1994. At that time, President Yang Shuzi took the lead in carrying out cultural quality education in the university in response to the problems of weak humanities education across universities in China. The humanities education seminar series was one of its main contents.

The school collated and published the speeches from the seminars, and published them in a book series titled *Zhongguo Daxue Renwen Qisi Lu* (*Humanities Enlightenment Records of Chinese Universities*). This series consisted of six volumes, and is known as "the masterpiece for reshaping the humanities spirit of Chinese universities." From a cultural point of view, humanities seminars, as an important form of humanities education at HUST, exemplified the ideals of HUST. Specifically: In terms of its purpose, the humanities seminar series was intended to subtly improve students' cultivation by creating a good campus cultural atmosphere. In terms of its content, the humanities seminar and a large amount of Chinese classical cultural knowledge are important ways to promote and spread traditional Chinese culture. In terms of its value, humanities lectures in the increasingly utilitarian society impart humanistic knowledge to students, which is beneficial to purify students' minds and guide students to read and learn with tranquillity. In short, the purpose of the humanities seminars is to be "student-oriented." Taking the "humanities" as its content also highlights the unique "scholarship" spirit, which is the external expression of HUST's cultural character.

2. Off-campus social practice activities.

The students' rich and colorful off-campus social practice activities are HUST's major "attraction." Social practice activities are mainly based on students, and their purpose is to improve the students' personal qualities through social service experience. Gathering information about off-campus social activities of HUST, the most impactful ones were mainly social service activities such as the "Long March of Public Morality,","The Search for Red History" and "Helping Western China with Clothes" that were sequentially launched since 2005. Here, we will use "Long March of Public Morality" as an example. According to the description, the "Long March of Public Morality" activities mainly included three steps: the first was the "Declaration of Polite Behaviors" based on transportation etiquettes, classroom etiquettes, and canteen etiquettes, and the second was self-discipline education with citizen morality as the core, while the third was responsibility education which focused on the cultivation of social responsibility. The school stated that this activity was applied in the form of academic credits, requiring students to participate in various practical activities that focused on cultivating public awareness. The university did not hold these activities on a whim. In an interview with a reporter, Ouyang Kang, the deputy secretary of the school, pointed out the reason behind them was that there was a pandemic of declining moral quality among contemporary university students. The core of humanistic education was moral education. The moral education work of HUST was not limited to textbooks. The "Long March of Public Morality" was its attempt at a new form of practical moral education. Overviewing the many social practice activities of HUST, it can be observed that they were based on the basic positioning of comprehensive education. It showed that HUST indeed put in much effort for the sake of realizing its educational philosophy of "student-orientedness." HUST's practice has proven that students will become the ultimate beneficiaries of such activities, and the school's education philosophy will keep on developed along with the growth of students.

How did HUST earn its reputation? It was not the social effect of media propaganda, nor the bragging of HUST itself. From the university-running concept to the design of the system to the symbol of campus culture, when the cultural character of HUST was interpreted from the inside out, a unique Chinese cultural feeling could always be found within it. HUST's rapid rise since the Reform and Opening Up can be largely credited to this feeling. The upsurge of Sinology in the new century was on the rise. A new generation of intellectuals was rising. HUST was not just a special case of Chinese universities. There are now more and more universities in China exploring the formation of ideal cultural characters in their practice.

Summary

Since the Reform and Opening Up, there have been several characteristics in the formation of the cultural character of Chinese universities.

1) Chinese culture: The evolution of Chinese culture has basically shown a gradual upward trend during the 30 years of Reform and Opening Up. From the cultural upsurge during the period of ideological emancipation to the upsurge of Sinology in the economic era, to then the full arrival of today's globalization era, Chinese culture has moved from modestly learning from the West to a state of profound cultural self-consciousness, all while working towards its comprehensive revival.
2) New intellectuals: After the Cultural Revolution, the rise of new intellectuals showed a great "compassion of understanding" for Chinese culture. During this

period, although the "total Westernization" ideal has re-emerged, it had no appeal. The "World Cultural Integration Theory" emerged and became the direction of the future development of Chinese culture. At present, the "Chinese and Western Cultural Integration Theory" has become the mainstream of modern Chinese society.

3) Chinese universities: With the rise of new intellectuals, the cultural character of Chinese universities has demonstrated a relatively good development trend. Being "people-oriented," "building on humanities," and "looking beyond in tranquillity" have gradually become the distinctive characteristics of Chinese universities' cultural characters.

In general, although the development of the cultural character of Chinese universities since the Reform and Opening Up has faced many challenges, it has still been developing and has gradually shown an ideal possible trend. On the one hand, it has been affected by several cultural waves since the 1980s. On the other, a new generation of intellectuals is now rising and becoming part of the important constructors of the cultural character of Chinese universities. But, it is also worth noting that most of this ideal development trend is still at the conceptual level and has not yet been fully established.

Notes

1. Huntington, S. Clash of Civilizations and the Reconstruction of the World Order. Trans. Zhou, Q., et al. Beijing: Xinhua Publishing House, 1998: 67.
2. Liu, D., & Zhou, Y. Xixue Dongjian Yu Dongxue Xijian (Eastward Spreading of Western Learnings and Westward Spreading of Eastern Learnings). Beijing: China Social Sciences Press, 2000: 169–170.
3. Ibid, p. 170.
4. Gan, Y. Bashi Niandai Wenhua Yishi (Cultural Consciousness of 1980). Shanghai: Shanghai People's Press, 2006: 542.
5. Ibid, p. 32.
6. Ibid, p. 546.
7. People's Education Press. Jiaoyu Gaige Zhongyao Wenxian Xuanbian (Selection of Important Documents regarding Education Reforms). Beijing: People's Education Press, 1988: 24.
8. Hayhoe, R. China's Universities 1895–1995: A Century of Cultural Conflict. Trans. Xu, J. Beijing: Educational Science Publishing House, 2000: 154.
9. Ibid, p. 157.
10. Hou, D. Zhongguo Daxue De Lixing Zhilu (The Path of Reason for Chinese Universities). Shanghai: East China Normal University Press, 2009: 101.
11. Gan, Y. Bashi Niandai Wenhua Yishi (Cultural Consciousness of 1980). Shanghai: Shanghai People's Press, 2006: Reprint Preface 4.
12. Yin, H. Zhongguo Wenhua De Zhanwang (Outlook of Chinese Culture). Beijing: China Heping Publishing House, 1988: 67.

13. Chen, P. Dangdai Zhongguo Renwen Guancha (Observation of Humanities in Contemporary China). Beijing: Peking University Press, 2010: 2.
14. Liu, D., & Zhou, Y. Xixue Dongjian Yu Dongxue Xijian (Eastward Spreading of Western Learnings and Westward Spreading of Eastern Learnings). Beijing: China Social Sciences Press, 2000: 196.
15. Ji, X. 21 Shiji: Dongfang Wenhua De Shidai (The 21st Century: An Era of Eastern Culture). Wenhui Daily, 1992: March 10th.
16. Fei, X. Fansi, Duihua, Wenhua Zijue (Reflection, Dialogue, Cultural Self-consciousness). Journey of Peking University, 1997 (3): 22.
17. Chen, P. Daxue Hewei (What University Does). Beijing: Peking University Press, 2006: 203.
18. Chen, P. Daxue You Jingshen (The Spirit of University). Beijing: Peking University Press, 2009: 163.
19. Hou, D. Zhongguo Daxue De Lixing Zhilu (The Path of Reason for Chinese Universities). Shanghai: East China Normal University Press, 2009: 110.
20. Chen, P. Daxue You Jingshen (The Spirit of University). Beijing: Peking University Press, 2009: 169.
21. Readings, B. The University in Ruins. Trans. Guo, J., et al. Beijing: Peking University Press, 2008: 3.
22. Coase, R., & Wang, N. Biange Zhongguo: Shichang Jingji De Zhongguo (How China Became Capitalist). Trans. Xu, Y., et al. Beijing: CITIC Press, 2013: 254.
23. Chen, P. Daxue You Jingshen (The Spirit of University). Beijing: Peking University Press, 2009: 193.
24. Shao, H. Zhongguo Wenhua Yanjiu Ershi Nian (20 Years of Chinese Cultural Research). Beijing: People's Publishing House, 2003: 603.
25. Liu, X. Yu Li Zehou Duihua – Ganxing, Geren, Wode Xuanze (A Dialogue with Li Zehou – Sensibility, Individual Person, My Choice). China, 1986 (10): 13.
26. Zhang, D., & Cheng, Y. Zhongguo Wenhua Lunzheng (Discussion and Debate of Chinese Culture). Beijing: China Renmin University Press, 2006: 321.
27. Ibid, p. 326.
28. Ibid, p. 322.
29. Luo, Z. Wenhua Pinglun Yu Zhongxi Wenhua Yitong (Culture Commentary and the Similarities and Differences Between Chinese and Western Cultures). Open Times, 1999 (2): 107.
30. Dong, X. Zhongxi Wenhua Gongxing Lungang (Outline for Common Grounds Between Chinese and Western Cultures). Journal of Northeast Normal University, 1999 (3): 7.
31. Chen, P. Daxue Hewei (The Tasks of University). Beijing: Peking University Press, 2006: 185–186.
32. Hou, D. Zhongguo Daxue De Lixing Zhilu (The Path of Reason for Chinese Universities). Shanghai: East China Normal University Press, 2009: Foreword 7.
33. Zhang, Y. Gaodeng Jiaoyu Xiandaihua De Fansi Yu Jiangou (The Reflection and Construction of the Modernization of Higher Education). Harbin: Heilongjiang Education Press, 2000: 166.
34. Wang, J. Daxue Zhidao (The Way of University). Beijing: Higher Education Press, 2005: 159.
35. Ibid, p. 162.
36. Sui, Y. Lixing Hanwei Daxue (Defending University with Reason). Beijing: Peking University Press, 2013: 36–37.
37. Chu, Z. Lixiang Daxue (Ideal University). Beijing: Beijing Normal University Press, 2012: 262, 268.
38. Li, W. Biange Zhong De Daxue – Li Wei Jiaoyu Wencun (University in Revolution – An Archive of Education Works of Li Wei). Beijing: Higher Education Press, 2012: 68.
39. Ibid.

40. Hou, D. Zhongguo Daxue De Lixing Zhilu (The Path of Reason for Chinese Universities). Shanghai: East China Normal University Press, 2009: 75.
41. Gan, Y. Daxue Renwen Jiaoyu De Linian, Mubiao Yu Moshi (The Idea, Goal, and Model of University Humanities Education). Peking University Education Review, 2006 (3): 64–65.
42. Chen, P. Dangdai Zhongguo Renwen Guancha (Observation of Humanities in Contemporary China). Beijing: Peking University Press, 2010: 237.
43. Editing Committee of Zhongguo Daxue Renwen Qisilu, Zhongguo Daxue Renwen Qisilu (Disi Juan) (Record of Inspirations and Thoughts regarding Humanities in Chinese University (Volume 4)). Wuhan: Huazhong University of Science and Technology Press, 2000: 253.
44. Sui, Y. Daxue Yongsuhua Pipan (Criticism of the Vulgarization of University). Peking University Education Review, 2003 (3): 32–34.
45. Chen, P. Daxue You Jingshen (The Spirit of University). Beijing: Peking University Press, 2009: 180.
46. Ma, G. Daxue Mingxiaozhang Fangtanlu (Record of Interviews with Famous Presidents of Universities). Beijing: Huaxia Publishing House, 2010: 67.
47. Chen, P. Dangdai Zhongguo Renwen Guancha (Observation of Humanities in Contemporary China). Beijing: Peking University Press, 2010: 228–229.
48. Sui, Y. Lixing Hanwei Daxue (Defending University with Reason). Beijing: Peking University Press, 2013: 37.
49. Sui, Y. Xuefu Zhihun – Zhongwai Zhuming Daxue Xiaozhang Jiaoyu Linian (The Soul of Institutions – The Education Ideals of Famous Presidents of Universities around the World). Nanchang: Jiangxi Education Publishing House, 2001: Preface 2.
50. Ma, G. Daxue Mingxiaozhang Fangtanlu (Record of Interviews with Famous Presidents of Universities). Beijing: Huaxia Publishing House, 2010: Preface 2.
51. Ibid, p. 16–17.
52. Ibid, p. 71.
53. Editing Committee of Zhongguo Daxue Renwen Qisilu, Zhongguo Daxue Renwen Qisilu (Disi Juan) (Record of Inspirations and Thoughts regarding Humanities in Chinese University (Volume 4)). Wuhan: Huazhong University of Science and Technology Press, 2000: 166–167.
54. Ma, G. Daxue Mingxiaozhang Fangtanlu (Record of Interviews with Famous Presidents of Universities). Beijing: Huaxia Publishing House, 2010: 192–194.
55. Liu, D. Zhongguo Gaoxiao Zhishang (The Regrets of Chinese Higher Institution). Wuhan: Hubei People's Press, 2010: 14.
56. Ma, G. Daxue Mingxiaozhang Fangtanlu (Record of Interviews with Famous Presidents of Universities). Beijing: Huaxia Publishing House, 2010: 83–84.
57. Editing Committee of Zhongguo Daxue Renwen Qisilu, Zhongguo Daxue Renwen Qisilu (Diwu Juan) (Record of Inspirations and Thoughts regarding Humanities in Chinese University (Volume 5)). Wuhan: Huazhong University of Science and Technology Press, 2002: 102.
58. Li, Z., Zhou, Q. Meiti Shiye Zhong De Huazhong Keji Daxue (1978–2008) (Huazhong University of Science and Technology in the View of the Media). Wuhan: Huazhong University of Science and Technology Press, 2008: 176.
59. Ouyang, K. Zizhu Chengzhang Yu Renwen Qinghuai – Huazhong Keji Daxue Wenhua Suzhi Shijian Jiaoyu Tansuo (Autonomous Growth and Feelings for Humanities – the Exploration of Cultural Quality Practical Education by Huazhong University of Science and Technology). Wuhan: Huazhong University of Science and Technology Press, 2012: 12.
60. Li, Z., Zhou, Q. Meiti Shiye Zhong De Huazhong Keji Daxue (1978–2008) (Huazhong University of Science and Technology in the View of the Media). Wuhan: Huazhong University of Science

and Technology Press, 2008: 243.

61. Ibid, p. 249.
62. Ouyang, K. Zizhu Chengzhang Yu Renwen Qinghuai – Huazhong Keji Daxue Wenhua Suzhi Shijian Jiaoyu Tansuo (Autonomous Growth and Feelings for Humanities – the Exploration of Cultural Quality Practical Education by Huazhong University of Science and Technology). Wuhan: Huazhong University of Science and Technology Press, 2012: 212.
63. Ma, G. Daxue Mingxiaozhang Fangtanlu (Record of Interviews with Famous Presidents of Universities). Beijing: Huaxia Publishing House, 2010: 71.
64. Li, Z., Zhou, Q. Meiti Shiye Zhong De Huazhong Keji Daxue (1978–2008) (Huazhong University of Science and Technology in the View of the Media). Wuhan: Huazhong University of Science and Technology Press, 2008: 172.
65. Ibid, p. 170.

CHAPTER 6

The Reflection and Construction of the Cultural Character of Chinese Universities

The development of the cultural character of Chinese Universities has a history of over 100 years, and it has always followed the basic path of "taking Chinese culture as the foundation" and utilizing "cultural inheritors" as its main body of practice. From the second chapter to the fifth chapter, this book sorted out, analyzed, and summarized, from a historical perspective, the path of development of the cultural characters of Chinese universities during the country's social changes since modern times. Yet, this book not only focuses on the fate of Chinese culture during the social changes in various historical periods, that is, the description of the social background that formed and developed the cultural character of Chinese universities but it also pays attention to the "living" Chinese culture, or the "cultural inheritors" of Chinese universities. The book discusses their cultural views and their views on universities, along with providing a detailed summary of the specific characteristics of the cultural characters of Chinese universities under their influence. The research content of this work covers the social background, specific characteristics, and formation mechanisms of the cultural characters of Chinese universities during the late Qing Dynasty, the Republican China era, the Seventeen Years, and the era since the Reform and Opening Up. These arguments are enough to prove that the cultural characters of Chinese universities are "inward" and "artificial." Since the late Qing Dynasty, they have seen no major interruptions, although there have been many twists and turns.

Based on the above research, this chapter will further clarify and interpret, under a modern context the development history of the cultural characters of Chinese universities, the construction of an ideal set of cultural characters for Chinese universities. It will also do so by critically reflecting on this question, which will involve two basic issues, the universities' standing points, and methodology. Specifically, there are two main tasks in this chapter: the first is to clarify the value of the historical reflection on the cultural characters of Chinese universities, and the second is the interpretation of building an ideal set of cultural characters of Chinese universities. This will be done by defining the question of "what is a good set of cultural characters of Chinese universities." Logically, conducting a historical reflection of the cultural character of Chinese universities means also defining the premise of what a good set of cultural characters of Chinese universities actually is. Plus, the construction of an ideal cultural character for Chinese universities is also the purpose of the well-defined set of the cultural character of Chinese universities.

Section 1: Reflections on the Cultural Characters of Chinese Universities

The cultural characters of Chinese universities are "inward" and "artificial," no matter strong or weak, beneficial or harmful, they all had their original intentions, their preferences, and their characteristics through various periods of history. Indeed, the formation and development of the cultural characters of Chinese universities are the products of specific eras, which possed certain inevitability and relative rationality. However, when all of these circumstances are left in the past, and the Chinese society enters a new period of development, it faces a new era of challenges, in addition to the "compassion of understanding." As such, it is now even more necessary to critically reflect on the cultural character of Chinese universities to avoid different strands of extreme tendencies that are caught in the waves of history. Starting from this point, this section intends to summarize the experience of the cultural characters of Chinese universities through the historical reflection of their types and characteristics.

1. Types of cultural characters of Chinese universities

Based on different historical situations, the cultural characteristics of Chinese universities in each period were unique in their own right. On the one hand, the cultural characters of Chinese universities were rooted in the Chinese culture, but it is obvious that the type of "Chinese culture" that prevailed during the different periods was inherently different. On the other hand, the cultural characters of Chinese universities were formed under the guidance of "cultural inheritors." However, the attitudes towards Chinese and Western cultures and the preferences of the Chinese culture of these "cultural inheritors" were still vastly different, and this was caused by the different sources of these inheritors' identities. Taking the three basic dimensions of comparison between Chinese-Western cultures, value, and power, the following part of the book analyzes the types of cultural characters of Chinese universities by studying the degree, the value distinction, and the nature of the cultural characters of Chinese universities through different eras.

a) The dimension of Chinese – Western cultures

The conflict and integration between Chinese and Western cultures were part of an important context that this book uses to historically study the cultural characters of Chinese universities. The cultural characters of Chinese universities are a specific Chinese concept that is separated from the Chinese and Western cultures.

The impact ofWestern culture on Chinese culture since modern times is unprecedented. The history of the modern development of Chinese culture is a "bifold" in the history of abandonment and revival. On the one hand, Chinese culture was gradually reduced to a derogatory term relative to Western culture during its forced input, and Chinese culture as a whole was drowned in excessive self-denial and self-criticism. On the other hand, the hegemony of Western culture incited the consciousness of Chinese literati, and the positive features of Chinese culture were further excavated and affirmed when it was forced to prove its legitimacy in the present-day society. As Hayhoe stated, "Throughout the 20th century, it was obvious that there were such contradictions and conflicts in China: it wanted the economic and social benefits that Western science and technology might bring, while at the same time it still tried to maintain the culture of the country knowledge traditions and its own national characteristics".[1] Subject to changes forced by Western culture, the development and evolution of modern Chinese culture were full of various variables.

Historically, the extent to which the cultural characters of Chinese universities can be established directly depended on the weight of Chinese culture in the process of conflict and integration between Chinese and Western cultures. Analyzing it from this extent, the late Qing period can be seen as an important period in which the traditional Chinese society began to transition to modernization while strengthening its roots and fundamental purpose. The scholars in the late Qing era especially emphasized the cultural concept of *Zhongti Xiyong*, and in the eastward spread of Western learnings, Chinese culture secured its dominant position in the wave of the times, and the cultural characters of Chinese universities were the most distinctive during this period. Further, intellectuals in Republican China were extremely active. They were knowledgeable in both ancient and modern studies, and Chinese and Western learnings, and advocated for the integration of Chinese and Western cultures. Even though the May Fourth Movement gave a fatal blow to Chinese culture, objectively speaking, Chinese culture and Western culture gradually achieved a dynamic balance during their many conflicts. Hence, the cultural character of Chinese universities entered a period of balanced development. During the First Seventeen years, Chinese culture was trapped in the political atmosphere with no clear path to escape. After the Reformation Movement against the intellectuals, Chinese culture fell into a state of weakness, and the cultural character of Chinese universities declined overall. Since the Reform and Opening Up, Chinese culture began to recover and rebuild in line with the era of cultural rejuvenation, and the cultural character of Chinese universities was gradually showing a trend of revival. Based on the comparison of differences, the cultural character of Chinese universities can be divided into three basic types: thick, roughly balanced, and weak, which correspond to the three historical stages of the late Qing Dynasty, the Republican China era, and the Seventeen Years era.

b) The dimension of value

Based on the positive and negative factors in Chinese culture, the cultural character of Chinese universities can be divided into two categories: its negative and positive sense. The cultural character of Chinese universities in various historical periods contains both positive elements and negative characteristics, which reflect the value conflicts within Chinese culture. Chinese culture is the root of the formation and development of the cultural character of Chinese universities. Based on the dimension of value, Chinese culture is divided into "good" and "bad." Chinese society underwent tremendous changes in modern times, and Chinese scholars are still engaging in more and more distinctive discussions regarding the value of Chinese culture, especially its negative elements. The endless cultural discussions in modern times are all aimed at this question, whether with negative or positive attitudes, of "how to judge the value of Chinese culture?" This has always been a problem in Chinese cultural research. It is true that based on different era's backgrounds and different positions, it is difficult to reach a consensus on the value distinction of Chinese culture. However, after a long period of historical accumulation, there are indeed certain absolute concepts of lasting value within Chinese culture, which are difficult to alter even with different times and positions. In the field of higher education, the excellent Chinese cultural tradition that was universally recognized, repeatedly discussed and demonstrated since modern times was the ancient Chinese "way of *daxue*," namely *Ming Mingde* (illustrating illustrious virtues), *Xinmin* (renewing the people), and *Zhiyu Zhishan* (pursuing absolute perfection).

During the era of Republican China, Mei Yiqi's *Daxue Yijie* pointed out that "Today's university education, at a glance, does not have much to do with the meaning of *Ming Mingde* and *Xinmin,* but if you look deeper, you can find out that today's university education measures are yet to exceed the scope of these couple of meanings."[2] Tu Youguang, in their study of the history of Chinese higher education, called it "the general law of Chinese higher education." In contrast to this, there is nothing more criticized by society than the educational idea of "excelling in academics to enter officialdom." Some scholars pointed out that "because of the influence of Confucianism, and against the backdrop of different social systems and ideologies," as well as compared with university autonomy and university freedom in the Western concept of universities, the 'university concept' in the development of Chinese universities can be summarized as "excelling in academics to enter officialdom, succeeding in officialdom to further pursue the academics." "As a result, universities are government-oriented, administrative-leveled, and the official-ranked orientedness prevails. Professors are unwilling to learn with their whole attention dedicated to politics, which seriously hinders academic development and progress."[3] The distinction between the so-called positive and negative senses of the cultural character of Chinese universities in this book is therefore mainly based on the two value traditions above. In a nutshell, the cultural character of Chinese universities in the positive sense is mainly based on the ancient *Daxue Zhidao,* and the book uses it as the fundamental value orientation. And the core of the negative sense is the idea of *Xueeryou Zeshi* and *Shieryou Zexue.*

Throughout the history of the cultural character of Chinese universities, some promote the ancient idea of *Daxue Zhidao.* For example, the universities of Republican China were characterized by the virtues of *Houde Zaiwu* and *Tianxia Weigong.* Since the Reform and Opening Up, people-orientedness has become the foundation of the Chinese universities' establishment. While other people were influenced by negative ideas such as *Xueeryou Zeshi*, for example, in the late Qing Dynasty, "integrating scholarship with officialdom" was the mainstream idea, and "government masters" flooded the Imperial University of Peking. During the Seventeen Years, "party-rule of universities" became the main characteristic of Chinese universities, and Renmin University was specifically designed to train national cadres. On the whole, the ancient "way of *daxue*" was well-preserved and was demonstrated in the universities of Republican China. As such, the positive characteristics of the cultural character of Chinese universities during this period were the most obvious. In comparison, the negative characteristics of the cultural character of Chinese universities' culture were more prominent during the late Qing and the Seventeen Years periods, while it had gradually shown a tendency to return to the ancient ways since the Reform and Opening Up. Of course, the cultural characters of Chinese universities during different historical periods were not only the successors of positive culture but also the inevitable carriers of the negative characteristics of Chinese culture. Therefore, the cultural character of Chinese universities may have had different degrees of negative and positive components during different periods, but there were no such things as cultural characters of Chinese universities that were purely positive or negative.

c) The dimension of power

Based on the identity characteristics of "cultural inheritors," the cultural character of Chinese universities can be divided into two categories, namely scholar-led and government-led. The conflict of power here is the key to understanding the concepts of these two categories. "Cultural inheritor" is also a key factor in the formation mechanism of the cultural character of Chinese universities. There are two different sources of power (or rights) in the development of modern Chinese universities. One is scholars from folk intellectual groups, and the other is government officials from state institutions. Focusing on the historical alternation of the two dominant forces, there are two important turning points in the historical evolution of Chinese universities.

The first turning point was the establishment of the Republic of China in 1912 when Cai Yuanpei served as the director of the Ministry of Education. Before this, the late Qing dynasty officials took charge of the Chinese universities, representing official power and interests. After this point, the intellectuals of Republican China who came from the traditional scholar class gained dominance in Chinese universities. After 1927, although the Kuomintang government tried to restrain universities, it did not fundamentally change the dominant position of university presidents throughout Chinese universities.

The second turning point was the establishment of the People's Republic of China in 1949. As Xie Yong stated, "the iteration of eras in 1949 was unprecedented in Chinese history. This could be observed through the impacts on the whole society's daily life brought by previous iterations of regimes that were not abrupt, and the basic structure and cultural traditions of the society that were continued in general. However, this time, the revolution of the times changed the basic structure and cultural traditions of Chinese society."[4] With the loss of the leading position of intellectuals in Chinese universities, government domination once again became the fundamental characteristic of Chinese universities.

Based on the differences in the identity of university leaders, the types of cultural characters of Chinese universities during various periods can be summarized through different categories. Before the first turning point in the late Qing Dynasty, the cultural characters of Chinese universities were influenced by the scholars in the late Qing Dynasty, which could be called the government-led cultural characters of Chinese universities. Following the establishment of the Republic of China, the power also shifted, and intellectuals, especially university presidents, replaced the late Qing dynasty scholars, which then constituted the core driving force for the formation of the cultural characters of Chinese universities of this era. After 1949, it entered the second turning point, the founding of the country. During the Seventeen Years, the government-led property was the root of the cultural characters of Chinese universities. Although new intellectuals had started to rise since the Reform and Opening Up, after all, the initiative in universities was still limited. The "party-committee-responsibility" system of university presidents was still the main feature of Chinese universities, and the type of cultural characters of Chinese universities could still be classified as government-led.

History had proven that when university dominance lay with scholars, the cultural character of Chinese universities was further highlighted. For example, in the conflict and integration of Chinese and Western cultures, the universities of Republican China shaped many positive cultural characteristics. On the contrary, when the power was excessively concentrated in the hands of the government, it did more harm than good for the development of the cultural characters of Chinese universities. For example, the monarchy reigned supreme during the late Qing Dynasty, as the power was controlled by the central royal family. As a result, the development of the cultural character of Chinese universities not only showed an imbalance in the choice between Chinese and Western cultures, but it also tended to be negative in its value orientation. From this perspective, the dominance of Chinese universities directly affects or even determines the differences in the extent and value orientation of the cultural characteristics of Chinese universities. In other words, the extent and significance of Chinese cultural factors that could legally enter Chinese universities depended on the identity and position of their "cultural carriers." Some scholars pointed out that, "Among the defects and negative factors of traditional Chinese culture, some were products of authoritarianism, and others were popularized by authoritarianism. The excellent and positive factors of traditional Chinese culture were either strangled or suppressed by authoritarianism, and could not be promoted."[5] This was also the key to understanding the differences in the values of the cultural character of Chinese universities during Republican China and the Seventeen Years.

2. *The cultural character characteristics of Chinese universities*

Based on the investigation into the typical characteristics of Chinese universities' cultural character over the various periods, it was mainly concentrated on the following three aspects: moral standards, humanistic spirit, and the tradition of *Shi* (scholars). As the essence of Chinese cultural traditions, they have become the fundamental connotations of Chinese universities, and they constitute the basic spirit and absolute value of the universities' cultural character. The cultural character of Chinese universities, whether positive or negative, can be explained within the context of these basic ideas of the spirit and its adaptations. As a practical sociological concept, the most subtle point of "adaptive" culture lies in its vague interpretation of the original system. In other words, on the surface, the principles it follows and the goals it tries to achieve are consistent with the original system, but the modified goals are not exactly the same as the original system goals. They may even be fundamentally different from the original system goals in terms of their deeper connotations.[6] Just as some scholars explain the negative effects of Confucianism, "Confucius thought was later used and distorted by the ruling class to become a state religion and a tool for the ruling class,"[7] this idea does make sense. Many of the negative characteristics in the cultural character of Chinese universities exist due to the fact that Chinese culture has been used by "cultural inheritors" in the process of transformation between tradition and modernity and it has therefore become "adaptive." However, it is undeniable that all kinds of modifications are based on moral standards, humanistic spirit, and the tradition of scholars. These historical clues are clearly visible.

a) Moral standards

"In the history of culture, although there is no national culture in the world that does not emphasize morality or doesn't want morality, it is true that no nation like China has elevated morality to such an important position in its cultural value system."[8] Even before Confucius, it was written in *Zuozhuan Xianggong* that, "The greatest achievement is to establish virtues, followed by outstanding feats and significant philosophies. For these shall not be abandoned with age, and therefore they are immortal." In *Analects of Confucius: Liren*, it was also written that "Wealth and fame are what people want, but you shouldn't keep them if you didn't acquire it by *Dao;* poverty and lowliness are what people despise, and you shall not rid yourself of them if not by *Dao.* A intelligentleman without benevolence is not a true intelligentleman." After Confucius, it was written in *Mencius: Gongsun Chou Section 2* that, "There are three greatest achievements in the world: title, age, and virtue. The title is the most valued within the court; age is the most valued in the neighborhood, and virtue is the most valued in governance. All three shall be respected, and we shall not focus on only one aspect among them." China's custom of respecting ethics and virtues has existed since ancient times, and one cannot ignore any of them even if he has none of them.

This was also explicitly included in the target range of higher education. In *Daxue* it said, "the way of *Daxue* is to illustrate illustrious virtues." In the book *Daxue Linian Zai Zhongguo (The Concept of University in China),* Wang Jisheng in detail explained the educational connotation of Confucianism based on ethics and morality. Its goal was to cultivate "intelligentlemanship and modesty" and its core was that "benign intelligentlemen should practice politics with good morals." Its highest moral standard was "the way of *Zhongyong*," combining good morals with good practices, while its basic principle of life was "seeking harmony in differences" (agreeing to disagree).[9] In this respect, the moral education in ancient China was essentially an intelligentleman education with the main characteristics of combining politics with virtue, and combining virtue with practice, and seeking common ground while reserving differences.

Since modern times, moral standards, as the core value of Chinese culture and the fundamental characteristic of classical higher education, had entered Chinese universities and had a huge influence on the cultural character of Chinese universities. Due to social changes, cultural conflicts, and regime shifts, values based on moral standards shaped the cultural character of Chinese universities with different characteristics throughout different eras. One situation was that under the leadership of traditional intellectuals, morality symbolized the noble traditional intelligentleman's character, emphasizing the improvement of personal character for the sake of fulfilling social responsibilities. For example, the cultural character of *Houde Zaiwu* and *Yourong Naida* of Republican China's universities interpreted the "intelligentleman" idea of Chinese traditional morality, which was to cultivate oneself, rule the country and seek common ground while reserving differences. By using the *Houde Zaiwu* as an example, Liang Qichao's *Intelligentleman* speech at Tsinghua University in 1914 explained the "intelligentleman" ethos of "cultivating oneself and governing the country." Liang pointed out, "The image of the hexagram Qian indicates that 'the Heavens are in motion ceaselessly; The enlightened exert themselves constantly;' [while] the image of the hexagram Kun indicates that 'the Earth is supportive and natural, only the virtuous can bear the utmost.' The meanings behind these two hexagrams could serve as the requirements for an intelligentleman." He also advised Tsinghua students to "regard virtues highly and commit to scholarship, so that they could be real intelligentlemen who are capable of bearing great responsibilities and can attain great achievements. Turn the tide of our country in danger and be the mainstay. It would be a fortune for our country to have you."

Another situation was that pressured by the authority, morality transformed into a a tool that was loyal to the ruler or served a specific group of interest, leading to a pan-politicized astray. For example, in the late Qing Dynasty, Chinese universities viewed loyalty to monarchs and respect for Confucius as their goal, and morality was strictly limited to staying loyal to feudal monarchs and the absolute belief in Confucianism. This was the official orthodox thought. Another example was during the Seventeen Years. The ideological revolution became a distinctive feature of the cultural character of Chinese universities. Moral education was limited to political moral education, which was strictly limited to Marxism-Leninism and Mao Zedong Thought. As a result, political demands overwhelmed moral enlightenment, and the tradition of moral standards was "adapted" to the opposite direction of human enlightenment and social harmony, which caused great harm to Chinese universities and the entire society.

b) Humanistic spirit

Chinese culture has a long history. The most distinctive feature is its humanistic spirit, and the core value of the humanistic spirit is humanism. Du Weiming believes that "the object of concern in Chinese culture is the people," and it can even be said that it is mainly "philosophical anthropology." Tang Yijie pointed out that in the traditional Chinese ideology and culture, a humanistic tendency can be easily observed. This humanism is different from the Western anti-theistic tendency from the Renaissance, which paid more attention to independent personality, natural human rights, and emphasized the liberation of personality. This kind of thought can be seen as humanism with strong individualism characters. The humanism of ancient China mainly started from this angle: The human has an important core position in the universe. The so-called *Sancai* means the coexistence of humans, heaven, and earth. Only humans can *Can Tiandi, Zan Huayu* (understand the mechanism of heaven and earth, and help their creation).[10] In traditional Chinese discourse, the word opposite to *Renwen* (humanities) is *Tianwen* (astronomy). *The Book of Changes* has a saying, "Study astronomy and you can observe the changes in time; study humanities and you can teach it to the world." Compared with "humanities," "astronomy" is a natural subject that is opposite to human resources and human theories. In the late Qing Dynasty, Western learning gradually spread eastward, and the word *Kexue* (science) was translated as a special vocabulary opposite to "humanities" in Japanese. Since then, the distinction between humanities and science incited countless discourse and controversies, but one point remained the same, that is, humanities were based on people. The inheritance of classical humanities depended on traditional classics. As some scholars believed, if education did not revive classical learning (traditional classics), the general education which would save humanities education could be left without roots.[11] Based on the above, the "humanities" mentioned in this book are mainly opposed to the "science" from the West in modern times. The humanistic spirit of Chinese universities mainly includes the following three elements. One was seeing people as the core, the second was using the traditional Chinese classics as the carrier, and the third was using the living traditional humanities knowledge-masters (intellectuals with profound knowledge of Chinese studies).

Based on the profound influence of the humanities stage of higher education (from the legend of the Five Emperors to the end of the Qing Dynasty), and although Chinese universities have been in the "science" stage since modern times, the cultural character of Chinese universities still has a long-lasting effect in the conflict and fusion of Chinese and Western cultures. It exudes a feeling of "humanities" education. During the period of Republican China, Chinese universities practiced general education to realize the all-round development of human beings, that is, while introducing Western science and culture, they also developed humanities disciplines based on traditional Chinese humanities knowledge. The cultural character of *Wenshi Bingbao* interpreted exactly this kind of "fitting" of human feelings. From the School of Sinology at Peking University to the Institute of Chinese Studies at Tsinghua University, they collected the masters of the Qing Dynasty and the ancient classics, and the Chinese humanistic tradition was well-preserved and further inherited in Chinese universities. Since the Reform and Opening Up, Chinese universities have shown the cultural character tendencies of people-orientedness and humanistic orientedness. The fundamental starting point was to try to revive the Chinese humanistic tradition in the modernization process of scientism, to solve the difficulties of science bias in Chinese universities. In contrast to this, another fact of history was that the traditional humanistic spirit was moving towards "adaptation" throughout Chinese universities, and the humanistic tradition was seriously politicized.

For example, the humanities education of Chinese universities in the late Qing dynasty led people into politics by using the traditional humanistic spirit, and "adopted" them as tools for the rulers to exercise ideological control and political indoctrination of the people. Therefore, although there are many great masters and grand ceremonies in Chinese universities in the late Qing Dynasty, they had not inherited the tradition of the Chinese humanistic spirit. As a prominent feature of the cultural character of Chinese universities in the late Qing Dynasty, *Jingxue Weiben* did not focus on self-cultivation, but on stabilizing the core position of Confucianism in Chinese society. Fundamentally speaking, it was using traditional human knowledge to "teach" loyalty to the obedient people of the Qing Dynasty.

c) The tradition of Shi *scholars*

Shi is a special phenomenon in Chinese culture. Yu Yingshi once wrote a book called *Shi Yu Zhongguo Wenhua* (*Shi* and Chinese Culture), capturing the particularity of Chinese culture through the historical study of the *Shi* class. The book pointed out, "If you start counting from Confucius, the tradition of Chinese '*Shi*' has continued for at least 2,500 years, and it is still endured."[12] In the early years, Confucius ordered the *Shi* to practice *Shi Zhiyu Dao* (*Shi* should dedicate themselves to the *Dao*), which also meant for them to go beyond themselves and protect the society. And as the development progressed of *Xunzi*, the concept of *Shi Zhiyu Dao* became highly politicized.[13] Another term closely related to *Shi* was also the core concept of Confucian political thought, *Ren* (Benevolence). Therefore, the so-called *Shi* are often referred to as *Renren Zhishi* (Shi with benevolence and ambition). The old saying *Zhi Yu Ren* (dedication to benevolence) described a noble feeling of *Shi*. Li Zehou had a very good expression of this concept, "The kind of humane spirit and personality ideals derived from clan democracy, the kind of rational attitude that values reality and practical experience, the kind of practical spirit with optimism and aggressiveness... have all affected, educated and nurtured many people with lofty ideals in the long history of China." It is a tradition that often plays a progressive role in China's long history. Even in the late feudal society where Confucianism and the feudal ruling system were integrated, like Fan Zhongyan's *Xian Tianxia Zhiyou Eryou, Hou Tianxia Zhile Erle* (worrying the worries before the world, and feeling the happiness after the world), Zhang Zai's *Min Wutongbao, Wu Wuyu Ye* (all humans are my fellows, and all things in the world are our friends), Wen Tianxiang's *Kong Yue Chengren, Meng Yue Quyi* (Confucius taught us to achieve benevolence and Menfucius taught us to manifest righteousness), Gu Yanwu's *Tianxia Xingwang, Pifu Youze* (the prosperity and decline of the world lie in the hand of all of us), Wang Fuzhi's *Liujing Zewo Kaishengmian, Qichi Congtian Qihuomai* (I am tasked with drafting new understandings to the *Six Ancient Classics*, and I shall keep myself away from the world to achieve it)... all [of these sayings] shine with brilliant glory, forming the basic concepts, emotions, thoughts and attitudes of our nation, and they can all be traced to the structure of benevolence. Lu Xun said. 'Since ancient times, we have people who work hard, people who fight the tide, people who plead in the name of the people, people who sacrifice themselves for the right way ... even in the 'official records of history' which nobles and emperors treat as their family records, the glory of these people still often shines through the curtain. This is the backbone of China."[14] The tradition of Shi is the basic feature of Chinese culture and an important part of classical higher education. For example, the so-called concept of *Xinmin* in *Daxue* stipulates a kind of patriotism education full of the emotions for *Shi*, which laid the backbone of modern Chinese universities.

Modern China happened to exist amid changing times. The urgent need for education for the sake of saving the country made the cultural character of Chinese universities closely related to the salvation and redemption of the entire era. Therefore, the traditions of *Shi* always run through the development of the cultural character of Chinese universities. In different historical contexts, the traditional *Shi* spirit was derived from two different characteristics in the cultural character of Chinese universities. The first was the spirit of the *Shi*, whose main feature was the national morality beyond the individual, which manifested itself in the country's crisis as a strong sense of national duty and social responsibility. For example, one of the major characteristics of the cultural character of Chinese universities during the Republican China era was *Tianxia Weigong* (sharing the world equally with everybody). The so-called *Tianxia* (everything under Heaven) meant the Chinese people in a national sense, and the *Tianxia Weigong* of Chinese universities meant that the basic goals of Chinese universities were the independence of the people, the rising of China, and the happiness of the people, instead of simply serving a specific government. For example, the lyrics of the school song of the NSAU stated: *Qianqiu Chi, Zhongdang Xue; Zhongxing Ye, Xu Renjie* (the shame of centuries shall be cleared, and the duty of rejuvenation needs talents). Such was the spirit of the scholars of Republican Chinese universities to cultivate talents for the public. The other kind of *Shi* traditions were excessively politicized and became a narrow ruling tool to protect the interests of those in the power of authoritarian politics. Taking the cultural character of the "integrating scholarship with officialdom" in Chinese universities in the late Qing Dynasty as an example, the Chinese universities in the Late Qing Dynasty were created directly by the scholars of the era, and their basic purpose was to cultivate talents for the sake of protecting the rule of monarchy.

In summary, the characteristics of the cultural character of Chinese universities summarized in this book can be interpreted in the context of the core values of Chinese culture, which were moral standards, humanistic spirit, and the traditions of *Shi*. In the historical evolution of inheritance and adaptation, these absolute values endowed Chinese universities with different cultural characters during different historical periods. They were either actively interpreted or distorted, but the cultural character of Chinese universities remained the same. Overall, the cultural character of Chinese universities during the Republican China era adhered to the core connotation of Chinese culture through morality, humanistic spirit, and the traditions of *Shi*. However, the phenomenon of "adaptation" in the late Qing Dynasty and the Seventeen Years was more serious, and it mainly manifested in the pan-politicization of traditional values in Chinese universities. This had a significant negative impact. The humanistic spirit of Chinese universities during the Seventeen Years and the *Shi* traditions of Chinese universities since the Reform and Opening Up were not covered in this book. The reason for this is that during the Seventeen Years, humanities education used a political model with only ideological and political content. Since the Reform and Opening Up, the political order has been stable. Although Chinese universities still have a tradition of *Shi*, it is no longer a typical feature. The revival of humanities and moral traditions remain trends.

3. *The historical experience of Chinese universities' cultural character formation*

The above section clarified the history of Chinese universities' cultural character by analyzing its types and characteristics. Based on the above, we need to further think about the ideal cultural character of Chinese universities. Before we begin, the historical experience of the formation of the cultural character of Chinese universities can be summarized as follows:

First, the formation of the cultural character of Chinese universities is inevitable, and universities can achieve a good cultural character. The cultural character of Chinese universities is not only a fact that almost runs through their entire century of history, but it is also a part of their value. From the perspective of the formation mechanism, the cultural character of Chinese universities is formed in an "internal and artificial" process based on Chinese culture, with "cultural inheritors" as a communication bridge. Since Chinese universities were "born and raised" in China, it is historically inevitable for them to be influenced by Chinese culture. However, it is uncertain which Chinese culture and what persons had an impact on Chinese universities. In other words, the formation of the cultural character of Chinese universities has the dual characteristics of historical necessity and chance. History proves that there is a cultural character of Chinese universities during every period, but there is no established type or certain inevitable representations of this character. The cultural character of Chinese universities in different historical periods can only be seen as the unification of historical commonality and individuality of the times. The cultural character of Chinese universities is formed and developed based on the basic characteristics of traditional cultural and moral standards, humanistic spirit, and the traditions of *Shi*, and these are the common aspects of this culture. The cultural character of Chinese university culture also shows that various historical types and characteristics in different historical contexts, which could be considered as its unique character. This means that the development of the cultural character of Chinese universities is full of possibilities, and it can improve.

Second, the "good" cultural character of Chinese universities lies in the coordination of various special and contradictory relations. The analysis of the historical characteristics of the cultural character of Chinese universities shows that it contains various special contradictions, namely, the contradiction between Chinese and Western cultures, the contradiction between positive and negative factors in Chinese culture, and the contradiction between the intellectuals and the government. History proves that, in contradictions and conflicts, the cultural character of Chinese universities shall not simply choose between the two, but it must have a clear and firm fundamental position.

In other words, within the cultural character of Chinese universities, respect for Western culture is a precondition and the understanding of Chinese culture is its basis. All the while, distinguishing negative culture is also a precondition, and inheriting positive cultural elements is the basis. Acknowledging government power is a precondition, and safeguarding the subjectivity of scholars is the basis. Specifically, a "good" cultural character for Chinese universities should have at least the following points: First, the cultural character of Chinese universities should adhere to the general balance between Chinese and Western cultures. Second, it should be based on a positive sense of Chinese culture, adhering to the Chinese classical *Daxue*. Third, the cultural character of Chinese universities should be based on the dominance of scholars in Chinese universities, and use it as its primary condition. The idea of maintaining the balance of Chinese and Western cultures makes the concept of the cultural character of Chinese universities special but also wide. Taking the positive-sense of Chinese culture could be seen as the root of the cultural character to keep it noble and not vulgar while insisting on the dominant position of scholars in Chinese universities makes it possible to maintain a balance between Chinese and Western cultures, and gives space to enhance Chinese culture. In this context, a scholar-led cultural character of Chinese universities is the fundamental basis among the various types of cultural characters of Chinese universities. Chinese universities, no matter how good their administrative will is, will never have good cultural character under the control of the administrative will. In other words, if Chinese universities are not dominated by scholars, there will never be a "good" cultural character. Admittedly, scholars' authority does not necessarily mean that a good cultural character of Chinese universities will be produced, especially today, when traditional intellectuals from the past disappeared, and the bureaucratization of new intellectuals is becoming more and more serious, making the situation even more worrying. It is not accidental that the cultural character of Chinese universities during the Republican China era was outstanding in history. The fundamental point of the era was that educators ran schools during that time. Mencius said, "the so-called native country is not about taxes, but about generations of loyal subordinates." Mei Yiqi said: "the so-called university is not about buildings and campuses, but about generations of master scholars." In these remarks, the so-called cultural character of Chinese universities was not governed by the authority of the government but shaped by educators.

Third, the key to obtaining a good cultural character of Chinese universities lies in maintaining moderate principles. The so-called "moderate" idea, when discussing the problem of human virtue, is mainly used by Aristotle to describe a good quality or intermediate state of maintaining virtue in practical affairs, as opposed to inferiority and excessiveness. This book studies the cultural character of Chinese universities, mainly seeing it as the essence of a proper ideal state that obtains the truly good ideas, and which corresponds to the word "adaptive." Although the theoretical moralities, humanities, and scholar traditions are abstract values, they are also concrete practical activities in the historical characteristics of the cultural character of Chinese universities. The purpose of adhering to the principle of moderation in the cultural character of Chinese universities is to strike a balance between the abstract "moralities," "humanities," *shi,* and other basic Chinese cultural spirits and their specific practice. Aristotle said: "Since moral virtues are so modest, it is not easy to be a good person. This is because it is difficult to find the midpoint in everything."[15] In the same way, it is not easy to form a good cultural character of Chinese universities, because it is difficult to grasp this moderate midpoint in practice.

Throughout the history of Chinese university's cultural character, the moral traditions of *Houde Zaiwu* (bearing the utmost with virtues) transformed into the concept of "loyalty to the emperor, respect for Confucius" and "ideological revolution." While the humanistic spirit of people-orientedness transformed into "Confucian-centric" ideas, and the scholar-official tradition of "sharing the world equally with others" transformed into "universities ruled by the Party." The cultural character of Chinese universities was never firm in choosing between moderation and adaption, and it often went down the wrong path. History has proven that a good cultural character of Chinese universities can only be formed if it maintains itself at an appropriate distance between its concepts and reality. The cultural characters of Chinese universities in the late Qing Dynasty and the Seventeen Years are worth pondering. Their negativity can be largely attributed to the excessive expression of the basic values of Chinese culture. For example, morality, as an ethical concept of teaching people to be good, is transformed into an extreme "respect to the higher tier" hierarchical order, or unconditional obedience to the monarch and authority ("respect for Confucius and loyalty to the emperor" in late Qing Dynasty), or even the absolute belief in "ideological revolution." Essentially, the extreme characterization of the basic characteristics of the cultural character of Chinese universities in practice is a pan-political problem. In this context, the way to obtain the "moderate" cultural character ultimately lies in their independence. In Republican China, Chinese universities benefited from Cai Yuanpei's idea of "education independence" and they insisted that universities should be independent of politics. The cultural character of Chinese universities was the least politicized during this period, and this was not just a historical coincidence.

Section 2: The Ideal Construction of the Cultural Character of Chinese Universities

Since the late Qing Dynasty, the cultural character of Chinese universities has persisted for over a hundred years. It has indeed reached a historical stage of value screening and critical reflection. However, it is difficult to clearly explain its merits and demerits due to the special setting of times. Besides, the purpose of this book is not to provide simple criticism or deconstruction, but to find an ideal path for the development of the cultural character of Chinese universities by digging out the internal factors that exist and continue to exist in their cultural character. Admittedly, never in history has the reality and the facts been ideal, but on the other hand, this ideal cultural character indeed has sparked or is still sparking to a certain point in our history and our reality to varying degrees. Similarly, although we admit that the ideal cultural character of Chinese universities is not only necessary based in reality but it is also possible in practice, it is a perfect interpretation of China's high-quality cultural traditions. Yet, this does not mean that the ideal cultural character of Chinese universities can be perfect on its own and exist completely independent of society. This book does not have the intention of absolutely beautifying and forcibly fulfilling the ideal construction of the cultural character of Chinese universities. It only hopes that the ideal cultural character of Chinese universities can be used as an ideological belief to provide a generally accurate direction for universities' future practices.

1. Why should we construct the ideal cultural character of Chinese universities

The ideal cultural character of Chinese universities is mainly worth pursuing for two reasons: one is that the cultural character of Chinese universities is important, and the other is that China needs an ideal cultural character of Chinese universities. Based on the international perspective, the importance of the cultural character of Chinese universities is self-evident. While based on the local situation, Chinese society urgently needs an ideal cultural character of Chinese universities.

a) The importance of the cultural character of Chinese universities from the international perspective

At present, "higher education revolves around knowledge production and extends to two dimensions at the same time: one is modernization and the time dimension, characterized by the applicative turn; the second is globalization and the spatial dimension, characterized by decentralization and networking."[16] As some scholars said, "Today, for universities, is both the best and the worst era."[17] As far as Chinese universities are concerned, the good news is that Chinese universities have achieved unprecedented development by taking advantage of the era of higher education modernization and globalization. The bad news is that the particularity of Chinese universities cannot be highlighted in the process of modernization and globalization of higher education, and this gets even more blurred in their process.

On the one hand, with the application turn brought about by the modernization of higher education, the utilitarian transformation and vulgarization of higher education have become profound prices for its modernization transformation. The characteristics of Chinese universities as China's *Daxue* are becoming less and less obvious. An outstanding feature of modernization is technology, but scientism ultimately alienates higher education modernization into utilitarianism. Daisaku Ikeda and Toynbee pointed out in *Forecast of the 21st Century:*

> "In a society of modern technological civilization, it is compelling to feel that education has become a servile maid and a tool for the pursuit of desire. [...] Modern education has fallen into utilitarianism, which is sad. This ethos has brought two disadvantages. One is that learning has become a tool of politics and economy, and the original initiative has been lost, and thus the dignity has been consequently lost. The other is that only knowledge and technology with practical benefits is deemed valuable, so those who are in the field of such knowledge have become slaves of knowledge and technology, and the result is the loss of human dignity.[18]

As a result, universities turned from independent higher education institutions to politicized state units, and to economize enterprise companies, and they increasingly deviate from the essence of higher education institutions. When the university is like everything, but not itself, the 'university-like university' begins to be constructed as a university ideal of the new era. Entrapped in the wave of times of modernization of higher education, Chinese universities are also facing the cost of modernization. "There are tall and full walls enclosing our campuses, yet we cannot shut the campuses away from the huge wave of commercialization. Secular slogans were all over the place."[19] Can Chinese universities still be regarded as "universities?" More and more people start to feel unsure about the answer to this question. Modernization is an inevitable stage of higher education's development, which means that Chinese universities are destined to modernize with the times. So, how can they adapt to the trend of modernization of higher education while at the same time demonstrate the uniqueness of Chinese universities as China's *Daxue*? Especially when *Daxue* has become an important proposition of the current Chinese university's construction.

On the other hand, in the process of globalization of higher education, the uniqueness of Chinese universities as a 'China's' universities were facing the challenge of homogenization of higher education around the world due to the advantages of the mature Western university model. "The danger of globalization is homogeneity, that is, media contents and the global system (including the higher education model we use and the international benchmarks we follow) will force everyone and every country to engage in a generalized higher education model. That is, rendering the idealized American university model into the only possible model."[20] This means that during the process of globalization of higher education, "most countries will be destined to become a failed imitator of 'a possible global model,' instead of a powerful producer of their native ethnic model that could possibly replace the global model."[21] Chinese universities were externally introduced and they still are retroactive. They are the product of modern Western colonialism. They indeed keep imitating the Western university model. However, Chinese universities are, after all, universities that grow within China. After a century of ceaseless transformation, Chinese universities gradually developed their characteristics. Because of that, some scholars have proposed the concept of a "Chinese model of the university." However, Chinese universities are once again in danger of being homogenized with the trend of higher education globalization. If we intend to make Chinese universities a permanent proposition, we must not only passively adapt to the commonalities brought by globalization. Instead, we must actively develop and maintain our personalities. Higher education globalization is an inevitable trend. Without it, it would also be impossible for Chinese universities to progress. What is worth investigating is the way of maintaining the uniqueness of Chinese universities as "universities of China."

In summary, in the era of higher education modernization and globalization, Chinese universities are facing the crisis of converging with other social institutions and homogenizing alongside the universities of other countries. Faced with such a complex external environment, how could the uniqueness of Chinese universities be established? From a cultural point of view, the cultural character of Chinese universities is an essential feature of Chinese universities that distinguishes them from other non-university institutions and other countries' various models of university organizations. It is the foundation of why Chinese universities could call themselves "universities of China." The construction of the cultural character of Chinese universities not only directly affects the unique existence and independent status of Chinese universities on the world stage, but also, to a certain extent, determines the rise of China in the world. At present, China could be regarded as a huge country of higher education, but not a strong country of higher education. This is largely due to the lack of creativity and uniqueness of Chinese universities. Coase, the Nobel-prize winning economist pointed out the weakness of China's economy: "Due to the lack of innovation and the lack of unique products, many Chinese companies rely on order-oriented production – accepting orders from overseas markets and selling them after attaching foreign trademarks. For the Chinese economy that aspires to return to the number one position in the world, we call this dilemma 'production without products,' I dare not to compliment this model."[22] From a cultural perspective, if Chinese universities can realize the importance of their cultural character, unique and highly creative Chinese universities would be just around the corner.

b) *The necessity of ideal Chinese universities' culture character within the Chinese context*

The current situation self-evidently highlights the importance of Chinese universities' cultural character. What kind of cultural character do we need, then? To answer this question, we must first find out what the current cultural character of Chinese universities is now. The fifth chapter of the present book deconstructs the Chinese university cultural character from the Reform and Opening Up. It summarized the development trend of Chinese universities' cultural character since the Reform and Opening Up with the main focus on its ideal and typical features. The purpose was to demonstrate that since the Reform and Opening Up, Chinese universities' cultural character has shown a better development trend than in the Seventeen Years. It has also provided a realistic basis for the ideal construction of the Chinese universities' cultural character in this chapter. However, an objective fact that could not be avoided in these idealistic and typical descriptions is that although the cultural character of Chinese universities today is not the same as it was in the Seventeen Years (which placed repeated emphasis on "Party-ruled universities"), and the government is indeed gradually decentralizing, some drawbacks of the existing system are still the most realistic problems of Chinese universities. At present, an important characteristic of the cultural character of Chinese universities is still the "integration of learning and officialdom," guided by the value of the "excelling in academics to enter officialdom" idea.

When referring to the problems of Chinese university education in this century, Chen Pingyuan pointed out that, "Chinese universities successfully transplanted the Western education system, but they have not succeeded in inheriting the ancient Chinese 'way of *Daxue*.'"[23] In the 100-year history of the cultural character of Chinese universities, overall, it was true that Chinese universities had not successfully inherited the ancient Chinese "way of *Daxue*." They had no consistency. However, it is also worth noting that Chinese universities have successfully interpreted the philosophy of "excelling in academics to enter officialdom" of Chinese culture. "Since modern times, Chinese universities have followed the Western institutional framework in form, but their spirits and ideas have not deviated from the 'excelling in academics to enter officialdom' mindset."[24] This trait is especially evident during the late Qing and the Seventeen Years, as it served as the basis of Chinese universities' cultural characters during these periods. Although today, the situation has changed slightly, it did not improve significantly. According to Liu

Xiaofeng, "In modern Chinese society, the imperial examination system has not actually been abolished. Instead, only the content of study, morality, and academic institution has changed. The 'Four Books and Five Classics' and their idea of self-cultivation have been replaced by 'Western learning;' traditional academies have been replaced by the university. A set of the modern cultural and educational system which adapts to the nation-state institution has been established."[25]

The cultural and educational policy under the feudal imperialism continued in different forms throughout modern Chinese universities governed by the party. Under the "integration of learning and officialdom" framework, they did not have any fundamental differences. Since the Reform and Opening Up, "excelling in academics to enter officialdom" has evolved into some new features of the times within the institutional framework of university administrative levels. "Under the administrative levels, the university itself has been gradually 'politicized.' Officials are becoming 'scholars,' while scholars are becoming 'officials.' More and more government officials are becoming doctors or professors in the universities, while more and more professors are pursuing officialdom after the administrative positions."[26] The fundamentals of these problems could be explained by the educational tradition of integrating learning with officialdom from which the modern party-ruled university system derived.

It might be reasonable for late Qing universities to inherit this tradition because they attempted to "reform in regards to ancient rules" to alleviate the incompatibility caused by the abolition of the imperial examination, or for universities during the Seventeen Years to strongly advocate the "party-ruled university system" and allocate jobs for graduates in a centralized manner to maintain the stability of politics during that special era and to revive their economics. However, the administrative and unit-system tendencies demonstrated by contemporary Chinese universities were constantly questioned because of their lack of credibility. The current educational system is not run by educators, but by the Ministry of Education.[27] The fundamental difference between the two is that if universities were run by educators, they would not evolve such an obvious tendency of excelling in academics to enter officialdom. For example, under the leadership of educators, the universities of the Republic of China temporarily dispelled or contained, to a certain degree, the cultural tradition of the integration of politics and education. When Cai Yuanpei became the president of Peking University, he opined, "Universities are places for advanced and profound studies. There is no room for the idea of getting into officialdom or gaining wealth."

In contrast, universities run by the Ministry provides a fertile ground for the comprehensive revival of the excelling in academics to enter officialdom idea. At present, under the system of ministry-run universities, this traditional mindset has not declined, but instead, flourished in Chinese universities. This is especially evident in the professors' strong will to getting administrative promotions and the students' obvious tendency of applying for official posts after graduation. If Chinese universities become trapped here in the long run, on the one hand, it would be hard for the implementation of the development trends of positive cultural characters such as people-orientedness, building on humanities, and looking beyond in tranquillity. On the other hand, if the generally desirable development trend is curbed, the opportunity brought by the times when Chinese culture is experiencing a comprehensive revival and the de-administration of Chinese universities could be gradually entered while the national regulations could be missed. The time when Chinese universities would rise again could never come. When reflecting on the disadvantages brought about by the universities' cultural character of "excelling in academics to enter officialdom," the necessity of the ideal Chinese universities' cultural character becomes even more prominent. This should be the instinctive response and the inevitable choice of Chinese universities to seek advantages and avoid setbacks.

2. *How to construct the ideal cultural character of Chinese universities*

The ideal construction of the cultural character of Chinese universities does not only depend on the social needs of the international and local perspectives but it must also be rooted in the possibilities provided by history and reality. Theoretically, the historical experience, realistic trends, and potential possibilities of the cultural character of Chinese universities are all important reasons for the possibilities of the ideal construction of the cultural character of Chinese universities.

First, to start with, historical experience is the most direct available resource for the ideal construction of Chinese universities' cultural character. As Tao Xingzhi said when talking about Chinese historical experience, "Given the previous experience of our nation, we shall keep all that's suitable and remove all that's inappropriate. As of the standard of removal and retainment, we shall only consider its suitability and appropriateness, not its age."[28] The ideal construction of the cultural character of Chinese universities is, first of all, a process of "removal and retainment" of historical experience, that is, inheriting the good cultural character that appeared in history and removing the subtly existent negative cultural character.

The first steps are that the ideal cultural character of Chinese universities should go through the affirmation and inheritance of history. There are many good examples of Chinese universities' cultural character's history. Judging from the historical achievements of Republican China's universities in the century-old history of Chinese universities, they were undoubtedly the most outstanding despite their many limitations of the historical era. From the previous discussion, we can see that the cultural character of Republican China's universities was remarkable in terms of moral standards, humanistic spirit, and the tradition of *Shi*. However, it is also regrettable that many high-quality cultural characters of Republican China's universities did not persist nor had a lasting impact, especially the core concepts such as "being inclusive to attain great achievements" and "practicing both idealism and realism." These almost disappeared during the Seventeen Years. Why were the outstanding cultural qualities of Chinese universities lost? The answer might be found in the inheritance of the classical cultural characteristics of Western universities. Also based on traditional culture, some well-known Western universities formed a long-lasting classical university character and passed it down to future generations, especially the concept of the German classical universities which had influenced the world's universities since its very formation. In contrast, for more than a hundred years, Chinese universities have rapidly reproduced various types of cultural characters during different historical periods, all while achieving nothing in terms of consistent characteristics of Chinese university culture. As some scholars have pointed out: "Our problem is: there is a long history of culture, but it is not easy to condense it into traditions. There are traditions, but it is not easy to spread them. This is a real cultural crisis that we have encountered for a long time."[29] As far as the cultural character of Chinese universities is concerned, Chinese universities have a long-standing Chinese cultural foundation, but they have not derived a specific and long-lasting Chinese university cultural tradition. They have a high-quality Chinese university cultural tradition, but it is difficult to condense it into a consistent core value system. Chen Hongjie once interpreted the unique charm of the German classical university view as an almost religious "nature of Karisma" that transcends all practical values, including political value.[30] The lack of vertical inheritance and excessive catering to society's reality was the fundamental reason why the cultural character of Chinese universities was destined not to gain the "nature of Karisma." From this perspective, inheriting beliefs rather than tools to form a stable core value system, in theory, was the fundamental way out for the reconstruction of the cultural character of Chinese universities.

Second, the ideal cultural character of Chinese universities should also go through historical denial and revision. Compared with the fact that some high-quality cultural characters cannot be spread, the influence of some negative cultural characteristics of Chinese universities was lasting and profound. From the "integrating learning and officialdom" in the late Qing Dynasty to the "party-rule of schools" in the Seventeen Years to the administration of Chinese universities today, all are epochal interpretations of the traditional value concept of "excelling in academics to enter officialdom." In theory, the elimination of these negative characteristics of the cultural character of Chinese universities is the essential requirement and the inevitable choice for the ideal construction of Chinese universities' cultural character. But trying to get rid of all the inappropriate parts in one fell swoop would be extremely unrealistic and impractical.

On the one hand, the cultural character of any Chinese university is based on deep-rooted Chinese cultural traditions, and it has therefore become a cultural characteristic of Chinese universities during a certain period after a stable formation and development process. As such, it is difficult to eradicate. On the other hand, while there are indeed certain incompatibilities, the cultural character of Chinese universities is still suitable for China's basic national conditions at present and they have been regarded as the common sense of Chinese universities in thought. So, they can't be immediately terminated. In this regard, in the process of the ideal construction of the cultural character of Chinese universities, to get rid of the background of negative culture in history, their character needs to go through a long and gradual fading process.

Second, the existing development trend is an important basis for the ideal construction of the cultural character of Chinese universities. Since the Reform and Opening Up, the cultural character of Chinese universities has shown a relatively good developmental trend, which is mainly characterized by "people-orientedness," "building on humanities" and "looking beyond in tranquillity." At present, the cultural character of Chinese universities has reached a critical period of transformation. The so-called transformation is the transformation from the declining, negatively dominant, and government-led cultural character of Chinese universities in the Seventeen Years to a balanced, positive, and scholar-led cultural character of Chinese universities now. This critical period means that the ideal possibility trend of the modern Chinese universities' cultural character has gradually matured in its ideas and is now seeking the support of the system and its implementation in practice. This means there are two possibilities, either for it to become a veritable good cultural character or for it to grow to be a short-lived phase, similar to the era of Republican China, and then quickly retreat into silence. Without the support of historical experience, the ideal cultural character of Chinese universities will become sourceless, and it will lack the echoing of the favorable trends of reality. Then, the ideal reconstruction of the cultural character of Chinese universities will not even start. From a practical perspective, these high-quality cultural trends have sprouted and developed during the trend of the times of Chinese universities' criticism and have had the greatest practical significance. "People-orientedness" means respecting human beings and respecting human relations, "building on humanities" brings about profound humanistic cultivation, while "looking beyond in tranquillity" prevents the universities' turn towards vulgarity. It can be said that these words are aimed exactly at the current situation of utilitarianism and the vulgarization of Chinese universities. As a cure for the problems of Chinese universities, it is undoubtedly fertile ground for the reconstruction of their cultural character.

Firstly, it is vital to use "people-orientedness" to cultivate the heart of the cultural character of Chinese universities. The Chinese classical philosophy of higher education emphasizes using people as the logical starting point, while Western higher education philosophy sees advanced knowledge as its logical starting point. This is the fundamental difference between ancient Chinese universities and Western universities since the Middle Ages. Therefore, the cultural character of Chinese universities is based on Chinese culture, by adhering to the people-oriented idea of Chinese classical higher education. Coupled with the impact of Western epistemology and the erosion of global utilitarianism since modern times, the return of Chinese universities to the people-oriented tradition seems even more valuable in a practical sense. Therefore, using "people-orientedness" to cultivate the heart of the cultural character of Chinese universities is the fundamental point of making Chinese universities "Chinese universities."

Secondly, it is vital to establish the cornerstone of the cultural character of Chinese universities with the idea of "building on humanities." Humanities are the main theme that runs through and supports Chinese classical higher education. As Qian Mu said, Chinese society gradually established the political system of the "literati-rule of the country" since the Qin and Han Dynasties. As part of the national cultural system, ancient Chinese higher education was indeed humanistic education. As Tu Youguang said: "The 'science' stage of Chinese higher education in the past 100 years was the denial of the 'humanities' stage of Chinese higher education over the previous 4500 years," but, "will the result of such a denial still be considered 'Chinese' higher education?"[31] From this perspective, if the cultural character of Chinese universities is the cultural character of "Chinese universities," it is correct to reconstruct the humanistic foundation of Chinese universities on the current occasion of humanistic traditions' revival.

Thirdly, growing the root of the cultural character of Chinese universities with the idea of "looking beyond in tranquillity." Ancient Chinese higher education has always had the tradition of "*Shi* shall not participate in trade," and it also saw countless hermits who refused to participate in politics. This was not the mainstream of ancient Chinese society, but it was an important feature of the "humanities" stage of Chinese higher education. In the century of Chinese universities, and the realistic situation of the marketization of higher education and administration of management of higher institutions, the dignity and duty of higher education had gradually faded. Against this backdrop, the value of "looking beyond in tranquillity" is contrary to the utilitarian values of Chinese universities. It has therefore become the main development trend of the cultural character of Chinese universities. Now it seems that it would be difficult for Chinese universities to uphold their essential identity themselves, without the university character of "looking beyond in tranquillity." Based on the above, the formation of an ideal cultural character of Chinese universities lies in the process of cultivating the heart, establishing the cornerstone, and growing the root of the cultural character of Chinese universities, and doing all on a realistic basis.

Finally, digging and confirming the high-quality cultural tradition that has not been effectively inherited since modern times is also the breakthrough point in the ideal construction of the cultural character of Chinese universities. Admittedly, it is of great value for us to use the historical experience and realistic development trends of the cultural character of Chinese universities since modern times as the ideal source of idea characters' reconstruction. Although, it may also inevitably limit our thinking. If the ideal cultural character of Chinese universities is to achieve the true ideal of "Chinese universities," it must not stop at the mere repetition of historical characteristics and the possible reiteration of reality. Instead, it should develop some cultural qualities that are above the hundred years of history and it should exceed the current reality. This requires that the cultural character of Chinese universities must be able to dig out some of the cultural resources with great practical value that is still almost lost in Chinese cultural relics. It is worth mentioning that the tradition of academy education is a kind of high-quality classical university education heritage that has been lost since the birth of modern Chinese universities. In the millennium history of Chinese universities, academy education has been abolished and promoted multiple times over a thousand years. However, in the process of the new-old changes during the eastward spreading of modern Western learning, the tradition of Chinese academy education disappeared within the century-old history of Chinese universities. If the abolition of the imperial examination system was purely a move of "abolishing the old," then the desolation of the academy system was more for the creation of a move of "establishing the new," and its occasionality outweighs its inevitability. Chen Pingyuan stated in *Zhongguo Daxue Bainian:*

> As Shu Xincheng, an education historian, put it, "No one who has participated in education reform since the twenty-fourth year of Guangxu has had a detailed attack or criticism on the academy system." The "abolishment of the old" of their time was mainly aimed at the imperial examination system. As for the pros and cons of various academies, they had no time to conduct further investigations. [...] As of the reason for not changing the academy system that has been followed for over a millennium, or letting the two co-exist, it is because the original money was supposed to be transferred to support the establishment of schools. By not seriously distinguishing the academy in front of our eyes and only talking about the "learning of previous generations" that is miles away, the reform of the school system since the late Qing Dynasty could merely "completely transplant the education system of the Western industrial society."[32]

Chinese universities were born in the demise of traditional academies, and the spirit of academies that have persisted in Chinese higher education for thousands of years was automatically hidden in the background of history. Objectively speaking, the spirit of the academy was not a concept that had completely disappeared in modern Chinese universities. Some specific characteristics of the cultural character of Chinese universities, such as "being inclusive to attain great achievements" and "the world being equally shared by all" can be explained with the spirit of traditional academies. However, it must be acknowledged that in modern times, Chinese universities have not been able to fully utilize and inherit the essence of Chinese academies.

Taking this as a point of inspiration, the ideal construction of the cultural character of Chinese universities must also be able to make up for the historical shortcomings, and the digging and confirming of the authentic value of the academy tradition are highly important points for this breakthrough. On the one hand, the academy culture has always been a Chinese tradition ever since ancient times, and it still exists today, even in its insignificance. On the other hand, today's traditional culture is showing signs of recovery in Chinese society, and this trend seems to be merely starting. Therefore, no matter in history or reality, it is a feasible idea to reshape the cultural character of Chinese universities today with the spirit of traditional academies.

3. The ideal cultural characters of Chinese universities

In the dual context of modernity and history, the ideal construction of Chinese universities' cultural character is not only necessary but also possible. How could a cultural character, as the subject of this ideal construction, become "ideal?"

The "ideal" character could be achieved by distinguishing the "good" aspects of Chinese culture from the "bad" ones, exploring the humanistic traditions embedded in ancient Chinese cultural classics, and deciding on their value orientation with realistic considerations.

An ideal character suitable for the modernization transformation of Chinese universities should not only include a sublation of Chinese culture but also have positive feedback with reality. It, therefore, covers multiple connotations such as the essential characteristics of the Way of ancient *Daxue,* the basic content of traditional Chinese humanistic knowledge, and the setting up of a foundation for the Chinese university model.

a) Ontology

Ontology is a prescriptive exposition of the nature of oneself, an explanation for the reasons why things exist. Chinese classical higher education philosophy was quite different from Western education philosophy. Unlike Western higher education philosophy that emphasizes epistemology and political theory, "the tradition of Chinese universities can be summarized as enlightenment theory or positional education theory," the fundamental difference between the two is that "it (Chinese higher education philosophy) is based on the self-improvement of human nature, and requires internal transcendence to drive external expressions."[33] It could be said that a core concept in Chinese classical higher education philosophy is the "people" or the "self," which is also part of its fundamental value. The cultural character of Chinese universities is essentially based on Chinese classical higher education philosophy. Therefore, if modern Chinese universities cannot inherit this basic traditional value, it is difficult to claim that they possess the cultural characters of Chinese universities. From this point of view, the ideal Chinese university cultural characters should essentially be a series of good Chinese *daxue* qualities that are built around this fundamental value.

From a traditional cultural perspective, what are the good qualities of Chinese *daxue?* The way of ancient *daxue – Ming Mingde, Xinmin* and *Zhiyu Zhishan* – as the basic laws and highest ideals of Chinese classical higher education, undoubtedly depict the core qualities of ancient Chinese universities. Since the birth of modern Chinese universities, the question of whether and how the ancient way of *daxue* could be applied to the modern university system has aroused reflections throughout academia. So far, there are two basic stands. The first stand is that, "Over two thousand years ago, the main purpose of *daxue* was to cultivate people. While now, universities not only cultivate people but also conduct academic studies. Only by proposing a new 'way of the university' could a scientific answer regarding the nature and university-running pattern of today's university be proposed. At first glance, this new 'way of the university' could be expressed as 'the way of the university that lies in the illustration of illustrious virtue, the advocation of learning, the intimacy with people, the renewal of people, the diversity, the excellence, and the pursuit of absolute perfection.' There are both inheritance and innovation."[34] Another stand states that "Chinese universities are basically in line with Western universities. However, they are moving towards another extreme. Humanities are gradually marginalized." That is, it was turned from "illustrating illustrious virtue and pursuing absolute perfection" to "illustrating rationality, that is, the rationality of science and new knowledge; and pursuing absolute truth." "Now the university has become a university that only seeks knowledge and truth, rather than a *daxue* that pursues the realm of beauty and goodness and the principle of being human. Although they have attained great achievements, it has lost its soul. The ancient Chinese 'way of daxue' cannot be abandoned."[35] The affirmative attitudes of the two viewpoints of the way of ancient Chinese universities are the same, but the difference is that the former emphasizes innovation while the latter pays more attention to the strengthening of their foundation. As far as the current status of Chinese universities is concerned, the present study believes that the strengthening of the foundation seems to be more important than innovation. As Irving Babbitt believed, the main purpose of university education is not to encourage innovation and independent thinking that people often say, but to reflect "conservative and unity factors in national life."[36] What Chinese universities urgently need is not the innovation of tradition, either. Perhaps it is most important to understand and inherit the true connotation of tradition.

In fact, the fundamental reason why Chinese universities are so easily polarized to become "soulless" on the path of innovation is the lack of faith in the traditional Chinese way of *daxue*. As the essence of Chinese cultural tradition, "the way of the university" is not only a philosophy of higher education institutions but also a philosophy of life and morality. This means that the ideal Chinese university's cultural character not only runs a higher education institution but also enlightens and shapes an ideal good or kind person. In this sense, the ideal construction of Chinese university's cultural characters could only reflect the people-orientedness of Chinese classical higher education and find out what it is when it returns to the "way of the university." In his article *Cong Wenhua Kan Fuxing Jueqi (Renaissance and Rise from the Perspective of Culture),* Luo Zhitian once mentioned such a viewpoint, "For some time, everyone is concerned about the 'rising of great powers' in Europe and the United States. In fact, the more suitable Western historical experience that we are supposed to be looking at is probably their Renaissance."[37] Similarly, perhaps the revival of classical higher education tradition is the most valuable for the rise of Chinese universities. Therefore, the cultural characters of Chinese universities is a proposition to revive the traditional values of Chinese higher education on the ontological level. That is, to adhere to the core concept of rejuvenating the Chinese *daxue* way of *Ming Mingde, Xinmin,* and *Zhiyu Zhishan,* covering ethics, politics, and pedagogy and multiple other Chinese classical philosophical values.

b) Knowledge Theory

In terms of knowledge type, classical humanistic knowledge is undoubtedly a significant characteristic of the cultural character of Chinese universities. Webber once defined the *Shi* (scholar-official) in traditional Chinese society as "*Shi* who had been through humanistic education" or "*Shi* who had been through humanistic education and examinations."[38] Historically, Chinese classical higher education has taken humanistic knowledge as its main content and regarded studying Confucian classics as the most basic educational method. Its fundamental purpose was to cultivate the *Shi* that a was government ruled by the needed culture. With the disintegration of the traditional political order in modern times, China's higher education began to change from classics to science and entered the "science" stage of higher education, yet the "humanities" tradition has still always existed. According to Ji Xianlin, "In terms of the traditional influence and future development of Peking University, literature, history and philosophy should be the most protected and valued, because humanities discipline represented by literature, history, and philosophy was not only the lifeblood of national cultural heritage but also, more importantly, the source of social value guidance."[39] From this perspective, humanistic knowledge is an important aspect of the cultural character of Chinese universities. The ideal Chinese university's cultural character should be based on the excellent Chinese classical humanistic knowledge, and feature itself in the revival of the Chinese humanistic tradition.

Traditions are fading away and so are the master scholars. For Chinese universities to revive the Chinese humanistic tradition, ancient classics carrying ancient text would undoubtedly become their only practical reference. Because "excellent classical literature always resorts to our higher rationality and imagination, forming the purest classical spirit to serve higher rationality, it leads us to a religious-like purpose and closely integrates with the one and only true self that hides within us and tunes up with Heaven and Earth."[40] This is a state where the so-called scientific works cannot reach, and it is also the fundamental reason for moral weakness in the age of science. Returning to ancient classics is the inevitable path for Chinese universities to reshape their humanistic character. From the perspective of the classification of traditional knowledge, classical Chinese philosophy and historical studies are indispensable within the knowledge system of Chinese university's cultural character. Furthermore, Chinese studies conducted by Republican Chinese master scholars are also of great reference significance. We could grasp some classic texts in Chinese culture from Liu Mengxi's advocation of reading classics:

> Philosophy is basically about the works of pre-Qin scholars. The most important ones are Confucius, Mencius, Laozi, and Zhuangzi. As of Xunzi, Mozi, Hanfei Zi, and Gongsun Longzi, their works could be left aside as of now. Even Mencius is not necessary to read. However, there are two articles in Liji of the Han dynasty that must be read: *Zhongyong* and *Daxue* [...] No matter who the author is, the explanations and interpretations of Confucian thought in these two articles are most explicit, which provides a well-written outline of Confucianism.
>
> In terms of historiography, literary and historical scholars study the "first four official histories," *namely Shiji (Records of the Grand Historian), Qian Hanshu (Book of Han), Hou Hanshu (Book of Later Han), and Sanguo Zhi (Records of the Three Kingdoms). Shiji* alone would suffice for casual reading. It is not only historical but also literary. The historical figures were well constructed, with a beautiful writing style. If you could learn *Shiji* by heart, you would get familiar with Chinese history, culture, characters, and political systems – kill multiple birds with one stone. Also, in the late Qing and early Republican Chinese period, works completed by 20th-century master scholars in the field of literature and history could also be regarded as classics, such as Yan Fu, Zhang Taiyan, Liang Qichao, Cai Yuanpei, Wang Guowei, Tschen Yin-koh and Ma Yifu's books. It would be a great loss if their books were left unread. The works written by master scholars in the 20th century are in fact a bridge, and possibly a shortcut, for us to approach ancient classics.[41]

From the perspective of the intrinsic value of knowledge, there are three basic points of traditional humanistic classics: moral standard, humanistic spirit, and the tradition of scholar-officials. Their essence lies not within the reading of traditional classics, but the absorption and inheritance of their spiritual connotations. Since modern times, with the abolition of the imperial examination system and the infiltration of Western scientific values, the classics listed above have been neglected and deemed as useless studies in Chinese universities. The traditional spirit of Chinese universities has declined.

Therefore, from the perspective of knowledge theory, the ideal Chinese universities' cultural character lies within the return to classics, and the re-cultivation of the traditional morality, as well as the humanistic and *Shi* spirit of Chinese *daxue* through the revival of humanistic education.

c) Axiology

The practical value of Chinese university cultural character is mainly manifested in two aspects. In terms of Chinese culture, the ideal cultural character of Chinese universities is the identification and re-confirmation of China's high-quality cultural tradition, which leads on to the path of Chinese culture's revival. In terms of universities, their ideal cultural character lies in the building of an ideal Chinese university model based on Chinese culture. The latter is the fundamental interest of the present book's study of the cultural character of Chinese universities. Based on the historical characteristics of the cultural character of Chinese universities, their development could also be divided into four stages, representing four different Chinese university models.

The first stage is "universities with Chinese style." This refers to the Chinese university's model of development from its birth to the demise of the Qing dynasty. During this period, Chinese universities were mainly designed to safeguard the late Qing regime. Under the control of late-Qing scholar-officials, Chinese universities had the most distinctive cultural character, which was mainly characterized by being loyal to the emperor and being respectful to Confucius. As well as excelling in academics to enter officialdom, and keeping a "Confucian-centric" stand. The present book calls this model "universities with Chinese style," signifying that they were universities of traditional Chinese society, with "integration of learning and officialdom" as their basic value-orientation.

The second stage is "universities of China." This refers to the model of development of Chinese universities across the whole of Republican China. This period was hailed as the golden age of Chinese universities. Under the leadership of Republican Chinese university presidents, the cultural character of Chinese universities showed a relatively good development trend in the conflict and integration of Chinese and Western cultures. It was characterized by "bearing the utmost with virtues," "being inclusive to attain great achievements," "practicing both idealism and realism" and "sharing the world equally with all." The present book calls this model "universities of China," signifying that it was a relatively more successful model. The universities were oriented around the values of the traditional Chinese "way of *daxue*," especially "illustrating illustrious virtues" and "renewing the people."

The third stage was "universities with Chinese characteristics." This refers to the development model of Chinese universities during the Seventeen Years. During this period, the development of Chinese universities hit rock bottom. Due to the forceful intervention of political power, the revolutionary character and politics of Chinese universities' cultural character were prominent. Its main characteristics were being people-oriented, party-ruled, and undergoing an ideology revolution. The present book calls this model "universities with Chinese characters," signifying that the value-orientation of Chinese universities during this era lies fundamentally in political values.

The fourth stage is the "Chinese model of the university." It refers to a possible model that has been brewing and developing in Chinese universities since the Reform and Opening Up. For now, on the one hand, Chinese universities have shown a relatively favorable development trend, which is evidenced by cultural qualities such as "people-orientedness," "building on humanities", and "looking beyond in tranquillity." On the other hand, Chinese universities still regard "integration of learning and officialdom" as their internal principle, demonstrating serious administrative and politics-centric tendencies. Therefore, at present, Chinese universities are in the transitional stage from "universities with Chinese characters" to the "Chinese model of the university."

In short, no matter what kind of labels are attached to Chinese universities, we must recognize the importance of Chinese cultural traditions to Chinese universities and the uniqueness of Chinese universities' cultural character at all their stages. At the same time, no matter what reasonable explanation we make for the cultural character of Chinese universities, we must realize that China has not yet formed a real Chinese university model. Transcending beyond history and reality, the value of the ideal Chinese university cultural character lies in the construction of the "Chinese model of the university," a model that is really "Chinese." At present, the academic discussions on the Chinese university model are mainly based on the cultural perspective, demonstrating two basic orientations.

Scholars who emphasize China's fine cultural traditions tend to assume that the Chinese university model possibly exists based on good Chinese cultural traditions. For example, Canadian scholar Hayhoe was one of the first scholars who linked Chinese universities with Chinese culture and put forward the proposition of the "Chinese model of the university." According to Hayhoe's explanation, the so-called "Chinese model of the university" needs to build on the criticism and reflection of Western universities, it needs to learn from the wisdom of Chinese civilization, achieve dialogues between civilizations and focus on promoting Chinese culture. Another example is the two propositions brought up by Tu Youguang in his book *Wenming Bentuhua Yu Daxue (The Localization of Civilizations and the Universities)*: "A university in China" and "a university of China."[42] The latter is a positive concept of Chinese universities characterized by Chinese culture. Second, are the scholars who emphasize the negative characteristics of Chinese culture and are more inclined to summarize the Chinese university model as a historical or realistic factual existence under the influence of negative cultural traditions. As Wang Jianhua mentioned in the article *Cong Zhongguoshi Daxue Dao Daxue De Zhongguo Moshi (From Universities with Chinese Style to a Chinese model of university)*, the concept of "universities with Chinese style" not only represents the form of higher education institutions or forms of organization in ancient China but also specifically refers to modern Chinese unit system of universities. Besides, there are some studies of the Chinese model of the university outside the cultural horizon. For example, in the article *Gaodeng Jiaoyu De Zhongguo Moshi: Laizi Riben De Guancha (Chinese Model of Higher Education: An Observation from Japan)*, Japanese scholar Motohisa Kaneko put forward the "Chinese Model of Higher Education Development," which mainly pointed to the development characteristics of China's higher education marketization and transformation to the unit system.

In a nutshell, there are positive and negative value divisions in the research of the Chinese model of the university. Any definition or name is a special concept that requires the author's targeted interpretation. The terms "universities with Chinese style, "universities of China" and "Chinese model of the university" defined in this book share degrees of similarity with the concepts mentioned by the aforementioned scholars. These include the negative cultural standpoint of "universities with Chinese style" and the positive cultural interpretation of "universities of China" and "Chinese model of the university." However, their differences are also prominent. Fundamentally, the four concepts mentioned in this book regarding the Chinese models of the university are mainly based on the historical research conducted in the previous chapters on the cultural character of Chinese universities. Each concept is based on a specific historical background and it echoes with the specific characteristics and unique formation mechanisms. Among them, the "Chinese model of the university" is a future model for the development of Chinese universities. It is a modern interpretation and ideal design based on the historical experience of the cultural character of Chinese universities. Of course, the ideal Chinese university model does not only mean maintaining a positive and firm Chinese cultural position in the cultural character of Chinese universities. History has proven that if there are no scholars who believe in Chinese culture, no university that establishes itself based on culture, or no open-minded government, then an ideal Chinese university cultural character would not be formed. Nor would there be talk about the realization of any form of the real Chinese model of the university. This involves the formation logic of the ideal cultural character of Chinese universities.

Section 3: The Formation Logic of Ideal Chinese Universities' Cultural Character

In theory, the ideal cultural character of a Chinese university should be a collection of good Chinese cultural traits, with idealized characteristics that transcend history and reality. In reality, the cultural character of Chinese universities could never achieve an optimum state, but it is still possible for it to obtain a good cultural character to the greatest possible extent.

Hence, how can one obtain or get as close as possible to an ideal Chinese university's cultural character? The answer includes some basic issues such as the university's key influencing factors, the ideal behavior of each factor, and their interrelationships. Over twenty years ago, American scholar Henry Eskowitz and others had introduced the innovation of biological principles into the field of social innovation. From the perspective of society, politics, and science, the key factors influencing social innovation were all comprehensively proposed. The three-in-one innovation strategy of "university-industry-government" was called the "triple helix model of innovation." The theory was mainly aimed at the weak research and development capabilities of enterprises, the serious disconnect between industry and education, the deviation from the reality of tertiary education, the lack of communication between university enterprises. It aimed to promote the effective interaction between the government, industry, and academia. As a unique innovation model, it not only emphasized the close cooperation and interaction among the university, industry, and government in the innovation process but also required each party to maintain its own independent identity. Summarizing the key factors that comprehensively affect the cultural character of Chinese universities, which are universities, scholars, and the government, and by applying Etskowitz's "triple helix" principle of social innovation to the study of Chinese universities' cultural character, we could see that the construction model of Chinese universities' cultural character could also be interpreted as a "triple helix" with "university-scholar-government" idea at its core. This is essentially a theme of the times in which Chinese universities rely on the scholars and the government to revive traditional culture in Chinese universities.

1. What kind of scholars are needed to form the ideal cultural character of Chinese universities?

Scholars are the lifeblood in the formation and development of Chinese universities' cultural character. Succeeding the late Qing scholar-officials, Republican Chinese intellectuals created the miracle of Chinese universities during the war years. They leveraged their dominance in Chinese universities and shaped their ideal character. However, after the founding of the People's Republic of China, an unprecedented ideological revolution forced the traditional intellectuals out of the stage. Since the Reform and Opening Up, new intellectuals have begun to rise, and to a certain extent, they have led a better trend for the development of Chinese universities' cultural character. But on the other hand, "the role of intellectuals in the information age has become more obscure (even messed-up): entertainment, politicization, commercialization. [...] They stray farther and farther from the social expectations and intellectual conducts they should bear."[43] This is contrary to the spiritual connotation of new intellectuals as cultural inheritors. Based on the consideration of history and reality, the formation of Chinese universities' cultural character requires a group of pure intellectuals who, on the one hand, believe in the Chinese culture, possess outstanding Chinese studies knowledge, and inherit Chinese culture. On the other hand, those that treat scholarship as their duty, distinguish themselves from government officials or enterprise beneficiaries and act as the "balancers" of the relationship between the government and the universities.

a) The inheritors of Chinese culture

Whether the intellectuals, as the main inheritors of Chinese culture and the main body of Chinese universities, could establish the foundation of Chinese universities based on Chinese culture, is very important for the formation of Chinese university cultural character. Taking Chinese culture as the core concept, intellectuals should possess the following basic qualities for the formation of Chinese universities' cultural character.

First, is a high degree of cultural self-awareness. A prerequisite for the formation of Chinese universities' cultural character is the spread of Chinese culture. "However, a necessary condition for the spread of tradition is that this tradition could gain wide support from society. It would inevitably weaken the extent to which the traditions are supported by the masses if the elites of this society stand up together to oppose their own cultural traditions."[44] The May Fourth Movement is an obvious example. Without support from the intellectuals, Chinese culture would inevitably decline. This also implies that the formation of the Chinese universities' cultural character relies on the intellectuals who drive the masses together and enlighten society by passing down culture. As a practical subject in the formation of the cultural character of Chinese universities, the precondition for intellectuals to exert their driving force on society is the fact that they possess a high degree of cultural self-awareness. The so-called cultural self-awareness is not only a simple identification of certain abstract cultural principles but also a deep understanding of Chinese culture based on historical traditions. It is this high degree of cultural self-awareness that injects a near-religious belief that is sufficient to compete with any historical nihilism in the spread of the good Chinese cultural traditions. Just like "the Long march – the Communists would not have survived if they did not have a belief."[45] History proved that if Chinese culture cannot truly penetrate the hearts of the intellectuals and become part of their beliefs in life, the fine traditions of Chinese culture could not be further passed on. Without the spiritual advocation of intellectuals, it would be hard for the cultural character of Chinese universities to form.

Second, rational cultural consciousness. Modern society needs cultural beliefs, while in the era of faith, rational checks and balances are necessary. Rational cultural consciousness and value of choice is an inherent prerequisite for the intellectuals to transmit culture. Judging from previous historical experience, neither excessive cultural criticism nor absolute cultural loyalty from the intellectuals could be considered a rational way for China's rising and cultural renaissance. Especially as evidenced by the extreme attitude of the May Fourth Intellectuals and late Qing scholar-officials towards Chinese culture, irrational emotional impulses could not alter the fate of Chinese culture's decline. From the cultural upsurge in the 1980s to the contemporary Chinese studies fever, the revival of Chinese culture has become a general trend. This means that the revival of Chinese culture in Chinese universities is no longer a yes-or-no matter. The key to the problem is the method of making cultural judgments and choices in this revival of culture. As far as the formation of Chinese university cultural character is concerned, intellectuals, as the internal driving force in the development of Chinese universities' cultural character, are not only inheritors of traditions, but also rational analysts and transmitters of traditions. They should fully excavate and acknowledge the good aspects of Chinese culture, while at the same time resolutely abandon and play down the negative Chinese cultural traditions.

Third, the excellent cultivation of tradition. The May Fourth Movement and the decade of the Cultural Revolution were both regarded as turning points in traditional Chinese culture. However, there is a fundamental difference in terms of the anti-traditional nature of the two. The former was mostly caused by "angered intellectuals," while the latter was a pure "destruction of tradition by the ignorant."[46] The decade of the Cultural Revolution caused unprecedented destruction of Chinese culture. This was in large part due to the Red Guards' ignorance of traditional culture. In contrast, would Republican Chinese intellectuals who have been indulged in traditional culture from their childhood ever give up on their belief in Chinese culture, even under intense political pressure? The lack of mastering traditional knowledge and its cultivation and the dominance of political ideology were crucial factors in the decline of modern Chinese culture, which has also become the most critical factor affecting the formation of Chinese universities' cultural character. Therefore, in the revival of Chinese culture today, cultural inheritors' good cultural cultivations are especially necessary. One must first be a master of tradition to gain real Chinese cultural consciousness. Only then would they become a rational critic of Chinese culture. In the traditional sense, intellectuals were the so-called scholars, therefore, the new generation of intellectuals should be able to read the classics for self-cultivation. Naturally, Chinese cultural classics are mostly about life philosophy and spiritual pursuit, they focus on establishing morality and cultivating oneself. Content-wise, the basic content of Chinese cultural classics is humanistic knowledge, stressing humanistic literacy rather than technological skills. Function-wise, a political consciousness that asks one to shoulder the world as one's responsibility permeates Chinese cultural classics, rendering self-cultivation and the betterment of the country as the life pursuit of ancient scholars. In this sense, aspiring in scholarship, intellectuals' acquisition of cultural literacy is mainly a process of enhancing personal moral quality, humanistic accomplishment, and political responsibility.

Finally, is a broad cultural horizon. The study of the cultural character of Chinese universities contains a proposition regarding the balance between Chinese and Western culture. Whether the proportion of Chinese and Western culture could be effectively adjusted in Chinese universities is an important factor that affects the ideal construction of Chinese universities' cultural character. This requires that the intellectuals, as inheritors of the cultural character of Chinese universities, not only have profound cultivation in Chinese culture but also possess broad cultural horizons to maintain a dynamic balance between Chinese and Western cultures. Some scholars believe that by tuning up with the world, the already scarred Chinese culture has suffered a whole new kind of damage.

In fact, Western culture is also the best reference for Chinese cultural consciousness. It could prompt intellectuals to liberate themselves from the cultural box that confines them. Taking this analysis even further, a broad cultural horizon is required not only because Chinese culture needs to be further inspired in the process of self-criticism and value clarification through the comparison with Western culture. At the same time, it also implies that Chinese culture, as the basic prerequisite for Chinese universities has to maintain the nature of its cultural character in the increasingly open dialogue between different cultures in the world. This would further strengthen it. "Cultural tradition is, in fact, the root of a nation's growth. For the intellectuals who bear the mission of inheriting cultural traditions, only when they adopt a national and cultural standpoint could they rejuvenate their spirit, maintain their weight in the fierce conflict between Eastern and Western culture and remain as an equal entity in the dialogue between world cultures."[47] From this perspective, the intellectuals must adhere to the stand of Chinese culture in a broad cultural horizon, so that Chinese universities' cultural character could be formed in a relatively balanced cultural environment.

b) The balance between the university and the government

The relationship between the university and the government plays an important role in Chinese universities' cultural character formation field. The key issue is, in the formation of Chinese universities' cultural character, what are the qualities that intellectuals should possess, or what are the roles they should play in the relationship between the universities and the government? Specifically, as a balancer between the university and the government, the function of intellectuals is mainly manifested in the following two aspects.

On the one hand, intellectuals' personalities should be independent, ones that transcend utilitarianism. They need to especially maintain a certain degree of independent spirit when it comes to politics. Some scholars pointed out, "In the 60 years since the founding of the People's Republic of China, intellectuals in academia have suffered two major shocks in terms of academics and morals: the continuous ideological and political movements before the Reform and Opening Up have generally impaired their academic character and moral dignity; and after the Reform and Opening Up, especially after the implementation of the market economy system, under the pressure of knowledge specialization and marketization, the professional conduct of intellectuals has been widely questioned and criticized both within and from the outside of the system."[48] In the decline of the role of intellectuals, external pressure plays an important part, but intellectuals themselves could also be blamed. In many cases, the loss of independence of the new generation of intellectuals is entirely their own self-determined and voluntary self-destruction. Looking throughout the history of the development of Chinese universities' cultural character, whenever intellectuals respected themselves, the cultural character would develop in an ideal manner. While whenever the intellectuals succumbed to power, conspiracy, and the market and submerged self-consciousness in utilitarian thoughts, the cultural character would decline. It is true that in a real society, it is difficult for intellectuals to separate themselves from socio-economics and politics. This is especially so because of individuals' strong political complex, and this is further strengthened by the absolute power of the government over intellectuals. It could be said that the relationship between Chinese intellectuals and politics is very special and unique. However, even if in reality what Hayhoe called the "eclectic freedom"[49] could be obtained, the spiritual independence and self-esteem are still worth defending, because this relative spiritual independence could at least guarantee that the cultural spirit of intellectuals themselves would continue.

On the other hand, intellectuals should also be the balancers between the university and the government. Whether the relationship between the university and the government can be effectively balanced is an important factor that affects the formation of Chinese universities' cultural character. According to historical experiences, only in the relatively balanced relationship between the university and the government can Chinese universities be respected by the government and gain relative freedom, which is crucial to the formation of the ideal Chinese universities' cultural character. Intellectuals standing between the university and the government are an important force in balancing the relationship between the two. Republican Chinese intellectuals demonstrated an illustrious effort in terms of coordinating the relationship between Chinese universities and the government. Xie Yong pointed out in the article *1949 Nian Qian Zhongguo Guoli Daxue Xiaozhang Yu Zhengfu De Guanxi (Relationship between the President of the National Universities of China and the Government before 1949):* "Before 1949, China experienced an era of great upheaval, with only pockets of stability. In this era, in addition to external problems, there are also constant internal disputes. It is not easy for China's higher education to develop in this era. This result was caused by the joint efforts of Chinese intellectuals, as well as the balance between the government and the universities, maintained by the presidents of Chinese national universities."[50] In a sense, it is precisely because of the balanced relationship between the university and the government that the intellectuals strived to maintain that the cultural character of the Republican Chinese universities demonstrated a relatively ideal status. Republican Chinese intellectuals managed to become the buffer between universities and the government largely because of their unique position – they relied on politics while basing universities. Since the founding of the People's Republic of China, due to the serious administrative levels of Chinese universities, the role of intellectuals as a balancer between universities and government has been greatly weakened. Over-obedience to political power made intellectuals diverge further away from the spiritual tradition of relying on politics and aspiring to academics. In the Seventeen Years, intellectuals were forcedly controlled by ideology. They did not enjoy the actual right to voice their thoughts, and therefore could assume the responsibility of coordination. In comparison, since the Reform and Opening Up, the administrative levels of intellectuals has become a major hindrance in them playing the role of balancers. Therefore, coordinating the relationship between the universities and the government under their dual identities, politics, and academia has become a more challenging task of the times.

2. *What kind of universities are needed to form the ideal cultural character of Chinese universities?*

More than ten years ago, Hayhoe pointed out that China can develop market-oriented higher education with serious polarization. The majors and courses offered would directly serve the economy, but it is far from enough to promote social change and cultural development.[51] This is in tune with Motohisa Kaneko's definition of China's higher education marketization development model. The practice has proved that what is needed for the formation of the cultural character of Chinese universities is not a so-called enterprise university or research university oriented by economy or market, but a social-cultural university. As some scholars have said, universities must always give society something that is not what it wants, but what it needs.[52] From a cultural point of view, if a Chinese university wants to become a university needed by society, it must be based on social-cultural value orientation.

a) Chinese university as a cultural entity

Liang Baoguo pointed out in the article *Da Wenhua Shi Daxue Fazhan De Zhexue Jichu (Big culture is the philosophical foundation of university development):* "The 21st century is the era of big culture. Being a part of the big culture, the universities, therefore, have big cultural concepts and a big cultural vision." He further pointed out that "universities of the 21st century would have big culture as their philosophical foundation and support the latest development of society."[53] Hou Dingkai wrote in the preface of *Zhongguo Daxue De Lixing Zhilu (The Rational Road of Chinese University):* "Only when we regard the university as a cultural being, rather than a political or economic being could we touch the essence of the universities – their openness, independence, and tolerance are all derived from their cultural genes."[54] The cultural positioning and interpretation of universities have become a common consensus in academia. A basic premise for the formation of the cultural character of Chinese universities is their cultural positioning. To build a "social-cultural university," the focus of this book is the question of how, as the main body of Chinese cultural character construction, should Chinese universities create the necessary conditions for the formation of the ideal Chinese universities' cultural character.

First, they must establish a university concept based on Chinese culture. The ideal construction of the cultural character of Chinese universities is inseparable from the support of Chinese universities. The establishment of a university concept based on Chinese culture at the university's institution level is of the utmost importance. "It is true that the times and society do change. Whenever the society and the culture change, the status and nature of the university would be affected, so would our opinions and expectations of universities. However, on the other hand, some of the basic ideas that the sages and philosophers bore regarding the universities... were the living source for the university today, and the conceptual force that continues to shape the character of the universities."[55] From this perspective, it is understood that the excellent cultural traditions leftover from ancient China would never be outdated for contemporary Chinese universities, and they would still have fundamental value in shaping the concept of Chinese universities. According to Wang Jisheng, "The idea of a university as a conceptual system is deeply rooted in the soil of national culture. The development of the idea of a university in China was based on the educational idea of the ethics- and moral-centric Confucianism, while also absorbing the Western university concept of 'emphasizing on rationality and academic freedom,' which strives to explore the concept of socialist education with Chinese characteristics, and takes the road of 'using the excellent culture of the Chinese nation as the main subject of the development of Chinese and Western innovation and harmonious development.'"[56] Chinese university, as a cultural entity, is fundamentally based on Chinese culture. And hence, a reliable habitat must be established for the ideal cultural character of Chinese universities.

Second, the institutionalization of high-quality Chinese university culture and building a university system with Chinese characteristics must be completed. The construction of a modern Chinese university system is a core issue in the reform and development of Chinese universities. Any kind of cultural character of Chinese universities that embodies the national characteristics and development logic would need a matching university system. Most of the high-quality concepts about the cultural character of Chinese universities are generated among intellectuals. These ideas would probably disappear if they were not supported or acknowledged by the universities on the institutional level. The ideological trend of humanistic education in Huazhong Technological University in the last century succeeded and generated a wide impact that was so large because of the university's top-down institutional support. As mentioned above, since the Reform and Opening Up, the cultural character of Chinese universities has shown a development trend characterized by people-orientedness, building on humanities, and looking beyond in tranquillity under the influence of intellectuals. However, on the other hand, these good ideas are theories. The level has gradually matured, but due to the lack of systematic institutional cooperation, it has not yet become a generally binding value and behavior program for Chinese universities. It is indeed true that the brewing and initial formation of Chinese universities' cultural character starts with a bottom-up theoretical and ideological construction, yet its final formation cannot be completed without top-down institutional support. Referring back to historical experiences, we could see that a lack of institutionalization could lead to the self-disintegration of an ideal cultural character. The development of the cultural character of Chinese universities is currently in a critical period. It would either stay within the discourse space of the scholars and eventually disappear over time, or be legalized by the universities' institutional guarantee and become the program of the behavior of Chinese universities. From this perspective, it is a decisive factor that the high-quality characteristics of the cultural character of Chinese universities have already started institutionalization steps as soon as possible. Also, this is the only way to imbue practical significance in the ideal trend of Chinese universities' cultural character.

b) Chinese university as a collection of scholars

The universities and intellectuals are interdependent within the institution of the university. According to Jaspers, the character of a university depends on its professors. Each university has to rely on the kind of people it recruits.[57] On the other hand, the fact is that scholars also rely on universities to survive. Without the support of universities, it is difficult for scholars to work alone. This is also a key point in the formation of Chinese universities' cultural character. In particular, the formation of Chinese universities' cultural character depends not only on talented scholars but also on the universities, which provide the necessary support for intellectuals. Therefore, Chinese universities should meet at least the following two requirements. First, the universities must respect intellectuals. Their attitude directly decides what role the intellectuals can play in the formation of Chinese universities' cultural character. Intellectuals hold the lifeblood of Chinese culture. In a sense, they are a symbol of culture and morality, and they are the theoretical source and practical subject of the construction of Chinese universities' cultural character. Therefore, scholars cultivated within Chinese culture could only be nurtured when the universities show enough respect to the intellectuals and provide them with free leisure space for academic activities. In contrast, without the support and respect from the university, especially in terms of institutionalized acknowledgment, it would be impossible for scholars to make a difference in the practice of Chinese universities' cultural character, no matter how talented they were. Second, universities should endow and protect intellectuals' due rights as much as possible. Intellectuals bear the responsibilities and obligations of the theoretical and practical construction of the cultural character of Chinese universities. Correspondingly, they must have certain rights and freedom. In practice, intellectuals' cultural stand cannot always be consistent with the consciousness of the government. Therefore, situations of conflict between the inherent formation pattern of Chinese universities' cultural character and some government policies would still arise. This requires that universities, as the place that sustains the intellectuals' existence, must not only give intellectuals their due rights within their authority but also strive to adhere to and protect the legitimate rights of intellectuals. And the universities need to be courageous in resolving the external environmental pressure with a firm Chinese cultural position and long-term vision to ensure that the rights of intellectuals are not threatened and persecuted under the temptation and pressure of economy and politics. Only in this way can we ensure that intellectuals play the most effective role in the construction of Chinese universities' cultural character.'

c) Chinese university as the coordinator between the government and the scholars

Intellectuals often have conflicts with the government's policy orientation. It is an important mission of universities to coordinate the conflicts between the two parties. From this point of view, the special connotations of Chinese universities are:

On one hand, Chinese universities should have their basic standpoints as universities. In particular, they should maintain political independence. There are two propositions as to why universities are "universities." The first proposition is: What is a university? That is, what is the nature of a university? According to Jacques Derrida, unlike other types of research institutions, universities, in principle (though not entirely), should be the place where questions like truth, the nature of people, humans, and the history of the human form could be raised independently and unconditionally. That is, "It is a place where everything can be challenged unconditionally and different ideas can be raised."[58] It could be said that the independence and freedom of thought of the universities are fundamental to their existence. The second proposition is: What do universities do? That is the function of the universities. Historically, "Whether before or after the emergence of a nation-state, an important task of the universities is to protect the universal culture and spirit. The preservation of culture is indefinite and non-utilitarian – neither the standards of politicians nor the standards of ordinary people are sufficient as a basis for judging whether a culture needs to be preserved. The respect for tradition can even exceed political interests."[59] From this point of view, for a university to be a "university," it has to be a place of cultural preservation rather than a vassal for politics. The relationship between universities and politics is indeed particularly complicated in China. But in any case, the fundamental precondition for the relationship between Chinese universities and the government must be the recognition of the independence of Chinese universities. A university without a spiritual backbone could only act as the government's follower, not a coordinator between the government and the intellectuals.

On the other hand, with independence as a precondition, Chinese universities are the coordinators of the relationship between the government and intellectuals. The game between the intellectuals and the government has always been one of the most complex factors in the development of Chinese universities, even before the founding of the PRC, when the two parties cooperated most of the time, to when the PRC was just founded when the conflict between the two parties reached its peak. As an independent educational institution, the university stands between the intellectuals and the government. It should not only listen to the voices of intellectuals and avoid becoming the government's microphone but also respect and understand the government so that it would not be used by intellectuals with mal-intent. However, in the real context of China, the plight of universities as the coordinator between the government and the intellectuals is obvious: First, the government exerts a strong restraining force on intellectuals, and intellectuals have long been weak in their relationship with the government. The second is that Chinese universities are dominated by politics, thus have limited rights and freedoms. However, just as absolute freedom does not exist, Chinese universities are never absolutely "unfree." Certain realistic effects of certain functions of the universities might be hindered by external pressures and obstacles, but the responsibilities of the universities and the intellectuals cannot be denied.

According to some scholars, "Universities are allowed to have academic freedom because society believes the university is honest and self-disciplined, as well as that the scholars in the universities are soberer, more conscious and have broader horizons than their ordinary contemporaries. Therefore, before accepting the trust and power given to the university by the society, the university needs to prove its moral credibility!"[60] In this sense, the coordinator function of the universities depends on whether it can maintain its moral integrity. Only in this way can the university gain the trust of the society and obtain more freedom, to shoulder the responsibility as a coordinator in the formation of Chinese universities' cultural characters.

3. *The government's role in the formation of the ideal cultural character of Chinese universities*

The rise of intellectuals and the independence of universities are the key elements of the ideal construction of Chinese universities' cultural character. Whether these elements can be effective also depends on the government's attitude or degree of respect for the intellectuals and the universities.

First, the government should respect the intellectuals and ensure their dominance in Chinese universities. There is a paradox in the revival of Chinese culture regarding the government. On the one hand, the government supports and encourages the revival of Chinese culture so much that it listed it as a national policy of China's revival. However, on the other hand, the government distrusts and applies many institutional restrictions on the main inheritors of Chinese cultural traditions – the intellectuals. In the current university system, "Many university presidents in China have been included in the administrative hierarchy, some with very high official positions. However, many of them are unwilling to address or see themselves as "government officials." This is probably a great uniqueness of Chinese universities. But in any case, the actual role of government officials still constrains the presidents' behavior to a large extent and affects the public image of this profession."[61]

This makes us worry about how effective the intellectuals of Chinese universities would be in the transmission of Chinese university culture when they are forced or even actively involved in politics. In the revival of Chinese culture in Chinese society, especially in Chinese universities, the question of how should the government deal with the relationship between intellectuals has become a key issue. Ultimately, full respect and trust in intellectuals is a basic precondition. According to Tu Youguang, during the Prosperity of Zhengguan (The Reign of Emperor Taizong of Tang), the reason why Confucianism flourished and reached a peak of influence was because of the scholars who descended from the previous dynasty. This shows that in the historical inheritance of higher education, not only the culture is inherited, but also the people. Culture is inherited via the inheritance of the people."[62] There have been a few thousand years of history of Chinese culture and traditions. Yet its decline is only a matter of more than a hundred years. This is largely due to the loss of intellectuals since modern times. There are also many lessons in history that we should reflect on. In the Seventeen Years, although the regime was passed to the Communist Party from Kuomintang, the Republican Chinese intellectuals were not inherited by the new regime. Traditional intellectuals were criticized and transformed. As a result, Chinese culture was almost completely broken apart. Most fundamentally, not only has the era of traditional intellectuals become history, but a great path of the development of Chinese universities' cultural character has also faded. Today, traditional intellectuals no longer exist, but intellectuals with traditional cultural characters have not lost their ground, especially since the Reform and Opening Up, after which some outstanding traditional literati appeared one after another in Chinese universities. History is a mirror, the formation of an ideal cultural character of Chinese universities would therefore have a basic guarantee if the government could acknowledge and respect the intellectuals, empower them to take the leading position in Chinese universities. As long as scholars gain independence, Chinese universities' cultural character would flourish. It was no coincidence that it demonstrated ideal characteristics during the Republic of China. As Xie Yong stated, "At the time of the Kuomintang government, regardless of the conflicts, the government generally cooperated with the liberal intellectuals and at the very least remained respectful to them. The government was the stronger party, while the liberal intellectuals were much weaker. The cooperation between the two could be regarded as the cooperation between the strong and the weak. As long as the relationship between strong and weak can maintain cooperation, the stronger side must have greater sincerity."[63]

Second, the government should grant and defend the freedom of Chinese universities and construct free Chinese universities. Karl Jaspers pointed out that universities can only survive under good political and societal conditions. Their existence relies on the government's care. A university may exist only when and where the country cares. The country makes universities possible, and the former defends the latter.[64] The existence of universities is inseparable from the support of the government, but this does not mean that the government can control and confine the universities, taking them for granted. In the process of formation of the cultural character of Chinese universities, government participation and support are necessary, but it also needs to be clarified that the ideal cultural character of Chinese universities needs an open political environment – not only to enable universities to enjoy certain freedoms, but to also defend the freedom of the university.

Historically, the ideal cultural character of any Chinese university resulted from the universities' independent construction. The government has played an important role as a defender of freedom rather than its controller. Specifically, in the formation of the cultural character of Chinese universities, there are at least two positive aspects to the government's act of granting the universities freedom and maintaining it. On the one hand, Chinese universities have freedom, which means that Chinese universities have greater independence and autonomy in the construction of their cultural character. For example, in the process of institutionalizing high-quality cultural characters, universities would have greater autonomy to formulate relevant rules and regulations. In coordinating the relationship between intellectuals and the government, universities can leverage on their independent position to protect the legitimate rights and interests of the intellectuals as much as possible. On the other hand, free Chinese universities nurture free intellectuals. American sociologists Lewis Coser pointed out that geniuses could occasionally break the boundary and work as per normal without the protection of the university, but normal intellectuals are just like other normal people – they need powerful protections from the institution. The university may continue to exist as such an institution in the future. The intellectuals would still have their opportunities open, as long as free universities exist.[65] The formation of the cultural character of Chinese universities depends on free intellectuals, and free universities are the fertile ground for the cultivation of free intellectuals. Historical experience proves that when government control weakens (or when it exerts occasional control or no control at all), the status of intellectuals in Chinese universities would be relatively strengthened. Relying on the asylum of universities, intellectuals can realize their potential in the construction of cultural character more easily. Of course, what needs to be clarified here is whether the university can effectively utilize freedom in the process of forming its cultural character. There might be some deviations from the facts, but the solution is not administrative intervention. The government needs to practice tolerance and guidance, apart from enforcement and supervision.

In summary, the triple helix of "scholars-university-government" constitutes an ideal special field for the formation and development of the cultural character of Chinese universities. The basic logic for the formation of an ideal Chinese university's cultural character is to base itself in the hearts of intellectuals, take root in the free soil of Chinese universities, and give full play to the government's role of macro-control in this process.

The most crucial point is to coordinate the relationship between the three. If good cultural belief is the inner spirit of the ideal cultural character of Chinese universities, then the independence and cooperation between the university, the scholars and the government is the external tool for Chinese universities to stand fast to their souls. When free scholars dominate Chinese universities, "purpose" would dominate the "means," creating the possible condition for the ideal cultural character of Chinese universities and the Chinese model of the university. When the government overrides the scholars to manipulate Chinese universities, the so-called cultural character would inevitably fall into pan-politicization and stray further away from becoming real Chinese universities. For now, in the process of comprehensively reinforcing the reform of higher education, it has already become a clear trend for the Chinese government to gradually granting the universities autonomy and paying attention to the intellectuals.

Conclusion

By using the theme of "the cultural characters of Chinese universities," the present study questions the methods of construction of an ideal "Chinese model of the university" based on Chinese culture.

Historically speaking, regardless of the setbacks and limitations of the cultural characters of Chinese universities, it is a necessary precondition for us to trace it back to its roots and find out its reasonable elements. In reality, regardless of the obstacles and pressures against the formation of the cultural characters of Chinese universities, it is still not without a basis that we must formulate an ideal design and plan for it.

Our reality is that due to historical coincidences, Chinese universities have been confined too much in the framework of horizontal transplantation since their founding. Moreover, in the era of globalization, the homogenization and marketization of higher education have intensified. Therefore, the uniqueness of Chinese universities has not been well demonstrated or sustained throughout history, while in modern society, it is urgently required that Chinese universities inherit Chinese culture to survive. History has proven that Chinese universities are, after all, "Chinese universities." Losing cultural self-esteem and blindly following the West would inevitably lead to the loss of self, let alone stop them from becoming real "Chinese universities."

Therefore, the basic position of this book is that in the future, Chinese universities must first strengthen the roots of high-quality Chinese culture. Thereby making it possible for the interaction and integration with Western culture, as well as the competition with university models across the world. As such, we can see the realization of China's dream of strengthening the country with higher education is on the horizon. According to some scholars, "A nation with 5,000 years of civilization should establish an internal power system with self-confidence and ease of action, not merely rely on the established results of others."[66] The rise of Chinese universities needs to rely on our cultural self-confidence to build a power system with intellectuals as their core. Only in this way can Chinese universities completely stop the plight of being "Western universities in China" and become more than the "universities of China in China." That is, they could finally become the "universities of China in the world."

Notes

1. Hayhoe, R. China's Universities 1895–1995: A Century of Cultural Conflict. Trans. Xu, J. Beijing: Educational Science Publishing House, 2000: 50.
2. Yang, D. Daxue Jingshen (The Spirit of Universities). Shengyang: Liaohai publishing House, 1999: 69.
3. Wang, J. Women Shidai De Daxue Zhuanxing (The Transformation of the Universities of Our Times). Beijing: Educational Science Publishing House, 2012: 298.
4. Chen, Y. Shiqu De Daxue (Dying Universities). Beijing: Tongxin Publishing House, 2005: 244.
5. Zhang, D., & Cheng, Y. Zhongguo Wenhua Lunzheng (Chinese Cultural Debate). Beijing: China Renmin University Press, 2006: 229.
6. Wu K. Zhiyue Zhongguo Jiaoyu Gaige De Teshu Changyu (The Special Field that Restricts the Reform of Chinese Education). Jiaoyu Yanjiu, 2008 (12): 19.
7. A Zheng. Duihua: Wenhua Shanbian Yu Zhongguo Mingyun (A Dialogue: Cultural Change and the Fate of China). Beijing: Xiyuan Publishing House, 2001: 12.
8. Zhong, M. et al. Zhongguo Chuantong Wenhua Jingyi (The Essence of Chinese Traditional Culture). Xi'an: Xi'an Jiaotong University Publishing House, 2001: 116.
9. Wang, J. Daxue Linian Zai Zhongguo (University Ideas in China). Beijing: Higher Education Press, 2007: 43–44.
10. Shao, H. Zhongguo Wenhua Yanjiu Ershinian (Two Decades of Chinese Culture Research). Beijing: People's Publishing House, 2003: 507–508.
11. Gan, Y., Chen, L., Su, L. Zhongguo Daxue De Renwen Jiaoyu (Humanities Education in Chinese Universities). Beijing: SDX Joint Publishing Company, 2006: 89.
12. Yu, Y. Shi Yu Zhongguo Wenhua ("Shi" and Chinese Culture). Shanghai: Shanghai People's Press, 1987: Preface 2.
13. Yu, Y. Shi Yu Zhongguo Wenhua ("Shi" and Chinese Culture). Shanghai: Shanghai People's Press, 1987: 42.
14. Li, Z. Zhongguo Gudai Sixiang Shilun (History and Comments on Ancient Chinese Thoughts). Beijing: People's Publishing House, 1986: 38–39.
15. Aristotle. Nicomachean Ethics. Trans. Liao, S. Beijing: The Commercial Press, 2013: 55.
16. Cai, Z., Mao, Y. Gaodeng Jiaoyu Quanqiuhua: Luoji Yu Neihan (Globolization of Higher Education: Logics and Connotations). Journal of Higher Education Research, 2013 (9): 10.
17. Wang, J. Women Shidai De Daxue Zhuanxing (The Transformation of the Universities of Our Times). Beijing: Educational Science Publishing House, 2012: 2.
18. Ikeda, D., Toynbee, A. Forecast 21st Century. Trans. Xun, C. Beijing: International Culture Publishing House, 1985: 61.

19. Chen, P. Daxue You Jingshen (The Spirit of University). Beijing: Peking University Press, 2009: 180.
20. Cai, Z., Mao, Y. Gaodeng Jiaoyu Quanqiuhua: Luoji Yu Neihan (Globolization of Higher Education: Logics and Connotations). Journal of Higher Education Research, 2013 (9): 13.
21. Cai, Z., Mao, Y. Gaodeng Jiaoyu Quanqiuhua: Luoji Yu Neihan (Globolization of Higher Education: Logics and Connotations). Journal of Higher Education Research, 2013 (9): 13.
22. Ke, S. & Wang, N. Biange Zhongguo: Shichang Jingji De Zhongguo Zhilu (How China Became Capitalist). Trans, Xu, Y., et al. Beijing: CITIC Press, 2013: 249.
23. Chen, P., Zhongguo Daxue Shijiang (Ten Lectures on Chinese Universities). Shanghai: Fudan University Press, 2002: 8–9.
24. Wang, J. Women Shidai De Daxue Zhuanxing (The Transformation of the Universities of Our Times). Beijing: Educational Science Publishing House, 2012: 288.
25. Liu, X. Jianjin Hanzhi (To Pick Up All The Frozen Branches). Beijing: Huaxia Publishing House, 2007: 5–6.
26. Wang, J. Women Shidai De Daxue Zhuanxing (The Transformation of the Universities of Our Times). Beijing: Educational Science Publishing House, 2012: 288–289.
27. Zhu, Y., Ma, G. Chongqi Jiaoyu Gaige (Restarting the Educational Reform). Beijing: SDX Joint Publishing Company, 2014: 139.
28. Cited From Zhang, R. Zhongguo Jiaoyu Zhexueshi Disijuan (History of Chinese Educational Philosophy, Volume 4). Jinan: Shandong Education Press, 1999: 412.
29. Liu, M. Dashi Yu Chuantong: Zhongguo Wenhua Yu Chuantong 40 Xiaojiang (Masters and Traditions: 40 Minor Lectures on Chinese Culture and Tradition). Beijing: China Youth Press, 2007: 30.
30. Chen, H. Deguo Gudian Daxueguan Jiqi Dui Zhongguo Daxue De Yingxiang (Classical German University View and Its Influence on Chinese Universities). Beijing: Peking University Press, 2002: 107.
31. Tu, Y. Zhongguo Gaodeng Jiaoyu Shilun (History and comments on Chinese higher education). Wuhan: Hubei Education Publishing House, 1997: 4.
32. Chen, P., Zhongguo Daxue Shijiang (Ten Lectures on Chinese Universities). Shanghai: Fudan University Press, 2002: 26–27.
33. Chen, G. Gaodeng Jiaoyu De Minzu Chuantong: Sange Weidu De Sikao (The National Tradition of Higher Education: Thoughts on Three Dimensions). Journal of Higher Education Research, 2014 (7): 4.
34. Wang, J. Lun Daxue Zhidao (On the Way of University). Fudan Education Forum, 2005 (1): 23.
35. Kim, Y. Chongsi Daxue Zhidao (Reflection on the Way of University). Exploration and Free Views, 2013 (9): 82.
36. Hou, D. Zhongguo Daxue De Lixing Zhilu (The Path of Reason for Chinese Universities). Shanghai: East China Normal University Press, 2009: 94.
37. Luo, Z. Cong Wenhua Kan Fuxing Yu Jueqi (Looking at Rejuvenation and Rising from A Cultural Perspective). Dushu, 2014 (8): 36.
38. Zhang, Z. Zhongguo Shenshi: Guanyu Qi Zai Shijiu Shiji Zhongguo Shehui Zhong Zuoyong De Yanjiu (Chinese Gentlemen: A Research on Their Function in Chinese Society in the 19th Century). Trans. Li, R. Shanghai: Shanghai Academy of Social Sciences Press, 1991: 3.
39. Li, X., Beida Binfen Yibainian (The Colorful Century of Peking University). Beijing: Peking University Press, 1999: 349.
40. Hou, D. Zhongguo Daxue De Lixing Zhilu (The Path of Reason for Chinese Universities). Shanghai: East China Normal University Press, 2009: 94.

41. Liu, M. Dashi Yu Chuantong: Zhongguo Wenhua Yu Chuantong 40 Xiaojiang (Masters and Traditions: 40 Minor Lectures on Chinese Culture and Tradition). Beijing: China Youth Press, 2007: 130–131.
42. Tu, Y. Wenming Bentuhua Yu Daxue (Civilization Localization and University). Journal of Higher Education Research, 1998 (6): 6–7.
43. Hou, D. Zhongguo Daxue De Lixing Zhilu (The Path of Reason for Chinese Universities). Shanghai: East China Normal University Press, 2009: Preface 6.
44. Liu, M. Dashi Yu Chuantong: Zhongguo Wenhua Yu Chuantong 40 Xiaojiang (Masters and Traditions: 40 Minor Lectures on Chinese Culture and Tradition). Beijing: China Youth Press, 2007: 42.
45. Yao, G. Quanqiuhua De Renwen Shensi Yu Wenhua Zhanlue Xiajuan (The Hunamistic Reflection and Cultural Strategies of Globalization Volume 2). Shenzhen: Haitian Publishing House, 2002: 503.
46. Liu, M. Dashi Yu Chuantong: Zhongguo Wenhua Yu Chuantong 40 Xiaojiang (Masters and Traditions: 40 Minor Lectures on Chinese Culture and Tradition). Beijing: China Youth Press, 2007: 42.
47. Liu, M. Dashi Yu Chuantong: Zhongguo Wenhua Yu Chuantong 40 Xiaojiang (Masters and Traditions: 40 Minor Lectures on Chinese Culture and Tradition). Beijing: China Youth Press, 2007: 38–39.
48. Hou, D. Zhongguo Daxue De Lixing Zhilu (The Path of Reason for Chinese Universities). Shanghai: East China Normal University Press, 2009: 82–83.
49. Hayhoe, R. China's Universities 1895–1995: A Century of Cultural Conflict. Trans. Xu, J. Beijing: Educational Science Publishing House, 2000: 176.
50. Chen, Y. Shiqu De Daxue (Dying Universities). Beijing: Tongxin Publishing House, 2005: 239.
51. Hayhoe, R. China's Universities 1895–1995: A Century of Cultural Conflict. Trans. Xu, J. Beijing: Educational Science Publishing House, 2000: 312.
52. Chu, Z. Zhongguo Daxue Jingshen De Lishi Yu Xingsi (History and the Spirit of the Chinese University of Reflection). Taiyuan: Shanxi Education Press, 2006: 341.
53. Liang, B. Dawenhua Shi Daxue Fazhan De Zhexue Jichu (Greater Culture is the Philosophical Basis of University Development). Fudan Education Forum, 2003 (2): 26
54. Hou, D. Zhongguo Daxue De Lixing Zhilu (The Path of Reason for Chinese Universities). Shanghai: East China Normal University Press, 2009: Preface 5.
55. Kim, Y. Daxue Zhi Linian (The Ideas of Universities). Beijing: SDX Joint Publishing Company, 2008: Self-preface 5.
56. Wang, J. Daxue Linian Zai Zhongguo (University Ideas in China). Beijing: Higher Education Press, 2007: Preface.
57. Jaspers, K. The Idea of the University. Trans. Qiu, L. Shanghai: Shanghai People's Press, 2007: 147.
58. Du, X., Zhang, N. Delida Zhongguo Yanjianglu (Collection of Derrida's Speeches in China). Beijing: Central Compilation & Translation Press, 2003: 61.
59. Hou, D. Zhongguo Daxue De Lixing Zhilu (The Path of Reason for Chinese Universities). Shanghai: East China Normal University Press, 2009: 41.
60. Hou, D. Zhongguo Daxue De Lixing Zhilu (The Path of Reason for Chinese Universities). Shanghai: East China Normal University Press, 2009: 13.
61. Hou, D. Zhongguo Daxue De Lixing Zhilu (The Path of Reason for Chinese Universities). Shanghai: East China Normal University Press, 2009: 51.
62. Tu, Y. Zhongguo Gaodeng Jiaoyu Shilun (History and comments on Chinese higher education). Wuhan: Hubei Education Publishing House, 1997: 164.

63. Chen, Y. Shiqu De Daxue (Dying Universities). Beijing: Tongxin Publishing House, 2005: 243–244.
64. Jaspers, K. The Idea of the University. Trans. Qiu, L. Shanghai: Shanghai People's Press, 2007: 173.
65. Coses, L. Men of Ideas: A Sociologist's View. Trans. Guo, F., et al. Beijing: Central Compilation & Translation Press, 2004: 322.
66. Yao, G. Quanqiuhua De Renwen Shensi Yu Wenhua Zhanlue Xiajuan (The Hunamistic Reflection and Cultural Strategies of Globalization Volume 2). Shenzhen: Haitian Publishing House, 2002: 20.

References

1. Compilations of Materials

First Historical Archives of China. *Xianfeng Tongzhi Liangchao Shangyu Dang [Archive of Orders from the Emperors Xianfeng and Tongzhi*]. Guilin: Guangxi Normal University Press, 2000.

The Second Historical Archives of China, *Zhonghua Minguoshi Dangan Ziliao Huibian Disanji Jiaoyu* [*Collection of Historical Archives and Materials of the History of Republic of China Vol.3 Education*]. Nanjing: Jiangsu Ancient Book Publishing House, 1991.

National Institute of Education Sciences. *Zhongguo Xiandai Jiaoyu Dashiji (1919–1949)* [*Chronicle of Contemporary Chinese Education (1919–1949)*]. Beijing: Educational Science Publishing House, 1988.

Editing Committee of Education Yearbooks, Ministry of Education, China. *Dierci Zhongguo Jiaoyu Nianjian (Diyibian)* [*2nd Yearbook for Chinese Education* (1st Edit)]. Shanghai: The Commercial Press, 1948.

Party Literature Research Center. *Guanyu Jianguo Yilai Dang De Ruogan Lishi Wenti De Jueyi Zhushi Ben* [*Annotated version of the Party's decisions on several historical issues since the founding of the country*]. Beijing: People's Publishing House, 1983.

People's Education Press. *Jiaoyu Gaige Zhongyao Wenxian Xuanbian* [*Selection of Important Documents regarding Education Reforms*]. Beijing: People's Education Press, 1988.

Faculty of Education Archive, East China Normal University. *Gaodeng Jiaoyu Wenxian Faling Xuanbian [Selection of Higher Educational Legal Documents]*. Shanghai: East China Normal University Press, 1981.

Research Office of School History, Peking University. *Beijing Daxue Shiliao Diyijuan: 1898–1911 [Historical Materials of Peking University, Vol. 1: 1898–1911]*. Beijing: Peking University Press, 1993.

Research Office of School History, Peking University. *Beijing Daxue Shiliao Dierjuan: 1912–1937 [Historical Materials of Peking University, Vol. 2: 1912–1937]*. Beijing: Peking University Press, 2000.

Research Office of School History, Tsinghua University. *Qinghua Daxue Shiliao Xuanbian Diyijuan [An Edited Selection of Historical Materials of Tsinghua University Vol.1]*. Beijing: Tsinghua University Press, 1991.

Research Office of School History, Tsinghua University. *Qinghua Daxue Shiliao Xuanbian Dierjuan [An Edited Selection of Historical Materials of Tsinghua University Vol.2]*. Beijing: Tsinghua University Press, 1991.

Chen, X. *Zhongguo Jindai Jiaoyushi Jiaoxue Cankao Zailiao Shangce [Referential Materials for Teaching the History of Modern Chinese Education Part 1]*. Beijing: People's Education Press, 1986.

Chen, X. *Zhongguo Jindai Jiaoyushi Jiaoxue Cankao Zailiao Zhongce [Referential Materials for Teaching the History of Modern Chinese Education Part 2]*. Beijing: People's Education Press, 1987.

Gao, S. *Zhongguo Jindai Jiaoyushi Ziliao Huibian: Yangwu Yundong Shiqi Jiaoyu [Collection of Materials regarding Modern Chinese Education History: Education of the Self-Strengthening Movement Era]*. Shanghai: Shanghai Education Press, 1992.

Tang, Z., Chen, Z. *Zhongguo Jindai Jiaoyushi Ziliao Huibian: Wuxu Shiqi Jiaoyu [Collection of Materials of Modern Chinese Education History: The Education of the Wuxu Era]*. Shanghai: Shanghai Education Press, 1993.

Qu, X., Tong, F. *Zhongguo Jindai Jiaoyushi Ziliao Huibian: Jiaoyu Sixiang [Collection of Materials regarding Modern Chinese Education History: Education Thoughts]*. Shanghai: Shanghai Education Press, 1997.

Qu, X., Tang, L. *Zhongguo Jindai Jiaoyushi Ziliao Huibian: Xuezhi Yanbian [Collection of Materials regarding Modern Chinese Education History: The Shifting of Education System]*. Shanghai: Shanghai Education Press, 1991.

He, D. *Zhonghua Renmin Gonghe Guo Zhongyao Jiaoyu Wenxian 1949–1997 [Important Educational Documents of People's Republic of China, 1949–1997]*. Haikou: Hainan Publishing House, 1998.

Zhang, J. *Zhongguo Jindai Chuban Shiliao Chubian [A Draft Edit of Published Historic Materials of Modern China]*. Shanghai: Qunlian Press, 1953.

Zhu, Y. *Zhongguo Jindai Xuezhi Shiliao Diyiji[Historical Materials of Modern Chinese Education System, Vol. 1]*. Shanghai: East China Normal University Press, 1986.

Association of Chinese Historians. *Wuxu Bianfa [The Wuxu Reform]*. Shanghai: Shanghai Bookstore Publishing House, 2000.

2. Chinese Books

Chen, Y., *Jinmingguan Conggao Erbian [The Second Editing of Articles from Jinmingguan]*. Shanghai: Shanghai Ancient Books Publishing House, 1980.

Qian, M. *Zhongguo Xueshu Tongyi [General Points of Chinese Academics]*. Taipei: Student Books, 1977.

Qian, M. *Zhongguo Wenhuashi Daolun [An Introduction of Chinese Cultural History]*. Beijing: Jiuzhou Press, 2011.

Liang, S., *Dongxi Wenhua Jiqi Zhexue [Eastern and Western Cultures and Their Philosophies]*. Beijing: The Commercial Press, 2010.

Liang, S. *Zhongguo Wenhua Yaoyi [The Key Idea to Chinese Culture].* Shanghai: Shanghai People's Press, 2011.

Feng, Y. *A Short History of Chinese Philosophy.* Trans. Tu Youguang. Beijing: Peking University Press, 2013.

Fei, X. *From the Soil—The Foundations of Chinese Society.* Beijing: Peking University Press, 2012.

Li, Z. *Zhongguo Gudai Sixiang Shilun [History and Comments on Ancient Chinese Thoughts].* Beijing: People's Publishing House, 1986.

Li, Z., *Zou Woziji De Lu [Going My Own Way].* Shanghai: Shanghai SDX Joint Publishing Company, 1986.

Yin, H. *Zhongguo Wenhua De Zhanwang [Outlook of Chinese Culture].* Beijing: China Heping Publishing House, 1988.

Liu, Y. & Lv, S. *Zhongguo Wenhua Shiliu Jiang. [Sixteen Lessons on Chinese Culture]* Beijing: Changzheng Publishing House. 2008.

Zhang, D., & Cheng, Y. *Zhongguo Wenhua Lunzheng [Chinese Cultural Debate].* Beijing: China Renmin University Press, 2006.

Qian, J., *Guoxue Bidu [Must-Reads of Sinology].* Shanghai: Shanghai Ancient Books Publishing House, 2011.

Feng, T. *Zhongguo Renwen Chuantong Yu Zhongxi Renwen Jingshen Jiangyan Lu [A Collection of Speeches regarding Chinese Humanistic Tradition and Chinese and West Humanistic Spirit].* Changsha: Hunan Education Publishing House, 2010.

Liu, M., *Chuantong De Wudu [Misinterpretation of Traditions].* Shijiazhuang: Hebei Education Press, 1996.

Liu, M. Dashi Yu Chuantong: *Zhongguo Wenhua Yu Chuantong 40 Xiaojiang [Masters and Traditions: 40 Minor Lectures on Chinese Culture and Tradition].* Beijing: China Youth Press, 2007.

Liu, M. *Zhongguo Xiandai Xueshu Yaolve [A Brief Framework of Contemporary Chinese Academics].* Beijing: Joint Publishing, 2008.

Jin, G., & Liu, Q. *Kaifang Zhong De Bianqian: Zailun Zhongguo Shehui Chaowending Jiegou [Transformation in Opening Up: Re-discussion the Super-Stable Structure].* Beijing: Law Press·China, 2011.

Zhong, M. et al. *Zhongguo Chuantong Wenhua Jingyi [The Essence of Chinese Traditional Culture].* Xi'an: Xi'an Jiaotong University Publishing House, 2001.

Wu, Y. *Daxue Wenhua: Lixiang Yu Xianshi De Chongtu [University Culture: Conflicts Between Ideals and Reality].* Guangzhou: Sun Yat-sen University Press, 2010.

Cao, X. *Zhongxi Wenhua Duibi Daolun: Guanyu Zhongguo Wenhua Xuanze De Zaijiantao [An Introduction to Comparison between Chinese and Western Cultures: Another Reflection on Chinese Cultural Choices].* Beijing: China Youth Press, 1992.

A Zheng. *Duihua: Wenhua Shanbian Yu Zhongguo Mingyun [A Dialogue: Cultural Change and the Fate of China].* Beijing: Xiyuan Publishing House, 2001.

Liu, D., & Zhou, Y. *Xixue Dongjian Yu Dongxue Xijian [Eastward Spreading of Western Learnings and Westward Spreading of Eastern Learnings].* Beijing: China Social Sciences Press, 2000.

Gan, Y. *Bashi Niandai Wenhua Yishi [Cultural Consciousness of 1980].* Shanghai: Shanghai People's Press, 2006.

Shao, H. *Zhongguo Wenhua Yanjiu Ershi Nian [20 Years of Chinese Cultural Research].* Beijing: People's Publishing House, 2003.

Zhi, J. *Zhongguo Jinbainian Shi [The History of China during the Recent 100 Years].* Harbin: Heilongjiang People's Press, 1983.

Lin, Z. *Zhongguo Jindaishi [Modern History of China]*. Changsha: Hunan People's Publishing House, 1979.

Lv, S. *Zhongguo Jindaishi [History of Modern China]* Changsha: Yuelu Publishing House, 2011.

An, Y. *Chongzhuang Yu Ronghe: Zhongguo Jindai Wenhuashi Lun [Conflict and Integration: A Discussion of Modern Chinese Cultural History]*. Shanghai: Xuelin Press, 2001.

Hu, F., *Shehui Biange Yu Wenhua Chuantong: Zhongguo Jindai Wenhua Baoshou Zhuyi Sichao Yanjiu [Social Changes and Cultural Traditions: As Research on the Conservatism Ideological Trend of Modern China]*. Shanghai: Shanghai People's Press, 2000.

Meng, S. *Qingshi Jiangyi [Lecture Notes on History of the Qing Dynasty]*. Hangzhou: Zhejiang People's Publishing House, 1998.

Wang, E. *Wanqing Zhengzhi Sixiang Shilun [History and comments on the Political Thoughts of the Late Qing Dynasty]*. Guilin: Guangxi Normal University Press, 2007.

Qi, Q. *Wanqing Shehui Sichao Yanjin Shi [The History of Ideological Trend Progression of the Late Qing Dynasty]*. Beijing: Zhonghua Book Company, 2012.

Xiao, G. *Weiji Zhongde Biange: Qingmo Xiandaihua Zhongde Jijin Yu Baoshou [Changes within Crysis: Radicalism and Conservatism within the Modernization of the Late Qing Dynasty]*. Shanghai: Shanghai Joint Publishing, 1999.

Bai, W. *Yingbian Yu Kunjing: Qingmo Xinzheng Shiqi De Yishi Xingtai Kongzhi [Adaption and Difficulties: The Ideological Control during the New Policies Reform Era of the Late Qing Dynasty]*. Beijing: Community University of China Press, 2008.

Xiong, Y. *Xixue Dongjian Yu Wanqing Shehui [The Eastward Introduction of Western Learning and the Society of the Late Qing Dynasty]*. Shanghai: Shanghai People's Press, 1994.

Lin, Y. *Zhongguo Yishi De Weiji: "Wusi" Shiqi Jilie De Fanchuantong Zhuyi [Crisis of Chinese Conscious: Vigorous Anti-Traditionalism during "May Fourth" Period]*. Guiyang: Guizhou People's Publishing House, 1988.

Liu, L., *Wusi Wenhua Baoshou Zhuyi Sichao Yanjiu [Research on the Cultural Conservatism Ideological Trend of May Fourth Period]*. Beijing: The China Social Sciences Press, 2006.

Zhao, C. *Wenhua Jiyin Yu Shehui Bianqian: Zhongguo Shehuizhuyi Lujing Zouxiang De Minzu Wenhua Jiexi [Culture Genes and Social Changes: Analysis on the National Culture Lead by the Chinese Socialist Path]*, 2010.

Zhang, Z. *Quanxue Pian [On Encouraging Learning]*. Guilin: Guangxi Normal University Press, 2008.

Zeng, G. *Zeng Guofan Quanji [Collected Works of Zeng Guofan]*. Changsha: Yuelu Publishing House, 1985.

Lu, X., *Lu Xun Quanji [Collected Works of Lu Xun]*. Beijing: The People's Literature Press, 1981.

Lu, X. *Qiejieting Zawen Mobian [Latest Edition of Qiejie Pavillion Essays Collection]*. Beijing: People's Literature Publishing House, 1973.

Li, D., *Li Dazhao Xuanji [Selected Works of Li Dazhao]*. Beijing: People's Publishing House, 1959.

Mao, Z. *Mao Zedong Zhuzuo Xuandu Xiace [Selected Readings of Mao Zedong, Part 2]*. Beijing: People's Publishing House, 1986.

Mao, Z. *Mao Zedong Xuanji Diwu Juan [Selected Works of Mao Zedong, Vol. 5]*. Beijing: People's Publishing House, 1977.

Academy of Literature and Arts, Ministry of Culture. *Zhou Enlai Lun Wenyi [Zhou Enlai's Duscussion on Literature and Arts]*. Beijing: People's Literature Publishing House, 1979.

Liu Shaoqi Division, Party Literature Research Center. *Liu Shaoqi Xuanji [Selected Works of Liu Shaoqi (Part 2)]*. Beijing: Central Party School Press, 1985.

Liu Shaoqi Division, Party Literature Research Center. *Liu Shaoqi Lun Jiaoyu [Liu Shaoqi's Remarks on Education]*. Beijing: Educational Science Publishing House, 1998.

Qi, X., Shao, Z., *Chen Duxiu Jiaoyu Lunzhu Xuan [A Selection of Works by Chen Duxiu on Education]*. Beijing: People's Education Press, 1995.

Xu, J., Tian, J., *Du Yaquan Wencun [Record of Works of Du Yaquan]*. Shanghai: Shanghai Education Publishing House, 2003.

Gao, P., *Cai Yuanpei Jiaoyu Lunji [Collected Works of Cai Yuanpei on Education]*. Changsha: Hunan Education Publishing House, 1987.

Bai, J., Liu, Y., *Hu Shi Jiaoyu Lunzhu Xuan [A Selection of Works by Hu Shih on Education]*. Beijing: People's Education Press, 1994.

Liu, S., Huang, Y., *Mei Yiqi Jiaoyu Lunzhu Xuan [Selected Works of Mei Yiqi on Education]*. Beijing: People's Education Press, 1993.

Cui, G., *Zhang Boling Jiaoyu Lunzhu Xuan [Selected Works of Zhang Boling on Education]*. Beijing: People's Education Press, 1997.

Pan, N., Zhang, H., *Xunqiu Zhongguoren Weiyu Zhidao: Pan Guangdan Wenxuan [Looking for the Way of Position Education for Chinese People: Selected Works of Pan Guangdan]*. Beijing: International Culture Publishing Company, 1997.Gu, M. *Jiaoyu Da Cidian [Dictionary of Education]*. Shanghai: Shanghai Educational Publishing House, 1998.

Gu, M. *Zhongguo Jiaoyu De Wenhua Jichu [The cultural foundation of Chinese education]*. Taiyuan: Shanxi Education Press, 2004.

Shi, Z. *Jiaoyuxue De Wenhua Xingge [Cultural character of pedagogy]*. Taiyuan: Shanxi Education Press, 1999.

Yu, J. *Kongzi Jiaoyu Xueshuo [Theories of Confucian Education]*. Beijing: Capital Normal University Press, 2010.

Li, H. *Xue Yiwei Ji: Chuantong Zhongguo De Jiaoyu [Studying for Self: The Education of Traditional China]* Hong Kong: The Chinese University of Hong Kong Press, 2012.

Zou, J. *Xue Er You Ze Shi [Do well in academics in order to pursue an official career]*. Beijing: China Federation of Literary & Art Circles Publishing Corp, 2006.

Liu, H., & Li, B. *Xue You Ze Shi: Jiaoyu Yu Keju [Do well in academics to pursue an official career: Education and imperial examination]*. Changchun: Changchun Publishing House, 2004.

Liu, H. *Liu Haifeng Yanjiang Lu [A Collection of Liu Haifeng's Speeches]*. Wuhan: Huazhong University of Science and Technology, 2012.

Office of Chinese Philosophy Research, Department of Philosophy and Religious Studies, Peking University. *Zhongguo Zhexueshi [History of Chinese Philosophy]*. Beijing: Peking University Press, 2003.

Zhang, R. *Zhongguo Jiaoyu Zhexueshi Disijuan [History of Chinese Educational Philosophy, Volume 4]*. Jinan: Shandong Education Press, 1999.

Li, G., Wang, B. *Zhongguo Jiaoyu Zhidu Tongshi [General History of Chinese Education System]*. Jinan: Shandong Education Press, 2000.

Chen, J. *Zhongguo Jindai Jiaoyushi [History of Modern Chinese Education]*. Beijing: People's Education Press, 2003.

Yu, Z., *Minzu Weiji Xiade Jiaoyu Yingdui [Educational Response during a National Crisis]*. Wuhan: Central China Normal University Press, 2001.

Su, Y., *Zhongguo Xinjiaoyu De Mengya Yu Chengzhang (1860–1928) [The Sprouting and Growth of the New Education of China (1860–1928)]*. Beijing: Peking University Press, 2007.

Yuan, Z. *Zhongguo Dangdai Jiaoyu Sichao 1949–1989 [Chinese Contemporary Educational Thoughts 1949–1989]*. Shanghai: Joint Publishing Company. 1991.

Tu, Y. *Zhongguo Gaodeng Jiaoyu Shilun [History and comments on Chinese higher education].* Wuhan: Hubei Education Publishing House, 2002.

Xiong, M., *Zhongguo Gaodeng Jiaoyushi [History of Chinese Higher Education].* Chongqing: Chongqing Publishing House: 1988.

Dong, B. *Zhongguo Jinxiandai Gaodeng Jiaoyu Shi [Higher Education History of Modern and Contemporary China].* Wuhan: Huazhong University of Science and Technology Press, 2007.

Liu, G. *Xin Zhongguo Gaodeng Jiaoyu Dashiji (1949–1987) [Chronicles of New China's Higher Education].* Changchun: Northeast Normal University Press, 1990.

Zhuang, Y. *Zuijin Sanwushinian Zhi Zhongguo Jiaoyu [Education of China during the Past 30–50 Years].* Shanghai: The Commercial Press, 1931.

Tian, Z., Shang, L. *Zhongguo Gaodeng Jiaoyu Bainian Shilun: Zhidu Bianqian, Caizheng Yunzuo Yu Jiaoshi Liudong [History and Comments of A Century of Chinese Higher Education: The Shifting of Institution, the Operation of Finance and the Turnover of Teachers]* Beijing: People's Education Press, 2006.

Zhu, G. *Xixue Dongjian Yu Zhongguo Gaodeng Jiaoyu Jindaihua [The Eastward Spreading of Western Learning and the Modernization of Chinese Higher Education].* Xiamen: Xiamen University Press, 1996.

Hu, J. *The origin of the modern Chinese university system: university reform in the early 1950s [M].* Nanjing: Nanjing Normal University Press, 2001.

Zhang, Y. *Gaodeng Jiaoyu Xiandaihua De Fansi Yu Jiangou [The Reflection and Construction of the Modernization of Higher Education].* Harbin: Heilongjiang Education Press, 2000.

Zhang, Y. *Wenhua Shiye Zhong De Gaodeng Jiaoyu [Higher Education in Cultural Perspective].* Nanjing: Nanjing Normal University Press, 1999.

Wang, H. *Dazhong Gaodeng Jiaoyulun: Gaodeng Jiaoyu Dazhonghua De Wenhua-Gexingxiangdu Yanjiu [A Discussion on Popularized Higher Education: The Culture of the Popularization of Higher Education – A Character-oriented Research].* Guangzhou: Guangdong Education Publishing House, 2004.

Yan, G. *Shidu Daxue: Zuzhi Wenhua De Shijiao [Recognizing and Understanding Universities-From an Organizational Cultural Point of View].* Beijing: Educational Science Publishing House, 2002.

Wang, J. *Women Shidai De Daxue Zhuanxing [The Transformation of the Universities of Our Times].* Beijing: Educational Science Publishing House, 2012.

Zhou, G. et al. *Zhongguo Jindai Daxue De Xiandai Zhuanxing: Yizhi, Tiaoshi Yu Fazhan [The Contemporary Transformation of Modern Chinese Universities: Adoption, Adaption, and Development].* Hangzhou: Zhejiang University Press, 2012.

Li, W. *Bange Zhong De Daxue – Li Wei Jiaoyu Wencun [University in Revolution – An Archive of Education Works of Li Wei].* Beijing: Higher Education Press, 2012.

Fan, Y. *Shuangchong Qiyuan Yu Zhidu Shengcheng: Zhongguo Xiandai Daxue Zhidu Qiyuan Yanjiu [Double Origins and Institutional Generation: A Research on the Origin of Modern Chinese University System].* Wuhan: Huazhong University of Science and Technology, 2011.

Chen, Y. *Shiqu De Daxue [Dying Universities].* Beijing: Tongxin Publishing House, 2005.

Zhou, C., *Huang, X., Bainian Zhi Gong: Zhongguo Jindai Daxue Xiaozhang De Jiaoyujia Jingshen [Effort of a Hundred Years: The Educator Spirit of Presidents of Modern Chinese Universities].* Fuzhou: Fujian Education Press, 2005.

Sui, Y. *Xuefu Zhihun – Zhongwai Zhuming Daxue Xiaozhang Jiaoyu Linian [The Soul of Institutions – The Education Ideals of Famous Presidents of Universities around the World].* Nanchang: Jiangxi Education Publishing House, 2001.

Sui, Y. *Lixing Hanwei Daxue [Defending University with Reason]*. Beijing: Peking University Press, 2013.

Hou, D. *Zhongguo Daxue De Lixing Zhilu [The Path of Reason for Chinese Universities]*. Shanghai: East China Normal University Press, 2009.

Kim, Y. *Daxue Zhi Linian [The Ideas of Universities]*. Beijing: SDX Joint Publishing Company, 2008.

Han, Y. *Daxue Linian Lungang [Outline of Theories Regarding University Ideas]*. Beijing: People's Education Press, 2003.

Xiao, H. *Daxue De Linian [The Idea of University]*. Wuhan: Huazhong University of Science and Technology, 2001.

Wang, J. *Daxue Linian Zai Zhongguo [University Ideas in China]*. Beijing: Higher Education Press, 2007.

Wang, J. *Daxue Zhidao [The Way of University]*. Beijing: Higher Education Press, 2005.

Yang, D., *Daxue Jingshen [The Spirit of University]*. Shenyang: Liaohai Publishing House, 1999.

Chu, Z. *Zhongguo Daxue Jingshen De Lishi Yu Xingsi [A Study on the Spirits of Chinese University History and Reflection]*. Taiyuan: Shanxi Education Press, 2006.

Chu, Z. *Lixiang Daxue [Ideal University]*. Beijing: Beijing Normal University Press, 2012.

Chen, P. *Zhongguo Daxue Shijiang [Ten Lessons on Chinese Universities]*. Shanghai: Fudan University Press, 2002.

Chen, P. *Daxue Hewei [What University Does]*. Beijing: Peking University Press, 2006.

Chen, P. *Daxue You Jingshen [The Spirit of University]*. Beijing: Peking University Press, 2009.

Chen, P. *Dangdai Zhongguo Renwen Guancha [Observation of Humanities in Contemporary China]*. Beijing: Peking University Press, 2010.

Zhang, J. *Minguo Daxue: Yaoxiang Daxue Dangnian [Chinese Republican Universities: Throwing Back to the Universities in the Past]*. Beijing: Orient Publishing Center, 2012.

Chen, H. *Deguo Gudian Daxueguan Jiqi Dui Zhongguo Daxue De Yingxiang [Classical German University View and Its Influence on Chinese Universities]*. Beijing: Peking University Press, 2002.

Liu, D. *Zhongguo Gaoxiao Zhishang [The Regrets of Chinese Higher Institution]*. Wuhan: Hubei People's Press, 2010.

Zhu, Y., Ma, G. *Chongqi Jiaoyu Gaige [Restarting the Educational Reform]*. Beijing: SDX Joint Publishing Company, 2014.

Ma, G. *Daxue Mingxiaozhang Fangtanlu [Record of Interviews with Famous Presidents of Universities]*. Beijing: Huaxia Publishing House, 2010.

Yao, G. *Quanqiuhua De Renwen Shensi Yu Wenhua Zhanlue Xiajuan [The Hunamistic Reflection and Cultural Strategies of Globalization Volume 2]*. Shenzhen: Haitian Publishing House, 2002.

Tang, Z., *Cai Yuanpei Zhuan [A Biography of Cai Yuanpei]*. Shanghai: Shanghai People's Press, 1985.

Yuan, Y., Liu, Y., *Wang Guowei Nianpu Changbian: 1877–1927 [A Chronicle Record of Wang Guowei: 1877–1927]*. Tianjin: Tianjin People's Publishing House, 2005.

Huang, Y., *Mei Yiqi Jiaoyu Sixiang Yanjiu [A Research on the Educational Thoughts of Mei Yiqi]*. Shenyang: Liaoning Education Press, 1994.

Huang, Y., *Qinghua Chuantong Jingshen [The Traditional Spirit of Tsinghua]*. Beijing: Tsinghua University Press, 2006.

Huang, Y., *Ersanshi Niandai Qinghua Xiaoyuan Wenhua [The Campus Culture of Tsinghua University in the 1920s and 1930s]*. Guilin: Guangxi Normal University Press, 2000.

Su, Y., *Cong Qinghua Xuetang Dao Qinghua Daxue 1911–1929 [From Tsinghua School to Tsinghua University 1911–1929]*. Beijing: SDX Joint Publishing Company, 2001.

Li, X., *Beida Binfen Yibainian [The Colorful Century of Peking University]*. Beijing: Peking University Press, 1999.

Mu, Z., Mu, X. *Beida Gushi [Stories of Peking University]*. Beijing: China Market Press, 1998.

Liu, K., Fang, M., *Beida Yu Qinghua: Zhongguo Liangsuo Zhuming Gaodeng Xuefu De Lishi Yu Fengge [PKU and THU: The History and Style of Two Famous Institutes of Higher Education in China]*. Beijing: National Administrative Academy Publishing House, 1998.

Liang, J., *Yungong Yunneng Rixin Yueyi: Nankai Daxue Xiaozhang Zhang Boling [Discipline and Practicality, New Progress by the Day: Zhang Boling, The President of Nankai University]*. Jinan: Shandong Education Press, 2003.

Editing Group of School History of Nankai University. *Nankai Daxue Xiaoshi (1919–1949) [The School History of Nankai University (1919–1949)]*. Tianjin: Nankai University Publishing House, 1989.

Zhang, A., Guo, J., *Guoli Xinan Lianhe Daxue Shiliao (Er) [Historical Material of National Southwestern Associated University Vol.2]*. Kunming: Yunnan Education Publishing House, 1998.

Beijing Alumni Club, National Southwestern Associated University. *Guoli Xinan Lianhe Daxue Xiaoshi: Yijiusanqi Zhi Yijiusiliu Nian De Beida, Qinghua, Nankai [History of National Southwestern Associated University: Peking University, Tsinghua University and Nankai University From 1937 To 1946]*. Beijing: Peking University Press, 1996.

Jiang, Y., Xinan Lianda: *Teding Lishi Shiqi De Daxue Wenhua [National Southwestern Associated University: The University Culture of a Specific Period of Time]*. Chengdu: Publishing House of UESTC, 2010.

Yang, L., *Xinan Lianda De Sifenkesi Zhimi [The "Mystery of Sphinx" of National Southwestern Associated University]*. Kunming: Yunnan People's Publishing House, 2005.

"History of China Renmin University Research Studies Series" Editorial Board. *Zhongguo Renmin Daxue Jishi (1937–2007) Shangjuan [Chronicles of China Renmin University, 1937–2007, Volume 1]*. Beijing: China Renmin University Press, 2008.

Liu, B. *Zai Shenzhou Dadi Shang Jueqi Zhongguo Renmin Daxue Huiyi Lu (1950–2000) Shangjuan [Rising from the Divine Land: Memoir of China Renmin University (1950–2000), Volume 1]*. Beijing: China Renmin University Press, 2007.

Li, Z., Zhou, Q. *Meiti Shiye Zhong De Huazhong Keji Daxue (1978–2008) [Huazhong University of Science and Technology in the View of the Media]*. Wuhan: Huazhong University of Science and Technology Press, 2008.

Ouyang, K. *Zizhu Chengzhang Yu Renwen Qinghuai – Huazhong Keji Daxue Wenhua Suzhi Shijian Jiaoyu Tansuo [Autonomous Growth and Feelings for Humanities – the Exploration of Cultural Quality Practical Education by Huazhong University of Science and Technology]*. Wuhan: Huazhong University of Science and Technology Press, 2012.

Editing Committee of Zhongguo Daxue Renwen Qisilu, *Zhongguo Daxue Renwen Qisilu (Disi Juan) [Record of Inspirations and Thoughts regarding Humanities in Chinese University (Volume 4)]*. Wuhan: Huazhong University of Science and Technology Press, 2000.

Editing Committee of Zhongguo Daxue Renwen Qisilu, *Zhongguo Daxue Renwen Qisilu (Diwu Juan) [Record of Inspirations and Thoughts regarding Humanities in Chinese University (Volume 5)]*. Wuhan: Huazhong University of Science and Technology Press, 2001.

Xu, J. *20 Shiji Zhongguo Zhishifenzi Shilun [Historical Comments on Chinese Intellectuals in the 20th Century]*. Beijing: New Star Press, 2005.

Feng, J. *Mingyun Yu Shiming: Zhongguo Zhishifenzi Wenti Shiji Huimou [Destiny and Responsibility: Rethinking the Problem of Chinese Intellectuals after a Century].* Beijing: Sino-Culture Press, 2006.

Gong, Y. *Dangshi Zhaji [Notes on the History of the Party].* Hangzhou: Zhejiang People's Publishing House, 2002.

Li, W. *Huiyi Yu Yanjiu [Recollection and Research (Part 2)].* Beijing: History of Chinese Communist Party Publishing House, 1986.

Lin, Y., & Zhang, G. *Kaige Xingjin De Shiji [Period of Triumphant March].* Zhengzhou: Henan People's Press, 1996.

Du, X., Zhang, N. *Delida Zhongguo Yanjianglu [Collection of Derrida's Speeches in China].* Beijing: Central Compilation & Translation Press, 2003.

3. *Chinese Translated Books*

Aristotle. *Nicomachean Ethics.* Trans. Liao, S. Beijing: The Commercial Press, 2013.

Benedict, R. *Patterns of Culture.* Trans, Wang, W., et al. Beijing: Social Sciences Academic Press, 2009.

Huntington, S. *Clash of Civilizations and the Reconstruction of the World Order.* Trans. Zhou, Q., et al. Beijing: Xinhua Publishing House, 1998.

Weber, M. *The Religion of China: Confucianism and Taoism.* Trans, Hong, T. Nanjing: Jiangsu People's Publishing House, 1997.

Weber, M. *The Protestant Ethic and the Spirit of Capitalism.* Trans, Ma, Q. et al. Beijing: Peking University Press, 2012.

Zhang, Z. *Zhongguo Shenshi: Guanyu Qi Zai Shijiu Shiji Zhongguo Shehui Zhong Zuoyong De Yanjiu [Chinese Gentlemen: A Research on Their Function in Chinese Society in the 19th Century].* Trans. Li, R. Shanghai: Shanghai Academy of Social Sciences Press, 1991.

Flexner, A. *Universities: American, English, German.* Trans. Xu, H. & Chen, X. Hangzhou: Zhejiang Education Publishing Group, 2002.

Jaspers, K. *The Idea of the University.* Trans. Qiu, L. Shanghai: Shanghai People's Press, 2007.

Coses, L. *Men of Ideas: A Sociologist's View.* Trans. Guo, F., et al. Beijing: Central Compilation & Translation Press, 2004.

Readings, B. *The University in Ruins.* Trans. Guo, J., et al. Beijing: Peking University Press, 2008.

Hayhoe, R. *China's Universities 1895–1995: A Century of Cultural Conflict.* Trans. Xu, J. Beijing: Educational Science Publishing House, 2000.

Yeh, W., *The Alienated Academy: Culture and Politics in Republican China, 1919–1937.* Trans. Feng, X. et al. Beijing: China Renmin University Press, 2012.

Ishijima, N., *History of the Second Sino-Japanese War.* Trans. Zheng, Y. et al. Changchun: Jilin Education Press, 1990.

Ke, S. & Wang, N. *Biange Zhongguo: Shichang Jingji De Zhongguo Zhilu (How China Became Capitalist).* Trans, Xu, Y. & Li, Z. Beijing: CITIC Press, 2013.

ABOUT THE AUTHORS

JIA JIA, A Ph.D. candidate at the School of Education Science, Nanjing Normal University, Jia Jia engaged in basic theoretical research in higher education and has published many CSSCI papers and participated in many research projects. His Master's thesis was selected as the top master's thesis of Jiangsu Province in 2016.

WANG JIANHUA, A professor and doctoral supervisor of School of Education Science at Nanjing Normal University, Wang Jianhua has published such monographs as *The Modern University System from the Perspective of Three Departments, The University Transformation in Our Era,* and *The Dilemma of Academic Disciplines and the Experience of Universities.* His achievements have won the second and third prizes in the scientific research achievement award (humanities and social sciences) of various colleges and universities, and the first and second prizes of the Philosophy and Social Sciences Achievement Award of Jiangsu Province. He has been selected as one of the "top young talents of the national special support plan for high level talent," second-tier training objects of "333 project" in Jiangsu Province, and the first "Jiangsu young social science talent."